After Certainty

CW00751000

No part of philosophy is as disconnected from its history as is epistemology. *After Certainty* offers a reconstruction of that history, understood as a series of changing expectations about the cognitive ideal that beings such as us might hope to achieve in a world such as this. The story begins with Aristotle and then looks at how his epistemic program was developed through later antiquity and into the Middle Ages, before being dramatically reformulated in the seventeenth century. In watching these debates unfold over the centuries, one sees why epistemology has traditionally been embedded within a much larger sphere of concerns about human nature and the reality of the world we live in. It ultimately becomes clear why epistemology today has become a much narrower and specialized field, concerned with the conditions under which it is true to say, that someone knows something.

Based on a series of lectures given at Oxford University, Robert Pasnau's book ranges widely over the history of philosophy, and examines in some detail the rise of science as an autonomous discipline. Ultimately Pasnau argues that we may have no good reasons to suppose ourselves capable of achieving even the most minimal standards for knowledge, and the final chapter concludes with a discussion of faith and hope.

Robert Pasnau is professor of philosophy at the University of Colorado Boulder. He is the founding editor of *Oxford Studies in Medieval Philosophy* and the author of many scholarly books and articles on the history of philosophy and its contemporary manifestations. His book *Metaphysical Themes 1274–1671* (Oxford University Press, 2011) traced the breakdown of Aristotelianism and the rise of early modern metaphysics. In 2014 he gave the Isaiah Berlin Lectures at Oxford University, which now appear as *After Certainty*.

After Certainty

A History of Our Epistemic Ideals and Illusions

ROBERT PASNAU

OXFORD
UNIVERSITY PRESS

OXFORD
UNIVERSITY PRESS

Great Clarendon Street, Oxford, OX2 6DP,
United Kingdom

Oxford University Press is a department of the University of Oxford.
It furthers the University's objective of excellence in research, scholarship,
and education by publishing worldwide. Oxford is a registered trade mark of
Oxford University Press in the UK and in certain other countries

© Robert Pasnau 2017

The moral rights of the author have been asserted

First Edition published in 2017
First published in paperback 2019

Published in the United States of America by Oxford University Press
198 Madison Avenue, New York, NY 10016, United States of America

British Library Cataloguing in Publication Data
Data available

Library of Congress Cataloging in Publication Data
Data available

ISBN 978–0–19–880178–8 (Hbk.)
ISBN 978–0–19–885218–6 (Pbk.)

PREFACE

My earliest ambition as a philosopher, which goes back to my undergraduate days, was to write about epistemology. Since the topic in its more recent manifestations looked (at that time, to my youthful eyes) as if it had been quite exhaustingly studied already, it seemed a sensible career move (at that time, to those youthful eyes) to go back to an era where there was evidently much room for new research: the middle ages. When I arrived there via upstate New York, I found, however, that I did not know how to talk about medieval epistemology and could not even find much epistemology from that era to talk about. Hence I settled for the theory of cognition.

Some years later I found myself aspiring to write a book on how metaphysics and epistemology changed in the four centuries between Aquinas and Locke. It eventually became clear, however, that metaphysics alone would put quite enough strain on whatever readership there might be for such a book (to say nothing of the strain it eventually put on the art of bookbinding). The research on epistemology never left my spiral notebooks.

Still more recently I was invited to spend a term at Oxford delivering the Isaiah Berlin Lectures on the History of Ideas. Thinking of those notebooks, I decided that I ought to try, one more time, to write about the history of epistemology. This book is the result.

Since delivering those lectures in the spring of 2014, I have rewritten the main text quite extensively, but I have endeavored, so as to preserve a sense of the occasion, to retain the prose style I had adopted then for a public audience. I have also steadfastly adhered both to the original number of lectures and to something like their original length, so that the sprawling material of the notebooks might be distilled into a concentrated argument of manageable size.

Yet, if brevity is the soul of wit, then either soulless or witless I must be, because I found myself unable to resist cheating on these self-imposed constraints in that most shameful and dreaded of ways: by adding endnotes. Very long endnotes. But, though lacking in soul, I am not lacking in heart; hence I have written the main text so that it can be read without the notes. Moreover, I have tried to write the notes so that they, too, can be read continuously, without any need to refer back to the corresponding lecture. Accordingly, readers should on no account attempt the maddening exercise of paging back and forth between lecture and notes. Each lecture should be read without interruption, and the notes for a given lecture should be consulted only after that lecture has been read to the end, and only by readers who want to see more of the dense and scraggly roots from which these lectures grew.

CONTENTS

Lecture One

The Epistemic Ideal

Introduction

Over the weeks ahead I will sketch a series of chapters in the history of our thinking about knowledge. Any serious attempt at such a history should confront, from the start, the surprising fact that, of all the main branches of philosophy today, epistemology is the most alienated from its history. In ethics, politics, metaphysics, and mind, even in logic and language, philosophers pursue themes that go back to antiquity and that run almost continuously over the subsequent centuries. Yet historical precedents are few and far between for the sorts of discussions that have largely animated epistemology over the last fifty years. Today the study of knowledge is one of the foundational subjects of philosophy. But this has not always been so—indeed, for long periods of time, epistemology can appear not to have been an important philosophical subject at all, let alone a foundational one.

It is symptomatic of these discontinuities that the very term 'epistemology' goes back only to the middle of the nineteenth century, before which time philosophers evidently felt no need for a special label to talk about the study of knowledge. Moreover, the ways in which philosophy has been divided over previous centuries have left no space for epistemology as a distinct field of inquiry. For Aristotelians as well as for Stoics, philosophy broke down into logic, physics, and ethics. (Aristotle's *metaphysics* was seen as furnishing a kind of appendix to the physical sciences.) Among Arabic philosophers, following the traditions of late antiquity, theoretical philosophy standardly divided into physics, mathematics, and metaphysics, logic being a further subject on the side. In the seventeenth century things were much the same. Thomas Hobbes divided the sciences that study natural bodies from those that study political bodies, including among the former physics, ethics, poetry, and logic, but not the study of knowledge itself.[a] John Locke distinguished "three great provinces of the intellectual world": the nature of things, moral philosophy, and the doctrine of signs.[b] He and his contemporaries conceived of his great *Essay* as falling into that last category—a treatise of logic. In none of these divisions is there any hint of epistemology—under any name—as a special subject, let alone as a foundational philosophical subject.[1]

---

[a] *Leviathan* 9; see also *De corpore* 1.9.   [b] *Essay* IV.21.5.

Still, it is by no means the case that premodern philosophy neglected epistemology. There were debates over skepticism, of course, and over the relationship between sense perception and knowledge; and there were extensive investigations into the cognitive mechanisms that gave rise to sensation and belief. What was very unusual, however, was to address at any length the problem that lies at the heart of modern epistemology: how knowledge is to be defined. To be sure, there was Plato in the *Meno* and the *Theaetetus*, and the casual follower of philosophy's history might be forgiven for supposing that his example carried forward more or less continuously until the present day. In fact, however, Plato has always been more honored than imitated, and this is particularly the case with respect to his interest in definitions. The Platonic dialogues, especially the early ones, are interested in defining all sorts of things: knowledge, piety, friendship, courage, justice, statesmanship, and so on. Most of these definitional projects no longer interest us. Although philosophers still think sometimes about friendship and courage and regularly about justice, it is rare to find attempts at definition. Knowledge is the exception. It is only recently, however, that the quest to define the term has been perceived as a central philosophical question. From Aristotle through the Middle Ages and well beyond, philosophers took an interest in carefully circumscribing one or another particular kind of cognitive grasp of reality—perception, imagination, assent, deduction, and so on—but showed little interest in defining the broad category of knowledge. That English contains this very general word of positive cognitive appraisal did not strike philosophers, even those who worked in English, as calling for any special definitional inquiry.

My aim over the course of these lectures is to consider the sorts of questions about knowledge that philosophy *has* asked for most of its history and to examine how the answers to those questions have changed. I will be particularly interested in what I take to be one of the pivotal moments in the history of philosophy—the seventeenth-century rejection of scholastic Aristotelianism—which I will explore by looking at both sides of that divide. Lying behind the more famous innovations of that revolutionary century are, I shall argue, a series of decisive transformations in the sorts of epistemic demands we make on ourselves.[2]

I have been invited to give these lectures in the name of Isaiah Berlin, the great Oxford historian of ideas. As fortune would have it, the theme that will run through the course of these six weeks—of the ideals and illusions that beset our cognitive enterprise—is one that permeates Berlin's own thought. Over and over, Berlin warns against a certain sort of idealizing tendency, the folly of supposing that "all the ideals of mankind" are compatible. Within both politics and metaphysics, this tendency looms, with respect to ideals like *justice, truth, liberty,* and *progress.* This faith—that we can achieve, all together, all the various ideals that we aspire to—"is perhaps one of the least plausible beliefs ever entertained by profound and influential thinkers."[a] Even so, this "one belief, more than any other, is responsible for the slaughter of individuals on the altars of the great historical ideals."[b] In these lectures I wish to trace the rise and fall of such ideals in the domain of epistemology. Over the weeks to come we will look at how certain

---

[a] *Concepts and Categories,* p. 198.   [b] "Two Concepts of Liberty," in *Four Essays,* p. 167.

ancient epistemic expectations coalesced in the Middle Ages around a comprehensive theoretical framework, and how those ideals gradually dissolved, piece by piece, in the seventeenth century. I will begin, this week and next, by characterizing these epistemic ideals in a general way. In weeks three and four I will focus on perception and illusion; and then, in the last two weeks, I will take up reason and its frailties, coming around finally, inevitably, to talk about skepticism.

By the end of today I hope to have explained how epistemology came to stand as a foundational topic in philosophy. To tell that story, I need to describe the rise of a distinction between knowledge and science, a development that has its origins in the breakdown of scholastic Aristotelian metaphysics. But before arriving at these famous episodes at the dawn of modern science, we need to consider the framework in which epistemology was pursued for most of its history. The story I wish to tell today and in the weeks ahead turns on reconceptualizing what a theory of knowledge might look like. If the history of epistemology looks strange to us, this is because we have lost sight of the subject's most prominent aim. Once that aim comes into clearer focus, we will be able to make much better sense of a great many episodes from the history of this subject. And, once we understand these episodes better, we will be in a position to ask whether this alternative epistemic framework might be an improvement on more recent ways of pursuing epistemology.

The framework I have in mind, and which I will argue dominated the history of our theorizing about knowledge, is what I call an *idealized epistemology*. Rather than take as its goal the analysis of our concept of knowledge, an idealized epistemology aspires, first, to describe the epistemic ideal that human beings might hope to achieve and then, second, to chart the various ways in which we commonly fall off from that ideal. As one might expect, it turns out to be fairly easy to characterize what we would ideally like to achieve in principle and quite hard to come to grips with what we might actually be able to achieve in practice.

Aristotle's Ideal Theory

To see an idealized epistemology in action, we should start by looking back to Aristotle, the ancient inspiration for so much of what gets said about knowledge during the first two millennia of philosophy in the Middle East and Europe. Like Plato, Aristotle devotes an entire treatise to investigating the character of something they both call *epistēmē*. But the results Aristotle arrives at, in his *Posterior Analytics*, are utterly different from what Plato had suggested in his *Theaetetus*. Whereas it might plausibly be thought that the *Theaetetus* has the same goal as that of many modern epistemologists—considering our ordinary way of talking about knowledge and of pursuing necessary and sufficient conditions for its satisfaction—it is clear from the very start of the *Posterior Analytics* that this is not Aristotle's aim. No conversation with an ordinary Athenian, no matter how one-sided, could plausibly have elicited the result that knowledge concerns a proposition that is necessary and universal, known on the basis of an affirmative demonstration in the first syllogistic figure, the premises of which are necessary and explanatory of the conclusion. This is not what even the most erudite Athenian could have meant by *epistēmē* before Aristotle came along, and if this is what *epistēmē* is, then we would have to conclude that it is something that hardly anyone has ever had, in any domain.

But if the *Posterior Analytics* is not analyzing the meaning of 'knowledge', then what is it doing? In what sense is this an epistemology at all? One line of answer to these questions has been to find some other English word that better fits Aristotle's project, the most prominent such suggestion being that this is a theory of *understanding*. Clearly this is a promising idea about how to translate *epistēmē* in the context of the *Posterior Analytics*. The agent who comes to understand a proposition in the way Aristotle describes goes well beyond simply *knowing* that proposition. One can come to know quite well that vines shed their leaves, for example, simply by observation.[a] But someone who grasps the general truth in the way Aristotle describes—on the basis of necessary principles grounded in the vine's essence—might plausibly be said to have a better *understanding* of that truth. Even so, as helpful as this may be as a translation, it does not go very far toward explaining what Aristotle is after. Is he simply engaged in his own linguistic project, trying to understand a Greek word for which 'understanding' is the closest English counterpart? Presumably there is something special about *epistēmē* as the *Posterior Analytics* conceives of it, something that makes it worthy of being singled out for special treatment. And understanding, to be sure, is eminently worthy of study. But why study this, rather than knowledge? And why develop the details in the way Aristotle does? Are the arcane requirements of his demonstrative method really intended as necessary and sufficient conditions for understanding a thing?

The traditional reading of the *Posterior Analytics* takes it to be a theory of scientific knowledge. This is another way in which *epistēmē* has been translated, and the treatise itself is almost always described in these terms, as offering a theory of knowledge or understanding *in the domain of science*. It is odd that this should be so, however, because it is apparent even on a casual inspection that the treatise's scope is much broader than science as we now conceive of it. Although scientific examples figure prominently, they are not its exclusive focus. The method is evidently meant to apply to mathematics too; there are, indeed, as many mathematical examples as there are scientific ones. There is also no reason to describe the method as scientific rather than philosophical, since it is completely unclear how we would mark the divide between science and philosophy at this early date. To be sure, various ancient authors use the plural form *epistēmai* to refer more or less to what we now think of as 'the sciences.' But it is highly misleading to describe the *Posterior Analytics* as a treatise on science, given how much more broadly the theory is meant to apply. A theory that does not discriminate between science and mathematics on one hand and between science and philosophy on the other is surely not a theory of science in our sense at all. Scholars will perhaps defend themselves on this point by insisting that, of course, they are using the term 'science' in the broad sense of the Greek *epistēmē*. But, once that is said, it becomes clear that characterizing the treatise as scientific in its concerns in fact explains nothing at all.[3]

To describe the *Posterior Analytics* as a theory of science is perhaps most charitably regarded as shorthand for the more complex idea that it aims at an account of *systematic theoretical knowledge*—the sort of thing one does in mathematics and philosophy just as

---

[a] *Post. An.* II.16.

much as in the sciences. One may speak of the project synecdochically as *scientific*, but that is just because, as in many other prominent cases, we do not have in English the right term for conveying what Aristotle is after. There is, however, more to be said here than this. Commentators have almost unanimously latched onto the notion that the *Posterior Analytics* offers a theory of science because they have not seen any other sort of enterprise in the vicinity that the treatise could be concerned with. It is not just that we lack a word for systematic theoretical knowledge, but that we lack any place in our conceptual scheme for the study of such a thing. However, philosophers do of course study the nature of science. Hence it has become an *idée fixe* in the recent literature that this is what the *Posterior Analytics* does.

Regardless of how the topic of the *Posterior Analytics* is to be characterized, there is a further puzzle concerning its methodological prescriptions: that the method described seems both impractical and in fact unpracticed by Aristotle. If possessing *epistēmē* requires grasping first principles and essences, then it seems unlikely that we have achieved this condition in more than a few domains. (Mathematics would be the most likely place to find such a methodology in place. But it is unclear whether mathematical proofs satisfy the requirement that one know a proposition through principles that explain the reason why it is so.) Perhaps unsurprisingly, Aristotle's own writings, including the *Posterior Analytics* themselves, contain no examples that satisfy all the necessary requirements. To be sure, his many examples serve individually to illustrate one or another dimension of the theory, but each seems incomplete in one regard or another. The prescribed method, then, seems to be one that he himself is incapable of fully putting into practice.[4]

All of these puzzles dissolve when one reads the *Posterior Analytics* as describing an epistemic ideal. Aristotle characterizes his subject matter as *epistēmē haplōs*, unconditionally or unqualifiedly knowledge, in contrast to various lesser forms of knowledge, which he is willing to count as *epistēmai* but which are in one way or another deficient.[a] According to this distinction, these lesser kinds are simply the ordinary sorts of knowledge that human beings regularly do possess, and unqualified knowledge is the ideal state that we should aspire to, even if its attainment is extremely difficult. This explains why Aristotle elsewhere seems not to practice what he preaches—not because it is not his goal, but because it is an idealized goal. For this reason, too, the *Posterior Analytics* itself gives us little more than fragments of what an *epistēmē* taken *haplōs* is supposed to be. This is not the perverse failing that it might seem, because Aristotle is describing the ideal aim of inquiry rather than something that he himself is in a position to achieve.

Aristotle nowhere says explicitly that *epistēmē haplōs* is an ideal that he has not yet realized. But he comes close in the *Metaphysics*, where he remarks:

> The study of truth is difficult in one way, in another easy. A sign of this is that no one is able to attain it completely, nor entirely misses it. But each individual says something concerning the nature of things, so that while he may individually contribute little or nothing, from the collaboration of all there comes a great amount. It is like the proverbial door: who can fail to hit it? In this respect it is easy; but being able to grasp the whole and not only a part makes the difficulty clear.[b]

---

[a] E.g. *Post. An.* 71^{b}10, 72^{b}30, 73^{b}17, 74^{a}33.   [b] *Meta.* II.1, 993^{a}30–^{b}7.

Aristotle does not use the term *epistēmē* here, but it seems clear enough that the study (*theōria*) he has in mind is just what he had described in rigorous detail in the *Posterior Analytics*. For what is most distinctive about Aristotle's conception of *epistēmē* is his insistence that it involve a grasp not just of a single isolated proposition, but of the whole causal and inferential network of propositions that lie behind it. Aristotle's ideal theory therefore requires a grasp of the whole door, not just a part, and what he tells us here is that it is easy to make a contribution to *epistēmē*, but very hard to achieve the complete ideal. Indeed, "no one" is able to do that.

As soon as one considers the possibility that Aristotle is offering not a theory of 'knowledge'—even for a special refined domain of inquiry—but an account of the ideal limit of human inquiry, it becomes easy to see why Aristotle would insist on the various details of his account. According to the canonical definition of *Posterior Analytics* I.2, *epistēmē* in the ideal, unqualified sense arises "when we think we know of the explanation [*aitia*] because of which the object holds that it is its explanation, and also that it is not possible for it to be otherwise."[a] This imposes two requirements on *epistēmē*: that it be grounded in an explanation; and that it concern what is necessary. Although, as we will see today and next week, both of these conditions become controversial in the seventeenth century, it is nevertheless easy to see why Aristotle would have taken each one to be an element of the cognitive ideal. And, when subsequent chapters introduce further conditions on *epistēmē*, these conditions are defended precisely as features of the cognitive ideal. In I.24, for instance, he offers a lengthy series of arguments as to why *epistēmē* should be of the universal rather than the particular. How do we choose between these options? By determining which achievement is superior. Thus, "if you know something universally, you know it *better* as it holds than if you know it particularly. Hence universal demonstrations are *better* than particular demonstrations."[b] The next chapter argues in similar fashion about the reason why *epistēmē* should be based on affirmative rather than negative premises: not because the latter fail to yield knowledge or understanding or science, but because "the affirmative, being prior and more familiar and more convincing, will be better."[c] And so I.26 continues by showing that positive arguments "are better" than arguments cast in the form of a *reductio*. Obviously, arguments that are deficient in these respects can significantly increase our understanding. Indeed, in other places Aristotle happily recognizes a wide variety of cognitive states that fall short of the ideal described here, such as grasping particulars and retaining them in memory, reaching conclusions in a nonexplanatory way (by way of the fact 'that', *hoti*, rather than by way of the reason 'why', *dia ti*), and achieving practical wisdom in action. We might reasonably describe all of these as kinds of knowledge. The point of the *Posterior Analytics* is simply that they are not ideal.[5]

Normative Ideals

Among authors writing in Latin, from antiquity to the seventeenth century, *epistēmē* becomes *scientia*, and *scientia* continues to be understood in terms of the cognitive ideal. Jumping ahead to the high Middle Ages, we can find Albert the Great, in the prologue to

---

[a] *Post. An.* I.2, 71^{b}9–12.   [b] I.24, 85^{b}13–15.   [c] I.25, 86^{b}29.

his *Posterior Analytics* commentary (1261), remarking of *scientia* that "this is the end and the most perfect and the sole unconditionally desirable thing among the logical sciences."[a] Thomas Aquinas, in his commentary, remarks that "to have *scientia* of something is to cognize it perfectly." From this principle he derives the twin features of the canonical definition: that what is known in this way must be necessary, and that it must be grasped through a grasp of its cause.[b] Describing Adam's condition in the Garden of Eden, he writes that "just as the first man was endowed in a perfect state with respect to his body . . . so too he was endowed in a perfect state with respect to his soul . . . And thus the first man was endowed by God so as to have *scientia* of all the things about which a man is naturally suited to be instructed."[c] Even after Aristotle's influence began to wane, authors continued to take for granted that *scientia* should be understood as the cognitive ideal. Francisco Sanches, for instance, a late sixteenth-century critic of Aristotelianism, puts in capital letters his definition of *scientia* as "the perfect cognition of a thing."[d] And René Descartes, in his early *Rules for the Direction of the Mind*, conceives of these rules as a guide for the achievement of *scientia*, and writes that they "will help us ascend to the peak of human cognition."[e] Descartes's case will be considered in some detail next week.[6]

Once we begin to think of *scientia* (née *epistēmē*) as the ideal, the peak of perfection, it becomes natural to worry that, however it is to be characterized, it will remain only an ideal, unattainable to us. We noticed already how, in Aristotle, it is hard to find a single conclusion that meets all the criteria of his ideal theory. And indeed, historically, it is very common to worry about how close human beings might be able to come to the cognitive ideal. Back in the second century, Ptolemy had remarked that, of the various theoretical disciplines, "only mathematics can provide sure and unshakable knowledge [*eidēsis*] to its devotees." As for physics and metaphysics, "they should be called conjecture rather than knowledge [*katalēpsis epistēmonikē*] . . . There is no hope that philosophers will ever be agreed about them."[f] Pietro Pomponazzi, in the Renaissance, similarly remarked that "philosophy would be beautiful, if it were as certain as mathematics. For metaphysics and philosophy are conjectural, and on almost any subject one may find different opinions, so that it is like playing with toys."[g] (This is one of two obstacles Pomponazzi describes as plaguing philosophy. The other, naturally, is that it does not pay.)

Although Ptolemy and Pomponazzi put their complaints in strong terms, their concern is one that nearly everyone has always shared about almost every area of human inquiry. So, if epistemology is to be conceived in ideal terms, it might seem that skepticism lies just around the corner. In fact, however, the strategy of idealization does not require identifying some sort of *absolute* ideal and then holding it fixed regardless of whether it can be obtained. The objective is not to identify standards that only a god could achieve. The point instead is to define what sort of knowledge *we* might be able to achieve, given the world we live in. Accordingly, if the highest cognitive ideal turns out to be one that can be achieved only in certain limited contexts, then an idealized epistemology had better be ready to make various retrenchments to the theory, as

---

[a] *Comm. Post. an.* I.1.1 (ed. Jammy, I: 514a).   [b] *In Post. an.* I.4.
[c] *Summa theol.* 1a 94.3c.   [d] *Quod nihil scitur*, p. 200.   [e] *Rules* 2 (X: 364).
[f] *Almagest* I.1, p. 36 trans.; see also Lecture Two, p. 27.   [g] See Perfetti, "Pietro Pomponazzi," §5.

required to identify a level of cognitive excellence that ordinary people can meet in ordinary circumstances. And this is in fact what we find happening, beginning with Aristotle. Although the *Posterior Analytics'* theory of demonstration sets a formidable standard for *epistēmē*, Aristotle elsewhere describes in considerable detail an epistemology of nonideal conditions, which he labels *dialectic*. The *Topics*, his treatise devoted to this subject, explains what one should do in cases where one or another component of demonstrative reasoning is not available, and considers what merit there is to arguments that fall short of the rigor of *epistēmē*. Although dialectic does not rise to the level of the ideal, it is appropriately deployed by certain kinds of people in certain kinds of situations and is a worthy subject of philosophical investigation.[7]

For the next two millennia, epistemology largely wrapped itself around these two frameworks, demonstrative and dialectical, and subsequent Aristotelians devoted considerable effort to investigating the conditions under which one or another method was most appropriately deployed. Accordingly, it became standard to register the different senses in which one might speak of *epistēmē* or *scientia*. In Themistius's fourth-century commentary on the *Posterior Analytics*, for instance, we are told that '*epistēmē*' is said in two ways, broadly and strictly. The strict sense is that of the *Posterior Analytics*. Broadly, in contrast, "we say that every apprehension [*gnōsis*] is knowledge [*epistēmē*], however it comes about, whether it be of accidental things, through whatever method [*tropos*]."[a] The first Latin commentary, that of Robert Grosseteste in the 1220s, distinguishes four ways of speaking of *scientia*: he begins with Themistius's very broad sense but arrives at the strictest sense only after registering two intermediary levels, one for natural science (where conclusions hold only for the most part) and one for mathematics (where Grosseteste thinks we lack a grasp of the reason why).[b] In one form or another, this four-fold division runs all through subsequent scholastic thought.[8]

If its goals are adjusted to fit the capacities of real agents and real circumstances, an idealized epistemology might seem to embrace a purely descriptive account of human cognitive activities. But in fact the theory is normative in its ambitions. In seeking to establish the cognitive ideal, the theory aims at a question that lies at the heart of epistemology: the question of when ordinary agents, in ordinary circumstances, should believe the things they believe. This way of proceeding insists that a normative account of our epistemic position, nonideal as it is, presupposes some conception of the ideal. Such a methodology– ideal theory as foundational for real-world applications— is familiar enough in other normative domains. In political philosophy, for instance, it is common to frame a theory of justice around an account of what an ideally just state would look like. The project is not, of course, to describe a form of government suitable only for the gods. Nor is it supposed that the only just state would be one that perfectly satisfies the ideal theory. The goal is an understanding of what a just state would be for beings such as we are, in a world like this one. With some such picture of the ideal, calibrated against what is actually possible, we are able to think about what sort of political structures we might reasonably demand. This is precisely what we find in an idealized epistemology: it begins with a conception of the human cognitive ideal, then applies it to the question of what we ought to believe.[9]

---

[a] *Paraphrasis Post. an.* I.2 (ed. Wallies, p. 5; ed. O'Donnell, p. 247).   [b] *Comm. Post. an.* I.2, p. 99.

In many ways, this is a more promising approach than what one finds in epistemology today. Rather than describe an ideal and then consider how close we might come to achieving it, the modern epistemologist has tended to begin with questions of threshold: exactly what divides knowledge from mere true belief? It would be as if political philosophers spent most of their time trying to define exactly where the borderline falls between the just and the unjust state, or as if ethicists focused on just precisely how good an act must be in order to count as praiseworthy. To be sure, there will be cases in the moral or political domain where such questions of threshold have practical relevance. But it would be odd to expect clear lines of demarcation, and odd to think that the principal task of normative theory is to discover those lines. In epistemology, too, boundary conditions clearly matter. We care about the theory of knowledge largely because we care about what we ought to believe and what we ought to do, and we think such questions of belief and agency are tied up with questions about what we know. Next week we will see why, beginning in the seventeenth century, epistemology becomes increasingly focused on whether our beliefs are *justified*. Once the issues are so starkly normative it becomes natural, as we will see, to look for the boundaries that demarcate knowledge. Even so, it is strange to embrace the widespread current assumption that the way to investigate such questions runs through language—as if finding necessary and sufficient conditions for the word 'knowledge' would show us what the proper standards are for belief and action.[a] A more meaningful way to proceed is to begin with an account of the epistemic ideals toward which we ought to aspire and then to reflect on how much progress toward those ideals we should demand of ourselves in one or another domain.

Like other normative disciplines, an idealized epistemology holds out the hope not only of clarifying our actual practices, but of putting us in a position to critique those practices. Mill's utilitarianism describes an ethical ideal, maximizing happiness, which does not immediately tell us exactly how much happiness an action must produce to count as morally good. All the same, even if Mill's theory does not mark the precise boundaries of right action, it has tremendous potential to influence society's conceptions of where those boundaries should be drawn, simply by winning people over to a new conception of the moral ideal. Something similar might happen in epistemology. A pessimistic conception of our epistemic prospects—of the sort we will encounter in Lecture Six—might encourage a more tolerant attitude toward belief. Instead of scorning those who hold various religious, ethical, and political views upon insubstantial evidence, we might indulgently regard such naïfs as being on more or less the same footing as everyone else. In contrast, optimism regarding the attainability of some epistemic ideal might lead us toward higher expectations in everyday life. Indeed, this may already have happened. William Whewell, in his nineteenth-century paean to the progress of science, argues for the larger social consequences of the scientific revolution: "an advance from the obscure to the clear, and from error to truth, may be traced in the world at large."[b] Whewell contends that rising standards of certainty and precision in science caused society to elevate its cognitive expectations more generally—a clear case of how an epistemic ideal, once seen to be realizable, might bring about a broader shift

---

[a] Lecture Two discusses the linguistic tendencies of much recent epistemology.
[b] *History of Scientific Ideas* I: 279.

in normative expectations. Even if Whewell's enthusiasm is misplaced, the phenomenon is not implausible. An idealized epistemology might be more than descriptive—it might also have normative force. So, even if recent theorists of knowledge have only interpreted the word in various ways, the point might instead be to change it.[10]

The Breakdown of Aristotelian Essentialism

It is relatively easy to describe the *absolute* epistemic ideal—the sort of knowledge that a god might have. The ideal would be to grasp, in a single glance, all of reality, with complete certainty, and to understand all the explanatory connections between things. Eventually, in my final lecture, I will consider whether there might be limits to this sort of absolute ideal, even for a god. The more pressing questions of an idealized epistemology, however, concern its application to this world. It is only here that the normative dimension of the theory comes into play, since one can reasonably insist that human beings *ought* to achieve a certain epistemic standing only if it is *possible* for us to do so. This is what I mean by the *normative* epistemic ideal.

To see what sort of epistemic ideal is possible for us requires taking into account two kinds of constraints: those imposed by our human limitations and those imposed by the character of the world in which we live. This is perhaps part of the reason why the theory of knowledge has not traditionally been conceived of as a distinct subject of inquiry. Epistemology, once idealized, can be developed only as part of a much broader theory. On one side, an account of the normative ideal must be embedded in a theory of our cognitive capacities. Such constraints will take center stage in later lectures. Today, however, I am concerned with those constraints that arise from the other side, from our conception of the world around us. Such metaphysical questions have, traditionally, gone hand in hand with epistemology. When Plato, for instance, discusses his theory of knowledge in the *Theaetetus* and the *Republic*, he does so in the context of his theory of Forms, which he regards as ideal objects of inquiry. Conceived of apart from the Forms, Plato's epistemology is unintelligible. Aristotle's epistemology, as set out in the *Posterior Analytics*, expressly sets itself against that Platonic conception of reality. In its place Aristotle offers a more down-to-earth but still ideal object: the inner essences of things. The details of Aristotle's theory of knowledge depend on his essentialism just as much as those of Plato's depends upon his Forms.

It was, of course, the Aristotelian framework that became dominant after antiquity. When this framework collapsed in the seventeenth century, it did so not mainly because of doubts specific to Aristotelian epistemology, but because of doubts over its metaphysical foundations. Specifically, seventeenth-century authors began to challenge the Aristotelian doctrine of essences. As long as that metaphysical doctrine had thrived, so had the *Posterior Analytics* framework, along with its conception of the cognitive ideal. But with the rise of the mechanical philosophy came a new metaphysics, and with it a new conception of knowledge. Or, to be more precise, as we will see, the seventeenth century gives rise to several distinct conceptions of the epistemic ideal, engendering new meanings for both 'knowledge' and 'science' and paving the way ultimately to our modern conception of epistemology as the foundational subject of philosophy.

For early chapters in this transformation, we can turn to Hobbes and Locke, authors of the first two great philosophical treatises of the English language. To understand their backstory, however, something should be said briefly about the history of English epistemic vocabulary. A theory of knowledge ought not to be a theory of 'knowledge.' But we can perhaps disrupt epistemology's preoccupation with language, at least for a short while, by reflecting on the historical contingencies that led to our current patterns of usage. When English began to take shape in its modern form, in the later Middle Ages, various options were available for talking about our epistemic achievements. There was our verb 'to know,' which is attested in Old English and is very common throughout all periods, along with the noun 'knowledge,' which begins in Middle English. Then, also going back to Old English, there is the verb 'witen' (from the same root as the German *wissen*). Finally, beginning in the fourteenth century, English starts to use the Latinate word 'science.' Each of these words might have come into prominence as our principal way of talking about epistemic achievements. Indeed, it is interesting to see that each of the three—'knowledge,' 'witen,' 'science'—predominates in one or another early translation of Boethius's *Consolation of Philosophy*, which was the first philosophical work to be rendered in English. By the early seventeenth century, 'witen' largely falls out of usage as a verb, whereas 'knowledge' and 'science' often seem quite interchangeable. In some texts, we find 'knowledge' where we would expect to find 'science.' Francis Bacon, for instance, in 1605, describes mathematics as "the most abstracted of knowledges."[a] Others use 'science' where now we would use knowledge, and still others switch back and forth even within the same sentence. Joseph Glanvill, for instance, in 1661, writes that "he is the greatest ignorant, that knows not that he is so: for 'tis a good degree of science, to be sensible that we want it."[b] [11]

Confronted with unsettled terminology and complex theoretical questions, philosophers naturally set about constructing systematic accounts. But by the time this started to happen in English, Aristotle's philosophy lay under a dark cloud, disreputable even if still enormously influential. Consider Hobbes's *Leviathan* (1651). Writing in English, Hobbes proposes that we think of "knowledge" as coming in two kinds: knowledge of fact and knowledge of the connection between propositions. The first "is nothing else but sense and memory." The second is "the knowledge required in a philosopher," and this is what Hobbes says should be called *science*.[c] On its face, this looks entirely un-Aristotelian, as one might expect, given that Hobbes has absolutely no sympathy for the broader metaphysical framework of Aristotle's epistemology. Moreover, quite unlike Aristotle's, Hobbes's account seems to make science rather easy to acquire; we need grasp only that one proposition entails another. But this turns out to be misleading, because Hobbes goes on to express considerable doubt about whether we often manage to achieve science. He remarks that geometry is the only science we have successfully attained[d]—ironically enough, coming from a man who would later spend years trying to persuade the leading geometers of his day that the circle can be squared. As for the natural sciences, they "cannot teach us our own nature, nor the nature of the smallest creature living."[e] The grounds for such pessimism are unclear from the *Leviathan* itself, but can be grasped from the earlier *De corpore*. There, writing in Latin, Hobbes lays out a

---

[a] *Advancement of Learning* Bk. II (*Major Works*, p. 235).   [b] *Vanity of Dogmatizing* ch. 23, p. 225.
[c] *Lev.* 9.1.   [d] 4.12.   [e] 21.33.

conception of *scientia* that turns out to be much more Aristotelian than one might have guessed, inasmuch as science arises out of a series of demonstrations grounded in initial definitions that establish "the causes and generation of things."[a] Chains of inference that do not bottom out in an understanding of ultimate causes do not count as science.[12]

Locke, the other great seventeenth-century fount of philosophical English, offers a similar picture of the epistemic landscape. On the one hand, he has a very demanding sense of 'knowledge,' which he associates with science and contrasts with a looser notion of assent based on probabilities. (But, as we will see next week,[b] Locke is unlike Hobbes in that he refuses to speak of such assent as knowledge.) Although Locke does not expressly define 'science' as a distinct kind of knowledge, it seems clear that, like Hobbes, he understands it in broadly Aristotelian terms, as requiring a grasp of the necessary connection from causes to effects. Also like Hobbes, Locke despairs of our being able to achieve any such thing, writing: "As to a perfect science of natural bodies (not to mention spiritual beings) we are, I think, so far from being capable of any such thing, that I conclude it lost labour to seek after it."[c] Locke's discussion of these matters goes one step further, however, inasmuch as his skepticism about the prospects for science results from a sophisticated refashioning of the Aristotelian doctrine of essences. Whereas Hobbes had retained the causal requirement without an Aristotelian metaphysics of essence, Locke maintains at least a vestige of that metaphysics, taking for granted throughout his writings that there are some such "real essences" or "real constitutions" that both define what a substance is and explain its various accidental features. Thus, he says, "'tis past doubt, there must be some real constitution on which any collection of simple ideas co-existing must depend."[d] To have scientific knowledge of the natural world, then, would be to grasp these ultimate causal principles. But Locke completely rejects our ability to do any such thing: "we in vain pretend to range things into sorts, and dispose them into certain classes, under names, by their real essences, that are so far from our discovery or comprehension."[e] Our conventional groupings of things into kinds—what he calls their *nominal essences*—have little connection to the actual distribution of real essences.

If Locke's view of real essences had been merely skeptical, then not much would have followed for the Aristotelian idea of *scientia*. After all, even for the Aristotelians, the essences of things are merely an ideal goal of inquiry. But Locke's account implies that essences are a false ideal —that we do not live in a world that clusters so neatly into kinds, and that what clusters there are may not reflect any deep metaphysical structure. At this point Locke might have articulated some other epistemic ideal, which is in effect what both Descartes and Newton did, albeit in very different ways, as we will see later today and next week. Instead Locke despairs of our achieving anything that would count as an epistemic ideal. Science, for him, is the epistemic ideal, and to possess it would be to grasp the real essences of things and to understand why those essences give rise to the various qualities and operations that we observe in the world around us. Yet, because of the "darkness we are involved in," such "connections and dependencies [are] not discoverable in our ideas." Accordingly, "we are so far from being able to comprehend the whole nature of the universe, and all the things contained in it, that we are not

---

[a] *De corpore* 6.13.   [b] Chapter Two, p. 41.   [c] *Essay* IV.3.29.
[d] III.3.15.   [e] III.6.9.

capable of a philosophical knowledge of the bodies that are about us, and make a part of us."[a] In part he blames the world for not having a structure that is readily discernible, and in part he blames our cognitive faculties: "the weakness of our faculties in this state of mediocrity . . . makes me suspect that natural philosophy is not capable of being made a science."[b] Locke is enthusiastic about the achievements of a few contemporaries: he describes himself as living "in an age that produces such masters as the great Huygenius, and the incomparable Mr. Newton."[c] But, by Locke's standards, even work such as this falls short of the ideal. We can see what that epistemic ideal is, Locke thinks, and we can see its unattainability.[13]

Hobbes and Locke stand at the brink of post-scholastic epistemology. Having rejecting Aristotelian metaphysics, they are unable to engage in the epistemic program that Aristotle had described. Yet, even so, they continue to accept that program as an ideal, insofar as they accept that genuine knowledge or science would require a grasp of the ultimate causes of things. That they hold such a view is really no surprise, because they thus follow the virtually unanimous verdict of the philosophical tradition. We have seen how the causal requirement appears in Aristotle's canonical definition of *epistēmē*. Indeed, Aristotle remarks that "study of the reason why is what reigns supreme in knowledge."[d] From antiquity through the Middle Ages and well into the seventeenth century, this requirement gets taken for granted. Plato had spoken of the need to grasp the "legitimate cause and reason" of natural phenomena.[e] From Peter Abelard to Pierre Gassendi, authors invoke Vergil: "Happy is he who has been able to grasp the causes of things."[f] When Aquinas comments on Aristotle's definition, he first insists that *scientia* is perfect cognition, then adds that "one who has *scientia*, if he is cognizing perfectly, must cognize the cause of the thing of which he has *scientia*."[g] Throughout the sixteenth century, and even among many of the most anti-Aristotelian seventeenth-century authors, this ideal remained firmly in place. Francis Bacon offers the epigram that "to know [*scire*] truly is to know through causes."[h] On these grounds Descartes criticizes Galileo's crowning masterpiece, the *Two New Sciences*: "without having considered the first causes of nature, he [Galileo] has searched only for the reasons beyond various particular effects, and so has built without any foundation."[i] [14]

Hobbes and Locke both follow this traditional conception of the epistemic ideal, but with the crucial difference that neither thinks that we can satisfy this ideal, not even in principle. What drove them to this conclusion was not some sort of generalized skeptical crisis or broad scruples over causality. Rather they came to have doubts of a much more specific kind, regarding Aristotelian essentialism. That doubts over essence should lead to despair over causal understanding may be surprising, but in fact it is a characteristic feature of late scholastic Aristotelianism to think of *causal* explanation almost exclusively in terms of grasping the *essences* of things. Strictly speaking, to be sure, the causal demand applies to all four Aristotelian causes: not just to the "internal" causes, material and formal, but also to the "external" causes, efficient and final. But scholastic philosophy put little weight on efficient causes as explanatorily significant and treated matter as

---

[a] IV.3.29. [b] IV.12.10. [c] *Essay* epistle.
[d] *Post. An.* I.14, 79ᵃ24. [e] *Timaeus* 28a.
[f] Abelard, *Logica "Nostrorum,"* pp. 505–6; Gassendi, *Syntagma* II.I.4.1 (I: 283a)—both quoting Vergil, *Georgics* ii.490.
[g] *Comm. Post. an.* I.4, n. 5. [h] *Novum organum* II.2. [i] To Mersenne, 1638 (II: 380).

simply the enduring background frame over which change occurred. Moreover, despite the famous controversy that surrounds final causes, in truth these too were rarely given much weight in scholastic natural philosophy. The governing program, instead, was to understand a thing's inner nature—its essential qualities and, above all, the substantial form that gave a substance its coherence and enduring character. Thus Henry Oldenburg, first secretary of the Royal Society, blamed substantial forms for having single-handedly "stopped the progress of true philosophy."[a] Even if formal causes were just one of the four scholastic types of causes, they still dominated theoretical inquiry, quite overshadowing material, efficient, and final explanations. Such an attitude endures even in Pierre Gassendi, who betrays his basically scholastic outlook on explanation when he remarks that "not much work needs to be expended on grasping the external causes, which experience itself and the senses reveal at once. The difficulty lies with the internal causes. Those who investigate these are rightly said to be searching deep into the secrets of nature."[b] For Gassendi, this characteristically scholastic program could still be carried forward within the atomistic Epicurean framework, shorn of Aristotelian forms. But when later seventeenth-century authors came to have fundamental doubts about essential explanations, the whole program came to seem a false ideal.[15]

And here is where things get really interesting. Hobbes and Locke have a traditional conception of the epistemic ideal and propose reserving the Latinate English word 'science' to pick this ideal out. If this usage had stood, it would have condemned "science" to a marginal existence, as the sort of knowledge we might imagine in our dreams of the life to come. We could praise the efforts of Newton and others for their practical benefits, but not for having attained the level of science. As Locke puts it, "how far soever humane industry may advance useful and experimental philosophy in physical things, scientifical will still be out of our reach."[c] What in fact happened, however, is that the great seventeenth-century figures whom we now think of as scientists, rather than despairing of success or reconciling themselves to mere practical benefit, articulated a new, post-Aristotelian conception of the epistemic ideal, one that relinquished the goal of causal understanding grounded in a grasp of essences. This is the next stage in our story.

Trading Depth for Precision

The history of modern science's turn away from causal explanation has been told many times and been much disputed, but it can be understood somewhat more clearly in light of the historical background we have been surveying. A key transitional figure is Galileo. In his third letter on sunspots (1612), he writes that "in our speculating we either seek to penetrate the true and internal essence of natural substances, or content ourselves with a knowledge of some of their properties [affezioni]." He goes on to set aside the ideal of grasping essences, judging it impossible for us to have such knowledge, and in its place he extols inquiry into the mere properties of both earthly and celestial phenomena: "location, motion, shape, size, opacity, mutability, generation, and dissolution."[d] On its face, this is not so far from what we have seen Hobbes and Locke later say, but what is

---

[a] *Correspondence* III: 67.   [b] *Syntagma* II.1.4.1 (I: 284a).
[c] *Essay* IV.3.26.   [d] *Discoveries*, p. 123 (*Opere* V: 187–8).

new here is Galileo's enthusiasm for a method that simply lets go of the old ideal. It is not that Galileo denies the desirability of understanding the causes of the phenomena under investigation. Indeed, one can sometimes find him speaking of such knowledge as his goal, and even boldly claiming to have achieved it. What motivates his new attitude, then, is neither metaphysical scruples over causation nor any principled methodological hostility toward causal explanation. Instead, his complaint is that philosophy has pitched its ideal at the wrong level, not because causal explanation is not desirable but because, in many domains, such explanations are not to be reasonably expected. As he remarks of his theory of comets in *The Assayer*:

I should not be condemned for being unable to determine precisely the way in which comets are produced, especially in view of the fact that I have never boasted that I could do this, knowing that they may originate in some manner that is far beyond our power of imagination.[a]

Philosophy is damaged, Galileo thinks, by demanding a goal that, often, cannot be achieved. Instead of pushing ourselves into speculation over causes we cannot understand, we should celebrate our ability to grasp the "properties" of bodies and the rules that govern them.[16]

In effect, Galileo is urging a recalibration of our epistemic ideal. This approach would go on to find its most illustrious proponent in Isaac Newton. In a famous query from the *Opticks* (Latin edition of 1706), he writes:

To tell us that every species of things is endowed with an occult specific quality by which it acts and produces manifest effects is to tell us nothing. But to derive two or three general principles of motion from phenomena, and afterwards to tell us how the properties and actions of all corporeal things follow from those manifest principles, would be a very great step in philosophy, though the causes of those principles were not yet discovered; and therefore I scruple not to propose the principles of motion above mentioned, they being of very general extent, and leave their causes to be found out.[b]

It would be hard to overstate the dramatic shift that this method represents, when contrasted with the prevailing approach of the Aristotelians. Aristotle had begun his *Physics* with the injunction to seek causes:

When the objects of an inquiry, in any department, have principles, causes, or elements, it is through acquaintance with these that knowledge [*eidenai*] and understanding [*epistasthai*] is attained. For we do not think that we know [*gignōskein*] a thing until we are acquainted with its primary causes or first principles, and have carried our analysis as far as its elements.[c]

The contrast is striking. The expectation Aristotle had announced with the very first words of his treatise would set the agenda in natural philosophy for two millennia. With Newton, that agenda collapses. The "two or three general principles" that he offers make no claim to take us all the way to Aristotle's "primary causes or first principles"; instead they merely describe "the phenomena."

Do Galileo and Newton truly renounce the search for causes? Sometimes they talk in this way, but elsewhere they seem to be still searching. Their attitudes become clearer when we think in terms of epistemic ideals. Neither author believes that a grasp of

---

[a] *Discoveries*, p. 258 (*Opere* VI: 281).   [b] *Opticks*, query 31, pp. 401–2.
[c] *Physics* I.1, 184[a]10–14.

causes is to be despised. *Everyone* would ideally wish to have such knowledge, if it were available. Nor is their point merely that such knowledge is not forthcoming any time soon. *Everyone*, even the most doctrinaire scholastics, acknowledges that much. Instead, what is new here is an enthusiasm for a new research project, one that neither resorts to fanciful causal speculation nor wallows in skeptical resignation. In part, what is new is the insight that there is quite a lot of work to be done in framing general principles to account for the phenomena. But of equal importance is the further thought that such work is a worthy end of inquiry. Galileo's *Two New Sciences* (1638), from the end of his career, remarks:

> The present does not seem to me to be an opportune time to enter into the investigation of the causes of the acceleration of natural motion, concerning which various philosophers have produced various opinions . . . Such fantasies, and others like them, would have to be examined and resolved, with little gain. For the present it suffices our Author that we understand him to want us to investigate and demonstrate some attributes [*passioni*] of a motion so accelerated (whatever be the cause of its acceleration).[a]

What Galileo is accomplishing "suffices," as he puts it, for present purposes. This is a normative claim about what human beings ought to be doing—indeed, what their "Author," God, wants them to be doing—by way of understanding the world around them. In the next life our aspirations can be higher. But, for now, in many domains, this is the appropriate normative ideal. Newton speaks in strikingly similar ways in the second edition of the *Principia* (1713). Famously abjuring the temptation to "feign hypotheses," he writes that "it is enough that gravity really exists and acts according to the laws that we have set forth and is sufficient to explain all the motions of the heavenly bodies and of our sea."[b] "It is enough," Newton says, not because there would be no value in learning more, but because in this life, with respect to much of the world around us, this is what we are capable of.[17]

For Newton in particular, an important part of what leads him to regard his approach as worthy of the appellation 'science' is that he sets for himself an alternative epistemic ideal, that of *precision*. In effect, what Newton gives up in speculative depth he compensates for through the precise accuracy of his mathematical methods. His brief preface to the *Principia* gives pride of place to this quest for accuracy: "Anyone who works with less accuracy is a less perfect mechanic, and anyone who could work with perfect accuracy would be the most perfect mechanic of all."[c] As an ideal, this is not wholly new. Plato had put considerable weight on the need for an *epistēmē* to be precise, and Aristotle, too, had spoken of this desideratum in various places. But Aristotle had expected full precision to be possible only in mathematics: "the precise reasoning of mathematics is not to be demanded in all cases, but only in the case of things that have no matter. Therefore its method is not that of natural science."[d] For Newton, in contrast, the ideal is one that can be insisted on across the sciences. If the natural sciences fail to be precise, "the errors belong not to the art, but to its practitioners."[e] Even in the formerly second-rate mechanical sciences, Newton thinks, the highest ideal can be achieved. In place of philosophical depth, he offers the precision of mathematics.

---

[a] Third Day, pp. 158–9 trans. (*Opere* VIII: 202).   [b] *Principia*, General Scholium, p. 943 trans.
[c] *Principia*, Preface, p. 381 trans.   [d] *Metaph.* II.3, 995[a]15–16.   [e] *Principia*, Preface, p. 381 trans.

This transposition of ideals is not coincidental. Scholastic philosophers went deep into identifying the substantial forms and elemental qualities that ground the natural world, but in so doing they made precision impossible, because they had postulated the existence of entities they were unable to characterize in any sort of accurate detail. In this respect one might say that their method in natural philosophy recapitulated their theology, where they likewise postulated ultimate entities (God and angels) about which very little could be said with any precision. For Newton, as a natural philosopher, to postulate such hidden principles is (as above) "to tell us nothing" (though famously, when it came to theology, Newton took a much more indulgent view). Inevitably, there is a trade-off here. We can seek precision about what lies close to the surface; or we can aspire, inchoately, to the murky depths. For us, just as much as for Newton and his scholastic predecessors, the goal of a fully precise account that goes all the way down remains a distant, merely absolute ideal. When it comes to the sort of ideal that might have normative force for our epistemic practices, we have to make a choice between the competing ideals of depth and precision.[18]

By the early eighteenth century it was clear that Galileo and Newton would carry the day, and the term 'science' would eventually come to be associated with the modes of inquiry they pursued rather than with the remote absolute ideal to which Hobbes and Locke had attached it. So, as the story goes, modern science is born. We rightly celebrate this development for the way it saved science from the limitations of speculative metaphysics, and we rightly see Galileo and Newton as its founding figures. If, in comparison, one reads William Gilbert's *De magnete* (1600), it is clear that *something* importantly new is happening. In place of armchair speculation, there is a striking emphasis on observation grounded in experiment. But Gilbert's conclusions in the end still strike a modern reader as something of an embarrassment, because he persists in taking as his ideal an account of the underlying causal explanation for magnetism; and, to satisfy that desideratum, he can do no better than to propose that magnets possess a soul. Similar complaints might be made—and were constantly made—about many stretches of Descartes's scientific writing: even if his explanations are wholly mechanical, still those explanations serve as the vehicle for speculative causal explanation. No wonder that (as we have seen) Descartes found Galileo's method so alien.

Yet, though we may admire the modern renunciation of causal depth and the precision that such a renunciation makes possible, it must be said that it exacts a price. For every Gilbert and Descartes whose work might have been improved as a result of less metaphysical speculation and more attention to precise data, we can cite in contrast a figure whose abjuration of explanation leads to absurdity. Consider Joseph Glanvill. In his *Vanity of Dogmatizing* (1661), he takes up the great question of why anointing a weapon helps cure the wound that the weapon had previously inflicted. Having learned from his peers at the Royal Society how science is to be done, Glanvill magisterially declines to frame hypotheses. "It is enough for me that *de facto* there is such an intercourse between the magnetic unguent and the vulnerated body, and I need not be solicitous of the cause."[a] Here, one may protest, we have neither explanatory depth nor precision. Sometimes the new method was clearly not "enough."[19]

---

[a] *Vanity of Dogmatizing* ch. 21, p. 208.

Even so, carried along by its successes, post-scholastic science made a virtue out of resignation. Locke had thought that the lesson of post-scholastic philosophy was that natural science is impossible, which is to say that, in the domain of nature, human beings simply cannot achieve their epistemic ideal. Events would develop otherwise, however, not by showing Locke to be wrong about what we are capable of, and not by reframing science as a nonideal discipline, but instead by reconceiving the ideal. Inspired by the brilliant examples of Galileo and Newton, natural philosophers by and large embraced a diminution of ambitions. They did so, in general, without any sense of having succumbed to skepticism, or even without any sense of having dethroned science from its traditional status as the ultimate goal of inquiry. By the time of David Hume's *Treatise of Human Nature* (1739), 'science' and 'knowledge' had so parted ways that, even while Hume judges knowledge to be largely unattainable, he takes science as the governing ambition of the whole project: "In pretending therefore to explain the principles of human nature, we in effect propose a complete system of the sciences, built on a foundation almost entirely new, and the only one upon which they can stand with any security."[a] Within this new framework science could carry on, radically transformed from the *epistēmē* of Aristotle or the *scientia* of the scholastics but still heir to those notions, inasmuch as science remained the normative goal of inquiry, the epistemic ideal to which human beings might aspire. So the scientific revolution begins from a revolution in our cognitive expectations.[20]

Epistemology in the Ascendant

If this was to be the fate of science, then where does it leave philosophy? Next week we will consider how, by the end of the seventeenth century, philosophers began to reconceptualize knowledge in response to a rising interest in probability. But even before looking into the changing fortunes of that concept, we are in a position here to consider the fate of epistemology in the modern era. The rise of modern science stripped philosophy of a large part of its traditional core, those fields once known as *natural philosophy* but now rechristened as *science*. Shorn of the new sciences, philosophy faced a choice. On the one hand, it could turn its back on the new scientific ideals, or at least insist on its autonomy in relation to science. In that case philosophy might continue its pursuit of deep causal explanations, not as a chapter of science but as metaphysics. Leibniz is the shining early example of this sort of approach, and his efforts at a metaphysics that could transcend natural philosophy would shape German philosophy through Kant and beyond. On the other hand, philosophy might embrace the new scientific conception of the epistemic ideal, and hence begin to assume a similar modesty regarding conjectural causal explanations. The early champion of this approach, which sets itself against the speculative metaphysics of the scholastics, was Locke. In one of his most familiar passages, he pronounced it "ambition enough to be employed as an under-labourer in clearing ground a little, and removing some of the rubbish that lies in the way to knowledge." Again, it is "enough" to do this, not because more would not be better, but because this is the most we should suppose possible. The ambition to do

---

[a] *Treatise*, Introduction, p. xvi. On Hume's skepticism, see Lecture Six.

more has made philosophy hitherto, in Locke's biting words, "the sanctuary of vanity and ignorance."[a]

With this dilemma in mind, we can return to the question with which I began this lecture. Why is it that epistemology—after so many centuries of not being a discrete subject at all—has now become a foundational subject within philosophy? The answer is that we have followed Locke's path through the dilemma, inasmuch as philosophers in the Anglo-American tradition have largely deferred to science on questions of what the world is like and why. Thus the dominant philosophical tendency for three hundred years, at least in the English language, has been to concentrate on those subjects that once comprised logic in its broad traditional sense: the study of knowledge, language, and patterns of inference. In place of explanatory depth, philosophy has come to prize, above all else, precision. As the young Wittgenstein wrote, "[t]he aim of philosophy is the logical clarification of thoughts . . . Philosophy should take the thoughts that are otherwise cloudy and blurred, as it were, and make them clear, giving them sharp boundaries."[b] Once subservient to theology—the reigning medieval project of under-standing the ultimate reasons why—modern philosophy has made itself handmaid, underlaborer, actuarial clerk to the scientist. As Voltaire, under the sway of the new English method, succinctly put it, "[p]hilosophy consists in stopping when the torch of science fails us."[c] So it has been, more or less, through Hume and Whewell, Mill and Moore, Davidson, Dummett, and Quine.

Except that, in recent years, there have been signs of change. Although long accus-tomed to the diminished Newtonian ideal of precision over explanatory force, philo-sophers of the past several decades have been increasingly unwilling to embrace their supporting role in that enterprise. Wittgenstein himself exemplifies one path of resist-ance, when in his later works he calls into question his youthful aspirations to logical precision: "we eliminate misunderstandings by making our expressions more exact; but now it can look as if we are moving towards a particular state, a state of complete exactness; and as if this were the real goal of our investigation."[d] The main line of Anglo-American development, however, has been not to challenge the ambition of scientific precision, but rather to disavow the metaphysical resignation of earlier gener-ations. And so in recent years there has been a recrudescence of speculative metaphysics, which has again become the central philosophical topic of our day. In keeping with this trend, historians of philosophy have increasingly found themselves drawn not to Locke and Hume, but to the metaphysically more adventuresome work of Spinoza and Leibniz, and even to the medieval metaphysics that Hume had long ago consigned to the flames.

Predictably, as philosophers have returned to their speculative enthusiasms of old, scientists have begun to complain in an increasingly acerbic voice. Stephen Hawking declares that "philosophy is dead."[e] Freeman Dyson, reviewing a book on that most ambitiously philosophical question of all—*Why is there something rather than nothing?*—calls philosophy today "a toothless relic of past glories."[f] Why such belligerence? For as long as philosophy played its subsidiary role, content to serve as handmaid to the

---

[a] *Essay* epistle, p. 10.   [b] *Tractatus* 4.112.
[c] *Philosophical Dictionary*, "Soul," VI: 168.   [d] *Philosophical Investigations* I.91.
[e] Hawking and Mlodinow, *Grand Design*, p. 5.   [f] "What Can You Really Know?"

restrained ideals of modern science, the scientists have been willing to tolerate the philosopher's ancient pretensions to wisdom. But if the philosophers are not going to abide by the old Newtonian code of resignation—if they are going to frame hypotheses about reality in all its depths—then it becomes necessary for the real lovers of wisdom, with their laboratories and government grants, to speak out against these pretenders. The philosopher, having given birth to and fostered the various sciences, is now sent off into the woods to die, yielding her lectureship and office space to worthier academic enterprises.

But perhaps we need not rush quite yet to throw up barricades between the arts quad and the science towers. The history of philosophy has its consolations, one of which is a vivid awareness of the way in which, in one form or another, this power struggle between science and philosophy is nothing new. Going back to antiquity, champions of an austerely empirical conception of inquiry have battled against proponents of a speculative rationalism. So it was between Plato and his unspeakable rivals, the Presocratic atomists; so it was between Newton and Leibniz. At issue, I have been arguing, is the nature of our epistemic ideals. What sorts of demands do we make of ourselves as we investigate the world around us? An answer to this question depends in turn on still deeper puzzles about what this world is like. If we suppose that all there is is particles in motion, subject to forces of various sorts, then the great task of speculative inquiry must be to measure those forces as accurately as possible. But what if there is more to the world than this? What if we live in a world with beings whose agency runs beyond anything hitherto imagined by science? What if these beings are sensitive to values that cannot be weighed in any laboratory? Who, then, will measure these things, and how much precision may we demand? Of course, these glimmers of transcendence are perhaps just illusions, destined to be assimilated to the ever-growing reductive empire of science. Yet who will decide when that reduction has succeeded? How will we know?[21]

Lecture Two

Evident Certainties

Last week I described the project of an idealized epistemology, focused not on the dividing line between what is and what is not knowledge, but on the ideal that agents like us might hope to achieve in a world like this. Following the course of this project, from Aristotle up to the seventeenth century, I described how modern science articulated its own epistemic ideal, one that parted ways in crucial respects with the traditional concerns of philosophy. Deferring to that scientific ideal, philosophers in modern times have tended to conceive of their discipline as essentially actuarial, balancing the ledgers as science rushes onward. On this new conception of philosophy, epistemology became newly ascendant.

But what exactly is epistemology? As fundamental to philosophy as this subject has become, it is surprisingly unclear what it is centrally about. Today I try to explain how our modern conception of epistemology grew out of the decline of scholasticism.

Lexicology

For the past half-century, epistemology has primarily aimed at conceptual analysis, first and foremost the analysis of *knowledge* itself. Its aim is conceptual analysis, but in truth its principal concern has often seemed linguistic: under what conditions is it true to say, in English, that someone knows something? Of course, one is free to choose between the formal and the material mode of exposition, but the modern field of epistemology in particular has often seemed to labor under the formal yoke, wishing to understand the structure of our central epistemic concepts but settling for the conventions of our ordinary epistemic vocabulary. Something about epistemology as it is currently conceived of seems to lure its practitioners into the trap of lexicology.

Epistemology is prone to lexicology because it lacks other sorts of stable grounds on which to build. Philosophers of mind do not belabor the ordinary English meaning of 'consciousness' but rather begin by disambiguating, and thereafter make no fuss over the word itself. It is quite unclear, in contrast, whether 'know' is similarly ambiguous. Theories of causation, likewise, do not care about the word 'cause'—they take as their starting point various paradigm cases and try to make those come out right. It is not so clear, however, what counts as a paradigm of knowledge, inasmuch as the most familiar cases, such as *2 + 2 = 4* and *this is a hand*, are notoriously problematic and heterodox in character. Unable to gain traction in these sorts of familiar ways, and yet looking for the boundaries that demarcate the domain of knowledge, epistemology tends toward lexicology. Few want such an outcome, but the modern history of the subject repeatedly displays this pattern, and it is unclear what alternative there is.

In all of this, epistemology suffers from an unfamiliarity with its history. In taking as its central mission the carving of boundaries for knowledge, epistemology cuts itself off from the main ways in which past philosophers have conceived of the field. A better understanding of this history and of its orientation toward the epistemic ideal would offer at least some stable ground from which epistemologists might escape from mere lexicology. So I argued last week. But this history also points the way toward something more. For, as we will see today, there are reasons why epistemology came to be concerned more with defining the scope of knowledge than with the epistemic ideal. Indeed, in the end, we will see that these reasons are not just a matter of historical accident but in fact help to vindicate, at least in part, our modern preoccupation with boundary conditions.

Still, to understand all this properly, one needs to see how the history goes. Last week, the main case study was Aristotle, and I argued that the *Posterior Analytics'* theory of *epistēmē* is not quite science, not quite understanding, and certainly not knowledge. What it is, instead, is an account of our epistemic ideal. This week I begin with Descartes and argue that he, too, should be read as offering not a theory of knowledge but an idealized epistemology, with this dramatic difference: that certainty is now central to the epistemic ideal. Not that Descartes marks the start of this tradition; on the contrary, he comes near its end. Indeed, it is the failure of his approach that leads to the first manifestations of epistemology in something like its modern sense. The crucial developments are the rejection of certainty as a normative epistemic ideal and a growing tolerance for the merely probable. With this there emerges a new-found interest in the question of just how much probability is good enough. Good enough, that is, to justify us in our beliefs and thereby to give us knowledge.[1]

Descartes's Ideal Theory

One hardly needs the background story of last week's lecture to see that Descartes takes *scientia* as the goal of inquiry and conceives of it in a way that is much indebted to the Aristotelian framework for *epistēmē*. To be sure, he rejects large swaths of what one finds in the *Posterior Analytics*, such as the syllogism and the restriction to universal premises, to say nothing of his rejection of the inner essences that ground Aristotelian explanation. But Descartes holds on to the general framework of an epistemic ideal at which theoretical inquiry should aim. One can find this assumption in place from his very earliest work. According to Rule 2 of his *Rules for the Direction of the Mind*, "we should attend only to those objects of which our minds seem capable of having certain and indubitable cognition."[a] He then immediately remarks, in discussing this rule: "All *scientia* is certain and evident cognition." A few lines below, he adds this: "So, in accordance with this Rule, we reject all such merely probable cognitions and resolve to believe only what is perfectly cognized and what cannot be doubted." These passages

---

[a] *Rules* 2 (X: 362).

suggest that *scientia* is the kind of cognition that is certain, evident, and indubitable. He goes on in this same section to characterize this and other rules as ones that "will help us ascend to the peak of human cognition."[a] It seems, then, that *scientia* is perfect cognition—or at least as perfect as a human being can achieve.

This impression receives confirmation at the start of the *Meditations*, when Descartes makes this famous pronouncement: "I realized it was necessary, once in the course of my life, to demolish everything completely and start again right from the foundations *if I ever wanted to establish anything in the sciences that was stable and likely to last*."[b] The italicized words announce Descartes's goal: attaining stable and lasting results in the sciences. Of course he does not here have in mind "the sciences" in our modern sense of the term; he is referring instead to the acquisition of *scientia*, and his ambition is to show how we can acquire *scientia* even in the hitherto murky domain of God and soul. His view, indeed, turns out to be that *scientia* is possible especially in these domains. The standard he holds himself to is remarkably high. In a letter to his disciple Regius written in May 1640, just after he had completed the *Meditations*, Descartes distinguishes between *scientia* and the conviction (*persuasio*) possessed by someone who cannot help but assent to the clear and distinct perception of some self-evident truth. "I distinguish the two as follows: there is [mere] conviction when there remains some reason that could lead us to doubt; *scientia* is conviction based on a reason so strong that it can never be shaken by any stronger reason."[c] Conviction is a state in which one cannot refrain from assenting to a proposition—in a purely subjective sense, the proposition is indubitable. Presumably, such conviction will be based on *some* reason. But it will not count as *scientia* unless it is based on *unshakable* reasons. This would seem to be indubitability in a stronger sense: it is not just that one is not presently able to doubt the proposition, but that there is no way in which one will ever be able to doubt the proposition, given the reasons one has for it. As he puts it in the Second Replies, "no cognition that can be rendered doubtful seems fit to be called *scientia*."[d]

These passages point toward the two best known characteristics of Descartes's conception of *scientia*: its emphasis on *certainty* and its *foundationalism*. The theory is foundationalist in the sense that, for a belief to count as *scientia*, its truth must either be certain in its own right or else be grounded in something else that is certain in its own right. What exactly it means for a belief to be certain is one of the central issues to be explored today. Setting that issue aside for the time being, we should notice a third feature of Descartes's account: its *internalism*, which is to say that the possession of certain, foundationally structured beliefs does not yield *scientia* unless the believer grasps the reasons that show beyond doubt the truth of the beliefs. This last feature is particularly clear in the following passage, where the requisite adequacy of reasons gets expressed in interpersonal terms.

Whenever two persons make opposite judgments about the same thing, it is certain that at least one of them is deceived, and it seems that neither has *scientia*. For if the reasoning of one of them were certain and evident, he would be able to lay it before the other in such a way as eventually to convince the other's intellect as well.[e]

---

[a] *Rules* 2 (X: 364).   [b] *Med.* 1 (VII: 17), emphasis added.
[c] III: 65.   [d] VII: 141.   [e] *Rules* 2 (X: 363).

As before, the evidentness that Descartes requires for *scientia* must be not just subject-ively persuasive, but objectively good, one test of which is whether these reasons would be able "eventually to convince" others. What we can now also say is that those reasons must be possessed by the agent—they must be *internal* to her. It is not enough that she be able to acquire reasons in principle, or even that she be *able* to understand them *if* they were shown to her. Instead, she must *have in hand* her reasoning to such a degree that, when she finds herself locked in disagreement, she can "lay it before the other" and thus dissolve the conflict. Descartes regularly expresses the utmost confidence that his views will pass just this test, once they are understood. Thus he tells his disciple Regius: "I consider my opinions to be so certain and evident that whoever rightly understands them will have no occasion to dispute them."[a]

Unlike Aristotle, Descartes is not ordinarily read as advancing a theory of science. Instead, though with no more plausibility, he is routinely thought to be advancing a theory of knowledge, and hence made into the archetypical proponent of foundation-alism, certainty, and internalism in epistemology. All of this is true enough, but only with respect to Descartes's ideal theory. As for what is commonly said about his theory of knowledge, most of it is entirely wrong. If our subject is 'knowledge' as that word is used today, then Descartes is neither a foundationalist nor an internalist, not even a strict advocate of certainty. Indeed, if epistemology is conceived of in its usual modern guise, then Descartes cannot be said to have a theory of knowledge at all. What he has is an idealized epistemology, a theory of *scientia*.

Two sorts of considerations make this quite clear. First, the theory is so demanding that virtually no one other than Descartes and his followers can be said to have achieved *scientia*. Descartes in fact claims that, up until his time, the only *scientia* possessed by anyone has been mathematical *scientia*. For instance, in explaining why we should attend only to what we can cognize with certainty, he remarks that, "if my reckoning is correct, out of all the sciences so far devised, we are restricted to just arithmetic and geometry if we stick to this Rule."[b] Years later, in *The Search for Truth*, he speaks of "the slight progress we have made in the sciences whose first principles are certain and known to all" and then adds:

In the other sciences, whose principles are obscure and uncertain, those who are willing to state their view honestly must admit that, for all the time they have spent reading many a vast tome, they have ended up realizing that they have *scientia* of nothing and have learned nothing.[c]

Of course, Descartes thinks that he himself has managed to push the bounds of *scientia* quite a bit farther. But did he really believe that, up until the middle of the seventeenth century, no one had *knowledge* of anything, except for a few claims in mathematics? A skeptic might be happy with this result, but Descartes was no skeptic, or so it is always supposed.

In fact Descartes goes even farther. He famously holds that "the certainty and truth of all *scientia* depends on the one cognition of the true God, to such an extent that I was incapable of perfect *scientia* about anything else until I recognized him."[d] If *scientia* were knowledge, then this would entail that the atheist lacks knowledge, as, apparently,

---

[a] Letter of July 1645 (IV: 248).   [b] *Rules* 2 (X: 363).
[c] *Search for Truth* (X: 526).   [d] *Med.* 5 (VII: 71).

would anyone who believes in the wrong God. Thus, in the Second Replies, in a passage quoted in part already, he remarks: "I do not dispute that an atheist can clearly *cognize* that the three angles of a triangle are equal to two right angles. I maintain only that his cognition is not true *scientia*, since no cognition that can be rendered doubtful seems fit to be called *scientia*."[a] Even in geometry, then, *scientia* is available only to someone who has the right religious beliefs and who uses those religious beliefs in just the right way to ground that *scientia*. All things considered, it looks doubtful that anyone other than Descartes (and his most devoted followers) has ever had *scientia* about anything. If we think of Cartesian *scientia* as knowledge, then we should think of Descartes as a fairly radical kind of skeptic. Insofar as that result seems obviously wrong, we should stop thinking of *scientia* as knowledge.

The second reason for denying that Cartesian *scientia* is knowledge is that Descartes denies that *scientia* should regulate belief. As observed last week, one of the reasons for caring about boundary conditions in epistemology is that what we know seems closely tied to what we ought to believe. For Descartes, however, the boundaries of *scientia* lie very far from the boundaries that should delimit belief. In the First Meditation he remarks that his habitual opinions "are doubtful in a way, but are nevertheless highly probable, and are such that it is much more reasonable to believe than to deny them."[b] Admittedly, this passage compares only belief and denial: it does not say that it is more reasonable to believe than to suspend judgment. But a passage from the Synopsis to the *Meditations* goes farther, remarking that "the great benefit of these arguments is not, in my view, that they prove what they establish—namely, that there really is a world, that human beings have bodies, and so on—things that no sane person has ever seriously doubted."[c] It would be insane to doubt these matters; yet it is also the case, according to Descartes, that no one has ever had a *scientia* of these things. Apparently, then, our lack of *scientia* concerning some proposition has no direct relation to whether we ought to believe it. This is quite alien to our modern conception of knowledge.

This aspect of Descartes's account is closely related to the first aspect. The skeptics of old had maintained that we ought to withhold assent. If we must act, we should act only *as if* we have beliefs about the world. Because Descartes sees no such connection between *scientia* and belief, his form of skepticism (if it should be called that at all) is of a purely theoretical sort. Hardly anyone has *scientia*, but this makes no real difference to anyone's life. For Descartes as a philosopher and scientist, the rarity of *scientia* is a depressing result, and one that he wants to change. But he has no expectation that his methods will lead everyone to acquire *scientia*, and no real interest in seeing that happen. Indeed, the preface to the *Meditations* explains that he wrote in Latin rather than in French "lest weaker intellects might believe that they too ought to set out on this path."[d] Now, we have seen Descartes say that those of us who seek the truth should believe only what we can grasp with certainty. But this advice applies strictly to those who are pursuing *scientia*. Those who have no interest in that project, or lack the ability to pursue it, or simply have not yet found the time to do so are certainly not supposed to give up all their beliefs. That, as Descartes says, would be insanity. Even in the absence of *scientia*, ordinary folk *ought* to go on believing what they do. Whether such beliefs

---

[a] Second Replies (VII: 141).   [b] *Med.* 1 (VII: 22).
[c] *Med.* synopsis (VII: 15–16).   [d] *Med.* preface (VII: 7).

should count as knowledge, in some more ordinary sense of the word, is not something that Descartes shows any interest in.[2]

The Ideal of Certainty

Our normative epistemic ideal, says Descartes, encompasses foundationalism, internalism, and certainty. All three of these notions have a long history, which might be profitably explored. But the story that I want to tell, of how an idealized epistemology began to concern itself with boundary marking, requires attending especially to the role of certainty.

Familiar as the demand for certainty is in epistemology, its historical roots are not at all easy to establish. Aristotle, surprisingly enough, says nothing about it in the *Posterior Analytics*. Yet if one jumps ahead to later medieval commentaries, certainty is treated as if it were an expectation rooted in the text itself. At the start of Albert the Great's commentary, for instance, he declares:

A human being ought to fill his soul not with what is [merely] plausible [*probabile*] and conjectural [*opinabile*], because they do not yield a stable [*stans*] disposition in the soul, but with things that are demonstrable and certain, which render the intellect certain and stable, because such things are themselves certain and eternally stable.[a]

Thomas Aquinas inserts the certainty requirement directly into his gloss on Aristotle's canonical definition of *epistēmē*;[b] and, when John Duns Scotus defines *scientia*, the certainty requirement appears as a fourth condition added on to the properly Aristotelian requirements that its object be (1) a necessary truth that is (2) evident through some prior cause that (3) entails its conclusion syllogistically.[c] All these authors explicitly link the certainty requirement with the notion that to achieve *scientia* is to achieve cognitive perfection.[3]

So where, if not from Aristotle, does the demand for certainty arise? Given my claim that premodern epistemology is largely idealized, and given how natural it is to build certainty into such an ideal, it should be no surprise that the demand for certainty arises all over the place. Without making any claim to completeness, let me here briefly describe three streams of influence. A first one is the Stoic tradition of distinguishing between mere impressions and the sort of cognition (*katalēpsis*) that is required for *epistēmē*, a distinction Zeno memorably pictured as the difference between an open hand and a closed fist. To have *epistēmē* is to have something beyond *katalēpsis*, something possible only for the wise man. It is to have a closed fist with the other hand wrapped around it and squeezing it tight. This requires a grasp of things that is "secure and firm and unchangeable by reason."[d] Moving into the Latin tradition, Cicero in his *Academica* first describes the Stoic criterion and then strategically deploys it on behalf of the Academic skeptic. A similar criterion appears in Augustine, who, despite writing *Contra academicos*, likewise starts from a position quite favorable to Academic skepticism:

---

[a] *Comm. Post. an.* I.1.1 (ed. Jammy, I: 514a).
[b] *Comm. Post. an.* I.4 n. 5, glossing *Post. an.* I.2, 71^{b}9–12, for which see Lecture One, p. 6.
[c] *Ordinatio* prol. part 4 qq. 1–2 (Vatican edn. I, n. 208).
[d] Sextus Empiricus, *Against the Logicians* I.153 (Loeb vol. 2).

I do not call anything *scientia* where the person who professes it is sometimes mistaken. *Scientia* does not consist merely in the matters that are apprehended. Instead, it consists in the fact that they are apprehended in such a way that nobody should be in error about it or vacillate when pressed by any opponents.[a]

That this notion comes from the Stoics is made clear when Augustine goes on to invoke "certain philosophers" who think that only the wise man has *scientia*.[4]

A second source for the emphasis on certainty in epistemology is the Alexandrian tradition of late antiquity. Last week we saw Ptolemy, near the head of that tradition, dismiss two thirds of theoretical philosophy as being "guesswork rather than know-ledge" and hold out only mathematics—which included astronomy—as providing "sure and unshakable knowledge to its devotees."[b] In that passage Ptolemy uses the phrase *katalēpsis epistēmonikē*, which points back to Stoicism; but the very different context of these remarks at the start of his famous *Almagest* warrants treating this passage as a distinct line of influence on later discussions of certainty. And it would indeed be influential, even many centuries later. The remark from Albert the Great quoted a moment ago, for instance, is explicitly presented as a gloss on this remark of Ptolemy's. But, whereas for Ptolemy the lesson is that only the mathematical sciences yield certainty, Albert expands this line of thought to embrace any conclusion that can be produced through Aristotle's demonstrative method. Albert thus looks not to mathem-atics for certainty but to the *Posterior Analytics*, concluding that, of the various branches of logic, "this alone is nobler and more excellent than the others on account of the certitude of its proofs."[c] In so doing, Albert is following later Alexandrian traditions, which embraced the Stoic–Ptolemaic quest for certainty but transposed into an Aristo-telian context. Consider the first surviving commentary on the *Posterior Analytics*—that of Philoponus, from the early sixth century—the very first words of which are that "this [subject] is the culmination [*telos*] of the study of logic."[d] A little later he adds: "Philosophers need demonstration as an instrument [*organon*] for the correct pursuit [*katorthōsis*] of the parts of philosophy . . . It is by the standard [*kanōn*] of demonstration that the philosopher distinguishes true from false in a theory and good from bad in action."[e] Later in that same Alexandrian tradition, Elias would distinguish the branch of philosophy dealt with in the *Posterior Analytics* from the other parts of philosophy by the fact that only it is comprised of "propositions that are true in all respects."[f] By this point, the sort of certainty that had seemed altogether impossible to the skeptics and that the Stoics had reserved for the wise man and Ptolemy for mathematics has come to be identified as the province of Aristotelian demonstration.

This late Alexandrian tradition was taken up directly into the foundations of early Arabic philosophy, beginning in the ninth century, and thus we arrive at a third stream of influence behind the later epistemic ideal of certainty. Al-Kindī, the fountainhead of Arabic philosophy, took Ptolemy's *Almagest* as his exemplar and sought to develop a philosophy that would live up to the standards of certainty exhibited by mathematics. Subsequently the association between knowledge and certainty would become virtually

---

[a] *Contra academicos* I.7.19.   [b] *Almagest* I.1 (p. 36 trans.); see Lecture One, p. 7.
[c] *Comm. Post. an.* I.1.1 (ed. Jammy, I: 514a).
[d] *Comm. Post. an.* (Commentaria in Aristotelem Graeca [= CAG XIII.3): 1.5; p. 15 trans. McKirahan.
[e] 2.24–3.1; p. 16 trans.   [f] *Comm. Categorias* proem (CAG XVIII): 117.2–3.

inevitable within the Arabic tradition, because Abū Bishr Mattā's standard tenth-century Arabic translation of the *Posterior Analytics* employs 'certainty' (*yaqīn*) quite liberally throughout the text, in places where Aristotle speaks simply of knowledge ('*ilm*) or demonstration (*burhān*). Al-Fārābī puts particular weight on the notion of certainty, describing "certain philosophy" as the culmination of a process that gets an imperfect start in sophistical and dialectical reasoning.[a] In his logical works he embraces the Alexandrian picture of the *Posterior Analytics* as the sole basis for certitude, and hence as the culmination of all reasoning. This picture subsequently runs through all of later Islamic thought. According to al-Ghazālī, for instance, "true demonstration is what provides necessary, perpetual and eternal certainty that cannot change."[b] [5]

Given how entrenched the notion of certainty had become in the later Middle Ages in such a wide range of places, it is no wonder that this notion gets taken for granted by Albert the Great and others, as an unquestioned element in their conception of the epistemic ideal. No wonder, either, that Descartes takes it to be perfectly obvious that *scientia* requires certainty. Taking up the torch of Ptolemy—though, to be sure, not under Ptolemy's now discredited name—he reconsiders the question of where outside mathematics certainty may possibly be found. Rejecting the Aristotelian tradition that ran from Alexandria through Baghdad and on to Paris, Descartes boldly replaces the *Posterior Analytics* with his own approach. The method changes, but the epistemic ideal remains the same.

Here, then, are the bare outlines of how the ideal of certainty has made its way across the centuries. But now, with all this history on display, a question I have hitherto avoided becomes inescapable. What exactly is this certainty that is so sought after? The question is not easy to answer. If we think of the English word and its Latin origins, we can say that 'certainty' has at its core the ideas of *fixedness* and *stability*. Applied to the case of belief, we can understand such stability to hold with respect to either the belief's subject or its object. Subjectively speaking, certainty requires a confidence so stable as not to admit of any doubt on the believer's part. Call this *indubitability*. Objectively speaking, certainty requires that the thing believed be sufficiently fixed in its existence as to be a stable object of knowledge. Call this *necessity*. Aristotle had insisted on this sort of object-side certainty, but what characterizes later philosophy is the expectation of a certainty that encompasses both of these components. In Albert the Great, for instance, as quoted above, the proper objects of *scientia* "render the intellect certain and stable," and do so "because such things are themselves certain and eternally stable." Within this framework, the great question, then, arises of how to tie these subjective and objective components together into a single, overarching expectation. Mere subjective confidence might rightly be described as a kind of certainty, but it hardly captures the ideal. Thus John Buridan begins his account of what it means to describe *scientia* as certain by insisting that certainty requires truth. "No one is certain of something through a false opinion, however firmly he may adhere to it."[c] But of course it would hardly count as ideal just to stumble upon a necessary truth and doggedly insist on it. Hence Albert says that certainty on the subject side arises "because" of certainty on the object side. This

---

[a] See e.g. his *Book of Letters* (*Kitāb al-ḥurūf*), n. 108 etc. (see Khalidi, *Medieval Islamic Philosophical Writings*, pp. 1 ff.).
[b] *Miʿyār al-ʿilm* (McGinnis and Reisman, *Classical Arabic Philosophy*, p. 239).
[c] *Quaest. meta.* I.3.

requires some sort of method of discovery that reliably takes us back and forth between truths in the world and belief in those truths: a bridge between objective and subjective certainty. Aristotle offers one such method, Descartes another. In each case, the ideal is a certainty that is more than merely subjective or objective, and indeed more than just the simple conjunction of the two. What we want is to have indubitable beliefs that are grounded in the truth in a way that makes those beliefs incapable of going wrong. Call this *infallible certainty*.[6]

Over and over in the weeks ahead such infallibility will appear as a perennial ideal, pursued but never attained. Part of what made its attainment particularly difficult is the abiding notion that such certainty, if it is to count as genuine, must be achieved at the ideal limit. Nicholas of Autrecourt, in the fourteenth century, makes this quite explicit: "the certainty of evidentness has no degrees. Thus, if there are two conclusions, and we are evidently certain of each, then we are no more certain of one than of the other."[a] Three centuries later, Thomas Hobbes would similarly conclude that "the certainty of all *scientiae* is equal, for otherwise they would not be *scientiae*, since to have *scientia* does not admit of more and less."[b] Such absolutism is natural enough, given certainty's role as a cognitive ideal. But, given that no one could reasonably suppose that we often reach that ideal, we should also expect authors to harp on such absolute certainty only when their aims are destructive. Thus Hobbes's remark comes at the start of a tract devoted to attacking the geometers of his day for their incompetence. And Autrecourt stresses that certainty is all or nothing along the way toward showing that his opponent grasps almost nothing with certainty.[7]

Where doubts arise over the attainability of an epistemic ideal, the natural response within the idealized framework is to reduce normative expectations. This is indeed what one finds time and again throughout the history of philosophy, even while one continues to find other authors—and sometimes the very same author—pursuing that same epistemic dream. Consider again Descartes. He claims quite explicitly that we have infallible certainty when we restrict ourselves to assenting to what we clearly and distinctly perceive; in such cases "it clearly cannot happen that I err."[c] But Mersenne pushes him, in the Second Set of Objections, on whether the certainty of clear and distinct perceptions can itself be supported by a noncircular certain argument. Without that, the objection charges, we can have "no degree of certainty."[d] Descartes responds, predictably, by invoking divine goodness, but he sees that more is needed, and so his next step is to shift the argument from infallibility to indubitability, "a conviction so firm that it can in no way be removed, and such a conviction is clearly the same as the most perfect certainty."[e] Has Descartes made a concession or has he not? The inability to doubt would seem to fall a long way short of the inability to be wrong, yet Descartes carries on as if he has delivered exactly the sort of perfect certainty that he promised, and subsequent works continue to make assertions of infallibility. Indeed, one might say that the very essence of his method of radical doubt is to help us distinguish the merely indubitable from the truly infallible and reframe our beliefs accordingly. Lecture Five will return to consider exactly why Descartes is unable to achieve that goal;

---

[a] Second letter to Bernard, n. 6.   [b] *De principiis et ratiocinatione geometrarum*, p. 2.
[c] *Med.* 4 (VII: 62); see also e.g. *Med.* 3 (VII: 35), Second Replies (VII: 144), *Principles* I.43.
[d] Second Objections (VII: 126).   [e] Second Replies (VII: 145).

but for now the point is just that infallibility is an ideal he can neither attain nor bring himself to abandon.

Consider Galileo, too. As a young man, he had lectured on the *Posterior Analytics*, and throughout his career he stressed the importance of achieving certainty. In a letter from near the end of his life addressed to an old Aristotelian rival, he praises the Aristotelian method of logic for providing "sureness of demonstration" and remarks: "up to this point I am a Peripatetic."[a] In his battles over the Copernican theory of the solar system, he embraces a principle he found in Augustine, to the effect that, where human inquiry is uncertain, we should follow biblical authority in reshaping it but, where human inquiry achieves certainty, we should use those certain results as a guide to interpreting the Bible. Hence his goal in astronomy has to be nothing less than a *demonstration* of the heliocentric model. Otherwise the Bible would trump. But just how much certainty can we expect? At the end of the first day of his *Dialogue concerning the Two Great World Systems* (1632), Galileo has Salviati make a remarkable speech that compares our epistemic perfection to God's. How well we fair in such a comparison depends, Salviati says, on whether we think about it extensively or intensively. Extensively, human beings do poorly, because there are infinitely many things that God understands, only a very few of which we understand. But intensively—that is, with respect to the certainty with which we can grasp a single proposition—our minds can be equal in perfection to God's. As Salviati puts it, "with regard to those few propositions that the human intellect does understand, I believe that its knowledge equals the divine in objective certainty, for here it succeeds in understanding necessity, beyond which there can be no greater sureness."[b]

"Very bold and daring," Galileo has Simplicio reply. Bold enough that, when the church began proceedings against Galileo a year later, this claim was considered among his suspicious teachings.

This distinction between two dimensions of the epistemic ideal, intensive and extensive, fits well with the diminished expectations we saw Galileo endorse last week: his willingness to relax the causal requirement in order to permit a mode of inquiry that describes the features of a given physical phenomenon, without entering into speculation about why or how things work as they do.[c] Leaving such extensive perfection to the metaphysician, Galileo contents himself with aiming at intensive perfection in a few well-defined areas of natural philosophy. The ambition of God-like certainty, he makes clear, can be humanly achieved only in one *scientia*—that of mathematics. Still, with respect to his insistence on such certainty as a normative ideal of epistemic inquiry, Galileo falls into line with a tradition we have seen stretch back to the Stoics and Ptolemy, through the schools of Alexandria, Baghdad, and Paris. Indeed, he and Descartes might be viewed as the last great champions of that tradition.[8]

At the end of today's lecture I will make a suggestion about why the ideal of infallible certainty has such a persistent hold on us, even while its attainability seems so obviously doubtful. But first we should consider what comes next in our story: how the idealized expectation of infallible certainty gave way to greater tolerance for mere probability, which led ultimately to a new concern with finding the epistemic boundaries of permissible belief.

---

[a] To Liceti in 1640 (*Opere* XVIII: 248).   [b] *Dialogue*, first day (p. 118 trans.; *Opere* VII: 128–9).
[c] See Lecture One, pp. 14–16.

Degrees of Evidentness

Conventional wisdom has it that the era of Descartes and Galileo suffered from a strange sort of epistemic malady, a *crise pyrrhonienne*. This notion is unfortunate in various respects: it gives too much weight to the influence of ancient skepticism; it exaggerates the degree to which there was anything approaching a skeptical "crisis" at the time; and it distorts the motivation of Descartes and others, as if their main project were the refutation of skepticism. Yet it is clear enough that the sixteenth and seventeenth centuries display a growing concern over whether the traditional epistemic ideal of certainty is achievable. Sometimes these doubts amount to an attack on philosophy itself—which means, for that time, also an attack on science itself. Of the greatest interest here, however, are those who responded to these currents by reframing the epistemic ideal around probability rather than around certainty.[9]

A great deal has been written about the rise of interest in probabilistic reasoning in seventeenth-century thought, but it is not easy to say exactly what is new here. What is most clearly new is a sudden flourishing of mathematical treatments of probability, running from the correspondence of Pascal and Fermat to the work of Christiaan Huygens and on to Jacob Bernoulli at the end of the century. The appearance of these and other works at this time coincides with a general rise in the professionalization and sophistication of mathematics, but it also reflects a wider cultural interest in the relationship between probability and certainty. Whereas, for centuries, the Aristotelian tradition had privileged an infallible grasp of necessary truth as the hallmark of *scientia*, the waning of scholasticism gave rise to an increasing interest in the contingent and the merely probable. One sees this in a wide array of domains, including law, medicine, ethics, religion, economics, and natural philosophy.[10]

To understand these events in their proper historical context, one needs to go back well before the seventeenth century. We have seen how medieval authors, both Latin and Arabic, took for granted that certainty is a key part of the epistemic ideal. They did so with little explicit encouragement from Aristotle. On the contrary, Aristotle had famously warned, near the start of the *Nicomachean Ethics*, that one should resist the temptation to apply the same standards to every domain: "precision [*to akribes*] is not to be sought alike in all discussions."[a] This passage was very regularly invoked by medieval Aristotelians, but with an important difference. When Robert Grosseteste, in the 1240s, produced the first Latin translation of the *Ethics*, he rendered the Greek *akribes* as *certum*. This had a decisive impact on how the *Ethics* passage would be understood. Here, for instance, is Aquinas:

According to the Philosopher in *Ethics* I, "certainty is not to be sought alike in all matters." For in the case of human actions . . . demonstrative certainty cannot be had, inasmuch as they concern contingent and variable matters. Hence probable certainty suffices, which attains the truth for the most part, even if in a few cases it falls short of the truth.[b]

---

[a] *NE* I.3, 1094^{b}13.   [b] *Summa theol.* 2a2ae 70.2c.

Aquinas and others regularly extended the point to natural philosophy, where one likewise has to be satisfied with conclusions that hold only "for the most part." Here too, it was understood that a lesser kind of certainty is enough.[11]

Aquinas offers only a fairly coarse-grained distinction between demonstrative certainty and probable certainty. But when we reach John Buridan in the mid-fourteenth century, we arrive at what would become the canonical three-level distinction between absolute, natural, and moral certainty. Because Buridan's discussion of these issues in his *Questions on the Metaphysics* (1340s) is both sophisticated and the forerunner of how epistemology would later develop, it is worth taking a little time to work through it. Tellingly, the question Buridan asks is not whether we have knowledge but whether a "comprehension of the truth" is possible for us. His initial response is that this is quite easy, because to comprehend the truth is simply to assent to a true proposition, and we all do this all the time. The hard question is whether we can do it *with certainty*. Here he draws the usual distinction between objective and subjective certainty. On the object side, what is needed is that the truth assented to be firm; and here, too, he thinks it uncontroversial that this condition can be met. He gives the example of the proposition that God exists, where such firmness holds *simpliciter*, "because in no case can it be falsified."[a] This last expression makes it clear that by "firmness" he means *necessity*—in no possible world can the proposition come out false. Another class of examples exhibits firmness *ex suppositione*—specifically, "on the supposition of the common course of nature." Here he gives various examples from natural science, which can be said to display firmness of truth "notwithstanding the fact that God could make fire cold and so falsify the proposition that *all fire is hot*." This is what we now call natural necessity.

Matters get more involved when Buridan turns to the subject side of certainty and to the need for what he calls "firmness of assent." This is understood in purely subjective terms, as "assenting to a proposition without any fear of the opposite."[b] Again, he says, there is no doubt that we can achieve this standard. Both Christians and heretics have been known to be so confident about the truth of their beliefs that they were willing to die for them. And we all achieve considerable subjective certainty all the time, in virtue of what he calls "natural appearances." But the final and hardest problem for Buridan is whether we can achieve such subjective certainty in a way that is *evident*. Even if a true belief is maximally certain both subjectively and objectively—as is the case, for instance, with the faithful's endorsement of church dogma—this will be mere faith, says Buridan, and not genuine *scientia*, unless we have the right sort of evidentness.

What is it to be evident? For Buridan and his contemporaries, evidentness is the bridge that connects the purely objective and the purely subjective senses of certainty. Roughly speaking, it is the all-important quality that distinguishes *scientia* from mere true belief. Indeed, although historians have paid it little systematic attention, evidentness is *the* central epistemic concept among both scholastic philosophers and their critics; it features prominently first among Aristotelians, then in Descartes and throughout the seventeenth century, and even up to the time of David Hume.

---

[a] *Quaest. meta.* II.1, f. 8vb (p. 145 trans. Klima, *Medieval Philosophy*).
[b] II.1, f. 8vb (p. 145 trans.). For "fear of the opposite," see Lecture Six, p. 136.

As a start at an analysis, we can distinguish three entwined notions:

A. The evidentness of a cognitive object; that is, *a thing's being evident.*
B. The evidentness of a cognition that grasps such an object; that is, *an evident cognition.*
C. That which makes something be evident; that is, *the evidence.*

The last of these senses is most deeply entrenched in epistemology today. Moreover, whether we are dealing with Latin (*evidentia*), French (*évidence*), or English (*evidence*), modern readers find it natural to suppose that we are talking about type-C evidence. In fact, however, it is not until the later eighteenth century that this third sense became prevalent in philosophical texts. Before that time, the predominant senses were A and B. In either sense, evidentness is widely understood to be what distinguishes *scientia* from lesser cognitive states. Thus Aquinas: "the certainty of *scientia* and understanding [*intellectus*] comes from the evidentness of the things that are said to be certain, whereas the certainty of faith comes from a firm adherence to that which is believed."[a] Skipping ahead four hundred years, we can find Thomas Hobbes, writing in English, still taking much the same view:

There are two things necessarily implied in this word knowledge; the one is truth, the other evidence; for what is not true can never be known…Likewise, if the truth be not evident, though a man holds it, yet is his knowledge of it no more than theirs that hold the contrary. For if truth were enough to make it knowledge, all truths were known: which is not so.[b]

Translated into modern English, 'evidence' in the first line would best be rendered as 'evidentness,' to make it clear that Hobbes, like Aquinas, is speaking in terms of sense A. That is, for both authors, and for a great many more in the centuries between them, the most general characterization of *scientia* or knowledge is that it is a firm belief regarding an evident truth.[12]

So it is that the most fundamental epistemic questions of these centuries concern what evidentness is and under what circumstances a proposition counts as evident. In the weeks ahead I will consider the second of these questions, looking at some of the ways in which perception and reasoning yield evidentness. Focusing for now only on the question of what it is, the start of an answer is to observe that things possess type-A evidentness when they are apt to produce type-B evidentness. A mark of the latter, in turn, is indubitability: someone who evidently cognizes a proposition cannot resist assenting to that proposition. But here we reach a crucial question: is such indubitability *sufficient* for evidentness, or is it a mere mark? The usual scholastic view seems to be that evidentness requires more than a subjective inability to doubt—that it further requires the proposition to be true, and indeed that we cannot go wrong about that truth. This is to say that evidentness yields infallible certainty.[13]

For a particularly nuanced example of how such a story goes in detail, let us return to John Buridan and his final and hardest problem: whether we grasp the truth with evidentness. His solution begins by distinguishing among three degrees of being evident. The first, unqualified degree (*evidentia simpliciter*) occurs "when, from the nature of sense or intellect, a human being is compelled or necessitated to assent to a

---

[a] *Sent.* III.23.2.2.3c.   [b] *Elements of Law* I.6.2.

proposition in such a way that he cannot dissent."[a] This applies to first principles and their logical consequences. Next comes natural evidentness, which likewise compels the intellect, but only on the supposition that "the common course of nature is observed."[b] So far, his account fits the analysis just offered. First, evidentness is grounded in things, but is relative to our human faculties. Only certain sorts of propositions are evident, and which ones count as evident depends on "the nature of sense or intellect" (as just quoted). Second, the reason why evidentness is observer-relative is that the mark of evidentness is cognitive compulsion. As is typical throughout this period, such evidentness is not characterized by concepts like *justification* and *warrant*. There is no suggestion that we achieve this sort of evidentness and thereby *earn the right* to form a certain belief. Quite to the contrary, Buridan—like others—describes evidentness as something that *compels* assent. That which is evident is indubitable, whereas nonevident propositions carry at least some measure of doubt. This is the sense in which evidentness yields certainty on the subject side. Third, Buridan wants more from evidentness than mere subjective compulsion; he wants a kind of objective infallibility, such that, as he puts it elsewhere, "someone cannot be deceived."[c] In cases of the first degree, the guarantee is absolute. In cases of the second degree, it holds only conditionally, yet he insists that this suffices for *scientia* regarding the natural world.

Buridan's discussion takes a dramatic turn, however, when he introduces his third degree of evidentness:

There is still another, weaker evidentness, which suffices for acting well morally. This goes as follows: if someone, having seen and investigated all the attendant circumstances that one can investigate with diligence, judges in accord with the demands of such circumstances, then that judgment will be evident with an evidentness sufficient for acting well morally—even if that judgment were false on account of invincible ignorance concerning some circumstance. For instance, it would be possible for a judge to act well and meritoriously by hanging an innocent man because through testimony and other documents it sufficiently appeared to him in accord with his duty that that good man was a bad murderer.[d]

In contrast to the first two degrees, this sort of evidentness is fallible. Indeed, in the example on offer, the judge's judgment is evident but false. Furthermore, such moral evidentness apparently does not compel assent. We are now instead in the domain of moral appraisal, where someone who assents and acts on the basis of what is morally evident is doing the right thing. With this, evidentness can play a role close to that of *justification*. Given the degree to which things are evident, we can be said to be within our rights to form such a belief.

This shift from compulsion to justification will loom large in what follows. In these brief remarks, however, Buridan offers just the barest anticipation of the changes that are to come. He says so little, indeed, that it is not even clear whether this weakest category of evidentness is enough for *scientia*. Given that evidentness is supposed to be what distinguishes *scientia* from mere faith, he is perhaps implicitly committed to broadening *scientia* that far. Yet he does not explicitly say so; and, before moving on

---

[a] *Quaest. meta.* II.1, f. 8vb (p. 145 trans. Klima, *Medieval Philosophy*).
[b] II.1, f. 8vb (p. 145 trans.).   [c] *Quaest. Post. An.* I.2c.
[d] *Quaest. meta.* II.1, f. 9ra (p. 146 trans.).

to discuss later chapters in our story, it is worth pausing to reflect on why he does not. As I have been stressing, it makes very little immediate difference, from within the idealized framework, whether moral evidentness is sufficient to make a firmly held true belief count as *scientia*. Buridan has told us what *scientia* in the strictest sense looks like, and we can see how, if we want to be able to speak of *scientia* with regard to the natural world, we need to weaken the requirements. Our having to presuppose the regularity of nature, to achieve certainty in that domain, is not something that Buridan finds worrisome—it is just a fact about our epistemic situation. Similarly, whether or not the judge knows—or has *scientia*—that the accused is guilty is simply not an interesting question from Buridan's point of view. Elsewhere Buridan is perfectly happy to acknowledge the *scientia* of wholly contingent propositions that are based on mere appearances: "everybody speaks in this way: that 'I know [*scio*] that this iron is hot, because I manifestly sense that it is hot,' and 'I firmly know that Socrates was running yesterday, because I saw him running.'"[a] Of course, from a more demanding point of view, such beliefs are markedly uncertain. But what matters, in the idealized framework, is simply to map the contours of our epistemic situation, not to draw arbitrary lines in the sand.

Again, then, we see early epistemology's lack of interest in the question of exactly where to place the boundaries between what is and is not knowledge. And this in turn helps explain why authors from this era tend to be so little worried about skepticism. For, without the sort of boundary mongering that is familiar today, it becomes unclear how one is even to describe the alleged crisis of skepticism. To say that human beings lack *scientia* in the strictest sense is virtually a truism, and hardly tantamount to skepticism. So presumably the skeptical challenge has to be made at some lower level of demandingness. But where? If one descends far enough—all the way, for instance, to Buridan's weakest form of evidentness—then skepticism seems to lose much of its force. Yet where in between these two extremes do we find some privileged focal point? Buridan himself attacks those who "speak very badly" by demanding absolute evidentness in all things,[b] but he does not fuss over the limits to *scientia*. And so it is that later medieval authors in general are remarkably unconcerned by the threat of skepticism. It is not just that their theological worldview gives them a ready response, since of course the skeptic will challenge that worldview along with all the rest. Rather, skepticism looks uninteresting from within an idealized framework, because it seems to collapse into either the platitudinous complaint that we can never have complete certainty or the unbelievable claim that we can never have even reasonable confidence.

Yet, alas, the moral of our story is not quite so simple and satisfying. With respect to skepticism, we will see in Lecture Six how an adversary as determined as Hume can raise deep skeptical problems even from within the idealized framework. And in what remains of this lecture I want to consider how the demand for epistemic boundaries starts to loom large even in the seventeenth century, as the notion of moral certainty, paired with an increased interest in the merely probable, leads to an increasing concern with identifying the point at which belief becomes warranted. Out of this is born the modern notion of justification, understood not as an intellectual compulsion in the face of an evident truth, but rather as an epistemic permission in view of what is sufficiently probable.[14]

---

[a] *Summulae* VIII.4.4 (p. 710 trans.).
[b] *Quaest. meta.* II.1, f. 9ra (p. 146 trans.); see also Lecture Six, p. 118.

Proportioned Belief

Although John Buridan did not use the phrase 'moral certainty,' his conception of a lesser degree of certainty would start to appear regularly, under just this label, within a few decades of his death. It seems to appear first in Jean Gerson and allied moral theologians of the fifteenth century, and thereafter becomes commonplace throughout scholastic discussions. These discussions continue into the early seventeenth century, both on the continent and in England, especially in Protestant apologetics. William Chillingworth, for instance, in his hugely influential *Religion of Protestants* (1638), defends the textual reliability of the Bible by appealing to a lesser kind of certainty.

But [you say that] we cannot be certain in what language the scriptures remain uncorrupted. Not so certain, I grant, as of that which we can demonstrate; but certain enough, morally certain, as certain as the nature of the thing will bear. So certain we may be, and God requires no more.[a]

Subsequent religious controversialists, notably John Tillotson, took up this same line, and from there it took on a prominent place in the scientific ideology of the Royal Society, particularly through the influence of John Wilkins, one of the founding figures of that society and also a keen participant in the religious controversies of his day. His *Principles and Duties of Natural Religion* (1675) begins with a beautifully clear little chapter on evidence and belief in which he draws the usual threefold distinction between what he labels mathematical, physical, and moral certainty. Like others before him, Wilkins urges that we should not expect greater certainty than the subject admits of. Similar ideas are advanced at length by a great many others.[15]

Recent scholars, unaware of the long history of such distinctions, have often been overly impressed with the novelty of these seventeenth-century developments. It becomes harder to say what exactly is new here, however, once we see that the notion of moral certainty can be found all throughout later scholastic discussions. The constantly heard seventeenth-century injunction to look for only as much certainty as is possible is nothing new either: as we have seen, one finds it all throughout the Aristotelian tradition, and it has roots in Aristotle's work itself. What changes most dramatically in post-scholastic epistemology is that the possibility of infallible certainty no longer gets taken for granted, even in the most ideal of cases. Thus, by the mid-seventeenth century, talk of levels of certainty is routinely accompanied by the proviso that even the highest sort of human certainty should not be regarded as absolute infallibility. Wilkins, for instance, describes it as "a blasphemous arrogance" to characterize even mathematical certainty as unerring. The best we can have is "a conditional infallibility, that which supposes our faculties to be true, and that we do not neglect the exerting of them."[b] Even more strikingly new is the readiness of so many figures to give up, in almost all cases, anything beyond moral certainty. Robert Boyle cautions, for instance, that "there are I know not how many things in physics that men presume they believe upon physical and cogent arguments, wherein they really have but a moral assurance."[c] Joseph Glanvill, in a similar spirit, writes:

---

[a] *Religion of Protestants* ch. 2, §55.   [b] *Principles and Duties* I.1, p. 9.
[c] *Excellence of Theology* pt. II, §3 (*Works* VIII: 66).

The best principles, excepting divine and mathematical, are but hypotheses; within the circle of which we may indeed conclude many things, with security from error. But yet the greatest certainty, advanced from supposal, is still but hypothetical. So that we may affirm that things are thus and thus, according to the principles we have espoused. But we strangely forget ourselves, when we plead a necessity of their being so in nature, and an impossibility of their being otherwise.[a]

This is worlds away from the confidence of earlier Aristotelians, including even Buridan, who thinks that in natural philosophy the *only* supposition we need to make is that nature will continue on in a regular way, unimpeded by God.[16]

What is new here is a kind of epistemic pessimism. This is not, however, the sort of pessimistic crisis that leads to skepticism, but rather one that yields a new description of the normative ideal. Even while stressing that moral certainty is often all we are capable of, these authors immediately have the further thought that *this is good enough*. Buridan himself had introduced the notion of moral evidentness in this way, remarking that this "suffices for acting well morally." In the seventeenth century, such pronouncements become routine and spread over all aspects of inquiry. Thus Chillingworth: "we pretend not at all to any assurance that we cannot err, but only to a sufficient certainty that we do not err."[b] And Boyle: "a rational assent may be founded upon proofs that reach not to rigid demonstrations, it being sufficient that they are strong enough to deserve a wise man's acquiescence in them."[c] Pierre Bayle, on the continent, arrives at a similar conclusion: "It does not matter much if one says that the mind of man is too limited to discover anything concerning natural truths, or concerning the causes producing heat, cold, the tides, and the like. It is enough for us that we employ ourselves in looking for probable hypotheses and collecting data."[d] We can see all these authors coalescing around a lesser goal for inquiry as they use that same phrase we came across over and over last week—"it is enough": this goal is not certainty in the sense that Aristotelians hoped for, but evidentness good enough to make belief reasonable. And with that shift in emphasis comes a corresponding shift away from a conception of evidentness as compelling or forcing assent, toward a conception of evidentness as justifying or warranting assent.[17]

As natural as these developments look in hindsight, at the time they looked radical. Descartes at several points had invoked the notion of moral certainty, but he would not allow himself to settle for that. He brags in the preface to the French edition of the *Principles* that the principles he has discovered "enable us to deduce the knowledge [*connaissance*] of all the other things to be found in the world,"[e] insisting on the word 'deduce' to mark the high standard he takes himself to have met. In his last year of life he writes to Henry More that "no arguments satisfy me in physics except for those that involve the necessity you call logical."[f] Even many of Descartes's followers found it hard to endorse their master's enthusiasm for this cause, but the banner would be raised in mid-seventeenth-century England by Thomas White as he argued for the infallibility of the Catholic Church. White mocks his Protestant opponents for lacking the convictions of the true heretic: "these delicate believers content their easy and civil natures with a

[a] *Scepsis scientifica* ch. 23, p. 145.   [b] *Religion of Protestants* ch. 3, §50.
[c] *Discourse of Things above Reason*, first advice (*Works* IX: 398).
[d] *Dictionaire*, "Pyrrho," note B (pp. 194–5 trans.).   [e] IXB: 10–11.   [f] V: 275.

dough-baked probability, as if they were little concerned whether the religion they professed were true or false."[a] Probability may be a useful guide when it comes to the forced choice between uncertain courses of action, but it should not be used to govern assent:

Probability signifies no more than a seeming gloss of truth rising from a heap of arguments, whereof no one proves the conclusion, nor is there such connection betwixt any two or more, that together they gain an irresistibility. Whence it is evident, there is nothing advanced towards the truth of the assent, since this remains known: that the position may be false notwithstanding all those appearances.[b]

Elsewhere, writing against Glanvill and, by extension, against the whole Royal Society, White condemns their attacks on Aristotle, through which they "tear science itself out of the hands of the learned, and throw it into the dirt of probability."[c] Throughout the seventeenth century such sentiments were a common response to the growing pessimism of the age and its attendant recalibration of our epistemic norms.[18]

For the pessimistic recalibrationists to win the day, it was not enough just for them to abandon the epistemic ideals of old. The reactionary champions of those ideals were fighting back in the name of certainty, and certainty could not simply be surrendered. It had to be reconceptualized. Throughout the Aristotelian tradition, as we have seen, certainty comes in two flavors, objective necessity and subjective confidence, which get tied together by evidentness to yield infallibility. This picture of certainty, though commonplace, omits something crucial: the possibility of a certainty that is conditional upon the information we hold, or what is now known as *epistemic probability*. One feels the absence of this notion all the way through the Aristotelian tradition. For, when its representatives are asked why the objects of *scientia* must be necessary truths, as stipulated in Aristotle's canonical definition,[d] their usual answer is that, if *scientia* were to concern things that are merely contingent, then we could never rule out their going out of existence undetected, in which case our epistemic condition would be nonideal. What seems obvious, at least in retrospect, is that such safety could be gained by requiring only a conditional epistemic necessity—that is, by requiring that, necessarily, the proposition is true *given the evidence that we have*. Then I can say that, although I do not know for all time that Socrates is running, I do know right now that he is, because I am watching him jog down the road.

The example is Buridan's but, even so, this notion of conditional certainty would be clearly articulated only in the seventeenth century, in the service of the new epistemology. That it would take so long is something of a puzzle, because scholastic authors in fact had all the resources they needed to articulate such a notion. First, as we have seen, it was quite common in the scholastic tradition to allow a broad sense of *scientia*, which was aimed at contingent events like Socrates's running. Second, the scholastics had a well-developed understanding of conditional necessity, which played an important role elsewhere in their thought (most famously with regard to divine foreknowledge). Finally, in the later Middle Ages, the conception of evidentness gave them something

---

[a]   Preface to William Rushworth, *Dialogues*, n.p. [5].
[b]   Preface to William Rushworth, *Dialogues*, n.p. [16].
[c]   *Exclusion of Scepticks*, eighth plea, p. 55.
[d]   *Post. An.* I.2, 71^{b}9–12, quoted in Lecture One, p. 6.

to conditionalize on in an epistemic context. So it ought to have been quite natural to say that I am certain that Socrates is running because I see him right there.

Yet, although one finds scholastic authors like Buridan talking that way, such remarks were treated as mere concessions to ordinary language, marginal to high theory, and hence marginal to epistemology. Part of the problem was a reluctance to admit contingent particulars into idealized epistemology. As discussed last week,[a] epistemology from its very start fell under the sway of the Platonic ambition to grasp the essences of things. Although Aristotle brought the Forms down to earth, he still assumed that the aim of epistemic inquiry is the necessary and eternal. That assumption dominated scholastic thought even while the resources became available within epistemology to accommodate the contingent. As a result, it is only in the seventeenth century, when philosophers finally overthrew the Aristotelian doctrine of essences, that they were able to rethink their epistemology along with their metaphysics, and in consequence to reformulate the epistemic ideal in a way that gave a central role to contingent particulars as worthy objects of knowledge.[19]

From this perspective Buridan is important because he lays the groundwork for a broader class of cases, which involve contingent objects that are not so evident as to compel assent. It is only in the seventeenth century, however, that this idea begins to assume a central place in epistemology. Hints appear in the theological writings of Chillingworth, Wilkins, and others, but the idea becomes wholly explicit only in more philosophically adroit writings, such as Arnauld and Nicole's *Port-Royal Logic*. The very end of that treatise distinguishes between two kinds of truths: "First are truths that concern merely the nature of things and their immutable essence, independently of their existence. The others concern existing things, especially human and contingent events."[b] What sorts of rules of reasoning can be framed for the second, less discussed sort of truth? It would be absurd, the authors say, to treat such cases on the model of necessary truths, or to ignore such a truth on the grounds that it is not necessary. Their solution is this:

One need not consider it nakedly and in itself, as one would a proposition of geometry. Instead, one needs to pay attention to all the accompanying circumstances, internal as well as external . . . Once one has done that, if all the circumstances are such that it never or very rarely happens that similar circumstances accompany the falsity of the belief, then our mind is naturally led to think that it is true.[c]

In other words, we should consider a contingent proposition in light of the surrounding facts, and then we can conclude that, conditional upon those facts, the proposition is either necessary or very likely to be true.

There is no great conceptual breakthrough here, inasmuch as all the pieces of this sort of analysis had long been available. Even so, the change in emphasis by the end of the seventeenth century is striking. Moreover—and this is the critical point—once the idea of epistemic probability achieves prominence, it becomes possible to stress an entirely different conception of the epistemic ideal, one grounded not in the elusive quest for infallible certainty, but in the more modest ideal of proportioning one's belief to the evidence. Chillingworth, for instance, writes that "God desires only that we believe the

---

[a]   Lecture One, p. 10.   [b] IV.13, p. 263 trans.   [c] IV.13, p. 264 trans.

conclusion as much as the premises deserve, that the strength of our faith be equal or proportionable to the credibility of the motives to it."[a] Glanvill likewise urges that "a man proportion the degree of his assent to the degree of evidence, being more sparing and reserved to the more difficult and not thoroughly examined theories, and confident only of those that are distinctively and clearly apprehended."[b] This is not wholly new either. The notion that assent can come in degrees had been the subject of careful analysis among scholastic authors, and anyone familiar with that notion will immediately recognize the virtue of proportioning one's assent to the likelihood of truth. But in the seventeenth century these ideas assume a prominence that they had never had before, and become among some authors the centerpiece of their epistemic theories.[20]

The most important example is John Locke. He begins his *Essay concerning Human Understanding* (1689) by announcing his purpose to "enquire into the original, certainty, and extent of human knowledge; together with the grounds and degrees of belief, opinion, and assent."[c] This immediately puts the reader on notice that the goal is not the Aristotelian–Cartesian one of assembling a body of certain knowledge, but the more modest one of assessing the extent to which such certainty can be acquired and the degree of belief that should obtain where certainty is lacking. When Book IV finally gets around to considering knowledge and assent, certainty remains only as a remote, absolute ideal. The focus shifts toward the new normative ideal of proportionality:

the mind if it will proceed rationally ought to examine all the grounds of probability, and see how they make more or less, for or against any probable proposition, before it assents to or dissents from it, and upon a due balancing the whole, reject or receive it, with a more or less firm assent, proportionably to the preponderancy of the greater grounds of probability on one side or the other.[d]

This *principle of proportionality*, as we can call it, describes an ideal that is perhaps not as inspiring as Aristotelian or Cartesian certainty but is at least, Locke thinks, something we are capable of. Because we are capable of it, it can plausibly be regarded as a normative epistemic ideal. But it is an ideal that needs to be urged upon us, because we are no longer in the domain of wholly evident truths that irresistibly compel assent. Here instead it begins to be proper to speak of justification: what we "rationally ought" to do is to proportion our beliefs to "all the grounds of probability." Such grounds now include not just the type-A evidentness of the proposition in question but the broader field of type-C evidence that must be brought into balance. This concern with what we are warranted to believe in light of the evidence takes us a step closer to modern epistemology. But we are not quite there, because within this Lockean Program there seems little reason to focus on epistemic boundaries, and indeed little reason to be interested in *knowledge* at all. Our final task, then, is to see how that begins to change.[21]

The Limits of Knowledge

Once proportionality starts to take hold as the new epistemic ideal, it becomes unclear what relevance is left to 'knowledge.' But this depends, of course, on how we want to

---

[a] *Religion of Protestants* ch. 1, §8.
[b] "Of Skepticism and Certainty" (*Essays*, p. 46).
[c] *Essay* I.1.2.   [d] IV.15.5.

use that word. Last week we saw how 'science' took on a new meaning in the seventeenth century, when figures like Galileo and Newton resigned themselves to uncertainty over causal explanations. We are now in a position to see how the meaning of that other great epistemic word in English also begins to change in a way that draws it to the heart of modern epistemology.

Throughout the seventeenth century, authors mainly assume that 'knowledge' properly speaking should be associated with 'science' and that both words should be used in the traditional manner, as demanding ideal certainty. According to Chillingworth, for instance, "science and knowledge, properly taken, are synonymous terms."[a] To the question of whether one can know that a distant, unseen city like Constantinople exists, he replies that "in propriety of speech I could not say that I knew it, but that I did as undoubtedly believe it as those things which I did know."[b] Locke too, late in the century, is adamant about reserving 'knowledge' for the absolute ideal: "the highest probability amounts not to certainty, without which there can be no true knowledge."[c] Even well into the 1700s, Hume still takes for granted that what is merely probable cannot count as known.[22]

This absolutist conception of knowledge, combined with the principle of proportionality, gives rise to what I am calling 'the Lockean Program.' On this picture, knowledge is not normally to be hoped for. As Locke puts it, "our knowledge, as has been shown, being very rare . . . most of the propositions we think, reason, discourse, nay act upon, are such, as we cannot have undoubted knowledge of their truth."[d] Yet this admission does not drive Locke into skepticism in any substantive way. Instead it drives him to reconsider our normative ideal, which turns away from the acquisition of knowledge toward the proper degree of assent.

Within the Lockean Program just as much as within the earlier Aristotelian framework, questions of where to mark the boundary between what is and what is not knowledge are drained of their significance. Locke does occasionally involve himself in such boundary disputes. The most prominent example is when he declares that we can be said to have sensory knowledge of "the particular existence of finite beings without us,"[e] even though the degree of certainty found in such cases is imperfect. To many modern scholars, this has looked like one of the most fraught episodes of the whole *Essay*—the crucial place where Locke attempts and pathetically fails to overthrow skepticism. Yet, once one understands the Lockean Program in its historical context, it becomes clear that there is scarcely here anything worth arguing about. Locke readily acknowledges that this "sensitive knowledge" is less certain than is the "intuitive knowledge" we have of our own ideas, and also less certain than the "demonstrative knowledge" we base upon those ideas. Is it certain enough to count as knowledge? Well, it is what it is, that being "not only as great as our frame can attain to, but as our condition needs."[f] Why argue over lexicology? Eschewing drawn-out battles over where to draw lines between vague categories, the Lockean Program focuses instead on cataloguing the different levels of certainty, so that our degrees of assent may be suitably proportioned. Once that is done, it scarcely matters how we assign the labels. Indeed, Locke's way of thinking about these issues is so different from ours that we should say of

---

[a] *Religion of Protestants* ch. 6, §2.   [b] *Works*, p. 740.
[c] *Essay* IV.3.14.   [d] IV.15.2.   [e] IV.2.14.   [f] IV.11.8.

him what I have already said of Descartes, and for much the same reasons: that he simply does not have a theory of knowledge in our sense of the term.[23]

In part, the issue here is just one of words. These were still early days for an English philosophical vocabulary, and the proper way to deploy that solid Anglo-Saxon word 'knowledge' was still very much in doubt. Across a wide range of domains, Locke is still searching for the right terms to replace the "uncouth, affected, or unintelligible" Latinizing vocabulary of the Aristotelians.[a] For most of the early English authors, the use of 'knowledge' that seemed most appropriate was limited to what was ideally certain; normal practice was to find other words to talk about nonideal cases. Yet the issues are far from being merely lexicological. For, if the Lockean Program had become ascendant, the recent history of epistemology might look quite different. Rather than framing itself around binary questions like *Is it justified?* and *Is it knowledge?*, epistemology might have focused on quantified degrees of credence. Questions of definition and problems of skepticism might have lost much of their force. As it happens, this is how many would like to see epistemology done today, in terms of formal, quantified methods rather than through absolute concepts like *knowledge* and *belief*. So what happened? Why, despite all this history, does modern epistemology find itself stubbornly drawn toward boundary conditions?

The trouble comes when three individually plausible ideas come together:

- the principle of proportionality;
- pessimism over our ability to achieve infallible certainty;
- the conviction that we are often entitled to believe absolutely, without doubt.

Any two of these three doctrines might be jointly maintained; but, together, they make for a highly unstable triad. Accordingly, various authors abandon one or another of the three. In Locke, as we have seen, it is absolute belief that gives way, except in those "very rare" cases where certain knowledge can be achieved. Others, such as Thomas White, optimistically insist on the prospects of certainty. But the most interesting response to the unstable triad lies with those who abandon the principle of proportionality. It is here that we find the seeds of modern epistemology.

I remarked already that proportionality appears in various authors before Locke. Yet these earlier treatments generally fail to adhere to the principle in any consistent way. For instance, even while Chillingworth denies having enough certainty to *know* that Constantinople exists, he adds: "I did as undoubtedly believe it as those things which I did know."[b] This flatly violates proportionality. Tillotson does just the same thing, now thinking of Jamaica: "I am as free from all doubt concerning it, as I am from doubting of the clearest mathematical demonstration."[c] In a way, these claims are not so far from how Locke himself would later talk. He writes, as we saw, that there are some propositions so close to being certain that we "assent to them as firmly . . . as if they were infallibly demonstrated."[d] But in Locke's hands this is a point about the difficulty of discriminating between near-identical cases. In other hands, the principle of proportionality is entirely set aside. Wilkins is especially explicit about this. Speaking of moral certainty, he writes that "the mind of man may and must give a firm assent to some

---

[a] *Essay* epistle, p. 10.   [b] *Works*, p. 740 (as quoted earlier).
[c] *Works* I: 16.   [d] *Essay* IV.15.2.

things, without any kind of hesitation or doubt of the contrary, where yet the evidences for such things are not so infallible, but that there is a possibility that the things may be otherwise."[a] This is quite unlike how Locke, later, would carefully categorize the different degrees of certainty and assent. For Wilkins, doubt-free assent requires not infallible certainty, but only freedom from "reasonable doubt."[b] Where we have this, we should assent undoubtingly and act accordingly.

Wilkins and others violate the principle of proportionality, at the upper limits of the range, in order to stake out a wider domain for unqualified belief. At what point is such belief licensed? Precisely where we attain moral certainty. And, since these authors contend that religious beliefs admit of moral certainty, they are thus able to defend the rationality of unqualified belief in Christianity. More generally, once this broader domain for absolute assent is identified, it becomes natural to think that the prime normative ideal in epistemology is to believe firmly all and only those things of which one is at least morally certain. This in turn leads to the great question of what exactly counts as moral certainty. Considerable debates arose in this regard, to the point where Jacob Bernoulli seriously proposed that legislative action be taken to fix moral certainty's exact limits: perhaps 99 out of 100, or 999 out of 1,000. Epistemology now begins to consider where to draw the line between what is and is not sufficiently certain to warrant firm belief.[24]

Wilkins in particular, in his small way, takes what can retrospectively be seen as a decisive step, because he both rejects the principle of proportionality in favor of a broad scope for absolute belief and identifies the whole range of such belief with *knowledge*. For, even as he continues to associate knowledge with certainty, he allows that mere moral certainty is good enough, treating mathematical, physical, and moral as three different kinds of knowledge and thus locating the threshold for knowledge not at intellectual compulsion but at the absence of reasonable doubt: "that kind of assent which does arise from such plain and clear evidence as does not admit of any reasonable cause of doubting is called knowledge or certainty."[c] This step is decisive, because it allows us to associate this new normative ideal of epistemology with the word 'know-ledge.' Henceforth, in looking for the boundary between what is and is not morally certain—the threshold for reasonable, warranted, justified belief—we can simply say that we are looking for the boundary between what is and is not known. Admittedly, the import of this step is hardly obvious. After all, from early on, *epistēmē* and *scientia* were commonly used in a very broad sense. But in these earlier authors, from Themistius through the scholastics and on to Hobbes, that vulgar usage was too broad to count as a normative ideal. As we saw last week, Themistius would count as knowledge in a broad sense "every apprehension...however it comes about...through whatever method."[d] There is nothing remotely ideal about this. On the other hand, those who insisted on using 'knowledge' very strictly could not think of it as furnishing a normative ideal either. Both Locke and Hume, for instance, are so strict in how they use 'knowledge' that it plays only a peripheral role in their epistemology. And, although earlier traditions—from Aristotle through Descartes—did think of *epistēmē* and *scientia* as normative ideals, they plainly did not take themselves to be fashioning a theory of

---

[a] *Principles and Duties* I.3, p. 27.   [b] I.1, p. 8.   [c] I.1, p. 5.
[d] *Paraphrasis Post. an.* I.2 (ed. Wallies, p. 5; ed. O'Donnell, p. 247); see Lecture One, p. 8.

what we should firmly believe. That is, in essence, why these authors cannot be said to have a theory of knowledge in our modern sense. It is only when knowledge gets linked to moral certainty that we arrive at something like our current epistemic framework.[25]

Again, it is not the word 'knowledge' that matters. To be sure, it is convenient to have a label for the domain of beliefs that are of sufficient certitude to be fully believed. But we could do without the word, or we could use another. The more substantive question is why it was Wilkins's program, rather than Locke's, that shaped modern epistemology. And the answer is that when faced with the unstable triad of proportionality, pessimism, and absolute belief, Locke chose the first two against the third, and this proved to be a road that, until recently, few were willing to travel. Instead, the main lines of debate formed over the prospects for certainty, as against the demand to respect the evidence. Insisting on a proportional respect for the evidence, Thomas White contends that "in all propositions, therefore, where we see no more than probability, it is our part to withhold our assent, till evidence or certainty deserve it."[a] To this Wilkins would reply that he, too, claims more than mere probability—he claims moral certainty. But to White it is all the same: "so long as the truth itself convinces not his judgment, what imports it him whether the probability be as 200 or 1,000 to one, since to him (all this notwithstanding) it is unknown whether it be truth or no."[b] Such strictures admit of no exception to the principle of proportionality, but require achieving perfect certainty. To White's opponents, this looked like madness. Chillingworth, decades earlier, had already confronted a similar line of thought and responded in this way:

Which assertion, because he modestly delivers as very probable . . . hereupon you take occasion to ask: *Shall I hazard my soul on probabilities, or even wagers?* As if whatsoever is but probable, though in the highest degree of probability, were as likely to be false as true! Or, because it is but morally, not mathematically, certain that there was such a woman as Q Elizabeth, such a man as H. the 8., that is in the highest degree probable, therefore it were an even wager there were none such![c]

This is rhetorically impressive, but in fact Chillingworth changes the subject, moving from the question of what we ought to believe to the practical domain of hazarding and wagering. White himself is ready to allow that we should often *act* in the absence of certainty. He offers the example of a general who must array his forces on the basis of what seems probable, even if the fog of war makes certainty impossible.[d] Where White digs in his heels is with respect to *belief*; here is where he and authors like Chillingworth fundamentally disagree. For, even if Chillingworth will not strictly apply the word 'knowledge' to a case of mere moral certainty, he sees no reason why he should not "as undoubtedly believe it as those things which I did know."[e] Wilkins concurs, and even wants to call it knowledge. And so modern epistemology begins to take shape, as a struggle between those who optimistically maintain high epistemic standards and insist that these standards can be met and those who pessimistically relax their expectations, give up on proportionality, and nevertheless claim that we are entitled to believe. Ultimately such entitled true beliefs are what came to count as knowledge.[26]

[a] Preface to Rushworth, *Dialogues*, n.p. [14].   [b] N.p. [14].
[c] *Religion of Protestants* ch. 4, §57.
[d] Preface to Rushworth, *Dialogues*, n.p. [13].
[e] *Works*, p. 740 (quoted earlier).

What joins this debate is a shared commitment to absolute belief, that remaining side of the unstable triad. White seeks certainty because he takes for granted that belief must be absolute, and it is this that, similarly, drives Chillingworth and others to violate proportionality at the top of the scale. So why not just relinquish absolute belief, and thereby avoid the whole protracted fight? This, the Lockean Program, represents the road not taken at the end of the seventeenth century, when the epistemic ideal of certainty began to give way to the ideal of proportionality. Although the advantages of this path are widely appreciated today, it is easy to see why it looked unattractive at the time. For one thing, it requires us to conceive of belief in a thoroughly alien way, as coming in degrees even amid life's absolute events. When rafting down the Colorado River, I must go either to the left of the rock or to the right. If I proportion my action to the probabilities and go dead center, the results will be disastrous. Now in one respect such a case makes it easy to see how we are able to distinguish between commitment in action and confidence in belief: I can go hard left, for instance, even while remaining quite doubtful about whether I have chosen correctly. But even here there are countless things that I do not doubt at all: that I am on a river, in a raft, confronted with a large rock, and so on. These are fixed points in my reasoning, and it is hard to accept that these and countlessly many other such beliefs are in any way qualified.

Moreover, seventeenth-century authors faced special pressure to think that many of our beliefs—even our most central ones—are absolute. For when it comes to the practice of religion, which is after all the central issue in many of these texts, all parties take for granted that unqualified belief is an essential, constitutive part of the activity. This may look like a doubtful assumption even in the case of religion, or it may look like a special case that will not generalize. But belief in God might also be thought of as part of a much broader phenomenon, which extends to other interpersonal relationships, where we would not want our commitment to those we love to be qualified by hesitations and doubts. And, once we go that far, we might go farther still and consider our commitments to ideals and institutions of all kinds. It is easy enough to see what it would be like to believe only partially in the people and things we care about. Indeed, we know just what such doubts are like, and most of us try to resist them. Accordingly, the case for absolute belief rests on more than the unreflective prejudice of common-sense. With respect to both backgrounded and foregrounded belief, we face pressure to treat those beliefs absolutely.[27]

There's the rub that makes calamity of modern epistemology. For, as soon as philosophy descends from the lofty heights of its absolute epistemic ideal and humbly addresses itself to real-world questions—to believe or not to believe—the principle of proportionality comes under intense pressure. That thesis tells us that we should give our absolute assent only to what is infallibly certain. Yet such certainty is something we have come to despair of achieving. So what are we to do? The principle of proportionality seems incontrovertible as a normative principle—it is how rational beings ought to conduct themselves. And still, even in the absence of certainty, we want to believe, and cannot help but believe. Hence the epistemologist is forever unsatisfied, in need of certainty but unable to have it.

Over the next three weeks we will go down some of the paths toward certainty that have been proposed over the centuries. Ultimately, however, in the final lecture, we will need to backtrack and consider what options are left in a world where uncertainty is inevitable.

Lecture Three

The Sensory Domain

In the previous two weeks we have looked in general at the ideals that have informed epistemology over the centuries and at how those ideals were recalibrated to reflect a changing conception of the world and of our place in it. Yet, even as we adjusted ourselves to lesser goals in one way or another, the expectation has remained that at least sometimes, in some domains, we can achieve the sort of evident certainty to which philosophy has traditionally aspired. Nowhere has this expectation been more doggedly pursued than in the domain of the senses. But where exactly that privileged domain is to be located has been the subject of endless dispute.

Sensory Ideals

As we turn to the domain of the senses, it is immediately striking just how indubitably we are drawn to relying upon them. Indeed, even among philosophers who disagree sharply with respect to their *theories* of perception, there is essentially no debate at all regarding our sensory *practices*. From every philosophical perspective, there is general agreement that, at the end of the day, we should all keep perceiving the world just as we always have. To be sure, some of us might like to have better vision or hearing, or a better sense of smell and taste. Even then, however, the ideal is simply to be normal. Technology allows us to detect the electromagnetic spectrum beyond the small fragment of humanly visible light, but no one has any real desire to *see* that wider range of frequencies. Bees see more and dogs hear and smell more, but no one would think this to be an ideal to which *we* ought to aspire. Who would want to smell all the things that a dog can smell? When it comes to perception, the normative ideal is just to be normal.

At the same time, the history of philosophy displays the most amazing diversity of views regarding just what sort of cognitive contribution the senses actually make. On one side, in the broadly rationalist camp, are those who profess to despise the cognitive value of the senses. This group has Plato at its head and extends to Cartesians such as Nicolas Malebranche:

I shall teach you that the world you live in is not such as you believe it to be, since it is not such as you see it or as you feel it. You judge all objects surrounding you on the basis of your senses, and your senses delude you a very great deal more than you can imagine. They are accurate witnesses only with regard to what concerns the good of the body and the preservation of life. As to anything else, there is no accuracy, no truth in their deposition.[a]

On the other side, in the broadly empiricist camp, one finds a shared sense of confidence that hewing close to the deliverances of sensation is the cornerstone of all sound reasoning. Aristotle belongs here, as do many of his medieval followers—and also John Locke, who describes the ideas of sensation and reflection as "the first step a man makes toward the discovery of anything, and the groundwork whereon to build all those notions which ever he shall have naturally in this world."[b] These debates are as familiar as anything in philosophy, but even so it is remarkable just how radically divided these two camps are, on what would seem to be the most elementary of questions.[1]

It is a curious fact about perception, then, that its objective value has been the subject of such fierce debate, even while, from a subjective point of view, we can hardly imagine what it would be like to deploy the senses any differently. Part of the reason for this puzzling duality is that, amid these dramatic disagreements, philosophers have shown over the ages a remarkably persistent tendency to maintain that the senses have *some* proper sphere of operation within which they reliably get *something* right. One finds this idea in Democritus and in the Epicureans, in Aristotle and in later Aristotelians, in Anselm, and even among seventeenth-century anti-Aristotelians. Thus Joseph Glanvill, a leading proponent of the Royal Society, even while speaking of the "grand deceit" of taking sensations in the mind for qualities of the world, writes that "to speak properly, and do our senses right, simply they are not deceived, but only administer an occasion to our forward understandings to deceive themselves."[c] Even Malebranche, despite claiming (above) that there is "no accuracy" and "no truth" in the senses, thinks that the fault does not lie with the senses themselves: "We are deceived not by our senses but by our will, through its precipitous judgments."[d] Given this assumption, it is natural that we would trust the senses even while quarreling fiercely over where exactly they are most to be trusted.[2]

Why would such disparate figures all suppose that there is any such privileged sensory domain? In some cases, the motivation is unmistakably religious: they believe that God would not have given us these senses unless they had some nearly flawless domain of application. But one can also discern a less theologically loaded source for the doctrine of a privileged sensory domain, one that grows out of reflection on the very nature of the senses. For it is perfectly clear that sensation is a natural phenomenon, one that we could not refuse to engage in even if we wanted, and one that we would not want to give up, inasmuch as it undoubtedly brings us great benefits. This makes it natural to suppose that there must be *some* level of sensory operation that is, at least in general, highly successful at grasping reality. After all, if this were not the case, then it would be hard to explain what the point of sensation would be and why we do find it to be of such extraordinary value.

My topic today and next week, then, is the long philosophical quest for that elusive domain of sensory privilege, the place where sensory indubitability finds vindication in

---

[a] *Dialogues on Metaphysics*, dial. 1 (in *Philosophical Selections*, p. 148).
[b] *Essay* II.1.24.   [c] *Scepsis scientifica* ch. 12, p. 67.
[d] *Search after Truth* I.5, p. 23 trans.

some measure of infallibility. As we will see, there have been the most dramatic disagreements, reversals, and confusions regarding where in the world this domain is to be found, disagreements that in turn fuel the notorious disputes over the cognitive value of perception. The focus today is on those who take it that there is some *external* locus of sensory privilege, beginning with Aristotle and later Aristotelians, who tell a surprisingly different story; then we will move on, toward the crisis that emerged when the privileged sensory domain of the scholastics turned out to be illusory. This will set the stage for next week, when we will consider those who think that the only true domain of sensory privilege is *within* the perceiver, in the domain of ideas. Running throughout these disparate accounts is the sort of Panglossianism that we will encounter again and again as the natural offspring of an idealized epistemology: here, it is the conviction that there must be *some* privileged domain where our subjective confidence in the senses finds validation in objective achievement. Here again we will confront the idealizing assumption that the world is knowable and that we are well positioned to know it. Looking back over the long course of our efforts to make good on that ideal, we will ultimately be in a position to consider whether this elusive domain of sensory privilege, in part or in whole, may in fact be illusive.

Domains of Privilege

To clarify this notion of sensory privilege, it is helpful to distinguish two levels of appraisal: the qualitative and the sentential. *Qualitatively*, we want the senses to show us features of the world—its color, its smell, its heat. *Sententially*, we want the senses to show us that things are so—that the leaves are green, that the smell is coming from over there, that the oven is hot. The skeptic finds insuperable obstacles at both these levels. For those who would surmount skepticism, these two domains require very different strategies.

At the sentential level, there is a robust consensus over the general trustworthiness of the senses. It is here that the normative ideal is just to go on perceiving normally and that our shared embrace of various empirical truths goes hand in hand with our practical reliance on sense experience. True, the ancient skeptics were so bold as to challenge even the most modest empirical claims about the world. Indeed, legend has it that Pyrrho led a life so much in keeping with his skepticism that he trusted nothing to the senses and "faced all risks as they came, whether carts, precipices, dogs or what not."[a] The story, however, is quite unbelievable. Are we to accept that Pyrrho lived to be ninety thanks only to his friends who, as the legend has it, followed him around all day, saving him from disaster? Later Pyrrhonists frankly admitted that they followed the appearances.[b] Whether or not this commits them to having beliefs, it is clear that the skeptics at least trusted the senses as guides to steer by. Not even they were prepared to use the senses any differently from everyone else.

Where massive philosophical disagreement arises is at the qualitative level. For, even if no one can help but trust her senses in her daily life, and even if nearly everyone endorses ordinary empirical sentences about the world around him, it is quite unclear exactly what the senses are showing us about the world. What is this green that characterizes the leaves, and indeed what are the leaves? That there could be

---

[a] Diogenes Laertius, *Lives* IX.62.   [b] E.g., Sextus Empiricus, *Outlines of Scepticism* I.vii, x, xi.

disagreement at this qualitative level and not at the sentential level might seem odd, since the latter evidently depends on the former. Indeed, a large part of what impels the long history of disagreement at the qualitative level is just a desire to find a firm foundation on which to ground our ordinary beliefs about the world. Still, such dependence is mediated by language, and this makes all the difference. Even Berkeley, with his radically inward-turned idealism regarding the immediate qualitative deliverances of the senses, accepts that, in the end, the senses do show us that the leaves are green—even if he understands such a sentence very differently from the rest of us. Language, with its quasi-magical ability to reach out and find suitable objects of reference somewhere, manages to smooth over disagreements that, at the qualitative level, seem to be quite intractable.

Of course, disagreement still arises at the sentential level, especially with regard to the issues at stake in last week's lecture. Does sensory perception yield the sort of evidentness that characterizes *scientia*? To be sure, the deliverances of perception are often indubitable, but are they also, in any respect, infallibly certain? Must we settle instead for mere moral certainty when it comes to empirical sentences? From questions such as these arises our modern concern with fixing the level of justification sufficient for knowledge. This week and next, however, I set aside these properly epistemic developments at the sentential level and focus instead on the senses' qualitative grasp of reality. For, even while a new epistemology emerges from the ashes of our long-burning desire for certainty, the abiding conviction remains that somewhere, somehow, the senses afford us access to a privileged qualitative domain.

As a first step toward demarcating that qualitative ideal, we can register two points of agreement. First, if there is going to be such a domain in the external world, it will be found only within a limited ontological sphere. No one, for instance, could suppose that the senses have any degree of privilege within the category of substance. The senses constantly misidentify things, taking one for another, confusing a friend with a stranger, an aspen with a birch, a violin with a viola. A fortiori, they go wrong about substance-level facts: whether that is Tommy biking down the street; whether the birch tree is common in the Rocky Mountains. To find the domain of sensory infallibility, we need to set aside such cases, which go beyond the narrow purview of sensation, and focus more closely on what the senses themselves show us directly about the world. Happily, there has been a fair amount of terminological continuity regarding what to call these features of the world. Sticking with Latinate terminology, we might speak of them as *qualities*, *modes*, or *properties*. Unhappily, as we will see, this verbal consensus conceals the most thoroughgoing disagreement as to which qualities are privileged.

This first constraint on our subject leads to a second. In order to find the right ontological sphere for our privileged domain, we need to distinguish between what the senses themselves reveal of the world and how we interpret that experience. How exactly such a distinction is to be drawn has proved endlessly controversial. But something of the kind seems necessary in order for us to distinguish between the immediate qualitative deliverances of the senses and those subsequent levels that culminate in a sentential judgment. At these higher levels, even if there is a baseline consensus that the senses are trustworthy, still the possibility of error is obvious. If there is going to be a domain of privilege, it will have to occur at an earlier stage. As Anselm put it back in the eleventh century,

When sight and the other senses seem to report that any number of things are otherwise than they really are, it is not the fault of the senses. They are reporting what they able to, since that is the ability they received. Instead, we should blame the judgment of the soul, which does not discriminate well what the senses are able to do or what they ought to do.[a]

This insistence on the distinction between sensation proper and sensory judgment runs all through the history of our theorizing about perception.[3]

For a typical example of the difficulties involved in discerning what belongs properly to sensation, we might briefly consider that old chestnut, Molyneux's problem. William Molyneux, whose wife became blind shortly after their marriage, famously put to John Locke the question whether someone born blind and then suddenly made able to see could visually distinguish between a cube and a sphere. Molyneux thought not, and Locke agreed.[b] Indeed, Locke argued that someone newly sighted might have *exactly* the same sensation as someone normally sighted, and yet be unable to discern cube from sphere. For, on his account, visual sensation itself conveys the ideas only of light and color. As for the rest of what vision reveals, this requires a further cognitive judgment, grounded in our perception of light and color, which the newly sighted would have to acquire through practice over time. For Locke, the great interest of Molyneux's problem, then, is that it makes explicit something we might otherwise not even notice:

This [judgment], in many cases, by a settled habit, in things whereof we have frequent experience, is performed so constantly, and so quick, that we take that for the perception of our sensation, which is an idea formed by our judgment; so that one, viz., that of sensation, serves only to excite the other, and is scarce taken notice of itself.[c]

The usual lesson taken from Molyneux's problem is that we are not immediately presented with visual information about depth. But, although that would be one place to draw the line between sensation and judgment, this is not where Locke himself draws it. For him, it is only light and color that are the "proper objects" of vision, and he contrasts this with the qualities of "space, figure, and motion."[d] This is to say that not only three-dimensional bodies, but even two-dimensional shapes must be conveyed through judgment. With respect to all such spatial qualities, we must learn how to perceive them, by seeing variations in light and color.[4]

For Locke, then, the proper domain of vision is quite narrow. One might expect that it would be here, if anywhere, that vision has its privileged domain. But in fact nothing could be farther from being the case, because Locke's proper domain of vision—light and color—also happens to be the domain of the secondary qualities, perception of which is fraught with controversy. Hence Locke faces a conundrum: those features of bodies that are the bedrock of his physical theory, his so-called primary qualities, are not the proper objects of sensation. But the secondary qualities seem to fare no better, and indeed sometimes he seems to think that they are not in the external world at all.

The puzzles that Locke and his contemporaries face in this regard are familiar; but, if we are to understand exactly why Locke finds himself in this bind, we need to go back not just to medieval Aristotelianism but even to Aristotle himself, and consider how he

---

[a] *De veritate* ch. 6, p. 127 trans.   [b] *Essay* II.9.8.   [c] II.9.9.   [d] II.9.9.

had dealt with a similar sort of crisis regarding the objects of perception. As we will see, history by no means repeats itself. But this is precisely what makes it is so interesting.

Aristotle's Relationalism

Prephilosophical reflection on perception takes for granted that the senses reliably show us the external world as it is. This is more or less true by definition, since to challenge our naïve assumption of sensory fidelity just is to commence philosophizing. And so it is that we find, even among the earliest philosophers, very clear attempts to shake off our pretheoretical naïveté. Here let me invoke only, very briefly, Democritus, whose best known words are these: "By convention sweet and by convention bitter, by convention hot, by convention cold, by convention color; but in reality atoms and void."[a] Too little of Democritus's work survives for us to have much confidence in how exactly to understand this remark, but close inspection of the fragmentary remains suggests that he did not mean merely to draw a distinction between what would become known as primary and secondary qualities; rather he wanted to undermine the reality of sensible qualities across the board. Thus, according to Sextus Empiricus (admittedly an unreliable source, since he saw skepticism everywhere), "Democritus overthrew all sensible reality."[b]

Knowing so little about Democritus's exact views, we cannot say exactly what influence they had on Aristotle. But it seems clear enough that the *De anima*'s theory of perception is framed in part as a response to Democritean subjectivism. Characteristically, that response begins by pulling apart several different kinds of sense objects. First, Aristotle distinguishes between those things that are sensible in their own right and those that are sensible only incidentally, as when we say that we see the son of Diares, whom we see only because he happens to have a color. Among things that are sensible in their own right, he distinguishes between the proper and the common sensibles. The proper sensibles (e.g., color, sound, flavor) can be perceived only through a single sense, whereas the common sensibles (e.g., motion, rest, number, shape, size) are common to all the senses.

In the midst of this discussion, Aristotle makes a further and quite surprising claim: that, when it comes to its proper sensibles, a given sense "does not admit of error."[c] This is, indeed, quite a bold assertion of sensory privilege. To see how Aristotle can maintain it, we need to look ahead to what the *De anima* says later on, in response to those who would deny that the sensible qualities are objective, mind-independent features of reality:

The earlier natural philosophers did not speak well when they supposed that nothing is white or black without sight, nor is there flavor without tasting. For though they were in one way right, in another way they were not right, since both sensation and sense object are spoken of in two ways, in some cases as potential and in others as actual. What was said by them applies to the latter, but does not apply to the former.[d]

[a] Taylor, *The Atomists*, n. 179.
[b] *Against the Logicians* II.355 (in Taylor, *Atomists*, n. 182d).
[c] *De anima* II.6, 418[a]12.   [d] III.2, 426[a]19–25.

The challenge in question is that sensible qualities might be entirely subjective, not even existing without the relevant sense. Although Democritus is not mentioned by name here, this is presumably intended, at least in part, as a response to his claim that these qualities exist only "by convention." Rather than dismiss this possibility entirely, Aristotle makes an important concession, saying that it is true with regard to actualized sense objects. What this amounts to had been explained earlier in the same chapter of the *De anima*:

The actuality of the sensible and of the sense is one and the same, though their being is different. I mean, for example, actual sound and actual hearing. For it is possible for someone who has hearing not to be hearing; and what has sound is not always making a sound. But whenever what is able to hear is actually hearing and whatever is able to sound is sounding, then actual hearing and actual sounding occur at the same time . . . And since the actuality of the sensible and the sensory power is one, though their being is different, it is necessary that what is spoken of in this way as hearing and sounding perish or be preserved at the same time, and so also for flavor and tasting, and similarly for the other cases. But this is not necessary for those things spoken of in terms of potentiality.[a]

This passage has been the subject of considerable disagreement and outright bafflement but, when these words are set alongside various other passages, a surprisingly nuanced view emerges. As Aristotle seems to understand sensible qualities here, they are actual only when actually sensed. Hence, at this level, we get the Democritean result that there is no color without sight. This outcome is not quite as radically subjective as it might appear, however, because we still have the color in potentiality, even when it is not seen. And it is the potential color, strictly speaking, that is the sensible quality. Hence colors do not exist merely by convention. Even so, by characterizing the actuality of a sense object as he does, Aristotle seems to commit himself to something remarkable. For, given that potentialities are defined in terms of the actualities to which they give rise, Aristotle suggests here that sense objects, by their very nature, are powers to produce certain kinds of sensory experiences. Thus sounds, to take Aristotle's earlier example, can exist without being heard. But, if one wants to know what a sound is, the Aristotelian answer is that it is a power (a potentiality) to produce the experience of hearing. So, instead of treating a sensible quality as entirely independent of perceivers, Aristotle makes its nature depend on its perceivers, whose actualization is its actualization. As I will henceforth put this point, rather than treat sensible qualities *absolutely*, he treats them *relationally*.

Aristotle's relational account holds only with respect to the proper sensibles. That in turn helps explain how he can suppose that the senses are infallible in this special domain. For, if the very nature of a proper sensible consists in its capacity to actualize certain sense powers, then those sense powers cannot fail to exhibit some reliability with regard to such an object, because we have simply stipulated that their object is *whatever serves to actualize them*. Just how much reliability this yields depends on exactly how tightly we circumscribe the relation. Aristotle says little about this, but it is at least easy to see the options. If a sensible is defined as that which produces *this sensation now*, then we have full-blown infallibility, because for every act of perception there will be—by

---

[a] 425^b26-6^a1, 426^a15-19.

definition—a corresponding power. But the price of such infallibility is Protagorean relativism: the way things look to me is correct for me and the way things look to you is correct for you. Since this is clearly not what Aristotle is after, we might consider a more loosely defined relation, according to which the sensibles are what produces determinate sensations in normal perceivers under normal circumstances. Still more loosely, the sensibles might be defined in terms of producing a merely determinable class of sensations. We might, for instance, say that being a color just is the power to produce visual sensations. On this last account, we might make mistakes about determinate hues even in normal circumstances, but at least it would be infallibly true that, when we have a visual experience, we are seeing color. That Aristotle himself is after something less than complete infallibility is suggested when he offers the concession that "perception of the proper objects of sense is true or is subject to falsity in the smallest degree."[a] But beyond this he has little more to say, leaving the details as an exercise in building your own Aristotelianism.[5]

In offering this sort of relational account of the proper sensibles, Aristotle concedes a great deal to the Democritean camp, allowing that color, sound, and the like, despite seeming to be absolute features of reality, are in fact real only by virtue of there being sensory beings like us, who are responsive to these objects. The proper sensibles depend on us in the way in which a joke's being funny depends on the sensibilities of its audience. This is a startlingly subjective view of the sensible qualities. Indeed, one might well doubt whether it could really be Aristotle's, were it not for the fact that he elsewhere seems to commit himself to such consequences. In *Metaphysics* IV, for instance, he argues for an underlying reality beyond sensible qualities, on the following grounds:

If only the sensible [*to aisthēton*] exists, then nothing would exist if animate things did not exist, for [in that case] there would be no sensation. Now it is likewise true [in that case] that there would exist neither sensibles nor sensings, since this is the affection of a sensory being. But, even in the absence of sensation, it is impossible for the substrata [*hupokeimena*] that cause the sensation not to exist. For sensation is not the sensation of itself, but there is something beyond the sensation, which must be prior to the sensation.[b]

The argument critically relies on the idea that, in a world without animate beings capable of sensation, there would be no sensibles—that is, apparently, no color, no sound, and so on. This surprising claim is exactly what one would expect to find if Aristotle defines the sensible qualities relationally, in terms of being perceived. So, he here reasons, if all things outside perceivers were sensible qualities, then if the perceivers were removed there would be nothing left. Since that is absurd, there must be "something beyond" sensations and sensibles, something "prior" to them.

Aristotle does not always characterize the sensibles in this relational way—some passages flatly contradict this approach—but the idea is repeated enough times in enough places to represent, at a minimum, one important strand in his thought. He is inclined to accept, for instance, the otherwise strange and unmotivated view that the proper sensibles can have no effect in the world beyond acting on their corresponding

---

[a] *De anima* III.3, 428[b]18.   [b] *Meta.* IV.5, 1010[b]30–11a1.

sense power.[a] And in the *De anima* itself, a chapter after having introduced color as something sensible in its own right, he draws yet another distinction:

The visible is color, and this rests on what is visible in its own right—in its own right not by definition, but because it contains within itself the cause of its being visible.[b]

Here we seem to have a new candidate for what is sensible in its own right: not color, but that which underlies color. The underlying body counts as visible, evidently, because it plays an underlying causal role. Color gets its title as the object of sight through metaphysical fiat, "by definition," through a relational account that guarantees the veridicality of perception. But if we want to understand the full causal story of what gives rise to color experiences, we need to consider not only the colors but also their underlying subjects.

As this last passage suggests, Aristotle sometimes describes the sensibles relationally and sometimes he does not. Like so many others in the history of philosophy, he seems to be of various minds with respect to how we should talk about color and the other sensibles, because such talk serves so many different sorts of purposes. We might, in particular, contrast two projects. One, that of the natural philosopher, is to tell the causal story of how qualities in the world give rise to sensations in the mind. This project fosters an absolute conception of the sensibles. A second project, that of the epistemologist, is to understand what the senses show us about the world. Such *objects* of sensation might simply be thought to be those absolute qualities in the world that *cause* our sensations. In a world like that, the senses would be quite ideal in what they reveal about the world around us. By Aristotle's time, however, the shadow of Democritus loomed over all these naïve accounts. The causes of sensation—atoms in motion, as Democritus had it—might be entirely different from what the senses show us about the world. Hence another great Democritean slogan: "In reality we know nothing, for truth is in the depths."[c] Aristotle's relationalism acknowledges the gravity of this charge. Ideally, the senses would reveal the fundamental qualities of the natural world. And Aristotle does seem to think that, when it comes to the tangible qualities hot and cold, the senses do just this. But in general there is no reason to suppose that the senses are showing us the world in its absolute character. This is not to say that they show us nothing about the world, only that their domain has as its defining feature the very fact of its being perceptible. (What do funny movies have in common? They make people laugh.) Ideally we might have hoped that the senses would take us deeper into reality than this. Yet, on reflection, why should they? Why should the world be so easy to grasp?[6]

Although such relationalism runs all throughout Aristotle's discussions of the sensibles, later Aristotelians failed to recognize it. Unconcerned by the sort of subjectivist challenge posed by Democritus, commentators in the Greek, Arabic, and Latin traditions were content to treat sensible qualities in absolute terms, as mind-independent objects, made evident through perception. This, as we will see, had profound consequences for the subsequent history of these discussions, because when seventeenth-century authors once again begin to take Democritus seriously, the only version of Aristotelianism they know is one that can offer them no help. Left to their own

---

[a] *De anima* II.12, 424^{b}3–5.   [b] II.7, 418^{a}29–31.   [c] Taylor, *The Atomists*, n. 179b.

resources, they go down dark and twisting paths of their own devising. But here, in my enthusiasm for the story I have to tell, I am getting ahead of myself. Let us turn to what becomes of Aristotelianism in the Middle Ages.

Aristotelian Realism

Medieval authors were so far from recognizing the relational thread in Aristotle's view that they generally did not even consider it a possibility. An exception is Averroes. In an intriguing passage from his *Middle Commentary* on the *De anima* (*c*.1190), he sheds some light on why relational accounts of the proper sensibles did not seem attractive. The passage concerns a remark in Aristotle's *De anima* (II.7) quoted once already:

The visible is color, and this <u>rests on</u> [*esti to epi*] what is visible in its own right—in its own right not by definition, but because it contains within itself the cause of its being visible.

This passage, as the Greek is now standardly construed, draws a distinction between color and its underlying subject and explains how they can both count as visible. Averroes, however, in line with standard medieval translations (Arabic and Latin), construes the passage differently:

The visible is color, and this <u>is</u> visible in its own right—in its own right not by definition, but because it contains within itself the cause of its being visible.[a]

The original texts, across the various languages, are close enough for the two passages to receive similar English translations, except for just the few critical underlined words. That slight difference transforms the meaning of the passage, so that the medieval version has color rather than its underlying subject as visible in its own right on account of its causal role. In explaining the passage so construed, Averroes distinguishes between what it is to be visible and what it is to be a color. Extensionally (as we now might put it) these two concepts are nearly equivalent, inasmuch as visible things, with few exceptions, just are colors. But the concepts themselves are different (again, as we might put it), because *visible* is a relational concept whereas *color* is absolute. In Averroes's own words:

The truly visible, then, is color, and it is color that exists in its own right outside the soul. As for the visible, it is visible only in connection with the viewer . . . For [the essences of] some things are said in their own right without relation to anything else, whereas the essences of other things are said in relation to something else. Color is among those things that exist in their own right, whereas the visible is among those things that are said in relation.[b]

Averroes's idea is that color counts as visible "in its own right" because the concept (or "essence") of color is absolute, inasmuch as a thing counts as a color "without relation to anything else." The concept of the visible, in contrast, is relational, inasmuch as it applies to a thing "only in connection with the viewer."

It is easy to see why Averroes thinks that *visible* should be understood relationally, inasmuch as a thing's counting as visible depends on its relationship with other things

---

[a] Quoting from the translation of Aristotle in Averroes's *Long Commentary on the* De anima II.66.

[b] *Middle Commentary on the* De anima II.7, n. 173.

that see it. But why not say precisely the same about color? Averroes immediately goes on to make the critical argument:

Color is the cause of the existence in a thing of this relationship—that is, of the thing's being visible. This is because a body becomes visible due to its surface, the surface becoming visible due to the color it possesses. It is color that moves a transparent body—a body that receives light—into actuality.[a]

Averroes thus treats *color* not as relational but as a natural kind concept: as picking out a class of physical agents in the world that produce a certain effect in the surrounding bodies and thereby make a body visible. If there were no perceivers, then nothing would count as visible. But there would still be things we might justly call colors, inasmuch as there would still be qualities of bodies playing this particular causal role. And it is because we conceive of colors in this way that we should think of them as the things that are visible in their own right. For, as the last clause in the original Aristotelian text makes clear, we want to identify that which is visible in its own right with that which is "the cause of its being visible."[7]

   This line of thought goes to the heart of the standard medieval version of an Aristotelian theory of sensation. The things that are visible in their own right are the colors, because these are the properties in the world that are in the right sort of causal relationship with our visual faculties. This is the domain of special visual privilege, because this is where the world rubs up against sight without any error-inducing mediation on the part of judgment. Hence this is the domain where the senses are infallible or, at any rate (as we saw Aristotle put it earlier), "subject to falsity in the smallest degree."[b] What does that mean, "in the smallest degree"? A relational account can attribute such guaranteed reliability to a conceptual link between the senses and their proper objects: the sensible qualities are defined in terms that guarantee veridicality more or less strictly. But on the usual medieval reading the guarantee is natural rather than conceptual: the senses are reliable because they have been designed that way, and their reliability in the case of the proper sensibles holds for the most part, which is as strong a claim of reliability as can be made for purely natural sublunary biological processes.

   So we arrive at what often gets labeled "Aristotelian realism" with regard to the sensible qualities: the view that the senses have a privileged domain in the external world, where they get things right for the most part, perceiving some of the principal qualities that are causally efficacious in the natural world. As we have seen, this picture does not do justice to Aristotle's own discussions of the subject but, even so, it aptly characterizes the Aristotelian framework, which would dominate philosophy until the seventeenth century.

   The collapse of Aristotelian realism would be a principal ingredient in the fascinating chaos that engulfs post-scholastic thought. But before turning to these developments we might glance at some early signs of the trouble to come, from back in the fourteenth century. This was itself an era of considerable philosophical turmoil. Skepticism had come into fashion in Europe, as had various kinds of reductive corpuscularianism. Philosophers hotly contested the nature of all sensible qualities, including motion,

---

[a] II.7, n. 174.   [b] *De anima* III.3, 428[b]18.

size, and shape, as well as color and the other proper sensibles. In short, movements were afoot in Paris and elsewhere that threatened to bring down the whole edifice of Aristotelian philosophy. Ultimately the church had to intervene aggressively, issuing a series of condemnations, in 1346 and 1347, which ended the teaching careers of Nicholas of Autrecourt and John of Mirecourt, two prominent iconoclasts. Subsequent scholars, on pain of heresy, were forced to adhere to traditional Aristotelian doctrines on topics like substantial form and real qualities. From this point forward, scholasticism was locked into its familiar form, until church authority weakened enough in the seventeenth century that it could, at least in certain parts of Europe, be safely questioned.

If external conditions had been different, the "modern" revolution of the seventeenth century might well have happened in the mid-fourteenth century. If it had, the vanguard of that movement would have been the two philosophical giants of the era, John Buridan and Nicole Oresme. But Buridan and Oresme stayed largely within the prescribed confines of orthodox scholasticism, and their works after 1347 were especially cautious with regard to the various condemned doctrines. Even so, the ideas they put forth raise a host of difficulties for orthodox perceptual theory. Both stress the long history of Aristotelian attempts to specify precisely the domain in which the senses are infallible with regard to their proper objects. Themistius, back in late antiquity, had required a well-disposed sense organ, a pure medium, and an appropriate distance.[a] Averroes would later qualify the doctrine so as to claim only that "the sense does not err for the most part."[b] Oresme invokes this history and then goes one step farther, contending that the thesis holds only at the determinable level. When we see that something is colored, Oresme says, we are very unlikely to be wrong. But when it comes to distinguishing between white and red, mistakes are quite possible, and mistakes become even likelier when we go down to determinate shades. Oresme even takes the extraordinary step of questioning whether color is the primary object of sight. Against the consensus that runs from antiquity all the way to the seventeenth century, he suggests that what we see is not colors on the surface of bodies, but rather reflected light, and that indeed there is no need to postulate any such thing as surface color, because what we call 'colors' is simply light as it is variably reflected off different surfaces.[c]

Buridan's challenge to the standard theory is even more radical, because he calls into question the very idea of a privileged qualitative domain. Reciting the various ways in which commentators have constrained Aristotle's avowal of infallibility, Buridan concludes that, once the theory becomes so thoroughly hedged, there is no longer any reason to privilege the proper over the common sensibles. Under the right conditions and for the most part, the senses do not err with regard to *any* of their sense objects. This is of course an embarrassment to the project of developing a faithful Aristotelianism, since it represents such a clear departure from the Philosopher, but Buridan is completely unconcerned by that. He simply follows the logic of the standard medieval view to where it naturally leads.

Indeed, Buridan goes farther still, challenging Aristotle's most fundamental distinction between kinds of sensibles. On the standard medieval view, as we have seen, the proper sensibles are privileged in virtue of a specially tight causal relationship between sensory

---

[a] *On the Soul* II.6, re. 418[a]8–13.   [b] *Long Commentary on the* De anima II.63.
[c] Nicole Oresme, *Quaest. de anima* II.10, II.16.

experience and a set of qualities in the world (color, sound, flavor, odor, heat). But Buridan claims, to the contrary, that sensation presents in a confused way all of the various external sensible objects, without having any sort of privileged access to any of them and without even representing any of them as distinct from any other:

Although an external sense cognizes Socrates, or whiteness, or something white, still this happens only through a species represented confusedly and all at once along with the substance, the whiteness, the size, and the location, in accord with how it appears in the cognizer's field of vision [in prospectu]. The sense cannot distinguish the confusion. If, that is, it cannot abstract from one another the species of substance, whiteness, size, and location, then it cannot perceive substance, whiteness, or something white, except in the way it exists in its field of vision.[a]

When we see Socrates, we are furnished with a confused representation of various things: color, size, shape, location, even Socrates himself. No one aspect of this confused representation is privileged. How could it be, at the sensory level, since the senses are incapable of pulling apart the various aspects of a single confused representation?

So much, then, for a privileged qualitative domain. Buridan allows the distinction between proper and common sensibles, but only at a very superficial level, as nothing more than the obvious contrast between those sensibles apprehended by a single, unique sense and those that are grasped by multiple senses. He undermines even the distinction between what is sensible in its own right (per se) and what is sensible only incidentally (per accidens). On the standard scholastic view, this distinction marks the difference between those features of the world that do and those that do not make a causal impression on the senses. But Buridan refuses to commit to any such neat link between sensory experience and the underlying causal reality. Instead he takes the distinction to arise from the conceptualization we impose on sensation at the intellectual level: "when we say that one thing is sensible per se and another per accidens, we do not intend a division or difference between things that are sensed, but rather we intend a distinction or difference between names or concepts by which the things we sense are named or conceived."[b] Across the board, he thinks that we have illicitly imported intellectual conceptualization into our account of perception, making it seem as if the senses have the conceptual resources to pull apart distinct aspects of what is given to them. At the strictly sensory level there is no domain where we are ideally capable of grasping the world as it is. On the contrary, sensory perception is always confused, in the technical sense that it is incapable of representing one sensible as distinct from another.[8]

Such claims spring quite naturally from doubts over medieval Aristotelian realism—that is, from doubts over whether the proper sensibles are causal features of the natural world to which our sensory powers give us privileged access. Although church authority deterred Buridan from attacking this theory directly, his qualms on this score led him to a theory of perception not held hostage to any doubtful story about how the sense powers interact with the physical world. Perhaps there are no such qualities as the senses allegedly detect. If there are, their nature is surely much too obscure to be grasped clearly by the senses. In any case, given the extreme uncertainty of all such stories, Buridan finds it quite natural to argue that the senses themselves—prior to the conceptualization of intellect—offer us no special window into reality. Hence there is no

---

[a] Buridan, Quaest. de anima III.8 n. 26.   [b] II.12 n. 12.

privileged domain of immediate sensory access. Even at the qualitative level, the workings of sensation are far less ideal than philosophers had hitherto supposed.

The Quantitative Turn

Although John Buridan was the most important philosopher at the most important university in the world for three decades in the mid-fourteenth century, his account of perception had little influence on subsequent developments. Aristotelian realism remained ascendant until the middle of the seventeenth century, when it came under fierce attack from a familiar roster of figures: Galileo, Descartes, Hobbes, Gassendi, and many others. The result was a radically changed understanding of how sense perception works and in what domain it has its special privilege.

The trouble begins with the scholastic theory of real qualities. As we have seen, the Aristotelian tradition—even if not Aristotle himself—treated color and the other proper sensibles as causal agents at work in the natural world. To be sure, not all of these qualities were regarded as equally fundamental. The elemental qualities—hot, cold, wet, dry—are most basic, and their various combinations give rise to the mixed qualities we actually perceive. Still, the various proper sensibles, even if they result from the elements, are nevertheless fundamental in something like the way in which we regard H_2O as fundamental. Just as we think of water as fundamental to life, so they thought of colors, sounds, and so on as fundamental to sensation, inasmuch as these are the physical agents that directly shape the contents of perceptual experience.

Of the various scholastic doctrines that came in for scorn in the seventeenth century, none fared worse than did these real qualities. Metaphysically, the theory was suspect because it claimed that such qualities could exist independently of bodies (at least miraculously, in the Eucharist). Thus Descartes mocked them as like "little souls attached to their bodies,"[a] and in place of such real accidents he and others introduced a metaphysics of *modes*. But quite apart from its doubtful metaphysics, the doctrine of real qualities was attacked as bad natural philosophy, precisely because it treated qualitative properties as fundamental. One of the principal goals of the mechanistic philosophers was to account for such qualities in wholly geometric–kinetic terms—as nothing more, in bodies, than particles of various shapes and sizes set in motion in various ways.

Beyond these questions of natural philosophy and metaphysics, the debate over real qualities also had an epistemic dimension. As we have seen in other cases, the epistemic ideal depends critically on how one conceives of the world, and so it is here that the rise of the mechanical philosophy yielded a revolution in perceptual theory. Around 1300 it was common wisdom that what a sense most reliably puts us in touch with is its proper sense object: color, sound, heat, flavor, odor. By the end of the seventeenth century, in contrast, opinion had turned upside down so much that this list of special sense objects came to describe precisely those cases where the senses were *least* to be trusted, and the cases where the senses got things right were instead the so-called common sensibles, the geometric–kinetic properties of motion, shape, and size.

---

[a] Letter to Mersenne in 1643 (III: 648).

These features of the world came to be honored as *primary qualities*, relegating the old proper sensibles to the class of mere *secondary qualities*.

The distance between these authors and the Aristotelian tradition is remarkable. On Aristotle's ranking, the perception of the proper sensibles "is subject to falsity in the smallest degree," followed by the perception that a proper sensible is to be attributed to one subject or another, followed at the least reliable tail end by the perception of the common sensibles, where "there is, most of all, error in the realm of perception."[a] For the mechanistic philosophers, in contrast, the proper sensibles are precisely the place where the senses go most disastrously wrong. When Malebranche writes, as quoted at the start of this lecture, that "your senses delude you a very great deal more than you can imagine," it is these secondary qualities that he has in mind above all else. Where the senses are at their best—where they most reliably capture the world as it is—is in their perception of the common sensibles, the so-called primary qualities. Yet these, strictly speaking, are not qualitative features of the world but rather quantitative ones. In the terms of Aristotle's *Categories*, they are *quantities* rather than *qualities*.

The trouble is that quantities are an extremely problematic place in which to locate the domain of sensory privilege. One obvious difficulty is that there seems to be no denying Aristotle's point that, when it comes to the perception of size, shape, and motion, the senses are indeed highly fallible. So, if this is the domain where the senses get things most nearly right, we must immediately lower our expectations considerably. Yet this is only the first of various difficulties for the theory. A further set of problems arises from the apparently continuous nature of the primary qualities. Although scholastic authors had considered in some detail the paradoxes of the continuum, in their view these worries did not raise any particular difficulties for perception, because their proper objects of perception were qualitative. Once real qualities are abandoned, however, the consequences for perception become hard to miss. Leibniz, for instance, flatly denies that bodies possess geometric properties of the sort usually supposed. He writes to Arnauld that, because of the infinite divisibility of continuous bodies, there is no fact of the matter at all about their shape; hence "the extensions we attribute to bodies are merely phenomena and abstractions."[b] In the seventeenth-century context, when such properties are supposed to be the *best* candidates for being objects of perception, this is a serious problem.

Most serious of all, however, was the question of how the primary qualities could play the causal role formerly played by secondary qualities. Color, on the usual scholastic account, is a real quality within bodies that can propagate itself through an illuminated medium, up to the sense of sight, thereby transferring information about the surface qualities of the original body. This was not a process riding on top of some more familiar mechanistic process, because the scholastics in general denied that the geometric–kinetic properties of bodies had any causal efficacy on their own. Hence Aquinas writes that "the common sensibles do not move the senses first and on their own, but by reason of sensible quality."[c] And "just as accidental sensibles are apprehended only insofar as proper sensibles are apprehended, so too for common sensibles. For sight never apprehends size or shape except insofar as it apprehends something

---

[a] *De anima* III.3, 428^{b}18–25.   [b] To Arnauld, April 30, 1687 (*Philosophical Essays*, p. 87).
[c] *Summa theol.* 1a 78.3 ad 2.

colored."[a] Across the natural world, the fundamental causal agents were not bodies in motion, but qualities spreading their influence on nearby bodies, making cold things hot, dry things wet, and so on. From the scholastic point of view, then, it would have been entirely mysterious how there could be any perception at all, if the proper sensibles were cut out of the story.[9]

Suppose, however, with the mechanistic philosophers, that we reject colors and so on as the scholastics conceived of them, and that instead shapes and the rest play the analogous causal role. How exactly is this supposed to work? Is there a property of a body, its *shape*, that propagates itself in the illuminated medium? Descartes describes shapes as modes of extension. Do these modes exercise causality on the surrounding bodies? The familiar mechanistic story was that causation occurs when one body comes into contact with another, somehow transferring a certain motion from cause to effect. Aristotle himself had likened perception to the impression of a stamp, which offers a serviceably mechanistic picture of the process. But can we really suppose that the motions of bodies act mechanistically on the surrounding air, all the way up to the eye, and then stamp the eye with an impression that yields a sensation of the object? Quite apart from the familiar worries about how conscious experience could arise from such a process, it would be natural to be seriously skeptical even about the purely physiological part of that story. On its face, the mechanistic philosophy offers only a very dubious alternative to the scholastic conception of perception.[10]

Descartes's Three Paths

And so we arrive at that welter of conflicting doctrines that is seventeenth-century philosophy of perception. The material world, for post-scholastic philosophers, is particles in motion, yet particles in motion are not what we perceive—not, at any rate, in a way that lives up to the ideal expected of the senses. And to the extent that we do perceive shapes and sizes and the other geometric–kinetic properties, it would seem that we do so through colors, sounds, and so on; yet these are only doubtfully features of the external world. To see the range of options that would emerge, we can turn to Descartes, whose complex and somewhat conflicted views point down the three quite distinct paths that shape modern philosophy of perception: subjective, reductive, and relational.

As both a rationalist and a scientist, Descartes writes about perception in ways that are, on the face of it, difficult to reconcile. On the one hand, he tells us that the senses "do not, except occasionally and accidentally, teach us what external bodies are like in themselves. So we will readily set aside the prejudices of the senses and rely here on intellect alone."[b] On the other hand, his most developed scientific treatise was a detailed investigation into optics, in which he sought to explain precisely how vision does yield an accurate account of the external world. Moreover, it would seem entirely bizarre if, as one of the founding figures of modern science, Descartes really wanted to rely on "intellect alone," forbidding experience from playing any kind of substantial role in our

[a] *Comm. de anima* II.13.75–9.   [b] *Principles* II.3.

understanding of the physical world. These seemingly distinct strands in his thought need unraveling.

Sometimes Descartes suggests that the role of the senses is simply to help the body navigate through the world. Thus, in the *Meditations*, "the proper purpose of the sensory perceptions given me by nature is simply to inform the mind of what is beneficial or harmful for the composite of which the mind is a part; and to this extent they are sufficiently clear and distinct."[a] This might suggest that Descartes is unwilling to recognize any domain of sensory privilege that extends beyond his body. In fact, though, his views are much more nuanced. In his most detailed analysis of the claim that the senses would have to be "clear and distinct," he offers this rule:

Sensations . . . can be clearly perceived provided we take strict care in our judgments concerning them to include no more than what is precisely contained in our perception, and no more than that of which we are intimately conscious.[b]

This does not mean that we clearly perceive only the ideas that are within us. Rather Descartes's point is that we have to be on guard against mistakenly supposing that the senses are showing us more than they in fact are. We have become accustomed "from our early childhood," he says, to misjudge the contents of the senses: in seeing a color, for instance, we take ourselves to see something outside us that "closely resembles" our idea of color.[c] In the case of this and other proper sensibles, the rule requires us to limit our perceptions to what lies within us: "pain and color and so on are clearly and distinctly perceived when they are regarded merely as sensations or thoughts."[d] Here, as we will see in detail next week, is where the story turns inward. But this is not what the rule dictates for common sensibles such as size, shape, and number. Here we perceive things as they are in the world. Thus, again, the Aristotelian story is inverted: the common sensibles turn out to be the good case, whereas color and the other proper sensibles have become the bad case.[11]

Lying behind Descartes's account of perception is the now familiar assumption that the senses themselves cannot be leading us astray. Indeed, "there is absolutely nothing to be found in sensations that does not bear witness to the power and goodness of God."[e] To help make good on this claim, Descartes distinguishes three grades of sensation, the first of which is purely physiological and the second purely phenomenal (that is, a bare experience in the mind), leaving the third to culminate in perception: seeing for instance a certain shape and size, or seeing that a stick is colored. He remarks of this last grade that "although such reasoning is commonly assigned to the senses . . . it is clear that it depends solely on the intellect."[f] No wonder that Descartes insists (above) that we "rely on intellect alone," setting aside the "prejudices of the senses." This, for him, does not imply giving up on sensation entirely, but only judging it aright. Nor do such remarks imply that the lower grades of sensation are flawed. On the contrary, by distinguishing between pure sensation and a higher level of sensory judgment, Descartes can say of the first two stages that "there can be no falsity in these grades."[g] Even so, this sort of guarantee at the pre-intellectual level, so familiar from earlier theories, does not yield any external domain of sensory privilege, because we arrive at a perception of the

---

[a] *Med.* 6 (VII: 83).   [b] *Principles* I.66.   [c] I.66.   [d] I.68.
[e] *Med.* 6 (VII: 87).   [f] Sixth Replies (VII: 437–8).   [g] VII: 438.

external world only at the third stage. And at that level there is no guarantee of infallibility, because there we are liable, of our own free will, to go beyond what our God-given powers show us about the world.[12]

With respect to what is now the good case, the geometric properties, Descartes is no more sanguine about sensory reliability than were the Aristotelians. His famous inventory of perceptual illusions bars him from claiming anything like infallibility regarding the common sensibles, no matter how carefully hedged. Hence, in distinguishing this case from the bad case of the proper sensibles, he puts his point carefully: "there are many other features, such as size, shape, number, etc., which we clearly perceive ourselves to sense or to understand in no other way than as they are in objects, or at least as they can be."[a] These final cautionary words underscore the difference between this case and that of the proper sensibles. Even if our perception of the geometric properties is not highly reliable, it is at least accurate about *how* the world is. In contrast, the situation with regard to the proper sensibles is so dismal that, when we take them to be features of the external world, we are giving that world features that it is not even *possible* for it to possess. We may wrongly judge the sun to be three-feet wide and flat. Well, at least it could be that way. When we judge the sun to be yellow, we are not even giving it a property that it could have.

Why this difference? That is, why does Descartes think that, whereas our perception of the geometric properties gets the world at least roughly right, our perception of the proper sensibles not only does not but also cannot depict the world as it is? The short answer is that he thinks that colors and the other proper sensibles, as we sense them, are mental phenomena. If so, then it follows not just that they *are not* in the external world, but that they *cannot* be out there, since for Descartes *res extensa* cannot have mental properties. This, however, leads only to another question: Why not say that geometric qualities, *as we sense them*, are also mental phenomena? The answer is that, as we have seen, Descartes thinks that the perception of geometric properties shows us something about the world as it is—the size, shape, and motion of things. To perceive the proper sensibles in that way, the senses would have to work quite differently. In the case of color, the eye would have to reveal to us the microscopic rotation of particles. In the case of sound, Descartes writes, "if the sense of hearing brought to our thought the true image of its object, it would have to be the case that, instead of making us conceive of sound, it made us conceive of the motion of the parts of the air that then vibrate against our ears."[b]

Yet if earlier philosophers went wrong here, were they not led astray by the senses? And in that case must we not reject Descartes's claim (above) that, if we focus strictly on the senses prior to judgment, they exhibit "no falsity" and "absolutely nothing" unworthy of God? To avoid this result, Descartes takes the remarkable step of claiming that, when it comes to the proper sensibles, the senses do not misrepresent the world because they do not represent it at all. Rattling off a nearly complete list of what would soon be called the secondary qualities, he remarks that "what we call the sensations of tastes, smells, sounds, heat, cold, light, colors, and the like—these sensations represent nothing located outside our thought."[c] Descartes is not claiming that sensation never

---

[a] *Principles* I.70.   [b] *The World* ch. 1 (XI: 5).   [c] *Principles* I.71.

represents the external world. Indeed, he immediately adds that "at the same time the mind perceived sizes, shapes, motions, and so on, which were presented to it not as sensations but as things, or modes of things, existing (or at least capable of existing) outside thought." Sizes and so on are of course in the world, and these are "presented" to the mind through sensation, again building in the proviso that, even if the senses are not entirely reliable about these geometric properties, at least they show that world in the way it is, as it is "capable of existing." For color and the rest, matters are quite otherwise. When we experience color, the sense does not represent to us that the world has such a quality. It is we who have fallen into the bad habit of understanding the world in that way.

Now we can see how Descartes stands on the brink of three paths: subjective, reductive, and relational. The first path, the one most associated with his name and that would have the greatest influence on subsequent thought, is the way of ideas. Rejecting the scholastic treatment of sensible qualities as falling into natural kinds, Descartes offers instead a subjective account of the proper sensibles. Indeed, he seems to go so far as to deny that the senses represent anything out in the external world. There is thus no problem of misrepresentation when it comes to the secondary qualities, because there is no representation. The privileged qualitative domain is internal. Yet this first and most prominent path is precarious. As we have seen, Descartes asserts that the senses' main function is to alert us to what is beneficial or harmful to the body. To do this, the senses presumably must represent the external environment in some way or another. Otherwise, what would they be alerting us to? And it seems that the senses must play this role not just with respect to the geometric properties, but also with respect to the proper sensibles. Heat, after all, is a paradigm case for the bodily-harm story. So, if the senses do not *somehow* represent the proper sensibles as things out in the world, then this part of Descartes' story seems to collapse. Hence he needs some way to identify an external sensory domain.

This brings us to the second, reductive path. Descartes offers detailed and ingenious accounts of the mechanistic processes that give rise to our sensations, making these the most obvious candidates for being objects in the world. Yet he consistently resists treating such processes as objects of perception. For, even if these are the *causes* of the physiological events that ultimately yield perception, he cannot regard them as the *objects* of such perception, because this would violate the cardinal principle "to include no more than what is precisely contained in our perception, and no more than that of which we are intimately conscious."[a] Vision simply does not reveal to us such things as the microscopic rotation of particles, and so this sort of reductive explanatory level is not a plausible candidate to serve as the object of perception.

This leaves Descartes with one final and subtler path, that of relationalism, which yields an external sensory domain of certain unspecified powers within bodies:

It is clear, then, that when we say that we perceive colors in objects, this is really just the same as saying that we perceive something in the objects whose nature we do not know, but which produces in us a certain very clear and vivid sensation that we call the sensation of color. But the way in which we make our judgment can vary very widely. As long as we merely judge that

---

[a] *Principles* I.66 (as quoted above).

there is in the objects (that is, in the things, whatever they may turn out to be, which are the source of our sensations) something whose nature we do not know, then we avoid error.[a]

The passage attempts the delicate balancing act that Descartes requires. Color sensations have a vivid qualitative feel that we have become accustomed to project out onto the external world. That is a terrible mistake. But it is not the fault of the senses that we do this, inasmuch as our visual powers themselves do not represent the world in this way. This is not, however, to say that vision does not represent the external world at all. It shows us that there is an external world that causes our color sensations, a world that has certain geometric and kinetic properties. Again, the senses do not represent these reductive mechanistic facts. Still, vision does represent something in the world, inasmuch as a certain color sensation is the sign of something in objects that is the cause of such a sensation. What the nature of that something is—or even what it is roughly like—cannot be determined by the sensation itself. Yet the senses do have a kind of external domain: they represent that there is *something* there, even if their deliverances at this level are opaque.[13]

With this we are on the brink of returning to Aristotle's relationalism, whereby the objects of perception are defined in terms of the response they produce in perceivers such as us. Descartes sees that we can say, of colors in objects, that they are "something . . . that produces in us a certain very clear and vivid sensation that we call the sensation of color" (as above). But, rather than embrace this as the foundation of a relational or dispositional theory of the sensible qualities, he sees it effectively as a dead end. Thus the very same passage holds that, when we talk this way, we are saying that "there is in the objects . . . something whose nature we do not know." Or, as he puts it elsewhere in that same discussion, "if someone says that he sees color in a body or feels pain in a limb, this amounts to saying that he sees or feels something there of which he is wholly ignorant."[b] This is the best thing to say, if we want to be able to explain the way in which colors and pains are outside the mind. But Descartes takes such remarks to signal the discouraging end of this third path, and so these halting steps toward relationalism ultimately amount to just a short side road off the main theory, which treats our internal ideas as the primary objects of perception. Next week we will explore why Descartes and his contemporaries found this way of ideas so appealing. In the time that remains today, I will try to get more clear about why these two external approaches—reductive and relational—failed to get more traffic in the unsettled context of seventeenth-century philosophy.[14]

The Ideal of Fidelity

Descartes was unusually optimistic in his pronouncements about the underlying mechanistic explanation for various macro-level phenomena. Most authors of the time were much less confident about their various reductive hypotheses, and this might seem like a good reason not to have embraced a reductive account of the objects of perception. In fact, however, such accounts do not require any degree of confidence in some one

---

[a] *Principles* I.70.   [b] *Principles* I.68.

particular story. If color turns out to be the microscopic rotation of particles, then particle rotation has *always* been the object of vision, for us and for other animals, regardless of whether science has advanced to the point of making this reductive identification. On views of this kind, *whatever* the true reductive story turns out to be about a given sensible quality, *that* is what we perceive.

The real objection to reductive accounts, which is at the same time the main objection to relational accounts, comes from their failure to satisfy the epistemic ideal that these authors continue to cherish. To see why this is so, we need a more nuanced account of our long quest for infallibility, one that pays heed to two different dimensions of appraisal, which I will refer to as *reliability* and *fidelity*. For a sense to exhibit reliability, as I will use the term, it must be the case that a sense's signaling the presence of a quality closely correlates with that quality's presence. Ideally, however, we would like more than mere reliability from the senses. We would also like fidelity, which is to say that the senses should tell us something about the character of what we perceive: not just *that* a certain quality is present to us, but *what* that quality is like.

In principle, a reductive account of the objects of perception can score quite well in terms of reliability. If blue just is a certain rotation of particles, then seeing blue reliably shows us that. But the account is disastrous when it comes to fidelity. Thus Descartes, seeking an account of what the senses show us clearly and distinctly and taking for granted that there is *something* the senses show us in that way, hardly even considers that the objects of perception might be found at the reductive mechanistic level. In the case of hearing, for example, we have seen Descartes say that, for it to have "brought to our thought the true image of its object," it would have to show us "the motion of the parts of the air that then vibrate against our ears."[a] This, of course, hearing fails to do. Berkeley seems to make a similar point when he has Hylas propose that "in the real and philosophic sense . . . [sound] is nothing but a certain motion of the air." To this Philonous responds that, since it is sight and touch rather than hearing that detect motion, we would face the absurd result that sounds "may possibly be seen or felt, but never heard."[b] This may look flat-footed, since it seems obvious that Hylas might just hold his ground and insist that part of what the new science has shown us is that, in fact, hearing *does* acquaint us with motions of a certain kind. But Berkeley's point, I think, is subtler. Although the reductionist can in principle insist that hearing acquaints us with nothing more than certain motions, this would require supposing that what it shows us is nothing at all like what it *seems* to show us. A "motion of the air" is simply not the sort of thing we *hear*. Neither Descartes nor Berkeley can tolerate a world in which the senses are so miserably unfaithful to reality.

Part of the appeal of Aristotelian realism was that it secures fidelity as well as reliability. At least for the most part, the senses reliably track the presence of their proper objects, and they do so in a way that faithfully captures what those qualities are. To see how fidelity obtains, consider John Buridan's commentary on an often quoted remark of Aristotle's: "if some perception is lacking, it is necessary for some knowledge to be lacking too."[c] Buridan notices that this remark might seem to be undermined by Aristotle's own reductive story about what grounds the various sensible qualities.

---

[a] *The World* ch. 1 (XI: 5).   [b] *Three Dialogues*, dial. 1 (II: 182).   [c] *Post. An.* I.18, 81^{a}38.

He wonders: "Why, through a knowledge of the [elemental] tangible qualities, can we not come to a knowledge of flavors or odors [for example], since these are their causes, just as in many other cases we go from knowledge of causes to knowledge of effects, and conversely?" Buridan's answer is that explanation in terms of the four elemental qualities would count as a *kind* of knowledge available through other sensory modalities, but not one that gets at the *nature* of the sensible qualities: "if we lack a sense from birth then it is impossible for us, with respect to the sensibles proper to that sense, to acquire naturally a knowledge of the quidditative concepts of those sensibles."[a] This is to say that each of the senses shows us something in high fidelity about its particular corner of outward reality—indeed, that each sense shows us the very nature of its proper objects.

But, as the world changes, so our epistemic ideals change with it. Hence post-scholastic philosophers, after their quantitative turn, can no longer suppose, unproblematically, that the senses show us external reality in high fidelity. Thus Descartes suggests that the most the senses can be said to show us, without infidelity, is "something whose nature we do not know." Relationalism is the best we can do, if we seek a privileged external domain for sensation; yet Descartes himself is no more interested in developing this sort of program than were the scholastics themselves. Scholastic Aristotelians had no need of relationalism because they took the senses to show us external qualities both reliably and faithfully. Descartes sees that he could purchase reliability at the cost of fidelity, by treating sensible qualities as unknown powers defined precisely so as to be that which the senses perceive. This was the price that Aristotle, at least at times, seemed willing to pay in order to respond to Democritean subjectivism. But Descartes, though he sees the possibility, also sees just how badly it would clash with his epistemic ideals.

The story does not end here, however, because just this kind of relationalist program would be articulated very clearly, a few decades later, by Robert Boyle. In the proem to his most important theoretical work, *The Origin of Forms and Qualities* (1666), Boyle announces that investigating forms and qualities is a topic "the knowledge of which either makes or supposes the most fundamental and useful part of natural philosophy."[b] Far from proceeding to expel color and other scholastic real qualities from the domain of natural philosophy, Boyle labors to make room for them in the external world, allowing them to count as qualities, albeit secondary ones, treating them as powers, and developing a rigorous account of their identity as defined in relation to their environment. It is Boyle, in fact, who first appropriates the common scholastic distinction between primary and secondary qualities and recasts it in its now familiar mechanistic shape, with secondary qualities understood as powers or dispositions in objects.

Elsewhere Boyle writes that explanations come in degrees, some more satisfying than others. Best is to ground a phenomenon in "the more primitive and catholic affection of matter—namely, bulk, shape, and motion." Yet sometimes we cannot go so far, and in those cases Boyle urges us not to despise explanations "wherein particular effects are deduced from the more obvious and familiar qualities or states of bodies, such as heat, cold, weight, fluidity, hardness, fermentation, etc., though these themselves do probably depend upon those three universal ones formerly named."[c] It is, then, a kind of progress

---

[a] *Quaest. Post. an.* I.28c. See Pasnau, *Metaphysical Themes*, pp. 491–9.
[b] *Selected Papers*, p. 2.   [c] *Certain Phys. Essays* (*Works* II: 21).

to characterize heat or color as a power, even without fully understanding it, and then to use the notion of such a power in analyzing various other features of nature.

Boyle's relationalist program comes into further prominence through John Locke. Whereas Descartes had recoiled from treating color as something we know not what, Locke simply embraces this strategy as an effective way to talk about colors as qualities in the world. He argues that, distinct from the primary, geometric–kinetic qualities, there are "secondly, such qualities, which in truth are nothing in the objects themselves but powers to produce various sensations in us by their primary qualities."[a] This way of talking allows Locke to hold on to some kind of external domain for sensation. Colors in the world may not be the *immediate* objects of perception, but, even so, this domain of external powers gives Locke something to serve both as the cause of our ideas of color and the rest and as something for those ideas to be about. It is as if Descartes had sneeringly described how one might think of color perception as representing reality, but only if one wanted to speak of its uncovering a mysterious *virtus colorativa*, and then Locke comes along and says, yes, quite right, that's exactly what we should say.

Yet, although Boyle and Locke articulate a program for treating sensible qualities relationally, they are unable fully to embrace it. In their case the problem is not the failure of fidelity, since this is an ideal that neither of them seems to expect the senses to achieve. Thus Locke contents himself with describing the ideas of secondary qualities as "true" in virtue of being "marks of distinction in things," even if the character of what is being distinguished is "beyond our capacities distinctly to know."[b] This is precisely to accept that the senses exhibit only reliability, not fidelity. The problem, for Boyle and Locke, is that they are unwilling to embrace the metaphysical commitments that a full-throated relationalism requires. This is clear when Boyle describes how a body's relation to a sentient being is like that of a key to a lock, each taking on powers in virtue of its relationship with the other. Although we can speak of powers here, in fact neither key nor lock acquires "any real or physical entity" simply because of the other's existence. Similarly, in the case of the secondary qualities, "they are not in the bodies that are endowed with them any real or distinct entities."[c] Locke makes much the same point when he speaks of these qualities as "bare powers,"[d] thereby stressing that this talk of powers is not a return to the scholastic doctrine of real qualities as fundamental causes in nature. Such remarks are just what one might expect from a dedicated proponent of the mechanical philosophy. Neither Boyle nor Locke is willing to treat their powers as anything like real dispositions, over and above the material particles out of which the world is constructed. But such metaphysical scruples hamstring the epistemic value of their program. For, if powers are not "real or distinct entities," then such relationalism, far from safeguarding an external domain for the senses, in fact seems to explain it away.[15]

Here is where Aristotle might have helped. Not the Aristotle of the Aristotelians, whose sensible qualities fall into mind-independent natural kinds, but the Aristotle who wrestled with Democritus. Following the thread we pursued earlier, post-scholastic authors might have taken inspiration from Aristotle to develop a more satisfactory relational account of the sensible qualities. In fact, however, the Aristotelianism they

[a] *Essay* II.8.10.   [b] II.32.14.
[c] Boyle, *Origin of Forms and Qualities* (*Selected Papers*, pp. 23–4).
[d] *Essay* II.23.8.

knew was the discredited Aristotelian realism of the scholastics. Perhaps if medieval Aristotelians, over their many generations, had themselves taken up the relational thread in Aristotle's thought and woven it into their broader tapestry of systematic metaphysics, then the second coming of Democritean subjectivism in the seventeenth century might have met with a more satisfactory response along relational lines. But medieval Aristotelians felt no threat from Democritus, because they took sweet and bitter, hot and cold, and all the rest to be real causes in nature. So, ironically, although many of these authors might happily have embraced an ontology of relationally defined powers, they had no need for that kind of story in the sensory domain. And by the time Descartes, Boyle, Locke, and others felt such a need, Aristotle looked far too disreputable to furnish a fully adequate account. They were mechanists, not Aristotelians, and so the privileged domain of sensation was not going to be a domain of powers.

Thus it was that history failed to repeat itself.

From here on, our story splits into two. In one direction lies the path of resignation, which admits that the senses show us nothing of how the world is in itself. Here lies the skepticism of Hume and the idealism of Kant, along with the halfway sort of bowdlerized idealism that comes from distinguishing between the manifest and the scientific image. Those who go down this path wholly abandon the ideal of fidelity and acknowledge with a sigh the passing of yet another of our Panglossian epistemic ideals.

But there is another way. For, as we will see next week, even while giving up on perceiving the external world in high fidelity, the mainstream of seventeenth-century philosophy did not abandon the ideal of fidelity altogether, but turned instead to another domain where that ideal could be preserved, a domain within ourselves, where objects are seen even more properly and immediately. And so we come to the way of ideas.[16]

Lecture Four

Ideas and Illusions

Here is a very simple story about how perception works: Conceive of seeing, hearing, and the like as nothing more than events that occur within a cognitive agent. Let these perceptual events be the causal product of other events that occur in the physical world around us: events such as a surface's absorbing and reemitting light of certain frequencies, or rapid bodily motions' producing compression waves in the air. One kind of event, outside us, causes events within us, and those internal events represent the external events. Perhaps this is all that perception is, and no more philosophical baggage is needed.

To be sure, there are details to be worked out. On the outside, the world is presumably more than just a collection of unfolding events, and so we would like to have a metaphysics that tells us about the *things* that undergo these events. Still, on this story, it is the events that we perceive, not the things. On the inside, the perceptual events are of course conscious, and we will want an account of that, but this view prohibits us from postulating any sort of inner object for perception to be conscious of. The event itself is the conscious experience and, however that is to be explained, the view insists that we should not purchase an explanation at the cost of ontological profligacy.

Pleasingly austere as it may be to account for perception in these terms—as simply one kind of event, in the world, giving rise to another kind of event, in the perceiver—it can be fairly said that the whole history of philosophy conspires against this simplest of stories. Last week's lecture traced one persistent line of thought that discouraged treating the external objects of perception as events. For it has been commonly supposed, from Aristotle onward, that the senses give us some kind of privileged access to various *persisting* aspects of reality—not merely to the passing events of bodies in motion, but to stable features of that world. Inasmuch as it was not generally supposed that we perceive the bodies themselves—that is, the *substances*—the common view came to be that the objects of perception are standing *properties* of those bodies. As for which properties those were, and whether they were qualitative or quantitative, that debate ran on for centuries and eventually got swallowed up by various forms of skepticism and idealism, leaving perception without any hold on reality.

But, when one perceives, one must perceive something, or so it is natural to suppose. Hence, as soon as one begins to doubt whether there is a privileged external domain where the senses achieve something approaching infallibility, the question is liable to arise of whether there is some sort of privileged internal domain. To take this step, however, makes it tempting to reject this simplest of theories from within, because now, in addition to the event of perception, one seems to need an internal object of perception, which will be the thing that is perceived most reliably and faithfully.

Last week I described the first stages in this story and suggested that a concern with the fidelity of perception drove seventeenth-century theorists inward. This week I will consider the details of this inward turn more closely. As familiar as the way of ideas is, its origins and motivations are in fact much more puzzling and interesting than has generally been recognized. I will begin by stressing just how radically transformative the seventeenth century's inward turn is, and then I will consider at some length exactly why that transformation occurred, in light of the available alternatives. Once we understand its motivation, we will see that the inward turn toward ideas is not nearly as disreputable as is often supposed, given certain assumptions. But we will also see that these are assumptions we should no longer make.

How Ideas Become Objects

First, some terminology. Let the *simple view* of perception be that the perceptual act alone represents external things, without any need for some further, distinct internal representation. Let the *dual view* be that perception should be analyzed into the act and a distinct internal representation. Historically, the dual view has been by far the more widely accepted. Thomas Aquinas, for instance, compares the act of seeing to the act of heating and holds that "each occurs in virtue of some form."[a] In the case of heat, there is a form in the fire that corresponds to the form produced in the water that is heated. In the case of vision, there is a form in the thing seen that corresponds to the form produced in the visual power. It is in virtue of that form, the so-called *sensible species*, that one sees. Because such events happen at a distance, the species is required as a causal intermediary, which in the context of cognition can be described as a representation. Four centuries later, Locke offers a rationale that is not so very different: "For since the things the mind contemplates are none of them, besides itself, present to the under-standing, it is necessary that something else, as a sign or representation of the thing it considers, should be present to it: and these are ideas."[b] Again, since the things we perceive are generally at a distance from us, the claim is that there must be some *representative* of them in virtue of which they are perceived.

Throughout the centuries on which I am concentrating, such dual accounts were widely but not quite universally embraced. In the later thirteenth century, Peter John Olivi rejects sensible species in favor of what he rather mysteriously calls a "virtual attention" of the soul outward toward objects, bypassing the usual theory of forms multiplied through the medium between object and perceiver. William Ockham, a few decades later, also rejects species in favor of the simple view, arguing that external objects can act directly, at a distance, on our cognitive powers. One need not subscribe to such eccentric causal theories, however, in order to reject the dual view. In the seventeenth century, Antoine Arnauld thinks, like Ockham, that the mind's act of

---

[a] *Summa theol.* 1a 85.2c.   [b] *Essay* IV.21.4.

perception can itself serve as a representation of the distant object: "ideas, taken as representative beings distinct from perceptions, are entirely unnecessary to our soul for seeing bodies."[a] And Thomas Hobbes is a rare proponent of the ultrasimple view described above, on which sensation involves, simply, motions in the world giving rise to motions in the brain.[1]

Such scattered defenses of the simple view were, however, never mainstream. Among scholastic Aristotelians this is perhaps not surprising, inasmuch as they might have been predicted to embrace species as yet another bit of formal apparatus, one that joins the ranks of substantial form, real qualities, and the like. But it should be quite surprising to find, even among seventeenth-century anti-Aristotelians, a great deal of sympathy for sensible species. Descartes, for instance, who popularized 'idea' as the standard post-scholastic term for inner representations, expressly states: "By the term 'Idea' I mean the form of any given thought."[b] In choosing to use the word 'form,' he directly associates his account with the scholastic theory of species as forms of the soul. Locke is even blunter. Quite contrary to his usual efforts to distance himself from scholastic approaches, he explicitly introduces the term 'idea' with this remark: "I have used it to express whatever is meant by *Phantasm, Notion, Species*."[c] Strangely, then, the main line of post-scholastic thought, rather than reject the doctrine of species, in effect embraces it.[2]

These intriguing developments are the sort of thing that makes seventeenth-century philosophy so enduringly appealing—much more so than if it had been merely a long drawn out attempt to shatter the edifice of Aristotelian hylomorphism with the wrecking ball of mechanism. But what makes the whole situation even more weird and wonderful is that seventeenth-century authors went one step beyond the usual scholastic view. For not only did so many insist on retaining the scholastic doctrine of species as inner representations, but they also treated those representations as themselves the immediate objects of perception. Thus Descartes's definition of 'Idea' from the Second Replies immediately continues, "the form of any given thought, immediate perception of which makes me aware of the thought." Malebranche similarly writes that "by the word 'idea,' I mean here nothing other than the immediate object, or the object closest to the mind, when it perceives something." That external objects are not seen of themselves is, according to Malebranche, something that *tout le monde* accepts.[d] Likewise, the passage from Locke just quoted comes immediately after his declaration that 'idea' is "that term which, I think, serves best to stand for whatsoever is the object of the understanding when a man thinks." And Berkeley, too, writes that, "when I speak of tangible ideas, I take the word 'idea' for any the immediate object of sense, or understanding—in which large signification it is commonly used by the moderns."[e][3]

Views of this kind are now widely scorned. As Gilbert Ryle put it, "nearly every youthful student of philosophy both can and does in about his second essay refute Locke's entire Theory of Knowledge."[f] Indeed, although each of the passages just quoted represents the author's official statement of his view, a whole scholarly industry has arisen trying to save each of these authors from such a disreputable doctrine—all but Berkeley, at any rate, who prudently removed all possibility of misunderstanding by

---

[a] *True and False Ideas* ch. 4 (p. 18 trans.).   [b] Second Replies (VII: 160).   [c] *Essay* I.1.8.
[d] *Search after Truth* III.2.1 (p. 217 trans.).   [e] *New Theory of Vision* §45.   [f] *Collected Papers*, p. 154.

repudiating a mind-independent world that might serve as the object of perception. Why one would choose to study the seventeenth century and then spurn the way of ideas is to me a mystery, since this is in fact one of the most unique and interesting features of the era. Instead of subverting the plain meaning of their words, we should be asking *why* authors of this time suddenly began to insist on ideas as mediating objects. That this claim has seemed so incredible to so many is a clear sign that we have not yet come to terms with why they made their inward turn.

To begin to understand their motives, we need to consider seventeenth-century thought in its broader historical context. Within that context, it marks the most radical of departures to announce, as Descartes does, that the immediate objects of perception are not anything out in the world, but something inside the mind. The ancient skeptics had not taken such a view, nor had the Epicureans, for all their talk of how the senses are always true. The view is not Augustinian, and it certainly is not scholastic. Even if the seventeenth-century doctrine of ideas is modeled on the scholastic theory of species as forms, still there is virtually no scholastic who treats species as the inner objects of perception. On the standard scholastic view, species are mere causal intermediaries, running from external objects, through the air or through another medium, into the sense organ and the brain, and ultimately into the mind. To say that they are forms is to treat them like other, perfectly ordinary sorts of causal vehicles. The species is not the thing perceived, but merely the causal vehicle for perceiving external objects at a distance.[4]

To mark this distinction, it will help to have one more pair of technical terms. Let *mediated views* be those on which we perceive external objects—if we do at all—only in virtue of perceiving something within ourselves. Let *diaphanous views* be those on which we perceive external things directly, in the sense that whatever internal intermediaries there may be are not themselves the objects of perception. What is in the mind is diaphanous, meaning that we see right through it, meaning that we do not see it at all. Although it is natural to associate mediation with the dual view and diaphanousness with the simple view, in fact the two pairs of terms carve out orthogonal distinctions. As we will see, diaphanous dual views are common, and the mediated simple view has also had prominent defenders.

To say that mediated views are distinctive of the seventeenth century is not to say that the thesis itself is an innovation. On the contrary, it is a very old and familiar view, but almost always an unpopular one—effectively a straw man. For instance, when scholastic authors insist that species be understood as diaphanous, they do so quite self-consciously, because they are under pressure from critics who charge that the doctrine of species entails a mediated view. Olivi, for instance, the first of those critics, writes that, "if something else were interposed between the power's attention and its object, that would veil the thing and impede its being attended to in itself as if present, rather than aid in its being attended to."[a] Many later scholastics consider similar arguments, but what is particularly telling, for present purposes, is that the conclusion—the species would be the object—is almost always regarded as sufficiently absurd, on its face, as to require no further comment. As Gerard of Bologna puts it in making a similar argument

---

[a] *Summa* II.58 ad 14 (II: 469).

in the early fourteenth century, "that which represents something is first cognized in itself... But everyone holds that the species is not cognized before the object."[a] When Descartes and others insist otherwise in the seventeenth century, they are doing something that, if not quite unprecedented, is at least highly unusual.[5]

There is an argument for ascribing the simple view to Descartes, in which case his theory of ideas would be less scholastic than I have suggested. But from my point of view that is a peripheral issue. Both the simple and the dual view are well attested among scholastic authors, and so, although it is interesting to consider which of these Descartes held, he is not in either case saying anything novel. Much more interesting is that, regardless of whether his view is simple or dual, it is *mediated*, which means that his ideas, whatever they are, are the objects of perception in virtue of which we perceive external things (if we do at all). I am not in a position to claim that this is always Descartes's view—the texts are complicated, and the scholarship on this issue is large and sophisticated—but, at a minimum, this is how Descartes describes his view in his major works, when attempting to offer a precise account. Thus in the Third Replies: "I am taking the word 'idea' to refer to whatever is immediately perceived by the mind."[b] This would of course make no sense if Descartes thought that external things were immediately perceived by the mind.[6]

Descartes's very use of the term 'idea' rather than 'species'—a terminological choice that would determine usage for centuries—reflects this change of perspective. Right after the passage just quoted, he explains why he chose the word 'idea': "I have used this term because it was already commonplace among the philosophers for signifying the forms of the perceptions of the divine mind, though we recognize no sensory images [*phantasia*] in God. I had nothing more appropriate." Descartes knew quite well, then, that by choosing to speak of "ideas" he was embracing scholastic vocabulary, using a word that had hitherto been associated mainly with mental representations at the divine level. Why not use instead the term 'species,' which would seem the much more obvious and "appropriate" choice, inasmuch as it was the word standardly used in talk about the human case? His motivation becomes clear if we look back to Aquinas's discussion of divine ideas. Aquinas explains that we should speak of God as having ideas rather than species because "the idea of an action exists in the mind of the agent as that which is understood, rather than as the species by which it is understood."[c] This matters to Aquinas, because it gives him an explanation of how a multiplicity of divine ideas is compatible with divine simplicity. For our purposes, though, the critical point is that what makes an idea fundamentally different from a species, in scholastic jargon, is that a species is that *by which* a thing is thought or perceived, whereas an idea is an *object* of thought or perception. In passing over the obvious term 'species' in favor of 'idea,' Descartes surely knew what he was doing: he was choosing a terminology on which the vehicles of mental representation are themselves objects.[7]

I will return shortly to an issue that may seem puzzling: how one can hold a simple yet mediated view. The point I wish to stress for now is that the interpretive dispute over exactly how to understand the doctrine of ideas in Descartes, Locke, and others has

---

[a] *Quodlibet* I.17, n. 20.   [b] VII: 181.   [c] *Summa theol.* 1a 15.2c.

obscured a broader and more interesting issue. It is somewhat surprising that these authors appear to hold a dual view like that of the scholastics. What is utterly fascinating, however, is that they turn such a view in a radically new direction, eagerly embracing the mediating role of their ideas in a way that is nearly unprecedented in scholastic discussions. At the end of this lecture I will argue that, once we understand why the doctrine of mediating ideas flourished in the seventeenth and eighteenth centuries, we will see that it could have flourished *only* then, and we will also understand why the doctrine has been generally rejected in modern times. But, to see why the doctrine flourished, we need to set aside two unsatisfactory explanations: first, that the case for mediation might be made on the basis of introspection alone; second, that it might be based on the argument from illusion.

Introspection

Judging from what seventeenth-century authors often tell us, the prime reason for treating ideas as the inner objects of perception is simply that we are directly aware of their existence. Locke, for instance, begins Book II of his *Essay* by proclaiming:

Every man being conscious to himself that he thinks, and that which his mind is employed about while thinking being the ideas that are there, it is past doubt that men have in their minds several ideas . . . it is in the first place then to be enquired, How he comes by them?

The first question Locke will consider, then, is not whether we have ideas, but where ideas come from. The "whether" question need not be asked, because its answer, as Locke puts it here, "is past doubt." The "fountain of knowledge" that Locke calls *reflection*,[a] an introspective grasp of the operations of our own minds, makes it quite unnecessary to offer any further evidence for the existence of ideas as inner objects of perception. Still, the course of Locke's reasoning here is not entirely obvious. He begins by saying that we are each conscious of thinking, which seems unobjectionable, and then he adds that, when we think, we think about ideas. He can safely say that much because, as we saw earlier, back at the start of Book I he has defined 'idea' as "whatsoever is the object of the understanding when a man thinks."[b] To be sure, it is hard to deny that, if we are conscious of thinking, then we are conscious of the object of that thinking. But what seems to get taken for granted here, and what is not at all past doubt, is that the object of thought is internal to the mind.

That ideas are intermediaries in this way was very much in doubt for some of Locke's contemporaries. Arnauld, in particular, in a work published seven years before Locke's *Essay*, challenges Malebranche's version of the view that ideas are "the immediate object" of perception:

If he had consulted himself and considered attentively what happens in his own mind, he would have seen clearly there that he knows bodies, that he knows a cube, a cone and a pyramid, and that if he turns toward the sun he sees the sun . . . He would never have found the least trace of that *representative being* of a cube or of the sun, distinct from the *perception*, and which was supposed to make up for the absence of the one object and the other.[c]

---

[a] *Essay* II.1.4.   [b] I.1.8.   [c] *True and False Ideas* ch. 7 (p. 33 trans.).

As will become clearer shortly, Arnauld does not dispute our ability to reflect upon our own thoughts and to become aware that we are having a perception. But in so doing, he thinks, we acquire no reason at all to postulate, in addition to the act of perceiving, a further internal "being" that is "representative" of the thing perceived. The perception itself, Arnauld thinks, simply is the representation. Malebranche's mistake, he charges, is to pay insufficient attention to the testimony of reflection and to let himself instead be influenced by "a prejudice that he had not taken care to cast entirely aside."[a] That prejudice is the metaphysical speculation of the scholastics, who postulated such representations—under the labels 'species' and 'phantasms'—in much the same disreputable way in which they postulated substantial forms. Just as Malebranche was an avowed opponent of substantial form, so, says Arnauld, he ought to have rejected ideas and other such internal representations, as the "fantastic assumption"[b] of scholastic Aristotelianism.

In a way Arnauld is right about scholastic views, in another way not. What is right is that both the scholastic doctrine of species and the typical seventeenth-century doctrine of ideas are versions of the dual view, which introduces a level of metaphysical apparatus into the theory of perception by treating representations as forms distinct from the act of perception. Arnauld's defense of the simple view avoids such commitments. But Arnauld is not right in supposing that the scholastics treat these representations as inner objects. Keen to use that despised tradition as a bogeyman, he reports that "the majority of philosophers"[c] have treated ideas as intermediaries in this way. In fact, however, the scholastics usually agree not just that species ordinarily are not objects of inner reflection, as we have seen, but that they *cannot* be introspected in this way. Francisco Suárez is typical:

Some say that intelligible species are cognized through themselves, for since they are the principles of cognizing other things, it would not be surprising if they are the principles of cognizing themselves, and it is superfluous to add on other things. But it seems to me that they are not cognized through themselves, for if so they would be cognized most evidently, which is not so. Hence I say that they are cognized through their effects—that is, through acts—since we infer in no other way than through our acts that species are to be posited.[d]

Suárez refers here to intelligible species within the intellect, but the same point holds for sensible species. Earlier we saw how scholastic authors take for granted that it is things in the world, not species, that are the primary objects of thought and perception. Here Suárez is saying something more: that in fact such species cannot be cognitive objects at all, except inferentially, insofar as someone sufficiently well versed in natural philosophy can infer that, if I am engaged in an act of cognition, then there must be a certain kind of species within me.

This passage might be read as supposing that at least our cognitive acts are "cognized through themselves," but many discussions go even farther and contend that, just as we cannot introspect the inner species, so we cannot introspect even the act of perception. Thomas Aquinas is the leading example of this approach. His governing methodology, in understanding the soul, is to work from the outside in:

---

[a] Ch. 7 (p. 34 trans.).   [b] Ch. 7 (p. 34 trans.).   [c] Ch. 4 (p. 15 trans.).   [d] *De anima* disp. 9 q. 5 n. 8.

In cognizing the soul we must advance from things that are more external, from which are abstracted the intelligible species through which the intellect cognizes itself. In this way, then, we cognize acts through objects, capacities through acts, and the essence of the soul through its capacities.[a]

The point is not just that we must do things in this temporal order: first focus on external things, then focus on our internal acts of cognition before turning to the soul's various powers and finally to its very nature. Rather the point is that we have no independent access to the later steps in the process, other than through the information we acquire about external things. Thus "the soul is present to itself... not as understood through itself, but from its object... The soul is cognized not through another species abstracted from itself, but through the species of its object."[b] Cognition occurs through species, but species are a vehicle for cognizing *external* things. There is no room in this story for "another species" that represents our inner states, and as a result there is no separate stream of cognitive access aimed within. This is not to say, absurdly, that we have no access to whether we are thinking and perceiving. The point, instead, is that such information is acquired by inference. The mind is diaphanous to itself, and so our only way in is to start with things out in the world and work backwards.[8]

Aquinas's views on self-knowledge are shared by a wide range of scholastic authors and represent the broadly Aristotelian side of the discussion. Psychology, on this picture, is a department of biology and requires the same sort of empirical methods, beginning with the patient observation of the outside world. Reflection along the lines Locke would later set out, a direct introspective access to our own mental states, is rejected as a myth. The human mind, far from being a privileged epistemic object, is just one more natural faculty to which we have no particular special access. Hence, as Aristotle warned at the start of the *De anima*, "grasping anything trustworthy concerning the soul is completely and in every way among the most difficult of affairs."[c]

So, despite Arnauld's rhetoric, something novel is at work in the later seventeenth century, when mediation becomes endemic to philosophy. Given the strikingly diaphanous conception of self-knowledge common among scholastic Aristotelians, it is natural to wonder whether the rise of mediation might be linked to innovations with regard to self-knowledge. Moreover, it is familiar enough that Descartes embraces a methodology that is radically opposed to the outside-in approach of the Aristotelians. But the first-person orientation of the *Meditations* is hardly original, inasmuch as Augustine had already urged his readers to work from the inside out: "Refuse to go outside. Return to yourself. Truth dwells within."[d] In works like the *Confessions* and the *De trinitate* he practiced this method at length, studying the workings of his own mind as a way to understand both human and divine nature. Might it be the case, then, that the seventeenth century's changing conception of perception reflects a shift away from Aristotelianism and toward Augustinianism?

There is no denying that Augustine's inside-out methodology takes on a special prominence in Descartes and many of his followers. But it does not seem plausible to suppose that this is what sparks the rise of their mediated views of perception. After all,

---

[a] *Comm. de anima* II.6.180–6.   [b] *Quaest. de veritate* 10.8 ad 4–5 sc.
[c] *De an.* I.1, 402[a]10–11.   [d] *On True Religion* 39.72.

Augustine himself did not embrace mediation. Moreover, Augustine's first-person methods were already massively influential throughout the Middle Ages. Anselm, for instance, grounds his famous ontological argument for God's existence not on the nature of the world around him, but on introspection: "Enter into the chamber of your mind; exclude everything but God and what helps you to search for him, and then search for him, with the door closed."[a] Even so, Anselm likewise shows no temptation to embrace mediation. And, even in the heyday of scholastic Aristotelianism, many authors are more Augustinian than Aristotelian when it comes to self-knowledge, and yet none of them is tempted by mediation. Olivi and Ockham, for instance, are two leading examples of later scholastics who take broadly Augustinian stances on self-knowledge. But they are among the most forceful opponents of anything that smacks of mediation in perceptual theory. So, although it might be plausible to suggest that the rise of such mediated theories in the seventeenth century makes Augustine's first-person method-ology particularly appealing, there is no reason to think that the explanation runs in the other direction.[9]

With this in mind, let us return to the puzzling case of Arnauld, who combines enthusiasm for Augustine with a commitment to the simple view that hearkens back to Olivi and Ockham. At the same time, however, Arnauld defends mediation, endorsing Descartes's claim that "it is our ideas that we see immediately and that are the immediate object of our thought."[b] Arnauld can say this, despite taking our ideas to be identical to our perceptions, because he holds perception to be reflexively self-conscious:

Our thought or perception is essentially reflexive upon itself: or, as it is more felicitously said in Latin, *est sui conscia*. For I never think without knowing that I think. I never know a square without knowing that I know it; I never see the sun or, to put the point beyond doubt, I never imagine I see the sun, without being certain that I imagine I see it.[c]

Reflexivity here is meant to be understood quite literally: the thought is aware *of itself*. Thus Arnauld insists that there is just one perception aimed reflexively at itself and also aimed outward:

Although I see this intelligible sun immediately by means of the virtual reflection that I have of my perception, I do not stop there; rather, this same perception in which I see this intelligible sun makes me see, at the same time, the material sun that God has created.[d]

The "intelligible sun" is within my mind and seen "immediately"; it, in turn, "makes me see" the "material sun" that is out in the world. The account is clearly mediated—and yet it is simple, because the act of perception somehow has itself as its object, and it is "by means of" such self-reflection that it immediately sees the intelligible sun and thereby sees the material sun. Here, then, is a way in which a theory can be both simple and mediated: it can be so if the act of perception reflexively mediates itself.[10]

Although Arnauld is best known for his defense of the simple view, in fact the most remarkable feature of his theory is this notion of self-reflexivity. The essentially meta-physical question of whether perception should be understood in simple or dual terms is

---

[a] *Proslogion* ch. 1.   [b] *True and False Ideas* ch. 6 (p. 26 trans.).
[c] Ch. 6 (p. 25 trans.).   [d] Ch. 11 (p. 52 trans.).

an old one, familiar enough to earlier generations. What is striking in Arnauld is that, even while defending the simple view, he still finds a way to embrace the Cartesian doctrine of mediation. Much more might be said about whether this mix of views is coherent, but the puzzle for now is why he, like his contemporaries, would strain so hard to defend mediation. Introspection does not seem to offer an answer. So let us turn to the argument from illusion.

The Argument from Illusion

In the popular imagination, the argument from illusion is "the Bad Argument" that laid "the foundation of modern epistemology."[a] And it is indeed true that one can find the argument popping up throughout the seventeenth century and finally reaching its apogee in Berkeley. One finds it in Hobbes, for instance, who mentions reflections in glass and water and the double image of a candle,[b] and again in Malebranche, who remarks that "it is certain that the material object is never the immediate object of the mind, since frequently this object does not actually exist, and never did exist, such as when we are sleeping or have a fever."[c]

The argument is so familiar as barely to need rehearsing: the mind perceives a certain sort of object; but the supposed external object is in fact not of that sort (or, worse, as in the case of hallucinations and dreams, it is entirely nonexistent); therefore there must be something other than the supposed external object that is being perceived. Accordingly, the process of perception cannot be diaphanous but must involve some kind of mediating object. Put so crudely, the reasoning seems obviously fallacious, but it continues to have its supporters to this day. The argument can also be found throughout medieval thought, as well as in antiquity. So it is not as if the argument from illusion were some kind of seventeenth-century discovery, leading the era away from the doctrine of diaphanous species toward the doctrine of mediating ideas. Moreover, even among medieval authors who accept the force of the argument from illusion, a very wide range of responses get deployed. Strikingly, however, even those who are willing to take quite extravagant measures to accommodate illusions do not think that the objects of perception are ordinarily internal to the perceiver. Here I discuss, briefly, four scholastic cases. Although discussion of these earlier views will lead us away, for a time, from our principal quarry, the detour will be warranted in the end by the perspective it affords on why ideas ultimately became objects of perception.[11]

Disjunctivism

According to Peter John Olivi, when we perceive things as they are, we perceive them directly, without the need for an intermediary. But what about those cases where the object of cognition is not present, either because it no longer exists or because it never did exist? In that case, Olivi thinks, the cognitive process works indirectly, through a mediating species:

---

[a] John Searle, *Seeing Things as They Are*, p. 23.   [b] *Elements of Law* I.2.4–5.
[c] *Réponse au Livre des vraies et des fausses idées* 9.12 (*Oeuvres complètes* VI: 78).

A species is not needed to represent an object, even though this is what it seemed most needed for . . . For when an object is present to an attention that is turned toward it and intent on it, then that object sufficiently presents itself to that attention through its very self—and indeed presents itself even better than through any created species that is deficient in the solid being and proper truth of that object. An absent object, on the other hand, is sufficiently represented to the attention through a memory species.[a]

As we saw earlier, Olivi thinks that, if species were to represent external objects, they would inevitably be the object of our attention. Supposing this to be obviously un-acceptable, he holds instead that the act of perception itself represents the object, and hence grasps it without any intermediary. But, if there is no external object, then our perceptual attention must be directed at an image of the thing:

To grasp or to think about absent objects, some species in place of the object is necessary. First, because every attention directed toward an object necessarily has its terminus in something. For one cannot attend to nothing nor have a terminus in nothing. Also, that in which the attention is terminated must be present to it, so that the attention itself attains it virtually. But when we think about something that is not actual (or if it is, is not present to our attention), then the attention cannot be attached to and terminated in that thing. Therefore in that case some image of the thing must be exposed to the attention and be its terminus.[b]

Olivi is particularly focused on cases of dreaming and memory, where one perceives or thinks of a thing that is wholly absent. But his rationale would seem to extend to illusory cases as well, if we think of illusions as cases where we perceive a sensible quality that is not there. In any case, the general strategy is disjunctive: that we should distinguish between two fundamental modes of cognition, one of which grasps things as they are, whereas the other fails to grasp what exists.

This disjunctive approach becomes enshrined in scholastic thought a generation later, thanks to John Duns Scotus, who coins the labels 'intuitive' and 'abstractive' to describe the difference. Not that Scotus shares Olivi's doubts over species in either case. If Scotus is going to err, it will never be on the side of parsimony. In the present case, he thinks that the doctrine of species is quite compatible with direct access to external objects: on my terminology, he holds a dual but diaphanous view. Scotus also, much like Olivi, thinks of cognition not as just the passive reception of information, but as an active, outward-directed grasping of things in the world: "a cognitive power must not only receive the species of its object, but also tend through its act toward the object."[c] This leaves him, just like Olivi, in need of some story about the object of cognition across all cases. His solution is to propose that cognition works in two fundamentally different sorts of ways. Intuitive cognition "attains an object in its proper actual existence, as for example with the vision of color, and generally in the sensation of the external senses." In contrast, although an abstractive cognition must have an object, "either the object does not exist, or at least the cognition is not of it as it actually exists."[d] He describes the difference between these two modes of cognition as follows:

These will be said to be distinct cognitions—distinct in kind [species]—because of the formal motive accounts [rationes] in the two cases. For in the case of intuitive cognition the thing in its

---

[a] *Summa* II.74 (III: 122–3).   [b] II.74 (III: 115).   [c] *Quaest. meta.* VII.14.29.   [d] *Quodlibet* XIII.27.

proper existence is in itself that which moves objectively, whereas in abstractive cognition that which in itself moves is something in which the thing has cognizable being, whether that be a cause virtually containing the thing as cognizable, or whether it be an effect, such as a species or likeness representatively containing that of which it is a likeness.[a]

This is a characteristically thorny Scotistic passage, full of opaque technical vocabulary, but the basic line of thought is tolerably clear. Cognition should be treated disjunctively, as involving two different kinds of operations: one that takes place when we grasp the thing itself and another that takes place via some intermediary representation, when we do not grasp the thing as it is.

In the wake of Scotus's innovation came a centuries-long debate over how to understand abstractive and intuitive cognition. That the distinction received such attention at all should be cause for surprise, because the doctrine as Scotus describes it looks rather pedestrian. His discussions of abstractive cognition focus on cases like imagination, memory, and abstract thought, with which he contrasts ordinary sense perception as his example of intuitive cognition. To suppose that a difference in kind among cognitions can be drawn along these lines is neither surprising nor very interesting. Recent scholarship has devoted loving care to this long fourteenth-century debate, but without considering why the distinction between intuitive and abstractive cognition mattered so much. The answer I am suggesting is that Scotus's distinction, although pedestrian on the face of it, in fact points to a much more radical view: that there is a difference in kind between those cases where we grasp existing things as they are and those cases where we fail to do so. This is surprising, because one would naturally suppose that the difference between such cases lies in how the external world is and that the process within us works much the same, in either case. By treating the processes disjunctively, Scotus initiates a fierce and protracted debate.[12]

Auriol's Apparent Being

Within a decade of Scotus's death in 1308, Peter Auriol mounts the first great reformulation of the intuitive–abstractive distinction, drawing largely on various arguments from illusion. The cases he inventories—a list that becomes canonical in later discussions—include afterimages, dreams, fear-induced apparent sounds and visions, sticks half-submerged in water, double vision, mirror images, and more. According to Auriol, all these examples show that Scotus's account of the intuitive–abstractive distinction leads to unacceptable consequences. One such consequence is just what I have stressed already: that vision (and other kinds of perception) would be split into two fundamentally distinct kinds, veridical and nonveridical. This, for Auriol, is unacceptable: "there is no act within the visual power that does not share the specific nature of vision."[b] Even worse, as a vision goes from being veridical to nonveridical—for example, the stick is first seen out of the water, and then seen half-submerged—we would have to suppose that the vision itself undergoes this kind of fundamental change in its nature, from being intuitive to being abstractive. But surely in such a case there is no fundamental difference in the vision itself; it is the outside world that has changed.

---

[a] XIII.33.   [b] *Scriptum* proem 2, n. 90 (p. 202 trans. Pasnau, *Cambridge Translations*).

As Auriol puts it, "true and false apply to numerically the same cognition without its undergoing any change, with only a change in the object."[a] That of course seems right. It is just hard to believe that, at the moment the stick enters the water, the process of perception, as it occurs within the mind, changes in any fundamental way.

At this point Auriol might just have rejected the intuitive–abstractive distinction entirely, but he proposes instead to reformulate it—not as a distinction between fundamentally different kinds of cognitive events, but as a phenomenological distinction.

In the case of one appearance, things appear as present, actual, and existent in reality, whether or not they exist. This is intuition. In the case of the other appearance, whether or not a thing exists, it does not appear as present, actualizing, and existent in reality, but in an imaginary and absent-like manner.[b]

Of course, no one could dispute that there is *this* sort of difference in cognition. Sometimes we take ourselves to see things and sometimes to imagine things. But the difference, for Auriol, lies on the surface, at the level of how things seem to us, and does not mark any fundamental divide in the way cognition occurs.

So much, then, for the disjunctive approach. But that approach was intended to *solve* the argument from illusion, and what Auriol has in effect done is to invoke the argument from illusion *against* disjunctivism. So the question then arises of how he himself thinks that illusory cases should be handled. Auriol agrees with Scotus and Olivi that cognition requires some kind of object, the thing that appears when one experiences a cognitive act. But, whereas Olivi and Scotus pursue divide-and-conquer strategies, Auriol insists on a unified account that covers even cases where there is no external object that really exists as it appears to exist. At this point the familiar seventeenth-century way forward would be to find some object within the mind. Auriol, however, like his contemporaries, judges it absurd to treat something within the soul as the object of cognition. (Moreover, he rejects the doctrine of species.) But what is left, then? His solution is to offer an extremely well-developed version of a theory that would surface over and over in later centuries: the doctrine that to perceive something is to grasp that thing in its apparent being.[13]

Auriol invokes apparent being to explain cognition of all kinds—sensation, imagination, dreams, intellective thought—regardless of whether or not this cognition is veridical. But it is the illusory cases that put the theory on best display. In the case of a mirror image, for instance, he begins by ruling out the possibility that the object is a species, or the vision itself, or any real external object (like one's own face). None of these can be the object, because none exists where and how the object seen exists, inverted and behind the mirror. So Auriol concludes that the image one sees is "only the appearance of the thing, or the thing with apparent and intentional being, with the result that the thing itself is behind the mirror in seen, judged, and apparent being."[c] Two points here are crucial. First, Auriol embraces a key assumption in the argument from illusion: that there is always something in existence that matches how things seem to be. When one sees a bent stick, there *is* a bent stick, half-submerged in water just as it appears to be. When you see a face in a mirror, there *is* a face literally "in" (or on the

[a] Proem 2, n. 91 (p. 202 trans.).   [b] Proem 2, n. 111 (p. 207 trans.).
[c] *Scriptum* d. 3 q. 3 [sct. 14], n. 31 (p. 223 trans.).

other side of) the mirror, its features the reverse of yours. Since Auriol rejects disjunctivism, he thinks that a similar story holds even in veridical cases, but in that case the apparent being lines up exactly with the real being, both in location and in qualities. As he puts it, in that case "we do not distinguish the image or thing in apparent being and in real being, because in the case of a true vision they occur together."[a] The second point to be stressed is that Auriol thinks he can say these things without losing his hold on reality, because he thinks that, in veridical cases, the apparent being somehow *is* the real object, even if it has another kind of existence. Thus it is "the thing itself" that has apparent being behind the mirror. And, in the case of one's veridical perception of a wall:

The thing that is seen, along with the fact that it really exists, also has a judged and seen existence. This does not impose on that reality any variety or distinction or number with respect to anything absolute; rather, it adds an intrinsic and indistinguishable relation that is called an objective appearance. Accordingly, sight is not terminated at the thing that is its object through the mediation of anything absolute, as if there were some cloak or intermediary between the vision and the wall that is seen.[b]

I will not try to do justice here to the metaphysical intricacies of this "intrinsic relation." For present purposes what matters is just that Auriol sees no need, neither in veridical nor in illusory cases, to postulate some intervening entity that would "cloak" external objects.[14]

The doctrine of apparent being came into prominence through Scotus. In the thorny passage quoted above, for instance, he speaks of "cognizable being" as the object of an abstractive cognition. In effect, Auriol takes this feature of abstractive cognition and invokes it to account for all cognition—indeed, it is for him the very mark of cognitive activity. By so reframing the intuitive–abstractive distinction, Auriol willingly gives up on a privileged domain where sensation infallibly shows us things as they really are. What he gains instead is an alternative domain where things are as they appear, a domain that would have a long and successful subsequent career, under many names: intentional being, objective being, fictive being, and so on. Extravagant claims are often made for the ability of such accounts to have their cake and eat it, too, by allowing the object of perception both to be as it is perceived to be and yet somehow also to be, at the same time, the external thing itself—even when the external thing itself (the real thing with so-called *subjective* being) does not exist as it is perceived to be. The view runs throughout later scholastic thought and would seem so useful that even leading critics of scholasticism, like Descartes and Arnauld, cannot resist appealing to it. Yet there is a striking difference. In Auriol, objective or apparent beings are out in the world, right where they seem to be, and in ordinary veridical cases they are aligned with real, subjective beings. When we look ahead to the post-scholastic philosophers of the seventeenth century, we find that their metaphysics is too narrow, and their conception of the physical world too austere, to countenance objective beings out in the world. But, rather than reject such things altogether, they turn inward and treat objective beings as creatures of the mind, a domain so mysterious already that it does no harm to introduce further exotica.[15]

---

[a] *Scriptum* d. 3 q. 3, n. 31 (p. 224 trans.).   [b] *Scriptum* d. 27 q. 2 art. 2 (ms Vat. Borgh. lat. 329, f. 302rb).

Ockham's Simply Unmediated View

We have now seen several examples of how the argument from illusion and its close relatives motivated scholastic theorizing about perception without precipitating an inward turn. Consider next the case of William Ockham, who flatly rejects the argument from illusion. This in turn positions him to reject both Scotus's disjunctivism and Auriol's apparent being. With respect to the latter, Ockham makes various predictable and decisive-looking objections. He argues, for instance, that if a color in its apparent being is numerically the same as a color in its real being, then it will be impossible for one to exist without the other. But the whole point of the theory is to allow for such a possibility, in illusory cases. Hence the two cannot be the same. But then the theory introduces the sort of veil between perception and reality that Auriol sought to avoid.

Ockham shares Auriol's aversion to disjunctivism. But, whereas Auriol had effectively treated all cognition on the model of Scotus's abstractive cognition, Ockham takes precisely the opposite approach, describing all cognition in the sort of terms Scotus had reserved for the intuitive case. This is to say that Ockham rejects mediation in favor of a simple and diaphanous view, across both intuitive and abstractive cases:

First, I say that in no intuitive cognition, sensory or intellective, is a thing constituted in any being that is intermediary between the thing and the act of cognizing. I say instead that the thing itself is immediately seen or apprehended, without any intermediary between it and the act . . . Second, I say that through an abstractive cognition immediately following an intuitive cognition, nothing is made nor does anything take on being beyond the abstractive cognition itself. For the object of an intuitive cognition and of an immediately following abstractive cognition are entirely the same, and under the same aspect. Therefore, just as there is no intermediary between an intuitively cognized object and the intuitive cognition, so there will be no intermediary between an object and an abstractive cognition.[a]

Ockham here rejects not only apparent being but also species of all kinds, and does so for both intuitive and abstractive cognitions. The resulting view is both simple and diaphanous.

Such an austere picture, though easy to state, is hard to square with the argument from illusion. Working through Auriol's various cases one by one, Ockham implements two kinds of strategies. The first, which he applies to cases like the bent stick, holds that we are seeing the stick, and seeing it just as it is, given that it is half-submerged in water. To be sure, a straight stick seen under these circumstances gives rise to a sensation equivalent to the sensation that would be produced by a *bent* stick wholly out of water. But nothing problematic is occurring at the sensory level, inasmuch as this sensation is just as it should be under the circumstances. The trouble is the potential for a failure in judgment at the intellectual level, if we believe the proposition *This stick is bent.* Ockham's other strategy applies to those cases of Auriol's that involve afterimages, such as the image of the sun that remains even after looking away. Here Ockham grants that what one sees is not in the external world. Such cases reveal something more general about how perception works: that sense objects make an impression on the

[a] *Ordinatio* I.27.3 (*Opera theol.* IV: 241–2; p. 229 trans. Pasnau, *Cambridge Translations*).

sensory powers. Hence, if the impression is strong enough and if one quickly averts one's gaze to a suitably neutral object, then one can actually *see* that leftover internal impression. So, again, there is no need for disjunctivism and no need for any special further object, inside or outside. The physical process itself explains what is going on.[16]

Rather than discard the intuitive–abstractive distinction, Ockham offers his own reformulation. The distinction is not, as Scotus had thought, between fundamentally distinct kinds of processes. Instead, both cases work much the same way, simply and without mediation. Nor is the distinction a matter of phenomenology, as Auriol thought. Instead, Ockham appeals to causal roles within the mind: intuitive cognitions are those that can give rise to an evident judgment as to whether or not a thing exists. Scotus himself had alluded to a link between intuition and evidentness; but, by putting the connection at the heart of his account, Ockham takes the controversy over the distinction to a whole new level. For, as we saw two weeks ago, where there is evidentness there is *scientia*. Thus Ockham is able to claim that, "if someone intuitively sees Socrates and the whiteness existing in Socrates, then he can evidently know [*scire*] that Socrates is white."[a] Indeed, where there is evidentness, Ockham thinks there is both indubitability and infallibility. This makes it look as if he is advancing an extraordinarily strong claim for a privileged domain of sensation. Yet Ockham of course knows that the senses are fallible. So, strictly speaking, the claim has to be qualified: under normal natural conditions—the right distance, the right medium, and so on, when the intuition counts as what Ockham calls a "perfect intuitive awareness"[b]—intuition leads directly to an evident judgment that things in the world are so. Now, to be sure, Ockham never suggests that we can be certain of being in this perfect condition. So, as usual, our epistemic state is not as ideal as it might be. Still, Ockham thinks, in the normal run of things, our sensory powers are a remarkably powerful tool for achieving a robust cognitive grasp of the world around us, one that he confidently includes within the domain of *scientia*.[17]

Does Ockham's brand of unmediated intuition deserve even this much? As we will see in two weeks, debate over this point continued throughout later scholasticism, as authors wrestled both with the argument from illusion and with the possibility of supernatural deception. For now, though, let us consider one last fourteenth-century proposal about how to secure perception of the external world even in the face of illusion: a proposal that turns in yet another direction but still resists turning inward.

Autrecourt's Platonism

Nicholas of Autrecourt is best known for the radically skeptical conclusions he advances in a series of letters; they argue that, if intuitive cognitions ever generate false judgment, then they can never yield certainty, evidentness, or *scientia*. Read in isolation, the letters might seem to suggest that there is no alternative to skepticism. But in his own systematic work Autrecourt vigorously strives to avoid such consequences, insisting on the principle that "everything that appears is true, when clear and evident in a full

---

[a] *Ordinatio* prol. q. 1 (*Opera theol.* I: 6).   [b] I: 31.

light."[a] The qualifying second half of that claim is meant to ward off various sorts of appearances that we have no business trusting; but, even so, Autrecourt is stuck with having to make good on the truth of quite a few appearances that we might suppose to be nonveridical. The strategy he adopts is not easy to discern from the winding course of his *Tractatus*, but ultimately amounts to a radically Platonic version of the objective-being strategy found in Peter Auriol.[18]

Auriol, as we have seen, must postulate that the very same object exists in different places at the same time: your face, for instance, really exists in one place, but when seen in a mirror it also exists, inverted, behind the mirror, in objective being. One reason for impatience with such a doctrine is that it would seem to require an extravagant ontology of universal entities, capable of such multiple instantiations. And yet Auriol, like the vast majority of scholastic Aristotelians, flatly rejects realism with respect to universals, insisting instead that everything that exists is particular. Apparently, objective being is supposed to be a special case, not subject to the usual considerations of parsimony. Autrecourt, in contrast, is willing to follow the argument from illusion all the way to the metaphysics it requires: he treats the objects of perception as universals, multiply instantiated outside the mind wherever they appear to exist. To reach this conclusion, he offers a fascinating argument. To begin, he introduces a simple and very common kind of illusion: differences in apparent color that result from different illuminations. Suppose that, at midday, I am looking at my bright blue house and you are looking at your pale blue house. We are, indisputably, looking at different colors. But now suppose I look at my house at dusk, and suppose it looks to have just the color your house looks to have at midday. Am I seeing the same color at dusk that I saw at midday? No, Autrecourt says, instead I am seeing at dusk the very same color that you were seeing at midday: I am seeing pale blue.

That this conclusion follows is doubtful, to say the least. But Autrecourt grounds it on an ingenious argument, driven by what we now call *internalism* with regard to mental content. What Autrecourt assumes is that mental representation must be a function of how a cognitive power is internally disposed. How could anything *outside* the mind have a bearing on how the mind represents the world to be, except insofar as that external environment makes a difference to the mind's *internal* states? This looks at least plausible, although the thesis was intensely controversial then, and remains so today. But suppose we grant it. Autrecourt contends that it yields the following, quite radical internalist principle:

A [cognitive] power having an act equivalent to the act of another power sees whatever the other power sees, and sees only that, since it has only an equivalent act.[b]

Take two perceivers who are exactly alike intrinsically with regard to the perceptions they are currently having. In light of his internalist principle, Autrecourt thinks that the two perceivers must be seeing *exactly the same thing*. This is, furthermore, hardly a remote possibility. In my example above, it would apply to me at dusk and to you at midday. His own example is of two observers, one in England and one in Paris, having an intrinsically exactly similar experience of whiteness. Given Autrecourt's radical

---

[a] *Tractatus* ch. 6 (p. 230.17–18).   [b] *Tractatus* ch. 7 (p. 238.41–3).

internalism, it must be the case that they are seeing *numerically the same color*. So if one insists, at this point, on the commonsensically nominalist position that there is one instance of the color in England and another exactly like it in Paris, then one would have to say that each observer sees both colors. But this is clearly absurd: it commits one to the possibility that, "if there were an object infinitely far away, it would be seen as clearly as if it were two feet away."[a] What seems much more natural, given these assumptions, is to say that there is only one color, existing simultaneously in both England and Paris. Hence, in Autrecourt's case, the argument from illusion yields a theory of universals as objects of perception.[19]

Autrecourt does not suppose, as Auriol does, that these universal objective beings are numerically the same as the thing itself in its real, subjective being. On the contrary, he regards it as quite difficult to know what to say about subjective being. His general picture is that, for any given thing in subjective being, there will be countless objects in objective being for each way in which that thing might be perceived. What we see is one or another of these objective beings. Who sees the thing itself, in subjective being? Not us:

We do not grasp that subjective being as it is in itself, but only according to some kind of objective being. Nevertheless we make affirmations about these objective beings according as they refer to or are taken for that subjective being that is one in itself.[b]

Of course we want to see the subjective being behind the appearances, and we talk as if we succeed in so doing, but in fact we fail. Does this mean that only God sees the things in themselves? That depends. If subjective beings are themselves finite, then the divine mind is of the wrong sort to see them. For God has his own mode of perceiving things, and he is constrained by the rules of mental representation just as we are. To see the objective beings that we see, God would need to assume a mental state just like ours, which he cannot. So, if subjective being is finite as well, then it seems that God cannot see that either. Better, Autrecourt says, to say that God perceives only himself—a conclusion that many more orthodox scholastic theologians had also affirmed. But now Autrecourt feels some pressure to conclude that the things themselves, in their subjective being, *just are God*.

What each objective thing seeks, and what it moves towards, is the one subjective being that is God. And this being understands himself by a cognition that is the same as himself in subjective being, and he attains [himself] in the subjective being according to which he exists.[c]

What the argument from illusion has now brought us to is something approaching Spinozistic monism. The only real, subjective being in the world is God. What we have access to is the world of appearances, and those appearances are universal properties, which have only objective being and are instantiated only where and when an appearance occurs. Even our own acts of perception, Autrecourt insists, are themselves universals—when two people see exactly the same color, they do so by sharing a single act.[d] Presumably that act is itself an objective being. Presumably, on this view, we ourselves are all objective beings, at least insofar as we are acquainted with ourselves and others. Autrecourt makes it clear that he is not committing himself to such a

---

[a] Ch. 7 (p. 245.6–8).   [b] Ch. 7 (p. 243.37–40).   [c] Ch. 7 (p. 262.20–3).   [d] Ch. 7 (p. 245.10–15).

thoroughly radical position, but he finds it hard to know what else subjective being could plausibly be said to be, if not the mind of God.[20]

Rather than commit himself one way or the other and then proceed to work out the details, Autrecourt comes to an abrupt halt at this point in the *Tractatus*. At any rate, in the sole surviving manuscript, housed here in Oxford at the Bodleian library (MS Canonici Miscellaneous 43), the text suddenly runs out, ending mid-sentence with the words *Et advertendum est* . . .—"It should also be noted . . ." This has often struck me as the perfect model for how all philosophical texts should end: not pretending to have reached any sort of closure, but in mid-thought, hopeful of taking yet another step forward.

The Quest for Fidelity

The variety of scholastic responses to the argument from illusion underscores the lengths these authors were willing to go to avoid treating the objects of perception as something inside the mind. The seventeenth century's inward turn is thus something new and strange, and this demands some explanation. Having now argued that neither introspection nor illusion, by themselves, can furnish such an explanation, I am left to pursue the line of thought begun last week: that, for philosophers from Descartes forward, transformations in metaphysics and natural philosophy leave the mind as the last remaining refuge for a domain of sensory privilege.

The age-old story about the five senses had been that we see colors, hear sounds, and so on. If such qualities are not outside the mind—or if they are there but not in the way they appear to be, which is just as bad—then we must either admit cognitive disaster or relocate the objects of perception. Admittedly, even when color, heat, smell, and so on are rejected as fundamental agents in the natural world, perception might still have some limited validity as a tool for grasping geometric and kinetic properties, the new primary qualities. But if sight gets color wrong, hearing gets sound wrong, smell gets odor wrong, and so on, then the senses would seem to be badly defective with regard to their central function. This is an outcome that seemed intolerable. According to Descartes, "it seems impossible that God should have placed in me a faculty that is not perfect in its kind, or that lacks some perfection that it ought to have."[a] Berkeley similarly appeals to divine goodness: "We should believe that God has dealt more bountifully with the sons of men than to give them a strong desire for that knowledge which he had placed quite out of their reach."[b] So, if the senses do not grasp external things in the way philosophers had always supposed, some other domain of privilege must be found. That the demotion of colors and so on to the status of secondary qualities played the decisive role is suggested by Malebranche, who insists that Augustine himself would have held a mediated theory of perception but for his being in the grip of "the prejudice that colors are in objects."[c] And no wonder that it later seems to Hume that "the fundamental principle" of the "modern" philosophy is "the opinion concerning colours, sounds, tastes, smells, heat and cold; which it asserts to be nothing

---

[a] *Med.* 4 (VII: 55).   [b] *Principles of Human Knowledge* Intro §3.
[c] *Réponse au Livre des vraies et des fausses idées* 7.12 (*Oeuvres complètes* VI: 68).

but impressions in the mind."[a] Although these post-scholastic philosophers were not the first to raise such doubts—in some form, they go all the way back to Democritus—this was the first time that such ideas became mainstream.

My thesis, then, is that perception became mediated as a direct result of the secondary qualities' losing their status as real, physical, external-world causes. But, to see exactly how this happened, we should get clear on where seventeenth-century proponents of the corpuscularian philosophy took their predecessors to have gone wrong. As we saw last week, Descartes contends that it is not even possible for the external world to have colors and other sensible qualities as they appear to the senses. He takes himself to have discovered what the external world is—simply bodies in motion—and takes it that there could be no room there for qualities like color as they are perceived. Implicit here is a criticism of earlier philosophers, who Descartes thinks made the mistake of supposing that "what is called color in objects is something exactly like the color we sense."[b] As should be clear by now, this cannot be right, inasmuch as for scholastic authors "the color we sense" *is* the color in objects. But such caricatures can be found throughout anti-scholastic writings. Locke, to take another example, writes that "qualities are commonly thought to be the same in those bodies that those ideas are in us, the one the perfect resemblance of the other, as they are in a mirror; and it would by most men be judged very extravagant if one should say otherwise."[c] This, too, distorts the standard scholastic view. Although it is true that species were thought to be likenesses of external objects, this holds no more for perception than it does for any causal relationship. The general causal requirement that an effect resemble its cause could scarcely have been enough to inspire the conclusion—bizarre on its face—that the inner character of a perception is exactly like the physical character of the world outside of us. Why would anyone suppose this? And this is a particularly bizarre conclusion to ascribe to scholastic philosophers, given that they generally denied that we have direct access to these species that are supposedly a mirror of external reality.[21]

Yet, even if scholastic authors were very far from supposing that what is out in the world is just like what is in our mind, they did accept that perception shows us the sensible qualities of things in *high fidelity*. This is to say, drawing on a distinction introduced last week,[d] that the senses not only serve as reliable detectors of what is in the world around us, but also faithfully show us what that world is like, by revealing to us the qualities that are the fundamental causal agents in nature. Prior to the seventeenth century, most took for granted that these two ideals—reliability and fidelity—are somehow satisfied by our perception of sensible qualities in the world. When metaphysically adventuresome fourteenth-century authors like Peter Auriol and Nicholas of Autrecourt did confront the fear of infidelity—that the world is not as the senses show it to be—they managed to find some other privileged sensory domain out in the world, possessed of some less than fully real mode of existence. But for post-scholastic authors of the seventeenth century, with their commitment to a narrowly mechanistic conception of the external world, no such outward solution was available. Moreover, with the rise of the new science, it began to seem as if all perception might be fundamentally illusory. In short, the austerities of the new metaphysics and the new

---

[a] *Treatise* I.4.4, p. 226.   [b] *Principles* I.70.   [c] *Essay* II.8.16.   [d] Lecture Three, p. 66.

natural philosophy formed an anabolic cocktail that nurtured a monstrous threat, the argument from illusion on steroids. The only defense consistent with their austere metaphysics was to seek shelter within the mind.

This historical saga suggests a general principle in the philosophy of perception:

> *The Fidelity Constraint.*   Where the senses reliably track the presence of two or more items along a single causal chain running from external object to perceiver, the item that is tracked with greater fidelity is that which is most properly the object of perception.

This principle tells us how to adjudicate between competing perceptual objects. Along any one causal chain from external object to perceiver, it may be that the senses reliably track various features of reality. My visual perception, for instance, may closely correlate with what is happening on the surfaces of the bodies I am looking at, and may also closely correlate with what is happening in my optic nerve or in some part of my brain. Which of those things am I seeing? The Fidelity Constraint asserts that what I am seeing—in the most proper, privileged, and primary sense of the term—is whatever the senses display most faithfully. Not the optic nerve, then, because vision does not even reveal that I have an optic nerve, let alone two of them; but maybe features of the surface of the object, if that is what wins out in terms of fidelity. If there is nothing else that the senses do a better job of revealing to us, then we should say that it is these surface features that I see.

Various examples illustrate the plausibility of this principle. When you see the headlights of a car in your rearview mirror, for instance, it would seem perverse to insist on the mirror as the proper object of vision, even if in some sense the mirror is a more immediate object. We say instead that you see *the car's headlights*, and that you see them *in the mirror*. What explains this verdict? According to the Fidelity Constraint, the explanation is that the car's headlights score much higher in terms of fidelity. In looking into a mirror, you learn little about the character of the mirror—only the bare fact that it is perfectly reflective—but you learn a great deal about the object that is reflected. Now consider, in contrast, seeing a tree in sunlight. The causal process is essentially the same, from light source to reflective surface to eye, but because ordinary objects are so poorly reflective we learn more about *them* when we see them in sunlight than we do about the sun whose light they reflect. So we properly say that you see *the tree*, and that you see it *in sunlight*.

There are many borderline cases. When you see a picture, for instance, it is unclear whether you primarily see the picture or the thing depicted in it. If the image is frozen, as in a painting or a photo, then that seems to decide the question in favor of the image. For, even if what is depicted is a still life or a landscape, the image is locked into a certain depiction, from a fixed vantage point, and this makes it much less tempting to say that we are seeing the thing depicted. With video, however, matters are quite different. If the image is clear and sufficiently life-like, then we feel considerable temptation to say that we are seeing the event itself, in the world, just as much as if we were watching in person. But the situation is tricky. The less clear the image, the more it seems right to say that we are seeing the video screen. Moreover, in person, we see the events as if they are taking place right in front of us, a certain distance away. When looking at a video screen, one might say that we see the events as if they are taking place behind the screen. (Compare Auriol's assessment of mirrors.) But perhaps this is not right. Perhaps looking at a screen is more like looking into a telescope, and we see right through it, as it were, to the events themselves, wherever they occur. But here another puzzle arises: Does it matter whether the event is being depicted live or is a recording of something that occurred earlier? (Compare the familiar worry that what we see in outer space happened minutes or even years before the light reaches our eyes.) Although it is unclear how to adjudicate these borderline cases, the Fidelity Constraint helps account for why they are unclear.

Once we see the critical role played by questions of fidelity, it becomes evident that other familiar ways of assessing these debates are misguided. First, it turns out to be quite unhelpful to focus on whether one or another object is perceived more *directly* or *immediately*. Although today's lecture offers many historical examples of authors who describe their views in these terms, in fact this way of talking threatens to obscure the issues. The rearview mirror fails to be an object of perception not because it fails to be sufficiently immediate from a causal point of view, but because it scores comparatively poorly in terms of fidelity. Similarly, the scholastics' sensible species may be intermediaries in perception, and one might even suppose, as scholastics occasionally did, that they are, in some sense, objects of inner attention. But should we properly speak of perceiving them? No, not if we perceive external things in higher fidelity. The occurrence of mediation in this causal sense has nothing to do with whether a theory should count as *mediated* in my technical sense of the term. This leads to a second point: that the debate over whether perception is focused within or without has little to do with the choice between simple and dual views. As stressed already, both of these views are compatible with locating the objects of perception inside the mind, and neither view entails that outcome. What matters, instead, is where fidelity obtains.

These two conclusions point toward a third mischaracterization. Despite the very common complaint, which runs from antiquity all the way to this day, that mediated views lead to skepticism, in fact there is no intrinsic connection. Even if the mind has a privileged domain of inner sensory objects that it grasps in high fidelity, nothing prevents it from being the case that, through these inner objects, we *also* grasp external things with quite good fidelity. For we could be living in a world in which outer reality matches up quite closely with the way our inner ideas are, meaning that anyone who grasps the one in reliably high fidelity will grasp the other with similar fidelity. If, in this matching world, the inner objects score highest in terms of fidelity, then the Fidelity Constraint holds that they should be regarded as the proper objects of perception. But even if, in such a world, perception were both dual and mediated, still the senses would provide perfectly good information about the outer world as well. Now, of course, one can always raise skeptical questions, and so in this case the question could arise of how we *know* that we are in a matching world. But the point is that there is nothing about how perception works in such a world that makes this question inevitably fatal. Skeptical queries like this can be raised just as easily for a perfectly simple and unmediated theory like Ockham's. The reason why there seems to be a special problem about skepticism for mediated theories of perception is not that they are mediated in my technical sense, but that the mediation is driven from the start by antecedent worries about outward fidelity. It is infidelity that breeds skepticism, not mediation.[22]

With all this in mind, let us return to the historical developments I have been tracing. For most scholastic authors, ordinarily perception seems unproblematic with regard to fidelity, and so external things go unchallenged as perceptual objects. Even if sensible species are likenesses of external qualities, these inner species cannot score as high with regard to fidelity, if for no other reason than that they are not located where the objects of perception seem to be. It is only once philosophers begin to doubt whether the senses faithfully depict external objects that they feel drawn toward treating inner representations as the things we primarily perceive. Unwilling to countenance a speculative metaphysics of apparent beings or other exotica out in the world, they locate that privileged sensory domain within the mind, and so our ideas become the primary objects of perception. But what this requires, the Fidelity Constraint predicts, is that these ideas are themselves grasped with the highest fidelity. This prediction in fact holds true. According to Descartes, "for as long as the mind merely contemplates these ideas and neither affirms nor denies that there is anything outside itself corresponding to these ideas, it cannot be deceived."[a] And Locke: an idea "can be no other but such as the mind perceives it to be."[b] And with this we really do have the sort of veil of ideas that brings skepticism in its wake—not because of the mere fact of mediation, but because mediation presupposes the thought that here and only here, in the inner domain of ideas, do the senses show us things as they really are.

Now I am in a position to make good on the claim I advertised earlier today: that the era of Descartes and Locke was not only the first, but in fact the *only* time in the history of philosophy when it could have seemed widely plausible that inner representations are the primary objects of perception. It was the first, because this was the first time in the history of philosophy when quite general doubts arose over whether there are suitable external objects for perception. But it was also the only time such views could flourish, because the days were quickly coming to a close when it could widely seem plausible to locate sensible qualities within the mind. Bodies cannot have "the color we sense," Descartes says (as above), because nothing like that could exist in the physical world. Hence the only place where we can locate color as it seems to be, in high fidelity, is within an immaterial mind. Descartes was right, or at least right enough, about the external world, but he was entirely wrong to suppose that it does any good to relocate the objects of perception within. For, once we learned that the mind itself is merely particles in motion, the cluster of interconnected neurons that we call the brain, it became hard to see how sensation could be said to reveal much of anything about what goes on within us. Fidelity fails to obtain for inner objects just as dramatically as it fails to obtain for external objects. Hence the same reasoning that led Descartes to judge it impossible for bodies to have "the color we sense" makes it natural today to conclude that colors cannot be in the mind either.

Does this mean there are no colors? No, no more than it means that we see nothing at all. Instead we have arrived back at a familiar theme: that philosophy has been searching for an epistemic ideal that, on reflection, we have no grounds for supposing ourselves to be able actually to achieve. The trouble with the seventeenth century's mediated theories is not that they are excessively skeptical in their implications, but that they are excessively optimistic, taking for granted that we can achieve an ideal of fidelity that in fact ought to have been abandoned. Descartes mocked the scholastics for thinking that

---

[a] *Principles* I.13.   [b] *Essay* II.29.5.

the external world is just as it seems to be, but it is equally problematic to suppose that our minds are just as they seem to be. There is nothing about the nature of perception that should encourage the Panglossian assumption that, when we perceive the world as being a certain way, there must be something, somewhere, that *is* that way. The ideas-first epistemology of the seventeenth century is thus an historical anomaly, a product of a time when the mind was thought to be specially mysterious and the outer world simple. Now that we understand the mind to be just another part of that world, we can recognize more clearly where the demand for high fidelity leads: not to the conclusion that we are trapped behind the veil of our own ideas, but to the conclusion that we are wholly blind—that we perceive nothing. The manifest absurdity of this result makes it obvious that what has to be rejected is the ideal of perception in high fidelity.

Even so, the search for a privileged sensory domain continues to this day. Although the Cartesian–Lockean way of ideas is now generally discredited, philosophers persist in offering a whole menu of options on which somehow, somewhere, whether within or without, something is just the way it seems to be. But we need not continue to search for this kind of magical domain of sensory privilege. Bearing in mind our long history of failure, we would do better to abandon the ideal of perception in high fidelity. Once we do this, the argument from illusion loses its power and we can be content with the way in which, under certain predictable circumstances, the senses reliably show us straight sticks as bent. More generally, we can be glad that a certain vibration of an object reliably generates a certain auditory response, and that a surface's being energized by light in a certain way reliably generates a certain visual response. Of course, it would better to perceive things exactly as they are, so that straight things always reliably look straight and vibrating things seem to vibrate. But philosophy should grow up and face the reality that perception just does not work like this, in any domain. No one guaranteed that our story would have an entirely happy ending.[23]

If we do still feel unhappy at this mixed outcome, it is because we are pursuing the wrong ideal. Vision may reveal nothing as it really is, in either mind or world, but yet we obviously do see something with a fair degree of reliability, and 'color' seems as good a word as any for the proper objects of visual perception. If we can agree on that much, then the best option is to put color back into the world and allow that the colors are the things we see, just not in the sort of privileged way philosophers have assumed. After all, in the end, there really is nothing that the senses reveal so well as they reveal the sensible qualities of bodies in the world. Applying the Fidelity Constraint here and more generally, we can reach the distinctly unmagical conclusion that of course we perceive things in the external world, albeit not as faithfully as we might have liked.

All of this may be a disappointment, but it really ought to be no surprise. The bad news of the seventeenth-century was that the senses fail to deliver the external world in high fidelity. The bad news of the twentieth was that they also fail to deliver the mind in high fidelity. As a result, science has turned out to be much more like theology than had been previously supposed: the first causes of things being themselves inaccessible, we must make inferences from their effects, through a mirror darkly. We should simply learn to live with that.

Lecture Five

The Privileged Now

After two weeks of looking at the sorts of ideals that philosophers have expected from our senses, today I ascend to the intellectual level, and consider our ability to reason from premises to a conclusion.

The final verdict of last week's lecture was that our quest for a domain of sensory privilege turns out to be illusory even when we attempt to turn within and reflect upon the mind's own ideas. With that last refuge abandoned, I concluded that there is nothing the senses reveal in high fidelity. Although perception may be reliable, it is very far from achieving the sort of ideal we have historically expected. Today I pose an analogous question regarding our ability to reason. Is there any domain of epistemic privilege where we can be certain that things are just as they seem to be? But, whereas last week's subject—the directness of our sensory access to the external world—was as familiar as anything in the history of philosophy, my topic this week is far less familiar: the extent to which we can or should attempt to encompass a whole chain of thoughts within the scope of the privileged now.

The Anselmian Glance

To begin to explain, let me turn to that great medieval figure, Anselm of Canterbury. Among the many hard questions that his fellow monks put to Brother Anselm, perhaps the most philosophically intriguing concerned the fall of the devil. About halfway through Anselm's intricate dialogue on this subject, he has the teacher warn his student that they need to take a step back and consider some more fundamental issues. He then remarks:

It is important for you not to be content merely to understand each of the things I say individually, but to gather them all up in your memory at the same time and see them in one glance, as it were.[a]

The imperative Anselm expresses can be readily appreciated: we often feel the need to get a course of thought into our heads all at once, so that we can see the argument as a whole. It is, however, quite obscure what is involved in this sort of all-at-once grasp of an

---

[a] *Fall of the Devil* ch. 12 (pp. 187–8 trans.).

argument and under what circumstances it is possible. It is also by no means clear what is lost when we fail to see the whole argument in what I will hereafter call a single *Anselmian glance*. My aim is to shed some light on these questions by considering the role this glance plays, first in later medieval debates and then in the post-scholastic era. As in previous lectures, we will find, now at the intellectual level, the recurring expectation of a privileged epistemic domain, and we will see how these expectations endure through the scholastic era, up to Descartes and beyond, even while considerations emerge that call some of this privilege into doubt.

Although the notion of an Anselmian glance may appear recondite, it can be seen as one aspect of the more familiar and much discussed phenomenon of first-person authority. Before plunging into the historical details, let me pause to situate the issues in that context. If the question arises of what I believe or feel, it is obvious that I myself am the best source of information. Not that my perspective is unimpeachable— sometimes, for instance, my wife is quicker than I am to recognize that I am in a bad mood. Still, I have some sort of authority when it comes to my own mental states. In an analogous sort of way, though no doubt with less justification, I privilege my own perspective when it comes to many matters outside myself. *Look, a bear!*, my wife says, but although she is surely as reliable a witness as I am, I do not quite believe there's a bear until I see it myself. There is much for the epistemologist to wonder about in the way we each privilege our own first-person awareness, and in the end I will call into question some aspects of this privilege, but for now let us simply mark the phenomenon.

Just as I give special weight to how things seem to me, so I give special weight to how things seem at the present time. Put slightly differently, I privilege not just the perspective that is right *here*, from where I am standing, but also the perspective that is right *now*, at this very moment. I may have taught Anselm's great dialogue a few years back and made careful and clear lecture notes, but I do not really trust those notes in the same way in which I trust my current impressions of the text. I do not think that I am any smarter now, but still, for whatever reason, I can hardly help but put greater trust in my present judgments. The existence of careful and clear notes is important to the example, because it shows that the main issue is not the reliability of memory. I do not doubt that I used to interpret the text in a certain way; the problem is that I do not wholly trust those old views. The analogy between the privileged now and the privileged self is again useful. My need to see the bear for myself is not brought on by worries about a communication breakdown. Her utterance was quite unambiguous, and so I have no doubt that she takes herself to see a bear. The problem is that I trust myself more than her, just as I trust my present judgments about the text more than my old judgments.

There is more than an analogy between these kinds of privilege; they are in fact mutually dependent. If my wife and I are comparing memories, I have little inclination to privilege mine over hers. It is only with respect to how things seem *now* that I favor my own perspective. Similarly, if my friend Christina offers me a choice between her old notes on Anselm and her current thoughts, freshly typed out, I will not have any immediate preference. Her present thoughts will seem more valuable only to the extent that I think she is wiser now than before, and it is easy to imagine cases where I would rather have those older notes. In general, it is only with respect to how things seem to *me* that I privilege the present. Putting these two lines of thought together, we can say that what I privilege is the first-person present perspective—how things seem to *me now*. Obviously, this sort of me–now privilege can be overcome, and frequently is, by the conflicting testimony of other people and of our own memories. But clearly a part of what we are trying to do when we seek to encompass some complex thought in a single Anselmian glance is to achieve a certain privileged grasp of that subject. In what follows I attempt to sort out the character of this privilege, first by assessing whether it is even possible, and then by considering why it is desirable—why it should be regarded as part of the epistemic ideal. Historically, we will see that the value of the Anselmian glance has been understood in various ways. Once we see that, we will be in a position to conclude that its desirability has been considerably overrated.

Many Thoughts at Once

The phenomenon of trying to grasp an argument in a single glance is familiar enough, but it is not at all easy to explain what it involves, and one might even doubt whether it is possible. In recent years, for instance, Tyler Burge has maintained that even the shortest of arguments rely on memory: that "even one-step demonstrations could go bad if the reasoner's short-term memory were defective enough."[a] This seems to accord with an older tradition in the philosophy of mind, according to which one can have only a single thought at a time. Thomas Aquinas articulates this thesis in some detail, devoting an entire article of the *Summa theologiae* to the question of whether our intellect can think about more than one thing at once.[b] His negative answer is grounded partly in the familiar experience of thinking, but he puts even greater weight on the metaphysical claim that the intellect thinks by taking on a certain sort of form, and that it can no more have two such forms at a single time than a body can have two shapes.

This analogy should give us pause, for several reasons. First, whereas a shape can be had all at once, in an instant, it is not clear that a thought can be. Thoughts might instead seem to be events that take place over time. In that case a view like Aquinas's might be expressed as maintaining that we can no more have multiple thoughts at once than we can utter multiple sentences at once. (We cannot literally speak out of both sides of our mouth.) The Anselmian glance, accordingly, would be understood as requiring multiple thoughts unspooling concurrently in the mind, in parallel. I will return later to this question of whether thought is instantaneous or successive, but for now let us just keep the issue in mind (whatever that turns out to mean).

Another difficulty with the analogy with shape is that it seems at first glance that my body has many shapes—one shape for my hands, one for my feet, and so on. Is there any basis for insisting that one body can have only one shape, albeit a very complex one? That is far from clear, because it is not clear how to individuate shapes. Similar trouble arises, however, over what counts as a single thought. Presumably I can have in my mind, all at once, a whole concept, even a rather complex concept. Can I have in mind a whole proposition? If so, how about a conditional proposition? If so, why not a one-step demonstration (something Burge rules out)? Aquinas discusses this issue in some detail. He thinks that one can consider a whole proposition at a single time, provided one

---

[a] "Content Preservation," p. 463.   [b] *Summa theol.* 1a 85.4.

considers it "as one."[a] Similarly, one can have in mind at once both some ultimate end and the means to achieve that end, "insofar as they are somehow one."[b] And although considering a premise and a conclusion individually requires two separate acts of thought, a single act of thought is capable of "assenting to the conclusion on account of the premises."[c] The governing idea, for Aquinas, is that one can think at once only of what can be encompassed within the content of a single cognitive form (an *intelligible species*, in his jargon). So one cannot have, at the same time, discrete thoughts about a premise and a conclusion—that would require two forms. But one can have the single thought that *a follows from b*, or that *to obtain c I should do d*. Such a thought can be had all at once, provided one does not attempt, at the same time, to form a discrete thought about any of the ingredients. It would take a separate thought, at a separate time, to consider on its own the *a* on account of which *b* obtains, or the *c* on account of which I should do *d*.[1]

I am not sure that Aquinas's discussion sheds much light on what is possible with respect to the Anselmian glance. Too much turns on the question of what can be represented by a single intelligible species, which seems only to postpone the issue. So far as I can find, more recent philosophers have not much concerned themselves with these questions. But psychologists have done so in considerable detail, under the heading of *working memory*. To understand the words of this paragraph, as they go rushing by, you must be able to hold a certain amount in your mind—otherwise the individual words could not be processed as sentences. This is just one example of working memory at work. Considerable ingenuity has been put into studying how much information we can hold onto in this way. In a famous paper from 1956, George Miller suggested that the answer is seven, plus or minus two. More recent research by Nelson Cowan has arrived at the number four, plus or minus one.

It is, however, not entirely clear what working memory is supposed to be. On some accounts, it is a system of short-term storage to which we have especially direct access. Others treat it not as a kind of memory, but instead as an extended conscious workspace, so that to hold multiple thoughts in working memory is to hold them in conscious awareness all at once. Thus, when Cowan argues that we can keep roughly four things in working memory, he explicitly indicates that he means this as an answer to the question "what is the limit on how much can be experienced at once or on how much we can be conscious of at once?"[d] This connection between working memory and consciousness goes back to William James, who offered this vivid account of the difference between true, long-term memory and what he calls "primary memory":

An object which is recollected, in the proper sense of that term, is one which has been absent from consciousness altogether, and now revives anew. It is brought back, recalled, fished up, so to speak, from a reservoir in which, with countless other objects, it lay buried and lost from view. But an object of primary memory is not thus brought back; it never was lost; its date was never cut off in consciousness from that of the immediately present moment.[e]

With this sort of picture in mind, one might appeal to working memory as an explanation of how it is possible for us to grasp a whole argument all at once, in a single Anselmian glance.

---

[a] *Quaest. de veritate* 8.14c.   [b] *Summa theol.* 1a2ae 12.3c.   [c] 1a2ae 12.4c.
[d] *Working Memory Capacity*, p. 3.   [e] *Principles of Psychology* I: 646–7.

These remarks about the relationship between working memory and consciousness bring out how the Anselmian glance tacitly presupposes our *conscious awareness* of several things at once. Anselm is not content with our having some stored disposition to assent to the premises of the argument; he wants us to be occurrently, consciously thinking about each of the premises right now. If a mere disposition sufficed, then it would be quite unproblematic to get a whole argument in mind all at once. For, whether one thinks of the mind as a soul or as a brain, it is clear enough that, at any given moment, the mind stands in countlessly many subconscious states, storing the traces of a lifetime of experience. Our interest is not in these vast, hidden regions of the mind, but in the highly constrained space where those resources become, for a brief time, consciously experienced. The authority of the first-person present perspective, however it is to be understood, rests precisely on such awareness.

Now it may be that philosophy does a disservice to cognitive science by constantly pushing to the fore this vexed notion of *consciousness*. That may prove to be too crude a tool for understanding phenomena such as working memory, where we seem to grasp thoughts in a way that rises to the level of consciousness but somehow just barely. Bernard Baars has influentially compared the mind to a theater and working memory to its stage, to which he further adds a spotlight that singles out a given idea for special attention.[a] Where is consciousness in this model? Perhaps it is best not to ask. But, whatever terminology and metaphors we choose, the phenomenon in question seems quite real. When I try to hold more than one thing in my head at once, it feels like what I am trying to do is, literally, to keep thinking about all of them at once. Up to a point, it seems to me that I can do that. There may be still more things that I am not consciously thinking about right now, but that lie waiting in the wings, in some kind of ready storage or short-term memory. Yet discussions of working memory seem to be grappling with a phenomenon that is not strictly a sort of memory at all, but rather the mind's ability to think more than one thought at once.

In reaching this conclusion, I mean to be rejecting views like those of Aquinas and Burge. Burge holds that "preservation memory . . . is epistemically necessary if we are to understand any argument as justifying beliefs through the steps of the argument."[b] No doubt memory is very often, even usually, required for an argument to have the sort of justificational force it is intended to have. But why suppose that memory is *always* required, for *every* argument, even for the *briefest* interval of time? No doubt our mind's awesome complexities can support only a very limited scope of conscious awareness. But what reason do we have for thinking that the scope is restricted to precisely a single thought, concerned with precisely one proposition? Why not allow instead that we can hold a whole argument in our mind at once, in a single Anselmian glance?[2]

Evidential Force

I would not wish to dwell too much on such obscure questions about the character of consciousness. Let us, then, take for granted only what is most obvious: that we do in some way seek to get the details of an argument to the forefront of our minds, whatever

---

[a] *In the Theater of Consciousness*, prologue.   [b] "Interlocution," p. 37.

that involves, and that we seek this because it is cognitively advantageous. Once we take for granted that we are in some way *capable* of the Anselmian glance, the question can be asked of just *why* this is advantageous. Here again recent work in philosophy is of limited help, but we can derive some inspiration from older material. For there was, in the later Middle Ages, a very lively debate over the importance of grasping a whole argument all at once.

As the first lecture discussed in some detail, scholastic Aristotelians conceived of the cognitive ideal for human beings in terms of the acquisition of *scientia*, understood along the lines of the *Posterior Analytics*. Knowledge of this sort comes through a syllogistic demonstration ultimately grounded in self-evident premises. For various fourteenth-century authors, the question thus arose of whether *scientia* requires that, in grasping the conclusion of a demonstration, one grasps the premises at the same time. Opinion was split on this matter and, for those who took the affirmative position, there was further disagreement over why exactly it is valuable to grasp a whole demonstration at once.

One way of accounting for the value of such a grasp is in terms of the contribution that the Anselmian glance makes to what we might characterize as our *understanding* of a conclusion. To understand a thing, on one prominent construal, requires grasping that thing in its larger context. Accordingly, someone who plods slowly and carefully through a complex argument may eventually reach the correct conclusion. But seeing the whole argument in a single Anselmian glance permits an understanding of why the conclusion holds in a way that would be impossible for someone unable to see the whole thing at once. This appears to be William Ockham's position. He reserves *scientia* for the dispositional grasp of the conclusion of a demonstrative syllogism. To grasp the whole argument at once is something that goes beyond *scientia*, something he calls *sapientia*.[a] This word would ordinarily be rendered as 'wisdom,' but in this context it might just as well be translated as 'understanding.' Anselm's own view seems similar. He famously takes as his slogan the phrase *fides quaerens intellectum*—"faith seeking understanding." This was in fact the original title of his masterpiece, the *Proslogion*, and he explains in the preface to that work that the inspiration for the ontological argument came from his desire to replace the "chain of many arguments" offered in the *Monologion* with "a single argument" that might, all by itself, establish God's existence and perfection. Similarly, when Anselm asks his student, who is considering the fall of the devil, to pull together all the threads of the argument and try to see them all at once, he wants to make sure that his student understands why the conclusion obtains. The student might instead simply trust his teacher, following step by step and seeing the truth of each step without seeing how it all fits together. This sort of progress toward a conclusion is like following detailed step-by-step directions from point A to point B—go left, then left, then right, then left. When carefully followed, this can be a perfectly reliable method for arriving at one's destination. But it is better also to have a map of the route, so as to be able to visualize the whole path all at once. That sort of perspective on an argument is not easy; but, insofar as it can be obtained, for beings like us it is surely a part of the cognitive ideal.[3]

It seems undeniable that such understanding is part of what makes the Anselmian glance valuable, and in what follows I will take as much for granted. Historically,

---

[a] *Ordinatio* I prol. q 8 (*Opera theol.* I: 222).

however, the debate over these issues has concentrated on a rather different source of value: not that grasping the whole argument allows us to *understand* the conclusion better, but that grasping the premises and the conclusion at the same time is essential for the *evidentness* of the conclusion. To say this, however, is to say that the Anselmian glance is critical to *scientia*, since evidentness plays the critical role in scholastic philosophy, as the added factor that turns merely true belief into *scientia*.[a] Peter Auriol, in the early fourteenth century, offers a good example of this sort of view. When we have *scientia* with regard to some proposition, he argues, we do so on the basis of prior propositions. Ultimately the foundational premises of a demonstration are self-evident, which is to say that their truth can be grasped in their own right, all at once, without reference to anything else. But *scientia* concerns the conclusion of a demonstration, which the intellect is led to embrace because of the premises. The crucial point, for Auriol, is that such a conclusion must be grasped *at the same time* as those premises.

It is impossible for the intellect to be drawn to the truth of a conclusion, judging it to be true, unless this happens through some cause of that truth existing outside that conclusion. This, however, is the truth of some principle. Therefore, it is necessary that the intellect reaches the truth of a conclusion only insofar as it simultaneously reaches the truth of the principle.[b]

Auriol insists here that conclusion and premises must be grasped "simultaneously." He goes on to argue that all this must be grasped in a "singular and simple" act of intellect. It must be "numerically the same intellection" that reaches the truth of both a conclusion and its premises, or there would be no way to explain how "the intellect is drawn to the truth of a conclusion."[c] For the premises to have the requisite *evidential force*, which yields an indubitable intellectual assent to a conclusion, both premises and conclusion must be grasped in a single Anselmian glance.

As an analogy, Auriol considers desire. Just as the intellect grasps a conclusion on account of the premises that make it evident, so the will is drawn to one thing on account of being drawn to some further end. Ends are the sort of thing that are desired in their own right, and so one's appetite for an end need not be explained by anything else. But when we desire something that is not an end in its own right—say, we want a donkey—that desire can arise only when accompanied by a desire for some end. Something similar holds for rational argument: "a conclusion has truth only from the truth of the premise, and the intellect is drawn toward it only to the extent it has been drawn to the truth of the premise."[d] This analogy is liable to mislead, because it is obviously not the case that when one desires a thing one must constantly keep the end in mind as well. In the course of my search for a donkey whole stretches of time might pass during which I give not the slightest thought to why I want that donkey. Auriol can grant this. What he must maintain is that the rationality of a desire for some means can be vindicated only if—at some point—we are able to hold that desire in mind together with the desire for the end that motivates it. Similarly, a conclusion can of course be believed without giving any thought to the premises that led to the conclusion. Indeed, one can believe a conclusion dispositionally—and have *scientia* of it dispositionally—without presently thinking about it at all. But, for that conclusion

---

to be truly evident, for it to compel assent, the whole argument must be grasped within a single Anselmian glance.[4]

For an interestingly different perspective we can turn to Francis of Marchia, who lectured in Paris around 1319—just a few years after Auriol. Marchia argues, contrary to what Auriol and others had assumed, that the intellect cannot grasp a whole argument in a single act. That would require too many diverse objects to fit into one thought. Marchia, however, in contrast to the usual view, thinks that the intellect can have more than one occurrent thought at once. That leaves room for a version of the Anselmian glance: one might grasp a whole argument at once by simultaneously having discrete thoughts about the argument's different parts. Yet, although Marchia thinks that it may be *possible* to apprehend a whole argument all at once, through multiple concurrent thoughts, he insists that doing so would not facilitate the acquisition of *scientia*.

Devoting an entire question to the topic, Marchia accepts that the whole point of a demonstration is to extend the scope of what is intellectually evident, beginning with the self-evident and working outward from there through valid inferences that yield further evident conclusions. But he argues that, for premises to have this sort of evidential force, a temporal element is required. In order for the premises to *motivate* the conclusion in the desired way, compelling the mind to assent, they must *not* be grasped at the same time as the conclusion. To spell out why this is, Marchia contrasts grasping a whole argument with grasping a whole sentence. In the case of understanding a sentence,

Our intellect does not run [*discurrit*] from a grasp of the terms to a complex grasp of the proposition. Instead, it understands both the proposition itself and each of its terms on its own [*per se*] and absolutely, rather than one from another, and so it is not moved from one understanding to another.

A whole sentence, then, is grasped all at once. But this is not how it works for an argument, as he immediately goes on to explain:

Things are different for a conclusion and its premises, because our intellect understands the conclusion on the basis of its premises. Since it is moved from these actually cognized premises to the conclusion, and since it is impossible for the same thing at the same time to rest in something and be moved from it, therefore [the premises cannot be understood at the same time as the conclusion].[a]

When we conceive of a proposition, we are able to do so all at once, simultaneously grasping the terms of the proposition through discrete intellectual acts, acts that are somehow coordinated in such a way as to yield a single, complex thought. When it comes to a whole argument, however, Marchia takes a very different view. If what we are after is the state of mind that involves understanding a conclusion *on the basis of* more evident premises, then this should be understood as the temporally extended process of considering an argument's premises and letting those premises compel the mind's assent to a conclusion. This is how it works, not just for human beings but for any finite intellect. Even the angels, he says, must take time to grasp an argument, if that argument is to supply the evidential force that motivates the conclusion.[5]

Marchia thus disagrees with Auriol over whether the Anselmian glance should be considered a normative ideal, but he does so because of a more fundamental disagreement over a question broached near the start of this lecture: whether thought takes place at an instant or over time. Auriol assumes that thought is synchronic—occurring at an instant—and so concludes that, if an argument is to have evidential force, it must be grasped all at once. As we have seen, Marchia accepts that this is so when it comes to entertaining a single proposition. But he thinks that matters are quite different for whole arguments. Here there is an evidential process at work that begins with seeing that the premises must be true and that they entail their conclusion, which *then* induces us to embrace the conclusion as itself evident. The evidential force of a demonstration thus requires a diachronic process.

This is an old debate. Although Marchia cites no authorities, in taking the diachronic side he is unwittingly following in Plato's footsteps. As Plato had put it in the *Theaetetus*,

It seems to me that the soul when it thinks is simply carrying on a discussion in which it asks itself questions and answers them itself, affirms and denies. And when it arrives at something definite, either by a gradual process or a sudden leap, when it affirms one thing consistently and without divided counsel, we call this its judgment.[a]

Auriol, in contrast, is tacitly taking Aristotle's side. Aristotle had expressly rejected Plato's position with the remark that "reasoning is more like resting or dwelling upon something than like moving, and the same holds for a syllogism."[b] If we accept this Aristotelian picture, then it is natural to think that the syllogism ideally demands an Anselmian glance over the whole. If, instead, we follow Plato and conceive of discursive thought as essentially a motion through premises toward a conclusion, then we would expect it to be this diachronic process that culminates in the conclusion. The Anselmian glance may well still have value, in that it may foster our subsequent understanding of the conclusion we have reached, but what initially makes that conclusion evident is an intellectual process that necessarily takes time.

Insofar as one can speak of a consensus arising over this debate, it seems to lie with Auriol's synchronic approach and its appeal to the Anselmian glance. Thought can occur all at once, without motion, and when an argument is grasped in this way we have the most ideal sort of *scientia*. Marchia himself in fact tells us that this is the *opinio communis*.[c] And we can see a later instance of this consensus in Adam Wodeham, who enters into the discussion a decade or so later, around 1330. In the usual way, Wodeham conceives of *scientia* as requiring that one assent to a proposition "firmly and without hesitation," which he associates with evidentness. This leads him to resolve the question of whether *scientia* requires grasping the premises and the conclusion all at once by distinguishing between two levels of evidentness. At the first, higher level, the evidentness must arise all by itself: "actually having *scientia* can be taken in one way for an evident judgment such that, when it is posited in the soul with everything really distinct set aside, it is a contradiction for the soul not to assent evidently that things are as the conclusion signifies."[d] Taken in this way, an occurrent act of *scientia* requires grasping the conclusions

---

[a] *Theaetetus* 190a.   [b] *De anima* I.3, 407^{a}32–4.
[c] *Reportatio* I.1.2 art. 2, n. 8; *Scriptum* I.1.8 (in *Quodlibet*, p. 304, line 23).
[d] *Lectura secunda* d. 1 q. 1 art. 2 §14 (p. 348 trans. Pasnau, *Cambridge Translations*).

and the premises all at once. If not, then that assent would not be evident all by itself, apart from everything else. Its evidentness would instead depend on some prior grasp of the premises. In a weaker sense, however, Wodeham allows that such dependence on prior cognitive states is perfectly acceptable. Here it is enough for *scientia* to be evident not in itself, intrinsically, but because "it has an evident act attached to it regarding that same conclusion."[a] This attachment is presumably an historical, causal connection: assenting to the premises, at some previous time, has brought me to my present assent to the conclusion. For Wodeham, this counts as *scientia*, but in a lesser way, since "it will not be evident through any intrinsic evidentness but through extrinsic denomination, because if all else were set aside, then even if the firmness of its adherence remains, it does so without being evident."[b]

Wodeham's distinction between intrinsic and extrinsic evidentness serves as a useful reminder that, as usual, the term *scientia* is not what matters. Like scholastic authors in general, Wodeham is content simply to register its multiple meanings. The deeper question is what our normative epistemic ideal should be, and here Wodeham takes Auriol's side. The Anselmian glance is better, because it allows our grasp of a conclusion to be evident intrinsically, not just in relation to some other mental state that has previously obtained. So there is a commitment to an ideal here, in which one's first-person present mental state affords a certain kind of epistemic privilege, because that state, all by itself, renders a certain proposition indubitable. It is precisely this kind of ideal that I mean to argue against. But first we should look ahead to the seventeenth century, where we will find that this somewhat obscure scholastic discussion takes on a new prominence in Descartes.[6]

Descartes's Privileged Now

Descartes gives a critical place to the Anselmian glance throughout his writings, and explicitly ties its achievement to the successful acquisition of *scientia*. Predictably, he is not much concerned with the more abstruse aspects of the scholastic debate, such as whether thought is synchronic or diachronic, or whether we can, strictly speaking, think more than one thought at once. Indeed, it is possible that Descartes was unaware of the existence of these earlier discussions. Even so, he regularly insists on the importance of grasping an argument as a whole. In his early *Rules for the Direction of the Mind*, for instance, he writes that "for a complete *scientia*, every single thing relating to our undertaking must be illuminated in a continuous and wholly uninterrupted sweep of thought."[c] The *Principles of Philosophy* (1644) likewise distinguishes between the certainty of the privileged now and the worrisome fallibility of past judgments:

The mind, then, knowing itself, but still in doubt about all other things, looks around in all directions in order to extend its cognition further. First of all, it finds within itself ideas of many things . . . Next, it finds certain common notions and from these it constructs various demonstrations, and for as long as it attends to them it is completely convinced of their truth . . . Yet it cannot always attend to them. As a result, when it later recalls that it still lacks *scientia* regarding

---

[a] §14 (p. 348 trans.).   [b] §14 (p. 350 trans.).   [c] Rule 7 (X: 387).

whether it may have been created with a nature such as to be mistaken even in matters that appear most evident, the mind sees that it has just cause to doubt such conclusions.[a]

So long as we are working within the privileged now, we can build up from the *cogito*, adding introspective judgments and then a priori proofs based on self-evident principles. All of this will satisfy the highest standards for *scientia*—at least the highest humanly attainable standards—provided that we can grasp it all in a single Anselmian glance.[7]

Yet it takes enormous mental energy to get a whole argument in view and keep it there, and even the best of us can do it for only a short time. Eventually the practical demands of life force us to let go; and, even if we were to manage somehow to keep those demands at bay, there would be other arguments we would want to consider, each one crowding out the last. What happens, then, when we let go of an argument that we have so painstakingly gathered into our mind? Descartes is centrally concerned with this question, particularly in the *Meditations*. As he writes,

My nature is such that so long as I perceive something very clearly and distinctly I cannot but believe it to be true. But my nature is also such that I cannot always fix my mental vision on the same thing so as to perceive it clearly. Often the memory of a previously made judgment comes back when I am no longer attending to the arguments on account of which I judged that things were so.[b]

Given the *Meditations'* aim of achieving stable and lasting *scientia*, this is potentially a disaster. Descartes insists, however, that we can hold on to our privileged state of certainty so long as we hold on to the conclusion that there is a God who is no deceiver. Thus *Principles* I.13, quoted just above, concludes that "the mind sees that it has just cause to doubt such conclusions and that it cannot have certain *scientia* until it has come to recognize the author of its being." The Fifth Meditation passage just quoted immediately continues:

Hence other arguments can arise that would easily undermine my opinion, if I were unaware [*ignorarem*] of God, and I should thus never have true and certain *scientia* about anything, but only shifting and changeable opinions. For example, when I consider the nature of a triangle, it appears completely evident to me, steeped as I am in the principles of geometry, that its three angles are equal to two right angles; and so long as I attend to the demonstration, I cannot but believe this to be true. But as soon as I turn my mind's eye away from the demonstration, then in spite of still remembering that I perceived it with complete clarity, I can easily fall into doubt about its truth—if, that is, I were unaware of God. For I can convince myself that I am made by nature in such a way as to go wrong occasionally in matters that I take myself to perceive as evidently as can be—particularly since I remember that I have often held as true and certain many things that I have later, on the basis of other arguments, judged to be false.

Now, however, I have perceived that God exists, and at the same time I have understood that everything else depends on him, and that he is no deceiver. From this I have drawn the conclusion that everything I clearly and distinctly perceive is of necessity true. Accordingly, even if I am no longer attending to the arguments on account of which I have judged that this is true, as long as I remember that I clearly and distinctly perceived, no counter-argument can be adduced to make me doubt. On the contrary, I have true and certain *scientia* of it. This is so not

[a] *Principles* I.13.   [b] *Med.* 5 (VII: 69).

just for this conclusion, but for all the other conclusions that I remember ever having demonstrated, in geometry and similar domains.[a]

While still within the privileged now, our evident perceptions are epistemically ideal—as certain as is humanly possible. Indeed, for as long as we occurrently possess what he describes more precisely as a "clear and distinct perception" of an argument, we are not even capable of doubting it: "so long as I attend to the demonstration, I cannot but believe this to be true." Yet, as soon as our grasp of the demonstration recedes into memory, room for doubt arises. Once that happens, "I can convince myself" of having possibly gone wrong.

Descartes's intense concern with the Anselmian glance goes well beyond merely wanting us to *understand* an argument better. As in the earlier scholastic tradition, he thinks that an argument must be brought within the privileged now if it is to yield *scientia*. And here the critical point is that, as we saw in Lecture Two, *scientia* for Descartes requires the kind of certainty associated with the indubitability of evidentness, such that "no counter-argument can be adduced to make me doubt." Like Auriol and Wodeham, then, Descartes is concerned with the evidential force of a deductive argument, which he takes to decay once the argument falls into the past. If I am to be certain of a conclusion, I must see right now that those premises entail the conclusion. Moreover, I must be certain of the premises too, and so they, too, must be evident and that evidentness must obtain for me right now. And so it is that the Cartesian epistemic ideal requires that the whole argument be grasped all at once insofar as this is possible—in a single Anselmian glance.

Where Descartes goes beyond earlier discussions, however, is in proposing a remedy for the inevitable reality that we cannot hold a single argument in thought, all at once, for long. His remedy is to establish God's existence. This explains why the long Meditation Five passage just quoted culminates with this conclusion: "Thus I see plainly that the certainty and truth of all *scientia* depends on one cognition, of the true God, to such an extent that I could have perfect *scientia* about nothing else until I knew him."[b] This claim has struck readers from the start as being embarrassingly circular (and obviously so), inasmuch as it would seem that Descartes cannot achieve a perfect grasp of God's existence without already having reached a perfect grasp of much else. From our present vantage point, however, we can see why Descartes sees no difficulty here. In remarking that *scientia* requires knowledge of God, he is counting on his reader to have something like the Aristotelian understanding of *scientia* as a stable disposition lodged within the mind. Within the privileged now, the arguments of the first three meditations go through with the highest level of human certainty, without our having to presuppose the truth of their ultimate conclusion, which is that God exists. That ultimate conclusion is required, however, in order for these evident perceptions to be preserved beyond the privileged now, as stable, certain dispositions within the mind.

Descartes himself makes it quite clear that it is this sort of appeal to the privileged now that enables him to avoid circular reasoning. Mersenne had raised the circularity worry in the Second Objections, and gotten this reply from Descartes:

[a] *Med.* 5 (VII: 69–70).   [b] *Med.* 5 (VII: 71).

When I said that we can have certain *scientia* of nothing until we have cognized that God exists, I expressly declared that I was speaking only of *scientia* of those conclusions whose memory can recur when we are no longer attending to the arguments through which we deduced them.[a]

Descartes's interview with Frans Burman makes the same point. Burman worries: "It seems there is a circle, since in the Third Meditation the author uses axioms to prove the existence of God, even though he has not yet established that he is not deceived about these." To this Descartes is reported to have replied: "He does prove this, and he knows [*scit*] that he is not deceived about the axioms, because he is attending to them. For as long as he does this, he is certain that he is not deceived, and he is compelled to assent to them."[b] This is almost exactly what we should now expect Descartes to say, all the way down to the notion of intellectual compulsion within the privileged now. Moreover, Burman goes on to raise just the worry we might expect, that "our mind can conceive of only one thing at a time, whereas the proof in question is fairly long and is built up from multiple axioms." Descartes responds:

First, it is not true that the mind can conceive of only one thing at a time. To be sure, it cannot conceive of *many* things at a time, but still it can conceive of more than one. For example, I am right now, at the same time, conceiving and thinking of my talking and of my eating. Second, it is false that thought occurs instantaneously, for all my acts occur in time, and I can be said to continue and carry on with the same thought over a period of time... Therefore, since our thought is able to grasp more than one item in this way, and since it does not occur instantaneously, it is clear that we can grasp the entire demonstration about God. For as long as we do this, we are certain that we are not deceived, and thus every difficulty is removed.[c]

Here Burman reports Descartes to have gone out on a limb regarding the character of thought, saying that yes, we can have more than one thought at a time, and taking the diachronic Platonic side in the old debate over whether thought occurs instantaneously. But the main point is that, one way or another, there is a kind of certainty that can be had only when we "grasp the entire demonstration." All these passages make it plain that what has appeared to generations of readers as a circle is in fact a consequence of Descartes's distinguishing between the privileged status of an all-at-once Anselmian glance and the shakier epistemic status of evidence retained over time. His concern with such a distinction is not at all surprising, given the long history of such debates.[8]

Memory's Testimony

There are good reasons to be suspicious of the supposedly privileged epistemic status of the me–now. But before airing those suspicions let us look a little more closely at what good it does Descartes to appeal to God's existence. The present is supposed to be epistemically privileged on his view because it can, in the special circumstances of a clear and distinct perception, yield certainty. Descartes's further idea is that a certainty sufficient for *scientia* can be retained over time, outside the privileged duration of the Anselmian glance, provided that one recognizes that God exists and is no deceiver.

---

[a] Second Replies (VII: 140, responding to VII: 124–5).   [b] Conversation with Burman (V: 148).
[c] V: 148–9.

So how exactly does this help? Consider a range of cases that fall progressively farther from the Anselmian ideal:

A. Holding a whole argument in mind at once.
B. Holding the conclusion in mind and being able to produce the supporting argument at will.
C. Holding the conclusion in mind and being able to produce the supporting argument with effort.
D. Holding the conclusion in mind and remembering that the supporting argument was once grasped, but no longer being able to produce that argument, even with effort.
E. Holding the conclusion in mind without any memory of its evidential basis.
F. Having forgotten both the conclusion and its supporting argument.

Grade A describes the Anselmian glance. Grade F, at the opposite extreme, represents the case of complete loss, and here there is not much to say. Since there would remain not even a dispositional belief in the conclusion, we are not even in the domain of knowledge, however imperfect. We can, then, focus on the middle four grades. As always, let us eschew the tedious game of assigning the silent-K word to one or another grade. Suffice it to say that each of the grades is better than the ones beneath it and that we should, all else being equal, desire to maintain the highest grade possible.

But of course we must make choices. I once knew how to prove the soundness and completeness of first-order logic, but I couldn't do that now. I am at grade D and not ashamed to admit it, because this isn't information I feel any obligation to have retained. But there are other matters where grade D would be embarrassing—matters relating more closely to my professional work, and matters of such import that all educated people ought to be able to justify themselves. It would, for instance, be a serious intellectual deficiency to be unable to account for one's political or religious views—I do not of course mean to provide a sound *proof*, but at least to say something cogent about the reasons that incline one in a certain direction. To be sure, a great many people are sadly deficient in this regard, but the point is just that there *is* something sad about that state of affairs. In certain domains, then, we think it important to maintain grade B, or at least grade C. That in turn requires that we spend some time at grade A or close to it, getting in our head the whole course of an argument and understanding why we believe what we do.

In the very most important sorts of cases, then, the question arises of what we can do to maintain ourselves in a state as close as possible to grade A. For the sake of concreteness, let us concentrate on a falling off from grade A to grade B. Descartes, for one, saw quite a sharp decline even here. He supposed that the certainty of the privileged me–now is left quite behind when the moment passes—unless we hold firmly in mind certain facts about God. To assess this thought, we need to get clear about why the present is supposed to be epistemically privileged in this way and why the mere memory of having grasped an argument puts us in a significantly less good epistemic position.

The most obvious thing to say about such a case is that, outside of the privileged me–now, reliance on memory introduces a further risk of error. This is no doubt part of the story, but it seems to be only a small part and far from what is most interesting here. After all, we could reduce the risk of memory error to an absolute minimum by writing down a precise account of our thoughts within the privileged now. This might take the form of a signed affidavit:

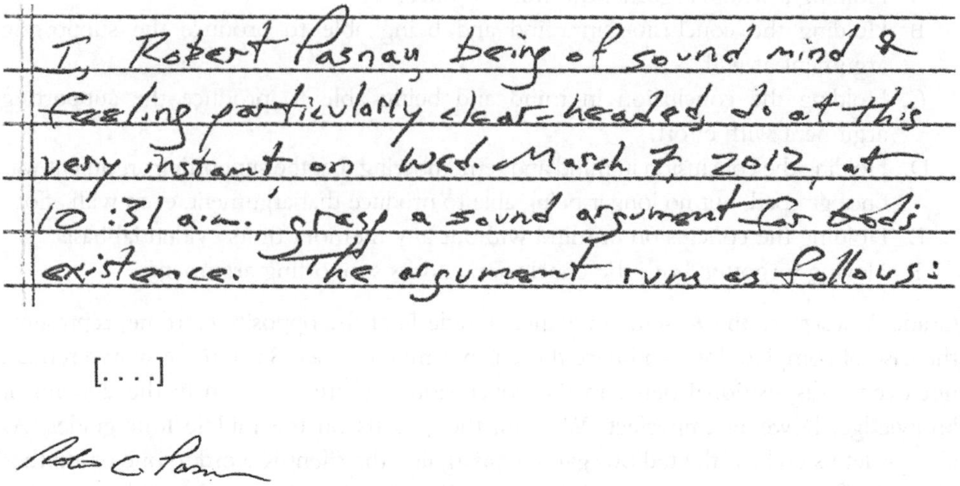

I, Robert Pasnau, being of sound mind & feeling particularly clear-headed, do at this very instant on Wed. March 7, 2012, at 10:31 a.m., grasp a sound argument for God's existence. The argument runs as follows:

[. . . .]

Figure 5.1. Sample Memory Affidavit

Provided I do not lose this rather valuable piece of paper, I will have taken the vagaries of memory largely off the table. Not entirely off the table, admittedly, since it would be desirable to remember having written down this statement. Inevitably, too, my written account of the argument will fail to be wholly precise about some of the details, and it will be useful to have some memory of the event to guide my future interpretation. Still, in view of a document such as this in combination, let us suppose, with a vivid apparent memory of the event, it would take quite a remote and dubious skeptical hypothesis to cast doubt on the fact that I did in fact take myself to have in mind a sound argument for God's existence. Such far-fetched skeptical doubts about memory are not what is of interest here. For, even if we take for granted the accuracy of memory, a gap still remains between my epistemic status at the moment of grasping an argument and my subsequent epistemic status, which relies only on my memory of having once seen that the argument is sound. In a case where I am seeing, right now, that an argument is sound, I regard myself as having the strongest possible reasons for embracing the conclusion. Once that privileged moment has fallen into the past, I may still feel justified in my belief, but the strength of my evidence feels diminished and subject to doubt. This privilege of the me–now does not depend on doubts about the reliability of memory.[9]

   Once we grant the reliability of memory, we are left with the task of explaining the disparity between our attitudes at different times toward the very same belief-generating process. At the moment the process is taking place within us, we supposedly have the strongest possible reasons for accepting its reliability. Retrospectively, however, we are said to have some good reason to doubt the process. Does this make any sense? If I will have good reason for doubt retrospectively, then should I not, even from within the privileged now, providently anticipate those reasons and commence to doubt, even while the argument is vividly in front of me? Conversely, if I am right to privilege my present grasp of the argument, then should not that attitude remain in place even after the moment has passed? Worries about memory aside, it is hard to see why the passing of time should make a difference.

Here it is useful to compare our epistemic attitudes toward our past selves with our epistemic attitudes toward others. If you tell me that you have grasped a demonstration of some momentous claim—showing me your signed affidavit or, even better, insisting that you have the whole thing in mind right now—I will be interested but skeptical. If I antecedently hold you in sufficient respect, I may take the time to work through your argument and may try to get it within the field of my own Anselmian glance. Or, if it is a claim that lies outside my own competence, I might seek confirmation that you are to be trusted in this domain. The point is that, one way or another, it would be reasonable for me to seek supporting evidence before accepting your claims, at least in cases of great import. In effect, this is how we treat our past selves. If I remember having reached some important conclusion some time ago, I am likely to respect my past self enough to take this information seriously, but I may not trust myself enough simply to accept that verdict without further investigation. I may well need to get it all in front of my mind again, just as I would if some trusted colleague had told me of the result. The parallel seems to show that we demand evidence of the reliability of our past selves in much the same way we demand evidence of the reliability of others.

Michael Dummett has suggested, along similar lines, that "memory may be said to be the testimony of one's past self."[a] But this way of describing the situation does not fully illuminate the phenomenon. To trust one's memories is indeed analogous, in a certain way, to trusting the testimony of another. But in trusting my memory what I trust is that my memory is accurately transmitting how something seemed to me in the past. The analogous case for testimony would be to trust that someone is accurately reporting how it seems to her. Although that can of course be in question when it comes to accepting testimony, it is not the central issue. We generally take for granted that our interlocutors are speaking accurately and sincerely about how things seem to them, and we focus on whether how it seems to them is in fact how it is. Returning, then, to the privileged me–now, the analogous situation is to take for granted that our memories are accurate and to focus on whether how it seemed to us is in fact how it is. This is why testimony, rather than memory, makes for the best analogy with the first-personal disparity between the privileged now and the underprivileged past. In just the way we may ask what warrants our trust in the testimony of others, so we may ask what warrants our trust in the testimony of our past selves.

With all this in mind, consider again Descartes. He contends that we can have confidence in the reliability of our evident perceptions in the past, provided that we attend to the nature of God. His reasoning is that, if God is no deceiver, then God would not have made us to be fallible in these most favorable cases. That we might be fallible even in our clear and distinct judgments is a worry that it becomes possible to have when looking retrospectively at our past thoughts. We can rule out such doubts, however, provided that we bear in mind that God exists and is no deceiver. Appealing to God in this way is thus simply Descartes's way of mounting an argument for the

---

[a] "Testimony and Memory," p. 412.

diachronic reliability of our cognitive faculties. One might attempt much the same thing today in terms of evolutionary theory. The general idea is to produce an argument for the reliability of our faculties under certain conditions, and then to wield that argument whenever retrospective doubts about the outputs of those faculties arise. Let us call such an argument a Reliability Proof.

From our present vantage point, the critical thing to understand about Descartes's strategy is that it rests entirely on the epistemic privilege of the me–now. Accordingly, if his Reliability Proof is to assuage our doubts over the remembered dictates of past reasoning, that proof must not itself be part of the remembered past, but must instead be lodged in my privileged now. This is not something that Descartes himself makes entirely clear, but the logic of his position requires it. Given that the whole point of the Reliability Proof is to yield justification for beliefs whose evidence has fallen into the remembered past, that proof itself will have evidential force only if it somehow retains its me–now privilege. This is not to say that the quest for *scientia* requires its devotees to retain a monomaniacal obsession with the Reliability Proof for the remainder of their lives, never letting it out of their minds. What Descartes's system requires of mere mortals like us is just that the proof remain at grade B, or at least at grade C, able to be brought up to grade A should doubts arise.[10]

In this way Descartes's whole strategy depends on the fact that he accords special epistemic status to first-person conclusions reached within the privileged now of the Anselmian glance. There cannot be a Reliability Proof for everything, unless we are to supply proof beyond proof *ad infinitum*, or else go round in a circle. Descartes's strategy for avoiding these familiar bad options is to base everything on the epistemic privileges of the present moment. If my present clear and distinct perceptions are ideally warranted—at least according to the human ideal—then there is no possibility of shoring them up with any further evidence or argument, nor any possibility of knocking them down with doubts. Hence a Reliability Proof grasped in the privileged now requires no further proof; it is the solid foundation of which epistemologists dream at night. Provided that we are able to keep this proof in mind, or at least within ready reach, it can serve to justify the many other beliefs that were once privileged but now have fallen into the underprivileged past. Crucial to the strategy, then, is the requirement that we be capable of grasping a whole argument all at once. If we cannot do that, then the whole strategy collapses, because we would then have only some worthless fragment of a sound argument within the scope of the privileged me–now.

Disprivileging the Present Self

Now that we have identified how Descartes's whole argumentative strategy turns on the privilege he accords to the first-person present, we are in a position to see just what is wrong with that strategy. The problem is that, on reflection, the supposed privilege of the me–now turns out to be nothing more than a groundless cognitive bias. What is plausible about Descartes's position is that, as a descriptive matter, we *do* privilege our present judgments. When I introduced the phenomenon at the start of this lecture, for instance, I described how in fact I do give special weight to what *I* can see right *now*, or how some philosophical matter seems *at this moment* to *me*. Nothing at all has been said, however, about whether I ought to favor these sorts of first-person present judgments. Descartes, indeed, seems to rest his case on nothing more than facts about how we are prone to reason. He remarks, as quoted already, that "so long as I perceive something very clearly and distinctly I *cannot but* believe it to be true."[a] This is how things are in the privileged me–now. In contrast, "as soon as I turn my mind's eye away from the demonstration . . . I *can* easily fall into doubt about its truth."[b] Such remarks are descriptive, not normative. Descartes is pointing to the psychological fact that we are unable to doubt things that we presently grasp with complete clarity, whereas we can doubt those same things once our clear and distinct perceptions have passed. Even if this is true, it does not show that the evidential force of such present beliefs is unassailable. And, even if we are prone to doubt perceptions that have slipped into the past, this does not show that their evidential force has decayed.

The privilege Descartes accords to the me–now, then, is not so much an epistemic ideal as it is an artfully constructed version of what philosophers now refer to as *dogmatism*. According to the dogmatist, we accord default epistemic privilege to selected beliefs and rely on them to serve as the foundation for everything that is to come. Beliefs that fall into this select class count as evident from the start, and so do not require any further marshaling of the evidence for them. But the reason why such beliefs do not require further evidence is not that they in fact have some sort of objectively infallible status; it is rather that in practice we treat them that way, and rightly so, because there has to be *something* that has this sort of default privilege. Dogmatism comes in various flavors, more and less restricted. Descartes is very far from being the sort of unrestricted dogmatist who would privilege by default all of our established beliefs. He is dogmatic only in a very limited way, with regard to the privileged me–now, and only with respect to a certain class of perceptions, those that are evident or, in his proprietary terminology, clear and distinct. So understood, his approach has an undeniable appeal. For if we can construct, within this privileged moment, a Reliability Proof—an engine that we can wield in justifying the rest of what we believe—then we will have refuted the skeptic in a way that is much more satisfying than by simply embracing unrestricted dogmatism. We will not have declared victory over the skeptic by mere fiat but would have claimed instead only a small island of epistemic privilege, which we subsequently leverage to achieve total victory.

As intriguing as this strategy may be, we should register just how far short it falls of the sort of ideal that earlier generations had sought to achieve. When scholastic philosophers insisted that *scientia* requires evidentness, they characteristically demanded both indubitability and infallibility, thereby expecting our beliefs to exhibit both subjective and objective certainty.[c] Descartes's privileged domain of the first-person present seizes on the subjective compulsion associated with evidentness, but without providing for any higher perspective from which infallibility could be assured. On its face, the whole point of the *Meditations* is to embrace doubt, so that we may transcend our merely subjective confidences and achieve true infallibility. But one might suspect that, in the end, the *Meditations* does nothing more than show us which beliefs are truly indubitable.

---

[a] *Med.* 5 (VII: 69).   [b] VII: 70, emphasis added.   [c] See Lecture Two, p. 29.

When pressed by his critics to defend the privilege he accords to the me–now, Descartes, rather than offer an objective defense, makes the move characteristic of dogmatists everywhere: he threatens his opponent with skepticism. His conservative Dutch critic Voetius, for instance, charged that Descartes's method would inevitably lead to skepticism by insisting on a standard of evidentness too high to be ever satisfied. To this Descartes responds that Voetius is in reality the skeptic:

If you are referring here to *the very time* at which an act of faith or some natural cognition arises, it is *you* who are destroying all faith and human *scientia*, and *you* who are in fact a skeptic, since you maintain that no cognition free from doubt can ever be had. But if we are talking about *different times*—for someone who at one time has true faith or evident *scientia* of some natural thing may at another time not have it—this merely shows the weakness of human nature, which does not always remain fixed on the same thoughts, and it does not follow that there should be any doubt in the *scientia* itself. Hence you prove nothing against me, for I was speaking not of any certainty that would endure through an entire human life, but merely of the kind of certainty that is achieved *at the moment* when some *scientia* is acquired.[a]

Rather than seeking to establish infallibility, Descartes carefully focuses his response on subjective indubitability. Invoking the privileged me–now, he contends that the only way to avoid doubt is to focus on the evidentness of our current thoughts.

As an argumentative strategy, this is ingenuous, but it leaves open the question of whether we have any principled reason for the particular sort of restricted dogmatism to which Descartes appeals. Why should I privilege today's beliefs rather than yesterday's? Why should I privilege my beliefs rather than yours? The only thing Descartes has to say is that we find these beliefs irresistible. Insofar, then, as the Anselmian glance is founded on the Cartesian line of thought we have been exploring—on the subjective certainty of our present first-person judgments—its value is doubtful. Rather than accord some kind of default epistemic privilege to our present self, one might suggest that we should be impartial between present and past, treating the judgments of our past self as just as reliable, on their face, as our present judgments. Of course, special considerations may tilt the scales in one direction or another, toward either our older, wiser present selves or our younger, keener youth. We may also, of course, have reason to doubt that we remember accurately how things used to seem. But in cases where we can be reasonably confident of our past judgments, it may be that we should, *prima facie*, give those judgments the same weight that we give our present judgments.[11]

If we seek an interlocutor with the sophistication to raise these sorts of worries about Descartes's position, we need look ahead only as far as John Locke. Having relinquished the Cartesian dream of perfect certainty,[b] Locke feels no particular pressure to embrace the sort of me–now dogmatism we have found in Descartes. Indeed, when he considers cases that fall away from the ideal grade-A Anselmian glance, he is prepared to allow that grades B and C have sufficient certainty to count as knowledge:

For our finite understandings being able to think, clearly and distinctly, but on one thing at once, if men had no knowledge of any more than what they actually thought on, they would all be very

---

[a] *Epistola ad Voetium* (VIIIB: 170), emphasis added.   [b] See Lecture Two, p. 40.

ignorant: and he that knew most, would know but one truth, that being all he was able to think on at one time.[a]

What about grade-D cases where we retain only the conclusion and have entirely forgotten the supporting argument? Locke expressly considers this case at some length, and remarks that he had at one time regarded it as a borderline case between opinion and knowledge, like cases of testimony. But he then declares that "upon a due examination I find it comes not short of perfect certainty, and is in effect true knowledge." My memory of having been demonstratively certain, he goes on to argue, should count for just as much, epistemically speaking, as having the demonstration itself before me. To ask for more than that is to demand what is "beyond the reach of human faculties."[b] Locke thus tempers the absolute ideal of the Anselmian glance through reflection on what is humanly possible, and sees no particular advantage to the privileged now.[12]

These considerations in favor of disprivileging the present suggest how we might likewise disprivilege ourselves. Just as it would make good epistemic sense, *prima facie*, to cast aside our biased preference for our present judgments over our past judgments, so it would make sense to cast aside our self-biases and treat others as, *prima facie*, just as likely to get things right as we ourselves are. It certainly is true that we find it psychologically difficult to give up these biases. There may even be values to self-trust and faith in others that have nothing to do with their epistemic value. But, judged from a strictly epistemic point of view, there is no reason to suppose that self-trust is more likely to yield true belief.

Yet Descartes is, if anything, even more committed to self-privilege than to the privileged now. His *Discourse on Method* describes how, "as soon as I was old enough to emerge from the control of my teachers, I entirely abandoned the study of letters, resolving to seek no knowledge other than that which could be found in myself or else in the great book of the world."[c] At the start of the *Meditations* he declares: "I am here all alone." The very idea of doing philosophy by meditation is worlds away from the interactive methods of the ancient academies or of scholastic disputations. Admittedly, Descartes did take the extraordinary step of publishing seven sets of objections along with the *Meditations*, but those many pages of criticism yielded few substantive reversals of his own views. The objections are useful, from Descartes's point of view, mainly for illuminating how others might misread his work, and for furnishing Descartes with the opportunity of a public triumph over his critics.

As it happens, however, the very terms of Descartes's system offer some reason for disprivileging the self. For if the Reliability Proof that I construct on the basis of God's existence works to secure the trustworthiness of *my* past beliefs, in a first-person way, then the logic of Descartes's position requires that it should work interpersonally. This is to say that the same line of thought that shows *my* past true and distinct perceptions to be reliable shows that *yours* are likewise reliable. Hence if I, with the Reliability Proof in mind, can be possessed of "true and certain *scientia*"[d] in virtue of remembering *my own* clear and distinct perceptions in the past, then I should be able to achieve the same results in virtue of *your* clear and distinct perceptions, if you communicate

---

[a] *Essay* IV.1.8.   [b] IV.1.9.   [c] *Discourse* pt. 1 (VI: 9).   [d] *Med.* 5 (VII: 70), quoted earlier.

them to me. To be sure, not everyone is equally reliable when it comes to identifying clear and distinct perceptions. But there is in principle no reason for me to privilege my own past perceptions. I am undoubtedly more reliable than some people, but others are surely more reliable than me. So, although it would be foolish to accept indiscriminately others' testimonies regarding their clear and distinct perceptions, there will surely be many cases where I have just as much reason to embrace the reports of others as I do to embrace the testimony of my own memory. If I have in hand a Reliability Proof that applies to all clear and distinct perceptions, for any of God's creatures, then I should count myself in possession of knowledge of a very elevated sort *whenever* I get a trustworthy report of some proposition's having been clearly and distinctly perceived, whether by my past self or by anyone else. Outside of the privileged now, the logic of Descartes's position does not support any sort of first-person privilege.

As we might expect, Locke has little sympathy for this sort of first-person privilege. What makes disagreement between people so intractable, he argues, is our inability to collect all our reasons before us at once and reconsider the grounds for our conclusions. Only those who are capable of this superhuman task should presume to tell others what to think. As things are, "in this fleeting state of action and blindness we are in," the best course is not to expect others to give up their opinions for our own, but rather "to commiserate our mutual ignorance."[a] On Locke's account, just as there is no good epistemic reason to privilege the present over the past, so there is no good epistemic reason to privilege ourselves over others. To be sure, he does not go so far as to say that we should adopt an attitude of impartiality between ourselves and others, giving equal weight to their opinion and to our own. He thinks that we have no real choice other than to embrace the conclusions that strike us as correct, even if our views are merely long-settled habits based on evidence we no longer recall. No one should be expected to "obsequiously quit his own opinion." As for our understanding, "however it may often mistake, it can own no other guide but reason."[b] In the end, Locke thinks such reasoning can take us quite a long way. Trusting our past judgments while being open to the views of others, there are some things that we can know and even more things that we can believe with some measure of probability. Without following Descartes's unwarranted privileging of the me–now, we can still describe an epistemic ideal that is both within human reach and worth reaching for.[13]

In Locke, then, we find a clear rejection of the sort of epistemic ideal that runs through late scholastic philosophy and then lodges itself in Descartes: the assumption that we should privilege our first-person present thoughts. But it cannot be said that Locke's views make a decisive difference to the subsequent debate. On the contrary, the ideal of the Anselmian glance seems to persist in philosophy into the eighteenth century and beyond, even while being put to very different sorts of uses. A particularly remarkable example is the case of David Hume. His skeptical arguments from the last part of Book I of the *Treatise* (1739) show that reason "leaves not the lowest degree of evidence in any proposition."[c] These notorious pages are never refuted or retracted, and

---

[a] *Essay* IV.16.4.   [b] IV.16.4.   [c] *Treatise* I.4.7, p. 267.

yet Hume is able to set them aside. How? He can do so precisely because he endorses a Cartesian conception of the privileged now, according to which the force of rational argument extends only for as far as we are able to keep these thoughts in our head. Thus, for as long as these arguments hold sway, Hume finds himself quite in their grip: "I am confounded with all these questions, and begin to fancy myself in the most deplorable condition imaginable."[a] Expecting at the outset to vindicate the senses against the attacks of the Pyrrhonists, Hume feels instead forced to confess: "to be ingenuous, I feel myself *at present* of a quite contrary sentiment, and am more inclined to repose no faith at all in my senses." The italics here are Hume's own, because his very point is that the force of rational argument lasts only for as long as we are able to keep these considerations in mind. Thus,

> It is impossible, upon any system, to defend either our understanding or senses; and we but expose them further when we endeavour to justify them in that manner . . . Carelessness and inattention alone can afford us any remedy. For this reason I rely entirely upon them; and take it for granted, whatever may be the reader's opinion at this present moment, that an hour hence he will be persuaded there is both an external and internal world.[b]

There is no response to skeptical arguments, and yet they can be resisted, not by methods that have any rational merit, but simply by letting nature take its course. Thus "nature breaks the force of all sceptical arguments in time."[c]

In Hume, then, Descartes's insistence on the privileged me–now gets strangely transmogrified, embraced not as the foundation of reason but instead as the only escape from rational self-destruction. The first-person present is where rational arguments have their full force, but what those arguments show, on close inspection, is that reason "entirely subverts itself."[d] Rather than arriving at an ideal *scientia* of ourselves and of the world around us through the Anselmian glance, Hume thinks that such intense reflection leads us to recognize the groundlessness of all reasoning. Accordingly, whereas Descartes must take measures to shore up our accumulated certainties against the ravages of time, Hume positively welcomes "carelessness and inattention" as the sole "remedy" against skepticism. Escaping the destructive influence of critical reflection, Hume contends that the best we can do—the only ideal to which human beings can and ought to aspire—is to follow the sensitive part of our nature: "'tis not solely in poetry and music we must follow our taste and sentiment, but likewise in philosophy."[e]

The epistemic privilege of the first-person present is thus no longer an ideal for Hume, but a welcomed check on the force of reason, without which we might have no option but to succumb to total skepticism. Yet this leaves us in a curious position. Locke's rejection of the privileged me–now ought to have made epistemic progress easier, since we no longer need to adhere to the obsessive rigors of the Cartesian method. From a Humean point of view, however, abandoning the privileged me–now yields just the opposite result. Far from relaxing our epistemic standards, Locke makes it harder to embrace Hume's remedy of "carelessness and inattention." Now the arguments of the skeptics, if they do indeed have weight, will retain that weight over time

---

[a] I.4.7, p. 269.   [b] I.4.2, p. 218.   [c] I.4.1, p. 187.   [d] I.4.7, p. 267.   [e] I.3.8, p. 103.

and across persons. And even if Hume is right that our nature is prone to "break the force" of such arguments, still what we *ought* to do, as a matter of our normative ideal, is take these arguments as seriously as we can. And with this we are ready to take up the subject of my final lecture, which will begin by considering whether the familiar arguments of the skeptics actually do have the sort of force that Hume ascribes to them. My answer will be that yes, quite plausibly they do, but we still have reasons for hope.[14]

Lecture Six

Deception and Hope

Five weeks ago I invoked a theme from Isaiah Berlin: the tendency of philosophers, over the ages, toward a kind of Panglossianism writ large in various moral and metaphysical domains, an "ancient faith," as he called it, in our ability to achieve the best case scenario identified through pure philosophical reflection.[a] We have now seen how this sort of faith has shaped the history of our epistemic ideals. Yet we have also witnessed an ongoing retrenchment in these expectations over the centuries, a steady diminishment in the sort of ideal that could be regarded as normative, given our actual abilities and circumstances. What remains to do in this final lecture is to consider just how bad things ultimately are. Bad indeed, my answer will be, so long as we still aspire to our historically lofty ideals. But once we allow ourselves to give up those vainglorious expectations, we need not feel bad at all, provided that we are still able to hope.

God the Deceiver

Consider, to begin with, that most venerable and seemingly powerful skeptical scenario of all: the possibility of divine deception. Despite the tendency toward optimism that runs throughout the history of philosophy, the possibility of a deceiving deity looms over many traditions, calling into question just how secure our epistemic situation really is. Yet while God may deceive us, as the story goes, we certainly cannot deceive him. His epistemic situation is ideally secure, even while ours is fraught with peril. Today I want to begin by challenging several aspects of this seemingly unexceptionable story. On the one hand, I will argue, there is a surprising constraint on our vulnerability to deception, even at the hands of God. On the other hand, God himself faces a surprising vulnerability to deception, which makes even his position far less ideal than has always been supposed.

Previous lectures have focused on the seventeenth century's role in breaking free from the epistemic ideals of earlier centuries. Yet medieval authors too, despite their generally Panglossian perspective, give considerable attention to our precarious state. Siger of Brabant, for instance, in the later thirteenth century, considers in detail the possibility that "all things that appear to us are simulacra and like dreams, so that we are

---

[a] "Two Concepts of Liberty," in *Four Essays*, p. 167 (see Lecture One, p. 2).

not certain of the existence of a single thing."[a] At around the same time, Thomas Aquinas discusses at length the ways in which demons might mislead us, concluding that they cannot act directly on our immaterial minds but can quite easily distort our material sensory powers. Among fourteenth-century authors, a long and lively dispute arises over the possibility of divine deception. Some appeal to the distinction between God's absolute and ordained power, allowing that divine deception is possible only in the absolute sense, but not in light of what God has ordained to be done. Others, most notably Gregory of Rimini, argue that not even God's absolute power permits deception. Still others contend that God's deceiving us is possible not just absolutely but even in light of what God has ordained, though of course the deception would have to occur for the sake of some good, never maliciously. This last view is taken by John Rodington in the course of his extended argument for the startling thesis that "the intellect cannot know something without doubting whether it knows it."[b] This conclusion applies, according to Rodington, to all cases of *scientia*. It is not that we cannot know, but that our knowledge is never perfectly free from doubt—in particular, from the possibility that "God can make one thing appear to be another."[c] [1]

The prospect of divine deception is in some ways the most fearsome sort of skeptical scenario, given the deceiver's presumed omnipotence. What recourse is there? Most familiar is the strategy we now associate with Descartes: prove that there is a God, and that God is good; conclude that God would not deceive us. Admittedly, this strategy, all by itself, cannot rule out the occasional beneficent case of divine trickery of the sort Rodington describes. But it does arguably preclude *systematic* deception on God's part. As Descartes himself carefully puts it, "Since God is the supreme being, he must also be supremely good and true, and it would therefore be a contradiction that anything should be created by him that positively tends towards falsehood."[d] This Cartesian strategy was already common among scholastic authors, who saw that it might serve as a general-purpose tool for combatting skeptical scenarios of all sorts, whether or not the threat comes directly from God.

Another common approach is to concede that human knowledge is only conditionally certain. By the later seventeenth century, such concessions are commonplace,[e] but one finds the idea in the fourteenth century as well. Rodington takes this view, and so does John Buridan when he argues that, with regard to knowledge of the natural world, one can speak of certainty only on the supposition that "the common course of nature is observed."[f] To insist on a higher ideal is a disaster:

Some people have wanted to destroy natural and moral *scientia*, on the grounds that in many of its principles and conclusions there is no absolute evidentness [*evidentia simplex*], but that instead these principles and conclusions can be falsified through supernaturally possible cases. They speak quite badly, because such *scientia* does not require absolute evidentness; it suffices for there to be the aforesaid qualified [*secundum quid*] evidentness, based on a supposition.[g]

---

[a] *Impossibilia* II (*Écrits*, p. 73).
[b] *Sent.* I.3.3 (in Nardi, *Soggetto e oggetto*, p. 80; Tweedale, *John of Rodynton*, p. 427).
[c] I.3.3 (Nardi, p. 80; Tweedale, p. 427).   [d] Second Replies (VII: 144).   [e] See Lecture Two, p. 36.
[f] *Quaest. meta.* II.1, f. 8vb (p. 145 trans. Klima, *Medieval Philosophy*); see Lecture Two, p. 32.
[g] II.1, f. 9ra (p. 146 trans.).

Rather than *prove* that there is a God and that it would be contradictory for God to fashion us or the world in a way that makes certainty systematically impossible, the strategy of conditionalization requires that we relax our expectations for what human beings can ideally achieve. Here lies the beginnings of the path traced in Lecture Two, away from absolute certainty and toward the more modest ideal of probability.

There is, I will argue shortly, something inevitable about these concessions to our limited epistemic condition. But the history of these debates is full of attempts to preserve the lofty ideals we find it so natural to expect. Last week we saw how Descartes's appeal to the privileged first-person present ultimately rests on an artfully delimited dogmatism. Medieval authors, of course, had their own solutions. Lecture Four considered the case of Nicholas of Autrecourt, whose letters confront an opponent who would safeguard knowledge of the external world through the sort of condition-alization that Buridan would later champion, by stipulating that the object of perception "has not been produced or conserved supernaturally." Autrecourt mocks this approach on the grounds that, if a conclusion must be based on a premise that is not evident, then the conclusion itself cannot be evident, a result he seemingly embraces.[a] Yet these skeptical letters serve merely as Autrecourt's first meditation, as it were, laying the groundwork for his *Tractatus*, where he advances a positive account of how certainty can be acquired. By embracing an unconventional ontology of universal, intentional objects, Autrecourt makes perception logically immune to error, and thus gets the much sought result that evidentness is not just subjectively indubitable but also infallibly certain.[b]

Another way forward is suggested by Autrecourt's near contemporary in the mid-fourteenth century, John of Mirecourt. Unwilling to embrace the sort of intentional beings that Autrecourt appeals to, Mirecourt accepts that there can be no absolute certainty regarding the *existence* of anything other than oneself. One's own existence can be established with complete certainty, Mirecourt thinks, on the basis of Augustine's *cogito*, but our grasp of the existence of anything beyond oneself must inevitably be subject to some qualification. He expressly includes God's existence within the scope of this claim, which makes it clear that Mirecourt is not going to follow the Cartesian strategy of grounding certainty in the existence of a benevolent deity. The only sort of certainty he allows here is, once again, conditional, dependent on the supposition that the course of nature holds constant.[2]

Mirecourt's originality emerges when he argues that we can have absolute certainty in the limited case of first principles and conclusions derived therefrom. Descartes would later suggest in the First Meditation that error could arise even here, if God, or at least an evil demon, were to make me "go wrong every time I add two and three or count the sides of a square."[c] Mirecourt sees this worry: he considers the objection that "God can cause someone's soul to dissent from *anything*, and therefore that person can err."[d] His response turns on an earlier disputation where he had analyzed the nature of a mental act. According to what he calls the standard view, the soul thinks something when it has within itself, in addition to the power of intellect, a distinct entity that is the thought. When intellectual cognition is so conceived, the door is open to divine deception, because God can simply create whatever thought he likes within the soul, and then

---

[a] First letter to Bernard, n. 7.   [b] See Lecture Four, pp. 28–9.
[c] *Med.* 1 (VII: 21).   [d] *Sent.* q. 6, p. 439.72–3.

the power of intellect will necessarily think it. But Mirecourt urges the adoption of a view on which there is no real distinction between a thought and the power of thought. On this sort of account, God cannot simply put the thought into someone's mind and then have that person think it. To give a person a new thought requires changing a person's intellect. Of course, God can create wholly new intellects, and create them so that they are, right now, having a certain thought. But, if God decides to give me a whole new intellect that has a certain thought as its content, it would evidently not be *me* who is having that thought. Perhaps God can also simply reach in and change my intellect. But in that case the thought imposed would seem to be an alien one, not my own. Mirecourt thus reaches the striking and surprisingly plausible conclusion that "God cannot, by himself, cause any error within the soul."[a]

To be sure, it is still possible for God to deceive us, through secondary causes. If God wants to trick me into thinking that a dragon lies ahead, he can easily create a pattern of light and color that produces in the eye the impression of such a monster. But when it comes to first principles—paradigmatically, the principle of noncontradiction—Mirecourt insists that not even God can cause me to err. For, no matter what sorts of perceptual illusions he might produce, together with the false judgments these would inspire, there is nothing that could lead me to question the principle of noncontradiction. In this limited domain, human beings are capable of perfect, completely infallible certainty, such that "it is not possible for someone to affirm that a thing is so and for the thing not to be as he affirms it to be."[b] As with Autrecourt, then, evidentness here yields both subjective indubitability and full-blown infallibility.[3]

Clever as Mirecourt's argument is, the result he obtains is quite limited. First, he gets infallibility at most for self-evident principles. Second, more subtly, what Mirecourt shows is that, when a higher power seeks to deceive me directly, it is not *I* who committed the error. But, even if God cannot directly cause me to judge wrongly, God can still cause a false judgment to occur within me. It would not be *my* judgment, to be sure, but there would still be falsehood here, and it might *seem* as if it were my judgment. That, by itself, is a serious problem. For what good does Mirecourt's infallibility do for me, if I am unable to tell whether or not a particular judgment is true? Even if the judgment is not mine, still a false judgment is occurring within me. Hence Mirecourt has not actually eliminated the possibility of falsehood.

Moreover, even if Mirecourt has blocked supernatural deception in certain cases, this fails to address the most powerful sort of skeptical scenario. Much worse than the prospect of externally induced error is the prospect of internal error arising from a radically flawed cognitive power. This is the worry that David Hume would make much of in the eighteenth century, but the idea is thoroughly familiar well before that. Consider John Tillotson:

Infallibility is an absolute security of the understanding from all possibility of mistake in what it believes. And there are but two ways for the understanding to be thus secured: either by the perfection of its own nature, or by supernatural assistance. But no human understanding being absolutely secured from possibility of mistake by the perfection of its nature . . . it follows that no man can be infallible in any thing, but by supernatural assistance.[c]

[a] *Sent.* q. 6, p. 440.120.   [b] *Sent.* q. 6, p. 438.20–1.   [c] *Works* Preface (I: vi).

The specter Tillotson raises is that our minds might be imperfect in ways we could never know. This, even more fundamentally than divine deception, undermines every pretention to certainty, leaving us with nothing better than merely moral certainty.[a]

Tillotson here registers another possibility: that certainty might be achieved through supernatural means. This is not an option that he himself relies much on. Yet there is a long medieval tradition, associated especially with Augustine, of supposing that some kind of divine illumination plays an ongoing role in our cognitive lives. Indeed, even in classical antiquity, one finds Socrates invoking a "divine or spiritual sign" that speaks to him when he is on the verge of acting wrongly.[b] Let us turn, then, from the question of divine deception to the question of divine assistance. Unfashionable as such appeals may now be, we will find that the topic nevertheless carries an important lesson. For, just as there is a surprising constraint on God's ability to deceive us, so there is also a surprising limit to how far God can help, and this limit reveals something about our own circumstances.

God the Deceived

It is the most common of tropes to contrast the human case with the divine and to insist on our inferiority by comparison with the absolutely ideal epistemic position that is God's. Buridan begins his discussion of certainty with the remark that "there is the certainty and evidentness of divine wisdom, to which no created cognition can attain."[c] Three centuries later, Joseph Glanvill distinguishes the sort of certainty we are capable of from

certainty infallible, when we are assured that it is impossible things should be otherwise than we conceive and affirm of them. This is a sort of certainty that humanely we cannot attain unto, for it may not be absolutely impossible but that our faculties may be so contrived as always to deceive us in the things which we judge most certain and assured.

Again, we see the worry about internal error. Who then can achieve infallible certainty? It "perhaps is proper only to Him, who made all things what they are, and discerns their true natures by an infallible and most perfect knowledge."[d]

Every so often, one does find a demurral. Galileo is so committed to the ideal of certainty as to insist, as we saw in Lecture Two, that, when it comes to those few things we do understand, our objective certainty is equal to God's.[e] John of Mirecourt had claimed something similar with respect to the evidentness of first principles. These were, however, decidedly minority views. Even Descartes, when pressed on this point by Mersenne in the Second Objections, acknowledges that the certainty he claims for himself is merely "human certainty," not that of God or an angel.[f][4]

Yet, while it might seem the merest of truisms to reserve to God alone the honor of having perfect certainty, this way of talking obscures something important about the epistemic ideal. To see as much, it will be helpful to spend a few minutes contemplating the surprising fact that not even God's knowledge could be entirely certain. Consider, to

---

[a] See Lecture Two, p. 36.   [b] *Apology* 31d.   [c] *Summulae* 8.4.4, p. 709 trans.
[d] "Of Scepticism and Certainty" (*Essays*, pp. 49–50).   [e] See Lecture Two, p. 30.
[f] Second Replies (VII: 144).

start with, any sort of being that regards itself as cognitively ideal in every respect. Not the *human* ideal—such cases of cognitive hubris are familiar enough in university faculties everywhere. This being, instead, takes itself to satisfy a *divine* standard of epistemic perfection—to be, in short, God. So thinly described, one may again suppose that such cognitive agents are to be found living among us, in our local asylums and on the backstreets of London. These people, however, are crazy. What we want is a being who has very good reasons to regard itself as divine. Admittedly, it is not at all easy even to begin to describe what this would be like. But if we follow the mainstream of theologians working in one or another of the monotheistic traditions, we can say that such a being would take itself to grasp everything that is true, and to do so not over time, taking things one by one, but in an instant. The infinite and eternal mind of God does not make inferences, though it sees the validity of all inferences, and does not come to know anything but rather has always, eternally, changelessly grasped everything that can be grasped. The truth of all this, for such a being, will seem completely self-evident.

We might flesh out this picture of a perfect cognitive agent in various familiar ways. Let it seem to this being that it is capable of doing anything that can be done; that it creates and sustains everything else that exists; that it providentially cares for its creatures, disposing all things for the best. Supplement and revise this picture in whatever way strikes you as plausible; the details are in general not important. Keep in mind, however, the precise nature of the task. I am not asking you, in Anselmian fashion, to conceive of a perfect being. I am instead asking you to conceive of a being that takes itself, with good reason, to be perfect in all these ways.

If we could know what it is like to be such a being, then we would know what it is like to be God. But my contention is that, whatever such a state of mind is, it should inevitably contain some degree of doubt. Take this being we have considered. So as not to foreclose any possibilities, simply call it G for now. If G's epistemic situation is as it seems to it, then G is God. Let us, at any rate, concede this much, supposing for the sake of argument that the sort of all-at-once omniscience we have described is sufficient for divinity. My question is whether G can be completely certain that its epistemic situation *is* as it seems. And my contention is that no such certainty is possible, not even for G. Consider, to start with, whether G might be deceived by some super-powerful agent. If G is God, then this is of course not possible—no one can deceive God, at least not as we have agreed to think of God. But is there not room for G to wonder whether it is so deceived? To be sure, it would take a very powerful being indeed to sustain the illusion of eternal, infinite omniscience. But if it is an illusion, then it would not necessarily take a being of infinite power to produce it, or a being of infinite capacity to experience it. Perhaps, indeed, it is *easier* to create that sort of illusion than to create the sort of ever-fluctuating experience that philosophers commonly imagine mad scientists to simulate. We can imagine that this is not how things seem to G—that to G it seems that only a perfect being would be capable of producing and experiencing a state of mind such as *this*. But such confidence is of course just the sort of illusion we might expect our superdeceiver to bring about within his unwitting victim. So, just as it seems epistemically possible that we are the victims of some sort of evil demon, the same appears to be true of G. If G is God, then most assuredly G is not floating in some mad scientist's vat. But how can G ever be in a position to be sure of its true identity?

Might G have more cognitive resources than I have hitherto allowed for, which would make its situation disanalogous to our own? Perhaps. At first glance, however, some of the most evident points of dissimilarity between us and G seem not to be to G's cognitive advantage. Consider, first, how G's apparent eternality makes it unable to compare its present cognitive state to past ones. Even if G's one, eternal cognitive act feels utterly all-encompassing in its grasp of the world, still G cannot take reassurance from the regular repetition of that act. Its singular mental experience is quite unrepeatable. G also lacks the ability to make another kind of comparison, across persons. To be sure, we should imagine that G grasps not just the existence of all other persons, but also their mental states. Even so, G's own epistemic state is (seemingly) solitary and unique. G (takes itself to) grasp how the world seems to finite minds and how they respond to the world, but G knows of no other infinite mind with which it might compare notes. Like Ḥayy ibn Yaqẓān in Ibn Ṭufayl's famous allegory, G must come to grips with the world entirely on its own, aided by nothing but its own ideas and impressions of the world. To be sure, such a solipsistic existence may be no real obstacle to a mind as powerful as G's, but it is a point of disanalogy with the human case that does not work to G's advantage.

The most obvious respect in which G stands at an advantage by comparison to us is in the apparent infinity of its cognitive powers. Even if our minds can go only so far before running out of time and cognitive resources, we might suppose that G can, all at once, go all the way down, infinitely far. This is, however, not as helpful as one might suppose. First, the possibility of making this sort of infinite, all-at-once descent presupposes that G's mind is in fact infinite, which is part of what, for G, should remain in doubt. But even if we were to grant that G is capable of infinitely many thoughts all at once, it is not clear what advantage this would offer. It is not as if grasping the infinite allows G to reach some sort of magical place of certainty not accessible to our merely finite minds. The infinite is simply one thing after another, unendingly; and, even though an infinite mind actually has one thought on top of another, without end, that does not help at all with the project of finding some sort of stable, completely certain resting point. Even if for every p there is some supporting q repeated endlessly, there is still room for doubt over whether any given q really does decisively support some p. An infinity of such supporting relations is no more certain than our paltry finitude.

If introspection fails to show that G must be God, might it be possible for G to construct an a priori proof? After all, many mortal philosophers have supposed themselves able to establish God's existence through reason alone. Hitherto, such efforts have proved unsuccessful. But perhaps G could find such a proof, even if we cannot. The first thing to be said is that any such a priori proof would itself be vulnerable to the usual sorts of skeptical objections from external deception, unrecognized internal flaws, and so forth. But, even if we were to grant that G grasps God's existence as an a priori necessary truth, it does not follow that G is God. Something that would follow is that G either is God or was created by God. This is true simply in virtue of how we have agreed to think of God, as the creator of the universe. But even if G is smart enough to grasp something that we cannot—that the universe has a creator—and even if G takes itself, with good reason, to be the creator of the universe, G is still not in a position to be completely certain of this. For it could be—for reasons that are hidden even to G—that God willed to create a being such as G, a being so cognitively powerful as to be tempted to mistake itself for God.

Perhaps this last scenario will not seem very likely. Why would God create such an excellent being, and then allow it to be deceived in this way—not just by letting it seem to be omniscient but also, remember, by letting it seem to be the omnipotent creator and sustainer of everything? Since we have agreed to think of God in traditional monotheistic ways, we must agree that God is perfectly good, and surely a perfectly good creator would not allow this state of affairs. Well, tell that to the men and women locked up in asylums as suffering from one or another illusion of grandeur. Tell that to Satan, who according to the story was the greatest of God's creatures, and somehow made the mistake of supposing that he could be greater than God. Satan, we may suppose, in his pride, felt quite confident about his place in the universe. Such examples illustrate that, even if God would not let all of humanity suffer from systematic deception, it is by no means out of the question that this might happen in isolated cases. Hence, even if G has very strong reasons to believe that God exists, some doubt must still remain over whether G is God. That piece of *de se* information—information not of what the world is like, but of where G fits into it—must remain at least somewhat open to doubt.

If G's place in the universe remains, for G, a matter of some uncertainty, then the same must be true of God. This must be so, because we are imagining G as standing in precisely the same cognitive state that God would stand in, if there is a God. Therefore, just as these familiar skeptical arguments apply to G, so they apply to God. This will perhaps be a difficult conclusion to swallow. Surely, it may be thought, it is ridiculous to suppose that a perfect being—omniscient, omnipotent, and infinite—could be in doubt about its very nature. Even if it is not clear exactly *how* God might rule out the familiar skeptical scenarios canvassed above, surely we ought to be confident that God some-how has a way of removing all doubt. The trouble with this confidence is that it relies on the sort of Panglossian epistemic faith that we should by now be ready to abandon. In particular, it assumes that there is, at least in principle, a way to escape the gap between seemings and reality. The point of these musings about the prospects for divine certainty is to show that the epistemic difficulties raised by this gap are purely conceptual, since they arise for any cognitive agent whatsoever. After all, nothing in the line of argument just advanced depends on any special feature of God's epistemic situation. The argument applies not just to human beings and God, but to any cognitive being that might be imagined in between the two, in any part of the universe you care to consider. God, like everything else in the universe, has no way to take up an epistemic position outside of himself from which to confirm that things are as they seem. The point, then, is that it is just not conceptually possible to achieve complete cognitive certainty; the very nature of cognition precludes this outcome. Insisting that divine certainty must be possible some way or another is thus rather like insisting that God must somehow be able to make $2 + 1 = 4$. Well, perhaps God *can* make $2 + 1 = 4$; and perhaps, equally, God can achieve complete certainty. Given the course of the argument so far, I am hardly in a position myself to claim anything like complete confidence regarding such matters. Still, from our finite, imperfect perspective, these do not look to be open possibilities. We should therefore not expect even the most perfect cognitive being to be capable of perfect certainty.

If this much is right, then something more follows about our own epistemic predica-ment. Suppose the road to certainty is blocked in the way I have just argued, as a truth of logic rather than as a consequence of our special cognitive predicament. In that case it turns out that there is no one else in the universe, not even God, who could enable *us* to bridge the gap between seemings and reality. After all, if this gap is a conceptual truth, then not even God would be able to cross it, let alone show us the way. This is not to say, absurdly, that God could not teach us anything. God might, in countless ways, reveal things to us and thereby lead us to true belief. We might reasonably pray for illumination and receive it, becoming aware in this way of how the world is. But, if the divine mind is itself blocked from attaining objective certainty, then, no matter how much we pray, God cannot make us objectively certain either. As far as that goes, appealing to God is no better than appealing to the Wykeham Professor of Logic.[5]

The Dismal Verdict

Have we just discovered that even an all-powerful God would lack knowledge, and so landed ourselves in the most global of skepticisms? I hope that, by this point, no one will find such a thought very tempting. My argument from the start has been that we ought to avoid setting some sort of absolute ideal as the threshold for knowledge, prior to reflection on what is actually possible for beings such as ourselves. Not even an ideally perfect being, it turns out, is ideally certain. It does not follow that God lacks knowledge, or even that God fails to be omniscient. To deny omniscience on these grounds would be as puerile as to insist that God is not omnipotent because he cannot create a rock too heavy for him to lift. It may be, as Aquinas says, that "*scientia* exists most perfectly in God."[a] We need not conclude that this is wrong, only that it amounts to less than one might have supposed.

The main interest of the divine case lies in what it shows about ourselves: how it highlights the absurdity of the skeptic's demand for certainty. Reflection on the case of God shows that the skeptic must take the word 'knowledge' to be categorically inapplicable, not just to us as a species, but to any species. This is an intolerable result. It is perfectly useful and apt to be able to say, in a wide range of circumstances, that people *know* one thing or another. It would be the most wildly absurd of overreactions to allow the bare logical possibility of error—grounded in nothing about the human condition—to shut down such ways of talking. The verb 'to know' is so indispensable, indeed, that, if on skeptical grounds we were not allowed to use it, we would have to go out and find some other word to take its place.

The word 'knowledge,' however, can take care of itself. It needs no defense from us and deserves to be left in peace by the philosophers for a while. Of more interest is the question I have been asking from the start: what should we regard as the normative epistemic ideal for us, given our capacities and circumstances? The Aristotelian ideal was that the senses would show us the real qualities of nature from which we might derive the true essences of things, and that these conclusions might all be made evident in a way that is both subjectively indubitable and objectively infallible. We have now watched as one, and then another, part of this story have fallen apart, only to be replaced by some more restricted domain of epistemic privilege, be it our inner sensory states or

[a] *Summa theol.* 1a 14.1c.

our first-person present thoughts. The lesson of the previous two lectures was that even these privileged domains offer no assurance of certainty. This seems to leave us only one option: that, instead of certainty, we should expect just a reasonable degree of probability. Yet what if not even this much is possible? This is the dismal possibility I will explore through the remainder of this final lecture.

Again, the case of God is particularly instructive. I assumed earlier that, even if God's beliefs are not certain, God still has good reasons for believing himself to be God. But the sorry truth is that, given everything we have seen, it is hard to see how God is in a position to assign any objective probabilities to his beliefs. What is the probability of his being nothing more than a deceived brain in a vat? If he is God, we can say that the probability is zero, but what if God is not allowed the dogmatic assumption that he is God? What probability, then, can he assign to the brain-in-a-vat hypothesis? As before, there seems to be in principle a barrier to any noncircular solution to this problem. Any line of reasoning that might lead God to regard himself as having strong evidence for the divinity hypothesis against the vat hypothesis could get started in one of two ways: either by assuming that the divinity hypothesis is true or by relying on other premises, which are themselves subject to being undermined by the vat hypothesis. Earlier I remarked that it would be quite extraordinary for a being to have a divine-like mental experience and yet not to be God. Well, indeed, that would be an extraordinary experience to have. But is it *more* extraordinary to take oneself to be God and to be wrong, or to take oneself to be God and to be right? Which of these states of affairs is objectively more likely? How could anyone, even God, answer these questions? And even if, to God's infinite mind, an answer immediately suggests itself, what basis would there be for confidence that this is the *right* answer—unless God takes for granted that he is God? The dismal verdict is that God lacks not only the capacity for certainty, but even the ability to construct any sort of positive, non-question-begging rationale for his beliefs. And if this is true of God, then without doubt it is true a fortiori of us, and of any finite minds. Accordingly, the skeptical scenarios do more than preclude certainty; they preclude our ability to construct any kind of noncircular argument for any of our beliefs.

Obviously, if my intent were to establish such a grandiose claim, then I ought to have gotten started on the job somewhat earlier in these lectures. Anyway, to *establish* that such a claim is true would be self-defeating. The most I could do would be to rebut the many attempts that have been made over the centuries to defuse the threat of skepticism. I will not even pretend at this. Instead I want to suggest only that we ought to take much more seriously the threat of the dismal verdict. For what remains of these lectures, then, I simply will take that threat quite seriously and devote myself to articulating its nature and the options that remain in its wake.

Of course, it is hardly the case that the dismal verdict has been ignored. On the contrary, one might say that it is something of a truism to acknowledge that all arguments bottom out somewhere. As Aristotle put it in one of the earliest attempts to defeat the skeptic, "their mistake is that . . . they seek a reason for that for which no reason can be given; for the starting-point of demonstration is not demonstration."[a] But

---

[a] *Meta.* IV 6, 1011[a]12–13. See also *Post. An.* I 3, 72[b]7–16.

the point of the dismal verdict is not just the truism that any argument must start somewhere, but the more aggressive claim that, ultimately, this lack of foundations undermines any evidence for thinking that a given proposition is more likely than its alternative. The sort of doubt at issue here is not the mild sort of skepticism made famous in Descartes's First Meditation: that we cannot know anything with certainty, and hence we lack all knowledge (or, to be precise, all *scientia*). This was the sort of worry, considered in Lecture Two, that led to the Lockean Program and eventually to a looser conception of the epistemic ideal that requires only moral certainty, or freedom from reasonable doubt, rather than absolute certainty. The present worry is that, if we honestly consider our situation without presuppositions, we ought to admit that no belief is free from reasonable doubt, and that indeed there are equally legitimate doubts on each side of every proposition.[6]

With this, we have arrived at the central principle of Pyrrhonism: equipollence—the dismal verdict that, in the words of Sextus Empiricus, "to every account an equal account is opposed."[a] Admirably careful to avoid any positive assertions that go beyond the appearances, the Pyrrhonists offer this only as a report about how things seem to them. So, as Sextus more precisely puts it, "to every account I have scrutinized . . . there appears to me to be opposed another account . . . equal to it in convincingness or lack of convincingness."[b] Of course, as the Pyrrhonists know perfectly well, this is not how things appear to the vast majority of us, entrenched as we are in our dogmatic world-views. But the idea for which they tirelessly argue is that, if we step back from our particular worldviews and consider without prejudice the totality of the evidence, all the way down to the ground, in fact nothing appears more likely to be the case than anything else. Or, more cautiously, no claim that the skeptic has ever considered appears any more likely to be true than its opposite.[7]

Pyrrhonism is of course regarded as a form of skepticism—that is to say, a knowledge-denying theory. In this capacity, the view is almost universally rejected. A 2009 PhilPapers survey found that less than 5 percent of professional philosophers identified themselves as embracing or even leaning toward skepticism about our knowledge of the external world. More than 80 percent embraced antiskepticism—a higher degree of consensus than was found on any of the other 29 questions asked. Given the amount of attention that skepticism has received over the centuries, such consensus may seem surprising; but in fact this is as it should be. It is not that the skeptical scenarios have been refuted or that basic self-confirming first principles have been discovered. Rather, it has long seemed apparent on all sides that, if we cannot achieve the sort of epistemic ideal that philosophers have classically aspired to, then the right thing to do is to move the goalposts and focus on the sorts of epistemic goals that are achievable. As an historical matter, it turns out that our linguistic usage has been to hold on to the word 'knowledge' even after the goalposts have moved. But, as I keep arguing, the word itself is not really that important. What matters is just that we have some way of characterizing our manifest achievements in grappling with the world around us.

The near universal rejection of skepticism is justified, but what tends to get lost amid the fuss over what counts as knowledge is the important but dismal verdict suggested by

---

[a] Sextus Empiricus, *Outlines of Scepticism* I.vi.12.   [b] *Outlines*, I.xxvii.203.

the skeptic's position: that ultimately there are no good noncircular, non-question-begging reasons for anything. This thesis has been so neglected as not even to have a name, so let us give it one. Let *epistemic defeatism*, in its most global form, be the view that, in the final analysis, we have no good evidence for the truth of any proposition. Put a bit more carefully, we can think of "good" evidence as evidence that is undefeated, where evidence can be defeated by being either rebutted through further evidence that denies a given proposition or undercut by further evidence that undermines the force of the original evidence. Epistemic defeatism holds that "ultimately" there is no good evidence in the sense that, for any subset of evidence that supports a proposition, additional evidence is always available that, in the end, wholly defeats the original evidence, entirely canceling its evidential weight. Epistemic defeatism need not deny that, in actual practice, given the many assumptions we make about the world, we have a great deal of evidence. But the view insists that such evidence is ultimately not good, because it is always conditional on taking for granted certain things or ignoring others, and that these assumptions, tacit or explicit, cannot themselves ultimately be supported by good evidence.

I have not argued for the truth of this dismal verdict and I am not sure whether I myself believe it, but I do think it is a possibility that deserves serious attention. Remarkably, the Pyrrhonists advanced their cautious version of a defeatist epistemology not so as to breed dismay, but because they thought it would make us happy. In this I think they were surely mistaken. It really is quite depressing to think that our epistemic situation might be so nonideal. Perhaps it provides some consolation to recognize that even a perfect being would suffer from similar limitations, but we might have hoped for better. Indeed, we do hope for better, and here again is where our Panglossian tendencies reassert themselves. Although the history of philosophy displays a steadily diminishing optimism with regard to our epistemic prospects, few have been willing to confront squarely the ultimate epistemic disillusionment: that in the final analysis we have no good noncircular reasons for believing anything. That our situation could be so nonideal has simply not been a possibility that many people have been willing to take seriously.

We should, then, pull apart the different strands of thought that get run together under the heading of skepticism. Once epistemic defeatism is marked off as a distinct thesis, one finds it being advanced, over and over, throughout the history of philosophy, by figures who otherwise have very little in common. From antiquity it moves to the Islamic world, where al-Ghazālī describes having suffered a skeptical crisis that came to an end only when God "cured" him. "This did not come about by composing a proof or by arranging some words [كلام], but rather by a light that God Almighty cast into my breast, this light being the key to the greater part of knowledge [المعارف]."[a] In medieval Europe, Petrarch reports being similarly enmeshed in doubt (as we will see later), and by the sixteenth century such views were common in Europe. Montaigne takes inspiration from Pyrrhonism, and in this he is followed by Pierre Charron and Pierre Bayle. The trend culminates in Hume, whose views I will take up shortly.[8]

---

[a] *Rescuer from Error* n. 86 (p. 63, trans. Khalidi, *Medieval Islamic Philosophical Writings*).

Although these various strands of thought are commonly jumbled together under the heading of *skepticism*, in fact these authors stake out radically different positions. The ancient skeptics argued for the consequence that we should suspend belief, something that seemed quite intolerable to later figures in this tradition. The denial of knowledge is central to some discussions, whereas that claim matters not at all to Sextus Empiricus. Al-Ghazālī is clearly quite earnest in thinking that God provides the cure for our epistemic predicament, and Montaigne and Bayle similarly claim that Pyrrhonism opens the mind to God's grace. It has been doubted, however, whether Montaigne is entirely sincere about this, and in Bayle's case such doubts loom even larger. By the time one reaches Hume there is barely any pretense of an appeal to the divine. What all these authors nonetheless share is the commitment to a certain conception of the place of human beings in the world, a pessimism over our ability to find ultimate reasons for the things we believe. In embracing epistemic defeat, they relinquish our cherished assumption that we can achieve anything at all approaching that ideal.[9]

Hume's Quietism

The threat of defeatism in epistemology parallels the recurring suspicion in other philosophical domains that we are unable to produce a robustly satisfying, realistic explanation of our most ordinary assumptions. Such doubts are, indeed, one of the hallmarks of modern thought across all the most basic philosophical questions that range over the nature of morality, freedom, perception, truth, and language. Consider in particular the moral domain. The moral realist, seeking to capture the assumptions embedded in our ordinary lives, thinks that the rightness of an action has some kind of objective ground, something that makes it morally good independently of contingent facts about what human beings happen to care about. For the moral antirealist, in contrast, there is no such objective ground. If we can aptly speak of moral rightness at all, it is a function only of what we in fact happen to value. Epistemic defeatism poses an analogous challenge. Those who deny defeat hold that there are ultimate, objective evidential grounds that make some beliefs more rational than others. According to the epistemic defeatist, in contrast, if one can aptly speak of beliefs as being rational at all, those beliefs must ultimately take their rationality from subjective facts about what believers happen to think. In place of objective evidential grounds, the best we can do is make dogmatic assertions of privilege. Just as the moral antirealist despairs of any argument that runs from *is* to *ought*, so the epistemic defeatist despairs of our ability to go from *seems* to *is*.[10]

Through these last remarks I have invoked the specter of Hume, the greatest historical proponent of moral antirealism, who first spoke of the gap between *is* and *ought*.[a] Hume deserves a prominent place in this story, because he is the first great philosopher after the ancient skeptics to give a systematic defense of epistemic defeatism. As he puts it, "'tis impossible upon any system to defend either our understanding or senses."[b] Hume is not simply making the Cartesian complaint that our beliefs, although highly likely, have not yet been put on a certain foundation. By Hume's time,

---

[a] *Treatise* III.1.1, p. 469.   [b] I.4.2, p. 218.

that mild form of doubt was scarcely threatening, since it could be so readily handled by Lockean proportionality. Nor is Hume focused on whether or not we have knowledge. He accepts the traditional view that knowledge requires complete certainty, thereby taking the opportunity for knowledge off the table, in most domains, right from the start. If Hume were only making a claim about knowledge in his sense of the term, then again the Lockean Program of proportioning one's beliefs to the evidence would be sufficient to address his concerns. As usual, Hume's aims are much more radical: he seeks to undermine not just certain knowledge but also probable warrant, so that we are left with "not the lowest degree of evidence in any proposition, either in philosophy or common life."[a]

Like the Pyrrhonists, Hume takes such defeatism to make the rational demand that we should suspend belief. It is, however, the Pyrrhonists' subscription to this corollary that leads Hume to react to their view with such scorn, referring to ancient skepticism as a "fantastic sect"[b] and calling its proponent an "absurd creature"[c] who need not be refuted because the skeptic's claims are impossible for us to accept. Yet Hume hardly takes any consolation in this. His conclusion that we ought not to form any beliefs about anything is made no more tolerable by the observation that we cannot help but form such beliefs. As a result, for Hume, Pyrrhonism brings none of the tranquility its ancient proponents advertised. Instead, "I am confounded with all these questions, and begin to fancy myself in the most deplorable condition imaginable, invironed with the deepest darkness, and utterly deprived of the use of every member and faculty."[d]

Hume himself is of limited help in thinking about how to escape epistemic defeat. To be sure, he has a great deal to say about the sources and structure of the beliefs that we do hold. Just as his moral antirealism accompanies well-developed ideas about our moral practices, so his epistemic defeatism stands alongside an extended account of our cognitive psychology, an account that he thinks rises to the level of science.[e] Even so, Hume has no principled way to reconcile these paths, and so his mood fluctuates between lighthearted carelessness and hopeless despair. For the most part, however, rather than dwell on the darkness, he prefers to concentrate on the fact that we do continue to form beliefs, and he accordingly turns his attention to a theory of how nature makes this happen. This ability simply to ignore skepticism is made possible, as we saw last week, by his dogmatically privileging the now. As he says, with regard to his defeatist conclusions, "I know not what ought to be done in the present case. I can only observe what is commonly done; which is, that this difficulty is seldom or never thought of; and even where it has once been present to the mind, is quickly forgot."[f] His attitude here is rather like the way so many of us treat death: we know what is coming, but we are by nature mercifully unable to dwell on it. Yet if we agree, as I argued last week, that it is a groundless bias to privilege the first-person now, then there should be no comfort in our natural propensity, over time, to find skeptical arguments "cold and strained and ridiculous."[g] We might find it hard to persist in the philosophical conclusions we have taken pains to reach, but we have no good reason not to make every effort to try, rather than to settle complacently for how things seem to us now.

---

[a] I.4.7, pp. 267–8; see also I.4.1, p. 182.   [b] I.4.1, p. 183.
[c] *Enquiry concerning Human Understanding* 12.1, p. 149.   [d] *Treatise* I.4.7, p. 269.
[e] See Lecture One, p. 18.   [f] *Treatise* I.4.7, p. 268.   [g] I.4.7, p. 269.

If our goal is an honest and grown-up appraisal of our epistemic situation, then Hume's approach can hardly count as a step in the right direction, inasmuch as he counsels a childish insistence on living in the present.[11]

But then what alternative is there to despair? Hume's conclusion that our beliefs are ultimately groundless leads to epistemic despair when joined with the doctrine that now goes under the name of *evidentialism*: that we should form a belief only when we possess sufficient evidence. Since epistemic defeatism contends that we never possess sufficient evidence, defeatism conjoined with evidentialism yields the Pyrrhonian demand that we give up our beliefs. This combination of views leads Hume to despair, which he overcomes only by ignoring the evidentialism he never renounces. What Hume might have done, at this point, is to have disclaimed evidentialism as yet another absolute ideal that we are incapable of achieving in practice. Like Aristotle after Plato, Buridan after Aquinas, or Locke after Descartes, Hume could then have offered up his own more modest normative ideal, one we would actually be able to achieve. Thus Hume might have been the hero—or antihero—of this final chapter in our long journey away from the ideal of certainty.

Alas, history does not unfold so neatly. It is, to be sure, easy to see how Hume might have won the laurels in this our dismal race to the epistemic bottom. His writings are full of suggestions about principles of belief formation grounded in something other than ultimately undefeated evidence. Yet this is not how the story goes. After setting out with great vigor the impossibility of achieving the evidentialist ideal, Hume finds himself unable to follow evidentialism down the road to Pyrrhonian suspension, but equally unable to abandon the evidentialist ideal. Unwilling to take recourse in supernatural assistance either, he is left at an impasse.

Why not abandon evidentialism, as just one more fallen idol along humanity's long road toward intellectual maturity? I suspect that Hume's reason for not doing so is ultimately the same as ours: that neither he, nor we, can abandon our claims to have grasped what is true. The discussion of skepticism in the *Treatise* begins by describing reason as "a kind of cause, of which truth is the natural effect," but then immediately cautions that such an effect "may frequently be prevented."[a] If epistemic defeatism is correct, then we ultimately have no solid basis for determining just how frequently and when such disruptions occur. In fact, Hume quickly reaches the conclusion that "our judgment is not in *any* thing possessed of *any* measures of truth and falsehood," but then immediately withdraws the claim as "entirely superfluous," given that nature's "absolute and uncontrollable necessity has determined us to judge as well as to breathe and feel."[b] In judging, as in believing, we make claims about what is true. Accordingly, the necessities of nature conflict not only with the Pyrrhonian suspension of belief, but also with the self-conscious embrace of epistemic defeat, given that defeat undermines any objective claim to the likelihood of truth. Thus Hume finds himself in hopeless conflict as he approaches the end of Book I of the *Treatise*, desiring to embrace what is "natural and agreeable" while recognizing that the pursuit of truth might require that he "strive against the current of nature," and yet wondering why "I must torture my brain with subtleties and sophistries, at the very time that I cannot satisfy myself concerning

[a] I.4.1, p. 180.   [b] I.4.1, p. 183.

the reasonableness of so painful an application, nor have any tolerable prospect of arriving by its means at truth and certainty."[a] Hume's principles demand that he either follow the Pyrrhonsts to suspension of belief or abandon the "tolerable prospect" of truth as an epistemic ideal—neither of which he is able to do. This is the Humean predicament, and if epistemic defeatism is correct then it is our predicament as well.[12]

Hume's way forward is to embrace a kind of quietism: he simply stops striving after such ideals and focuses his attention instead on how in fact nature operates. Abandoning the hope of grounding our beliefs in reason, he thinks that we need to begin by registering the fact that we *do* form certain sorts of beliefs, and that we cannot do otherwise. Remarkably, rather than relinquish at this point the traditional terminology of 'evidence,' Hume accommodates evidentness within the context of his diminished expectations. Given that the necessities of nature have fixed in us the propensity to regard various connections between ideas as more or less likely to obtain, we can speak of the evidentness of these connections and characterize the various "degrees of evidence"[b] in virtue of which the mind assents with greater or lesser confidence. All of this gives us grounds (albeit of a purely subjective sort) for reaching normative conclusions about how the mind ought to operate. Thus Hume can accept the cardinal Lockean principle: "a wise man, therefore, proportions his belief to his evidence."[c] And, although—following Locke's demanding usage—he thinks that our beliefs almost never rise to the level of knowledge, he still thinks that we can achieve science. Both "evidence" and "science" are possible, even though Hume admits that, viewed from a strictly rational point of view, "the understanding...leaves not the lowest degree of evidence in any proposition."[d]

In making this descriptive, naturalistic turn, Hume crystalizes a tendency that had been developing for centuries. When John Buridan, back around 1350, offered his influential distinction between levels of certainty and evidentness, he sought infallibility but recognized that what we in fact mostly achieve is an indubitability that reaches the truth only given certain assumptions.[e] And when, some three hundred years later, John Wilkins argues for the pivotal thesis that we can have knowledge on the basis of such merely moral certainty, he appeals to psychological facts about the frame of our nature:

I appeal to the common judgment of mankind, whether the human nature be not so framed as to acquiesce in such a moral certainty as the nature of things is capable of; and, if it were otherwise, whether that reason which belongs to us would not prove a burden and a torment to us, rather than a privilege, by keeping us in continual suspense, and thereby rendering our conditions perpetually restless and unquiet.[f]

Wilkins declines to rest his argument on what reason shows must be the case, because he thinks that if we follow strict reason we could never have more than "a conditional infallibility," dependent on the assumption that our faculties are properly working.[g] Tacitly rejecting Lockean proportionality, he holds that we "may and must give a firm assent...where yet the evidences for such things are not infallible."[h] To do otherwise

---

[a] I.4.7, pp. 269–70.   [b] E.g., I.3.11, p. 124; I.3.13, p. 153.   [c] *Enquiry* 10.1, p. 110.
[d] *Treatise* I.4.7, p. 267.   [e] See Lecture Two, pp. 33–5.   [f] *Principles and Duties* I.3, pp. 29–30.
[g] I.1, p. 9.   [h] I.3, p. 27 (see Lecture Two, pp. 42–3).

would run entirely against the grain of our nature and would leave us burdened with perpetual fear.

Over the course of these six lectures, we have seen many other examples of this same dynamic: how, for instance, our supposedly fail-safe domain of sensory privilege becomes so qualified as to be trivial;[a] how the special privilege of the first-person present rests on little more than dogmatic bias;[b] how our immunity to divine deception turns out to be so narrow as to yield no certainty at all.[c] In each case, the initial appearance of objective infallibility turned out to be nothing more than subjective indubitability, and the aspiration for certainty reduced to a hope of reasonable probability. In this historical context, there is nothing surprising about Hume's continuing to insist on the evidentness of our beliefs. Evidentness had always, first and foremost, been a matter of subjective compulsion.[d] That it might also be a mark of infallible certainty was the pious hope of many generations, culminating in Descartes's *Mediations*. By calling everything into doubt, the *Meditations* forces us to confront the gap between indubitability and infallibility, and so to consider what is left of our supposedly infallible knowledge once we strip away the veneer of indubitability. Yet as Descartes's last burst of epistemic optimism gave way to the more measured ambitions of later generations, it became inevitable that someone would ask whether, without the veneer, the whole house might fall.

Here is where Hume comes in. While engaged in his positive, naturalistic program, he finds it quite unproblematic to encourage us to match the degree of our belief with the (subjective) evidentness of a proposition, even if that evidentness entirely collapses when subjected to rational reflection. From that strictly rational perspective, we should either abandon all belief or give up on one last epistemic ideal: that of achieving the truth. But Hume finds himself unwilling—or unable—to do either of these things. He is committed to an ideal that he thinks we cannot achieve, even while he develops a naturalistic methodology that he thinks cannot bear rational scrutiny. His only way out is a kind of philosophical quietism, according to which we just carry on as nature intended, without attempting a theoretical resolution.[13]

Believing Hopefully

Is there really nothing more to be said? Suckers for a happy ending, we keep waiting for some charismatic philosopher to appear on the scene, take us in hand, and heroically guide us through the gap from *seems* to *is*. What we have been given instead—so far, over the brief recorded history of our civilization—is two radically different and decidedly unheroic ways out: naturalism and idealism. The naturalistic tradition, as it runs from Hume to Quine, eschews all attempts to answer skeptical worries over epistemic defeat. Judging those matters to be best left in silence, the naturalist shifts our attention toward the work of biologists and psychologists in order to describe our cognitive faculties as they actually are. Epistemology, thus naturalized, becomes "a chapter of psychology and hence of natural science."[e] For the idealist, in contrast,

---

[a] See Lecture Three, esp. p. 57.   [b] See Lecture Five, esp. p. 111.
[c] See this lecture, p. 120.   [d] See Lecture Two, p. 33.   [e] Quine, "Epistemology Naturalized," p. 82.

the way forward in epistemology runs through a revisionary metaphysics that relocates the objects of knowledge to a privileged mental domain. From the early eighteenth century forward, the idealist's main goal has been to escape epistemic defeat. As Berkeley put it, "we should believe that God has dealt more bountifully with the sons of men than to give them a strong desire for that knowledge which he had placed quite out of their reach."[a] Relying explicitly on this Panglossian assumption—that ours at least cannot be the *worst* of all epistemic worlds—Berkeley and his descendants avoid epistemic defeat by relocating the world.[14]

Both naturalism and idealism, in their own ways, change the subject of epistemology. But what if we wish to continue thinking of epistemology as an essentially normative discipline, concerned with what we ought to believe about the mind-independent world? And what if we see no heroic solution to epistemic defeat, and yet are unwilling or unable to follow the Pyrrhonian's suspension of belief? We might then despair, in Humean fashion, or else affect a careless quietism. Yet there is another option: we might assume an attitude of hope with respect to our epistemic prospects, self-consciously granting just how nonideal our cognitive situation is, and yet expressing hope, all the same, that our beliefs hit their mark. In what remains of these lectures I want to explore this possibility. That requires returning to some earlier history.

Hume marks the end of a post-scholastic tradition that runs from Montaigne through Bayle, embraces defeat, and then seeks epistemic salvation in God. In effect, such fideism is the last chapter in the earlier mentioned Augustinian tradition of divine illumination. Consider the beginning of Augustine's great early work, the *Soliloquies*, which prays that he may find God in one way or another:

Teach me how to come to you. I have nothing else but the will to come. I know [*scio*] nothing save that transient dying things are to be spurned, certain and eternal things to be sought after. Knowing this alone, Father, I act as I do, but as for how to come to you, of this I am ignorant. Tell me. Show me. Provide for my journey. If those who take refuge in you find you by faith, give me faith; if by virtue, give me virtue; if by knowledge [*scientia*], give knowledge. Increase in me faith, hope and charity.[b]

As usual, Augustine shows remarkable philosophical sophistication even in a passage that looks superficially like a mere expression of piety. Augustine tells us exactly what he has (the knowledge and the will to seek God) and what he lacks (the knowledge of how to find God). Ideally, we can suppose, he would like to attain that knowledge; but Augustine does not assume that this will be possible, so he asks for whatever works, whether that be knowledge, faith, or virtue.

Part of what would later make Hume so original in epistemology, but also so despairing, is that, even while he accedes to epistemic defeat, he refuses to avail himself of this sort of Augustinian appeal to God. Moreover, as we saw earlier, it is doubtful that divine assistance could help in this way, given the impossibility of epistemic certainty even for God. To be sure, God might have various ways of instilling confidence within us about how things are. But this is not the help we need; as Hume stresses, nature itself takes care of sustaining our confidence. The sort of divine help that would be useful is a strategy for defeating the ultimate defeaters of the skeptical scenarios. But if epistemic

---

[a] *Principles* Intro, section 3 (see Lecture Four, p. 88).   [b] *Soliloquies* I.1.5.

defeatism holds globally, as a conceptual truth, then not even God could enable us to defeat these defeaters, because God himself is unable to do that, even in his own case.

Still, even if God cannot provide the ultimate cure for epistemic defeat, Augustine's invocation of the three theological virtues points toward the two most promising non-Humean strategies for reconciling defeatism with our ordinary beliefs about the world. First let us consider faith, then hope (saving charity, as usual, for another day). To hold a proposition on faith, as I will here use that term, is to believe it firmly, and thus to attach high credence to it, even though one does not suppose that the evidence warrants such confidence. Believing on faith, so understood, directly clashes both with evidentialism and with Lockean proportionality, which is why it strikes so many as utterly disreputable. Moreover, inasmuch as we are not seeking to follow the path of Humean quietism, we should not suppose that such agents hide from themselves the sorry evidentialist situation. On the contrary, the faithful (as I am conceiving of them) adhere to their firm convictions even while maintaining a self-consciously grown-up awareness of how poor the evidence is. This is liable to make their stance look even more disreputable, if not flatly incoherent, insofar as one might think that no agent *could* self-consciously maintain one credence while recognizing that the evidence warrants a different credence. But the fideistic epistemic defeatist will reply that such charges need to be evaluated in light of the other options we face. To be sure, ours would be a better world if we never needed to take anything on faith. Yet if we find that our world is not so ideal, then we must work with what we have. Even God must take something on faith.[15]

There is, however, a better option, one that depends not on faith but on hope. To hold a proposition on hope, as I use the term, involves believing that proposition without having a high credence in its truth. To explain how this can work, I need to be more explicit about the distinction between credences and absolute beliefs. A credence is a level of confidence in a proposition, or what Locke called a degree of assent. A belief is something different: to believe a proposition is to be committed to its truth, where such commitment can be understood in terms of a cluster of dispositions involving both practical reasoning and affective states, as well as dispositions toward various actions in certain circumstances. Typically, beliefs accompany high credences. But the two attitudes are capable of independent variation. So, today, I might have a fairly high credence in one proposition, and believe that proposition. But I might have an even higher credence in another proposition, and not believe it. Tomorrow, credences unchanged, I might cease believing the first proposition and begin believing the second.

In light of these distinctions, consider a remark from around the turn of the eighteenth century by Jacob Bernoulli, one of the leading exponents of the sort of probabilistic evidentialism found in Locke and others. Bernoulli's interests are mainly mathematical: he seeks precise quantitative measurements of what expectation an agent should have in various sorts of situations, particularly situations involving games of chance. To take one of his simplest examples, if I am to choose either what is in your left hand or what is in your right hand and I know there are seven coins in one hand and three in another (but I do not know which is where), then I can expect $(7+3)/2$, and so my expectation should be five coins. But what is an expectation? Bernoulli writes:

It can be seen from what we have said that we are not here using the word 'expectation' in its ordinary sense, according to which we are commonly said to expect or to hope for what is best of all, though worse things can happen to us. Here we are speaking insofar as our hope of getting the best is tempered and diminished by the fear of getting something worse. Thus the value of our expectation always signifies something intermediate between the best we hope for and the worst we fear.[a]

Bernoulli is describing an epistemic ideal that we would now characterize in terms of rationality. Although you might hope for seven coins, and although you might fear receiving only three, what you can rationally expect is five.

In positioning rational expectation halfway between hope and fear, Bernoulli self-consciously builds on a scholastic framework that treats the presence and absence of fear as a defining feature of our various doxastic states. Thus, says Albert the Great, "opinion, when it is inclined to a thing by [merely] plausible reasons, fears the contradictory on account of the weakness of its reasons."[b] Scholastic discussions standardly distinguish two ways of escaping from this state of doxastic fear. One way is for a proposition to be made evident, in which case one has *scientia* of it. The other way is to embrace the proposition on faith, without evidentness.[c] But if we distinguish between credence and belief, a third possibility opens up: that, without elevating one's credence through faith, one might simply stop fearing that one is wrong. Instead of fearing and hoping in equal measure, one places one's hopes entirely in being right, and hence one believes.[16]

It may seem strange to imagine hope and credence parting ways like this, but in fact this can readily happen. The critical thing to notice is that hope and fear are affective rather than cognitive states. As such, they not only can but regularly do run in different directions from our cognitive judgments. One may have an extremely high credence that a thing is so, and yet fear that it is not. Or one may have a fairly low credence in a proposition, and yet regard it with sunny optimism. As an illustration of the role such affective attitudes can play in shaping belief, consider one of the very few medieval expressions of skepticism, that of Francesco Petrarca:

So much do I fear to become entangled in errors that I throw myself into the embrace of doubt instead of truth. Thus I have gradually become a proselyte of the Academy . . . I give no credit to myself, do not affirm anything, and doubt every single thing, except for what I believe is a sacrilege to doubt.[d]

Giving greater weight to the risk of error, Petrarch takes the side of fear rather than that of hope. This leads him to a skeptical suspension of belief—nearly a global skepticism, but for his prudent exception for religious belief. Yet we can imagine that, without any change on the cognitive side in his credences about the plausibility of skeptical arguments, he might instead have taken up an attitude of hope. This would mean setting aside his worries about being "entangled in error" and optimistically dwelling on the prospects of being right. To become optimistic in this way does not require supposing it more likely that one is right: the initial change required is affective rather than cognitive. Where optimism is diluted by fear, according to the medieval analysis, there can be at most uncertain opinion. Hence Petrarch is a skeptic. But where there is hope, fear is assuaged, and hence there can be confident belief. Here, then, is a way to escape

---

[a] *Art of Conjecturing* pt. 1, p. 134.   [b] *Ethica* VII.1.2.5 (ed. Borgnet VII: 467).
[c] See Lecture Two, pp. 32–3.   [d] Cassirer et al., *Renaissance Philosophy of Man*, pp. 34–5.

Pyrrhonian belief suspension indirectly, not by intellectually refuting epistemic defeatism or by ignoring it in Hume's manner, but simply by ceasing to worry about it.

Among epistemic defeatists, these noncognitive aspects of belief formation did not go unnoticed. Montaigne amusingly wonders whether passionate hostility to authority or love of one's own reputation "has not sent some men all the way to the stake to maintain an opinion for which, among their friends and at liberty, they would not have been willing to burn the tip of their finger."[a] For him, the entanglement of belief with passion is one more reason why we should be suspicious of our beliefs. In Hume, such noncognitive influences play a central role in explaining why we continue to maintain our beliefs even in the face of epistemic defeat. Indeed, he says that the whole point of his lengthy discussion of skepticism is to make clear that the real grounds of belief lie in nonrational influences:

My intention then in displaying so carefully the arguments of that fantastic [skeptical] sect is only to make the reader sensible of the truth of my hypothesis, that all our reasonings concerning causes and effects are derived from nothing but custom; and that belief is more properly an act of the sensitive than of the cogitative part of our natures.[b]

Hume is not implying that the skeptical arguments are unsound. On the contrary, it is their very soundness that gives him the result he is after. For, if they are sound, the question then arises of why we do not follow them. The answer, he thinks, can only be that our beliefs are governed by something other than reason. Indeed, he concludes that, if belief were based on pure reason, "it must infallibly destroy itself, and in every case terminate in a total suspense of judgment."[c] [17]

Hume's own explanation runs through the natural force of sentiment and custom, and nothing could be more alien to his purposes than to take refuge in one of the theological virtues. For a more helpful precedent, then, we might look back to Aquinas, who takes the theological virtue of hope to be an affective confidence, within the will, in our achieving the ultimate end of human life: eternal union with God. Where does that confidence come from? According to Aquinas, it comes from the cognitive side: "hope tends with certainty toward its end, as if taking part in the certainty of faith, which is in the cognitive power."[d] This is to say that Aquinas is too much of an intellectualist to approve of hope—even divinely infused hope—without any cognitive underpinning. Moreover, he thinks that hope, if it is to be virtuous, must be balanced by a corresponding fear of divine punishment. Too much hope, unalloyed by fear, results in the vice of presumption.

What I propose, in effect, is epistemic presumption writ large: that we hope for, and so believe in, many things that we do not rationally suppose to have a high degree of likelihood. Of course, as in the case of faith, hope must be constrained. Too much hope, or the wrong kind of hope, will strike everyone as absurd. Given the thesis of epistemic defeatism, the sorts of constraints available cannot be evidential. But that does not mean that there can be no constraints—only that the constraints will ultimately be grounded in something other than objective evidence. Whatever those constraints may be, believing out of hope is quite different from believing out of faith, because to have faith is not just

---

[a] "Apology for Raymond Sebond" (*Complete Essays*, p. 426).   [b] *Treatise* I.4.1, p. 183.
[c] I.4.1, p. 184.   [d] *Summa theol.* 2a2ae 18.4c.

to believe, but also to have a very high credence in the likelihood of a thing's being so. Hope, as I am thinking of it, requires no such cognitive confidence. It requires merely an optimism on the affective side—a cheerful willingness not to worry about the all-too-possible bad scenarios. This has a considerable advantage over its fideistic counterpart, because it comes much closer to adhering to the cardinal principle of evidentialism. The hopeful agent honors the evidence, through her credences, even while she takes liberties with her beliefs. Fideism requires a worrisome lack of integrity on the cognitive side, assigning probabilities in a way that the evidence does not warrant. The hopeful defeatist, in contrast, exploits the affective aspect of belief formation by letting her sentiments lead her to belief, even while her credences reflect the depressing limits on our overall evidence.[18]

In extoling such an attitude I do not mean to suggest that it is within our voluntary control. Petrarch describes himself as too enmeshed in doubt to be hopeful, which suggests that it was not possible for him to see things otherwise. Hume makes it similarly clear that his conduct is governed by nature. Outside of his study, he just cannot help but believe things that, earlier on, he had been capable of doubting. In this regard we are almost all Humean rather than Petrarchian. Even if, on philosophical grounds, we find epistemic defeatism cogent, it would be almost impossible for most of us to cease believing the various familiar propositions about the world that we take for granted. Unlike Petrarch, we are by nature not able to sustain the sorts of fears that would cause us to suspend belief.

If epistemic defeatism is true, then Petrarch's "embrace of doubt" is in a sense the most rational choice. But the sense in which this counts as rational is quite circumscribed: it is rational only given the evidentialist constraint that all belief be based on sufficient evidence. If the only thing in life that we value is maximizing our ratio of true to false beliefs, then evidentialism is undoubtedly rational and suspension of belief would seem to be the only rational response to epistemic defeat. But, inasmuch as we care about many things other than truth and falsity—inasmuch as we want to live rich, engaged lives—an attitude of hope recommends itself. To be hopeful is to take a step beyond Hume and to make the grown-up acknowledgment that our present, irresistible attitudes are not ones that can be sustained in the cold light of reason. Yet we still move ahead with life, hopefully, even while remembering the disappointing verdict of philosophical reflection on our epistemic predicament.

To be sure, the outcome we have finally reached is far from ideal. Our beliefs, governed by our natural tendency toward hopefulness, turn out to be quite out of sync with our rational credences regarding what is likely to be the case. For anyone committed to the traditional ambitions of philosophy, this is deeply depressing. We had aspired to do better. But if nature leaves us no choice with regard to the vast majority of our beliefs—if we are unable to fear, and hence unable to doubt—then these nonideal circumstances are ones we had better get used to. We have no choice but to settle for considerably reduced ambitions in epistemology. Perhaps the only good news here is that settling for less is something we find it remarkably easy to do. It is simply not within our nature to worry about such matters for very long.[19]

NOTES

Caveat lector. The endnotes for each lecture are meant to be read after having read the whole of that particular lecture, and are intended only for readers who want a more fine-grained historical account than what the lectures themselves provide. These notes have been written so as to be read continuously, without referring back to the lecture. So, although superscript numbers have been used in the usual way, to connect the notes to particular places within each lecture, first-time readers are urged not to skip back and forth until the lecture has been read to the end.

Notes to Lecture One

Introduction

The Place of Epistemology

Note 1 (p. 1). According to the usual textbook version of philosophy's history, the so-called "early modern" era is characterized above all by its newfound interest in problems of knowledge. For Julia Annas and Jonathan Barnes, this is "the age of epistemology" (*Modes of Scepticism*, p. 4). Says John Searle: "after Descartes, the central problems of philosophy were epistemic" (*Seeing Things as They Are*, p. 29). Yet the experts recognize that this is a difficult judgment to sustain. John Carriero remarks in a recent essay that the differences in thinking about knowledge, then and now, "are gross enough that we might wonder about the extent to which seventeenth-century philosophers and modern philosophers are interested in the same thing. We might also wonder about the extent to which it is helpful to apply the same label— say, epistemology—to both sets of interests" ("Epistemology Past and Present," p. 175).

There is certainly something to the idea that the seventeenth century witnesses a new emphasis on issues broadly conceived of as epistemic. This emphasis is on display in Locke's magnum opus, *An Essay concerning Human Understanding*, whose title would later be emulated in Berkeley's *Principles* and in Hume's first *Enquiry*. Descartes's interest in matters that are broadly epistemic is similarly plain. Yet for none of these authors is *knowledge* a particularly central issue, at least not as we think of knowledge today. The first two lectures explain why this is so.

The first occurrence of 'epistemology' known to the *Oxford English Dictionary* dates to 1856. In other languages, terminology remains unsettled to this day. In French, for instance, *épistémologie* is, traditionally, the philosophy of science, and it is not really clear how to refer to the modern Anglo-American tradition of epistemology, since neither *connaissance* nor *savoir* exactly matches the range of the English word 'knowledge.' Yet, if it is *Descartes* who supposedly turned philosophy toward epistemology, then how strange that the *French* would find themselves at a loss for the proper words to track this development! Or might it be that the anomaly of usage lies on the side of English? This lecture attempts to show how a distinctively English conception of epistemology grows from the soil of Newtonian science and Lockean philosophy.

At issue is not just the proper words, but the character of the subject itself. For it is only very recently that epistemology (under any name) has become a distinct philosophical subject. According to the standard ancient classification, philosophy divides into logic, physics, and ethics. This is how the Stoics divided the subject (see Cicero, *Academica* I.5.19, where he attributes this tripartition to Plato, and II.36.116, where he attributes it to the Stoics and "most others") and how Aristotle's corpus would come to be organized. Augustine takes this division for granted as he works through the case against skepticism in *Contra academicos* Book III.

In the Alexandrian tradition of late antiquity it becomes standard first to distinguish between practical and theoretical philosophy and then to divide each branch in a more fine-grained way. Ptolemy, for instance, invoking Aristotle, divides theoretical philosophy into physics, mathematics, and theology (*Almagest* I.1, trans. p. 35), the last of these sometimes being referred to as metaphysics. In later discussions within the Alexandrian tradition, logic is often added as a fourth category. This way of dividing the field ultimately made its way into the Arabic tradition. Al-Kindī, for instance, similarly distinguishes between practical and theoretical philosophy, and then divides the latter into logic, physics, metaphysics, and psychology (see Peter Adamson, *Al-Kindī*, pp. 30–2). For further details on this period, see Dimitri Gutas, "Paul the Persian" and Christel Hein, *Definition und Einteilung der Philosophie*.

In the Latin West, Boethius adopts the Alexandrian tradition and reports a dispute over whether logic should be judged to be a part of philosophy or merely a tool with which to do philosophy (*Comm. Isagogen* vers. 2, I.3). Boethius himself takes the latter view, but subsequent authors in the Latin tradition split over this question. In the early twelfth century, Hugh of Saint Victor divides philosophy into theoretical, practical, mechanical, and logical parts, remarking that "these four contain all *scientia*" (*Didascalicon* II.1). Later in that same century, Dominicus Gundisalvi, the Spanish scholar with a foot in both the Latin and the Arabic traditions, describes logic as preparatory to the traditional three parts of theoretical philosophy: physics, mathematics, and theology/metaphysics (*De divisione philosophiae*, trans. Grant, *Source Book*, p. 61). For details regarding the medieval Latin tradition, see James Weisheipl, "Classification of the Sciences." On Hobbes's division of the sciences, see Tom Sorell, "Hobbes's Scheme."

In the preface to the French edition of the *Principles*, Descartes writes that "the whole of philosophy is like a tree. The roots are metaphysics, the trunk is physics, and the branches emerging from the trunk are all the other sciences. These reduce to three principal ones: namely medicine, mechanics, and morals" (IXB: 14). In Jean le Rond d'Alembert's compre-hensive chart of the various *connoissances humaines*, from the Diderot–d'Alembert *Encyclopédie* (1751–72), philosophy has five parts: the science of God, logic, morality, mathematics, and physics (vol. 1: 10b). Throughout all these texts, it should be noted, there is no discernible difference between a division of philosophy and a division of the sciences.

Despite all the interesting variation over the centuries in how the parts of philosophy get counted, there is no sign of anything that corresponds very closely to epistemology as we now think of it. But this is not to say that the concerns of epistemology find no place at all in these older divisions. For it is clear enough that they belong in the category of logic. Consider, for instance, Dominicus Gundisalvi: "Some truth is known [*notum*], some unknown [*ignotum*] . . . Anything at all that is unknown becomes known only through something that is known. Therefore, logic is the only science that teaches how by means of the known to arrive at a cognition of the unknown" (trans. Grant, *Source Book*, p. 62). This sort of robustly epistemic understanding of logic is entirely normal. Aquinas, to take another example, remarks at the start of his commentary on the *Posterior Analytics* that "an art is necessary that serves to direct the act of reason, through which we proceed in that act of reason in a way that is orderly, without difficulty or error. And this art is logic, i.e. *scientia rationalis*."

Much the same understanding of logic runs through the post-scholastic era. On Locke's *Essay* as a work of logic, see Kenneth Winkler, "Perception and Ideas," p. 234. The *Port-Royal Logic* defines its subject as "the art of conducting reason well in knowing [*connaissance*] things, as much to instruct ourselves about them as to instruct others" (trans. p. 23). According to

John Sergeant, at the end of the seventeenth century, "logic is the proper art" that yields "a certain method to arrive at truth and attain knowledge, without which all our studies are to no purpose" (*Solid Philosophy* preface, n. 11). Hume writes in the introduction to his *Treatise* that "the sole end of logic is to explain the principles and operations of our reasoning faculty, and the nature of our ideas" (p. xix; cf. *Treatise*, Abstract, p. 646). Norton and Norton's edition offers this annotation: "Note that Hume's conception of logic is a broad one, roughly equivalent to what many philosophers would now call epistemology" (p. 424). Perhaps not *equivalent*, but at any rate certainly *encompassing*. Indeed, Hume describes all of Book I of the *Treatise* as his logic (Appendix, p. 657). And in thinking of logic this way Hume is simply following a very old tradition, a tradition that would endure all the way to Frege's blistering attack on psychologism and insistence that the laws of logic are "the most general laws, prescribing how to think wherever there is thinking at all" (*Basic Laws*, p. xv).

Plato's Limited Influence

Note 2 (p. 2). The casual assumption that the Platonic definitional quest informs the whole history of philosophy is so rampant that it might seem unfair to single out individual scholars. Yet examples must be made:

> Ever since Socrates, philosophers have made various attempts to explain what this tether [cf. *Meno* 98a] is made of and what it is tied to at the other end, for it is through the tethering that beliefs become justified, and it is only through justification that the value of knowledge can accrue to beliefs.
> (Philip Olson, "Putting Knowledge in Its Place," p. 244)

> Whatever else we may or may not say of the theories of Heraclitus and Parmenides, Plato and Aristotle, the Stoics and the Epicureans, the Skeptics and most of the other philosophical sects or schools of antiquity, it is true that they were fundamentally concerned with the definition of genuine knowledge and the establishment of its relation to mere beliefs.   (Manfred Kuehn, "Knowledge and Belief," pp. 389–90)

It is worth pausing over such claims for a moment, because there is more at work here than just the persistence of a particular bit of misinformation that has somehow become entrenched in our textbook histories. The irresistibility of such "ever since the dawn of philosophy" claims attests to our vulnerability to a cognitive shortcut we might call the heuristic of historical continuity: our propensity to take data points scattered across an historical timeline and to fill in the gaps on the assumption that things have always been so. As vision fills in for the blind spot where the optic nerve meets the retina, so our historical imagination fill in the inevitable gaps in our knowledge with an assumption of homogeneous continuity. In the present case, then, even if all we know is that Plato wanted a definition of knowledge and that philosophers today similarly seek such a thing, those two data points alone are enough to foster the conclusion that this quest must have continued uninterrupted over millennia about which we are wholly uninformed.

This propensity counts as a heuristic in the psychologist's technical sense, because it offers an easy shortcut past the hard work of historical research. That work requires not just painstaking scholarship and a facility with other languages, but also the kind of historical imagination that sets aside the heuristic of historical continuity and opens itself up to the possibility of radical discontinuity. Compare Isaiah Berlin:

> [R]econstructing what occurred in the past in terms not merely of our own concepts and categories, but also of how such events must have looked to those who participated in or were affected by them...This kind of imaginative projection of ourselves into the past, the attempt to capture concepts and categories that differ from those of the investigator by means of concepts and categories that cannot but be his own, is a task that he can never be sure that he is even beginning to achieve, yet is not permitted to abjure.
> (*Concepts and Categories*, pp. 135–6)

I know of no better expression of just how difficult a task confronts the historian of ideas.

For doubts as to whether even Plato is concerned with defining knowledge in the ordinary sense, see Myles Burnyeat, "Aristotle on Understanding Knowledge," pp. 133–6, and Mark Kaplan, "It's Not What You Know," pp. 351–3. See also Hugh Benson, *Socratic Wisdom*, which argues that the early dialogues should be read as concerned not with knowledge but with understanding. In contrast, see Gail Fine, "Knowledge and Belief," pp. 114–15, who warns against the overhasty assumption that Plato's topic is not knowledge in our sense. It should also be noted that other Platonic dialogues, in particular in the *Republic*, might be read as being oriented more toward the epistemic ideal than toward boundary conditions.

Aristotle's Ideal Theory

Note 3 (p. 4). It is now widely accepted that ἐπιστήμη in the *Posterior Analytics* should be conceived of as *understanding*. The case has been most influentially made by Burnyeat ("Aristotle on Understanding Knowledge") and put into practice by Jonathan Barnes in his standard translation.

The older Oxford translation (by Mure) renders ἐπιστήμη as "scientific knowledge," an association that continues to be made in virtually every discussion of the topic. Terence Irwin, to take one prominent example, offers this general characterization: "the *Posterior Analytics* describes the structure of a science and of the content of scientific propositions" (*Aristotle's First Principles*, p. 118). And Christopher Taylor remarks that "the *Posterior Analytics* ... gives a detailed account of the conditions necessary and sufficient for the achievement of ἐπιστήμη in the context of an exact science, but this appears to the modern eye as at best one kind of knowledge, *scientific* knowledge, among others" ("Aristotle's Epistemology," p. 116). Both Burnyeat and Barnes, though shying away from the term 'knowledge,' take for granted that the treatise's subject is science, and Burnyeat even ultimately allows "that in the end it will not do too much damage to go back to the traditional rendering of ἐπιστήμη as 'scientific knowledge'" ("Aristotle on Understanding Knowledge," p. 132). For ἐπιστήμη in the plural, ἐπιστῆμαι, as meaning something close to *the sciences*, see for example Plato, *Republic* VII, 522c. But arithmetic and geometry are also paradigms of ἐπιστῆμαι (e.g. Arist., *Post. An.* 75^{a}39, 76^{b}8–9, and see the tabulations in Barnes, "Aristotle's Theory of Demonstration," p. 129). So, even as the account gets described as a theory of science, it seems clear that this is not science in our modern sense. Thus Barnes cautions: "'science' is here of course to be understood in the broad sense of the Greek ἐπιστήμη" (p. 123).

Note 4 (p. 5). H. S. Thayer refers to "the extraordinary fact that no one completely satisfactory scientific syllogism fulfilling the requirements Aristotle prescribes for scientific demonstration can be found in *Posterior Analytics*" ("Aristotle on the Meaning of Science," p. 100). Barnes goes even farther, remarking that "in the whole of the Aristotelian *corpus* there is not, as far as I am aware, a single example of a demonstration" ("Aristotle's Theory of Demonstration," p. 124). Others have, in the face of this worry, sought to find more extensive signs of demonstration in the *corpus*. Focusing in particular on the biological works, Allan Gotthelf makes a persuasive case that their structure "is at least amenable" to the framework of the *Posterior Analytics* ("First Principles," p. 178). (Other essays in that same volume reach a similar conclusion.) But the point remains that, if we take the *Posterior Analytics* seriously as a guide to what ἐπιστήμη requires, it is hard to see anywhere in Aristotle where ἐπιστήμη has been achieved.

Even given the idealized character of Aristotle's proposal, it is not quite right to conclude that no one has ever achieved that ideal or ever will. On the contrary, Aristotle takes the striking view that philosophy has in the past "probably often been developed as far as possible and then perished" (*Meta.* XII.8, 1074^{b}10–11; see also *Politics* VII.10, 1329^{b}25–35). But this reflects no particular optimism regarding past cultures; instead, it is simply an implication of his belief that the world's past history is *infinite*. For, given an infinity of past human civilizations, there is a probability approaching 1 that, whatever cognitive achievements are possible for human beings, they have in fact been achieved, and indeed not just "often" but even infinitely many times.

Mathematical cases might seem to be the best candidates for successful demonstrations. But there was a long history of debate over whether mathematical demonstrations show the reason why the conclusion holds. Aristotle clearly thinks that this causal condition is satisfied in mathematics (see e.g. *Post. An.* II.11, 94^{a}27–35). But this was contentious both in antiquity and among later commentators; it is denied, for instance, by Robert Grosseteste, as this lecture mentions in passing (p. 8). For discussion of the situation in Aristotle, see Barnes's commentary at pp. 92–3, 107–8. For later antiquity, see Orna Harari, "Proclus' Account of Explanatory Demonstrations." For the particularly rich history of Renaissance discussions, see Neal Ward Gilbert, *Renaissance Concepts of Method*, pp. 86–92, Anna De Pace, *Le matematiche e il mondo*, Paolo Mancosu, *Philosophy of Mathematics* ch. 1, and Peter Dear, *Discipline and Experience* ch. 2.

With respect to the general question of what the *Posterior Analytics* is proposing, Barnes has suggested that it gives us not a method for acquiring knowledge, but a method for presenting it in systematic form (see "Aristotle's Theory of Demonstration" as well as his commentary at pp. xii, xviii–xx). But, as others have observed (e.g. Burnyeat, "Aristotle on Understanding Knowledge"), this hardly seems to solve the puzzle, inasmuch as Aristotle's actual method of presentation seems just as far from his prescriptions as does his method of discovery. It is hard to believe, moreover, that the complex strictures of the *Posterior Analytics* are intended primarily as a strategy for presenting one's research.

Note 5 (p. 6). I am hardly the first to suggest that Aristotle is describing an epistemic ideal. J. H. Lesher, for instance, argues, against Burnyeat, that the achievement of ἐπιστήμη goes beyond understanding and is in fact "a complete grasp of a subject" ("On Aristotelian ἐπιστήμη," p. 49), amounting to "expert knowledge" or "disciplinary mastery" (p. 54). This is clearly in the neighborhood of my proposal. These remarks, in turn, are perhaps not far from what Burnyeat himself thinks, inasmuch as he too concludes that "Aristotle's thought is concentrated on the τέλος, the achieved state of understanding which is the end and completion of the epistemological process" ("Aristotle on Understanding Knowledge," p. 133). This is, quite precisely, my own view. Taylor, similarly, holds that "*nous + epistēmē* is the ideal type of knowledge" ("Aristotle's Epistemology," pp. 121–2). But because none of these scholars conceives of idealized epistemology as a central epistemological project in its own right, they are unable to give these thoughts their proper prominence and significance. Thus Burnyeat continues to think of the treatise as "a contribution to the philosophy of science" ("Aristotle on Understanding Knowledge," p. 97), as does Taylor (note 3 here), and Lesher puts all of the weight on the too narrow idea of ἐπιστήμη as expertise within a discipline.

On the broader context of demonstration in ancient Greece as a kind of ideal, see G. E. R. Lloyd, *The Ideals of Inquiry* ch. 1. On how even demonstration itself is a highly flexible notion in Aristotle, see also Lloyd, "The Theories and Practices of Demonstration."

Normative Ideals

The Epistemic Ideal after Aristotle

Note 6 (p. 7). Among later Aristotelians, it becomes commonplace to conceive of ἐπιστήμη/ *scientia* as the epistemic ideal. Albert the Great's discussion in the prologue to his commentary on the *Posterior Analytics*, as quoted in this lecture (pp. 6–7), is a prime example from the start of the scholastic era, and there is nothing particularly original about the way he frames the issues.

On the contrary, he is simply giving voice to an epistemic framework that is already widely shared. Lecture Two will offer more information on developments between Aristotle and the thirteenth century, focusing on the rise of the expectation of certainty. In this note I focus squarely on the conception of *scientia* as an epistemic ideal and offer more examples from the later Middle Ages and beyond.

Thomas Aquinas regularly characterizes *scientia* as perfect cognition (see, e.g., *Summa theol.* 1a2ae 67.3c; *Quaest. de veritate* 11.1 sc 5; *Sent.* III.31.2.1.1 obj. 4; and *Quaest. de virtutibus in communi* 7c: "someone is said to understand or know inasmuch as his intellect is perfected for cognizing what is true"). Aquinas discusses in some detail the case of Adam and Eve: it is theoretically important that, as this lecture notes (p. 7), he describes them as existing in a state of cognitive perfection. For further details, see Philip Reynolds, "Infants of Eden," and Edmund Byrne, *Probability and Opinion*, pp. 85–9.

John Duns Scotus similarly invokes epistemic perfection when he seeks to explain why *scientia* requires certainty:

The first condition, that this *scientia* or cognition be certain, excluding all deception, opinion, and doubt, applies to every intellectual virtue, because every intellectual virtue is a perfection of intellect, disposing intellect for its perfect operation, and a perfect intellectual operation is a certain* cognition of what is true. Hence every intellectual virtue is a disposition for determinately saying what is true. For this reason opinion and mistrust, which can extend to what is false, are not intellectual virtues. (*Reportatio* prol. 1.1 [Wolter and Bychkov n. 9; Wadding XI.2, n. 4]) [*'certain' is printed only in the Wadding edition (and is not found in the manuscripts), but the addition is plainly required for the argument's validity]

Scotus's appeal to *scientia* as an intellectual virtue draws on *Nicomachean Ethics* VI, where Aristotle includes ἐπιστήμη among the intellectual virtues. Scotus is also presupposing a broader tradition of treating the virtues as perfections. So, as Aquinas puts it, "virtue perfects a power as regards its perfect act" (*Quaest. de virt. comm.* 2c). Accordingly, "a speculative intellectual virtue is that through which the speculative intellect is perfected in its consideration of what is true" (*Summa theol.* 1a2ae 57.2c).

These remarks help make explicit something that really ought to have been obvious before now. For, if anyone were to have approached the history of theorizing about knowledge not from the peculiar perspective of epistemology today, but rather as a special subject within the history of virtue theory, then it would have seemed just obvious that *scientia* is an epistemic ideal. But, even if there are many today who study epistemology from a virtue-theoretic standpoint, these historical connections have not been properly appreciated.

The conception of *scientia* as an ideal persists throughout later scholasticism. John Buridan, for instance, remarks that, in the context of the *Posterior Analytics*, "*scire* is described not as it is generally taken, but most strictly and powerfully" (*Quaest. Post. an.* q. 7c). See also Domingo de Soto, *De demonstratione* q. 2, p. 295B: "to know [*scire*] is to cognize perfectly the truth of a thing."

The story remains unquestioned among post-scholastic authors. This lecture quotes Descartes's early *Rules* (p. 7), but might just as well have cited the preface to the French edition of the *Principles of Philosophy*: "the word 'philosophy' means the study of wisdom [*sagesse*], and by 'wisdom' is meant not only prudence in our everyday affairs but also a perfect knowledge [*parfaite connaissance*] of all things that mankind is capable of knowing [*savoir*]" (IXB: 2). This sets the agenda for philosophy as the pursuit of perfect knowledge, which is what Descartes, writing in Latin, refers to as *scientia*.

As with the *Posterior Analytics*, it is easy to find recent discussions of seventeenth-century thought noting that *scientia* serves as a kind of ideal. But here too there has been no attempt to situate such an observation within a broader systematic framework, and so the significance of the observation has not been grasped. As a typical example of how limited these discussions tend to be, consider Sorell, Rogers, and Kraye's recent, state-of-the-art collection of essays *Scientia in Early Modern Philosophy*, which begins with the following remark: "In early modern philosophy, *scientia* is an honorific term" (p. vii). This is about as satisfactory as beginning a book on early modern political institutions with the remark that, "in early modern Europe, *king* is an honorific term." As the notion of *monarchy* stands to political theory during this time, so *scientia* stands to epistemology: it is the central organizing notion in relation to which every lesser condition assumes its position.

Nonideal Cases

Note 7 (p. 8). Once one sees how *scientia* lies at the summit of the idealized framework for epistemology, it becomes possible to fit other pieces into that framework, as ways of theorizing about cognition in nonideal cases. I offer some suggestions about how to do this in a scholastic context in my paper "Medieval Social Epistemology."

In thinking along these lines, there is much more to say than merely that the various lesser forms of *scientia* and *cognitio* mark diminished levels of achievement on the way to the ideal. Dialectics in Aristotle, for instance, plays something like that role, in as much as it provides guidance on forming beliefs in nonideal circumstances. But it also plays a more practical role in various arenas that Aristotle was concerned with, such as the art of examining others (see *Soph. Ref.* 11, 172ª22). Beyond dialectics lies rhetoric, the focus of which is even more practical and less oriented toward the acquisition of truth and the production of knowledge. What dialectics and rhetoric share, in contrast to the demonstrative method of the *Analytics*, is that they "are concerned with such things as come, more or less, within the general ken [γνωρίζειν] of all men and belong to no one ἐπιστήμη" (*Rhetoric* I.1, 1354ª2).

When epistemology is conceptualized to cover this sort of terrain, it can be allowed to expand into fields that currently lie at the neglected fringes of the discipline, such as the philosophy of education. Indeed, we ought to ask ourselves what sort of discipline philosophy has become, when questions about education are scorned as marginal while we valorize those who devote their careers to puzzling over the Gettier problem.

Ordinary Language

Note 8 (p. 8). The idealized framework requires taking an epistemic term—ἐπιστήμη, علم, *scientia*—and making it stand for the cognitive ideal. Of course, one could use a neologism for this purpose, but the universal practice, in both ancient and modern languages, has been to take a perfectly ordinary term and give it this technical sense. Inevitably, however, such a way of proceeding leaves in its wake the problem of what to say about ordinary, nontechnical uses of the term. For those who think of epistemology as mainly an exercise in linguistic analysis, such difficulties are liable to dominate the whole field. But even philosophers with no particular interest in mapping the contours of ordinary language need some story about how their way of talking relates to the ordinary idioms of their listeners. Augustine, for instance, writes as follows:

> When we speak strictly [*proprie*], we say that we know [*scire*] only that which we grasp through the mind's firm reason. But when we speak with words better suited to custom, as even divine scripture speaks, then we should not hesitate to say that we know [*scire*] both the things we perceive with our bodily senses and the things we believe on faith through worthy witnesses—provided we understand what the difference is between the one and the other.   (*Retractationes* I.14.3 = trans. I.13.3)

Although Aristotle himself did not expressly address this issue, one finds it in his commentators. Philoponus, author of the earliest surviving commentary on the *Posterior Analytics*, flags this issue by using the language of καθ' αὑτό and κατὰ συμβεβηκός (*per se* and *per accidens*:

CAG edn. p. 28, trans. p. 38). Themistius, as cited in this lecture (p. 8), distinguishes between ἐπιστήμη spoken of broadly (κοινῶς) and ἐπιστήμη spoken of strictly (κυρίως).

Themistius's discussion would come to influence the scholastic tradition through Gerard of Cremona's twelfth-century Latin translation of an earlier, no longer extant Arabic translation. Grosseteste, author of the first Latin commentary on the *Posterior Analytics* (a work from the 1220s), develops still further the broad–strict distinction of Themistius. The passage is so influential as to be worth quoting in full:

> It does not escape us, however, that having *scientia* is spoken of broadly, strictly, more strictly, and most strictly. [1] *Scientia* commonly so-called is [merely] comprehension of truth. Unstable contingent things are objects of *scientia* in this way. [2] *Scientia* strictly so-called is comprehension of the truth of things that are always or most of the time in one way. Natural things—namely, natural contingencies—are objects of *scientia* in this way. Of these things there is demonstration broadly so-called. [3] *Scientia* more strictly so-called is comprehension of the truth of things that are always in one way. Both the principles and the conclusions in mathematics are objects of *scientia* in this way . . . [4] *Scientia* most strictly so-called is comprehension of what exists immutably by means of the comprehension of that from which it has immutable being. This is by means of the comprehension of a cause that is immutable in its being and its causing. (*Commentarius* I.2, p. 99)

On Grosseteste's reliance in general on Themistius, see Rossi, "Robert Grosseteste and the Object of Scientific Knowledge."

Later versions of Grosseteste's fourfold distinction are legion; and they often cite Grosseteste ("the Bishop of Lincoln") as their source. See, e.g., Albert the Great (*Comm. Post. an.* I.2.1), Henry of Ghent (*Summa quaest. ord.* 1.1c), William Ockham (*Summa logicae* III-2.1), Buridan (*Summulae* 8.4.3–4), John Wyclif (*Tractatus de logica* ch. 13 [vol. 1: 177]), Paul of Venice (*Summa phil. nat.* I.1 and *Exp. Post. an.* I.2, quire b3r), and de Soto (*De demonstratione* q. 2, pp. 294–5).

In the seventeenth century, Gassendi indicates the breadth of ordinary usage when he invokes "the familiar and common manner of speech, by which we are said to know [*scire*] many things." In this sense, "experiences or appearances can be called *scientia*." As for the objection that an experience should be called opinion rather than *scientia*, he remarks that "we speak indifferently of opining or knowing [*opinari vel scire*], as even the custom of speech of the vulgar supports" (*Exercitationes paradoxicae* II.6.6, p. 499). This is similar to the broad usage of 'knowledge' that this lecture (p. 11) quotes Hobbes as later proposing: that knowledge "is nothing else but sense and memory" (*Lev.* 9.1; see also *Lev.* 5.17).

On Ideal Theory

Note 9 (p. 8). Recent epistemology, in its quest to map the lower end of Grosseteste's spectrum, has lost historical interest in describing the ideal. In calling for an idealized epistemology, then, I am calling for a return to what has been, historically, the dominant way of theorizing about knowledge. This is also a call to take seriously the normative aspect of epistemology: as not simply a special kind of linguistic–conceptual inquiry but, in its widest generality, an attempt to understand how we ought to function as cognitive beings. When epistemology is so conceived, it becomes natural to begin with ideal theory. The classic modern statement of the case for beginning here is found in John Rawls:

> Obviously, the problems of partial compliance theory are the pressing and urgent matters. These are the things that we are faced with in everyday life. The reason for beginning with ideal theory is that it provides, I believe, the only basis for the systematic grasp of these more pressing problems . . . At least, I shall assume that a deeper understanding can be gained in no other way, and that the nature and aims of a perfectly just society is the fundamental part of the theory of justice. (*Theory of Justice*, p. 9)

Descartes offers an earlier, even more ambitious formulation when he identifies "morals" as one of the principal parts of philosophy and then remarks that "by 'morals' I understand the highest and most perfect moral system, which presupposes a complete knowledge of the other sciences and is the ultimate level of wisdom" (IXB: 14).

For an interesting recent discussion of utilitarianism as specifying an ideal, see Alastair Norcross, "Reasons without Demands." He argues that a proper formulation of the theory tells us what the ideally right action is (maximizing goodness) and how to rank the alternatives, but remains silent on the question of where the boundary is between right and wrong. There is no such boundary, on Norcross's view, only a scale of goodness.

In associating my proposal with ideal theory in the political domain, I expose it to the sorts of criticisms that are raised against that way of proceeding. Ralph Wedgwood, for instance, has argued against ideal theory on the grounds that it invites a confusion between questions about what is normative and questions about what is possible. On his view, "the fundamental normative and evaluative questions are not about what is ideal, but about what is better and what is worse" ("Against Ideal Theory," §4). A different sort of criticism has been voiced by Charles Mills. Citing Rawls, he goes on to comment:

What was originally supposed to have been merely a tool has become an end in itself; the presumed antechamber to the real hall of debate is now its main site. Effectively, then, within the geography of the normative, ideal theory functions as a form of white flight. You don't want to deal with the problems of race and the legacy of white supremacy, so, metaphorically, within the discourse of justice, you retreat from any spaces worryingly close to the inner cities and move instead to the safe and comfortable white spaces, the gated moral communities, of the segregated suburbs, from which they become normatively invisible.

("Lost in Rawlsland")

As Mills elsewhere puts it, "ideal theory can only serve the interest of the privileged" ("Ideal Theory," p. 172).

This last sort of objection can be somewhat eased, I hope, by stressing the way an idealized epistemology has to be calibrated to the world we actually live in, which in turn opens the door to attending to the many nonideal aspects of the human epistemic predicament. But, rather than engage with these concerns directly, let me just note that there is one politically charged dimension on which ideal theory in the specifically epistemic domain might in fact be better suited to serve the interests of someone other than the privileged. For in setting aside ideal theory, modern epistemology has focused instead on normal theory and on the minimal conditions necessary for someone to count as a knower. This, if we follow the argument of Lennard Davis ("Constructing Normalcy"), corresponds to a general societal preoccupation, from the nineteenth-century on, with what counts as "normal" in society, a preoccupation that replaces an earlier cultural focus on the ideal. A society that fixates on the normal, however, is one where disability becomes especially marked with disapproval. In contrast, Davis argues, a culture focused on the ideal rather than the normal has much less reason to distinguish certain individuals as deficient. In such a culture we are all more or less deficient, inasmuch as no one attains the ideal. Hence, in the cognitive domain, ideal theory has at least some prospects of escaping the sorts of "gated communities" and "segregated suburbs" that Mills decries. (The start of Lecture Three, however, discusses why normal conditions have a particular grip on our theorizing in the case of sense perception.)

Calibrating the Ideal

Note 10 (p. 10). If epistemology is in danger of walling itself off from issues that matter, the danger lies not in idealization, but rather in its obsessive attention to linguistic usage. Hence, although questions about what we ought to do are as meaningful as any other we may ask, and although such questions are closely linked with questions about what we know, it is not terribly useful to debate over whether only what we "know" should count as a reason for action (see John Hawthorne and Jason Stanley, "Knowledge and Action"). Our fragile linguistic habits will simply not bear that sort of weight. (Similarly for the claim that one should assert only what one "knows," although the well-known defense of this thesis in Timothy Williamson, *Knowledge and Its Limits* ch. 11 is a special case, because it is grounded in Williamson's idiosyncratic understanding of *knowledge* as conceptually basic.)

This lecture suggests that substantive, real-world questions about what we ought to believe (and assert) can be engaged through reflection on the epistemic ideal, once that ideal has been calibrated to beings like us, in a world such as this one. The example given in this lecture (p. 9) is of how the scientific revolution (allegedly) led to more rigorous epistemic standards in domains outside natural science. W. K. Clifford's famous essay "The Ethics of Belief" is in effect a call for applying such standards in a more thoroughgoing and rigorous manner. The opposite sort of case—an argument for lower standards—can be found in authors like Montaigne and Bayle, for whom skepticism leads not to suspension of belief but to a recalibration of our normative epistemic ideal, opening up room for Christian faith (see Lecture Six, p. 129 and note 9 there). A somewhat similar modern example is William Alston. His book *Perceiving God* argues at length for the unattainability of noncircular arguments for the reliability of sense perception. Alston's conclusion is that, rather than give up on the possibility of perceptual knowledge, we should relax our epistemic demands. Once we do that, he thinks that even many forms of mystical religious experience will count as sources of knowledge.

Yet another historical example of recalibration appears in John Wyclif, back in the later fourteenth century. It is often the case, Wyclif argues, that ordinary folk have *scientia* where philosophers do not, because philosophers fail to have the requisite confidence:

For some seek a middle premise that is infallibly conclusive and known *per se* in such matters, to the extent that they doubt, whatever substance or sensible thing is pointed out, whether it now exists, and so whether they are asleep or awake. And in short [they doubt] every sensible since, as they say, any given appearance could be created even while it is an illusion. Ordinary folk, however, do not seek any such middle premise, but instead they adhere without fear and without worrying about a premise, and so they know [*sciunt*] well enough. For otherwise such matters are not now knowable by us.   (*Tractatus de logica* ch. 13 [vol. 1: 179–80])

The key move comes at the very end. If one holds out for an "infallibly conclusive" middle premise, "known *per se*," which will get us from appearances to reality, then one will never have *scientia*, because such an argument is not within our grasp. One could, then, land in skepticism and conclude that *scientia* regarding the external world is impossible. But Wyclif here takes for granted that this is the wrong conclusion to draw. *Scientia* describes an ideal, but it is an ideal calibrated against what is possible for us in a world such as this one. So, if the philosophers are seeking something that is unachievable, then the trouble lies with them and not with *scientia*. We should, then, attend to the example of ordinary folk.

The Breakdown of Aristotelian Essentialism

The History of 'Knowledge'

Note 11 (p. 11). Historians of philosophy have ignored the various English translations of Boethius's *Consolation of Philosophy*. Given that text's prominence, however, and its interest in questions of knowledge (especially foreknowledge), it is a particularly useful source of information about how epistemic terms changed over time. The Old English translation (*c*.880–950), traditionally (but probably falsely) ascribed to King Alfred, consistently uses the verb 'witen' for verbs of knowing, e.g.: "þu sægst þæt God <u>wite</u> ælc þing ær hit geweorðe" ("you say that God <u>knows</u> everything before it happens": prose 32 par. 1, no exact correspondence in Boethius).

Given that 'witen' has, among its core meanings, 'certain knowledge' and 'understanding,' it makes for an excellent word for talking about the epistemic ideal—but, alas, it has disappeared from modern usage and I will not try to revive it, tempting as that is.

In Geoffrey Chaucer's translation (c.1380), *scientia* is generally rendered as 'science,' for example: "yif þat any wy3t wene a þing to ben oþer weyes þan it is, it nys nat oonly <u>vnscience</u>, but it is deceiuable oppinioun ful diuerse and fer fro þe soþe of <u>science</u>" (*si quid aliquis aliorsum atque sese res habet, existimet, id non modo <u>scientia</u> non est, sed est opinio fallax ab <u>scientiae</u> ueritate longe diuersa*; Bk. V prose 3, p. 156). Compare John Lydgate (1430s), discussing the appointment of judges: "Thei ouhte . . . To have <u>science</u> off philosophie, And <u>knowe</u> ther textis off canoun & cyvyle" (*Fall of Princes* Bk. III, p. 416). This usage of 'science,' as roughly equivalent to 'knowledge' in the modern sense, endures into the seventeenth century. A 1697 English translation of Franco Burgersdijk's logic, for instance, renders the different grades of *scientia* like this: "The word science is either taken largely to signify any cognition or true assent; or strictly, a firm and infallible one; or lastly, an assent of propositions made known by the cause or effect" (*Monitio logica* II.20).

By the time of Queen Elizabeth's 1593 rendering of Boethius, *scientia* is generally translated as 'knowledge.' Here is how she renders the previous passage: "yf any man think awry of that that is, not only that is not a <u>knoledge</u>, but is a false opinion, furr diffrent from the trouth of <u>knowledge</u>" (lines 43–45). But sometimes Elizabeth switches between 'knowledge' and 'science' as a rendering of *scientia*, for example: "Wherefore if thou woldest way his <u>fore-knoledge</u> by which he all understandith, thou woltst Iudge that he hath not <u>aforeknowledge</u> of thinges to come, alone, but rightlyer a <u>science</u> of neverworn contynuance" (*Itaque si <u>praeui-dentiam</u> pensare uelis qua cuncta dinoscit, non esse <u>praescientiam</u> quasi futuri sed <u>scientiam</u> numquam deficientis instantiae rectius aestimabis*; Bk. V prose 6, lines 55–9). Compare Thomas Starkey, a chaplain to Henry VIII, who in a letter from 1534 describes his education as follows: "Fyrst, here in oxforth a grete parte of my youthe I occupyd my selfe in the study of philosophy, joynyng therto the <u>knolege</u> of both tongys bothe latyn & greke, and so aftur passyd ouer in to Italy, whereas I so delytyd in the contemplacyon of natural <u>knolege</u>" (Herrtage, *England in Reign of Henry the Eighth*, p. x). Here at the end 'knowledge' is used where one would expect 'science.'

Another early English epistemic verb is 'kennen,' but this seems less well suited to describe the epistemic ideal of *scientia*. Its usage, instead, seems rather like our modern use of 'to know.' But 'kennen,' for whatever reason, lacked a corresponding noun in common usage, just as 'science' lacked a corresponding verb. It was presumably a competitive advantage of 'know' that it was in wide currency in both nominal and verbal form.

Yet another early English epistemic term is 'cunning,' which seems to serve in early English as a generic cognitive category. Thus Reginald Pecock, circa 1454, speaks collectively of the "six intellectual, knowal, or kunnyngal vertues" (*Folewer to the Donet*, p. 63). Surprisingly, however, as this passage suggests, Pecock treats 'knowledge' as a similarly broad term. Thus the six intellectual virtues he describes—"intellect, science, prudence, craft, opynyoun, and feiþ"—are all kinds both of 'kunnyng' and of 'knowyng,' for example: "opynyoun is a <u>knowyng</u> wherbi we <u>knowen</u> not certeynli and vndoutabili, but oonli likli." (p. 64). It is "science," on Pecock's usage, that is known certainly and indubitably. This is close to the opposite of how Hume would come to use these terms three centuries later (see this lecture, p. 18).

For detailed information about the early history of all these words, see Kurath and Kuhn, *Middle English Dictionary*, in many volumes (and freely available online), which expands considerably upon the more limited information in the *Oxford English Dictionary*.

These lexical issues remained unsettled for some time. In his *Traité philosophique de la foiblesse de l'esprit humain* (c.1690), Pierre-Daniel Huet considers whether his skeptical views have the consequence of "extinguishing the light of science" (start of III.10). The French word here is just *science*. So how should this be translated into English? One anonymous early eighteenth-century translator renders it as 'knowledge,' whereas Edward Combe, from the same period, sometimes translates it directly as 'science' and other times as 'knowledge.' Moreover, Huet himself sometimes speaks not of *science* and *savoir*, but of *connaissance*, and both English translations regularly translate this as 'knowledge'; nor is it clear that Huet uses these French terms in substantially different ways. Huet himself flags the fact that *savoir* is "equivocal" between the ideal sense, where one finds "full evidentness and perfect certainty," and the ordinary case of "knowing with probability" (III.10, trans. anon., pp. 188–9). For further information on Huet's skepticism, see Lecture Six, note 8.

One might say, indeed, that these lexical issues still remain unsettled. For, even if 'knowledge' and 'science' eventually go in different directions in English, the result is that we now simply lack a word for talking about the epistemic ideal. Hence there is no real alternative to leaving *scientia* untranslated throughout these lectures. It is not just that 'knowledge' is equivocal or imprecise, but that 'knowledge' today can hardly even bear the weight of the epistemic ideal described by *scientia*. This is so despite the best efforts of some philosophers to train us to think of 'knowledge' as describing a remote, unattainable ideal: see, in particular, Peter Unger, *Ignorance* and, more recently, Laurence BonJour, "The Myth of Knowledge."

Hobbes's Various Epistemic Positions

Note 12 (p. 12). Hobbes is an interesting, early case in the development of a standard modern epistemic vocabulary. Much of what he says arises quite predictably from earlier usage. Thus he distinguishes between a broad and a strict sense of 'knowledge,' and he associates the strict sense with 'science.' But it is difficult to get clear on the precise nature of his views, because he seems to offer at least three not easily reconcilable accounts of knowledge and science: one in his *Elements of Law* (1640), a second in the *De corpore* (mid-1640s), and a third in the *Leviathan* (1651). The first of these divides knowledge into two kinds, but seemingly in quite a different way from the later works:

> By this we may understand there be two sorts of knowledge, whereof the one is nothing else but sense, or knowledge original . . . and remembrance of the same; the other is called science or knowledge of the truth of propositions, and how things are called, and is derived from understanding. Both of these sorts are but experience; the former being the experience of the effects of things that work upon us from without; and the latter the experience men have of the proper use of names in language.   (*Elements of Law* I.6.1)

Compare this to how the terms are set out in the *Leviathan*:

> There are of KNOWLEDGE two kinds; whereof one is knowledge of fact: the other knowledge of the consequence of one affirmation to another. The former is nothing else but sense and memory, and is absolute knowledge; as when we see a fact doing, or remember it done: and this is the knowledge required in a witness. The latter is called science; and is conditional; as when we know that, if the figure shown be a circle, then any straight line through the center shall divide it into two equal parts. And this is the knowledge required in a philosopher; that is to say, of him that pretends to reasoning.   (*Lev.* 9.1)

In effect, the *Leviathan* elevates science from a knowledge of the meaning of words to a knowledge of the connection between words. And neither of these seems to impose the demanding Aristotelian expectation that we grasp the causes of things.

It seems clear, however, that at least the *Leviathan* needs to be understood in the light of the fuller story, insisting on causal understanding, that the *De corpore* makes explicit. This seems required by *Leviathan* 46.1, which, though it does not mention science, does define 'philosophy' as knowledge acquired through reasoning about the causes of things. And perhaps the

Elements of Law should be likewise tied to this stricter theory, in which case all three versions might be brought together as a single doctrine. But at any rate the causal requirement is clearly in place in Hobbes's later works. For in various places he makes it clear that his pessimism regarding the prospects of reaching scientific knowledge arises from our failure to understand causes. A particularly telling passage comes from a 1656 disputation with the geometers:

> The science of every subject is derived from a precognition of the causes, generation, and construction of the same; and consequently where the causes are known, there is place for demonstration; but not where the causes are to seek for. Geometry therefore is demonstrable, for the lines and figures from which we reason are drawn and described by ourselves; and civil philosophy is demonstrable because we make the commonwealth ourselves. But because of natural bodies we know not the construction, but seek it from the effects, there lies no demonstration of what the causes be we seek for, but only of what they may be.
>
> (*Six Lessons to the Professors of Mathematiques*, epistle, in *English Works* vol. 7: 184])

Here, flush with success from the *Leviathan*, Hobbes adds "civil philosophy" to geometry as subjects admitting of science. But natural science is still not possible, because in that domain we have no way of grasping ultimate causes.

An idiosyncratic feature of Hobbes's view, suggested in the passage just quoted, is that he thinks that the reason why science is possible in the cases of geometry and politics is that these are subjects we *construct* rather than discover in nature. The passage just quoted from *Six Lessons* is immediately prefixed by this remark: "Of arts, some are demonstrable, others indemonstrable; and demonstrable are those the construction of the subject whereof is in the power of the artist himself; who in his demonstration does no more but deduce the consequences of his own operation."

A further complication in working out Hobbes's views is that the *De corpore*, unlike the other two works, was written in Latin, and the anonymous 1656 translation that even specialists tend to treat as if it contained Hobbes's own words is not by Hobbes; nor is it philosophically careful. Here is how the translation renders the *De corpore* version of a distinction between two kinds of knowledge:

> But we are then said to <u>know</u> [*scire*] any effect, when we <u>know</u> [*cognoscimus*] that there be causes of the same, and in what subject those causes are, and in what subject they produce that effect, and in what manner they work the same. And this is the <u>science</u> [*scientia*] of causes, . . . All other <u>science</u> [*cognitio*] . . . is either perception by sense, or the imagination, or memory remaining after such perception.   (*De corpore* 6.1, in *English Works* vol. 1: 66])

I have supplied the original Latin in parentheses, so that the translator's carelessness becomes evident. The first two sentences are discussing *scientia*, which in English Hobbes calls 'science,' but the translator first uses 'know' and then 'science' to render the word. Then, even worse, he uses 'science' to render *cognitio*, after having previously used 'know' to render that word, even though in this final sentence Hobbes has plainly switched over to talking about the kind of knowledge that does not rise to the level of science.

For further discussion of Hobbes's overall view, see Douglas Jesseph, "*Scientia* in Hobbes" and "Hobbes and the Method of Natural Science," which opens with the remark that "Hobbes's philosophy of natural science is dominated by the idea that all true knowledge must arise from an understanding of causes" (p. 86). For Hobbes and geometry, see Jesseph, *Squaring the Circle*.

Locke's Pessimism regarding the Ideal

Note 13 (p. 13). Locke expresses his skepticism regarding our prospects of attaining science so often, in so many places, and so eloquently that is difficult to forebear from quoting him at considerable length. Here, for instance, is a passage from *Some Thoughts concerning Education* (1693):

Natural Philosophy, as a speculative science, I imagine we have none, and perhaps, I may think I have reason to say, we never shall be able to make a science of it. The works of nature are contrived by a wisdom, and operate by ways too far surpassing our faculties to discover, or capacities to conceive, for us ever to be able to reduce them into a science.   (§190)

Locke goes on to suggest, as a strategy for working around this deficiency, that children be given Bible readers that should teach them the fundamentals of what revelation reveals, especially with regard to the world of spirits.

It is important, in these remarks from Locke, to separate out the epistemic and the lexical aspects. As an epistemic matter, there is something that Locke is saying we cannot do: we cannot grasp the real nature of the world around us. As a lexical matter, he wants to reserve both 'knowledge' and 'science,' in the natural domain, for this lofty achievement. Yet at the same time, as the example of Newton shows, there is much that we can do in studying nature, and this is worthy of celebrating, even if it is far from ideal. But it is easy to lose sight of that positive side of what Locke is saying, because he has reserved the words we care about ('science' and 'knowledge') for making only the negative point. Here, for instance, is a passage where he contrasts the negative and the positive message:

We are able, I imagine, to reach very little general knowledge concerning the species of bodies and their several properties. Experiments and historical observations we may have, from which we may draw advantages of ease and health, and thereby increase our stock of conveniences for this life; but beyond this I fear our talents reach not, nor are our faculties, as I guess, able to advance.   (*Essay* IV.12.10)

So is Locke a skeptic? Better to eschew that word entirely and say that he retains a traditional conception of the epistemic ideal, yet is extremely pessimistic about our ability to achieve it.

Such pessimism is not a complete departure from mainstream scholastic views. Roger Bacon, for instance, had remarked back in the thirteenth century that "no one is so wise regarding the natural world as to know with certainty all the truths that concern the nature and properties of a single fly, or to know the proper causes of its color and why it has so many feet, neither more nor less" (*Opus maius* I.10). Aquinas, at around the same time, says almost exactly the same thing: "our cognition is so weak that no philosopher could have ever completely investigated the nature of a single fly" (*In symbolum Apostolorum* prol., in *Opusc. theol.* II, n. 864). For a discussion of Aquinas's views, see Reynolds, "Properties, Causality, and Epistemic Optimism." In the next century, Ockham would express great skepticism regarding our ability to distinguish differences in species (*Quodlibet* III.6), as would Francis of Marchia (*Reportatio* I.3.1), among many others. In the early sixteenth century, Gianfrancesco Pico's attack on scholasticism takes for granted that *scientia* must grasp the essences of things, but he argues at considerable length that Aristotle gives us no method for doing so (*Examen vanitatis* V.7–13). For the general skepticism across the centuries with respect to our grasp of essences, see Pasnau, *Metaphysical Themes* §27.2; for a more extensive discussion of Locke's views regarding essences and of the basis for his pessimism, see §27.7.

Locke's pessimism regarding knowledge, it should be stressed, does not extend every-where. So, although "in the greatest part of our concernment, he [God] has afforded us only the twilight . . . of *Probability*," still God "has given us some certain knowledge, though limited to a few things in comparison" (*Essay* IV.14.1). So what are the limits? According to his canonical formulation, knowledge is "nothing but the perception of the connexion and agreement, or disagreement and repugnancy of any of our ideas. In this alone it consists" (IV.1.2). This should be read not as a definition (which would advert to certainty and evidentness; see Lecture Two, note 22) but rather as an attempt to fix the extension of the concept, the first 13 chapters of Book IV being subsequently devoted to fleshing out the details. Paradigmatically, knowledge extends to our grasp of our own ideas and of their similarity and dissimilarity and to the conceptual connections between them. This gets mathematics into the domain of knowledge. Surprisingly, it also allows it in ethics, because "morality is capable of demonstration as well as mathematics" (*Essay* III.11.16), on the basis of "self-evident propositions, by necessary consequences, as incontestable as those in mathematics" (IV.3.18). Hence, although natural science is not possible for us, moral science is: "morality is the proper science and business of mankind in general" (IV.12.11). See also *Conduct of the Understanding* §43, where the Golden Rule is described as a foundational truth on a par with Newton's law of universal gravitation. (On the status of morality in Locke, see Richard Ashcraft, "Faith and Knowledge in Locke's Philosophy" and Steven Forde, *Locke, Science, and Politics*.) Finally and most notoriously, Locke thinks that we can have knowledge of the existence of God and of an external material world (on which see Lecture Two, p. 41).

Causal Understanding

Note 14 (p. 13). In insisting that causal understanding is a key part of the epistemic ideal, Hobbes and Locke align themselves with a tradition that goes back to antiquity. Many aspects of this tradition have been documented in detail by William Wallace, in his two-volume *Causality and Scientific Explanation*. Here I offer my own *précis*.

In the *Gorgias*, Plato's Socrates had attacked rhetoric for being "unable to state the explanation (αἰτίαν) of each thing" (465a). Accordingly, he holds that it fails to count even as a τέχνη, let alone as an ἐπιστήμη—for which, among other things, a higher degree of precision would be required (see note 18 here). In Aristotle, the causal requirement is not just one among various features of the *Posterior Analytics'* conception of ἐπιστήμη; it is the central, organizing demand. The very reason why ἐπιστήμη requires a grasp of the essences of things is this causal requirement. And the requirement appears not just in the *Posterior Analytics* but in the most prominent other places. This lecture (p. 15) quotes the opening words of the *Physics*; and the idea likewise appears in the first chapter of the *Metaphysics* (981^{a}27), then again at II.2, 994^{b}30, and at *Historia animalium* I.6, 491^{a}11. Michael Ferejohn writes that "the central insight that drives the entire project of Aristotle's *Analytics* is the Platonic idea, briefly floated in *Meno* 98A, that what distinguishes knowledge from other types of true belief is that it is somehow 'tied down' by the possession of an explanatory account" (*Formal Causes*, p. 66).

This same insistence on grasping causes also appears right at the head of the Arabic tradition, in al-Kindī, who writes at the start of *On First Philosophy* that "knowledge [علم] of the cause is more noble than knowledge of the effect. For we know each of the effects completely only when we comprehend the knowledge of its cause" (*Philosophical Works*, p. 10). Later appeals to this requirement appear passim in the Arabic tradition—on this see Jon McGinnis, "Scientific Methodologies."

Indications of the causal requirement among Latin scholastic authors are everywhere. One forceful statement comes in the prologue to Buridan's questions on the *Posterior Analytics*: "it is plain that it is through knowledge of the cause or causes, and not otherwise, that certain, perfect *scientia*, excluding all ignorance, is acquired and maintained." In the early fifteenth century, Paul of Venice offers a particularly full account of the varieties of causal knowledge and why it is required (*Expositio in Posteriorum Aristotelis* re. I.2, quire b3r-v). In the early sixteenth century, de Soto writes that, "since to know [*scire*] is to cognize perfectly the truth of a thing, one can know a thing only if one cognizes its cause that are the causes of its truth" (*De demonstratione* q. 2, p. 295D).

The story is no different for preeminent early figures in the new science. William Harvey is quite explicit about his commitment to the *Posterior Analytics* framework (see Wallace, *Causality and Scientific Explanation* vol. 1: 184–93). Francis Bacon writes that "it is from ignorance of causes that works fail" (*Novum organum*, p. 45 [plan of work]; see also *Novum organum* I.3 and *Phaenomena universi*, in *Philosophical Studies*, p. 5). And even in astronomy, as this discipline started to come into its own in the late sixteenth and early seventeenth century, the causal requirement endures. Indeed, Kepler entitles his most important work *The New Astronomy Based upon Causes*. (For more on Kepler, see Edwin Burtt, *Metaphysical Foundations*, p. 64 and Wallace, *Causality and Scientific Explanation* vol. 1: 168–76. For sixteenth-century astronomy more generally, see Barker and Goldstein, "Realism and Instrumentalism.")

Throughout the first half of the seventeenth century such remarks remain entirely uncontroversial. Daniel Sennert, in 1636, mirrors the start of Aristotle's *Physics* when he writes: "Since to know [*scire*] is to cognize a thing by its cause, we must work with all our might in physics to grasp the true and proper causes of the operations and effects that occur in the natural world" (*Hypomnemata physica* II.1, p. 43 = *Thirteen Books*, p. 430). Kenelm Digby, in 1644, writes that "it belongs only unto a philosopher to examine the causes of things. Others are content with the effects" (*Two Treatises* I.6.2, p. 40).

Earlier on, in note 6, Descartes was quoted describing the goal of philosophy as "a perfect knowledge [*parfaite connaissance*] of all things that mankind is capable of knowing [*savoir*]." He says this so as to be able to stress that the epistemic ideal involves a grasp of causes: "In order for this kind of knowledge [*connaissance*] to be perfect it must be deduced from first causes; thus, in order to set about acquiring it . . . we must start with the search for first causes or principles" (*Principles*, preface to French edn., IXB: 2). This lecture (p. 13) reports his criticism of Galileo in this regard—a complaint repeated in a subsequent letter to Mersenne (II: 433), on which see William Shea, "Descartes as a Critic of Galileo." On Hobbes's traditional insistence that science must grasp the causes of things, see Jesseph, "Hobbesian Mechanics," esp. pp. 120–9 and 143–4, and Daniel Garber, "Natural Philosophy," pp. 117–18. For Hobbes's later criticisms of the Royal Society on account of its willingness to set aside causal explanation, see Steven Shapin and Simon Schaffer, *Leviathan and the Air-Pump*, pp. 19–20, 306.

Moving into the later seventeenth century, Arnauld and Nicole still take it for granted that knowledge is knowledge of causes. They mock, for instance, those who invoke powers and thereby pretend to have causal knowledge (*Port-Royal Logic* III.19, trans. p. 193). And they criticize geometers for their failure to give proofs that explain why a conclusion holds: "in order to have perfect knowledge [*une parfaite science*] of some truth, it is not enough to be convinced that it is true if we do not also penetrate into the reasons, taken from the nature of the thing itself, for why it is true" (IV.9, trans. p. 254). Similarly, arguments that work by reductio ad absurdum "can convince the mind but do not enlighten it at all, which ought to be the principal fruit of knowledge [*science*]. For the mind is not at all satisfied unless it knows [*sait*] not only that something is, but why it is" (trans. p. 255).

Isaac Barrow, lecturing on mathematics in Cambridge in the 1660s, writes that "it is the aim of all *scientiae* to investigate the principal properties, affections, and passions of their object, together with its essence, as they flow from it either immediately or mediately, and to show that they necessarily agree with it by an evident and certain discourse . . . Such a discourse is customarily called an ἀπόδειξις [demonstration]" (*Usefulness of Mathematical Learning*, lecture 4, trans. p. 52). Glanvill, at around the same time, declares:

we cannot properly and perfectly know anything in nature without the knowledge of its first causes, and the springs of natural motions: and who has any pretense to this? Who can say he has seen nature in its *beginnings*? We know nothing but effects, nor can we judge at their immediate causes, but by proportion to the things that do appear, which no doubt are very unlike the rudiments of nature. (*Essays*, pp. 15–16)

Note 15 (p. 14). Wallace concludes that "the early modern period, for all the protestations of reaction against late scholastic and Renaissance methods, was dominated by the same search for causes and thus was in recognizable methodological continuity with the medieval period" (*Causality and Scientific Explanation* vol. 1: 22–3). Edward Grant, "Late Medieval Thought," goes farther: he argues that both Copernicus and Newton were *more* focused on grasping true causes than many later medieval authors, who were content to proceed hypothetically.

I myself would say that, while the ideal of causal explanation remains constant throughout these centuries, the method of achieving it changes markedly. Inasmuch as a grasp of the true causes of things is an obvious and indisputable epistemic ideal, it should be no surprise to find philosophers and sciences across the ages aspiring to such a thing, in one way or another. Yet there is a model of explanation, distinctive of scholastic Aristotelianism, that we can see slowly give way over the course of the seventeenth century; and this model is related to the method of grounding one's explanation in the inner qualities of a things, which are in turn grounded in the thing's essence. Aristotle provides the broad license for this approach, for example at *Metaphysics* XIII.4, 1078^{b}24: "the essence is the starting-point of deductions." On this framework, and its origins in Socrates and Plato, see Ferejohn, *Formal Causes*. For the shift in focus that occurs in post-scholasticism, see Ian Hacking: "the old causes got at the essence of things. The new causes were efficient causes, explaining how things were made to work" (*Emergence of Probability*, p. 37). So it is, one might add, that our modern notion of cause came to be solely that of Aristotle's efficient cause.

Both Gassendi and Locke hold on to something like the scholastic model, as a condition on the epistemic ideal; but each has grave doubts about our ability to grasp the essences of things, doubts that render the scholastic project untenable *ab initio* for both. For Gassendi, the way forward is Epicurean atomism (see the next note). For Locke, it is not clear whether there is a way forward to natural knowledge and science, and so he contents himself with the role of "underlabourer" (*Essay*, epistle, p. 10). Going into print less than three years after Newton's *Principia*, Locke was hardly in a position to see how epistemic methodologies were about to be transformed, making the ideal of science once again look within reach.

The start of Roger Cotes's preface to the second (1713) edition of the *Principia* distils exactly the point where scholastic philosophy had seemed most deeply flawed:

There have been those who have endowed the individual species of things with specific and occult qualities; on which, in a manner unknown, they make the operations of the individual bodies depend. The whole [*summa*] of scholastic doctrine derived from Aristotle and the Peripatetics is based on this: for they affirm that the individual effects of bodies arise from the individual natures of those bodies, but whence those natures arise they don't teach us; and therefore they teach us nothing. And being entirely concerned with the names of things, and not with the things themselves, they must be regarded as having invented a philosophical way of talking, but not as having imparted any philosophy.   (Cotes in Newton, *Principia*, trans. p. 385)

Inner qualities and essences: this is just where Descartes had found fault with scholastic philosophy, seventy-five years earlier: "compare my assumptions with the assumptions of others. Compare all their *real qualities*, their *substantial forms*, their *elements* and countless other such things with my single assumption that all bodies are composed of parts" (to Morin in 1638 [II: 200]). But Descartes, in this regard, is not trying to do anything different from the scholastics: he simply wants to substitute one set of principles with another that reaches the same level of explanation. For the fundamental shift in epistemic expectations that gives rise to the new science, we have to look elsewhere.

Trading Depth for Precision

Relinquishing Causal Understanding

Note 16 (p. 15). There is no doubt that the first great challenger of the causal expectation is Galileo Galilei. But the details are contentious. The standard view, for most of the twentieth century, was that Galileo unequivocally rejected the traditional causal demand in favor of a mathematical account of the laws that nature follows. The trajectory that culminates in Galileo is described by A. C. Crombie as follows: "The metaphysical question about *why* things happen, which was answered in terms of substance and causes, in terms of *quod quid est*, gradually gave place to the scientific question about *how* things happen, which was answered simply by a correlation of the facts by any means, logical or mathematical, that was convenient" (*Robert Grosseteste*, p. 11).

There is a substantial textual basis for this straightforward reading. The passages quoted in this lecture might suggest as much, as do various remarks in Galileo's *Dialogue concerning the Two Chief World Systems* (1632). Here he has the Aristotelian Simplicio extol the importance of the question of what motion in general is, "leaving to mechanics and other low artisans the investigation of the ratios of such accelerations and other more detailed features." To this, Galileo has Sagredo simply shift the focus to the question he cares about by asking Salviati whether "you, descending sometimes from the throne of His Peripatetic Majesty, have ever toyed with the investigation of these ratios of acceleration in the motion of falling bodies?" (second day, trans. p. 190; *Opere* vol. 7: 190). For statements of this standard reading of Galileo, see Stillman Drake, "Galileo's New Science of Motion"; Maurice Clavelin, *Natural Philosophy of Galileo* ch. 8; and Peter Machamer, "Galileo and the Causes."

The standard reading can easily go too far, however, as when Drake remarks that Galileo's work, even if not an explicit attack on causal explanation, "at least implied that everything of lasting value in physics could be presented in the form of precise laws, experimentally confirmed" ("Galileo's New Science of Motion," pp. 153–4). This is clearly not Galileo's view. Causal understanding is of enormous value, when it can be had, and it is part of the epistemic ideal, when that ideal is unconstrained by the reality of our circumstances. Recent scholarship has shown that, early in his career, Galileo was thoroughly engaged in the traditional Aristotelian conception of *scientia*—see, in particular, the early material translated in *Galileo's Logical Treatises*, along with the accompanying discussion by Wallace. And it cannot be denied that, even in his mature work, Galileo at times claims to have arrived at causal knowledge. In the *Discourse on Bodies in Water* (1612), for instance, he writes: "I conceive, I have by this time sufficiently declared and opened the way to the contemplation of the true, intrinsic, and proper causes of diverse motions, and of the rest of many solid bodies in diverse media and particularly in water" (trans. p. 18). The third letter on sunspots criticizes "not a few Peripatetics on this side of the Alps who go about philosophizing without any desire to learn the truth and the causes of things" (*Discoveries*, p. 140). And, near the start of the fourth day of the *Dialogue*, he remarks that "before all else it is necessary to have a knowledge of the effects whose causes we are seeking" (trans. p. 484; *Opere* vol. 8: 443). He then goes on to promise this:

> Still, from those accounts which we are sure of, and which happen to cover the principal events, it seems to me possible to arrive at the true and primary causes. I do not presume to be able to adduce all the proper and sufficient causes of those effects which are new to me and which consequently I have had no chance to think about. What I am about to say, I propose merely as a key to open portals to a road never before trodden by anyone, in a firm hope that minds more acute than mine will broaden this road and penetrate further along it than I have done in my first revealing of it.   (*Dialogue*, trans. p. 485)

Here, then, Galileo thinks there is hope for causal explanation, and hope down the road of doing even better than he has done. Passages of this sort can be marshaled against every passage where Galileo relinquishes the prospect of causal understanding. What this shows is that Galileo has no principled metaphysical or methodological objection to causal explanation, when available. *Of course* such explanations are desirable, and sometimes they can be had. But what is critically new in Galileo's approach is the rejection of the assumption that all knowledge, if it is to count as worthy of the label 'scientific,' must reach such heights.

The case for reading Galileo's later work as still committed to causal explanation is made in Wallace, "The Problem of Causality in Galileo's Science," and, still more persuasively, in

Ernan McMullin, "The Conception of Science in Galileo's Work." In part, Galileo can hold on to the causal expectation because he thinks that his mathematical accounts can serve as causal explanations (see Joseph Pitt, "Galileo: Causation," esp. pp. 192–3). But it is not as if everything stays the same, with mathematics substituted for hylomorphism. (Compare Burtt's remark on Kepler: "This notion of causality is substantially the Aristotelian formal cause reinterpreted in terms of exact mathematics," *Metaphysical Foundations*, p. 64.) So what, then, has changed? According to McMullin, "there is every reason to suppose that Galileo simply took for granted that science has, in fact, the logical structure Aristotle supposed it to have. Were this not to have been the case, he would assuredly have given us more clues than he did about a new and different conception of science" ("The Conception of Science," p. 218). But this is misleading, if "logical structure" is meant to suggest that the relevant issues involve logic or metaphysics. At issue instead is the ideal goal of inquiry. As far as the absolute ideal goes, Galileo is perfectly traditional in supposing that we ultimately seek a grasp of the reason why. He departs from tradition in giving a larger role to mathematics, but he departs as well in offering a reappraisal of what is possible. This leads him to think that a modest conception of the ideal, stripped of its causal pretensions, still describes a kind of knowledge worth celebrating.

Why this reappraisal? Because Galileo is watching Aristotelian natural science crumble around him, and so he cannot hold onto the optimistic scholastic expectation that our inquiry into nature will get us down to the bottom of things, all the way to first principles and elemental causes. It was by now a familiar criticism of Aristotelian *scientia* that, if it really is going to insist on a grasp of causes, then such explanations would have to go down impossibly far, to the very foundations of things (see Lecture Two, note 7). For all the delight he took in his empirical and mathematical discoveries, Galileo found such pretensions absurd: "It always seems to me extreme rashness on the part of some when they want to make human abilities the measure of what nature can do. On the contrary, there is not a single effect in nature, even the least that exists, such that the most ingenious theorists can arrive at a complete understanding of it" (*Dialogue*, first day, trans. p. 116; *Opere* vol. 7: 126–7). Such complete understanding is possible for God, but not for us (see Lecture Two, p. 30), and so we have to adjust our normative expectations accordingly. It is in this spirit that *The Assayer* had extoled "I do not know" as an honest reply, in contrast to the duplicity of invoking occult phenomena (*Discoveries* p. 241; *Opere* vol. 6: 244).

If this is right about Galileo, then it puts us in a better position to look for other early examples of a turning away from the causal expectation. Hacking's *Emergence of Probability* concludes with a sketch of how knowledge and *scientia* get transformed in the post-scholastic era (pp. 179–85). On his story, the decisive event is the metaphysical challenge to causality, as it appears in Malebranche and Berkeley and culminates in Hume. Yet, as brilliant as Hacking's discussion is, it seems to me to misidentify the fundamental issue. The normative expectation of reaching causes is compatible with all manner of unorthodox theories about what causation is. Hence, as Hacking himself says, it is Leibniz who mounts "one of the last desperate defenses of the old category of knowledge" (p. 185)—despite Leibniz's thoroughly idiosyncratic views about causation. The issues here are not metaphysical, but epistemic, and concern the degree to which authors are sufficiently optimistic to suppose that causal explanations should be part of the normative ideal.

Accordingly, there is some plausibility in Richard Westfall's finding in Gassendi "a redefinition of science. Nature is not completely transparent to human reason; man can know her only externally, as phenomena. It follows that the only science possible to man is the description of phenomena, a new ideal of science which found its earliest statement in Gassendi's logical writings" (*Construction of Modern Science*, p. 40). Gassendi is a reasonable contender because, even though he has perfectly orthodox views about causation, he does have very pronounced doubts about our ability to grasp the essences of things (see Antonia

LoLordo, *Pierre Gassendi*, pp. 213–17, and my *Metaphysical Themes*, pp. 116, 636, 652–3). Still, Gassendi's doubts are not really all that different in kind from the perennial doubts of philosophers that stretch back into the early scholastic era (see note 15 to this lecture). For, despite Gassendi's pessimism (on which see also Lecture Six, note 8), and despite his commitment to an atomistic version of the mechanical philosophy, he nevertheless holds on to the traditional Aristotelian epistemic ideal, beginning the long treatment of physics in his *Syntagma* with the traditional invocation of the need to grasp the causes of things:

> So it seems that Physics can be defined as the contemplative *scientia* of the nature of things, inasmuch as, through it, we explore the composition of all things, as well as each thing specifically, inquiring, as much as is permitted, whether and from what principles they arise, whether and from what causes they are produced, whether and for what end they are made, whether and with what powers and properties they are endowed.
>
> (*Syntagma* pt. II proem, in *Opera* vol. 1: 125b)

This is entirely conventional, as a statement of the epistemic ideal, and nothing suggests that Gassendi's pessimism leads him to recalibrate these normative expectations. For the causal requirement in particular, see Gassendi's extended treatment at *Syntagma* II.1.4.1 (*Opera* vol. 1: 283 ff.).

A more straightforward example of the causal expectation coming under question in France can be found in Mersenne, who concludes his brief *Traité des mouvemens* (1634)—an essay on falling bodies—with a few methodological remarks. "We do not know the true reason for the fall of earthly bodies," he writes, although we can offer various reasons that might satisfy many people (p. 23). Still, other explanations might just as well be offered, and finding the true cause here "is no less difficult than demonstrating whether the earth is at rest or in motion" (p. 24). And so he concludes the essay with these words: "This is why it is enough to explain the phenomena of nature, because the human mind is not capable here of grasping the causes and principles" (p. 24). No educated reader at this time would fail to register the allusion to the start of Aristotle's *Physics*, where proper methodology requires precisely an inquiry into causes and principles (as quoted in this lecture, p. 15). But even if that would be ideal in absolute terms, "it is enough" [*il suffit*] to account for the observable features of nature, "the phenomena," and leave the speculative metaphysical questions for another time—just as, during this era, it was prudent to leave the question about the earth's motion for another time. So this is a clear early case of relinquishing causal explanation, but it is in fact an example that further illustrates Galileo's centrality, because Mersenne here is expressly writing as a champion of Galileo. That the treatise concludes with this remark shows just how much importance Mersenne attaches to these methodological claims. On Mersenne's connections to Galileo more generally see Peter Dear, *Mersenne*, Daniel Garber, "On the Frontlines," and John Lewis, *Galileo in France*, ch. 5.

Hacking sees Boyle as a crucial figure in these developments: "Robert Boyle, in making the low science of alchemy into the high science of chemistry, had much to do with that erosion" of "the scholastic goals of high science." "If I may be forgiven the crudeness in such a brief sketch, Boyle, for the first time succeeding in getting behind the phenomena, found no scholastic causes. He speculated about primary qualities, but necessary connections were nowhere in sight" (*Emergence of Probability*, p. 182). Boyle too, however, is a mixed case. Although it is true that his reductive treatment of the Aristotelian qualities—what he denigrates as "secondary qualities"—undermines the foundations of the Aristotelian causal story (for details, see my *Metaphysical Themes* chs. 19–23 and the discussion here in Lecture Four, p. 67), Boyle remains quite committed to the aim of achieving causal understanding. Thus he criticizes contemporary chemists for forsaking "the investigation of the true and fundamental causes" (*Producibleness of Chemical Principles*, in *Works* vol. 9: 23). In the preface to *The Sceptical Chymist* he worries that it "may prove somewhat prejudicial to the advancement of solid philosophy" to embrace the modern assumptions of chemists with respect to "their notions about the causes of things, and their manner of generation" (*Works* vol. 2: 208). Solid philosophy, for Boyle, is understood in traditional terms, as requiring a grasp of causes.

Causal Understanding in Newton

Note 17 (p. 16). Of the various figures after Galileo who contribute to the rise of the new philosophy and science, it is Newton, more than anyone, who shifts normative expectations for epistemology. He remarks in his exposition of definition VIII of the *Principia* that his concept of force "is purely mathematical, for I am not now considering the physical causes and sites of forces" (trans. p. 407). Responding to Leibniz, he writes:

Gravity without a miracle may keep the planets in. And to understand this, without knowing the cause of gravity, is as good a progress in philosophy as to understand the frame of a clock and the dependence of the wheels upon one another, without knowing the cause of the gravity of the weight which moves the machine, is in the philosophy of clockwork; or the understanding of the frame of the bones and muscles and their connection in the body of an animal and how the bones are moved by the contracting or dilating of the muscles, without knowing how the muscles are contracted or dilated by the power of the mind, is in the philosophy of animal motion. (*Philosophical Writings*, p. 117)

Newton's first communication to the Royal Society, in 1672, offers an argument for the presence of colors in light before striking a prism, but then declines to speculate about what light is and how refraction occurs: "I shall not mingle conjectures with certainties." But this would lead to subsequent controversies, within the society, as to whether Newton's limited claims were themselves certain consequences of his experiments or merely "hypothetical" (see, recently, Andrew Janiak, *Newton* ch. 3 and Gábor Zemplén, "Newton's Strategic Manoeuvring"). McMullin frames Newton's attitude nicely: "The properties of the nature under investigation are to be determined directly by experiment. The further matter of explaining the properties in causal terms is an optional affair, one that he is happy to leave until later" ("Conceptions of Science in the Scientific Revolution," p. 69). McMullin goes on to discuss, in fine-grained detail, how Newton consequently faced the temptation to offer explanatory causal hypotheses, resisting it more or less in various places.

For further, old but still useful discussions of Newton's views in this regard, see Westfall, *Force in Newton's Physics* and Bernard Cohen, *Newtonian Revolution*. But there seems to me no reason to accept Westfall's conclusion that, for Newton, "nature is ultimately opaque to human understanding" (*Construction of Modern Science*, p. 159). That itself is a hypothesis about the future prospects of inquiry on which Newton takes no stand. Here it is better to follow E. J. Dijksterhuis: "Newton wants to confine himself at first to discovering the forces governing the motions of the heavenly bodies, not because he is convinced that a profounder knowledge of the way in which these forces are exerted is ruled out in principle, but because the only evidence we have about it comes from the imagination and is unverifiable" (*Mechanization*, p. 482). McMullin likewise speaks of "a deferral, not an abandonment, of that quest" ("Impact," p. 299). For a thorough recent discussion of these issues, see Steffen Ducheyne, *The Main Business of Natural Philosophy* ch. 1.

In any event, Newton plainly does take himself to have reached *some* causal understanding of the phenomena described in his *Principia*, in virtue of having described the laws that gravity follows. Accordingly, one of the main turning points in the work occurs when Newton announces, some pages into Book III, that "above, we considered these motions on the basis of the phenomena. But now that the principles of motions have been found, we deduce the celestial motions from these principles a priori" (prop. 13, trans. p. 817). Newton is not using a priori in the later Kantian sense, as if the celestial motions could be deduced using pure reason alone. Instead, the deduction is a priori in the Aristotelian sense—that is, having previously worked from observable effects back to the causes (the "principles of motions"), Newton is now in a position to proceed in proper Aristotelian manner, producing a deduction that runs from causes to effects. What bothered his critics is that he thought it "enough" to offer an explanation that stopped at such principles, without going on to ground gravitational force in some deeper physical or metaphysical explanation.

The Ideal of Precision

Note 18 (p. 17). Newton's refusal to feign hypotheses has received vast amounts of attention, in comparison to which the foregoing remarks amount to the briefest of sketches. Much less discussed is his concern with precision and the larger context of this ideal. The preface to the *Principia* puts particular weight on this ideal, rejecting the received view of mechanics as the less accurate cousin of geometry. If that has been so, Newton writes, it is not because of any intrinsic defect in mechanics. Geometry itself, in fact, is simply a part of "the universal mechanics," and Newton's ambition is to develop a "rational mechanics ... accurately set out and demonstrated." The subject of this new mechanics will be "the *scientia* of the motions that result from any forces whatsoever, and of the forces that are required for any motions whatsoever" (*Principia*, preface, trans. p. 382). Regarding the standards of precision that in fact Newton achieved, Westfall has made a well-known remark: "Not the least part of the *Principia*'s persuasiveness was its deliberate pretense to a degree of precision quite beyond its legitimate claim" ("Newton and the Fudge Factor," pp. 751–2). For more recent and more enthusiastic appraisals, see William Harper, *Newton's Scientific Method* and George Smith, "How Newton's *Principia* Changed Physics." On the *Principia*'s first-edition preface and the relationship between geometry and mechanism, see Katherine Dunlop, "What Geometry Postulates" and Newton's more extensive comments in an unfinished treatise from the 1690s, where he describes the "stupid" (*crassa*) view of the "common" (*vulgi*) that "regards as geometrical everything that is exact, and as mechanical all that is not like that, as though nothing could be mechanical and at the same time exact" (*Geometria* Bk. I, in *Mathematical Papers* vol. 7: 289). On the status of mechanics in the seventeenth century and its antecedents back to antiquity, see Alan Gabbey, "Newton's *Mathematical Principles*" and "Between *ars* and *philosophia naturalis*," and Domenico Bertoloni Meli, *Thinking with Objects*.

It would be highly desirable to have a clearer sense of the antecedents to Newton's focus on precision, but almost no work has been done on the issue, and so here I can offer just a few preliminary indications. Precision (ἀκρίβεια) is extoled by Plato in various passages (e.g. *Theaetetus* 184c, *Republic* 504de, and esp. *Philebus* 55d–59d), along with at least the suggestion that what lacks in precision cannot count as ἐπιστήμη, and that therefore we need to choose suitable subjects of enquiry, namely subjects that are sufficiently separated from matter to admit of precision. Even mathematics, for Plato, suffers from being too closely tied to the visible domain of figures drawn by hand; the highest cognitive ideal would go from form to form, completely free of any link to images (*Republic* VI, 510b–11e).

Aristotle, unlike Plato, thinks that mathematics represents the highest ideal of precision, but he does not suppose that this ideal can be imposed across the board. Thus he carves out room for a broader domain of enquiry with the remark, quoted in this lecture (p. 16), that "the precise reasoning [ἀκριβολογίαν] of mathematics is not to be demanded in all cases, but only in the case of things that have no matter" (*Meta.* II.3, 995^{a}15–16). This is the point, too, of his famous remark at the start of the *Nicomachean Ethics*: "precision [τὸ ἀκριβές] is not to be sought for alike in all discussions" (I.3, 1094^{b}13). So, whereas Plato seems to have been the leading ancient champion of precision as a normative ideal, Aristotle attempts to moderate the expectation.

Among the sixth-century Alexandrian commentators on Aristotle, precision still looms large as a desideratum. Both Elias and David, in prolegomena that set out the different branches of philosophy, extol mathematics for its precision, and so treat it as the exemplary discipline to be used as a model in other areas (see Gutas, "Paul the Persian," pp. 247–8). The tenor of these remarks looks to achieve something of a compromise between Plato and Aristotle: they follow Plato in treating abstract precision as an ideal with some normative force, but allow that the ideal is not completely reachable in other fields.

Given the waning influence of Plato in the later Middle Ages, it is no surprise to find that the prevailing attitudes toward precision are more Aristotelian than Platonic. It is, however, hard to find much concern for precision as any sort of ideal at all, in part because those passages in Aristotle that might have transmitted this notion were obscured in the Latin translation. For instance, as Lecture Two discusses (p. 31), the remark on precision at *Nicomachean Ethics* I.3 went into Latin as a remark about degrees of *certainty*. Meanwhile, the passage at *Metaphysics* II.3 was not properly translated at all; it merely offered a transliteration, *acribologia mathematica*, where the first word meant nothing at all in Latin. Aquinas, for one, sees that Aristotle is distinguishing between an absolute and a normative ideal, and so he glosses the passage as a whole as arguing that "this mode [of inquiry], which is absolutely best, should not be sought in all things." But Aquinas seems to have no sense of an ideal in the neighborhood of precision as we would think of it, for he glosses *acribologia* as "diligent and certain reasoning" (*Comm. Meta.* II.5.336). Albert the Great's earlier commentary offers the gloss "demonstration or close scrutiny" and then proceeds to assimilate this notion to degrees of demonstrative certainty (*Metaphysica* II.13 [Cologne edn. vol. 16.1: 104a]). Albert's treatment closely follows Averroes's *Long Commentary* on the *Metaphysics*, which in Latin offers "close scrutiny" (*perscrutatio*) as a translation of ἀκριβολογία, and then goes on to gloss the point as one about different levels of certainty in demonstration (Bk. II text 16). (The passage is missing entirely from Bouyges's edition of the Arabic text.)

When one comes to sixteenth-century Italy, scholastic authors begin to look at the underlying Greek text. Hence Jacob Zabarella can remark that "the Greek word ἀκριβέστερα is read as *certior* in the Latin text, even though more properly speaking it should be rendered as *exactior*." Zabarella goes on to argue that 'more certain' and 'more exact' are two different things, but he does not make this point in the way we might expect. The senses grasp things "most certainly" but not "most exactly," for the reason that "the senses do not penetrate into the causes and nature of things" (*Comm. Post. an.* I ch. 23, in *Opera logica* col. 981B). So, again, *precision* in our sense of the term does not seem to be at issue.

It is not entirely clear just how off base these scholastic interpretations are, however, because it is far from clear just what "precision" amounts to in the ancient context. And here, happily, there is some solid scholarship to be leaned upon. The term ἀκρίβεια has been studied in some detail, up through Aristotle, in Dietrich Kurz, *AKPIBEIA*. Moreover, there is a very extensive discussion of Aristotle's case in Georgios Anagnostopoulos, *Aristotle on the Goals and Exactness of Ethics*, which also contains some very useful pages on Plato (pp. 47–56). These studies make it plain that great caution should be exercised in connecting the ancient term ἀκρίβεια with our modern concept of *precision*. Focusing solely on the case of Aristotle, it is evident that the term means quite different things in different contexts. In some cases, for instance, it seems to refer to a detailed examination as opposed to a mere sketch (e.g., *Topics* 101^{a}22). Elsewhere it seems to mean argumentative rigor (e.g., *Rhet.* 1396^{a}33), and still elsewhere it describes σοφία in comparison to ἐπιστήμη, because σοφία grasps both premises and conclusions (NE 1141^{a}16; see Lecture Five, note 3). Still, it seems right to insist that ἀκρίβεια, in at least many of its core usages, is closely related to our modern conceptions of precision, exactness, and accuracy. Consider again *Metaphysics* II.3, 995^{a}15–16: "the precise reasoning [ἀκριβολογία] of mathematics is not to be demanded in all cases, but only in the case of things that have no matter." No doubt mathematical reasoning can be considered more *certain*, and more *rigorous*, and more *detailed*. But Aristotle is telling us that ἀκρίβεια is found here because it has no matter. Why should that be the critical difference? Presumably because abstraction from matter seems to allow something in the neighborhood of what we now call precision (and see *De generatione animalium* IV.10, 778ᵃ4–9). Indeed, this assumption that precision is not to be had in the natural world is exactly what one finds Newton protesting against in the preface to his *Principia*.

Yet, even if this much is right, it remains unclear what sort of precision is at issue. Is this a matter of precision in the sense in which we can say that 180° is the *exact* sum of the interior angles of a triangle? Or is it precision in the sense in which we can say that 180° is *in every case* the sum of the interior angles of a triangle? Newton's concern seems to be mainly with accuracy in the first sense, in as much as he wanted to get the laws *exactly right*. But it may be that Aristotle, to the extent that he is talking about precision at all, is mainly talking about accuracy in the second sense. For in the much quoted passage from the start of the *Ethics* where each field of inquiry is said to have its own level of precision, he goes on to excuse ethics on the grounds that it is "only for the most part true" (1094ᵇ21). And this is how Aquinas understands the link between matter and imprecision at *Metaphysics* 995ᵃ15–16, commenting that "those things that have matter are subject to motion and variation. And so complete [*omnimoda*] certainty cannot be had in all of these things. For in them one asks not what is always the case, of necessity, but what is the case for the most part" (*Comm. Meta.* II.5.336; for more in this same vein, see *Summa theol.* 1a2ae 105.2 ad 8 and *Super Ioannem* 8.2).

Although these remarks provide just the barest sketch of a start toward an adequate discussion of the ideal of precision, they point toward an interesting possibility: that the sort of precision associated with mathematical accuracy is a desideratum that becomes widely sought, as a generalized epistemic ideal, only with Newton in the later seventeenth century. Perhaps this thesis unfairly neglects Kepler (see e.g. James Franklin, *Science of Conjecture*, pp. 149–50), and doubtless others might be mentioned as well. A useful paper by Westfall traces the developing interest in precision—and the developing instrumental ability to achieve it—from Tycho Brahe up to the time of Newton, concluding that, in the century *before* Newton, "scientific thought had moved from one world into another, and the central characteristics of the new world were mathematics and quantitative precision" ("Making a World of Precision," p. 84). But, although Newton's concerns certainly do not arise *ex nihilo*, it seems to be *his* example, and *his* rhetoric, that made precision, by the end of the seventeenth century, a widely sought ideal. The well-known mathematical turn of modern science is one indication of how such precision was becoming increasingly sought after; but to embrace precision is not the same as to embrace a mathematical vocabulary and to render one's conclusions in quantitative terms. Consider, for instance, how talk of "accuracy" makes its way even into Hume's ambitions to construct a science of human nature: "'tis at least worthwhile to try if the science of man will not admit of the same accuracy which several parts of natural philosophy are found susceptible of. There seems to be all the reason in the world to imagine that it may be carried to the greatest degree of exactness" (*Treatise*, Abstract, p. 645). Throughout the eighteenth and nineteenth centuries, one finds the sort of emphasis on precision that is a familiar feature of science today (see, e.g., Thomas Hankins, "Newton's Mathematical Way," and the essays in Norton Wise, *The Values of Precision*).

To the extent that later seventeenth-century scientists and philosophers exhibit a newfound enthusiasm for precision as an epistemic ideal, it becomes natural to wonder whether there is something about their conceptions of the world that fuels this development. To consider this issue, contrast the precision that our *descriptions* of the world might have with the precision that *the world itself* might have. (For this distinction, see Anagnostopoulos, *Aristotle on the Goals and Exactness of Ethics*, pp. 122–5.) The first may be an epistemic ideal, but it will have normative force only if the world cooperates. This was Aristotle's point about natural philosophy: that it cannot be made precise in the way that mathematics can, not because of any limitation on our part, but because material things do not admit of such precision. To this Newton responds (though perhaps not with Aristotle in mind, or even with quite the same notion of precision in mind) that, yes, such precision is to be found in the world, and that if we fail to grasp it, the fault belongs "not to the art, but to its practitioners" (as quoted in this lecture, p. 16). Here is a clear example of how an idealized epistemology must consider both what we are like and what the world is like.

Precision can be a normative ideal only in a world that admits of precise characterization. With this in mind, one might wonder whether the broader mechanical philosophy of the seventeenth century plays an important role in these changing epistemic ideals. For Newton, part of what underlies his commitment to precision is his conception of the world as governed by laws of nature (see, e.g., J. R. Milton, "Laws of Nature" and Walter Ott, *Causation and Laws of Nature*). Might the mechanistic philosophy in general lend itself to treating precision as a normative ideal? Michael Mahoney remarks that "nature was mathematised in the seventeenth century by means of its extensive mechanisation" ("Mathematical Realm," p. 705), and Roy Sorensen suggests that "mechanism is a metaphysics of precision because it narrows down the possible behavior of things" ("Metaphysics of Precision," p. 358). But matters are more complicated than this. To be sure, the mechanical philosophy lends itself to mathematical precision insofar as it reduces phenomena to features of things that are readily quantified, in particular to size, shape, and motion. Yet, as soon as one attempts to apply this mechanistic framework to a question that lies beyond the narrowly mechanistic, imprecision in the form of vagueness immediately results. What, for instance, are the substances, and what are their properties or modes? What counts as one thing's being the same as another, and what counts as a causal relationship between two things? For the mechanical philosopher, all these familiar questions suddenly become mired in obscurity, and the prospects for precision in these domains look hopeless. Mechanism lends itself to precision, then, only if one is willing to quash every line of inquiry that goes beyond its narrowly demarcated bounds.

For scholastic philosophers, in contrast, many philosophical questions could admit of perfectly precise answers, inasmuch as they could be defined in terms of the formal features of things. A substance, for instance, in the material domain, just is that quantity of matter that is actualized by a substantial form. In principle, moreover, such accounts might be expressed in rigorously precise mathematical terms. For instance, according to the standard scholastic view, the four elemental qualities (hot, cold, wet, dry) determine the physical character of all sublunary bodies (see my *Metaphysical Themes* ch. 21). So what are flesh and bone? This question could in theory be answered quite precisely, because scholastic authors might have made claims about exactly what ratio of these four elements yields one or another kind of flesh or bone. In practice, however, little effort was made to investigate such matters. An exception, in the early fourteenth century, was the rise of a movement centered around Merton College to develop just this sort of formal–quantitative framework, in domains ranging from natural philosophy to psychology, ethics, and theology (for a good overview, see Edith Sylla, "Oxford Calculators"). Yet this program never advanced very far—this was not to be the 'new science'—in part because few of its practitioners seemed to have any serious desire to apply this methodology to the real world. Perhaps they could not even imagine how it might be done, since for so many of the things they wanted to quantify—such as color or other qualities, and virtues of the soul—it was hard even to imagine how measurements might be made. Or, better, they had *only* their imagination, in as much as they commonly worked under the injunction to proceed "according to imagination," without trying to fit their mathematical accounts to reality (see Thomas Dewender, "Imaginary Experiments").

One sort of doubt about the possibility of precision at this time was the thought that quantities, even if they could be measured, would turn out to be incommensurable and so describable only approximately. Nicole Oresme in particular stressed this as an obstacle to developing the Mertonian project fully, writing in this connection that "precision transcends human ingenuity" (*Tractatus de commensurabilitate*, pp. 284–5). On this see Grant, "Buridan and Oresme on Knowledge," Franklin, *Science of Conjecture*, pp. 141–5, and Joel Kaye, *A History of Balance*, pp. 429–35. A more common worry was our inability to measure precisely the inner workings of nature. On this see Anneliese Maier, *Metaphysische Hintergründe*, pp. 397–8, who describes later medieval physics as "a physics without measuring" and goes on to discuss why this was so, concluding that later medieval authors assumed that "truly exact measurement, even in the simplest cases, is impossible in principle." See also Maier, *Zwischen Philosophie und Mechanik*, p. 24 n. 16, which quotes an interesting passage from Robert Grosseteste regarding the puzzle of what it is that one measures when one measures distances or times. (For an English version of some of this, see Maier, *On the Threshold*, pp. 168–70.) Such worries help explain how Cesare Cremonini from around the turn of the seventeenth century, the last of the great Paduan scholastics, could warn his students that "those who are too practiced in mathematics are deficient in physics" (in Meinel, *In physicis*, p. 25n).

Into the early days of the new science, these sorts of worries about measurement endured. Guidobaldo dal Monte, whose late sixteenth-century work led the way to a mathematical treatment of the science of mechanics, cautioned against supposing that instruments could be built to test the theorems of his system, because the requisite level of precision could not be attained in the material world: "matter allows this with difficulty" (*Mechanicorum liber* prop. 4, f. 22r; trans. Drake and Drabkin, *Mechanics*, p. 285). A lost letter from dal Monte to Galileo elicited this remarkable reply from Galileo in 1602: "when we commence to deal with matter, because of its contingency, the propositions abstractly considered by the geometer begin to be altered. Since it is impossible to formulate a certain science [*certa scienza*] of those propositions, being so perturbed, the mathematician is released from having to study them" (Galilei, *Opere* vol. 10: 100). Both of these passages are helpfully discussed in Bertoloni Meli, *Thinking with Objects*, pp. 26–35. At around the same time, the Jesuit Giuseppe Biancani defends the perfection of mathematical *scientia* by divorcing the objects of mathematics from the domains of both nature and art, on account of "the crudity and imperfection of sensible matter, which is incapable of taking on entirely perfect shapes" (*De mathematicarum natura*, p. 6; trans. Klima in Mancosu, *Philosophy of Mathematics*, p. 180). It was at this time far from clear, then, even among the leading proponents of the mathematical sciences, that such precision could be fruitfully applied to the natural world. Galileo, by the time of his *Dialogue* (1632), is putting worries of this kind into the mouth of the Aristotelian Simplicio: "these mathematical subtleties do very well in the abstract, but they do not work out when applied to sensible and physical matters" (second day, trans. p. 236). The whole method of the *Dialogue*, and of the later *Two New Sciences*, serves as a rebuttal to this charge, though these sorts of worries endure even in later figures like Robert Boyle (see Boyle, *Works* vol. 5: 196, vol. 11: 241) and Pierre-Sylvain Régis (*Cours entier de philosophie* pref., quire **4r). For an illuminating account of some of the gains in precision made over the course of the seventeenth century, see Alexandre Koyré, "An Experiment in Measurement." For a recent collection of papers that call into question the centrality of mathematics for seventeenth-century natural philosophy, see Geoffrey Gorham et al., *The Language of Nature*.

Interestingly, one of the first domains where one finds instruments capable of precise measurement is medicine, where around the turn of the seventeenth century Sanctorius of

Padua developed tools capable of measuring pulse, body temperature, and perspiration in quantitative terms (see Ian Maclean, *Logic, Signs and Nature*, p. 29). Yet, while the inroads of mathematics across the sciences made their mark on medicine (pp. 171–81), it was far from clear that medicine advanced in such a way as to vindicate that approach. A more robust source of inspiration was the concept of a *scientia media*—a 'middle' or 'in-between' *scientia* that encompassed optics and mechanics, where natural philosophy had long been developed in quantitative terms (see Nicholas Jardine, "Demonstration, Dialectic, and Rhetoric," James Lennox, "Aristotle, Galileo, and 'Mixed Sciences,'" and Garber, "Descartes, Mechanics, and the Mechanical Philosophy"). But even here it had to be shown that precision is both attainable and desirable, and it was part of Newton's great achievement to show both that it is and that such work could inform—indeed, revolutionize—the most fundamental fields in physics. This was slow to happen. The Cartesian tradition did not champion mathematical precision (see Roger Ariew, "Mathematization of Nature"). And even in the mid-eighteenth century Jean-Antoine Nollet could write that "it is dangerous for a physicist to develop too great a taste for geometry," since in physics "one never finds either precision or certainty" (in Yves Gingras, "What Did Mathematics Do to Physics?" p. 389). Yet Kant, a few decades later, held that "in any special doctrine of nature there can be only as much *proper* science as there is *mathematics* therein" (*Metaphysical Foundations of Natural Science*, p. 6). In the mid-nineteenth century, James Clerk Maxwell still felt that he had to make the case for mathematical precision:

> Vague ideas may possibly give picturesqueness to a declamation, but we must be very careful of them when they are disguised in the forms of exact science. To avoid this vagueness ourselves, we must eventually make use of that method of expression which, by throwing away every idea but that of quantity, arrives at the utmost limit of distinctness. We cannot express physical facts except in a mathematical form.
> (Inaugural lecture [1860], in *Scientific Letters* vol. 1: 671)

The case for a mathematical physics had to be argued, over the course of many years, both because of skepticism as to whether the natural world would admit of such precision and because of resistance to the forbiddingly technical character of the approach. Denis Diderot, editor of the eighteenth-century *Encyclopédie*, quarreled with his collaborator d'Alembert over whether the elaborate mathematical treatments of the *Principia* were really necessary. Diderot suggested that Newton might have saved himself and countless others a great deal of time if he had put his ideas into a more accessible, less mathematically dense form. So here we have another epistemic ideal, in competition with the ideal of precision: the ideal of *accessibility to a broad audience*. (On this see Gingras, "What Did Mathematics Do to Physics?" esp. pp. 391–8). One finds worries of a broadly similar kind in antiquity, in the frequent complaint that there is something base about an excessive concern with accuracy (as reported, e.g., in Aristotle, *Meta.* II.3, 995^{a}8–12). It is a familiar feature of much seventeenth-century philosophy and science that it puts as much weight on accessibility as it does on precision. Yet, familiar as this feature of the period is (especially to anyone who has ever taught the subject), there has been little theoretical attention paid to the epistemic costs and benefits of such an approach, as compared to the less accessible but more theoretically precise writings of the scholastic era or of philosophy and science today.

Precision versus Depth

Note 19 (p. 17). Gilbert's treatise on the magnet is famous for its concern with careful observation, seemingly on the basis of actual experiments. Yet at the same time he displays little concern for precise measurement or argument and reaches bold speculative conclusions about unobservable causes. Indeed, the very first words of the book speak of "the discovery of secret things and the investigation of hidden causes" (preface). And, although he goes on to compare his method to that of geometry (trans. p. xlviii), he ultimately feels the need to introduce a theory of souls to explain the underlying basis for magnetic phenomena (*De magnete* V.12). Thus Galileo, even while praising Gilbert as "worthy of great acclaim for the many new and sound observations that he made," complains that he puts forward claims about *verae causae* even though "his reasons, candidly speaking, are not rigorous, and lack that force that must unquestionably be present in those adduced as necessary and eternal scientific conclusions" (*Dialogue*, third day, trans. p. 471; *Opere* vol. 7: 432).

Galileo might have said much the same thing about Descartes. For that, though, we need look ahead only to Pascal, whose *Pensées* contain this note to self: "Write against those who delve too deeply in the sciences. Descartes" (n. 462, trans. p. 148). Or, in another remark on Descartes, he writes: "we must say in general: 'This happens through shape and motion,' because it is true. But to say which shapes and motions and to constitute the machine is ridiculous, for it is useless, uncertain, and laborious" (n. 118, trans. p. 25). The useless uncertainty here arises in part from delving too deeply, and in part from a lack of precision. As Dijksterhuis has remarked in modern times, speaking of both Descartes and Gassendi: "everything remains in the vaguely qualitative sphere, so that there is no question of an experimental verification of the truth of the theories in question" (*Mechanization*, p. 430). On the rising tide against Cartesianism in the late seventeenth century, see Peter Anstey, "Experimental versus Speculative Natural Philosophy," pp. 230–2. By the time of Cotes's preface to the second edition of Newton's *Principia* in 1713, the Cartesian philosophy, "even if it proceeds according to the most accurate mechanical laws," still deserves to be called "a fable, elegant and charming perhaps, but a fable nevertheless" (trans. p. 386). Several decades later, Émilie du Châtelet is unstinting in her praise of Descartes but admits that the example he set was pernicious in the long run: "he gave the whole learned world a taste for hypotheses, and it was not long before they fell into a taste for fictions" (*Selected Writings*, p. 147). Voltaire similarly admired Descartes but harshly criticized his speculative hypotheses: "Would one watch with sadness the greatest geometer of his time abandon geometry, his guide, in order to lose himself in the abyss of his imagination? Would one watch him create a universe rather than study the one that God created?" (*Oeuvres complètes* [Institut Voltaire edn.] vol. 15: 700).

In discussing the practice of anointing weapons to cure wounds, Glanvill appeals to Kenelm Digby, whom Glanvill credits with having "put out of doubt" the efficacy of such measures. Glanvill reports on how Digby offered a speculative mechanistic account of the causal mechanisms at work in such a case, in contrast to others, who had appealed here to the *anima mundi*. And indeed Digby did publish, a few years before Glanvill's treatise, an entire lecture on the subject of cures made by acting on objects at a distance from the wound: *A Late Discourse . . . Touching the Cure of Wounds by the Powder of Sympathy with Instructions how to make the said Powder; whereby many other Secrets of Nature are unfolded*. This might sound bizarre, even borderline insane, but the lecture itself—which went through at least four editions—is actually quite sensible, at least up to a point. Digby cautions from the start that "in matter of fact, the determination of existence, and truth of a thing, depends upon the report which our senses make us" (*A Late Discourse*, p. 4). He then proceeds to set out the evidence in some detail, on the basis of eyewitness accounts given by himself and other very prominent people. (This is an excellent example of the role that fame and privilege play in vouchsafing the authority of witnesses; on this, see Dear, *Discipline and Experience*, and Steven Shapin, *A Social History of Truth*.) Digby registers the worry that such cures at a distance might seem "either ineffectual or superstitious" (p. 8), but he carefully lays out the empirical—indeed, experimental—evidence. Then he takes one step farther, admitting that his listeners may not be persuaded by mere testimony and proposing to give them a "demonstration" that is "built upon certain and approved principles" (p. 17). From here Digby proceeds not to engage in special pleading on behalf of a bizarre thesis, but rather to take as given a puzzling but well-confirmed phenomenon and then to construct a plausible story about how things must be in the natural world in order to explain that phenomenon. Reading Digby's account is rather like reading modern attempts to account for the EPR paradox in quantum mechanics.

Developments after Newton

Note 20 (p. 18). Quantum mechanics is invoked by Bernard Cohen as a parallel for the situation of post-Newtonian physics: the *Principia*'s theory of universal gravity manifestly worked, and was embraced, but no one could understand how it worked (*Newtonian Revolution*, p. 147). There is a very large body of literature on the critical contemporary response to Newton, and especially to his insistence that science could proceed without framing hypotheses about ultimate causes. An emblematic example is a brief anonymous review from 1688 in the *Journal des sçavans*, which begins by praising Newton's *Principia* profusely, but merely as a mechanic, "the most perfect that one could imagine, it not being possible to make demonstrations more precise or more exact than those that he gives... In order to make a work as perfect as possible, Mr. Newton has only to give us a physics as exact as his mechanics. He will give it when he substitutes true motions in place of those that he has supposed" (Aug. 2, 1688, pp. 237–8; trans. Koyré, *Newtonian Studies*, p. 115). Leibniz too was unsparing in his criticisms, charging Newton with having returned to "occult qualities or scholastic faculties" (*Antibarbus physicus* [*Phil. Essays*, p. 313; *Phil. Schriften* vol. 7: 338]). For recent philosophically inclined essays on Newton's conception of force and its critique by Leibniz, see Janiak, "Newton and the Reality of Force" and Garber, "Leibniz, Newton and Force." For the earlier historical context behind the Newton–Leibniz dispute, see my *Metaphysical Themes*, pp. 541–6.

Despite such criticisms, and despite less effective apostles of the new method, such as Glanvill, the combined example of Galileo and Newton was so overwhelmingly impressive that it could hardly help but carry the day. As Garber concludes about one leading competitor, "the ultimate success of the Newtonian program has all but driven Leibniz's conception of force off of the playing field" ("Leibniz, Newton and Force," p. 41). For Newton's influence in natural philosophy more generally, see McMullin, "Impact." But one should not overstate the methodological influence of Newton, because to some extent he himself was responding to broader intellectual currents. As far back as 1667, Glanvill writes to Margaret Cavendish that "we have yet no certain theory of nature ... All that we can hope for, as yet, is but the history of things as they are, but to say how they are, to raise general *axioms*, and to make *hypotheses*, must, I think, be the happy privilege of succeeding ages" (in Cavendish, *Letters and Poems*, p. 124). Anstey ("Experimental versus Speculative Natural Philosophy" sections 5–6) shows how this rhetoric of eschewing hypotheses was commonplace by the 1690s, well before Newton's famous refusal to feign hypotheses, which appeared only in the second (1713) edition of the *Principia*.

Hume provides a particularly clear example of how the new methodology's influence was felt outside of natural philosophy:

> Nothing is more requisite for a true philosopher than to restrain the intemperate desire of searching into true causes, and having established any doctrine upon a sufficient number of experiments, rest contented with that, when he sees a farther examination would lead him into obscure and uncertain speculations. In that case his enquiry would be much better employed in examining the effects than the causes of his principle.
>
> (*Treatise* I.1.4, p. 13; and see the Introduction to the *Treatise*, p. xviii)

It is not that Hume is averse to grasping the causes of things when he can. Thus "we must endeavour to render all our principles as universal as possible, by tracing up our experiments to the utmost, and explaining all effects from the simplest and fewest causes" (p. xvii). Yet this sentiment gets sharply qualified: although we must do this, he immediately adds that "'tis still certain we cannot go beyond experience; and any hypothesis, that pretends to discover the ultimate original qualities of human nature, ought at first to be rejected as presumptuous and chimerical" (p. xvii).

On Hume's conception of science, see John Biro, "Hume's New Science of the Mind." For his relationship to Newton in particular, see Yoram Hazony, "Newtonian Explanatory Reduction," who remarks that "the heart of the enterprise of science" for Hume is to reach "those few causes or principles that are capable of explaining 'all effects'" (p. 163). That this is what the heart of *science* has become around 1740 is noteworthy, but it is hardly notable that Hume might hold this as an epistemic ideal. *Everyone* has *always* had this as an epistemic ideal. What is distinctive about Hume, beyond how he wants to regiment his English epistemic vocabulary, is that this ideal has come to seem so remote as no longer to be normative. Indeed, not surprisingly given his overriding skepticism, Hume shows signs of going beyond Galileo and Newton and of regarding the deepest reaches of the natural world as inaccessible in principle. This is in fact a conclusion he associates with Newton: "While Newton seemed to draw off the veil from some of the mysteries of nature, he shewed at the same time the imperfections of the mechanical philosophy; and thereby restored her ultimate secrets to that obscurity in which they ever did and ever will remain" (Hume, *History of England* LXXI [vol. 6: 542]). His first *Enquiry* endorses the sort of mitigated skepticism that calls for "the limitation of our enquiries to such subjects as are best adapted to the narrow capacity of human understanding" (12.3, p. 162). Such limitations make *knowledge* impossible, except in a few special cases, but remarkably they are consistent with the development of his new *science*, "which will not be inferior in certainty, and will be much superior in utility to any other of human comprehension" (*Treatise*, Introduction, p. xix). Still, as Lecture Six considers (p. 131), even if Hume's attentions are devoted primarily to establishing a new science, he is not able entirely to relinquish the ambition for knowledge. This old ideal has too strong a hold on him to be easily forsaken.

On the continent, at around the same time as Hume, Voltaire champions the sort of philosophical resignation that grows out of Galileo, Newton, and Locke. See, for example, the claim in his *Traité de métaphysique*: "I do not know [*connais*] the how, it is true: I would rather stop than go astray" (*Oeuvres complètes* [Institut Voltaire edn.] vol. 14: 434). The Newtonian physics, "founded on facts and the calculus, rejecting all hypotheses, is consequently the sole true physics" (vol. 15: 729). For a useful summary of Voltaire's restraint regarding causal knowledge, see J. B. Shank, "Voltaire" §2.5. The remark quoted in this lecture (p. 19) about the torch of science—*la philosophie consiste à s'arrêter quand le flambeau de la physique nous manque*—is in fact offered "in the spirit of wise Locke," and Voltaire goes on to exhibit the proper Newtonian restraint: "I observe the effects of nature, but I confess to you that I grasp no more than you their first principles" (*Philosophical Dictionary*, s.v. "Soul," p. 168; *Oeuvres complètes* [Garnier edn.] vol. 26: 234). The passage is not, however, included in modern editions and translations of the *Philosophical Dictionary*, which restore that work to its originally intended, more modest size, and hence remove various miscellaneous texts added by later editors.

Voltaire's restraint regarding causal claims was formed in opposition to the rather different attitude of his long-time collaborator, Émilie du Châtelet, whose *Institutions de physique* (1740) attempts to ground Newton's physics in a Leibnizian metaphysics. Against the Newtonian injunction not to feign hypotheses, du Châtelet offers a sophisticated defense of hypothetical reasoning as critical for scientific progress, provided that hypotheses are not given any more credence than the available evidence warrants (see *Selected Writings*, pp. 147–55). For discussion, see Karen Detlefsen, "Émilie du Châtelet" and "Du Châtelet and Descartes."

In the later eighteenth century, resistance to the English spirit of metaphysical resignation reaches its highest pitch of vehemence in Kant. In the forward to his *Metaphysical Foundations of*

Natural Science (1786), for instance, Kant insists on an older, full-strength epistemic ideal, grounded in foundational principles, and reserves for this the term *Wissenschaft*: "only that whose certainty is apodeictic can be called *Wissenschaft* proper; a cognition [*Erkenntnis*] that can contain mere empirical certainty is only improperly called science [*Wissen*]" (trans. p. 4). There is no very satisfactory way of rendering Kant's epistemic terminology into English, but in various places he makes it quite explicit how his German terminology connects to earlier Latin usage: *Wissenschaft* to *scientia*, and *Erkenntnis* to *cognitio*. These connections are readily drawn and quite illuminating, because Kant is still adhering to older traditions of usage as well as to the older normative ideals that attend upon those usages. His terminology resists English translation precisely because he refuses to fall into step with the revised epistemic expectations that grow out of Newton, Locke, and Hume. Those changing ideals caused the very meanings of these English words to change, at least within philosophy and science. We have seen in this lecture something of how the story goes for 'science.' Lecture Two concentrates on the case of 'knowledge' and its changing relationship with certainty.

Epistemology in the Ascendant

Note 21 (p. 20). Even as knowledge distances itself from certainty (see Lecture Two, pp. 40–4), science retains that association. Looking ahead to the nineteenth century, William Whewell begins his magisterial *History of Scientific Ideas* by equating science with "real knowledge" and goes on to write that "there do exist among us doctrines of solid and acknowledged certainty, and truths of which the discovery has been received with universal applause. These constitute what we commonly term Science" (vol. 1: 3). Whewell—who is generally credited with having coined the term 'scientist'—retains for science that part of the epistemic ideal that demands certainty and precision, and extols how

the progress of knowledge upon the subject of motion and force has produced, in the course of the world's history, a great change in the minds of acute and speculative men; so that such persons can now reason with perfect steadiness and precision upon subjects on which, at first, their thoughts were vague and confused; and can apprehend, as truths of complete certainty and evidence, laws which it required great labour and time to discover.   (*History of Scientific Ideas* vol. 1: 279)

It is at this juncture that, as reported in this lecture (p. 9), he proceeds to argue that such developments within science and mathematics have an "effect upon more common and familiar trains of thought" by setting a standard for certainty and precision that then leads to a broader elevation in cognitive expectations.

Celebratory rhetoric like Whewell's regarding the practices and institutions of science has come in for much criticism among recent philosophers and sociologists of science. Philip Kitcher, in *The Advancement of Science*, brands such triumphalism "the Legend of Science." Accordingly, those who promote the scientific ideal today are generally more cautious in the story they tell. Still, if the ideal of science has been somewhat downgraded in modern times, philosophy has generally seemed unable to meet even that standard, or any other reasonable standard. This was already Whewell's judgment regarding pretty much the whole history of philosophy: "We now proceed to examine with what success the Greeks followed the track into which they had thus struck. And here we are obliged to confess that they very soon turned aside from the right road to truth, and deviated into a vast field of error, in which they and their successors have wandered almost up to the present time" (*History of Inductive Sciences* vol. 1: 32–3). Philosophy may have earned some credibility in the eyes of science by resigning itself to the Lockean role of underlaborer. But not even this has saved the field from suspicion. Larry Laudan, switching metaphors, writes that, "for a very long time, philosophers have been regarded as the gatekeepers to the scientific estate. They are the ones who are supposed to be able to tell the difference between real science and pseudo-science." But he goes on to say that "it seems pretty clear that philosophy has largely failed to deliver the relevant goods" ("Demise of the Demarcation Problem," p. 111).

Most memorable of all the ruminations of the scientists on philosophy is this oft-quoted remark of the geneticist Steve Jones: "For most wearers of white coats, philosophy is to science as pornography is to sex: it is cheaper, easier, and some people seem, bafflingly, to prefer it." It is worth looking back to the original context of this remark, which is, if possible, even less friendly to the philosophical enterprise than the witticism taken in isolation suggests. Jones goes on to wonder about the way psychologists do not seem to be able to do without the philosophers. What does this show? "The cynical view that if their science needs philosophy they should do better science is less than reasonable. It may mean, though, that large parts of their enterprise are for the time being beyond the limits of science altogether...Some questions of the mind remain unanswered and perhaps unanswerable" ("The Set Within the Skull," p. 14).

Reflecting on this remark, one might say that the great question of philosophy today is just how far such unanswered questions extend. Jones seems to think that the mind is the unique place in nature where there might be some legitimacy to the efforts of "Thinkers... mystics...philosophers...the arts faculty." (He evidently treats these groups as coextensive.) So have the scientists figured out everything else, or at any rate nearly so? If they have, they really ought to share these results with the rest of us, because to the outside observer it looks as if the sciences have no clue with regard to many of the features of reality that matter most. Of course, it may be that these questions the philosophers ask—about truth and goodness and all the rest—are ultimately "unanswerable." In that case we should modify our epistemic expectations and recognize that the ideal of deep philosophical understanding is hopeless. But at what point do we give up? It is worth remembering that, at the dawn of the scientific revolution, Locke (as quoted in this lecture, p. 12), was prepared to pull the plug on natural science: "As to a perfect science of natural bodies...we are, I think, so far from being capable of any such thing, that I conclude it lost labour to seek after it" (*Essay* IV.3.29). Over the next century, such blanket pessimism would be shown to be misguided, but only in certain domains. Thus Kant still felt confident, at the end of the eighteenth century, that there would never "arise a Newton who could make comprehensible even the generation of a blade of grass according to natural laws that no intention has ordered" (*Critique of the Power of Judgment* §75, p. 271). Reflecting on such examples, we ourselves might want to think twice before rendering a final verdict as to when our epistemic ambitions reveal themselves as illusory.

Notes to Lecture Two

Lexicology

Note 1 (p. 22). Some epistemologists positively celebrate the tight link between epistemology and language. Peter Ludlow, for instance, extols "the new linguistic turn in epistemology" and remarks that "first, and most obviously, any investigation into the nature of knowledge which did not conform to some significant degree with the semantics of the term 'knows' would simply be missing the point...[E]pistemological theories might be rejected if they are in serious conflict with the lexical semantics of 'knows'" ("Contextualism and the New Linguistic Turn," pp. 12–13). We should wonder what "point" epistemologists are missing when they ignore the term 'knows.' Are they missing a similar point when they ignore the semantics of the Arabic word علم? Or is there something special about English? On its face, Ludlow's remark seems just as doubtful as saying that ontology—the study of what things there are in the world—must conform to the semantics of the term 'things.'

Linguists sometimes argue for the universality of the concept *know*. One leading figure, Cliff Goddard, remarks that "most cognitive scientists underestimate not only the scale of semantic variation across languages, but also the theoretical and methodological challenges it poses. In theorizing and discussing emotional states, they tend to take English for granted, effectively absolutizing the English lexicon of emotion and cognition" ("Universals and Variation," p. 72). Yet Goddard thinks that "a very small number of simple meanings connected with cognitive processes are shared across languages" and that *know* is among these. What does this remarkable claim amount to? In part, it is a claim about compositionality: that "all the thousands of complex word meanings in the world's languages can ultimately be paraphrased into configurations of semantic primes" (p. 74). But Goddard also makes the stronger claim of universality: "semantic primes are lexical universals in the sense of having an exact translation in every human language" (p. 75). An exact translation in every language? So what is the exact Arabic translation of the word 'know'? Is it علم or عرف? How about Latin? Is it *scire* or *cognoscere*? In any case, if Goddard is right, then why is epistemic vocabulary so devilishly difficult to translate across philosophical languages? Goddard does not really think, however, there is an exact translation in every language, because he recognizes that *the words* that express *know* vary semantically across languages. What he thinks is that the concept is shared. But how can anyone be in a position to be confident of this, since philosophers cannot even agree on exactly what concept is expressed in English by 'know'? Goddard seems to think that, whatever that concept may turn out to be, we can be confident that speakers from other linguistic communities will have just the same concept. And this seems to be the premise of much of modern epistemology. But it is hard to see how linguistics, given its methods, could establish more than that speakers across languages share something *roughly* like the concept *know*. Roughly alike, however, is not enough for the epistemologist who seeks precision.

For more credulous reflections on the universality of *know*, see Jennifer Nagel, "Defending the Evidential Value of Epistemic Intuitions." Nagel shares the usual misimpression that the methods of modern epistemology reflect the way philosophers have always gone about things. Thus she begins this paper as follows:

> Epistemology is difficult. In the ongoing struggle to improve our understanding of knowledge, epistemologists have used a variety of methods, including the method of eliciting intuitive reactions to particular cases. This method has been used for centuries, both by Western philosophers . . . and by Eastern philosophers.
>
> ("Defending the Evidential Value of Epistemic Intuitions," p. 179)

At least in the case of western philosophy, it is really quite unusual to find discussions where a particular puzzle case gets advanced and authors then search their intuitions to decide whether or not it counts as *knowledge*. Of course, it is common enough to find remarks like *This is not true, and therefore cannot be known*. But the historical practice is not one of using one's intuitions to demarcate the concept; it is rather to make lists of the various ways in which the word might be used and not to worry about which usage is somehow correct (see Lecture One, p. 8). The sort of conceptual analysis Nagel has in mind, guided by "intuitive reactions" to puzzle cases, is simply not a prominent method in the history of epistemology. For better or worse, this is a distinctive feature of modern analytic philosophy.

Of course, even on the modern scene, there are many and diverse research programs in epistemology that eschew finding the boundary conditions for knowledge. Prominent recent examples include the following books:

- Richard Foley, *The Theory of Epistemic Rationality*, which turns from knowledge to epistemic rationality;
- Edward Craig, *Knowledge and the State of Nature*, which focuses on social function;

- Stephen Stich, *The Fragmentation of Reason*, which would replace analytic epistemology with a pragmatic approach to cognitive success;
- William Alston, *Beyond "Justification,"* which turns from knowledge to justification, and then argues for a pluralistic conception of the latter.

Above all, as the end of this Lecture discusses, there is the Bayesian program of shifting from full belief to degrees of credence.

No doubt, conceptual analysis is an indispensable part of philosophical inquiry. But when we begin with lexicology, it becomes natural to suppose that the goal of inquiry is simply to analyze the stock of concepts that align with how we talk. This task poses such substantial challenges across many domains that it threatens to obscure the ultimately more important question of how we *ought* to conceptualize a given domain. Here I am much indebted to conversation with John Bengson, Herman Cappelen, and David Plunkett. For a nuanced recent discussion of the relationship between studying language, studying concepts, and studying the world itself, see Jonathan McKeown-Green, Glen Pettigrove, and Aness Webster, "Conjuring Ethics from Words."

Descartes's Ideal Theory

Note 2 (p. 26). It is uncontroversial that Descartes aims at the epistemic ideal of certainty, but many of the surrounding details are contentious. Central to my interpretation is that certainty counts as Descartes's standard for belief only in the special context of theoretical inquiry. Outside that unusual context, we should—and indeed must—form beliefs even when they are not perfectly certain. So I understand the start of part IV of his *Discourse*:

> For a long time I had observed, as noted above, that in practical life it is sometimes necessary to act upon opinions that one knows to be quite uncertain just as if they were indubitable. But since I now wished to devote myself solely to the search for truth, I thought it necessary to do the very opposite and reject as if absolutely false everything in which I could imagine the least doubt, in order to see whether, after that, I was left believing anything that was entirely indubitable.   (VI: 31)

And *Principles* I.3:

> This [global] doubt, while it continues, should be restricted solely to the contemplation of the truth. For with regard to the course of life, the chance for action would frequently pass before we could free ourselves from our doubts, and so we are not infrequently compelled to accept what is merely truth-like [*verisimile*].

The same point is made repeatedly in the *Meditations*. In addition to VII: 15 and VII: 22–3 (both quoted in this lecture), see VII: 247, VII: 350–1, and VII: 460. And see a 1641 letter to Hyperaspistes (III: 422–3), and the French preface to the *Principles* (IXB: 7).

A very different reading of Descartes is developed at some length by David Owens. He contends that, once we distinguish the lower standards applicable to "practical affairs" from the higher standards applicable to belief, we find that for Descartes "belief or judgment is...governed in all contexts by the rule of certainty" ("Descartes's Use of Doubt," p. 165). As evidence he cites many of the same passages that I have just cited. The difference is that he takes these passages to distinguish between what we should believe and how we should act. But to read Descartes in this way is, in effect, to make him into a kind of neo-skeptic, someone who thinks that the vast majority of people know nothing or almost nothing and should suspend their beliefs until acquainted with the Cartesian method. It seems to me that the main current of the texts runs strongly against this conclusion.

Gail Fine reads these passages the same way as Owens does, since she takes it as a "point of similarity" between ancient skepticism and Descartes that "both challenge not only knowledge but also belief" ("Descartes and Ancient Skepticism," p. 212). To cope with this, says Fine, Descartes "constructs a code of conduct by which to live: a code he accepts for the purposes of action, but to whose truth he is not committed" (p. 218). The distance between my reading and Fine's is striking. I claim Descartes challenges neither belief nor knowledge, but seeks only to elevate our epistemic state to the highest obtainable ideal, which he calls *scientia*, and which readers today, for lack of a better word, mistranslate as "knowledge."

(It is worth noting, in connection with ancient skepticism, that even when Descartes is working inside what we might call the epistemology room, he does not always think that the right course of action is to suspend all beliefs. Instead, at least in the First Meditation, the meditator decides to form quite new and exotic skeptical beliefs to the effect that all of his former beliefs are false. See Lecture Six, note 6, for discussion.)

For a reading of Descartes like my own, see Janet Broughton, *Descartes's Method of Doubt*, pp. 46–9. But Broughton does not have a worked-out account of what Descartes is after. She compares the method of doubt to a game in which one "winds up suspending judgment about things it would be quite reasonable to believe." Why? "The answer must be that the meditator wants what he thinks the method of doubt can give him: a way to achieve sturdy and lasting results in the sciences" (*Descartes's Method of Doubt*, pp. 49–50). Broughton is paraphrasing the start of the First Meditation, but why speak of the "sciences," when Descartes's immediate aim in the *Meditations* is declaredly philosophical? The problem, as in the literature on Aristotle, is that without the notion of an idealized epistemology we lack any better conceptual framework in which to locate Descartes's project.

Lex Newman's *Stanford Encyclopedia* entry is notably sensitive to whether Descartes's epistemology is a theory of knowledge in our sense of the term. Newman settles on the convention of referring to 'Knowledge' with a capital K, thereby marking, but not settling, the question of what such a thing is supposed to be ("Descartes' Epistemology"). Christopher Hookway remarks of the *Meditations* that "the modern concern with 'knows' and its cognates is almost entirely absent" there, but offers no alternative picture of Descartes's project other than the statement that "his aim seems to be to show that he can contribute to scientific inquiry successfully" ("How to Be a Virtue Epistemologist," p. 196). For Descartes's continuity with the Aristotelian conception of *scientia*, see e.g. Nicholas Wolterstorff, *John Locke and the Ethics of Belief*, though he overstates the situation when he remarks that "Descartes took over intact the traditional medieval tripartite scheme of knowledge, faith, and opinion, offering no substantial innovation in how these are to be understood. His attention fell almost entirely on that species of knowledge which is *scientia*" (p. 182).

A reading of Descartes's conception of *scientia* that is fairly close to my own is Ernest Sosa's. He finds in Descartes two levels of knowledge: an ordinary level of mere *cognitio* and a higher grade of *scientia*, which he describes as "reflective, enlightened knowledge" ("How to Resolve the Pyrrhonian Problematic," p. 240; see also *A Virtue Epistemology*, pp. 126–33). The result is that, for Descartes, not all knowledge rises to the level of *scientia* and, accordingly, much of what ordinarily gets said about Cartesian epistemology applies in fact only to one particular, high-grade kind of knowledge. Sosa sees Descartes as the forerunner to his own project, which is to identify two levels of epistemic goodness that might be worthy of the term 'knowledge,' depending on how strictly one understands that term. Although I am broadly sympathetic to all of this, I understand these two levels differently. Descartes is not giving us two ways to understand what it is to know something, nor is he marking two particularly salient boundaries of epistemic excellence. Instead, one finds in Descartes various casual assumptions, almost entirely undeveloped, about what it is to know something in some more ordinary sense. Then one finds in Descartes an ideal theory, which he thinks he can attain in certain domains, as described in the *Meditations* and elsewhere. This is, if you like, a kind of knowledge, but it has little to do with 'knowledge' as we now use that term.

More recently, Sosa has made it clear that he does not suppose there are exactly two well-defined conceptions of knowledge, low and high. Rather, there is a spectrum of worse and better cases, and the question of where to apply the label 'knowledge' is, for Sosa, "largely verbal" ("Replies," p. 430). This is appealing in its attempt to escape the lexicology trap, but does not bring us any closer to the lecture's main point, which is that Descartes is describing not one or another threshold along a spectrum, but the ideal attainable limit of that spectrum.

The Ideal of Certainty

Note 3 (p. 26). Legions of modern epistemologists have described how certainty is treated in a few canonical texts, such as the *Meditations*, and extrapolated from there to the whole history of philosophy. In so doing, they are not, as it happens, far from the truth. Thus Michael Williams writes: "For much of its history, our epistemological tradition tended to insist that knowledge properly so-called requires absolute certainty" ("The Agrippan Argument," p. 123). This is roughly right, but needs tweaking. It would be hard, first, to find anyone—except perhaps an acknowledged skeptic—who has supposed that human beings ought to aim for "absolute" certainty. Second, the demand for certainty did not generally arise because of some notion of how we should "properly" speak of 'knowledge'—unless 'properly' means just *strictly*. Instead the demand arose because of the assumption that a theory of knowledge should focus on the ideal case.

Among later medieval authors, one can find the connection between *scientia* and certainty in Peter Abelard: "*scientia* is neither thought [*intellectus*] nor estimation; instead it is the soul's very certainty, which endures even without estimation or thought (*De intellectibus*, n. 27). But this seems to refer to the stability of *scientia* as a disposition, as contrasted with occurrent thoughts.

The first Latin commentary on the *Posterior Analytics*, that of Robert Grosseteste (*c.*1228), has very little to say about certainty. The most developed passage is this one:

> Things are said to be certain by virtue of a relation they bear to cognition or mental sight. Therefore I hold that there is a spiritual light that floods over intelligible objects and the mind's eye, a light that is related to the interior eye and intelligible objects just as the corporeal sun is related to the corporeal eye and corporeal visible objects. Therefore intelligible objects that are more receptive of this spiritual light are more visible to the interior eye, and things the natures of which are more nearly like this light are more receptive of it. And so things that are more receptive of this light are penetrated more perfectly by a mental acuity that is likewise a spiritual irradiation. This more perfect penetration is greater certitude.   (*Comm. Post. an.* I.17.39–46)

Grosseteste does not build certainty into his account of *scientia*.

Albert the Great takes the certainty of *scientia* to establish its perfection. Thus the passage quoted in this lecture (p. 26) immediately goes on to conclude (as partly quoted in Lecture One, p. 7): "And from this it is clear that this alone is unconditionally desirable among the logical sciences. It is, therefore, the end and most perfect and the only unconditionally desirable thing among the logical sciences, and is alone nobler and more excellent than the others on account of the certitude of its proofs" (*Comm. Post. an.* I.1.1, in *Opera* [ed. Jammy] vol 1: 514a).

Aquinas's gloss on Aristotle's canonical definition of *scientia* at *Posterior Analytics* I.2, 71^{b}9–12 goes as follows, certainty being invoked at (c):

> When [Aristotle] says **We think we have** *scientia*, etc. [71^{b}9], he offers a definition of having *scientia simpliciter*. With respect to this we should consider that to have *scientia* of something is to cognize it perfectly. This, however, is to apprehend its truth perfectly, for the same things are principles of a thing's existence and of its truth, as is clear from *Metaphysics* II [993^{b}23–30]. Therefore [a] one who has *scientia*, if he is cognizing perfectly, must cognize the cause of the thing of which he has *scientia*. [b] If, however, he were to cognize the cause only, then he would not yet cognize the effect actually (which is to have *scientia simpliciter*), but only virtually (which is to have *scientia secundum quid* and as it were *per accidens*). Hence he who has *scientia simpliciter* must also cognize the *application* of cause to

effect. But [c] since *scientia* is also a certain cognition of the thing, and someone cannot cognize with certainty a thing that possibly stands otherwise, it thus must further be the case that an object of *scientia* cannot stand otherwise. Therefore, since [a] *scientia* is perfect cognition, he thus says **When we think we cognize the cause**; but because [b] it is an actual cognition through which we have *scientia simpliciter*, he adds: **And that it is its cause**; and because [c] it is a certain cognition, he adds **And it is not possible for it to stand otherwise**.

(Comm. Post. an. I.4 n. 5)

Compare Aquinas's remark at *Comm. Phys.* I.1.18: "*scientia* requires not just any sort of cognition, but the certitude of cognition." Part of what motivates Aquinas's thinking here is the Aristotelian assumption (following *Nicomachean Ethics* VI) that *scientia* is an intellectual virtue, supplemented by the Augustinian understanding of a virtue as infallible. See, for example, *Summa theol.* 1a2ae 57.2 ad 3, and compare Aquinas's gloss, at *Comm. Ethic.* VI.3, n. 1145, on Aristotle's remarks on ἐπιστήμη at *Nicomachean Ethics* VI.3: there Aquinas weaves *certitudo* through the whole discussion. For a very helpful study of Aquinas's thinking about certainty and probability, see Edmund Byrne, *Probability and Opinion*.

By the later thirteenth century, the certainty requirement is everywhere. See Bonaventure: "For scientific [*scientialem*] cognition there is necessarily required unchanging truth on the part of what is knowable and infallible certainty on the part of the knower" (*Sermones de diversis* 33.6). Scotus repeats his own favored definition in various places, certainty being listed as the first requirement from which the other features of *scientia* follow; see *Ordinatio* prol. p. 4 qq. 1–2 (Vatican edn. vol. 1, n. 208); *Reportatio* III d. 24 q. unic. (ed. Wadding vol. 11.1, n. 16); *Reportatio* prologue 1.1 (Wolter and Bychkov edn. vol. 1: n. 9; quoted in Lecture One, note 6). Scotus's broader views on *scientia* are discussed in some detail in Eileen Serene, "Demonstrative Science."

In Buridan, matters become more complex, as this lecture discusses, but at any rate the connection between *scientia* and certainty endures. See, for example, *Quaest. Post. an.* I.2, "*scientia* differs from opinion in this, that *scientia* requires certainty, which opinion does not," and I.7, "here 'to have *scientia*' is taken not broadly [*communiter*] but in the most proper and strong sense. Having *scientia* in this way requires evidentness, certainty, and firmness."

For useful overviews of medieval conceptions of certainty, see Joël Biard, "Certitudo" and Rudolf Schüssler, *Moral im Zweifel*, vol. 1, pp. 51–4. For a broader picture, see James Franklin, *Science of Conjecture*, who aptly remarks that "philosophy and religion are old enemies of probability" (p. 195).

Certainty in Antiquity

Note 4 (p. 27). In a book-length two-part article on the history of the notion of certainty, Andrea Schrimm-Heins claims that *certitudo ist kein Begriff der klassischen Latinität* ("Gewißheit und Sicherheit" 1991: 141, 1992: 198). Does she mean that "*certitudo* is not a word in classical Latin," or that the very concept is missing? To be sure, the abstract noun is rarely or never used before we find it fourth-century Christian authors. Even so, the adjective *certus* is very common in antiquity and regularly has an epistemic sense. Perhaps it is significant that ancient speakers felt no need to employ an abstract noun and that early Christian speakers (or authors) did. But the idea or concept of certainty is not alien to antiquity, even if classical Latin authors contented themselves with the adjectival form of the word.

It is, however, an exceedingly large and difficult matter to trace the certainty requirement through ancient thought, a task made considerably harder by the tangle of different things one might mean by 'certainty.' Arguably, the notion appears in Plato. Relevant passages include *Theaetetus* 152c, where ἐπιστήμη is "inerrant" (ἀψευδές), *Republic* V, 477e, where it is "infallible" (ἀναμάρτητον), and *Philebus* 59c, where the goal of inquiry seems to be "certainty, purity, truth and what we may call integrity" (τό τε βέβαιον καὶ τὸ καθαρὸν καὶ ἀληθὲς καὶ ὃ δὴ λέγομεν εἰλικρινές). Similarly, Socrates challenges Theaetetus to do better than "arguments from plausibility and likelihood" (πιθανολογίᾳ τε καὶ εἰκόσι) (162e). See also the famous passage at *Meno* 98a where true beliefs are said to "wander" until they are tied down. That discussion is particularly striking because it seems to go beyond the familiar notion that the *objects* of knowledge ought to be unchanging. It seems to demand, further, that we have some means of connecting our beliefs to those objects.

As Lecture One discusses (p. 6), Aristotle puts great weight on the necessity of the objects of ἐπιστήμη. In that sense, his theory demands certainty on the side of objects. But where medieval translations render him as appealing to a further sort of certainty, on the agent's side, the Greek shows him to be saying something rather different. In particular, the varying standards for "certainty" described at *Nicomachean Ethics* I 3, 1094^{b}13 are in fact better rendered as a claim about "precision" (τὸ ἀκριβές; see Lecture One, note 18). Presumably beliefs that are precise with regard to necessary objects will be highly stable. Thus, in contrast with ἐπιστήμη, whose objects are necessary, opinion (δόξα) concerns things that can be otherwise, and thus is "unstable" (ἀβέβαιον; *Post An.* I.33, 89^{a}6). For a recent attempt to make a case for the role of certainty in Aristotle's epistemology, see David Bloch, "Aristotle on the Exactness or Certainty of Knowledge."

Certainty plays a more pronounced role in Stoic thought, as is manifest from the Stoics' way of distinguishing between κατάληψις and ἐπιστήμη. Thus Stobaeus: "ἐπιστήμη is a κατάληψις that is secure [ἀσφαλῆ] and unchangeable by reason" (Long and Sedley, *Hellenistic Philosophers* 41H). Cicero sets out the Stoic criterion through Lucullus: "it cannot be doubted that no decision of the wise man can be false, nor is it enough for it not to be false, but it must also be stable, fixed, and established (*ratum*)" (*Academica* II.9.27). The metaphor of a closed fist is reported at *Academica* II.47.145 (Long and Sedley 41A). By the time of Lactantius in the early fourth century, it is a commonplace that, as he puts it, "*scientia* concerns what is certain and opinion what is uncertain" (*Divinae institutiones* III.3).

The ancient skeptics were happy enough to follow the Stoics in their quest for certainty and then fight back judo-style, as Broughton describes it, "using the strength of the Stoic's own maxim to flip him into suspense of judgment" (*Descartes's Method of Doubt*, p. 37). In their own right, however, the ancient skeptics generally did not endorse any particular standard for belief, weak or strong, nor did they focus on any particular cognitive state that we might dub "knowledge" and then make trouble over its possession. Rather, they pushed things all the way to the radical juncture of what Lecture Six (p. 128) calls *epistemic defeat*, arguing that neither side of any given question is more likely than the other.

There is, however, an intriguing exception to this pattern. Philo of Larissa, generally considered the last of the Academic skeptics, seems in the final stages of his career to have positively rejected the Stoic doctrine that κατάληψις cannot be false and embraced instead a fallibilist theory of knowledge, which he argued could be achieved. (The textual evidence regarding Philo is limited, making interpretation contentious, but see Charles Brittain, *Philo of Larissa*, esp. ch. 3, for a compelling account.)

Certainty in Classical Arabic Philosophy

Note 5 (p. 28). For a guide to the late antique intellectual world of Alexandria, see Edward Watts, *City and School in Late Antique Athens and Alexandria*. On the connection between these Alexandrian traditions and early Arabic thought, see Dimitri Gutas's reconstruction of the views of Paul the Persian. Paul is a pre-Islamic Syriac author whom Gutas shows to have drawn on David, a late Alexandrian Aristotelian. Paul's views, in turn, appear in the tenth-century Islamic scholar Miskawayh. In Miskawayh's account, which apparently derives from

Paul and ultimately from David, demonstrative syllogisms "are all undoubtedly true and certain" (Gutas, "Paul the Persian," p. 243).

Al-Kindī is remarkable for wanting to apply to philosophy the standards for certainty that he found in mathematics, particularly in Euclid and Ptolemy. One of his (regrettably) lost works was entitled *That Philosophy Can Be Acquired Only through the Science of Mathematics*. For further information see Peter Adamson, *Al-Kindī* ch. 2; Dimitri Gutas, *Greek Thought, Arabic Culture*, pp. 119–20; Roshdi Rashed, "Al-Kindī's Commentary on Archimedes," pp. 7–9 and "The Philosophy of Mathematics." Interestingly, al-Kindī shows no signs of familiarity with later Alexandrian Aristotelianism and only the most cursory familiarity with the *Posterior Analytics*, which was translated into Arabic too late to figure prominently in his thought. His influences are the mathematical traditions of antiquity.

It is only in the generations after al-Kindī that certainty comes to be joined to the method of the *Posterior Analytics* in the Arabic tradition. On the appearance of يقين ('certainty') in the Arabic *Posterior Analytics* and on its subsequent importance within al-Fārābī, see Deborah Black, "Knowledge and Certitude," who writes (p. 2):

Despite the prevalence of certitude in Arabic accounts of demonstration, one would be hard pressed to identify a specific counterpart in Aristotle's own presentation of his theory of demonstration in the *Posterior Analytics*. Indeed, one of the features that makes the Arabic conception of certitude important and philosophically interesting is it that it is unprecedented in the underlying Aristotelian theories that it is meant to explicate.

The last claim is too strong in light of the way certitude appears in the Alexandrian tradition, but clearly the Arabic tradition is original in the stress it gives this notion within an Aristotelian context. On the *Posterior Analytics* in the Arabic tradition more generally, see Michael Marmura, "The *Fortuna* of the Posterior Analytics."

For al-Fārābī's conception of demonstration, see his *Kitāb al-burhān*, an excerpt of which is translated in McGinnis and Reisman, *Classical Arabic Philosophy*, pp. 63–8. That text begins with the words "Perfect assent is certainty." See also David Reisman, "Al-Fārābī and the Philosophical Curriculum," pp. 66–7. On the link to Alexandria, Reisman remarks: "The al-Fārābīan corpus is almost single-mindedly driven by the combined goals of rehabilitating and then reinventing the scholarly study of philosophy as practiced by the Alexandrian school of neo-Aristotelianism" (p. 55).

Paul Heck, *Skepticism in Classical Islam*, p. 70, quotes Abū al-Ḥasan al-ʿĀmirī (d. 992):

it is impossible to decide the truth of matters that are disputed without the scale of logic, which is reliable for its justice and brings certainty. The art of logic is the intellectual tool by which the rational soul distinguishes between true and false in theoretical matters, between good and evil in ethical matters. Its place in souls that make use of it is like a straight standard by which knowledge is weighed in the balance.

Avicenna characterizes metaphysics as "the best knowledge [علم]—that is, certainty [اليقين]—of the best thing known—that is, God and the causes after him" (*al-Shifāʾ*, Metaphysics I.2 n. 18). At the start of his treatment of demonstration in *al-Shifāʾ*, he writes that its benefit is "to arrive at knowledge [العلوم] that is certain and conceptions that are true and beneficial, indeed necessary, for us" (trans. Marmura, "Fortuna," p. 92). Deborah Black shows that Avicenna grounds even testimony-based knowledge on its ability to engender certainty ("Certitude, Justification," pp. 132–3). More generally on Avicenna, see Jon McGinnis, "Avicenna's Naturalized Epistemology." For al-Ghazālī, see Farid Jabre, *La notion de certitude selon Ghazali*. For a broader discussion of the Islamic tradition, see McGinnis, "Scientific Methodologies in Medieval Islam."

There is also strong support within the Islamic religious context for the importance of certainty. An often quoted hadith has it that "certainty is the whole of faith" (الْيَقِينُ الْإِيمَانُ كُلُّهُ) (Aḥmad ibn al-Ḥusayn Bayhaqī, *Shuʿab al-īmān*, n. 9083).

Subjective versus Objective Certainty

Note 6 (p. 29). The distinction between subjective and objective senses of certainty can be found throughout scholastic authors. See, e.g., Thomas Aquinas: "Certainty can be considered in two ways. First, from the cause of the certainty, and in this way a thing is said to be more certain when it has a more certain cause . . . Second, on the part of the subject, and in this way a thing is said to be more certain when someone's intellect follows it more fully" (*Summa theol.* 2a2ae 4.8c). Aquinas insists on this distinction because it helps him sort out the different ways in which faith and *scientia* count as certain. Still, with respect to *scientia* itself, Aquinas thinks that the subjective and objective senses are two sides of the same coin. At a subjective level, certainty requires confidence, but this confidence must be grounded in a fixed reality, which gives it sufficient stability to make it count as objectively certain. Much the same distinction between subjective and objective senses of certainty (اليقين) can be found earlier in Avicenna (see McGinnis, "Avicenna's Naturalized Epistemology," pp. 131–2).

William Ockham briefly remarks that "certainty is taken either for adherence or for evidentness" (*Ord.* prol. q. 7 [*Opera theol.* vol. 1: 200]). Buridan too recognizes a distinction between subjective and objective: "certainty requires two things. One is on the part of the proposition assented to, that it is true . . . The other is on our part, namely that our assent is firm, without doubt or fear of the opposite" (*Summulae* VIII.4.4, trans. p. 707). But Buridan does not regard a purely subjective conviction as true certainty. As he goes on, "the credulity with which we assent to something false is not certain, but uncertain and fallacious." This is a common view. Durand of St. Pourçain had earlier drawn his own version of a distinction between an objective certainty ("certainty of evidentness") and a subjective one ("certainty of adhesion") and then insisted that the latter counts as certainty only in an improper sense (*Sent.* [3rd vers.] III.23.7 n. 7). Adam Wodeham describes it as contradictory for a false judgment to be described as certain (*Lectura secunda* prol. q. 2 §3 [vol. 1: 37]). Before that, one can find Scotus similarly taking for granted that certainty entails truth (*Ord.* I.3.1 qq. 1–2 [Vatican edn. vol. 3, n. 29; trans. p. 52]). Others, however, are more inclined to think of certainty, at its core, as a subjective state of mind. Thus Aquinas: "certainty is nothing other than the intellect's being determined to one thing" (*Sent.* III.23.2.2.3c). Domingo de Soto, in his remarkable sixteenth-century discussion of the question "Is *scientia* rightly defined?" writes that "certainty is the same as the firmness of assent from which someone is unable to be moved or can be moved only with difficulty" (*De demonstratione* q. 2, p. 303A).

Degrees of Certainty

Note 7 (p. 29). It is common enough, historically and today, to find authors insisting that certainty does not admit of degrees. In addition to the examples quoted in this lecture, see al-Ghazālī: "certainty cannot be weak or strong, because there is no more or less in the absence of doubt" (in Jabre, *Notion de certitude*, p. 439). Nicole Oresme, similarly, holds "as plausible" the claim that "assent with evidentness cannot be intensified or diminished," which he explains as the claim that an evident cognition cannot be made "more certain," because when something is evident then "no argument can incline it to believe the opposite" (*Quaest. de an.* III.16, p. 437). For modern examples, see Peter Unger, *Ignorance*, and Franklin, *Science of Conjecture*: "just as a suspected criminal is not a kind of criminal, so moral certainty is not a kind of certainty" (p. 70). Even so, since it is hard to find anyone who wants to hold human beings to anything like the perfect ideal of certainty, this invites the thought that there must be degrees of progress toward the ideal. Thus Scotus remarks that "there is nothing wrong [*non est inconveniens*] with some beliefs [*credita*] being more evident than others" (*Ordinatio* I.42c [Vatican edn., vol. 6, n. 15]). Peter of Ailly considers some interesting arguments for the view that certainty and evidentness cannot come in degrees (*Sent.* prol. q. 1 art. 1, pp. 147–8), but ultimately he concludes that they can (pp. 155–6). Buridan too, as discussed later in this note, allows for degrees of certainty in various domains.

Nicholas of Autrecourt makes for an interesting example. As noted in this lecture (p. 29), his most famous work, the letters, seem to insist on something like the perfect ideal. (For a series of arguments in response, claiming that "the certainty of evidentness" does come in degrees, see Giles's letter to Nicholas, in the *Correspondence*, pp. 84–7, nn. 13–16.) But even Autrecourt, in his less studied *Tractatus*, which in fact captures more of his own views, settles for the heavily qualified claim that, "if we have any certainty about things, I say that it is plausible that everything that appears to be is" (*Tractatus* ch. 6, p. 228). Autrecourt's views in this area are rich and important but difficult to discern, especially because the *Tractatus* itself seems to shift in its views over the course of its various chapters. For a detailed discussion, see Christophe Grellard, *Croire et savoir*, which reads Autrecourt as abandoning the requirement of certainty and allowing that the best we can do is construct an epistemology grounded upon a form of probabilism. Also on this theme, see Dallas Denery, "Autrecourt on Saving the Appearances" and Dominik Perler, "Relations nécessaires ou contingentes?"

If this is indeed Autrecourt's considered view, then it is ironic for several reasons. For one thing, Buridan's notion of moral certainty is generally thought to have been formulated as a response to Autrecourt's absolute conception of certainty, in his letters. But if Autrecourt himself embraces the merely probable, then their views, at least in this regard, are not as far apart as it would seem judging only from Autrecourt's letters. Second, Autrecourt would be condemned in 1346 for various theses found in his letters, including the claim that "the certainty of evidentness has no degrees" (*Correspondence*, appendix A, n. 1.6). But, in light of Autrecourt's views in the *Tractatus*, it seems that his broader aim was to show precisely how our cognitive achievements come in degrees and how a theory of knowledge could be framed around something less than the absolute ideal. Lecture Four returns to Autrecourt's views in some detail.

Higher Order Certainty

There are two interesting further features of the certainty requirement that are associated with its absolute character, and hence deserve mention here. The first is the common expectation not just of certainty with respect to the first-order belief in P, but also of some kind of higher order certainty with respect to that first-order certainty. This is especially characteristic of Arabic philosophy, and al-Fārābī seems to be its source:

Certainty means that we are convinced, with respect to what we assent to, that it cannot possibly be different from our conviction. Moreover, we are convinced that this conviction about it also cannot be otherwise, to the point that when one reaches a given conviction concerning his initial conviction, he maintains that it, too, cannot be otherwise, and so on *ad infinitum*.

(*Kitāb al-burhān*, trans. McGinnis and Reisman, *Classical Arabic Philosophy*, p. 64)

Although al-Fārābī's formulation is couched in subjective terms—what we are "convinced" of—it is clear from the broader context of his views that he means the test to be understood in objective terms as well. At the first-order level, this means that the proposition in question cannot be otherwise—it is objectively necessary, at least given that we are assenting to it. Second-order certainty, according to al-Fārābī, further requires that one's conviction itself cannot be otherwise. For more information, see Deborah Black, "Knowledge and Certitude."

Within the Arabic tradition, the persistence of this focus on higher order certainty is quite striking. Avicenna, for instance, shares al-Fārābī's commitment to an infinite series of higher level beliefs: "certitude is to know that you know, and to know that you know that you know, *ad infinitum*" (in Black, "Knowledge and Certitude," p. 44; more recently, see Black's discussions in "Avicenna on Self-Awareness and Knowing that One Knows," esp. pp. 76–81, and "Certitude, Justification," esp. pp. 122–3). Maimonides invokes the higher order require-ment at *Guide for the Perplexed* I.50: "If, together with this belief, one realizes that a belief different from it is in no way possible and that no starting point can be found in the mind for a rejection of this belief or for the supposition that a different belief is possible, there is certainty (يقين)." (For the broader context here, see Josef Stern, *The Matter and Form of Maimonides'* Guide, pp. 137–48.) Averroes, discussing the possibility of a regress of higher order knowledge (علم), remarks that "the second knowledge is one of the conditions of the first knowledge" (*Incoherence of the Incoherence* VI.81, trans. p. 212).

It is interesting to consider what this insistence on higher order certainty amounts to. The respective belief contents at issue seem to be that (1) it must be the case that P (first order), and (2) it must be the case that I am convinced that it must be the case that P (second order). What (2) seems to yield, most directly, is indubitability: I cannot doubt my first-order judgment, because I judge (at the second order) that the first-order judgment cannot be otherwise. If at least that much is right, then two further questions arise. First, as this lecture considers in other contexts, we can ask whether the demand is for mere indubitability, or also for infallibility. Second, we can ask why exactly all these authors are so convinced of the need for such higher order certainty. Perhaps one reason is that they all aim to block the possibility that one might come to a right conviction about the necessity of a certain fact, but might do so accidentally, as a matter of luck rather than in a way that is itself necessitated. One might, for instance, be lucky in choosing whose testimony to trust, or lucky in the sorts of particulars one observes, or lucky in the sort of community one grows up in. Higher order certainty bars all such cases, by requiring that one's conviction itself be stably arrived at, in a way that, as al-Fārābī puts it (above), "also cannot be otherwise." To get this payoff, it is critical that the sort of certainty at issue should be not just a subjective confidence, but an objective fact about the way the belief has been formed.

Although other traditions do not tend to speak expressly of second-order beliefs, they effectively insist on the same sort of higher order stability. This lecture (p. 27), for instance, quotes Augustine echoing the Stoics in his insistence that "nobody should be in error about it" (first order) "or vacillate when pressed by any opponents" (≈second order) (*Contra academicos* I.7.19). Descartes, too, holds that "*scientia* is conviction based on a reason so strong that it can never be shaken by any stronger reason" (to Regius, III: 65). Admittedly, it is not entirely clear that this sort of freedom from vacillation is equivalent to the Arabic demand for higher order certainty. This is the reading of the Stoic doctrine that one finds in Lloyd Gerson, *Ancient Epistemology*, p. 110. But there are, presumably, ways to secure such stability other than the request for higher order knowledge.

Occasionally, one does find Latin authors expressly invoking the need for higher order certainty. Thomas Wylton, for instance, seeking to establish the possibility of multiple concurrent thoughts (see Lecture Five, note 1), remarks that "if someone actually knows [*sciat*] some conclusion necessarily . . . then at the same time he knows that he knows it" (in Stella, "Quaestiones de libero arbitrio," p. 507). Durand of St. Pourçain remarks that "we adhere more firmly to that from which we withdraw with greater difficulty; but one withdraws with greater difficulty from *scientia* than from faith—assuming he truly has *scientia* and knows [*sciat*] that he has it" (*Sent.* [3rd vers.] III.23.7 n. 7). Autrecourt offers this definition of certainty: "when someone has a clear and evident cognition of some proposition, that it is so, and also perceives that he has such a clear and evident cognition, then one says that he is certain" (*Tractatus* ch. 6, p. 235).

Some scholastic authors, however, reject a higher order requirement. In note 13 to this lecture I argue that Buridan rejects it. Claude Panaccio, for different reasons, has claimed that Ockham rejects the requirement ("Savoir selon Ockham," p. 100). Peter of Ailly seems to be inconsistent on the question. He denies that first-order knowledge entails an actual higher order knowledge, on the grounds that this would require infinitely many acts of knowledge. But Ailly grants that "it is absurd for someone to know (*sciat*) and consider actually whether he knows and not know that he knows" (*Sent.* prol. q. 1 art. 1, p. 159, taken verbatim from John of Mirecourt, *Sent.* q. 5, p. 437). Yet elsewhere in that same discussion Ailly waffles on this issue. He considers the objection that, if a false appearance can be indistinguishable from an evident appearance, "then we would never be certain or evident that something is evident, and then we could doubt whether such an appearance *is* evident, and consequently we would have to doubt whether it is *true*" (*Sent.* prol. q. 1 art. 1, p. 147). This seems to show, quite effectively, that the absence of second-order certainty entails an absence of first-order certainty. In response, Ailly grants that this argument establishes that "it is not consistent for someone to have an evident awareness of something and to doubt whether he has an evident awareness of that thing" (p. 154). Accordingly, he holds that, "although it is not necessary that everyone having an evident awareness of something experiences it or knows it to be evident, neverthe-less everyone having such an evident awareness *can* experience this, and can know it to be evident without any new motive" (p. 154)—by which he seems to mean that the original experience itself bears the information that it is indeed evident. Yet later he seems to accept the initial premise of the objection, that it can be indiscernible to us whether or not an experience is evident (pp. 168–9). If he is prepared to allow this, then his insistence on higher order certainty falls back into doubt.

Late in the seventeenth century, Pierre-Daniel Huet contends that "to know [*connaitre*] the truth, without knowing [*savoir*] that you know [*connaissez*] the truth, is just as if you do not know [*connaissiez*] it" (*Philosophical Treatise* II.1, trans. p. 135). But Huet's purposes are skeptical (or at least somewhat so: see Lecture Six, note 8).

Causal Understanding and Certainty

A second interesting feature of the certainty requirement is that it demands a grasp not just of a single proposition, but of a much wider explanatory framework. This demand typically arises when the certainty requirement gets connected to the causal requirement discussed in Lecture One (p. 13). Buridan, for instance, discussing the phrase from Aristotle's canonical definition that "to have *scientia* is to grasp the cause of a thing" (*Post. An.* I.2, 71^{b}9), reasons as follows:

It is clear that ignorance is the opposite of *scientia* as its privation, and so it is impossible for any ignorance of a thing to coexist with perfect *scientia* about it. It is also clear that doubt never arises without ignorance . . . But doubts about a thing are removed only when its causes are grasped. Hence those who see the moon's eclipse, in ignorance of its cause, have the greatest doubts over how it could happen, whereas, by knowing the cause, all such doubt is removed. Hence it is plain that it is through knowledge of the cause or causes, and not otherwise, that certain, perfect *scientia*, excluding all ignorance, is acquired and main-tained.   (*Quaest. Post an.* proem)

Here we are told that certainty requires more than simply the infallible grasp of a given fact— for instance, that the moon is presently eclipsed. It also requires grasping other facts, in particular, the explanation of why the moon is eclipsed, in terms of the earth's shadow. Structurally, this further demand works much like the demand for higher order certainty. In grasping not just the fact that a thing is so, but also the reason why it is so, the agent is able to attain a more perfect degree of certainty about the original fact, ruling out the doubts that inevitably arise when one does not understand *how* such a thing can be happening.

Domingo de Soto likewise stresses the link between certainty and the causal requirement. Puzzling over how to square the modern focus on certainty and evidentness with the canonical Aristotelian definition that mentions neither of these things (*Post. An.* I.2, 71^{b}9–12, as quoted in Lecture One, p. 6), de Soto suggests that it is the causal part of Aristotle's definition that captures both certainty and evidentness: "it is the very same thing to cognize a thing through its cause and to judge the truth of a thing certainly and evidently" (*De demonstratione* q. 2, p. 295D).

Once one begins to insist that certainty requires causal knowledge, it becomes hard to know where to stop. Given that we are describing the ideal, it is natural to suppose that one's grasp of the reasons why must go all the way back, however far that may be. Indeed, Aquinas makes this quite explicit, glossing the start of Aristotle's *Physics* with the remark that "we all take ourselves to apprehend a thing when we have *scientia* of all its causes, from the first to the last" (*Comm. Phys.* I.1.5; compare the start of Aristotle's *Physics*, as quoted in Lecture One, p. 15). This is again analogous to higher order certainty, in particular to al-Fārābī's insistence that our convictions about our convictions go on upward, *ad infinitum*. In that case, however, the regress is perhaps less troubling, because the farther one goes into higher order thought, the less there seems to be to think about, and eventually the inquiry runs out in a way that may seem benign. In the case of prior explanations, in contrast, the regress from explanation to explanation never leaves us less to think about, and it seems quite hopeless to think we can ever come to grips with the whole explanatory framework behind any phenomenon.

Here we face again the distinction between the absolute ideal, fit for a god, and the normative ideal that we might recognize as having regulative sway over ourselves. One way in which the framework of the *Posterior Analytics* attempted to bring the causal require-ment down to the human level was to introduce a structural distinction among different epistemic domains (i.e., so-called "sciences") and then to require explanation only in a particular domain. The biologist, then, would be expected to understand the first principles of biology and the reasons why the phenomena of biology occur as they do, but would not be expected—*qua* biologist—to be able to explain the first principles of biology in terms of physics. Likewise, physicists need not ground their theories in the principles of theology. This sort of familiar balkanization of the "sciences" helps, but still goes only so far. As Lecture One discusses (p. 5), the Aristotelian corpus hardly provides much encouragement for the dream of filling in this sort of explanatory framework even within a single epistemic domain.

Buridan's way of handling such concerns is to admit that different *scientiae* can be more or less certain (*Quaest. meta.* I.3, and also *Quaest. phys.* I.5). He offers a detailed account of how the certainty of *scientia* increases to the extent that (i) its objects are firm and immutable, (ii) it leaves fewer doubts about those objects; (iii) its principles are evident, (iv) it is evident how to construct demonstrations, and (v) it is easy for us to pursue it. Each of these various conditions favors a different kind of *scientia*. Metaphysics does well on the first condition, mathematics on the fourth, and natural philosophy on the last. The condition he discusses at greatest length is the second, which turns out to involve causal understanding. *Scientia propter quid* (which reaches the reason why) is more certain that *scientia quia* (which grasps only the fact that something is so). Similarly, a *scientia* that goes deeper into the "specific reasons" (*rationes speciales*) for a thing counts as more certain. In both cases, certainty increases in proportion to explanatory power. Here too, he argues, metaphysics delivers the most certain *scientia*.

Scholastic authors from Albert the Great to the Coimbrans (i.e., the Jesuits at Coimbra University) devote entire disputed questions to whether or not *scientia* demands that one grasp *all* of a thing's causes. In the fourteenth century, see John of Jandun (*Quaest. phys.* I.3), Ockham (*Quaest. phys.* q. 137), Buridan (*Quaest. phys.* I.5), Albert of Saxony (*Quaest. phys.* I.2–3), and pseudo-Marsilius of Inghen (*Quaest. phys.* I.2–3). For sixteenth-century discus-sions, see Benedictus Pererius (*De communibus principiis* III.5) and the Coimbrans (Colle-gium Conimbricense, *Comm. Phys.* I.1.1). In parallel with those disputes, one finds the critics of scholasticism, from Nicholas of Cusa to Marin Mersenne, casting doubts on the

Aristotelian framework, on the grounds that to have *any* such knowledge would require knowledge about *everything*. Not surprisingly, the scholastic discussions proceed by drawing many nuanced distinctions. But, in the hands of their critics, the issues get treated with less finesse. Cusa, for instance, concludes categorically that, "if *scientia* of one thing is to be possessed precisely, then *scientia* of all things is necessarily to be possessed" (*Idiota de mente* III.3). Francisco Sanches similarly invokes the causal requirement to argue that *scientia* of anything requires *scientia* of all things, which makes any *scientia* impossible (*Quod nihil scitur*, pp. 196–207). The complaint turns up over and over, e.g. in Marin Mersenne (*La verité des sciences* I.2), Pierre-Daniel Huet (*Philosophical Treatise* I.7), and Joseph Glanvill: "We cannot properly and perfectly know anything in nature without the knowledge of its first causes, and the springs of natural motions. And who has any pretense to this? Who can say he has seen nature in its beginnings?" (*Essays*, p. 15). (On Mersenne's shifting attitudes toward certainty and the Aristotelian tradition, see Peter Dear, *Mersenne and the Learning of the Schools*, pp. 28–42, and Daniel Garber, "On the Frontlines.")

Within scholasticism, concerns of this kind gave rise to a strand of thought that treated *scientia* as obtaining only *ex conditione*, on the grounds that, at least in natural philosophy, there is no way of establishing that the postulated cause is the only possible cause. This doctrine has received attention, especially as it was boldly presented in Agostino Nifo, on which see A. C. Crombie, *Robert Grosseteste*, pp. 297–9 and Nicholas Jardine, "Epistemology of the Sciences," p. 689. The general idea has antecedents in Buridan, for whom, as this lecture discusses (p. 32), the certainty of natural philosophy holds only *ex suppositione*. For Buridan and for earlier scholastics, see Hans Thijssen, "Buridan and Autrecourt on Causality," pp. 250–4.

Certainty in the Seventeenth Century

Note 8 (p. 30). Descartes's attitude toward certainty is consistently unsettled, promising infallibility and then conceding that we may have to settle for indubitability. *Principles* I.43 is typical. Here he offers an important and straightforward statement of his foundational methodological rule: "it is certain that we will never mistake anything false for the true, provided we give our assent only to what we clearly and distinctly perceive." This is as clear a claim of infallible certainty as one could want. He goes on to argue for this claim in the way one might expect, through divine goodness. But then, remarkably, he hedges: "And even if there were no way of proving this, the minds of all of us have been molded by nature so that whenever we perceive something clearly, we spontaneously assent to it and can in no way doubt that it is true." So Descartes asserts infallibility and is prepared to argue for it; but he is also prepared to offer a lesser guarantee of indubitability, should the proof of infallibility seem inadequate. The reasons for that inadequacy will be considered in Lecture Five. For now, the main point is just that he very regularly does limit himself to that lesser guarantee. Indeed, if one looks at the way this lecture characterizes his commitment to certainty (pp. 22–3), it is almost always in terms of mere indubitability, not infallibility. Thus, to give just one example, the difference between mere *persuasio* and *scientia* is that in the first case "there remains some reason that could lead us to doubt," whereas *scientia* is "based on a reason so strong that it can never be shaken by any stronger reason" (to Regius in 1640 [III: 65]).

Descartes's fullest discussion of this issue comes in the Second Set of Replies, where he famously remarks that the certainty he claims for himself is merely "human certainty," not that of God or an angel: "What is it to us if someone imagines that something whose truth we are so firmly convinced of appears false to God or to an angel, and so *is* false, absolutely speaking? What do we care about this 'absolute falsity,' given that we do not in any way believe it or even have the slightest suspicion of it?" (VII: 144–5). Descartes is not saying that such doubts are incoherent or unintelligible, only that we do not put any credence in them: we lack, as the Latin more literally puts it, even a *minimum* suspicion of this possibility. But to say that our credence here is at zero is, again, to appeal to subjective indubitability rather than objective infallibility. And such a response is liable to seem worrisomely *ad hoc*, particularly coming from the author of the notorious skeptical arguments of the First Meditation. It may seem that one should either insist on certainty or not; and, if one cannot achieve it, one should simply say so rather than waffling over the distinction between absolute and human certainty. Yet, once one sees Descartes's project as a version of ideal theory, such worries should somewhat lessen. It is no part of an idealized epistemology to engage in a quixotic search for the absolute, divine ideal. The point is to understand what *we* are capable of, and then consider the circumstances and domains in which that might profitably be achieved. Only once allowances are made for the human predicament can we arrive at the sort of normative ideal that has implications for our cognitive ambitions. From Descartes's point of view, then, it is just tedious and misguided to make objections that turn on requiring a sort of certainty that is not within our power. It is in this spirit that he goes on to insist in this passage, as quoted in this lecture (p. 29), that the sort of complete indubitability he offers "is clearly the same as the most perfect certainty" (VII: 145). Yet, plainly, this is not so. Indubitability is good, but infallibility would be still better, particularly when combined, along the lines of the previous note, with a higher order, infallible grasp of that infallibility. Descartes cannot quite bring himself to admit that his method has no way of delivering that result. But, since he is the most careful of philosophers (even if not the most honest), he carefully and repeatedly flags the possibility of this lesser result. His view seems to be as follows: he *has* established infallibility but, if he has not, then no one can—and in that case the highest normative ideal would be indubitability, and he has plainly achieved that. Either way, he thinks he has achieved his ambition. (Thanks to Tad Schmaltz for pushing me on how I want to read this difficult passage from the Second Replies.)

Turning to Galileo, it is not clear whether his aim is infallibility or mere indubitability, but it is clear enough that, in some form or another, he is committed to the traditional ideal of demonstrative certainty. See, for example, the third letter on sunspots—"I do not wish to mix dubious things with those that are definite and certain" (*Discoveries*, p. 140)—or this remark from an unpublished note: "Not to believe that a proof of the earth's motion exists until one has been shown is very prudent, nor do we demand that anyone believe such a thing without proof... If these men [who, with Copernicus, argue for the earth's motion] are only ninety percent right, then they are defeated" (*Discoveries*, p. 169). In the *Two New Sciences*, Salviati remarks: "You reason from good probability [*probabilmente*]. But apart from mere truth-likeness [*verisimile*], I wish to increase the probability so much by an experiment [*una esperienza*] that it will fall little short of equality with necessary demonstration" (Third Day, trans. p. 162).

Critical to Galileo's position on the heliocentric model vis-à-vis church authority is a distinction between two levels of certainty:

Among physical propositions there are some with regard to which all human speculation and discourse cannot supply more than a probable opinion and a truth-like conjecture [*probabile opinione e verisimil coniettura*] in place of sure and demonstrated science [*sicura e dimostrata scienza*]; for example, whether the stars are animate. Then there are other propositions of which we have (or may firmly believe that we can have) undoubted certainty [*indubitata certezza*] through experience, long observation, and rigorous demonstrations; for example whether or not the earth and sun move, or whether or not the earth is spherical. As to the first sort of proposition, I have no doubt that where human reasoning cannot reach—and where consequently we can have no science [*scienza*] but only opinion and faith—it is necessary in piety to comply absolutely with the strict sense of scripture. But as to the other kind, I would believe, as said before, that first we are to make certain of the fact, which will reveal to us the true senses of the Bible, and these will most certainly be found to agree with the proved fact, even though at first the words sounded otherwise, because two truths can never contradict each other.

(Letter to the Grand Duchess Christina, in *Discoveries*, p. 197; *Opere* vol. 5: 330)

Given these two options, Galileo could advocate for the Copernican model only if he could achieve something very much like the epistemic ideal. Thus Ernan McMullin writes: "Part of the problem was that he [Galileo] admitted only two categories of suppositions: true and fictive; the all-important third alternative of 'highly likely' (or 'well-supported' or 'best available') is not mentioned by him and would hardly have been admissible as yet in natural philosophy, since it would have suggested opinion, not science" ("Conceptions of Science," p. 63). See also Edith Sylla, "Galileo and Probable Arguments" and A. C. Crombie:

> I should argue that Galileo aimed in the end at total certainty, that it was Aristotle and no other who provided him with the ideal of truly scientific certain knowledge, and that he retained this ideal from his earliest to his latest writings, even as he rejected the methods and destroyed the content of Aristotle's physics, and even when he recognized that demonstration truly scientific by Aristotelian criteria eluded his grasp.
>
> ("Sources of Galileo," pp. 158–9)

Compare Nicolaus Copernicus, who was more ready to settle for something less: "You see from all of these, then, that the earth's motion is more plausible [*probabilior*] than its rest" (*De revolutionibus* I.8).

Still, not even Galileo expected natural philosophers to achieve the highest level of certainty, as found in mathematics. Thus he has Sagredo remark: "I suppose Simplicio is also convinced as fully as permitted by natural science, in which he is aware that geometrical evidentness cannot be demanded" (*Dialogue*, trans. p. 475; *Opere* vol. 7: 436). On the claim of God-like certainty in a limited domain and on the appearance of this doctrine in the church's inquisition against him, see Ursula Goldenbaum, "The Geometrical Method," p. 277.

Degrees of Evidentness

From Certainty to Probability

Note 9 (p. 31). Newton counts as another post-scholastic proponent of certainty. Indeed, McMullin speaks of his "almost obsessive attachment to the ideal of certainty, an attachment which grew stronger, rather than lessoning, as he grew older" ("Impact," p. 295). Francis Bacon is sometimes also put in this camp. According to Barbara Shapiro, "Baconian science aimed for the certainty of mathematical demonstration via empirical data and proper scientific procedure" (*Probability and Certainty*, p. 24). And Franklin: "on the whole Bacon is the most insistent on certainty of all the founders of the scientific revolution" (*Science of Conjecture*, p. 217). On close inspection, however, Bacon can be seen to fall into a somewhat different category. To be sure, the goal of his efforts is certainty, as he signals in the preface to the *Novum organum*, with its call to those who seek *non belle et probabiliter opinari, sed certo et ostensive scire* ("not to believe prettily and plausibly, but to know certainly and definitively" (trans. p. 59). But the spirit of Bacon's work seems notably different from that of Galileo and Descartes: it seems much more inclined toward a fallibilist incrementalism. Its method is to "establish degrees of certainty" (p. 53) from sensation up through the various stages of his peculiar method of induction. A characteristic passage, tending toward fallibilism, is this: "Now the senses, though they often deceive us or fail us, can nevertheless, with diligent effort, suffice for knowledge [*scientias*]" (*De augmentis* V.2 [*Works* vol. 1: 622; trans. vol. 4: 412]).

An earlier warning of the challenges to come, with regard to the expectation of certainty, is Gianfrancesco Pico's *Examen vanitatis* (1520), which painstakingly attacks the possibility of attaining scientific certainty. But Gianfrancesco (nephew of the more famous Giovanni Pico della Mirandola) does not advance this charge as a skeptic who would abandon all belief. Instead, he takes himself to be attacking the institution of philosophy and putting in its place "the dogma of Christian doctrine" (*Examen vanitatis* epilogue, p. 1264). A century later, Pierre

Gassendi is similarly scornful of the scholastic quest for certainty. His youthful *Exercitationes paradoxicae* (1624), an extended attack on Aristotelianism, mocks scholastic authors for putting the greatest weight on the most obscure parts of philosophy and for neglecting the most certain areas, like mathematics: "it is through mathematics that we have *scientia*, if we have any *scientia*" (I.1.6). If people were better trained in mathematics from an early age, they would be better able to resist the obscurities of philosophy. No wonder, Gassendi says, the scholastics neglect mathematics. As this work unfolds, however, it turns out to be an attack on the very possibility of *scientia* (II.6ff.) as the Aristotelians define it, that is, a *scientia* that requires the grasp of essences grounded in a demonstrative syllogism. Not even mathematics can measure up to this standard (see *Exercitationes* II.6.8, p. 511). Still, there can be *scientia* of a non-Aristotelian kind: "we are not one of those who reject the familiar and common manner of speech, by which we are said to know [*scire*] many things" (*Exercitationes* II.6.6, p. 499). For a useful overview of this work, see Richard Popkin, *History of Scepticism*, pp. 91–6 and 120–4. For Gassendi's views on mathematics in particular, see Bernard Rochot, "Gassendi et les mathématiques."

By the time of his magnum opus, the *Syntagma philosophicum* (published posthumously, in 1658), Gassendi has developed his own, positive, Epicurean-influenced philosophy. Yet he maintains an underlying current of doubt over the degree of certainty that might be claimed on its behalf. Thus he argues that, although the ancient skeptics were wrong to render everything a matter of controversy, they were certainly right to question much of what the dogmatists maintained. The lesson is that, at least in physics, "we should be happy if we achieve not what is true, but what is truth-like [*verisimile*]" (*Syntagma* pt. I, De logicae fine ch. 5, in *Opera Omnia* 1: 79b). Samuel Sorbière remarked of Gassendi that "this learned man does not assert anything very affirmatively" (quoted in Popkin, *History of Scepticism*, p. 93). Notice, however, that Gassendi *does* make assertions, just not very confident ones. This, then, is not skepticism. What has fallen away is the expectation of certainty.

John Wilkins's career also reveals the transition at work. While still in his twenties, Wilkins writes (in 1640) that "in those natural points which carry with them any doubt or obscurity, it is the safest way to suspend our assents: and though we may dispute *pro* or *con*, yet not to settle our opinion on either side" (*Discourse* II.1, p. 7). Several decades later, however, as this lecture discusses (p. 43), Wilkins would become a prominent advocate of diminished standards for certainty and knowledge.

The classic case for the centrality of a Pyrrhonian crisis is Richard Popkin, *The History of Scepticism*. For a measured assessment, see Perler, "Was There a 'Pyrrhonian Crisis' in Early Modern Philosophy?" On the intellectual context behind such doubts over certainty, see Schüssler, *Moral im Zweifel* vol. 2, and see the further remarks in note 14 here and throughout Lecture Six (especially note 9).

Note 10 (p. 31). The emergence of a broader cultural interest in questions of probability has been well documented. See in particular Henry van Leeuwen, *The Problem of Certainty* and Barbara Shapiro, *Probability and Certainty*—as well as her later book *A Culture of Fact*, which gives particular prominence to the influence of legal thought.

For an engaging overview of the mathematical achievements of seventeenth-century discussions of probability, see Ian Hacking, *Emergence of Probability* and, for more technical detail, Anders Hald, *A History of Probability*. It is clear, however, that the central thesis of Hacking's book cannot be sustained: that these mathematical developments arose out of a conceptual breakthrough in the understanding of what evidence is. On this, see Ilkka Kantola, *Probability and Moral Uncertainty*, and Garber and Sandy Zabell, "On the Emergence of Probability." Garber and Zabell suggest that the mathematical breakthroughs of the later seventeenth century just happened and require no further explanation. This seems unnecessarily cautious. We can certainly say (with Franklin, *Science of Conjecture*, pp. 331–8) that part of the story is the notable rise in the sophistication of mathematics during this time. E.g., John Wallis, speaking of the 1630s at Cambridge, writes that "mathematics (at that time, with us) were scarce looked upon as Academical studies, but rather mechanical; as the business of traders, merchants, seamen, carpenters, surveyors of land, or the like" (quoted in Feingold, *The Newtonian Moment*, p. 87). Even in the 1630s, however, the increasing complexity of the subject is reflected in Gabriel Naudé's 1637 apology for his ignorance of mathematics, where it is remarked that these subjects "require the whole of a man to themselves" (quoted in Joy, *Gassendi*, pp. 114–15). Such remarks give a sense of how what made the proverbial "Renaissance man" possible was not the greatness of men during that earlier era but the relative poverty of the sciences then available.

Lorraine Daston reports on the craze, around the end of the seventeenth century, for applying probabilistic reasoning to far-flung questions in theology and law ("Probability and Evidence," p. 1126). A striking example is when, in 1699, John Craig proved by strict and precise quantitative mathematical reasoning that "it is necessary for Christ to return before 1454 years have passed" (*Theologiae christianae principia mathematica* ch. 2 prop. 18, p. 24). That gives us until the year 3150. How did he arrive at that number? By determining the point at which, given the slow decline in the credibility of historical evidence, it would cease to be probable to believe in his initial incarnation. Craig assumes both that God would not expect us to believe something that is not sufficiently supported by the evidence and that God will not make available new evidence between now and 3150.

The Meanings of 'Probable'

Note 11 (p. 32). The English word 'probable' simply renders the Latin *probabilis*, but that is the only straightforward aspect of the situation. Part of the complexity arises from the Latin term's covering for three different Greek technical terms. First, in Cicero it serves as a translation of πιθανός, which refers to what is persuasive or plausible (see Gisela Striker, "Sceptical Strategies," pp. 70–4). This meaning is retained in the classical Latin usage of *probabilis* (see Brittain, *Philo of Larissa*, p. 95 n. 32), and also in I Corithians 2.4, where Paul uses the technical terms of philosophy to explain that his message was conveyed "not in the persuasive words of wisdom but in the demonstration of Spirit and power" (*non in persuasibilibus sapientiae verbis* [πειθοῖς σοφίας λόγοις] *sed in ostensione* [ἐν ἀποδείξει] *Spiritus et virtutis*). Second, Boethius's translation of the *Topics* uses *probabilia* to render ἔνδοξα, those beliefs that have been accepted by either the many or the wise. Third, *probabilis* also gets used for εἰκός, which in Aristotle is what happens for the most part (e.g., *Rhetoric* I.2, 1357^{a}23–^{b}23). One can find later Latin usage adhering, in various contexts, to each of these three senses. Thus John of Salisbury follows the usage of the *Topics*: "*Logica probabilis* concerns what seems so to everyone or to the majority or to the wise—and concerns either all or most or the best known and most *probabile* claims, or their consequences" (*Metalogicon* II.3; cf. Arist. *Topics* I.1, 100^{b}21–3). Aquinas can sometimes be found offering the same definition (e.g., *Comm. Post. an.* I.8 n. 5), but elsewhere invokes the third sense, remarking that the nature of *probabile* is "what seems to be true in all or many cases" (*Comm. de caelo* I.22 n. 9).

The most common sense of the term in medieval scholastic texts is the first, and so *probabilis* there is generally best translated 'plausible.' Still, there is a subtle shift at work from Greek to scholastic Latin. The meaning of the original Greek word is largely subjective, inasmuch as it refers to what is persuasive *to someone*. (Hence Paul's pejorative usage above.) Scholastic texts shift to a more objective sense, according to which there are effective arguments available that would make a certain thesis plausible *to anyone* (anyone, at any rate, who is sufficiently fair-minded and well informed). Even on this objective sense, however, there is no expectation that what is *probabilis* should be more likely than not. Hence it is quite common, in scholastic texts, for an author to judge each one of two contradictory theses to be *probabilis*, though one may be more so than the other. Schüssler describes the late scholastic category of the *dubium probabile*, when "the probable arguments on each side are in effect [*quasi*] equal" (*Moral im Zweifel* vol. 1: 61n).

Among Latin Aristotelians, *probabilis* is the domain of dialectical reasoning as against demonstrative reasoning, which yields certainty. Of course, the ideal is the demonstrative; it yields, as Bonaventure puts it, "a certainty that cannot be resisted, to which a human being is compelled to assent, willingly or not [*velit nolit*]" (*I Johannem* proem, in *Opera* vol. 6: 243). Where this is not available, as it often is not, the best that can be hoped for is a dialectical argument that yields merely plausible results, where assent is not compulsory, and where there may be room for a voluntary act of faith (see note 13 to this lecture). It is critical to scholastic epistemology to stress that this usage is quite distinct from the modern usage of 'probable' as *more likely than not*. Among scholastic authors, what is *probabilis* need not be probable in our sense, given that, as noted above, respectable dialectical arguments can often be framed on rival sides of a question. In such a case, authors may or may not hazard a claim about which side is more plausible, but they will always do so with some fear of the contrary (on such fears, see Lecture Six, p. 136).

It is interesting to consider why the demonstrative ideal is not always available. Often this is because the argument is infected with probability in the second or third of the above senses—that is, because the premises available are mere ἔνδοξα rather than self-evident principles, or because the conclusion is merely something εἰκός, holding only for the most part. Aristotle's much quoted remark at *Nicomachean Ethics* I.3 speaks of degree of precision, but Lecture One (note 18) discusses how this was commonly understood in terms not of mathematical accuracy, but rather of the search for what is always and invariably the case. As for conclusions that hold only "for the most part," see *Post. An.* I.30 and the helpful remarks in Barnes's commentary, pp. 191–3. For much useful information on scholastic conceptions of "probability," see Schüssler, "Scholastic Probability as Rational Assertability," "Probability in Medieval and Renaissance Philosophy," and *Moral im Zweifel*, esp. vol. 1: 58–60. On what changes in the seventeenth century, see the overview in Daston, "Probability and Evidence."

For a remarkably readable, wide-ranging, well-researched, and generally accurate overview of the changing conceptions of certainty and probability from antiquity into the seventeenth century, see Franklin, *The Science of Conjecture*.

Evidentness

Note 12 (p. 33). What marks the difference between the merely plausible and the certain? For authors of the later medieval period, up through the time of David Hume, the answer is evidentness, which marks the domain both of certainty and of *scientia*, and hence plays a critical role in articulating the epistemic ideal.

As a technical term, *evidentia* goes back at least to Cicero (*Academica* II.6.17), who offers it as a translation of the term ἐνάργεια, which the Stoics had used to refer to those impressions that infallibly show us how the world is (see Ierodiakonou, "Notion of Enargeia"). The term is common in Augustine (both the noun and the corresponding adjective) and occurs occasionally in Anselm but does not seem to have a precise technical sense in either author. In the twelfth century, however, one begins to see signs of such a usage. Peter Abelard, for instance, remarks that Aristotle's distinction between perfect and imperfect syllogisms should be understood as a distinction in evidentness (*Dialectica* 257.25–8). This logical sense gets taken up in the thirteenth century, for instance in Albert the Great: "through this, syllogisms of the second and third imperfect figure are reduced to the first figure, whose syllogisms are perfect according to the evidentness of the necessity of the inference" (*Comm. Anal. pr.* I.1.8 [ed. Borgnet, p. 469a]), and also in the fourteenth century, for instance in Wodeham (*Lectura secunda* prol. q. 6 §13 [vol. 1: 164]). This might seem a rather narrow window for the term to enter through, but it would make perfect sense for *evidentia* to establish itself as a technical epistemic term first in the context of the syllogism, which, for an Aristotelian, is the paradigm of what generates *scientia*. (On this usage, see Peter Vier, *Evidence and Its Function*, pp. 111–16.) Yet, outside logic as well, *evidentia* quickly makes inroads as a canonical epistemic term, as when William of Auvergne (around the 1230s) contrasts the weakness of opinion with the strength that comes from "evidentness of truth and demonstrative proof" (*De fide* ch. 1, in *Opera*, p. 4bG).

In Aquinas, 'evidentness' is used to distinguish *scientia* of all kinds from mere opinion or faith: "Certainty can imply two things. First, it implies firmness of adherence . . . It also implies the evidentness of what one assents to, and in this way it is not faith that has certainty, but *scientia* and understanding" (*Quaest. de veritate* 14.1 ad 7). See also the commentary on Hebrews: "intellectual assent can happen in two ways: in one way, because the intellect is moved to assent from the evidentness of its object . . . in another way, it assents to something not on account of the evidentness of its object" (11.1). The first of these yields *scientia*, whereas the second yields only opinion and faith. For another mid-thirteenth-century example, see Bonaventure, *Sent.* I.8.1.1 q. 2c. For further useful remarks about the early history of the term, see Joseph Geyser, "Zur Einführung in das Problem der Evidenz."

The role of *evidentia* in scholastic thought is enormously complicated and in need of much further study. Clearly it wildly oversimplifies matters to say simply that, for Aquinas or later authors, evidentness is what distinguishes *scientia* from mere true belief. But, as a rough first approximation, this is how epistemology goes between Aquinas and Hume. And this is something new: it does not seem to be part of the Arabic tradition, or in Aristotle himself, or even in Robert Grosseteste's influential inaugural Latin commentary on the *Posterior Analytics* from the early thirteenth century, which defines *scientia* in the broadest sense as simply "comprehension of the truth" (*Comm. Post. an.* I.2, p. 99) and marks stricter senses of *scientia* according to the increasing immutability of its objects. Nor is it found in Henry of Ghent's well-known discussion of skepticism, which defines *scire* broadly as "every certain awareness [*notitia*] by which a thing is cognized as it is, without any mistake or deception" (*Summa quaest. ord.* I.1; trans. Pasnau, *Cambridge Translations*, p. 97).

From the end of the thirteenth century forward, however, evidentness nearly always accompanies discussions of *scientia*, whether that be understood broadly or narrowly. According to Scotus, "the *scientia* of conclusions depends only on the evidentness of the principle and the evidentness of the syllogistic inference" (*Ord.* I.3.1.4 [Vatican edn., vol 3, n. 224; trans. p. 120]). Elsewhere "*scientia* is a certain cognition of a necessary truth that is suited to have evidentness through something else that is necessary, prior, and evident, connected to it through syllogistic discourse" (*Rep.* IA, prol. q. 1 [Wolter and Bychkov edn. vol. 1: n. 8]; see also *Ord.* prol. p. 4 qq. 1–2 [Vatican edn. vol. 1, n. 208]). Ockham's own prologue to his *Sentences* commentary reuses this same language in fewer words: "What is *scientia*? . . . It is the evident awareness [*notitia*] of a necessary truth, suited to be caused through premises connected to it through syllogistic discourse" (*Ord.* prol. q. 2, in *Opera theol.* vol. 1: 87–8; cf. vol. 1: 76). Elsewhere Ockham reframes Grosseteste's multilevel account, describing *scientia* in the broadest sense not simply as any comprehension of the truth, but as "an evident comprehension of the truth" (*Summa logicae* III-2 ch. 1, in *Opera phil.* vol. 1: 506). According to Durand of St. Pourçain, "what one has *scientia* of is evident, but what one believes is not" (*Sent.* [3rd vers.] III.23.7 n. 7).

John Rodington writes that "where there is *scientia*, there there is evidentness with respect to its object" (*Sent.* prol. q. 1, in Tweedale, *John of Rodynton*, p. 277). Peter of Ailly characterizes Academic skepticism as the view that "no truth can be evident to us" (*Sent.* prol. q. 1 art. 1, p. 139). For a great deal of useful information on Scotus's conception of evidentness, see Vier, *Evidence and Its Function*. For Ockham, see T. K. Scott, "Ockham on Evidence," Panaccio, "Savoir selon Ockham," and Elizabeth Karger, "Ockham's Misunderstood Theory."

Buridan similarly describes *scientia* in the broadest sense as "the steadfast cognition of a proposition with certainty and evidentness" (*Summulae* VIII.4.3, trans. pp. 705–6). Autrecourt, in the prologue to his *Tractatus*, rejects arguments from authority as unsuited to make their conclusions evident. "In speculative matters we seek nothing other than to have *scientia*, so that things become apparent within the soul . . . Here we seek nothing other than evidentness, and so it does not seem worthy to use such arguments [from authority], but rather we seek the truth of what we ask in propositions that are known *per se* and in experiences" (p. 184). This is strikingly similar to something that Aquinas had said earlier:

> The disputation of a teacher, in the schools, has the purpose not of eliminating error but of instructing the listeners so that they may be led to understand [*ad intellectum*] the truth that the teacher puts forward. And here one must rely on arguments that investigate the basis for the truth, and that make it be known *how* what is said is true. Otherwise, if the teacher determines the question based on bare authorities, the listener will be made certain that the thing is so, but will acquire no *scientia* or understanding and will go away empty.
>
> (*Quodlibet* IV.9.3c, in *Opera omnia* vol. 25)

Aquinas does not expressly mention *evidentness* here, but we know from elsewhere (see this Lecture, p. 33) that he takes this to be the distinctive feature of both *scientia* and understanding. Without evidentness, one's epistemic position is very far from ideal. Hence Oresme, in his famous discussion of whether the earth moves, dismisses the accumulated arguments in favor of a diurnal rotation, with the remark that "these are persuasions that fail to be evidently conclusive" (*ce sont persuasions qui ne concludent pas evidanment*). Still, he says, one *could* believe that it is the earth that moves and not the sky, because "it is not evident to the contrary" (*Livre du ciel* II.25, pp. 536–7).

All the way through later scholasticism, the connection between *scientia* and evidentness gets taken for granted. Domingo de Soto offers this as an "exposition" of Aristotle's account of *scientia*: "*scientia* is a disposition that is true, certain, and evident, arising from the proper causes of a thing" (*De demonstratione* q. 2, p. 295F). Indeed, he holds that "among philosophers, who speak in accord with the propriety of names, we are said to have *scientia* of that alone . . . which we grasp with the mind's firm reason—namely, that which the intellect intuits with a manifest vision. Thus *scientia*, in its general name, is the same as evidentness" (p. 294L). This last remark may seem overstated, but in fact there is a case to be made for simply identifying *scientia* and evidentness, since if *p* is evident it is true and, if *p* is evident for S, then S is compelled to believe P. At a minimum, then, *scientia* and evidentness might be thought to be mutually entailing. (But not everyone treats evidentness as truth entailing, as this lecture points out with regard to Buridan's conception of moral evidentness [p. 34]. See the following note.)

Given this scholastic background, it is unsurprising to find post-scholastic authors of the seventeenth century using *evidentia* in the same way. According to Descartes, as quoted in this lecture (p.22), "all *scientia* is certain and evident cognition" (*Rules* 2, X: 364). He continues to use this formula all throughout the *Meditations*. The prefatory letter to the Sorbonne brags that his arguments are "the most certain and evident demonstrations . . . They leave no room for the possibility that the human mind will ever discover better ones" (VII: 4). He goes on to label the *cogito* as "the most certain and evident thought of all" (VII: 25), and concludes the Second Meditation with the remark that "nothing can be perceived by me more easily or evidently than my mind" (VII: 34). He tells us that the Third Meditation has demonstrated God's existence "most evidently" (VII: 51) and that "nothing can be cognized more evidently and certainly by the human mind" than God's existence and our dependence on him (VII: 53). In response to the initial dreaming doubt, he eventually concludes that "even if I am dreaming, if there is anything that is evident to my intellect, then it is altogether true" (VII: 71). This talk of "evidentness" has been overshadowed, among commentators, by his distinctive demand for "clarity and distinctness." As far as I can tell, the formulations are essentially equivalent, *clarity and distinctness* serving as a more precise account of how Descartes thinks that we should understand the traditional notion of *evidentness*. Indeed, the standard modern English translation of Descartes often simply renders the various forms of *evidens* as "clear" (e.g., at *Principles* I.21, I.50, I.54 and at *Med. 3*, VII: 51).

Other post-scholastic examples abound. According to Richard Hooker's *Laws of Ecclesiastical Polity* (1593), "to make nothing evident of itself unto man's understanding were to take away all possibility of knowing anything" (I.8, p. 63). Gassendi lays it down as a canon of his logic that "the certainty of a proposition depends on the evidentness from which its necessity is clear" (*Syntagma*, Institutio logicae pt. 2, canon 13, in *Opera* 1: 103). The next canon then defines probability in terms of the proportion of evidentness to obscurity. Then there is Hobbes, writing in English: "knowledge, therefore, which we call science, I define to be evidence of truth, from some beginning or principle of sense" (*Elements of Law* I.6.4). And, according to Isaac Barrow, "what else signifies a certainty of knowledge, but that the thing known seems evidently true to the mind of the knower" (*Usefulness of Mathematical Learning*, lecture 5, p. 69)? For John Wilkins, "that kind of assent which does arise from such plain and clear evidence as does not admit of any reasonable cause of doubting is called knowledge or certainty" (*Principles and Duties* I.1, p. 5). According to Thomas White, beliefs based on testimony count as a "kind of knowledge [which] may arrive to a *certainty*, if the authority assumed be out of all question [i.e., reliable beyond a doubt]: yet it is not Science, because not *evident*, since the thing appears but in the knowledge of *another*, and is undiscernible in *itself*, being it moves not the understanding by itself and things naturally connected with it" (*Peripateticall Institutions* I.2.10). And then there is Locke, for whom "probability [is] wanting that intuitive evidence, which infallibly determines the understanding and produces certain knowledge" (*Essay* IV.15.5). When Locke considers "the degrees of our knowledge" (IV.2), he begins, as if that were the obvious place to begin, by working through the "the degrees of its [the mind's] evidence" (IV.2.1). The term remains central to Hume, who describes "those philosophers who have divided human reason into knowledge and probability, and have defined the first to be that evidence which arises from the comparison of ideas." Hume goes on to suggest that we "mark the several degrees of evidence" that "distinguish human reason into three kinds, viz. that from knowledge, from proofs, and from probabilities" (*Treatise* I.3.11, p. 124). (On Hume's usage, see David Owen, *Hume's Reason*, pp. 185–8 and Frederick Schmitt, *Hume's Epistemology*, p. 79, and the further discussion in Lecture Six, p. 132.)

In all these English-language passages, 'evidence' refers to the evidentness of things, or else to the evidentness of the mind when confronted with things that are evident (types A and B in this lecture, p. 33). *Evidentness* is in fact the prime historical sense of 'evidence' in the *Oxford English Dictionary*: "The quality or condition of being evident; clearness, evidentness." The *OED*'s second sense is the more familiar, type-C sense: "that which manifests or makes evident." This second meaning is well attested even in medieval English, and can be found in medieval Latin philosophy as well. Blasius of Parma, for instance, defines *scientia* as "the firm assent, without fear, to a proposition that signifies things entirely as they are, based on the possession of evidence" (*Quaestiones de anima* I.8, p. 69). Here, in the early fifteenth century, we seem to have *evidentia* in the modern type-C sense of 'evidence,' since Blasius is speaking not of the evidentness of the main proposition, but of other evident propositions or experiences that ground our knowledge of the main proposition. This seems clear because he goes on to say that, on this definition, there is no *scientia* of first principles, since there is nothing else that makes them evident. John Wilkins, in the seventeenth century, also clearly has the type-C sense in mind when he writes that "the mind of man may and must give a firm assent to some things . . . where yet the *evidences* for such things are not so infallible, but that there is a possibility that the things may be otherwise" (*Principles* I.3, as quoted in this lecture, p. 43). Even so, it seems clear that *evidentness* is the dominant meaning in philosophical texts all through the seventeenth century and into the eighteenth. The situation has perhaps changed by the time of Thomas Reid, whose *Essays on the Intellectual Powers of Man* (1785) states that "we give the name of evidence to whatever is the ground of belief" (II.20 [*Works* vol. 1: 328a]). Even here, however, such evidence may just be the *evidentness* of the proposition in question. (For some of these same points about the meaning of 'evidentia,' see Jack Zupko, *John Buridan*, p. 360 n. 43. Similar conceptual issues are also discussed in a nonhistorical context by Patrick Rysiew, "Making It Evident.")

I have said that, roughly speaking, evidentness is what distinguishes *scientia* from mere true belief. Matters are, however, far from straightforward, because some authors think that knowledge can come apart from evident true belief in various ways. Scotus, for instance, insists that faith should count as being evident: not because it has the sort of evidentness that qualifies it as *scientia*, which would be "the evidentness of its object," but rather because it is "evident from authority" (*Reportatio* IA prol. q. 2 [Wolter and Bychkov edn. vol. 1: n. 176]). But why is this not good enough for *scientia*? If sense experience, induction, and deduction suffice to make the object evident, in a *scientia*-producing way, then why cannot testimony do the same? Scotus's position is unusual, inasmuch as authority-based beliefs are generally treated as the paradigm of nonevident beliefs. But is authority, then, not a source of *scientia*, not even broadly speaking? That would go against Augustine's familiar dictum: "Let it be far from us to deny that we know (*scire*) what we have learned from the testimony of others" (*De trinitate* XV.12.21). Perhaps this is why Ockham, in one of his discussions of the different degrees of *scientia*, defines it most broadly as follows:

> *Scientia* in one way is a certain awareness [*notitia*] of something true. And thus some things count as *scientia* through faith alone, as when we say that we have *scientia* that Rome is a large city, even though we have not seen it, and similarly I say that I have *scientia* that he is my father and she is my mother, and so on for other things of which we are not evidently aware (*nota*). But because we adhere to them without any doubt, and because they are true, we are said to have *scientia* of them.
>
> (*Exp. phys.* prologue, in *Opera phil.* vol. 4: 5 = trans.
> *Phil. Writings* p. 4; see also *Summula phil. nat.* III.22, in *Opera phil.* vol. 6: 317)

This is surprising, because authors generally seek to exclude faith from the domain of *scientia*, and indeed Ockham elsewhere (as noted earlier in this note) treats *scientia*, even in its broad sense, as requiring evidentness. Some of what is perplexing here can be finessed by insisting that it is not important, on the idealized approach, to draw lines between what is real *scientia* and what is not. But these recalcitrant passages point to deeper questions about what it is for a thing to be evident and whether or not there is a conceptual connection between *scientia* and *evidentia*, as authors from Aquinas to Hume understand these concepts.

Note 13 (p. 33). I expect it will take much of the twenty-first century for scholars to come to grips with the place of evidentness in the history of philosophy. Here, having just documented its relationship to knowledge, let me try to say something more about what evidentness is. The lecture (p. 33) distinguishes the type-A evidentness of an object from the type-B evidentness of a cognition and suggests that the first should be defined in terms of the second. This is to say that the evidentness of objects is response-dependent—dependent on the capacity of the relevant cognitive agents to grasp that object. Accordingly, it is standard to distinguish between things that are self-evident in their own right (*secundum se*) and things that are self-evident in relation to us (*quoad nos*). God's existence, for instance, is said by Aquinas (*Summa theol.* 1a 2.1c) to be *per se nota* absolutely speaking, but not *to us*, because we do not have the cognitive capacity to grasp a being whose nature is existence itself. (If you find yourself puzzled by how a thing's nature could be existence itself, then that just proves the point.) What makes faith fail to be evident, and hence fail to count as *scientia*, is not that its objects lack evidentness in absolute terms, but that they are not evident to us, in our middling epistemic state.

Yet, if *evidentness* is a response-dependent concept, it becomes unclear what it means to speak of evidentness "in absolute terms." Aquinas seems to think that a proposition is absolutely self-evident (his terms are *per se nota in se*) when it is self-evident to any mind that fully grasps the meaning of the terms. But this generated controversy, because Scotus argues that one either grasps a proposition or does not. If someone grasps a self-evident proposition, then it will seem self-evident to that person. If not, one simply has not grasped that proposition but has grasped some other proposition instead. Clearly this debate turns in large part on what counts as a "proposition" or, more generally, what the objects of assent are. For Scotus see for instance *Ordinatio* I.2.1 qq. 1–2 (Vatican edn vol. 2, nn. 15–26) and the discussion in Vier, *Evidence and Its Function*, pp. 88–94. The dispute reappears in Wodeham, who endorses Scotus's position (*Lectura secunda* I.3 §3).

What exactly is it, then, to have an evident cognition? This is far too large and fundamental a question to admit of any satisfactory answer here. One aspect of the problem concerns the sources of evidentness, which divide into sensory and intellectual. Lecture Four takes up the first of these, in discussing how an intuitive cognition gives rise to an evident grasp of contingent truths. Lecture Five takes up the second, discussing how the evidentness of a demonstration requires grasping a whole argument at once. More fundamentally, however, we should consider just what evidentness is. The natural place to take up that question is to consider the way an evident cognition is said to be one that compels assent. Aquinas suggests this sort of picture when he associates faith with a lack of evidentness, from which he takes it to follow that its "certainty and firm adherence [arise] through a voluntary choice" (*Commentary on Hebrews* 11.1). The implicit point here becomes explicit in Scotus, for whom "the intellect's assent is not within its power, but arises from the evidentness of its object, to which it must, through an act of intellection, necessarily assent or adhere more than it does to an object that is non-evident" (*Reportatio* IA.1.1.1 [Wolter and Bychkov edn. vol. 1: n. 17]; see also *Ord.* I.1.1.1 [Vatican edn. vol. 2, n. 22]). Ockham puts the point similarly: "whoever has evident *scientia* of some proposition cannot dissent from it solely on the will's command, but must be persuaded through a reason that moves its intellect more strongly to dissent, or else it must forget what it evidently knew [*noti*]" (*Ordinatio* prol. q. 7 [*Opera theol.* vol. 1: 192]). And again Buridan: "human evidentness is that in virtue of which a cognitive power by its nature or through evident reason is determined to assent to the truth" (*Summulae* VIII.4.4, trans. p. 709). For still more examples, see John Rodington, *Sent.* prol. q. 2 (in Tweedale, *John of Rodynton*, p. 309), Wodeham, *Lectura secunda* prol. q. 6 §13 (vol. 1: 163–4), and John of Mirecourt's First Apology, n. 44. Alexander Broadie shows that this conception remains in force among many late scholastic authors (*Notion and Object* ch. 6); and it continues to play a central role in Descartes: "The minds of all of us have been molded by nature so that whenever we perceive something clearly, we spontaneously assent to it and can in no way doubt that it is true" (*Principles* I.43). Here Descartes uses his proprietary idiom of 'clarity,' but in a letter written later, to a correspondent perhaps less familiar with Cartesian jargon, he happily describes such compulsion as the result of "a thoroughly evident argument" (*valde evidens ratio*) (letter of

1645, in IV: 173). As note 2 above discusses, Descartes regularly frames the certainty of clear and distinct perceptions in terms of such indubitability. On intellectual compulsion in Descartes more generally, see C. P. Ragland, "Descartes on the Principle of Alternative Possibilities." Many of these passages treat evidentness as a feature of objects (sense A), but even in this case they seek to define it in terms of an intellectual response: irresistible assent.

Here looms the crucial question flagged in this lecture (p. 33): is such indubitability *sufficient* for evidentness, or is it a mere mark? The lecture reports that the "usual" scholastic view treats evidentness as infallible, but the story here is quite complicated. One thing that is clear is that evidentness is generally regarded as factive, which means that if a proposition (or judgment) is evident then it is true. Ockham, for instance, takes it as clear that "an evident assent denotes that things are in reality as is indicated by the proposition that is assented to" (*Quodlibet* V.5 ad 4, in *Opera theol.* vol. 9: 499). Likewise, according to Oresme, "the false cannot be evident" (*Quaest. de anima* III.16, p. 436). This continues to be regarded as uncontroversial among later scholastics (see, e.g., the passages quoted in Broadie, *Notion and Object*, pp. 150–1). Even so, not everyone treats *evidentia* as invariably a success term. Buridan's moral evidentness, for instance, is compatible with false judgment. And, even before that, Wodeham distinguishes between three senses of evidentness, the first of which is not factive (*Lectura secunda* prol. q. 6 §13 [vol. 1: 163]). Still, as standardly understood, what is evident is true. Even so, this does not yield infallibility in any interesting sense. To be sure, factivity yields the result that, necessarily, if I evidently assent to *p*, then *p*. In that sense, an evident assent cannot be false. But one might equally say, in our modern idiom, that, necessarily, if I know *p*, then *p*. This does not make me infallible; it is just a cheap logical consequence of factivity. Nor does one get any closer to infallibility by insisting on *p*'s necessity. Buridan, for instance, writes that evidentness in the strongest sense occurs when "a cognitive power by its nature or through evident reason is determined to assent to the truth or to a true proposition that cannot be falsified by any power" (*Summulae* VIII.4.4, trans. p. 709). This promises indubitability, but not infallibility in any interesting sense, because it gives us only the cheap guarantee that, *if* a thing is evident, then it is necessarily true.

Infallibility in the robust, epistemically ideal sense is an invulnerability to error such that one will not go wrong whenever it *seems* that a thing is evident. And Buridan does appear to be committed to this, judging from the passage quoted already in this lecture (p. 34): "natural evidentness is rightly so-called, because according to it someone *cannot be deceived* so long as the common course of nature remains the same" (*Quaest. Post. an.* I.2c). Although this could be read as merely the cheap logical entailment, the word 'deceived' suggests that Buridan has in mind robust infallibility. And this is clearer still from the way he handles the ever present prospect of deception in such cases, for instance if God were to change the workings of nature or distort our vision by implanting a hallucinatory image in our eye (*Summulae* VIII.4.4, trans. p. 708). These sorts of possibilities have no impact on the cheap logical guarantee that what is evident is true, because Buridan could simply hold that, although such cases render judgment false and therefore nonevident, they have no bearing on the good cases where we *do* have an evident judgment. But Buridan sees perfectly clearly that this is not the issue. The issue, instead, is that these bad cases threaten to undermine the good cases by leaving us in doubt as to whether our seemingly evident judgments are in fact evident. Thus he has the skeptic conclude, invoking factivity, that "the judgment would be false and consequently it would be neither certain nor evident" and then immediately add: "And consequently nor would it be evident now, since it is not evident to you whether God so wills or not" (p. 708). Here it is clear that evidentness (and so *scientia*) requires more than mere indubitability plus truth. According to the skeptic, it further requires an evident higher order grasp that the first-order judgment is in fact evident. (On such higher order judgments, see note 7 here; on divine deception, see Lecture Six; on sensory illusions, see Lectures Three and Four.) In response, Buridan resists this final claim, because he hardly thinks that we can have an evident grasp of the divine will. Yet he is unwilling to abandon the claim of robust infallibility, and so his solution is to continue to insist that we "cannot be deceived," but to do so conditionally—"so long as the common course of nature remains the same" (as quoted). It is enough for *scientia naturalis* if we have evidentness under this condition, even if it is not evident to us whether or not the condition is satisfied.

Scholastic authors in general seem conflicted—at odds with themselves—over how hard to push for infallibility. John of Mirecourt insists on it, defining *evidentia specialis* as "that by which someone affirms that a thing is so, without any fear, through an affirmation caused naturally within him, from causes necessitating him to that affirmation, *and it is not possible for someone to affirm that a thing is so and for the thing not to be as he affirms it to be*" (*Sent.* q. 6, p. 438). But Mirecourt at the same time recognizes a weaker "natural assent," where the claim of infallibility is conditioned on "God's general influence and the nonoccurrence of any miracle" (p. 438). As we will see in Lecture Six (pp. 119–20), Mirecourt thinks that the claim of unqualified infallibility can be defended in certain cases. In opposition to this sort of approach stands Domingo de Soto, who wants to allow a *scientia* of contingent propositions grasped through perception (see Lecture Three, note 3). De Soto raises the objection that such cases cannot count as evident (and hence fail to count as *scientia*) because they are fallible, whereas "evidentness is an assent through which there is no room (*non stat*) for the cognizer to be deceived" (*De demonstratione* q. 2, p. 296K). As a response, De Soto considers Mirecourt's two-level approach (which he knows because it was taken over, verbatim and uncredited, in Peter of Ailly [*Sent.* prol. q. 1 art. 1, p. 143]), but he rejects it in favor of the view that "a judgment is evident *simpliciter* when it is, of its own nature, not deceptive, even if someone could supernaturally be deceived through it" (*De demonstratione* q. 2, pp. 296–7). This makes no claim to infallibility even in the best of cases, but merely to an intrinsic propensity not to deceive. Lecture Three considers in some detail how this sort of strategy gets applied to the domain of sensory knowledge.

Later scholastic authors often take for granted that evidentness entails infallibility. According to John Major, for instance, absolute evidentness (*evidentia simpliciter*) "is defined as a true assent without fear caused by principles necessitating the intellect, to which it is not possible for the intellect to assent and to be deceived in so assenting" (*Sent.* prol. q. 3, f. 6va). John goes on to register the possibility of a conditional infallibility that excludes the possibility of miraculous intervention. See Broadie, *Notion and Object*, p. 150, for this and other sixteenth-century references.

Although the relationship between evidentness, infallibility, and indubitability has received only slight attention from historians of medieval thought, the issue makes its way, as usual, into post-scholastic discussions and has thereby occasioned considerable discussion in recent scholarship on that period. For the connection between evidentness and intellectual irresistibility in Descartes, see Charles Larmore, "Descartes' Psychologistic Theory of Assent" (and, for a dissenting view, with attention to the background in Ockham, see Lilli Alanen and Mikko Yrjönsuuri, "Intuition, judgement et évidence"). In Hume this issue has received very extensive attention. The classic statement of the case for irresistibility as the critical epistemic standard in Hume is Norman Kemp Smith, *The Philosophy of David Hume*. For criticism, see, for example, Louis Loeb, *Stability and Justification*, pp. 20–5. For further references to post-scholastic appeals to intellectual irresistibility, in Locke and others, see Lecture Six, note 13.

Whatever exactly the relationship is between evidentness and indubitability, the interconnection of these two concepts has far-reaching implications. On one side, it has important repercussions for the contrasting case of faith, where assent is correspondingly said to be not compulsory but instead voluntary. These issues were debated at considerable length in the fourteenth century (see Grellard, *De la certitude volontaire*). The implications for epistemology are equally important. As long as evidentness is conceived of in terms of compulsion, there is little room for the normative idea of justification. Or, to be precise, there is little room for conceiving of knowledge—or of the epistemic ideal—in normative terms, because that is supposed to be the domain where we cannot help but believe the things we believe.

Closely related to these difficult questions is the one about the sort of access we must have to the evidentness of our beliefs. Of late it has become fashionable to assimilate one or another scholastic account to recent externalist approaches to epistemology, on which one need not have access to the evidence in virtue of which a belief counts as knowledge. (For Aquinas, see Eleonore Stump, *Aquinas* ch. 7; for Ockham, see Claude Panaccio, "Ockham's Externalism"; for Buridan, see Zupko, *John Buridan* ch. 12.) To be sure, there is an element of externalism in the attempt to save infallibility by imposing a condition (e.g., no divine intervention) that the believer has no ability to confirm. But, once one sees the role played by evidentness in these accounts, it becomes clear that scholastic theories are fundamentally internalist in spirit. The sort of irresistible assent associated with *scientia* is that which arises through the *awareness* of a proposition's evidentness. If you just suddenly form an irresistible, inexplicable compulsion to believe *p*, this would not count as *p*'s being evident, no matter how reliably caused that compulsion might be. The notion of evidentness comes out of the idea that there must be an intellectual seeing (*videns*) of the objects of knowledge, which is a paradigmatically internalist notion. This fits with the widespread view that certainty at one level entails higher order certainty (see note 7 here). And, since this is very much the tradition that Descartes's views grow out of, it also fits with the way in which his theory of *scientia* is a classic example of internalism in epistemology (see this Lecture, p. 23). (I am much indebted here to conversations with Philip Choi.)

If scholastic accounts must be likened to some modern framework, it would be better to think of their approach as allied in a certain sense with the modern movement toward a naturalized epistemology. Quine, the founder of this movement, took as his project a description of our cognitive apparatus rather than an evaluation of it. For the scholastics as for Quine, it would be arbitrary and hence pointless to pick some determinate level of epistemic success and then anoint that as the dividing line between knowledge and skepticism. Our cognitive abilities are plainly sufficient to warrant action on the basis of their guidance, and they plainly do not achieve anything like an ideal grasp of reality. No one has ever denied either of these claims. For Quine, the interesting project that remains is the biologists' and psychologists' work of describing these faculties as they are. On the scholastic *scientia* framework, the interesting project is to describe what sort of epistemic success we might ideally hope to achieve, so as to provide a kind of road map for intellectual inquiry. On either picture, debates over skepticism and how to define knowledge become hard to motivate. See Quine's response to a question about how we know that one theory is true and another false: "There is an obstacle in the verb 'know.' Must it imply certainty, infallibility? Then the answer is that we cannot. But if we ask rather how we are better warranted in believing one theory than another, our question is a substantial one" (*Theories and Things*, p. 180). Here Quine is identifying the top of the sliding scale, surrendering it, and then suggesting that what is left is simply comparative judgments. Are we better warranted here or here? There is no question of identifying a cutoff point where knowledge begins and mere true belief ends.

Compare Henry of Ghent, author of the most substantial thirteenth-century discussion of skepticism (*Summa quaest. ord.* I.1–2). Ghent is no one's idea of a naturalist. Even so, like Quine, he proceeds by dividing and conquering. Can we have *scientia* broadly speaking, where that refers to a certain awareness of what is true? Clearly we can, he thinks, simply by using our senses. But what about "an altogether certain and infallible awareness of the truth"? Here, at the top of the scale, Henry too just surrenders, arguing that we cannot achieve such perfection—or at any rate cannot achieve it on our own, without divine illumination (trans. Pasnau, *Cambridge Translations*, pp. 119–21). Now consider Descartes, who might at first glance look like a counterexample to this lecture's insistence (p. 35) that the idealized framework is skepticism-resistant. Here too we see the same strategy of distinguishing between cases. Do we have good reasons to believe what we ordinarily believe? Yes, and in general these are things that "no sane person has ever seriously doubted" (*Meditations* synopsis, VII: 15–16). At this modest level, skepticism is not worth taking seriously. The sort of skepticism that Descartes does take seriously is that which applies to high-grade, ideal *scientia*. Here, of course, Descartes does not surrender in Quinean fashion, or hide behind divine illumination, as does Henry of Ghent, or make knowledge conditional on an assumption we cannot affirm. Instead, he stands his ground even on that terrain most favorable to his enemy and insists on the most perfect certainty available to beings such as we are. Such heroism is, historically speaking, quite unusual. Most of those who work within the idealized framework are happy enough to make a tactical retreat. But Lecture Five discusses how even Descartes's stance is not quite as heroic as it initially seems, inasmuch as he appeals to a kind of resigned dogmatism, even at the high end of the theory.

Eventually, in Lecture Six, we will see how this tendency toward a naturalistic resignation culminates in the work of Hume.

Buridan's Three Degrees

Note 14 (p. 35). An understanding of the historical role of evidentness in epistemic theory helps explain what is important in Buridan's discussion. Evidentness in the strict sense, on his account, belongs to first principles. Or, to be exact, it belongs to *the* first principle, the law of noncontradiction. Lesser first principles, such as the first principles of physics, might be doubted. (Think of Zeno's denial of motion.) So beneath the strict evidentness of the first principle there is a lesser category of natural evidentness:

> In a second way one speaks of evidentness because it appears to everyone and there is no human reason (except a subjective one) through which the opposite could appear, and in this way natural principles and natural conclusions exhibit evidentness. Note that this evidentness is not *strictly* called evidentness, because the intellect *could* be deceived about such evident propositions through a supernatural cause. For God could make fire without heat, and could make and conserve in my senses a sensible species without an object, and so from this evidentness you would judge as if the object were present, and your judgment would be false. Still, such natural evidentness is rightly so-called, because according to it someone cannot be deceived so long as the common course of nature remains the same—although one would be deceived by a supernatural cause—and this evidentness suffices for natural *scientia*.   (*Quaest. Post. an.* I.2c)

Here we see the resigned pragmatism that the idealized framework lends itself to. Things are what they are. Our grasp of the natural world is neither ideally evident nor ideally certain, but that is not to say that it is worthless. It is good enough; it "suffices for natural *scientia*."

The real novelty in Buridan's account comes from his third category of evidentness, one that is good enough for practical affairs, even practical affairs of the greatest import, as when a judge considers whether to hang a man. The idea seems to be original to Buridan. Certainly it flies in the face of the most prominent earlier accounts, of Aquinas, Scotus, and Ockham, all of whom denied that cases of this kind could count as evident. Ockham, for instance, although he is willing in one discussion to count them as *scientia* in the broadest sense, specifically denies that such propositions are evident (*Exp. phys.* prologue, as quoted in the previous note). But Buridan's discussion of this lowest level of evidentness is too brief to make clear exactly how he thinks about such cases. For instance, does he think that moral evidentness compels assent?

Seemingly he does not, but he is not wholly explicit. Nor is it clear whether he thinks that such evidentness, when conjoined to a true belief, suffices for *scientia*. One could make an argument that he does, on the basis of the fact that he treats evidentness as a distinguishing mark of *scientia* (see note 12 to this lecture), and on the basis of what he says after introducing his three grades of evidentness: "Some speak very badly, wanting to destroy natural and moral *scientiae* on the grounds that there is no absolute evidentness [*evidentia simpliciter*] in many of their principles and conclusions." This is wrong, Buridan concludes, "because absolute evidentness is not required for such *scientiae*, but instead the aforesaid kinds suffice—evidentness that is qualified or based on a supposition [*secundum quid sive ex suppositione*]" (*Quaest. meta.* II.1, f. 9ra; trans. Klima, *Medieval Philosophy*, p. 146). Does this mean that mere moral evidentness suffices for *scientia*? It is not clear. In a way, this is just another distracting question of lexicology. Even so, the present lecture argues (p. 43) that this small point of usage ultimately becomes important to modern epistemology.

Buridan's views on the various degrees of certainty and evidentness are set out not just in the text I have focused on here, *Questions on the Metaphysics* II.1, but also at *Summulae* VIII.4.4 and in *Questions on the Posterior Analytics* I.2. There is now a fairly substantial secondary literature on the topic. See Biard, *Science et nature*, pp. 23–38, Grellard, *Croire et savoir*, pp. 262–72; Gyula Klima, *John Buridan*, pp. 234–58; Annaliese Maier, "Problem der Evidenz," Perler, *Zweifel und Gewissheit*, pp. 363–96, Jack Zupko, "On Certitude" and *John Buridan*, pp. 183–202. More generally, see Peter King, "Jean Buridan's Philosophy of Science."

For a criticism of my view that the importance of skepticism is exaggerated throughout the history of philosophy, see Julien Dutant, "Legend of the Justified True Belief Analysis," who speaks of "intense debates over whether we know," such that "skeptical views were taken much more seriously in history than they are now" (p. 113). I simply deny that this is the case. Moreover, even in places where skepticism flourished, it does not tend to be knowledge that is centrally at issue. This is so in Descartes, for reasons this lecture explains (pp. 24–6), and in Hume, whose use of 'knowledge' is so strict that it has only a marginal role to play in his epistemology (see note 22 here and Lecture Six, note 9). Not even the ancient skeptics are focused centrally on knowledge—the term barely appears, for instance, in Sextus Empiricus (see Lecture Six, note 7).

For a different account of the status of skepticism in the later Middle Ages, see Dominik Perler, *Zweifel und Gewissheit* and, more briefly in English, "Skepticism."

Proportioned Belief

Moral Certainty

Note 15 (p. 36). Buridan's notion of "another, weaker evidentness, which suffices for acting well morally" seems to have no exact precedent. It is common enough, as this lecture indicates (p. 31), to invoke Aristotle's dictum in *Nicomachean Ethics* I.3 about different standards in the moral domain. Aquinas, for instance, glosses the passage as saying that "the same certainty is not to be sought in all things" and adds: "Thus in contingent things, such as *naturalia* and *res humanae*, the certainty suffices that is such that something is true for the most part, even if it falls short occasionally, in a few cases" (*Summa theol.* 1a2ae 96.1 ad 3). But there is quite a distance from this remark, which merely invokes the familiar Aristotelian notion of what is true *in pluribus*, to Buridan's idea of there being a third category, beyond the natural domain, where there is sufficient evidentness for human affairs. Closer to the mark is Aquinas's notion of *probable certainty* (*Summa theol.* 2a2ae 70.2c, as quoted in this lecture at p. 31). Or consider this passage from Aquinas: "in human dealings we cannot have proofs that are demonstrative and infallible. Instead, conjectural plausibility [*probabilitas*] suffices, which is how the rhetorician persuades. And so, although it is possible for two or three witnesses to collude in a lie, it is not easy, nor is it plausible [*probabile*] that they are colluding, and so their testimony is accepted as true" (*Summa theol.* 1a2ae 105.2 ad 8). Here what counts as epistemically sufficient gets extended to exactly the sort of case that would later be treated as morally certain. Bonaventure similarly speaks of probable certainty, to explain how some of the angels could have fallen from heaven: "Certainty on the cognitive side comes in two kinds. One kind is infallible, as when one knows something in such a way that he cannot be deceived. The other kind is probable, as when one has truth-like reasons for one side, such that one has none or few reasons for the opposite" (*Sent.* II.4.2.1 ad 2). Scotus, too, speaks of "knowing certainly, at least with the certainty sufficient for human acts" (*Ordinatio* IV.29 [Vatican edn. vol. 13, n. 24). These passages are not far from Buridan's idea, but in the thirteenth century they come in at the periphery, without being put to any substantial theoretical work. Among Aristotelians, the ideal of demonstrative certainty remains in the ascendant as a normative ideal.

Even with these earlier intimations, Buridan's talk of moral evidentness does not seem to have had any immediate influence on his contemporaries. The figure who served to popularize the notion, half a century later, was Jean Gerson, the highly influential moral theologian and chancellor of the University of Paris. In his *De consolatione theologiae* (1418), he distinguishes between spiritual, natural, and moral certainty, the last of which he describes as follows:

Next, there is a certainty that can be called moral or civil, which is touched upon by Aristotle along with the preceding [natural] certainty at the start of his *Ethics* [I.3]. His words are that "it is proper to one who is educated to seek certainty in each thing in accord with the requirements of the material." It is equally wrong, he says, "to seek mathematical persuasion and moral demonstration" [1094^{b}24–7], since moral certainty arises not from the evidentness of demonstration but from plausible [*probabilibus*] conjectures, "roughly and broadly" [*grossis et figuralibus*] [1094^{b}20], more on one side than on the other. Suppose the Academics had entirely rejected such certainty, and that they had not gone on to declare it sufficient for moral action. If so, they would have seen what reason they had to presume that something good was to be done or something bad to be omitted, in conformity with the judgment of reason, with the sort of certainty it needs to have—just as virtue in itself is certain, or otherwise it is not virtue.   (Bk. IV, prose 2, trans. pp. 233–4)

Gerson here makes it clear that he takes the *Nicomachean Ethics* as his inspiration (supposing, for reasons explained in this lecture, p. 31, that Aristotle is talking there about *certainty*). Indeed, Gerson may not have had Buridan's earlier discussion in mind, although Buridan was then a very famous figure. For further details on moral certainty in Gerson, see Thomas Deman, *Probabilisme*, cols. 442–4, and Sven Grosse, *Heilsungewißheit und Scrupulositas*, pp. 83–4.

At any rate, after these tenuous beginnings, the idea spreads very quickly, and the lines of influence are clear. Antoninus of Florence, the greatest moral theologian in the generation after Gerson, explicitly invokes Gerson ("the Chancellor") and writes that "the certainty that is required in moral matters is not the certainty of evidentness, but of probable conjecture" (*Summa theologica* I.3 ch. 10, col. 203C). This illustrates the fluidity of the various terms in play and the hazards of generalization. Buridan had introduced the category as a species of evidentness, where evidentness was itself a kind of certainty. Gerson coined the term 'moral certainty,' but contrasted it with evidentness. Antoninus follows Gerson. So, whereas in Buridan it is natural to suppose that moral evidentness can give rise to *scientia*, in Antoninus it is natural to suppose that it cannot. None of these authors, however, explicitly says one way or another, in keeping with the general lack of interest in drawing such boundaries.

In the early sixteenth century, Gianfrancesco Pico distinguishes five levels of certainty: probable, moral, physical, mathematical, and divinely illuminated (*Examen vanitatis* V.4, p. 1095). Among late scholastics, the notion of moral certainty is commonplace. It is present, to give some examples more or less at random, in Suárez (*De fide theologica* VI.5 [*Opera* vol. 12:

n. 6]; *Disp. meta.* 29.3.36), Roderigo de Arriaga (see Curley, "Certainty," pp. 16–17), Juan de Lugo (*Disputationes scholasticae* I.13.4 nn. 311, 317), and André Dabillon, whose example is that there is a city named Constantinople, "although absolutely speaking it could be that all the historians are wrong" (*Nouveau cours*, Logique Bk. IV disc. 2 q. 3 n. 6, pp. 433–4). For further references, see Sven Knebel, *Wille, Würfel und Wahrscheinlichkeit*, p. 55 n. 263.

Outside of scholastic philosophy too, in the early seventeenth century, the notion is pervasive. Hugo Grotius's *Truth of the Christian Religion* (1627), responding to those still not satisfied with the arguments he had marshaled up to that point, invokes the idea of "different kinds of proofs for the variety of things" and lists mathematical, physical, moral, and testimonial (end of Bk. II). Jean de Silhon, writing in 1634, argues that, whereas a physical demonstration of God's existence is possible, we can have only a moral demonstration of the Christian faith and the soul's immortality (*Immortalité de l'ame* discourse 2, pp. 188–233). Silhon holds that mere moral demonstrations lack evidentness and complete infallibility, but "they are more than sufficient to oblige us to act in conformity with the information [*connaissance*] that they convey and the impression that they give us" (p. 224). It was this sort of thing that inspired Descartes's attempt in the *Meditations* to put the soul's immortality on a more solid footing than that of mere moral certainty. Indeed, inasmuch as Descartes and Silhon were acquaintances, this very work may well have had a direct impact. (For Descartes on moral certainty, see note 18 here.)

The role of moral certainty in seventeenth-century English thought has been studied in some detail, particularly in Henry van Leeuwen, *The Problem of Certainty*, Richard Popkin, *History of Scepticism* pp. 65–6, 208–18, and Barbara Shapiro, *Probability and Certainty*, esp. pp. 32–7. William Chillingworth's massive *Religion of Protestants* invokes the notion repeatedly—e.g., at 2.24, 2.154, 4.57, 6.6, 6.9, and 6.39 (and see Robert Orr, *Reason and Authority* ch. 3). Chillingworth may have acquired this usage from a brief period spent among the Jesuits in France. But in any case, from Chillingworth, the idea spread out to a broader circle in England. John Tillotson characterizes moral certainty as "a firm and un-doubted assent to a thing upon such grounds as are fit fully to satisfy a prudent man" (*Works*, preface, vol. 1: vi). It was Tillotson who edited Wilkins's *Of the Principles and Duties of Natural Religion* for posthumous publication in 1675. The notion of moral certainty is likewise important in both Joseph Glanvill (see pp. 36–7) and Robert Boyle, who writes:

Perhaps I shall not need to tell you that, besides the demonstrations wont to be treated of in vulgar logic, there are among philosophers three distinct, whether *kinds* or *degrees*, of demonstration. For there is a *metaphysical* demonstration, as we may call that, where the conclusion is manifestly built on those general metaphysical axioms that can never be other than true, such as *Nihil potest simul esse et non esse*; *Non-entis nullæ sunt proprietates reales*, etc. There are also *physical* demonstrations, where the conclusion is evidently deduced from physical principles; such as are, *Ex nihilo nihil sit; Nulla substantia in nihilum redigitur*, etc, which are not so absolutely certain as the former, because, if there be a God, He may (at least for ought we know) be able to create and annihilate substances; and yet are held unquestionable by the ancient naturalists, who still suppose them in their theories. And lastly, there are *moral* demonstrations, such as those where the conclusion is built either upon some one such proof cogent in its kind; or some concurrence of probabilities that it cannot be but allowed, supposing the truth of the most received rules of prudence and principles of practical philosophy.   (*Reconcileableness of Reason and Religion* pt. I sct. 8 [*Works* vol. 8: 281–2])

Note 16 here shows how widely Boyle wishes to deploy this last category of moral demon-stration.

The word 'moral' is itself of some interest in these contexts. In Latin as well as in the various vernaculars, *moralis* becomes so associated with the notion of moral certainty that the adjective takes on what is in effect a whole new meaning, detached from its association with ethics and human conduct. There are, for instance, moral impossibilities—where a thing is possible, absolutely speaking, but that it should obtain is "altogether incredible" (Seth Ward,

Philosophical Essay 3.3, p. 105). Descartes thus tells a correspondent that it would be possible, "metaphysically speaking," to build a machine that could fly like a bird, but that it is not possible "physically or morally speaking" (III: 163–4; for more details see Brian Embry, "Descartes on Free Will"). And so there are moral necessities too, e.g., in Sebastian Izquierdo: "something is morally necessary when, by way of inclination, that which usually, or always, or almost always is accustomed to occur cannot fail to happen, even if it can fail absolutely or in light of a law of nature" (in Michael Murray, "Pre-Leibnizian Moral Necessity," p. 14; for more details, see Knebel, *Wille, Würfel und Wahrscheinlichkeit* ch. 3). Then again, coming back full circle to the original usage of Buridan, there is moral evidence, as when Hume speaks of "all imaginable degrees of assurance, from the highest certainty to the lowest species of moral evidence" (*Enquiry concerning Human Understanding* 10.1, p. 110). One could go on and on citing examples. In all these contexts, 'moral' has come to be entirely unmoored from its association with ethics and human conduct. And, although in special contexts (especially the free will debate) the term can take on other shades of meaning, the core extended sense of 'moral' is quite plain and well established through centuries of perfectly ordinary scholarly usage. In this common and familiar sense, that which is *morally* φ is that which is nearly but not quite absolutely φ.

This broad usage of 'moral' is indeed so well established that one might suppose there must be some independent etymological origin for that non-normative sense. It seems clear, however, that there is not. The *Oxford English Dictionary* is characteristically helpful in establishing this point, but we have seen enough here to go farther still. The Latin *moralis* was coined by Cicero to talk about the branch of philosophy concerned with mores—that is, ethics. This has always been the primary sense of the term. How it came to have its broad non-normative sense is explained precisely by the history that has been set out here—the early hint at *Nicomachean Ethics* I.3, followed by the prominent examples of Buridan and Gerson. In the earliest examples, *moralis* still has some connection with the domain of human action, but philosophers gradually extended its application in the following centuries, presumably because they needed the word. For, whereas there were many familiar Latin terms for talking about the absolute—*absolute, simpliciter, proprie, stricte*—there were few good word for talking about what is nearly but not quite absolutely the case. (In English we can now speak of a thing as *virtually* or *practically* φ, but although these are words of Latin origin, they did not take on this extended meaning in Latin.)

Recalibrating the Ideal

Note 16 (p. 37). It is easy to talk about the way words are used, but much harder to understand why certain ideas become so prevalent at certain periods of time. In particular, it is natural to wonder whether the apparent rise of epistemic pessimism in the later Middle Ages and in the Renaissance can be connected to broader cultural events. Is the pessimism of Buridan and his contemporaries tied to the condemnations of 1347? (See my *Metaphysical Themes* §19.3.) Did the papal schism of the late fourteenth century produce still more pessimism in the ethical and religious domains? Is what we see in the sixteenth and seventeenth century the result of the instability of that era, as regards both the foundations of religion and the foundations of philosophy? These are fascinating questions to ask, but I do not pretend to have any good answers to them.

What can be asserted with some confidence is that there *is* a rising sense of epistemic pessimism in the centuries after Aquinas. But even here there is room for doubt about exactly where it starts. Barbara Shapiro, whose work is authoritative for the seventeenth century, summarizes her perspective with the remark that, "by the end of the seventeenth century, most English thinkers, no matter what their field of inquiry, had ceased to believe that their labors would produce the certitude or 'science' that had for centuries been the goal of the philosopher" (*Probability and Certainty*, p. 4). But William Wallace has objected that this gets the story quite wrong: "my thesis is that certitude was not seriously claimed for natural science during the late Middle Ages and the early Renaissance, but that it began to be claimed again in Italy in the early seventeenth century, precisely when Shapiro says it was being rejected in England" ("Certitude of Science," p. 281).

No doubt the truth is somewhere in between, but it is clear enough that the fourteenth century displays a marked rise in worries about the degree to which certainty is an achievable epistemic ideal. The topic is a vast one, and subsequent lectures will consider various further examples, but here I will mention just a few instances. Buridan's mid-fourteenth-century interest in the various degrees of evidentness is of course a leading example, and these concerns reappear, in various forms, in many of his near contemporaries. For instance, Albert of Saxony's commentary on the *De generatione et corruptione* begins with the routine question of whether anything can be absolutely generated or corrupted. But his way of dealing with the issue is anything but *pro forma*. After giving a very full and sympathetic statement of the case against substantial change, he distinguishes between two kinds of evidentness: *summa* and natural. One who has *evidentia summa* cannot be deceived, but Albert gives only examples of things we do not grasp in this way—for instance, "whether you are a man or a donkey, or whether you are the Creator or his creature." Natural evidentness, in contrast, "comes with verisimilitudes more on one side than the other, and such evidentness ought to suffice for natural cases, and if it does not suffice for someone, then he is not fit for philosophy" (*Quaest. de gen. cor.* I.1, f. 132vab). For similar remarks, see Marsilius of Inghen, *Quaest. de gen. cor.* I.2, f. 66vb. In one way these discussions do not go as far as Buridan, because they do not invoke moral evidentness, but in another way they go farther, because they allow a natural evidentness that is far weaker than Buridan's, who had made an exception only for the possibility of divine interference. See Maier, *Metaphysische Hintergründe*, pp. 388–97, for further examples in this area.

In a different context, Nicole Oresme considers whether motion is a common sensible. Whereas earlier treatments might have been expected to work through familiar Aristotelian points about the variety of senses and sense objects, Oresme takes the occasion to raise some deeper epistemic concerns, regarding whether we can be certain that there is motion at all. There are, he says, two kinds of certainty: "one kind is exact and perfectly evident [*praecisa et evidentissima*], so that the opposite is not imaginable; the other is sufficient and plausible [*probabilis*], even demonstrable, as in natural subjects when one proceeds in good faith." It is only in the second sense that we can be certain of anything's motion (*Quaest. de anima* II.15, p. 238). For further discussion of Oresme's views in this regard, see Grellard, "Théorie de la croyance."

There is nothing conceptually new in these remarks. Aquinas, for instance, as quoted in note 15, makes remarks of a similar kind. The difference is in the intensity and frequency with which prominent fourteenth-century authors advance such concerns regarding certainty and evidentness. What for Aquinas is a peripheral issue becomes, less than a century later, a central theoretical concern.

Anyone today who attempts to generalize over the dark philosophical ages of the fifteenth and sixteenth centuries is making it up. The enormous amount of material, almost none of it familiar to modern scholars, defies summary, and may do so forever. My tentative impression, however, is that the pessimism of many fourteenth-century authors working within the scholastic tradition moves outside that tradition. This leaves the field of scholastic philosophy (i.e., those working within an Aristotelian framework, within the universities) to be dominated by a generally conservative line of figures, who were generally optimistic about the sort of epistemic ideal we could attain through scholastic philosophical inquiry. This is, however, little more than a hypothesis.

Outside the scholastic tradition there are fewer sources, but they are better understood. The tendencies here toward epistemic pessimism—if not outright skepticism—are especially well known. Gianfrancesco Pico is an early instance of a Renaissance figure doubting the attainability of certainty through philosophy. His long attack on Aristotelianism seeks not to invalidate it entirely, but only to show that the Aristotelian method "is the faculty not of achieving *scientia*, but of well and plausibly conjecturing" (*Examen vanitatis* Bk. V, p. 1176). If we want "exact, wholly certain and pure certitude regarding the truth" (p. 1095) then we must have recourse to divine illumination. Later in the fifteenth century, Francisco Sanches writes a treatise *Quod nihil scitur* (1576) and, most famously, Michel de Montaigne writes his *Apology for Raymond Sebond* (1575–80).

When we enter into the seventeenth century, the story can be told in much greater detail. Gassendi's epistemic pessimism has been described in note 9 here. Also on the continent, consider Christiaan Huygens in 1673:

I do not believe we know [*que nous sachions*] anything with great certainty, but everything by verisimilitude, and that there are degrees of verisimilitude that are quite different—some as 100,000 to 1, as in geometrical demonstrations, which could be false, but which have been examined so often and for so long that there is hardly any reason [*presque point de raison*] to suspect their truth, and especially those that are short. (To Perrault, in *Oeuvres* vol. 7: 298)

According to the notorious seventeenth-century proponent of moral laxism, Juan Caramuel y Lobkowitz, "since we are not angels, but men, we have evidentness of scarcely four things, and so we are required to act according to probable opinions" (in Franklin, *Science of Conjecture*, p. 89).

It is in England, however, where this attitude becomes most pronounced. It is not, in any way, an attitude of skepticism, but rather an attitude of reduced ambitions, which highlights the impossibility of infallibility even in the best of cases. Thus Chillingworth distinguishes between "actual certainty" and "absolute infallibility" and holds that not even geometers are "infallible in their own science, yet they are very certain of those things which they see demonstrated, and carpenters are not infallible, yet certain of the straightness of those things which agree with the rule and square" (*Religion of Protestants* ch. 3 §26). John Wilkins similarly denies that we are capable of "absolute infallibility"—not even God can give us this, not even in mathematics. The best we can have is a "conditional infallibility, that which supposes our faculties to be true, and that we do not neglect the exerting of them" (*Principles and Duties* I.1, p. 9). And Robert Boyle brings virtually all knowledge down to the level of moral certainty: "there are I know not how many things in Physics that men presume they believe upon physical and cogent arguments, wherein they really have but a moral assurance" (*Excellence of Theology* II.3, in *Works* vol. 8: 66). Henry More, in his *Antidote against Atheism* (1653), insists that his goal is not demonstration, if by that one means "such arguments that the reader shall acknowledge so strong as he shall be forced to confess that it is utterly unpossible that it should be otherwise" (ch. 2, p. 4). Indeed, "there is nothing at all to be so demonstrated" (p. 3). And there is Robert Hooke's *Micrographia* (1665):

If therefore the reader expects from me any infallible deductions, or certainty of axioms, I am to say for myself that those stronger works of wit and imagination are above my weak abilities; or if they had not been so, I would not have made use of them in this present subject before me: wherever he finds that I have ventured at any small conjectures, at the causes of the things that I have observed, I beseech him to look upon them only as doubtful problems, and uncertain guesses, and not as unquestionable conclusions, or matters of unconfutable science. (*Micrographia*, preface, quire b1r)

For further references along these same lines, see Lecture Six, note 8.

It is tempting to see the Reformation's hand in all these developments. Richard Popkin puts this idea in strong terms: "The Reformers' challenge of the accepted criteria of religious knowledge raised a most fundamental question: How does one justify the basis of one's knowledge? This problem was to unleash a sceptical crisis not only in theology but also, shortly thereafter, in the sciences and in all other areas of human knowledge. Luther had indeed opened a Pandora's box at Leipzig in 1519" (*History of Scepticism*, p. 15). But it is hazardous to generalize. Luther himself was on the side of certainty, and his rival Erasmus on the side of plausible opinion (see Shapiro, *Probability and Certainty*, pp. 75–6 and Schrimm-Heins, "Gewißheit und Sicherheit," part 1: 190–203). Chillingworth and his followers in England are ranged against Catholics like Thomas White, but Pascal's Catholicism is even more severely pessimistic than is the English tradition (see Lecture Six, note 15). Of course, all this might still spring from the turmoil of the Reformation, and it is clear that a great many epistemic disputes did spring from that source (see, e.g., chapter 4 of Popkin's *History of Scepticism*). But even granted that there is some connection here, it is hard to discern cause and effect. If it was Luther who opened Pandora's Box, who was it who dragged the box down from the attic?

It is also tempting to conceive of a divide here between scholastic and post-scholastic authors, but that is even harder to establish. It is true that it is easy to find late scholastic authors insisting on certainty in very strong terms, as when John Case affirms our capacity to achieve "absolute *scientia*" (*In universam dialecticam*, p. 178). Or consider Johann Scharff, who complains about Joachim Jungius's diminished standards for *scientia* that "the end of demonstration in logic is indeed *scientia*, but not just any *scientia*, as Jungius's ambiguous usage here has it, but that true *scientia* that is far removed from the *Topics* and from what is plausible and contingent, and that is altogether evident and necessary" (in Clucas, "*Scientia* and *Inductio Scientifica*," p. 55). Still, the notion of moral certainty, which Chillingworth and others make so much of, got its start in a thoroughly scholastic context: at the University of Paris, with Buridan, in the mid-fourteenth century. Indeed, as we have seen, the locus classicus for such diminished expectations is a passage from Aristotle. And two of the most iconic anti-Aristotelians, Galileo and Descartes, were leading proponents of the certainty ideal. It is therefore hard to see these debates over our proper epistemic expectations as helping to mark the decline of scholasticism.

Note 17 (p. 37). Scholarly discussions of these debates tend to categorize them as episodes in the ongoing skeptical crisis of early modernity. But this miscategorizes and hence distorts what is most distinctive and theoretically interesting about these developments: the rise of a new normative ideal in epistemology. Here is Chillingworth, echoing Aristotle: "Nor yet was I so unreasonable as to expect mathematical demonstrations from you in matters plainly incapable of them . . . For he is an unreasonable master, who requires a stronger assent to his conclusions than his arguments deserve" (*Religion of Protestants* preface, quire §§1v). What is new here is not the concept of a less demanding standard, but its broad application, even to the domain of faith: "faith, which is not a most certain and infallible knowledge, may be true, and divine, and saving faith" (*Works*, p. 431). Robert Boyle later concurs: "those articles of the Christian religion that can be proved by a moral, though not by a metaphysical or physical demonstration, may without any blemish to a man's reason be assented to" (*Reconcileableness of Reason and Religion* I.8, in *Works* vol. 8: 282). Tillotson contrasts "infallible assurance" with "undoubted certainty" and says of the latter that "an undoubted certainty does not exclude all possibility of mistake, but only all just and reasonable cause why a prudent and considerate man should doubt" (*Works* vol. 3: 429). Joseph Glanvill proposes essentially the same distinction and urges that sensory perception and the testimony of others can count as undoubtedly certain, meaning that "there is no reason of doubt" ("Of Scepticism and Certainty" [*Essays*, p. 47]). Wilkins writes: "men ought to rest satisfied in the best evidence for it, which that kind of things will bear, and beyond which better could not be expected, supposing it were true" (*Principles and Duties* I.3, pp. 24–5). Henry More, in his *Antidote against Atheism* (1655), explains that demonstrations are not to be expected because "we may give full assent to that which notwithstanding may possibly be otherwise" (ch. 2, p. 4); "it is manifest that there may be a very firm and unwavering assent or dissent, when as yet the thing we thus assent to may be possibly otherwise" (ch. 2, p. 7). Walter Charleton, similarly, at the conclusion of his *Immortality of the Human Soul* (1657), insists that his arguments, even if established to a lesser degree of certainty than that of a geometric demonstration, are good enough: "everyone ought to seek for the best assurance of which the nature of that thing into which he enquires will possibly admit" (p. 187). In the present case, Charleton says that we have been given "good and important reasons, as well physical as moral, such as are not much inferior to absolute demonstrations" (p. 188). On the continent, similarly, Arnauld and Nicole write: "we should be satisfied with moral certainty in matters not susceptible of metaphysical certainty" (*Port-Royal Logic* IV.15, trans. p. 270). Joseph Butler puts these ideas into memorable form decades later, when he writes that "probability is the very guide of life" (*Analogy of Religion*, introduction, p. iv).

This new normative ideal—in effect, the modern ideal of justification—represents a change on several distinct levels. Most strikingly, it embraces a lesser standard of certainty, satisfying itself with that which is virtually or morally certain. But with this shift comes the less obvious but in some ways even more important shift from compulsion to warrant or justification, which critically depends on the idea that belief in what is merely morally certain is voluntary rather than compulsory. To see the difference here, compare Richard Hooker. Writing at the end of the sixteenth century, he is still thinking in terms of compulsion: "the truth is, that how bold and confident soever we may be in words, when it comes to the point of trial, such as the evidence is which the truth has either in itself or through proof, such is the heart's assent thereunto, neither can it be stronger, being grounded as it should be" (*Laws of Ecclesiastical Polity* II.7, p. 117). Here we have the usual scholastic connection between evidentness and compulsion, but now applied to a sliding scale of evidentness, which yields a version of the principle of proportionality conceived of as a binding psychological law. By the time we get to Locke, in contrast, proportionality has become a normative rule in need of constant urging, precisely because it is so prone to being violated. Thus the chief concern in *Conduct of the Understanding* is with the regulation of assent:

In the whole conduct of the understanding, there is nothing of more moment than to know when, and where, and how far to give assent, and possibly there is nothing harder. It is very easily said, and nobody questions it, that giving and withholding our assent, and the degrees of it, should be regulated by the evidence which things carry with them; and yet we see men are not the better for this rule; some firmly embrace doctrines upon slight grounds, some upon no grounds, and some contrary to appearance. Some admit of certainty, and are not to be moved in what they hold; others waver in everything, and there want not those that reject all as uncertain.

(*Conduct of the Understanding* §33)

This statement of the principle of proportionality is telling in two ways. First, far from treating the principle as a novel and exciting doctrine, Locke considers it rather obvious and banal—as he should, given its long history. Second, the passage makes clear that, in contrast to Hooker, Locke does not think of evidentness as compelling belief. On the contrary, for all its banality, the principle of proportionality is very regularly violated, which makes it a considerable normative challenge to regulate our assent accordingly.

Elsewhere, and perhaps inconsistently with this last passage, Locke accepts the scholastic point that, when something is perfectly evident, then "our will has no power to determine the knowledge of the mind one way or another" (*Essay* IV.13.2). Locke even extends such compulsion to cases of very high probability—for example, that "there is such a city in Italy as Rome" (IV.16.8). Here "probability upon such grounds carries so much evidence with it, that it naturally determines the judgment, and leaves us as little liberty to believe, or disbelieve, as a demonstration does" (IV.16.9). The present lecture (p. 42) suggests that we need not think of this as a violation of proportionality, because the difference between probability and demonstration in such cases is so slight and gradual as to leave no scope for differing proportions of belief (and see note 23 here). But, regardless, the compulsion Locke sees here applies only to the top of the scale, leaving the principle of proportionality in general as a rule that is normally within our power to respect or not, but that is far from compulsory. (For a sophisticated recent discussion of the extent to which Locke treats his principle as compulsory, see Mark Boespflug, "Locke's Principle of Proportionality.")

With respect to moral certainty, at the high end of probability, it is common in the seventeenth century to hold both that it *should* be fully endorsed and that it *will* be fully endorsed by anyone who is at all rational. But the very persistence with which these claims are urged indicates that the matter is at least somewhat in doubt. The risk seems to be real in the minds of these authors that remote skeptical scruples might overcome our natural epistemic tendencies. Thus Chillingworth holds:

> Moral certainty is begot in us, by presumption and probabilities, which either by their strength . . . or by their multitude, make up a moral demonstration, to which being well considered . . . *no prudent and sober man can possibly refuse* to yield a firm, certain, undoubting, reasonable assent and adherence.
>
> (Quoted in Orr, *Reason and Authority*, p. 51; emphasis added)

Although it would be deeply irrational to reject what is morally probable, Chillingworth does not think that the mind is literally compelled. Wilkins later writes: "I appeal to the common judgment of mankind, whether the human nature be not so framed as to acquiesce in such a moral certainty as the nature of things is capable of," adding that anyone who would do otherwise would "be generally accounted out of their wits . . . Is there anything imaginable more wild and extravagant amongst those in Bedlam than this would be?" (*Principles and Duties* I.3, pp. 29–30). Yet, though it would be irrational, perhaps even insane, to doubt what is morally certain, Wilkins makes clear that it is not compulsory:

> Though they [moral certainties] are not capable of the same kind of evidence with the former, so as to necessitate every man's assent, though his judgment be never so much prejudiced against them, yet may they be so plain, that every man whose judgment is free from prejudice will consent unto them. And though there be no natural necessity that such things must be so, and that they cannot possibly be otherwise, without implying a contradiction; yet may they be so certain as not to admit of any reasonable doubt concerning them.
>
> (*Principles and Duties* I.1, pp. 7–8)

In place of compulsion, Wilkins offers an absence of reasonable doubt, and this marks the start of the modern program in epistemology.

In reaching this conclusion, I disagree with the interesting recent work of Julien Dutant, who argues that, "far from being a long-held conception, the Justified True Belief analysis's shelf-life was a mere eleven years" ("Legend," p. 115). Although Dutant is right to question just how much continuity there is between modern epistemology and earlier centuries, in fact the continuities are there to be found, if one knows where to look. I must also disagree with John Carriero's general conclusion about epistemology during this time: "The seventeenth-century discussions do not, for example, invoke juridical terminology—evidence, justification, warrant, and so on" ("Epistemology Past," p. 188); "Justification and warrant and their relation to knowledge are not yet being explored for their own sake" (p. 192). Although 'justification' and 'warrant' are not yet terms of art in the seventeenth century, this is precisely the period when these modern epistemic concepts first begin to take hold. Thus I also have to say that Frederick Schmitt is wrong to credit Hume on this score: "he is the first philosopher self-consciously and systematically to recognize a status, justified belief, spanning knowledge and probability and to provide a substantial, if unannounced and usually implicit, account of this status" (*Hume's Epistemology*, p. 18). To be sure, Hume plays an important role in the story, as Lecture Six argues, but this is not the place to look for the rise of the justified true belief framework. That framework is already prominent in the later seventeenth century, even if not put in quite those terms, and even if not usually offered as a definition of 'knowledge.'

The Banner Raised for Certainty

Note 18 (p. 38). There are various stories about Descartes's early years, according to which he championed the prospects for philosophical certainty against the advocates of mere probability (see Popkin, *History of Scepticism*, pp. 143–6, 174–5). And it is clear enough in his early writings, particularly the *Rules* and the *Discourse*, that this is his goal. For instance:

> The *literati* are perhaps convinced that there is very little indubitable knowledge, since, owing to a common human failing, they have disdained to reflect upon such indubitable truths, taking them to be too easy and obvious to everyone. But there are, I insist, a lot more of these truths than they think—truths that suffice for the certain demonstration of countless propositions that so far they have managed to treat as no more than probable. (*Rules* 2, X: 362)

The *Discourse* distinguishes moral and metaphysical certainty and allows that we ordinarily have a moral certainty about the world outside us, but insists that we require a new method to rise to the level of metaphysical certainty (VI: 38–9). For a discussion of the different kinds of certainty in Descartes, see Peter Markie, *Descartes's Gambit*, and the critical remarks in Edwin Curley, "Certainty."

Daniel Garber has argued that Descartes's epistemic ambitions slacken as time goes on. "We began in the early *Regulae* and the later *Discours* with certain knowledge, and progressed in the *Principia* to mere moral certainty and genuine ignorance; from the certainty of intuition to the lesser grade of certainty associated with the senses, good enough for guiding life, but not for finding truth" ("Descartes on Knowledge and Certainty," p. 128; see also John Morris, "Descartes and Probable Knowledge"). This seems to me an overstatement. Although Descartes's epistemic ambitions become more nuanced over time, the main line of his thought insists on something at least close to the sort of certainty he brashly promised as a younger man. Thus the end of the *Principles* acknowledges that one might think that his arguments achieve only moral certainty (IV.205). But Descartes does not leave things there. The next section goes on to describe a certainty greater than moral, an "absolute" certainty grounded in metaphysics, of the kind that can be achieved in mathematics and in demonstrating that an external world exists. "Perhaps" the arguments of the *Principles* will be judged to meet this standard. Indeed, "it seems they can be understood hardly otherwise [*vix aliter*] than as they have been explained by me" (IV.206). And even if these qualifications hint at a willingness to settle for something short of the highest ideal, the mood does not last. By the time of the preface to the French edition three years later, Descartes is back to full-blown triumphalism:

> Admittedly, I have not dealt with all things, for this would be impossible. But I think I have explained all the things I have had occasion to deal with in such a way that those who read the book attentively will be convinced that there is no need to look for any principles other than those I have provided in order to arrive at *all the highest knowledge* that the human mind can achieve. (IXB: 11)

Toutes les plus hautes connaissances . . . It is hard to see any retreat from the ideal here.

Subsequent Cartesianism is unsettled in its willingness to follow Descartes in this ambition. A particularly full-throated endorsement comes in Ludwig Meyer's preface to Spinoza's

Principles of Descartes's Philosophy (1663), which depicts "the wretched plight of philosophy," which exposes "the mind eager for eternal truth" to "storms of contending beliefs" and "waves of uncertainty." Meyer's story casts Descartes as its hero; he is the "most splendid star of our century," who managed to establish much of philosophy with "mathematical order and certainty" (Spinoza, *Works* vol. 1: 225–6). Malebranche, in contrast, is less enthusiastic about this aspect of Descartes's thought: "God speaks to the mind and constrains its belief in only two ways: through evidentness and through faith. I agree that faith obliges us to believe that there are bodies, but as for evidentness, it seems to me that it is incomplete and that we are not invincibly led to believe there is anything other than God and our own mind" (*Search after Truth*, Elucidation 6, trans. p. 573). Arnauld, however, appends to his treatise *On True and False Ideas* a final chapter that responds to Malebranche on this score, arguing at length that an external world can be *très-bien démonstré* (ch. 28, trans. p. 176). Looking ahead to the end of the seventeenth century, one finds Pierre-Sylvain Régis admitting the merely "problematic" status of speculative physics. "It would be as unreasonable to seek demonstrations in physics as to settle for probability in mathematics. Just as the one should admit nothing but what is certain and demonstrative, so the other is obliged to accept all of what is probable, provided that it is deduced from the one sole system founded on the first truths of nature" (*Système de philosophie*, La physique, avertissement, p. 275).

In England, Thomas White is no Cartesian. And he is aware that the notion of moral certainty goes back farther than Chillingworth and his followers. Reaching for nothing less than Jesus's prophecy of end times (Mark 13: 14), he writes that "some of our divines . . . seem to have unawares contributed to the hatching of this dangerous cockatrice, incertitude, which these bold Reformers have at least showed to the world, like the 'abomination of desolation' standing in the Temple, to be abhorred by all Christian hearts and true lovers of virtue" (preface to Rushworth, *Dialogues*, n.p. [5–6]). As one reads White's mockery of his opponents for their "dough-baked probability" (as quoted in this lecture, p. 38), it is pleasant to imagine that he is alluding to Plato's mocking comparison of rhetoric with pastry baking (*Gorgias* 463ab)—but the parallel is probably accidental.

On White's career, see Beverley Southgate, *Covetous of Truth*. More recently, see Harry Pearse, "Historical Faith," which contains an interesting discussion of how White is willing to lower his high standards when it comes to the uneducated masses. On the contested doctrine of church infallibility, which lies at the heart of what White defends here, see Orr, *Reason and Authority* ch. 3, and Frederick Beiser, *Sovereignty of Reason*, pp. 104–16.

White is developing views that go back to earlier figures like the English Jesuit Edward Knott, to whom Chillingworth's *Religion of Protestants* is a reply, and White himself was at the center of a larger circle that included Kenelm Digby, Henry Holden, and John Sergeant (on which see Stefania Tutino, *Thomas White and the Blackloists*). Digby's *Conference with a Lady* contains an extended argument for the unique infallibility of the church in contrast to the various protestant sects, whose doctrines "float always in a great deal of incertitude and anxious apprehension and fear of error" (p. 79). A brief *Approbatio doctorum* prefixed to Digby's *Two Treatises* commends the author for his lofty epistemic ideals:

Whether it has hit or missed of the truth, we must needs esteem and highly extol the author's manly design to aim at evidence. Especially in this skeptic age, wherein so few profess or think it possible to know with certitude. Yea wherein even many of those, who to the vulgar seem Masters of learning, acknowledge all philosophy's decisions only problematical, and thence laboring to make their voluminous relations of each other's fancies and opinions pass for science, have quite banished her their schools. But here we find a large and lofty soul, who not satisfied with unexamined words and ambiguous terms, longing to know, dives deeply into the bowels of all corporeal and compounded things, and then divinely speculates the nature of immaterial and subsistent forms.   (*Two Treatises* quire ūii r)

The doctors who praise Digby for diving so deeply are Henry Holden and a certain "E. Tyrrel." Holden was a student of Thomas White's, and he himself wrote a *Divinae fidei analysis* (1652), translated into English (very poorly) in 1658. In the first chapter of this long treatise, Holden takes the traditional view that faith is distinguished by its subjective certainty in the absence of evidentness. He then turns to considering what such certainty is and takes up the distinction of "philosophers and divines of these later times" between metaphysical, physical and moral certainty, "which terms, because they do not exactly discuss and distinctly explicate, they make all things uncertain" (I.1.1, trans. p. 5). Holden dismisses this whole way of talking, remarking that such distinctions can mark only a difference in subject matter, not a difference in certainty: "unless certainty reach to its utmost height, we cannot say that it is absolute and complete" (p. 6). Yet such absoluteness is what we mean when we speak of certainty: "'tis nothing else but to have our mind or understanding so firmly, constantly, and immovably fixed in its adhesion to any subject whereof it judges, as that there remains no hesitation, no doubt, no wavering in his judgment, nor the least fear of being deceived" (p. 6). And this then leads him to attack those "who have banished all science, especially moral, and consequently all perfect and absolute certainty out of their schools" (p. 6).

John Sergeant is best known as a critic of Locke's way of ideas. But in the preface to his *Solid Philosophy Asserted against the Fancies of the Ideists* (1697), he protests against these same trends that White had earlier attacked: "For, alas!, how few men are there who will profess to *demonstrate* in philosophy, or to reduce their discourses to *evidence*? Without doing which, and abiding by the trial, perhaps there is not *one word of truth* in all philosophy, nor anything but *learned romance* in all the universities of Europe" (n. 10). He goes on and on in this vein. For more information on Sergeant's epistemology, see John Henry, "Testimony and Empiricism" and Southgate, "Beating down Scepticism."

Certainty Conditionalized

Note 19 (p. 39). Locke is indeed a worthy target of Sergeant's invective. It is a remarkable feature of his *Essay*—though hard to appreciate when read outside its larger philosophical context—just how centrally concerned it is with an epistemology of variable and contingent particulars. Moreover, inasmuch as Locke does concern himself with essences, he does so mainly in order to subvert our knowledge of them. Indeed, our very ideas of essences are diverted away from the necessary and eternal forms of things, toward the merely nominal essences that in fact our words describe. "Our faculties carry us no farther towards the knowledge and distinction of substances than a collection of those sensible ideas which we observe in them" (*Essay* III.6.9).

Descartes, too, makes an important contribution to an epistemology of contingent particulars. For, even if his ultimate ambition is to identify the first metaphysical principles from which he can derive "all the highest knowledge that the human mind can achieve" (IXB: 11), still his method requires beginning with certainty about contingent particulars: that I exist, that I am experiencing various sensations, that I have the idea of God. As we will see in Lecture Four, it is Descartes who inaugurates the strategy of an ideas-first epistemology, treating ideas as the immediate objects of knowledge and thereby privileging the contingent particular.

There are also broader cultural trends at work in this epistemic shift toward the particular, such as the rise of the new science, an increasing interest in historical research, and a maturing legal system. (For much interesting information see Shapiro, *Culture of Fact*, esp. pp. 30–1, 46–7.) It is no accident, either, that, when scholastic authors consider lower epistemic standards, they tend to think of legal contexts. This is how Buridan had introduced the notion of moral evidentness; and earlier we saw Aquinas introduce conjectural plausibility in a similar way (see note 15). Given that the law was, within the medieval university, one of the principal subjects of theoretical inquiry, this is a natural place to look for a theoretical framework that demands less than Aristotelian *scientia*.

The Islamic Aristotelian tradition is more open than its Latin counterpart to allowing *scientia* (علم) in its strict demonstrative form to concern itself with contingent particulars. Avicenna flatly advises, "do not pay attention to what has been said, namely, that the demonstrative syllogisms are necessary" (*Remarks and Admonitions* I.9.1, p. 149). Instead, he claims, syllogisms count as demonstrative when their premises "must be accepted" (الواجب قبولها) (p. 148). This seems to rely on the idea of conditional epistemic probability. For the broader context, see Marmura, "The *Fortuna* of the Posterior Analytics," pp. 94–6. For similar views in al-Fārābī, see Black, "Knowledge and Certitude," pp. 26–8. But the tendency to embrace the conditional within the epistemic ideal did not go uncriticized within Islam. Insisting that "true demonstration is what provides necessary, perpetual, and eternal certainty that cannot change," al-Ghazālī complained that "some of the theologians said that knowledge is a kind of ignorance" (*Miʿyār al-ʿilm*, trans. McGinnis and Reisman, *Classical Arabic Philosophy*, p. 239).

Avicenna says that Aristotle himself did not intend to limit demonstrative knowledge to necessary truths (*Remarks and Admonitions* I.9.1, p. 149). But consider this passage from the *Nicomachean Ethics* on the nature of ἐπιστήμη:

> Now what ἐπιστήμη is, if we are to speak exactly and not follow mere similarities, is plain from what follows. We all suppose that what we have ἐπιστήμη of is not capable of being otherwise; of things capable of being otherwise we are unaware, when they have passed outside our observation, whether they exist or not. Therefore the object of ἐπιστήμη holds of necessity. Therefore it is eternal; for things that hold of necessity in the unqualified sense are all eternal; and things that are eternal are ungenerated and imperishable.
>
> (NE VI.3, 1039^{b}18–24; see also Meta. VII.15, 1039^{b}31–40^{a}8)

This is the sort of context in which it is so natural to look for the notion of epistemic probability, which would allow for an ἐπιστήμη of observables, provided that our acceptance is conditional upon our evidence. So, given that I see Socrates running right now, the fact of his running is not capable of being otherwise. But once he has "passed outside our observation" we make no claim. Of course, Aristotle does not neglect the importance of reasoning about contingent objects. But he does insist on distinguishing this from ἐπιστήμη. "Let it be assumed that there are two parts that possess reason—one by which we contemplate the kind of things whose principles cannot be otherwise, and one by which we contemplate variable things...Let one of these parts be called the scientific (ἐπιστημονικόν) and the other the calculative [λογιστικόν]" (NE VI.1, 1139^{a}6–12).

Themistius' paraphrase of the *Posterior Analytics*, which would be influential in the Latin tradition, puts the link between ἐπιστήμη and necessity in clear terms: "the subject of ἐπιστήμη is something necessary that cannot be otherwise, whereas the subject of opinion possibly is otherwise, and ἐπιστήμη arises through necessary premises, whereas opinion arises through possible ones" (I.33).

For better or worse, Aristotle's line of argument gets taken up directly into the Latin tradition. Discussing the canonical definition of ἐπιστήμη (Post. An. I.2, 71^{b}9–12), Aquinas reasons that, "because *scientia* is also a certain cognition of a thing, and what possibly stands otherwise cannot be cognized with certainty by someone, so it must further be the case that what we have *scientia* of cannot stand otherwise" (*Comm. Post. an.* I.4 n. 5). The same idea appears in Scotus:

> The second condition, that *scientia* concerns what is necessarily true, follows from the first [*sc.* certainty]. For if *scientia* were of something contingently true, it could extend to something false, on account of its object's undergoing change, as happens with the object of opinion. *Scientia*, however, necessarily, is a disposition that is essentially cognitive of what is true. Therefore it necessarily includes essentially not only a general relation

between disposition and object but also a special one—namely, one of conformity to that object. But if that object were not necessarily true then the disposition, while remaining the same, could sometimes be in conformity to that object and sometimes not, on account of that object's undergoing change. And then it could be sometimes true and sometimes false.   (*Reportatio* IA, prol. q. 1, in Wolter and Bychkov edn. vol. 1: n. 10)

There seems to be simply no room in these passages for the notion that a cognitive state might be perfectly ideal and yet concern contingent events. For a thorough discussion of the objects of *scientia* among thirteenth-century Latin authors, see Amos Corbini, *La teoria della scienza* ch. 1.

One might think that these authors fail to grasp the very concept of epistemic probability. This, however, seems to me quite implausible. Aquinas, for instance, is perfectly clear on the difference between "absolute necessity" and "necessity under a condition"—or, in more technical terms, "necessity of the consequent" versus "necessity of the consequence." Indeed, his example of conditional necessity is that "it is necessary that Socrates is sitting given that he is seen to be sitting" (*Summa contra gentiles* I.67.565). This is precisely the idea of epistemic probability, and it would have been easy enough to wield this notion to broaden the strict Aristotelian conception of *scientia*, if Aquinas and others had so desired. The fact is, however, that they did not desire, for reasons that are ultimately more metaphysical than epistemic. Scholastic authors adhered to Aristotle's vision of a cognitive ideal aimed at unchanging essences because they accepted this metaphysics, and in consequence treated a grasp of such essences as that which specially deserves to be called *scientia*. So here we see, as Lecture One stresses, how an idealized epistemology rests heavily on a background metaphysics. In turn, the seventeenth century displays how epistemology changes when metaphysics changes.

The Principle of Proportionality

Note 20 (p. 40). To go from epistemic probability to the normative principle of proportionality requires supposing that our credences come in degrees. This, too, was a familiar enough idea for scholastic authors (see e.g. the discussion of Buridan in Grellard, "Science et opinion"). The very notion of subjective certainty immediately suggests that it must admit of more or less. And, by the fourteenth century, proto-quantitative discussions of the intensification and remission of forms can be found to extend such strategies to certainty and other such epistemic states (see, e.g., Oresme, *Quaest. de an.* III.16 and John Dumbleton, *Summa* I.29–31—not yet edited, but see James Weisheipl, "The Place of John Dumbleton," p. 451).

The naturalness of treating proportionality as an epistemic ideal is indicated by the fact that it can be found as far back as Philo of Larissa, in one stage of his development from Academic skepticism to a kind of fallibilism: "The sage is committed to his beliefs only to the degree that the evidence he has for them supports them" (Brittain, *Philo of Larissa*, p. 87; see note 4 here).

What is new in the seventeenth century, then, is not the very concept of proportionality, but a focus on this principle as the central epistemic norm. Chillingworth states it clearly:

You content not yourselves with a moral certainty of the things you believe, nor with such a degree of assurance of them as is sufficient to produce obedience to the condition of the new covenant, which is all that we require. God's Spirit, if he please, may work more, a certainty of adherence beyond a certainty of evidence: but neither God does, nor man may, require of us, as our duty, to give a greater assent to the conclusion than the premises deserve; to build an infallible faith upon motives that are only highly credible, and not infallible, as it were a great and heavy building upon a foundation that has not strength proportionable. But though God require not of us such unreasonable things, you [Edward Knott] do; and tell men they cannot be saved, unless they believe your proposals with an infallible faith.   (*Religion of Protestants* 2.154)

This notion of proportioning "certainty of adherence" to "certainty of evidence" raises the question of what the latter actually amounts to—that is, it leads to reflection on epistemic probability. Chillingworth points the way when he contrasts the limited evidentness of the

Christian faith with its objective certainty: "the articles of the faith be in themselves truths, as certain and infallible as the very common principles of geometry and metaphysics" (*Religion of Protestants* 6.3). Wilkins comes still closer to the notion: "such things as in themselves are equally true and certain, may not yet be capable of the same kind or degree of evidence as to us. As for instance, that there was such a man as King Henry the Eighth: that there are such places as America or China" (*Principles and Duties* I.3, p. 22). Advocates of certainty can be found exploring similar terrain. Here is Thomas White:

By the *Topics* of Aristotle, there's an ability to give us to bring arguments without end in favor of either side; whence for anything we know, what is more probable to day may be less tomorrow, if some great brain become affected to the contrary opinion and employ his wit to show what can be said for it. Thus to be more probable touches not the nature of the truth itself, but is wholly extrinsical, and signifies only that men have more labored on one side than on the other, and is as subject to mutability as the conceits of a sophister.

(Preface to Rushworth's *Dialogue*, n. p. [16])

To see how much progress gets made over the course of the century and how much more precisely such notions can be formulated, compare Jacob Bernoulli, around the turn of the eighteenth century. Contrasting objective and subjective certainty, Bernoulli remarks that "in themselves and objectively, all things under the sun, which are, were, or will be, always have the highest certainty" (*Art of Conjecturing* IV.1, trans. p. 315). But then, rather than simply treat subjective certainty as a measure of confidence, he defines it conditionally, as relative to the evidence:

Seen in relation to us, the certainty of things is not the same for all things, but varies in many ways, increasing and decreasing. Those things concerning the existence or future occurrence of which we can have no doubt—whether because of revelation, reason, sense, experience, autopsia [i.e., eyewitness], or other reasons—enjoy the highest and absolute certainty. All other things receive a less perfect measure of certainty in our minds, greater or less in proportion as there are more or fewer probabilities that persuade us that the thing is, will be, or was.

Even here, however, it is not entirely clear what Bernoulli is telling us. Objective certainty is plainly a feature of things in the world. He seems at first to treat subjective certainty this way too: it is *things* that are certain "in relation to us," when the evidence leaves us unable to doubt. But the last sentence in the quotation switches over to "certainty in our minds," suggesting that the relative probability at issue here is our subjective degree of credence conditional on the available evidence. Yet when Bernoulli frames his version of the principle of proportionality, he goes back to treating epistemic probability in objective terms, as the probability of a thing relative to the available evidence: "it is necessary that the confidence we ascribe to any particular thing be proportioned to the degree of certainty the thing has and also that it be diminished in proportion as the probability of the thing is diminished" (IV.2, p. 321). To this day, there remains dispute over which of these two ways is preferable for formulating the notion of epistemic probability.

The great champion of these notions, from the later seventeenth century, is Leibniz, whom Hacking describes as "the only man of his time regularly to declare the relational character of probability judgements" (*Emergence of Probability*, p. 135). This is overstated, but Leibniz certainly deserves credit for seeing how this kind of program could be systematically developed. As he remarks in the *New Essays concerning Human Understanding*,

I have said more than once that we need a new kind of logic, concerned with degrees of probability, since Aristotle in his *Topics* could not have been further from it: he was content to set out certain familiar rules...without taking the trouble to provide us with the scale that is needed to weigh the appearances and to arrive at sound judgments regarding them.   (IV.16, p. 466)

Leibniz is elaborating on Locke's remark that "exactness is required, to form a right judgment, and to proportion the assent to the different evidence and probability of the thing" (*Essay*

IV.16.9). Here the epistemic ideal of exactness (see Lecture One, p. 16) gets applied to epistemology itself. Locke himself takes some steps toward an exact account (see the following note), but Leibniz seeks to go much farther: he takes Locke's remark to license the development of "a new kind of logic," the descendant of Aristotelian dialectical (nondemonstrative) reasoning, but now offering exact "degrees of probability" rather than mere "familiar rules." The metaphor of a "scale ... to weigh the appearances" both suggests the quantitative nature of what Leibniz is after and assimilates this project to other domains, where better instrumentation had led to an increase in precision (see Lecture One, note 18).

Leibniz's close contemporaries recognized the significance of his ideas. Hume, for instance, in his abstract to the *Treatise*, specifically credits Leibniz with promoting the importance of "probabilities, and those other measures of evidence on which life and action entirely depend and which are our guide even in most of our philosophical speculations" (*Treatise*, p. 7). Building on these earlier developments on the notion of epistemic probability, Hume finds it natural to speak of probabilities as "measures of evidence."

Note 21 (p. 40). Epistemic probability is critical to the Lockean program. Locke defines probability in contrast with demonstration. The latter involves proving the agreement or disagreement of two ideas. In contrast, "probability is nothing but the appearance of such an agreement or disagreement, by the intervention of proofs, whose connection is not constant and immutable, or at least is not perceived to be so, but is, or appears for the most part to be so" (*Essay* IV.15.1). The discussion wobbles rather badly between thinking of probability as subjective and thinking of it as objective, but either way it is conditional on the available evidence. Hence even a theorem of geometry, although demonstratively certain to the expert, may be merely probable to the amateur. See also *Essay* IV.16.12, where Locke writes of unobservable phenomena that "these and the like coming not within the scrutiny of human senses, cannot be examined by them or be attested by anybody, and therefore can appear more or less probable, only as they more or less agree to truths that are established in our minds, and as they hold proportion to other parts of our knowledge and observation."

Although Locke's discussion is entirely nonquantitative, he nevertheless attempts to bring an impressive degree of rigor to it. In *Essay* IV.15.4, for instance, having just defined 'probability' in epistemic terms and explained its significance, he proceeds to set out in some detail the variables that determine how probable something will be in one's estimation. And in IV.16.1 he stresses that the sort of probability at issue is always relative to the available evidence: "whatever grounds of probability there may be, they yet operate no farther on the mind, which searches after truth, and endeavours to judge right, than they appear." He then runs through a whole series of cases, in an attempt to flesh out "the degrees of assent" that culminates in another statement of the proportionality principle:

This only may be said in general, that as the arguments and proofs pro and con, upon due examination, nicely weighing every particular circumstance, shall to any one appear, upon the whole matter, in a greater or less degree, to preponderate on either side, so they are fitted to produce in the mind such different entertainment, as we call belief, conjecture, guess, doubt, wavering, distrust, disbelief, etc.   (IV.16.9)

See also IV.17.24 and *Conduct of the Understanding* §33 (quoted at note 17 above).

The principle of proportionality is so important to Locke because he is so doubtful about achieving much of the sort of certainty required for knowledge. The *Essay*'s introductory chapter extols us to be grateful to God "for that portion and degree of knowledge he has bestowed on us ... how short soever their knowledge may come of an universal, or perfect comprehension of whatsoever is" (I.1.5). This culminates in a characteristic piece of Lockean rhetoric:

We shall then use our understandings right, when we entertain all objects in that way and proportion that they are suited to our faculties; and upon those grounds they are capable of being proposed to us; and not peremptorily, or intemperately require demonstration, and demand certainty, where probability only is to be had, and which is sufficient to govern all our concernments. If we will disbelieve every thing, because we cannot certainly know all things, we shall do much-what as wisely as he, who would not use his legs, but sit still and perish, because he had no wings to fly. *(Essay I.1.5)*

All by itself, this is not so very different from Aristotle's famous remark in the *Nicomachean Ethics*. But Locke treats the merely probable case as the central case, and demonstrative certainty as merely a remote aspiration, not a genuinely normative ideal:

Therefore as God has set some things in broad daylight; as he has given us some certain knowledge, though limited to a few things in comparison, probably, as a taste of what intellectual creatures are capable of, to excite in us a desire and endeavour after a better state: So in the greatest part of our concernment, he has afforded us only the twilight, as I may so say, of *Probability*. *(Essay IV.14.1; cf. IV.11.10)*

Locke does think, in contrast to the usual Aristotelian view, that we can have certain knowledge in ethics and that this can even be described as a science (see Lecture One, note 13), but in most of the "concernments" of ordinary people in ordinary life probability is the best that will be available.

Gilbert Ryle describes the principle of proportionality as "the central moral of his *Essay*" (*Collected Papers*, p. 160). As we have now seen, this is far from being Locke's most original idea, but Ryle's remark is fair enough in view of how important the principle is to the *Essay* and of how much more likely it is to be *true* than so much else that is in the *Essay*. For a developed discussion of Locke's thinking in this area, see Nicholas Wolterstorff, *John Locke and the Ethics of Belief*, esp. p. 182, and Larry Laudan, "The Nature and Sources of Locke's Views on Hypotheses." I follow Wolterstorff in speaking of Locke's "principle of proportionality."

The Limits of Knowledge

'Knowledge'

Note 22 (p. 41). Locke's strict usage of 'knowledge' is clear and consistent. In the *Essay*, he writes that "the mind has two faculties conversant about truth and falsehood. First, knowledge, whereby it certainly perceives and is undoubtedly satisfied of the agreement or disagreement of any ideas" (IV.14.4). The second faculty is judgment, which lacks certainty. See also IV.2.14, IV.3.6, IV.4.18, IV.6.3, IV.15.3, and IV.16.3. To Stillingfleet, he writes that, "with me, to know and be certain is the same thing; what I know, that I am certain of; and what I am certain of, that I know. What reaches to knowledge, I think may be called certainty; and what comes short of certainty, I think cannot be called knowledge" (*Works* vol. 3: 145). On the similarity of Locke's high standards to Descartes's, see Loeb, *From Descartes to Hume*, pp. 36–58. For a useful summary of the scope of knowledge in Locke, see Schmitt, *Hume's Epistemology*, pp. 62–4.

Although Locke uses 'science' and 'knowledge' as almost equivalent terms, they are not precisely synonymous. Instead, one can see in his work an early instance of the modern practice of treating *knowledge* as the specific tenet of an individual mind, whereas *science* is something like a body of propositions. Still, Locke seems to take for granted that, for a body of propositions to count as a science, these propositions must be *known* by us, and not merely held as probable judgments:

I deny not, but a man, accustomed to rational and regular experiments, shall be able to see farther into the nature of bodies, and guess righter at their yet unknown properties, than one that is a stranger to them. But yet, as I have said, this is but judgment and opinion, not knowledge and certainty. This way of getting and improving our knowledge in substances only by experience and history, which is all that the weakness of our faculties in this state of mediocrity, which we are in in this world, can attain to; makes me suspect, that natural philosophy is not capable of being made a science. *(Essay IV.12.10)*

This passage presupposes that science will meet the causal expectation discussed in Lecture One. But it seems to make the further point that our grasp of causes, to be adequate for science, would have to achieve the level of "knowledge and certainty."

Locke is sufficiently impressed with Newton's achievements to allow that he has achieved genuine knowledge in a few domains. See *Some Thoughts concerning Education* §194:

> Though the systems of physics that I have met with afford little encouragement to look for certainty or science in any treatise which shall pretend to give us a body of natural philosophy from the first principles of bodies in general, yet the incomparable Mr. Newton has shown how far mathematics, applied to some parts of nature may, upon principles that matter of fact justify, carry us in the knowledge of some, as I may so call them, particular provinces of the incomprehensible universe. And if others could give us so good and clear an account of other parts of nature, as he has of this our planetary world, and the most considerable phenomena observable in it, in his admirable book, *Philosophiae naturalis principia Mathematica*, we might in time hope to be furnished with more true and certain knowledge in several parts of this stupendous machine than hitherto we could have expected.

For a useful précis of Locke's views in contrast with his predecessors, see Margaret Osler, "John Locke and the Changing Ideal of Scientific Knowledge."

Matthew Hale's *Primitive Origination of Mankind* (1677) offers another instance of the strict usage of 'knowledge,' as he identifies it with "science" and distinguishes it from "opinion" on the one hand and from "faith or belief" on the other. "Science or knowledge [is] effected by such evidence *cui non potest subesse falsum*; as is the case of demonstrative evidence" (I.2, p. 57). Robert Hooke's usage is similar. Even though he extols the Royal Society for its "advancement of Natural Knowledge" (*Posthumous Works*, p. 329), he goes on to define knowledge in terms that make it hard to believe that the Royal Society could have achieved so much: "By Knowledge then in the highest idea of it, I understand a certainty of information of the mind and understanding founded upon true and undeniable evidence" (p. 330). Or, again, see John Toland in 1696: "since probability is not knowledge, I banish all hypotheses from my philosophy" (*Christianity Not Mysterious*, p. 15). Lecture One, esp. note 11, deals in greater detail with the use of 'knowledge' in early English texts.

For authors writing in other languages, different words yield different choices. Bernoulli, writing in Latin late in the seventeenth century, follows the traditional Aristotelian usage of *scientia* that we saw in Descartes: "we are said to know [*scire*] or understand [*intelligere*] those things that are certain and beyond doubt, but only to conjecture or have opinions about all other things" (*Art of Conjecturing* IV.2, trans. p. 317). But Leibniz, confronted with the French *connaissance* where Locke's *Essay* speaks of *knowledge*, seems to find it just puzzling that Locke would want to restrict knowledge to what is certain. Why not simply allow a "knowledge [*connaissance*] of likelihood," he wonders, with the result that there would be two kinds of knowledge (*New Essays* IV.2, p. 373)? Part of what makes this seem natural, presumably, is the gravitational influence of the Latin *cognitio*, which is always used quite broadly.

Hume, though impressed by Leibniz's work on probability (see note 20 here), retains the traditional English usage, so that 'knowledge' gets reserved for the ideal case: "knowledge and probability are of such contrary and disagreeing natures, that they cannot well run insensibly into each other, and that because they will not divide, but must be either entirely present, or entirely absent" (*Treatise* I.4.1, p. 181). Knowledge is possible only when we compare ideas (I.3.1, pp. 69–70), or when it comes to the existence and nature of our own ideas (I.4.2, p. 190). In the *Enquiry concerning Human Understanding*, "the sciences of quantity and number . . . may safely, I think, be pronounced the only proper objects of knowledge and demonstration" (12.3, p. 163).

The strict usage of 'knowledge' endures even into the twentieth century, for instance in John Maynard Keynes's *Treatise on Probability*, which reserves 'knowledge' for certain belief (II.2).

Fixing the Boundaries of Knowledge

Note 23 (p. 42). Naming the "Lockean Program" after Locke is warranted not because he was the first to conceive of things this way, but because he developed the program in the greatest detail and insisted on it as a central task for epistemology. Thus he writes:

> But there being degrees herein from the very neighbourhood of certainty and demonstration, quite down to improbability and unlikeness, even to the confines of impossibility; and also degrees of assent from full assurance and confidence, quite down to conjecture, doubt, and distrust. I shall come now (having, as I think, found out the bounds of human knowledge and certainty) in the next place to consider the several degrees and grounds of probability, and assent or faith.   (*Essay* IV.15.2)

Within this program, sensory knowledge is not an isolated borderline case. Having remarked that "most of the propositions" we embrace do not count as known, he adds that "some of them border so near upon certainty that we make no doubt at all about them, but assent to them as firmly, and act, according to that assent, as resolutely, as if they were infallibly demonstrated, and that our knowledge of them was perfect and certain" (IV.15.2). Well, do these beliefs count as knowledge or do they not? Locke's point is that the concept is a vague one, admitting of no precise demarcation. We cannot be *completely* certain of anything; only God can have that, or so Locke supposes. The highest certainty we can achieve lies in intuiting our own ideas and their connection. Beyond that there is a steady diminishment in certainty and no clear place to draw lines. That Locke's modern readers make such a fuss over which side of the line Locke puts sensory experience, even in the face of such remarks, is a testimony to the distorting influence of our modern boundary mongering.

On the vagueness of the boundary between what is known and what is merely probable, see also *Essay* IV.16.6, which describes "the first and highest degree of probability" as the testimony of general consent, supported by one's own experience, about what is always the case as a result of nature's causes—for example, that fire heats, iron sinks, and so on. "These probabilities rise so near to certainty, that they govern our thoughts as absolutely, and influence all our actions as fully, as the most evident demonstration: and in what concerns us, we make little or no difference between them and certain knowledge: our belief thus grounded, rises to assurance."

An earlier example of something close to the Lockean Program is the *Port-Royal Logic*. After setting out the notion of epistemic probability, Arnauld and Nicole remark of what is highly probable that

> we are right [*nous avons raison*] to believe in these events, if not with certainty, at least with high probability. This is enough when we are required to judge them. For, just as we should be satisfied with moral certainty in matters not susceptible of metaphysical certainty, so too when we cannot have complete moral certainty, the best we can do when we are committed to taking sides is to embrace the most probable, since it would be a perversion of reason to embrace the less probable.   (*Port-Royal Logic* IV.15, trans. p. 270)

Hacking identifies the *Port-Royal Logic* as the basis for Locke's discussion, in the *Essay*, of degrees of assent (*Emergence of Probability*, p. 86), but there is no reason to suppose that this French work had more influence on him than did Wilkins and other English authors who were saying the same sort of thing at around the same time.

Note 24 (p. 43). It can be a subtle matter to adjudicate apparent violations of the principle of proportionality. Authors who make this move tend to begin with the thought that different domains admit of different levels of evidentness (often invoking the *Nicomachean Ethics*). From this they go on to insist that, in these domains of lesser certainty, the best we can do is good enough (see note 17 to this lecture). The question then arises, good enough for what? In some cases, the idea is that such lesser degrees of evidentness are good enough for practical action.

This is the step that legal theory began to take at that time, when it settled on the reasonable doubt standard for a legal verdict (see Theodore Waldman, "Origins of the Legal Doctrine" and Shapiro, *"Beyond Reasonable Doubt"*). But in other cases such lesser evidentness is said to be good enough for full, unqualified belief; and here is where the principle of proportionality gets violated. Thus Tillotson, taking the existence of Jerusalem as his example, writes that

no man is blamed for this, as being over-credulous, because no man that will not take the pains to go thither can have any other greater evidence of it, than the general testimony of those who say they have seen it. And indeed almost all human affairs, I am sure the most important, are governed and conducted by such evidence, as falls very much short both of the evidence of sense, and of mathematical demonstration.   (*Works* vol. 3: 10)

It is not just that such evidentness is good enough for human affairs, but that it is good to ground full, indubitable conviction:

So that this is to be entertained as a firm principle by all those who pretend to be certain of anything at all: That when anything in any of these kinds is proved by as good arguments as a thing of that kind is capable of, and we have as great assurance that it is as we could possibly have supposing it were, we ought not in reason to make any doubt of the existence of that thing"   (*Works* vol. 1: 16).

Glanvill similarly approves of the fact that "we assent to such testimonies with the same firmness that we would to the clearest demonstrations in the world" (*Essays*, p. 49)—despite the fact that elsewhere, as this lecture shows (p. 40), he endorses proportionality. Boyle holds that "a moral certainty ... is enough in many cases for a wise man, and even a philosopher to acquiesce in" (*Excellence of Theology* pt. II sct. 3, in *Works* vol. 8: 65). Elsewhere, "those articles of the Christian religion that can be proved by a moral, though not by a metaphysical or physical, demonstration, may without any blemish to a man's reason be assented to" (*Reconcileableness of Reason and Religion* pt. I sct. 8, in *Works* vol. 8: 282).

There is a debate over whether John Wilkins violates the principle of proportionality. My own view concurs with that of Henry van Leeuwen, who finds Wilkins guilty of "breaking down the objective relation supposedly existing between evidence and assent" (*Problem of Certainty*, p. 70). More recently, however, Jamie Ferreira has denied this, on the grounds that Wilkins treats certainty as a threshold concept, meaning that, when one crosses the threshold into moral certainty, one arrives at *full* certainty. Hence full belief is appropriate (*Scepticism and Reasonable Doubt* ch. 2). Ferreira offers only very thin textual support for his reading; he seems to base his case instead on the thought that this is what Wilkins *ought* to say. (And he seems to take encouragement from the later case of Thomas Reid, who might more plausibly be thought to have held such a threshold view; see *Scepticism and Reasonable Doubt*, p. 77.) It seems clear enough, however, that Wilkins thinks of certainty as coming in degrees, given how he describes the different cases. Of moral certainties, he writes (as already quoted once) that, "though they are not capable of the same kind of evidence with the former, so as to necessitate every man's assent, though his judgment be never so much prejudiced against them, yet may they be so plain that every man whose judgment is free from prejudice will consent unto them" (*Principles and Duties* I.1, pp. 7–8). I take this to say both that moral certainties have a lesser kind of objective certainty and that it is unreasonable to be less than fully certain of them subjectively. This violates the principle of proportionality, which, if it is anything, is a rule for what levels of confidence and doubt are reasonable. One might object that 'certainty' just means *perfect certainty*, but the textual evidence is overwhelming that, over the centuries, this simply is not what the word means.

Wilkins goes on to describe the case of mere probability, where we assent even with some measure of doubt, because the evidence available is "not so weighty and perspicuous as to exclude all reasonable doubt and fear of the contrary" (*Principles and Duties* I.1, p. 11). That sort of partial belief contrasts with the case of doubt: "when the evidence on each side does equiponderate, this does not properly beget any assent, but rather a hesitation or suspension of assent" (p. 11).

Although Wilkins's philosophical ideas do not go very deep and, accordingly, have received little attention from historians of philosophy, his role in promulgating the new science is quite significant. Van Leeuwen describes him as "the person perhaps most responsible for the founding of the Royal Society" (*Problem of Certainty*, p. 49). Barbara Shapiro shows him to have been widely regarded as the "principal reviver of experimental philosophy" (*Culture of Fact*, p. 111). For detailed information, see the biography by Shapiro, *John Wilkins*.

Knowledge as Moral Certainty

Note 25 (p. 44). Despite looking rather hard, I have not found anyone before Wilkins who treats moral certainty as fixing the boundary of knowledge. The idea is not in Buridan or Gerson, nor does it seem to be in Chillingworth or other English enthusiasts of moral certainty. This is so even though it is easy to find authors who countenance a sense of 'knowledge' that includes what is morally certain. The trouble is that such authors, going back to Themistius in Greek and Grosseteste in Latin, let *too much* into the domain (see Lecture One, note 8). A good seventeenth-century example is Hobbes. As Lecture One discusses (p. 11), Hobbes treats 'knowledge' in its more demanding sense as synonymous with 'science,' but also allows a very weak sense of 'knowledge', as "nothing else but sense and memory" (*Lev.* 9.1). Similarly, Gassendi allows "the familiar and common custom of speaking, by which we are said to know many things," which lets "experiences or appearances be called *scientia*" (*Exercitationes para-doxicae* II.6.6, p. 499). And, even though Chillingworth requires that 'knowledge' be ideally certain, he registers the more casual usage that Wilkins would later endorse. Do I know that Constantinople exists, just from the testimony of others? Strictly speaking, no, says Chilling-worth. But "I deny not that the popular phrase of speech will very well bear, that we may say we know that which in truth we only believe, provided the grounds of our belief be morally certain" (*Works*, p. 740).

Shapiro, speaking of seventeenth-century England, puts great weight on this change in the use of 'knowledge': "'Knowledge' was no longer reserved for the logically demonstrable products of mathematical and syllogistic 'science.' The morally certain was also a form of knowledge, and the highly probable came close to being another" (*Probability and Certainty*, p. 4). And then: "What is interesting here is that the line between knowledge and opinion was becoming blurred. Where propositions attained moral certainty, they clearly passed over into the realm of knowledge . . . More and more, natural knowledge seemed to fall somewhere between mere opinion and moral certainty" (p. 33). Though I share her enthusiasm, it needs to be stressed just how unusual a usage this is for the seventeenth century. That Locke, in particular, does not fit into this story is something of an embarrassment for Shapiro, since she wants Locke to be "the most English of English philosophers" (p. 14). "Chillingworth, Glanvill, or Wilkins . . . collectively they indicate a shift in direction which culminated in the formula-tions of John Locke" (p. 32). No doubt the Lockean Program is important. But it is equally important to recognize that it is Wilkins, not Locke, who sets out the modern program for epistemology.

Even while the theory of 'knowledge' begins to assume its modern form, ways of talking about 'belief' (and the like, in other languages) remain notably disparate. One does find the now familiar usage in which knowledge is a kind of belief. See, for example, Chillingworth: "he that knows believes, and something more; but he that believes, many times does not know" (*Religion of Protestants* ch. 6 §2). Back in the fourteenth century, John Wyclif had similarly suggested that *scientia* might be "an aggregate of an act and a relation"—an *act* of believing (*credendi*) and a *relation* between the belief's content and how things are in the world (*Tractatus de logica* ch. 13 [vol. 1: 179]). Still earlier, Grosseteste (*Comm. Post. an.* I.19, pp. 278–9) had distinguished three senses of *opinio*. In the broadest sense, it is simply "cognition with assent" and, so taken, it is the "genus" of which *scientia* is one species. More narrowly, however, *opinio* involves assent together with some fear that the opposite might be true (on such fears, see Lecture Six, p. 136). In this sense, *opinio* and *scientia* are contrasted. This contrasting usage can be found in Aquinas with regard to *opinio* (e.g., *Summa theol.* 2a2ae 1.5 ad 4) and with regard to *credere* (2a2ae 2.1c). John Rodington expresses the contrast as follows: "to believe is to assent to something without evident awareness; to know is to assent with evident awareness" (*credere enim est assentire alicui sine notitia evidenti; scire est assentire cum notitia evidenti*: (*Sent.* prol. q. 1 dub. 7, in Tweedale, *John of Rodynton*, p. 305). The contrasting usage remains quite common through the seventeenth century, even in English texts that have adopted the terms 'belief' and 'knowledge.' According to Hobbes, for instance, "belief, which is the admitting of propositions upon trust, in many cases is no less free from doubt than perfect and manifest knowledge" (*Elements of Law* I.6.9). And, according to Locke,

The entertainment the mind gives this sort of propositions [*sc.* probable ones] is called belief, assent, or opinion, which is the admitting or receiving any proposition for true, upon arguments or proofs that are found to persuade us to receive it as true, without certain knowledge that it is so. And herein lies the difference between probability and certainty, faith and knowledge, that in all the parts of knowledge there is intuition; each immediate idea, each step has its visible and certain connexion; in belief, not so.   (*Essay* IV.15.3)

For these authors, believing *p* precludes knowing *p*.

Maria Rosa Antognazza treats such points as having profound significance for the history of epistemology, as showing why "the project of finding what should be added to belief in order to turn it into knowledge would have been regarded by much pre-twentieth century episte-mology as absurd" ("Benefit to Philosophy," p. 169; for similar remarks, in the ancient context, see Lloyd Gerson, *Ancient Epistemology* ch. 1). But this strikes me as misguided, inasmuch as the differences are wholly terminological. I do not know of any historical figure who resists the idea that we can identify a kind of mental state, in the vicinity of assent, which can serve as a component in analyzing what it is to be in some more exalted epistemic state, in the vicinity of knowledge. What that component state gets called varies from century to century and from author to author. For Buridan, for instance, it will not be called *opinio*, because "*opinio* signifies a defect from *scientia* in some way" (*Summulae* VIII.4.4, trans. p. 710). But this is just a point about that Latin word, as it gets used at that moment in time, and goes no deeper than the analogous observation today that a *guess* cannot count as *knowledge*, no matter what gets added to it. Accordingly, throughout these lectures, I use 'belief' to pick out the mental state that is a constituent in the epistemically ideal state of *scientia* and so on, without fussing over whether 'belief' corresponds to *assensus*, *credere*, *opinio*, and so on.

Still, the terminology itself matters. It points, for instance, to one reason why it is unfortunate that Richard Foley has found in *Essay* IV.15–16 the "Lockean thesis" that "it is epistemically rational for us to believe a proposition just in case it is epistemically rational for us to have sufficiently high degree of confidence in it, sufficiently high to make our attitude towards it one of belief" ("The Epistemology of Belief," p. 111). To be sure, this is a useful idea: that we think of 'belief' as the catchall term for all those credences ("degrees of assent" in Locke's terms) that rise above a certain cutoff point. But it ought to have been obvious that this cannot be *Locke's* notion, given that he does not even use 'belief' for the highest degrees of assent (those he counts as knowledge). Furthermore, the essence of the Lockean Program is to get away from thinking of belief and assent in absolute terms. This ought to be clear enough with regard to 'assent'—after all, the very title of Chapter 16 is "Of the Degrees of Assent." But it should also be plain that 'belief' is generally used as an approximate synonym for 'assent.' See, for example, *Essay* IV.15.5, speaking of testimony: "as the relators are more in number, and of more credit, and have no interest to speak contrary to the truth; so that matter of fact is like to find more or less belief." Nevertheless, and rather disgracefully, this inapt label—"the Lockean thesis"—has assumed a wide currency in recent formal epistemology.

Belief and Religion

Note 26 (p. 44). For seventeenth-century champions of absolute certainty, the violation of proportionality offered an obvious opening to attack. Henry Holden, for instance, utterly refuses to acknowledge the usefulness of the distinction between kinds of certainty, remarking that "what degree soever of certainty is wanting in any of these...the same degree of doubtfulness must needs be in our assent thereunto" (*Analysis of Divine Faith* I.1.1, trans. p. 5). As this lecture explains (p. 44), Holden, White, and others were happy to allow that mere moral certainty might be sufficient for action, in certain contexts. But they insisted that certainty of belief should arise only from a corresponding certainty of evidentness.

So where does that leave us in what was thought to be the most important case of all, that of religion? A century later, Immanuel Kant would suggest that religion requires not absolute belief but instead hope (see Andrew Chignell, "Rational Hope"). During the years we are considering, however, this radical proposal seemed quite unacceptable. Hence the debate circled around how to justify absolute belief. In general, the champions of moral certainty were inclined to violate proportionality, whereas their critics sought to achieve a loftier ideal. All parties to the debate agreed, however, that full belief in religious matters is obligatory. Thus Locke writes that "in some matters of concernment, especially those of religion, men are not permitted to be always wavering and uncertain, they must embrace and profess some tenets or other" (*Conduct of the Understanding* §6). Thomas White likewise considers whether we might act on the basis of probabilities, without assent. His answer is that surely God would not have it so: "this necessity binds God to put an inevitable certitude in the motives of faith and not a pure probability; else he would oblige us to this hard law, of hazarding our whole well-being on what we could not rationally believe to be true" (Preface to Rushworth's *Dialogues*, n.p. [14]). An ideal certainty must be possible for us, then, or else we would find ourselves in an untenable position.

Schüssler ascribes to Cajetan, an author from around the turn of the sixteenth century, the initial articulation of a distinction that is quite fundamental here, between speculative and practical doubt. One can remain speculatively in doubt about a proposition yet follow it in one's actions, "thus satisfying the formal requirements of sound moral reflection by remaining in speculative doubt about the right answer to a question but believing in the licitness of acting as if one answer were true. The whole edifice of Catholic casuistry after Cajetan rests on this possibility" ("Anatomy of Probabilism," p. 95). Cajetan is not thinking of moral certainty, but of cases where there are robust reasons for doubt. But part of what is at issue in the seventeenth century is whether even moral certainty ought to give rise to speculative doubts. No, says Wilkins—and others who deny the principle of proportionality. But, if proportionality holds and one's conviction must be diminished even slightly, then the question arises of whether such less than perfect subjective certainty can serve as a suitable foundation for religious belief.

We are now in the vicinity of Pascal's wager. For what if White's "inevitable certitude" is not available, and yet mere probabilistic "acting as if" is inadequate as a foundation for religious practice? In that case we might need some other reason to embrace religion. This is what Pascal famously offers us in his *Pensées* (n. 680, pp. 212–13), which were written around 1658 but not published until 1669. And not only Pascal. Tillotson, in a sermon delivered in the early 1660s, evokes an argument much like the wager against the atheist (*Works* vol. 1: 31), seemingly independently of Pascal (see Jeff Jordan, *Pascal's Wager*, pp. 149–54). Boyle, too, runs a version of the wager in 1675 (*Reconcileableness of Reason and Religion* I.8, in *Works* vol. 8:

283–5). Franklin credits Antoine Sirmond with the first "full version" of the wager back in 1637, and finds still earlier anticipations in Chillingworth and Silhon (*Science of Conjecture*, pp. 248–9). For a profound meditation on the philosophical implications of the wager, see Daniel Garber, *What Happens after Pascal's Wager*.

A very different way to defend moral certainty against proponents of a higher ideal would be to urge, as Locke suggests (see note 23 here), that gradations among high degrees of certainty are not even discriminable. Bernoulli says as much: "something is morally certain if its probability comes so close to complete certainty that the difference cannot be perceived" (*Art of Conjecturing* IV.1, trans. p. 316). If this were so, then the level of certainty present in the moral case would be so close to the absolute that we would be incapable of proportioning our beliefs accordingly. In that case there could be no objection to our violating proportionality, because we would not be able to modulate our credences finely enough. This strategy conflicts, though, with the widespread interest in calibrating the exact levels of moral certainty that obtain in various cases. Bernoulli himself, just a few pages later, suggests that we ought to try to draw such lines very finely indeed:

Because it is rarely possible to obtain certainty that is complete in every respect, necessity and use ordain that what is only morally certain be taken as absolutely certain. It would be useful, accordingly, if definite limits for moral certainty were established by the authority of the magistracy. For instance, it might be determined whether 99/100 of certainty suffices or whether 999/1000 is required. Then a judge would not be able to favor one side, but would have a reference point to keep constantly in mind in pronouncing a judgment.

(*Art of Conjecturing* IV.2, trans. p. 321)

A 1699 study by the Royal Society similarly attempted a precise mathematical calculation of the credibility of human testimony—by way of defending the moral certainty of scripture in matters of fact (see Shapiro, *Culture of Fact*, p. 175). Later, Georges Le Clerc Buffon, in his *Essais d'arithmétique morale* (1777), would suggest that the threshold for moral certainty should be fixed by the reasonable fear that a healthy person might have of dying within the next twenty-four hours. This was a convenient marker for Buffon, because he had done groundbreaking work on establishing empirically and statistically adequate mortality tables, and from those tables he concluded that the odds of a healthy fifty-six-year-old Frenchman's dying within the next twenty-four hours are 10,189 to 1. (This yields a credence of .000098.) Buffon concludes that "any equal or smaller probability must be regarded as null, and any fear or hope that falls below ten thousand must not affect us or even occupy for a single instant the heart or the head" (*Essais* §8, pp. 56–7). For this and other similar examples, see Daston, *Classical Probability*, pp. 90–3.

Note 27 (p. 45). My account of why the Lockean Program did not become ascendant depends on our inability to relinquish absolute belief. But what exactly is an absolute belief? The issue is much debated in recent epistemology. Here I assume that it is something different from a credence and that, in particular, it is not simply to be identified with any credence above a certain level of confidence. One promising account characterizes belief in terms of behavioral and cognitive dispositions—such as, for instance, a disposition to assert the proposition in question. See Mark Kaplan, *Decision Theory as Philosophy* ch. 4 and Keith Frankish, "Partial Belief and Flat-Out Belief" for rival attempts at developing this sort of distinction between full belief and credence. For a dispositionalist theory of belief more generally, see Eric Schwitzgebel, "A Phenomenal, Dispositional Account of Belief." Jacob Ross and Mark Schroeder, "Belief, Credence, and Pragmatic Encroachment," argue for an account of belief in terms of a disposition to hold a proposition true in reasoning. The distinction between credence and belief comes in for further discussion at the end of Lecture Six.

For a full-throated defense of "simple, all-out belief" see Richard Holton, who writes that "the Bayesian approach is not an idealization of something we actually do. Instead, it is quite foreign to us" ("Intention as a Model for Belief," p. 15). Many, however, dismiss the notion of absolute belief as something over and above credences. A classic statement of this view is Richard Jeffrey, "Dracula Meets Wolfman." His account of the "cultural evolution" (p. 171) that would result from replacing belief with degrees of credence amounts to a powerful argument for the Lockean Program. But the fact that Jeffrey still needs to argue the case so strenuously also testifies to how little influence Locke's program ultimately had on modern epistemology and how entrenched the notion of absolute belief remains.

Notes to Lecture Three

Sensory Ideals

Note 1 (p. 47). One of the most common of epistemic idealizations, throughout the history of philosophy, takes this schematic form: The senses *must* satisfy at least *this* ideal, or otherwise our epistemic situation would be hopeless. But of course it cannot be hopeless. Therefore etc.

Thus Walter Chatton (fl. 1320–30), against the possibility of a vision's naturally occurring in the absence of an object, argues that "otherwise all our certainty would perish, because our certainty concerning sensible things arises through our experiencing our sensations" (*Sent.* prologue q. 2 art. 2, p. 89). If the veridicality of the senses cannot be trusted, he goes on to argue, then "not even God can make us evidently certain that a thing exists" (p. 90).

Even in the seventeenth century, and even among those most familiar with the challenges posed by the new science, sensory certitude is often still held up as an ideal. Thus Joseph Glanvill writes that the Royal Society "deals in the *plain Objects* of *Sense*, in which, if anywhere, there is *Certainty*" (*Praefatory Answer*, p. 143).

Here is a place where it is tempting to think of the whole history of philosophy as dividing into empiricists and rationalists, starting with Aristotle versus Plato and moving on to Descartes versus Locke. Descartes signals his rationalist leanings right from the start of the *Meditations*: "Whatever I have up till now accepted as most true I have acquired either from the senses or through the senses. But from time to time I have found that the senses deceive, and it is prudent never to trust completely those who have deceived us even once" (VII: 18). Naïvely and pretheoretically, we all are empiricists, Descartes is saying, but the senses are not absolutely reliable and therefore should not be relied upon in absolute fashion. The project of the *Meditations* is to use reason to find something better and thus eventually to win the senses back, but in the qualified way that this Lecture describes. In contrast, the characteristic strategy of the empiricist is to *begin* by trusting the senses, on the grounds that, if we cannot start there, we cannot start anywhere. It is unclear, however, just how many examples there are of pure rationalists or pure empiricists, when the distinction is drawn in this way.

Malebranche builds on Descartes's critique of empiricism but pushes still farther, challenging our sensory grasp not just of secondary qualities but also of primary qualities. Thus he can conclude that "our eyes were not given us to judge the truth of things, but only to let us know which things might inconvenience us or be of some use to us" (*Search after Truth* I.6.1, trans. p. 30). This ultimately gets pushed all the way to its radical extreme, to doubts over the senses' testimony regarding the very existence of external bodies: "What evidentness do you have that an impression that is deceptive not only with regard to sensible qualities but also with regard to the size, shape, and motion of bodies, is not so with regard to the actual existence of these same bodies?" (*Search after Truth*, Elucidation 6, trans. p. 573). On Malebranche's doubts in this regard, see also Lecture Two, note 18.

Note 2 (p. 47). Despite his fairly extreme anti-empiricism, Malebranche does not think that the fault lies with the senses, as the lecture explains. In taking this line, he is following a tradition that goes all the way back to Democritus: "they say that what appears to our senses must be true" (Aristotle, *Meta.* IV.5, 1009^{b}14–15 [= Democritus in Diels and Kranz, *Vorsokratiker* 68A112]); "Democritus said straight out that truth and appearance are identical, and that there is no difference between the truth and what appears to the senses, but what appears and seems so to each individual is true" (Philoponus, *Comm. de an.* 71.25–8 [68A113]). After Democritus came the Epicureans. See, e.g., Lucretius: "whatever impression the senses get at any time is true" (*De rerum natura* IV.499 [in Long and Sedley, *Hellenistic Philosophers* 16A]).

Among scholastic authors, one more often finds the Aristotelian doctrine that it is only with regard to the proper sensibles that the senses are never in error. For the more general claim, see John of Mirecourt (1344): "No brutes are deceived, as is clear from the preceding, because every deception is an erroneous judgment, and brutes do not have judgment" (*Sent.* q. 5, p. 433). In modern times, Wallace Matson is fond of quoting Robert Frost on this score: "to err is human, not to, animal" (e.g., *Grand Theories*, p. 38). But Matson seems to have forgotten that Frost coins the phrase only to reject it: "Or so we pay the compliment to instinct, / Only too liberal of our compliment / That really takes away instead of gives" ("The White-Tailed Hornet," in *Poetry*, p. 279).

When Glanvill remarks, as quoted in this lecture (p. 47), that the senses "are not deceived, but only administer an occasion" for deception, he is invoking Descartes's remarks on the material falsity of our ideas of secondary qualities. For Descartes, it is not that these ideas are themselves erroneous, but that they "furnish judgment with the material for error" (Fourth Replies, VII: 231). For more on this, see note 13 to this lecture.

For a contrasting case, consider Francis Bacon: "the impressions of the senses themselves are faulty; for the senses fall short and they also deceive. But its shortcomings are to be supplied, and its deceptions are to be corrected" (*Novum organum* I.69). See also this marvelous passage:

> The senses deceive, but they supply the marks of their own errors. Yet while the errors lie in front of us, their marks must at length be sought out. The senses are faulty in two ways: either they fall short or they deceive us ... Where a sense does grasp a thing, its apprehensions are far from firm. For its testimony and information is always relative to man, not to the universe, and so it is a great error to assert that sense is the measure of things.   (*Instauratio magna*, Plan of Work, trans. p. 33)

And there is a lovely contemporary remark from Hugo Grotius: "very few facts are discernible through the senses, since we cannot be in more than one place at one particular time, and since the senses perceive only those things that are very close at hand. Yet there is no other way of attaining to true knowledge" (quoted in Franklin, *Science of Conjecture*, p. 80). It is subtle views such as this one that wreck the neat historical taxonomy of empiricists and rationalists.

Domains of Privilege

Note 3 (p. 50). In the scholastic context, as Lecture Two makes clear, questions about the sensory ideal can be asked in terms of the sort of evidentness they yield. In some respects, it is natural to suppose that the senses succeed in making things evident. After all, evidentness is associated with indubitability (see Lecture Two, note 13), and there is perhaps nothing more indubitable than the testimony of the senses, at least in favorable circumstances. Hence the expression "Seeing is believing." Moreover, the etymology of *evidentia* bears a direct link to vision and "seeing" (*videns*), which again creates an assumption that perceptual cases must count, and indeed perhaps ought to be treated as paradigms. On the other hand, evidentness is also associated with infallibility, and here sensory perception is obviously vulnerable.

Ockham sometimes suggests that there is no difficulty in sensory perception's ability to deliver the evidentness of *scientia*: "if someone intuitively sees Socrates and the whiteness existing in Socrates, then he can evidently know [*scire*] that Socrates is white" (*Ordinatio* prol. q. 1, in *Opera theol.* vol. 1: 6). In part he gets this result because of the distinctive way in which he thinks that perception is invulnerable to deception (see the lengthy discussion in note 17 to Lecture Four). The characteristic tendency among later scholastic authors, however, is to offer only a qualified embrace of the claim that the senses yield evidentness. Here is for instance Adam Wodeham: "although one does not have a categorical evident judgment that the moon is eclipsed, one does have a hypothetical evident judgment, namely, that this is so unless God deceives me" (*Lectura secunda* I.2.6 [vol. 2: 222]). Domingo de Soto takes a different route, contending that the senses yield evidentness without qualification—evidentness *simpliciter*— because such evidentness is always consistent with the bare logical possibility of deception: "a judgment is evident *simpliciter* when it is, of its own nature, not deceptive, even if someone could supernaturally be deceived through it" (*De demonstratione* q. 2, pp. 296–7). This allows De Soto to argue that perceptual judgments can count as *scientia*:

'To know' [*scire*] is taken in the first way, broadly [*communiter*], for the experience of merely contingent things that arise in our perceptual field [*in prospectu nostro*], as we are said to know [*scire*] that human beings are disputing (the ones we are hearing), and that a person is sitting (the one we see). And this, although it is in a way called *scientia*, because it is evident, nevertheless it is *scientia* not strictly but broadly, because it concerns things that are contingent and entirely variable, having no certainty. By its proper name, it is called *experience*.

(*De demonstratione* q. 2, p. 294M)

If De Soto had allowed for the sort of conditional epistemic probability discussed in Lecture Two (p. 38), he could have allowed that even this form of *scientia* counts as certain—we are certain given the testimony of the senses. But it would be another century before knowledge of contingent particulars was given this sort of analysis.

The very distinction between sensation and judgment, which is so fundamental to scholastic discussions, has its locus classicus in Ibn al-Haytham (Alhazen), *Optics* II.3.1–42. But the distinction is easy enough to find in earlier texts, for instance in Epicureanism. See, e.g., Epicurus, *Principal Doctrines* n. 24 (in Inwood and Gerson, *Hellenistic Philosophy*, p. 34) and Lucretius, *De rerum natura* IV.379:

Here, as always, we do not admit that the eyes are in any way deluded. It belongs to them to see where light is, and where shadow. But whether one light is the same as another ... that is something to be discerned by the reasoning power of the mind. The nature of things cannot be understood by the eyes. You must not hold them responsible for this fault of the mind.

For discussion, see Dominic Scott, "Epicurean Illusions."

The case of John Buridan, as discussed later in this lecture (p. 57), shows something of the variety of scholastic views on the relationship between sensation and higher level judgment. For discussions of various other aspects of the distinction among scholastic authors, see Katherine Tachau, "What Senses and Intellect Do" and Dominik Perler, "Seeing and Judging."

What are the objects of judgment? The usual scholastic answer is that they are *propositiones*, but that word, among scholastic authors, ordinarily refers to particular linguistic tokens (written, spoken, or thought), and hence is best understood as referring to what we now call *sentences*. There was, however, a lively debate over whether judgments indeed refer to such linguistic tokens or rather to the things themselves in the world—or perhaps instead to some kind of abstract entity, of the sort we now refer to as *propositions*. For a detailed history of these debates, see the series of volumes from Gabriel Nuchelmans, beginning with *Theories of the Proposition*.

In this lecture (p. 48) I prefer to contrast the qualitative with the *sentential* rather than with the *propositional* (as one might expect), in order to capture the baseline historical consensus over the value of the senses. What everyone accepts is that we can rely on the senses to show us that leaves are green—at least in the minimal sense of relying on such thoughts and utterances in our daily lives. Here is where even the most radical of ancient skeptics must grant something to the senses, on pain of giving up any vestige of a normal life. But, even if the skeptic must accept such thoughts and utterances, we still might wonder whether that skeptic must regard them as true. Perhaps this is a further theoretical claim on which the skeptic need not take a position. Hume, at his most skeptical, seems inclined to draw the line there: "If we believe that fire warms or water refreshes, 'tis only because it cost us too much pains to think otherwise" (*Treatise* I.4.7, p. 270). There are, then, empirical sentences—say, 'fire warms'— that Hume thinks we must accept on pain of giving up our normal lives, but that from a skeptical point of view are of doubtful truth. Such reservations, even at the sentential level, go beyond Berkeley, who harbors no such doubts: "Let me be represented as the one who trusts his senses, who thinks he knows the things he sees and feels, and entertains no doubts of their existence" (*Three Dialogues*, dial. 3, in *Works* vol. 2: 237). But Berkeley achieves such commonsense only at the sentential level. He firmly believes that fire warms and that the leaves are green, but only on a certain idealist understanding of what propositions these sentences pick out. In general, at the propositional level, there is the fiercest of disagreements among the philosophers, inasmuch as Berkeley accepts such empirical sentences on one construal of their meaning, Descartes on another, Buridan on a third, and so on.

Lecture Six discusses Hume's position in more detail. As to whether the ancient skeptics should be said to entertain any beliefs about the sentences they accept, see Lecture Six, note 8.

Molyneux's Problem

Note 4 (p. 50). The section of the *Essay* where Locke introduces Molyneux's problem begins by invoking the distinction between sensation and judgment: "We are farther to consider concerning Perception, that the Ideas we receive by sensation are often in grown people altered by the judgment, without our taking notice of it" (II.9.8). Indeed, Molyneux's problem is introduced only in the second edition, as an illustration of the distinction. Yet, as the long and lively subsequent history of the debate shows, it is not at all easy to decide just what light the problem shines on the nature of perception.

As Locke presents this problem, the central question, which he answers in the negative, is whether someone newly sighted would "be able with certainty to say which was the globe, which the cube, whilst he only saw them" (II.9.8). Yet a negative answer here is compatible with all sorts of views about the character of vision in the newly sighted. For it is possible that the newly sighted would see the objects just as we do, in perfectly vivid three dimensions, and yet would not be able to connect this experience with their tactile ideas of a cube and a sphere. Hence, along one vein of discussion, the central issue is the relationship between our tactile ideas and our visual ideas.

But this is not Locke's central concern: as noted, he takes the problem to show us something about the difference between sensation and judgment. Where, then, does Locke draw this line? It is clear, at a minimum (*pace* Laura Berchielli, "Color, Space and Figure"), that Locke thinks that sensation proper cannot convey three-dimensional information. In this respect he represents merely one instance of a view that has a long prior history (see Martha Bolton, "The Real Molyneux Problem") and runs on through the following two centuries (see A. D. Smith, "Space and Sight"). That not everyone would share this assumption is clear from the detailed historical account of Marjolein Degenaar, *Molyneux's Problem*, but this is a distinctive feature of most perceptual theories before the twentieth century.

In the lecture I claim that Locke further excludes spatial ideas (shape and motion) from sensation proper. This, admittedly, is not entirely clear. The best evidence for my reading is this:

Because sight, the most comprehensive of all our senses, conveying to our minds the ideas of light and colours, which are peculiar only to that sense; and also the far different ideas of space, figure, and motion, the several varieties whereof change the appearances of its proper object, viz. light and colours; we bring ourselves by use to judge of the one by the other. This, in many cases, by a settled habit, in things whereof we have frequent experience, is performed so constantly and so quick that we take that for the perception of our sensation, which is an idea formed by our judgment; so that one, viz. that of sensation, serves only to excite the other, and is scarce taken notice of itself.   (*Essay* II.9.9)

The passage takes for granted that sight gives rise to spatial ideas, but the last phrase underlined seems to make clear that these ideas are produced by judgment rather than by sensation itself. The case is trickier than this one passage suggests, however, because just a section earlier Locke had remarked:

When we set before our eyes a round globe, of any uniform colour, v.g. gold, alabaster, or jet, it is certain that the idea thereby imprinted in our mind is of a flat circle variously shadowed, with several degrees of light and brightness coming to our eyes.   (*Essay* II.9.8)

It is not easy to reconcile this sentence with the reading offered in this lecture. Still more passages might be cited, on both sides, and scholars have taken conflicting views on the matter. Against spatial qualities in sensation are, for example, Bolton, "The Real Molyneux Problem" and Vili Lähteenmäki, "Locke and Active Perception"; in favor are Bruno and Mandelbaum, "Locke's Answer" and Michael Jacovides, "Locke on Perception."

It might seem absurd to suppose that two-dimensional visual ideas are a product of judgment rather than immediately given in experience. After all, for sensation to have light and color as its content, it surely must have those colors spread out spatially, on a visual field. What would it even mean to deny this? In fact I think that Locke does not mean to deny it but means to insist that visual experience resolves itself into determinate spatial ideas, in two or three dimensions, only as a result of a judgment to which we grow so habituated that it becomes indistinguishable from the original sensation. Without that judgment, we would see the world to be colored, but we would be unable to make any sense of the actual arrangement of those colors, even if the colors themselves were somehow, confusedly, spread out in our visual field. When the thesis is so framed, it becomes perfectly natural to reach the same conclusion about two-dimensional shape that one reaches about three-dimensional shape. After all, to discriminate between whether a surface is circular or oval is to make a judgment, at the same time, about the three-dimensional disposition of that body, given that the one presupposes the other.

That Locke means to exclude even two-dimensional shapes from sensation is suggested by the way in which he seems to conceive of Molyneux's problem. Although the *Essay*'s report of the problem is not entirely clear, it appears as if the newly sighted person is meant to be aware that he is looking at a sphere and a cube and has been given the task of simply saying which is which. But, when the problem is so conceived, it would seem that the newly sighted person could pass the test. After all, he would be able to see that the one, being circular in aspect, lacks angles, whereas the other has spatial features consistent with being a cube. Of course, one might still object that our subject could not connect these visual ideas with his tactual ideas. But, even if the ideas are different, they would both presumably *resemble* the primary qualities they represent, and so it would seem reasonably easy for the subject to draw connections, given that he need only distinguish cube from sphere. This was precisely Leibniz's response to the problem in his *New Essays* (II.9, pp. 136–8). And, even if this was not quite how Locke was thinking of the case, he ought to have regarded the whole issue as far less easy to resolve, if he had thought that sensation immediately delivers even two-dimensional spatial information about the world. (Compare Ralph Schumacher, "What Are Direct Objects of Sight?".)

The claim that, one way or another, the vision of color has priority over the vision of shape goes back to Aristotle's insistence that color and shape belong to different categories of sensibles. The idea is variously developed among later Aristotelians and in the perspectivist tradition that runs through Ibn al-Haytham, and ultimately it shows up in Descartes: "size, distance, and shape can be perceived by reasoning alone" (Sixth Replies, VII: 438; and see Descartes, *Optics* 6). So it should hardly be surprising if Locke does exclude shape perception from the realm of immediate visual experience.

Whatever Locke's view was, the standard negative verdict to Molyneux's problem in subsequent generations clearly does involve a denial of spatial ideas within sensation proper. Thus Berkeley distinguishes primary and secondary objects of vision (*New Theory of Vision* §50, in *Philosophical Writings*, p. 24) and insists that "there is no other immediate object of sight besides light and colours" (§129, p. 55). This in turn leads to his own resolutely negative answer to Molyneux's problem, which he notes would not be so easy to maintain if sensation conveyed spatial ideas (§133, p. 57). Thomas Reid too, despite his enormous disagreements with Locke and Berkeley, similarly restricts the deliverances of sensation:

To a man newly made to see, the visible appearance of objects would be the same as to us; but he would see nothing at all of their real dimensions, as we do . . . He could perceive little or nothing of their real figure; nor could he discern that this was a cube, that a sphere; that this was a cone, and that a cylinder . . . In a word, his eyes, though ever so perfect, would at first give him almost no information of things without him. They would indeed present the same appearances to him as they do to us, and speak the same language; but to him it is an unknown language.   (*Inquiry into the Human Mind* VI.3, in *Works* vol. 1: 136–7)

The domain of sensation proper, on all these views, is radically restricted.

For all these authors it is critical to stress, as Reid makes explicit, that the newly sighted subject is having a sensory experience "ever so perfect," just as our own. The poverty of what such an experience turns out to involve, when shorn of our accumulated habits of observation, is what allows us to recognize the dramatic distance, even in normal perceivers, between pure sensation and our habitual sensory judgments. But this way of thinking about Molyneux's problem sits uneasily with another aspect of it: discussants regularly looked to confirm their answers through real-world medical cases. To see the tension here, we can distinguish two versions of the problem. Let us call "the easy Molyneux problem" the question of whether someone newly sighted can tell the difference between a cube and a sphere by using sight alone. As philosophical questions go, this is a relatively easy one to settle: just find some folk who are blind, give them sight, and run the experiment. Indeed, this has recently been done in India, and the results seem to establish fairly clearly that the negative answer is correct. Contrast this with what we might call "the hard Molyneux problem": Do newly sighted people have essentially the same visual experience of three-dimensional objects that ordinary perceivers have? This is a hard version of the problem because it is not clear how any experiment could resolve it. In particular, a resolution of the easy problem does not settle the hard problem. If the answer to the easy problem were yes, that might be because the cube and sphere appear to the newly sighted essentially as they do to ordinary observers. Or it might be because, despite profound differences in visual experience, the newly sighted are nevertheless able to discern cube from sphere. Nor does a negative answer to the easy problem solve the hard problem. The experience of the newly sighted might be fundamentally the same as that of normal observers, as far as the sensation itself is concerned, but the newly sighted might nevertheless be unable to connect that experience conceptually with their existing tactile experiences of cubes and spheres. This is the verdict that Molyneux, Locke, Berkeley, and Reid all seem to have reached. Their thought experiment simply stipulates a "yes" answer to the hard problem and contends that even then the answer to the easy problem would be "no."

Although this combination of views is philosophically coherent, it is not empirically testable. For, although we can easily enough ask newly sighted subjects to distinguish between a cube and a sphere, we cannot so easily ascertain whether they are seeing these objects in the way we suppose. Of course, we can ask them other questions, in an effort to learn about the character of their sensations; but, no matter what their answers to these other questions, the fact will remain that these are observers who cannot discriminate between a cube and a sphere. So the suspicion must always remain that their experiences are somehow stunted. As a result, the long history of disputes over whether one or another medical experiment vindicates Molyneux and Locke seems quite misguided, once we see that they seek an answer simultaneously to the easy problem and to the hard problem. That dynamic continues to this day. In 2011, Richard Held et al. published their exciting results from India, establishing in careful detail that Molyneux and Locke were right ("The Newly Sighted Fail to Match Seen with Felt"). They were, however, answering the Easy Problem, which opened the door for John Schwenkler ("Do Things Look the Way They Feel?") to object that the experimenters did not establish that their subjects were having sufficiently robust visual representations. Schwenkler has his own suggestions about how an experiment might confirm this, but if one thinks that Molyneux's problem presupposes an affirmative answer to the hard problem then all such suggestions are doomed to failure. And, if one follows Locke's assumption that in ordinary perceivers the processes of sensation and learned judgment are phenomenally indistinguishable, then the problem becomes doubly intractable. For now, in addition to the usual problems associated with intersubjective phenomenal comparisons, we face the difficulty of being unable to specify, even in the first person, what exactly it is like to have a raw visual sensation, unmediated by judgment. Unsure about our own case, how could we ever know whether someone newly sighted is having exactly that sort of experience? Nor do matters become any simpler if we reject Locke's assumption of indistinguishability, because then it is entirely unclear what sort of baseline perceptual experience we are counting on the newly sighted to have, in order to pose a theoretically interesting version of Molyneux's problem. (For somewhat similar concerns about whether the problem is empirically testable, see Alessandra Jacomuzzi, Pietro Kobau, and Nicola Bruno, "Molyneux's Question Redux.")

Aristotle's Relationalism

Note 5 (p. 53). This lecture oversimplifies, in several respects, Aristotle's relationship to Democritus. First, although Aristotle discusses Democritus at considerable length and in various contexts, it is not entirely clear how much his theory of sensible qualities is intended as a response to Democritus specifically, as opposed to subjectivist trends in Presocratic thought more generally. More importantly, it is quite unclear and controversial whether, as I argue, Aristotle is making a genuine concession to such subjectivism. On what is perhaps the more common modern reading (see the next note), Aristotle's concessions are merely verbal, leaving his view objective and absolute at its core. Given that there are texts pointing in various directions, one's interpretive choice here depends critically on how much one inclines toward thinking of Aristotle as yielding to the subjective concerns of Democritus and others. And here we face yet another difficulty, which is that we lack a clear sense of exactly what these "subjective concerns" are, in Democritus and others. This makes it hard to form a view about how seriously we should expect Aristotle to take such concerns. If we had a clearer sense even of what *Aristotle* took Democritus's arguments against the absolute reality of the sensibles to be, we would at least have some evidence for what Democritus's own views are. As things are, however, we have to rely on Democritean fragments such as this, reported by Sextus Empiricus:

There are two forms of judgment, genuine and bastard. To the bastard form belong all these, sight, hearing, smell, taste, touch. The form that is genuine, but separate from this one, is when the bastard form can no longer see in the direction of greater smallness nor hear or smell or taste or perceive by touch other things in the direction of greater fineness.   (Taylor, *The Atomists*, n. 179)

This fits well with the argument of the lecture, but it is an open question whether such concerns would have been enough to lead Aristotle to a relational view of color and other sensibles. A carefully extended argument for Democritus's influence on Aristotle across a variety of domains can be found in Mi-Kyoung Lee, *Epistemology after Protagoras*. I have tried to work out in detail Democritus's theory of perception in "Democritus and Secondary Qualities."

One thing, at least, that is clear about Aristotle's views in this domain is that he is committed to infallibility (or near infallibility?) with regard to our perception of the proper sensibles. It is a doctrine that he asserts over and over, in several different works. In addition to the passages quoted in this lecture (p. 51), see *De an.* III.3, 428^{a}11 and III.6, 430^{b}29; *De sensu* 4, 442^{b}8; *Meta.* IV.5, 1010^{b}2 and 1010^{b}24. What is unclear, unfortunately, is *why* he thinks this; it is unclear because he never even begins to explain himself. My own suggestion—that the result falls out of his relational view of the proper sensibles—is just one of many views. According to Anna Marmodoro, for instance, the unqualified guarantee holds only at the broadest determinable level of color, and only because "it is only color that can stimulate the sense organ of sight, so sight cannot be mistaken about that" (*Aristotle on Perceiving Objects*, p. 85). This lecture (p. 57) finds a similar view in Nicole Oresme. But Marmodoro also thinks that we can understand the guarantee in stronger terms, provided that we specify standard conditions (pp. 136–7; see also Justin Broackes, "Aristotle, Objectivity, and Perception," pp. 96–102 and Stephen Gaukroger, "Aristotle on the Function of Sense Perception").

On the most common reading, the guarantee holds not at the level of metaphysics, but because the proper sensibles are the kinds of objects that the senses are most naturally suited to perceive, and hence the domain where they come closest to being infallible. A key passage here is *De an.* II.6, 418^{a}24–5: "of the things perceptible in themselves, the proper objects are most strictly perceptible, and it is to them that the essence [οὐσία] of each sense is naturally suited [πέφυκεν]." This passage fits well with the usual medieval view, as described in this lecture (p. 56), according to which the proper sensibles are those natural quality kinds to which the senses are specially well attuned. Thus Aquinas writes:

A sense is always true with respect to its proper sense objects, or else has little falsity. For just as natural powers are deficient with respect to their proper operations only on rare occasions [*in minori parte*], because of some damage, so too the senses are deficient with respect to a true judgment concerning their proper sense objects only on rare occasions, because of some damage to the organ. This is evident in the case of the feverish, to whom sweet things seem bitter because of their tongue's disorder.

(*Commentary on the De anima* III.6.63–72 [on 428^{b}18])

My interpretation need not dismiss this idea entirely, but regards it as insufficient to explain the strength of the claim Aristotle makes and the insistence with which he makes it. This sort of natural suitability seems so common and familiar in the biological world as to deserve no special attention in the sensory context, and indeed, as John Buridan points out (this lecture, p. 57), it is not clear why it should particularly characterize our relationship to the proper sensibles.

One way to moderate Aristotle's remarks would be to treat them as generic. I may say, for instance, that "dogs make good pets," and this can be perfectly true as it stands, even though everyone knows that not all dogs make good pets. But this reading does not fit all the texts. *De anima* 428^{a}11, for instance, holds that "perceptions are always [ἀεί] true," which I think cannot be read generically (see also *Meta.* 1010^{b}20–4, as quoted in the next paragraph). It seems better, then, to follow Averroes's strategy of appealing to what is true for the most part, which would of course cohere with Aristotle's broader methodology in biology. But one might have qualms about this too, again citing the word 'always' at 428^a11 and 1010^b24.

Some modern scholars have read Aristotle's no-error doctrine as requiring that he identify sensible qualities with sensations. See in particular Terence Irwin, *Aristotle's First Principles*, who speaks in this connection of "purely phenomenal colour" (p. 314). This is evidently what one must say to maintain the strictest sort of guarantee, and it is the most natural way to understand *Metaphysics* IV.5, 1010^b20–4:

> not even at different moments does one sense disagree about the quality, but only about that to which the quality belongs. I mean, for instance, the same wine might seem, if either it or one's body changed, at one time sweet and at another time not sweet; but at least the sweet, such as it is when it exists, has never yet changed, but one is always right about it; and that which is to be sweet must of necessity be of such and such a nature.

It is hard to see what Aristotle could mean here, unless he embraces either a purely phenomenal understand of sweet or a relational account so tightly fixed as to yield full-blown Protagorean relativism regarding the sensibles. (See also *De sensu* 6, 446^b18–27, where something similar seems to be going on.) Still, the overwhelming current of the texts permits neither reading. Aristotle constantly speaks of the proper sensibles as distinct from sensations (on this, see Irving Block, "Truth and Error"), and the passage just quoted comes at the end of a denunciation of Protagorean relativism, even with regard to the proper sensibles. Indeed, the sensibles are even the same across species: "what is healthy or good is different for humans and for fish, but what is white or straight is always the same" (*NE* VI.7, 1141^a22–3).

Note 6 (p. 54). Interpretive disagreements over the proper sensibles ramify yet further when we consider Aristotle's remarks on the sensibles more broadly. Here interpretation runs the whole gamut from the extremely subjective to the extremely objective. In the end, it seems to me, one simply has to acknowledge that Aristotle speaks of the sensibles (τὰ αἰσθητά) in many ways, some of them contradictory. My heart goes out to the scholar whose area of specialization requires turning these texts into something more coherent.

The weight of scholarly authority, old and new, runs strongly against a relational interpretation. In addition to Arabic and Latin medieval authors, the ancient commentators also tend to treat the sensibles in absolute terms, holding for instance that visibility is an accident of color (see Broackes, "Aristotle, Objectivity, and Perception," pp. 58–60). Most modern scholars have reached the same conclusion. Stephen Everson, for instance, argues that the proper sensibles should be understood as "primary qualities," not defined in terms of their power to produce sensation but existing quite independently of sensation. He defends this interpretation by discarding *De anima* III.2 (quoted in this lecture, p. 52) as "incautiously expressed rather than . . . a statement of official doctrine" (*Aristotle on Perception*, pp. 105, 113). Allan Silverman similarly tries to work around the apparent implications of that passage in order to get the "objective existence" of colors ("Color and Color-Perception," pp. 271–3). Broackes takes more seriously the relationalism and, to account for it, he distinguishes between two ways of talking about redness ("Aristotle, Objectivity, and Perception," p. 67): as the power to produce perceptions of red (which he labels red$_p$), and as the objectively characterizable ground of that power (which he labels red$_g$). But it turns out in the end that Broackes thinks the proper sensibles, for Aristotle, are the objective grounds. The only significance he is willing to give the relationally defined red$_p$ is as a terminological nicety. Thus, in explaining *Metaphysics* 1010^b30 (quoted in this lecture, p. 53), Broackes holds that even in a world without perceivers, the sensibles still exist inasmuch as the qualities that cause sensation would still exist. What Aristotle means to call into question, Broackes argues, is merely the label we would attach to these qualities: "they merit the label 'sensibles' if and only if there are animals capable of perceiving them" ("Aristotle, Objectivity, and Perception," p. 93).

Such interpretations are prominent because there are texts supporting an absolute reading, texts in which the sensibles themselves clearly seem prior to sensation. I am not worried about a passage such as *Metaphysics* IX.10, 1051^{b}7: "it is not because we think that you are white, that you are white, but because you are white we who say this have the truth." This is consistent with relationalism in all but its most relativistic formulations, insofar as it is perceivers as a whole who determine what whiteness is, rather than some local subset whose members would count as the "we" in this passage. But a relational account does clash with *Categories* 7, 7^{b}35–8^{a}6: "the sensible would seem to be prior to sensation" inasmuch as "if animal is destroyed sensation is destroyed, but there will be something sensible, such as body, hot, sweet, bitter, and all the other sensibles." Nor is this an isolated passage. The discussion of relatives at *Metaphysics* V.15 makes similar trouble for the sort of relational view I am describing, because it, too, seems to characterize the sensibles as prior to the senses (1021^{a}27–^{b}3). And such priority seems required by the *De anima*'s methodology of defining faculties in terms of their objects (e.g., II.4, 415^{a}12–20). On this thread in Aristotle's thought, see Paula Gottlieb, "Aristotle versus Protagoras." She, too, recognizes a multiplicity of threads that seem difficult to reconcile.

It is not my responsibility to iron out all the wrinkles in Aristotle's various discussions, but I do mean to insist on the striking persistence of the relational thread. See, for instance, *Meteorology* IV.8, 385^{a}2: "for a thing is white, fragrant, noisy, sweet, hot, and cold in virtue of a power of acting on sense." And this helps explain why Aristotle finds some plausibility in the thesis that a sense object can have an effect only on its corresponding sensory power:

> Someone might raise a difficulty as to whether what cannot smell can be affected by scent in any way, or what cannot see by color, and similarly for the others. If the object of smell is scent, then if scent produces anything, it produces smelling, so that nothing incapable of smelling can be affected by scent; and the same argument applies to the other senses. (*De anima* II.12, 424^{b}3–5)

Aristotle quickly goes on to note that there are exceptions to this principle, at least for the objects of touch and taste. He can hardly suppose, after all, that the actions of hot and cold are limited to perceivers. And by the end of *De anima* II.12 it is unclear how much of the original thesis survives at all. (Compare *De an.* II.7, 418^{b}1, where we are told that the nature [φύσις] of color is to be "capable of setting in motion that which is actually transparent," a claim that gets reiterated at 419^{a}9–11. See also, more generally, *Phys.* VII.2, 244^{b}2–5^{a}12.) Still, it is significant that Aristotle finds the causal restriction thesis tempting at all. Ultimately there is no reason why a relationalist theory, just because it *defines* the sensibles in terms of their relation to the senses, must think that the sensibles have *only* this effect on the world. A funny movie, after all, can lower one's blood pressure. And indeed it is very hard to sustain the thesis that the sensibles—even setting aside heat and other tangibles—have an effect only on the senses. (On this point see Broackes, "Aristotle, Objectivity, and Perception," pp. 107–11, who is responding to Sarah Broadie, "Aristotle's Perceptual Realism." Broadie quite resourcefully defends this doubtful thesis but, tellingly, she does so not because she thinks that the sensibles are defined relationally, but because she thinks that Aristotle's broader natural philosophy commits him to it.)

If the sensibles are understood relationally, as mere powers to cause sensations, then Aristotle needs some sort of distinction between such powers and their underlying grounds. It is remarkable, then, that Aristotle seems to draw just such a distinction at *De an.* II.7, 418^{a}29–31, as quoted in this lecture (p. 54). The following note discusses the history of this vexed passage in some detail, but here let me just note the parallel with *De anima* II.10, where "the object of taste" (τὸ γευστόν) is said to be "the body in which the flavor resides" (422^{a}10–11). Marmodoro remarks of this passage that "Aristotle appears to vacillate between taking the object of perception to be the perceptible *quality*, and taking it to be the *entity* in the world possessing that perceptible quality" (*Aristotle on Perceiving Objects*, p. 82).

The most intriguing passage that invokes a ground beneath the sensibles is *Metaphysics* IV.5, 1010^b30–11^a1 (quoted in this lecture at p. 53), where Aristotle very explicitly distinguishes between the sensible (τὸ αἰσθητόν) and its substrata (ὑποκείμενα). This passage is perhaps the strongest textual evidence for a relational account, inasmuch as it makes quite explicit that the sensibles depend on perceivers. Naturally, however, interpretation of the passage is contested. On a rival interpretation, the sensibles here are not, as I understand the passage, the relationally defined sense objects, but rather the actualized sensibles described at *De anima* III.2 (where those might be either simple sensations or the sensible qualities themselves, *qua* perceived). If that is right, then room opens up for the substratum invoked here to be simply the sensible qualities, and an absolute account is thereby saved. Broackes points out, in favor of this sort of reading, that the substrata are characterized here as those things that "cause the sensation," and in his view this shows that the substratum must be the sensible quality ("Aristotle, Objectivity, and Perception," p. 93). But a relational account is going to need to have some story about powers resting on grounds, and it is to be expected that, in some way, the grounds play a crucial causal role as well. Of course, Aristotle offers no such account in detail. But his readiness to provide some such story is suggested by the account of color in *De sensu* 3, where, after explicitly invoking the *De anima*'s distinction between actual and potential color, he turns to describing the underlying physical theory, under the heading of "what each sensible must be, in order to produce actual sensation" (439^a13–17). That discussion does not settle much of anything, because his account of the physical theory is his account of *color*, and one might say the passage's precise task is to fill in the story of what potential color is. But that there is a distinction between color and its causal substratum seems clear from *De anima* II.7, as quoted in this lecture (p. 54), where "color rests on what is visible in its own right—in its own right not by definition, but because it contains within itself the cause of its being visible" (418^a29–31). Those who would deny the relational thread in Aristotle's remarks would do best to emend the usual translation of this passage, if not the underlying text itself (see the following note).

If the key passage from *Metaphysics* IV.5 is saying only that actual sensibles require perceivers, then it is saying something trivial. Those who read the passage in this way do not mind that implication, because what this means in context is only that Aristotle's concession to Protagoras and Democritus is trivial. But a further reason to doubt this reading of the passage comes from the character of the thought experiment being described. If Aristotle wanted to make only the trivial point that actual sensibles require actual perceptions, he could have said just that, by describing objects that no one is presently perceiving. Instead he goes one step farther, to imagine the remote world in which "animate things did not exist." In that scenario we get not just the trivial result that there are no actual sensibles, but the stronger and more interesting result that there are no sensibles at all, because there is nothing to define the sensibles in relation to. Consider, by contrast, *Metaphysics* IX.3, where we are invited to consider merely a sensible that is not presently being perceived. There Aristotle is attacking the Megarian view that denies unactualized powers. On a view of that sort, the mere absence of an occurrent perception is enough to yield the result that "nothing will be either color or hot or sweet or perceptible at all if people are not perceiving it" (1047^a4–5). But here at *Metaphysics* IV.5 he needs the more remote possibility that there are no perceivers at all, because here he wants to describe a world not just without actual sensibles, but without sensibles at all. (Notice, too, that *Meta.* IX.3 is yet another passage that brings out the relational character of the theory: it is because the sensibles are defined as powers to produce sensation that their persisting when they are not perceived serves as an embarrassment to the Megarian view.)

To define redness relationally is to think that what it is to be red is, most fundamentally, just to cause a certain kind of sensation. On this view, color perception does not seem to go as deeply into objective reality as we would ideally have hoped. But consider now the tactile qualities of hot and cold, the most fundamental physical properties in the natural world. Could Aristotle have understood them relationally? He might have, if he thought that, as it happens, the relationally defined tactile qualities are *also* the fundamental qualities of nature. And something like this seems to be at work in his derivation of the four elemental qualities at the start of *De generatione et corruptione* II.2, where he reasons that the principles of body will be sensibles and, in particular, tangible qualities. This leads him quickly to the famous foursome hot–cold–wet–dry. Why touch in particular? Evidently because this is the most fundamental sense power, found in all animals who possess any sort of sensation (see, e.g., the discussion of 316^b9 in C. J. F. Williams's commentary). Here is a place, then, where Aristotle leans quite heavily on the idealizing assumption that perception will show us the world in high fidelity, down to its foundations.

At the level of touch, then, Aristotle concedes nothing to Democritean subjectivism. Is it really plausible, then, that elsewhere his view is more concessive? One could try to hold on to the relational analysis *and* think that Aristotle treats all the proper sensibles along the same lines as touch. In that case the concession to Democritus would be largely verbal, acknowledging a sense of 'the sensible' ($\tau\grave{o}$ $\alpha\grave{i}\sigma\theta\eta\tau\acute{o}\nu$) that is relational and so subjective, yet insisting that in fact the proper sensible qualities are absolute features of reality. This is in effect Broackes's reading, and it is central to it that "Aristotle's world is one where there is no sense, I think, of a problematic relation between the sensible qualities and the objective world" ("Aristotle, Objectivity, and Perception," p. 102). Thus Broackes's Aristotle makes no real concessions to Democritean subjectivity. But on my reading the persistence of the relational thread shows that Aristotle was troubled by the relation between sensibles and the objective world and hence was prepared, at least sometimes, to make serious concessions to Democritus. Does this in turn make trouble for Aristotle's broader empirical methodology? Terence Irwin, who takes quite seriously the subjective tendencies in Aristotle's theory of perception, worries that it does. If the sensibles are defined relationally, as mere potentialities for activating the senses, then according to Irwin this would "raise grave doubts about how perception can yield any knowledge of external objects" (*Aristotle's First Principles*, p. 314). But here the silent-K word is especially unhelpful in pinpointing the precise trouble at issue. A more precise formulation would be that Aristotle's brand of subjectivism calls into question whether the senses show us the world in high fidelity, down to its foundations. And this indeed is a lesson worth learning from Democritus, one that unfortunately would be largely forgotten until the seventeenth century.

Aristotelian Realism

De anima II.7

Note 7 (p. 56). Averroes's rejection of a relational approach to color stems from a few lines of the *De anima* that present two fairly large textual difficulties. One issue, the lesser of the two, concerns the meaning of 'in its own right,' when Aristotle writes "visible in its own right not by definition, but because it contains within itself the cause of its being visible" (418^a30–1). The words 'in its own right' ($\kappa\alpha\theta$' $\alpha\grave{v}\tau\acute{o}$; *per se*) immediately suggest the discussion in *Posterior Analytics* I.4 (73^a35–$^b24$) of four ways in which a thing can be said of another "in its own right." In his Long Commentary on the *De anima* (II.66), Averroes argues that 418^a30–1 means to set aside the first of those four ways: that in which the predicate is contained in the definition of the subject. Instead, Averroes says, Aristotle has in mind the second mode of *per se* predication, according to which the subject is found in the definition of the predicate. Subsequent Latin discussions of the passage generally followed Averroes's lead. See for example Albert the

Great, *De anima* II.3.7 (Cologne edn. vol. 7.1: 108a) and Thomas Aquinas, *De anima Commentary* II.14.40–59.

In his Middle Commentary, however, which was not translated into Latin, Averroes reads the passage differently. Here, in line with the Greek commentators, Averroes takes Aristotle to be wholly setting aside the *Posterior Analytics'* account of the various ways in which a thing can be said of another in its own right. In place of that whole approach, which Averroes takes to rely on truth by definition, he suggests that Aristotle has in mind an entirely different notion of "in its own right," in which *per se* (بذاته) is contrasted with the relational mode (بالإضافة/بالقياس). This understanding of the passage is taken for granted in the parts of Averroes's discussion quoted in the lecture. (On the differences between these two commentaries at this point, see the note attached to this material in Alfred Ivry's translation of the Middle Commentary, p. 179 n. 2, and the response by Richard Taylor in his translation of the Long Commentary, p. 180 n. 165.)

The more fundamental textual difficulty of these lines from Aristotle concerns what it is that is supposed to be visible in its own right. Both the Arabic and the Latin traditions take it to be color that is visible in its own right. The Greek commentators, in contrast, along with modern scholars, read the passage quite differently. Here is the Greek as we have it from *De anima* II.7, 418^a29–31:

τὸ γὰρ ὁρατόν ἐστι χρῶμα, τοῦτο δ' ἐστὶ τὸ ἐπὶ τοῦ καθ' αὐτὸ ὁρατοῦ· καθ' αὐτὸ δὲ οὐ τῷ λόγῳ, ἀλλ' ὅτι ἐν ἑαυτῷ ἔχει τὸ αἴτιον τοῦ εἶναι ὁρατόν.

The standard modern way of taking this sentence runs along these lines:

The visible is color, and this rests on what is visible in its own right—in its own right not by definition, but because it contains within itself the cause of its being visible.

On this reading, color rests on top of that which is visible in its own right. This accords with the ancient Greek commentaries of Themistius, Philoponus, and pseudo-Simplicius.

Arabic and Latin commentators, however, translate the passage quite differently. Here is how an early Arabic translation renders the crucial first line:

لأن المنظور اليه لون ، واللون من الأشياء التى ترى بذاتها.

The visible is color, and color is among [*min*] the things that are seen in their own right.

(Aristotle, *Aristūtālīs fī al-nafs*, ed. Badawi)

Now here is the revised ninth-century Arabic translation of Isḥāq ibn Ḥunayn, which survives only in Latin translation:

Quoniam visibile est color, et hoc est visibile per se.
The visible is color, and this is visible in its own right.
(Quoted in Averroes, *Long Commentary*, p. 229)

And here is the Latin translation of William of Moerbeke in the thirteenth century:

Visibile enim est color, hoc autem est in eo quod secundum se visibile.
The visible is color, and this is in that that is visible in its own right.
(Quoted in Aquinas, *Comm. De anima*)

In contention here is really just one word from the Greek, the preposition ἐπί. Modern translations have Aristotle claiming that what is visible in its own right is the underlying subject of the color. The two Arabic translations preclude this reading of the text, forcing on us the idea that it is color that is visible in its own right. Moerbeke's more literal rendering leaves open the usual modern reading, but might also be read along the Arabic lines, and this is in fact how Aquinas does gloss the text:

He says first, then, that since color is something visible, being visible applies to color in its own right. For color, in that it is color [*in eo quod est color*], is visible.   (*Comm. De anima* II.14.40–2)

The usual modern translation makes better sense of the preposition ἐπί, which ordinarily has the spatial meaning of *on* or *in*. The overall thought of the passage, so read, is that, although color is of course visible, it is also the case that the subject of color, evidently the underlying substrate, is visible, and indeed visible "in its own right." But this, the passage hastens to explain, should not be understood as meaning that this substrate is *essentially* visible "by definition," but rather that it is "the cause" of its color, just as substrates are generally the causes of the qualities that inhere in them. This in turn coheres with *Metaphysics* IV.5, 1010^{b}34–5 (quoted in this lecture at p. 53), according to which the sensibles depend on perceivers, whereas "even in the absence of sensation, it is impossible for the substrata [ὑποκείμενα] that cause the sensation not to exist."

Although this reading makes good sense of *De anima* II.7, medieval translators and commentators could not accept it. In their eyes, Aristotle had already made it quite clear, at II.6, that color is what is visible in its own right, and so he could scarcely be saying something different here. Moreover, on this reading, colors are not the things that are visible by definition, through some sort of relational definition; they are rather the absolute features of the world that the sense organs are designed to detect. Finally, medieval authors saw no basis for treating any sort of underlying substrate as visible in its own right. The substrate, they unanimously supposed, is veiled from the senses. (On this last point, see my *Metaphysical Themes* chs. 6–9.)

Buridan and Oresme

Note 8 (p. 58). The general scholastic assumption of a veiled substratum is interestingly related to Buridan's discussion of sensory infallibility. Buridan writes: "There is indeed a difficulty in how to understand this famous authority [that the senses never err], since from the aforesaid arguments it appears that there are *many* sensory deceptions with regard to their proper objects" (*Quaest. de anima* II.11 n. 6). As the lecture discusses, Buridan holds that, if we provide enough qualifications, then we can arrive at a near guarantee that the senses are right both about the proper and about the common sensible (nn. 11–14). But he does not go so far as to extend infallibility to the sensibles *per accidens* (n. 15). No matter how reliably I am detecting qualities such as color, sound, size, and shape, this might not be my son biking down the street. Hence the traditional doctrine that, although the senses give us access to the sensible qualities of things, they cannot show us the thing itself, the substance beneath those qualities.

Yet Buridan's view of such matters is complicated and enriched by his further claim that the external senses themselves grasp their various objects confusedly. In addition to the passage quoted in this lecture (p. 58), see *Quaest. de anima* II.12 n. 8:

And it should be noted, as it seems to me, that since a quality and its subject—e.g., whiteness and the substance subject to it—exist at one time confusedly in location, sense does not have the power of distinguishing between them: it neither perceives that whiteness distinctly from the perception of its substance, nor perceives the substance distinctly from the perception of its whiteness. And so it does not perceive whiteness according to the concept according to which it is called whiteness.

This means that, at the strictly sensory level, all objects are perceived under a kind of veil, insofar as the external senses can no more distinguish the substance than they can distinguish the accident. Such distinctions come at a higher level of processing: either that of common sense or that of the intellect. This is not to say that, for Buridan, the various traditional distinctions between kinds of sensibles have no basis in what happens at the sensory level. He does think, as this lecture notes (p. 58), that the proper–common distinction can be based in whether or not a sensible is detectable by more than one sense. He also thinks that the *per se–per accidens* distinction has a basis in whether the concept in question is one "according to which a thing is sensed" (*Quaest. de anima* II.12 n. 12). His criterion for a feature's counting as sensible *per se* is whether, when something is changed only in that one feature, the change is sensible (see note 9 here).

Buridan's approach to these questions, so far as I know, has received no attention from modern scholars, perhaps because it did not become a standard scholastic view. It does show up later in that great recycler of others' ideas, Peter of Ailly: "sense does not sense abstractly, but the intellect understands abstractly. For sense, by seeing color or whiteness, does not distinguish between the subject and curvedness or whiteness, between which the intellect distinguishes by abstractly understanding this from that" (*Tractatus de anima*, p. 38, n. 11). And Nicole Oresme expresses a somewhat similar view: "no sensation occurs through an external sense alone; rather it is always more fundamentally the soul or its internal power. And so neither color nor sound nor local motion nor heat nor any other sensible is perceived unless the internal power actually attends and considers" (*De causis mirabilium* ch. 3 n. 7; cf. *Quaest. de anima* II.10, p. 192 and II.21, p. 300). But Oresme is making a different and stronger claim: not that the external senses sense all things confusedly, but that strictly they do not sense at all, until the "internal power" makes its contribution. This points ahead in the direction of Descartes's later insistence that perception occurs only in the mind, not in the physical senses. But Oresme is apparently not saying quite that: he seems to mean that it is the *internal senses* that are the proper locus of sensation. And the internal senses are a power of the brain rather than of the immaterial mind or intellect.

A still more striking parallel between these fourteenth-century authors and the seventeenth-century ones concerns their shared interest in whether the objects of sensation are grasped distinctly or confusedly. (For Descartes and Locke on the indistinctness, that is, confusion of our ideas of secondary qualities, see note 15 here.) Their similarity here is no accident; it emerges from the usual scholastic view that evidentness requires distinctness. This goes back all the way to Scotus, who writes for example that "theology is not perfect in such a way as to yield perfect and distinct knowledge [*notitiam*] through the evidentness of its object, as *scientia* does" (*Reportatio* IA prol. q. 2 ad 1, in Wolter and Bychkov edn. vol. 1: n. 205]). On this see the very useful pages in Peter Vier, *Evidence and Its Function*, pp. 51–3.

For Oresme's argument that it is only at the determinable level that the senses are infallible regarding the proper sensibles, see his *Quaestiones in De anima* II.10. This idea—that, say, sight does not go wrong about whether a thing is *colored*—would have wide currency. One finds it later in Francisco Suárez, for instance, who notices that such a guarantee seems to hold for both the proper and the common sensibles. In what sense, then, is there a special guarantee regarding the proper sensibles? Not because it is infallible in every particular case, but because "it is much more easily deceived with regard to common than with regard to proper sensibles" (Suárez, *De anima* disp. 6 q. 3 concl. 4). The same shift to the determinable level is defended by Franco Burgersdijk (*Collegium physicum* 25.14).

The need for some such stratagem is inevitable as soon as one turns away from a subjective, relational account of the proper sensibles and decides to treat them in absolute terms. So construed, the guarantee of infallibility inevitably came in for harsh criticism among those who rejected Aristotle's authority. Gianfrancesco Pico, for instance, claims that "all the teachings of Aristotle are grounded in the senses" (*Examen vanitatis* IV.12, p. 1058) and then proceeds to attack the guarantee of reliability. Does it depend on specifying just the right conditions, internal and external? In that case, how do we know what those conditions are and whether they obtain (p. 1062)? Does it hold only at the determinable level (e.g., of color in general)? Then the guarantee is too weak to be of any epistemic value (V.2, pp. 1077–8).

Oresme's proposed identification of color with reflected light is remarkable enough to deserve being translated at length:

The third conclusion that could plausibly [*probabiliter*] be sustained is that every color is light [*lux*], and that in the dark there is no color. This can be made persuasive, because one ought to posit only that which is apparent through experience or reason. But color cannot appear to experience in the dark, because it is impossible to see color in the dark, nor does it appear to reason, because it might be said that light is reflected from opaque bodies—from different bodies in different ways. Hence the light of the sun appears in one way when reflected by the moon, and in another way when reflected by another body. And likewise in *Meteorology* III [374ª8] it is said that the colors of a ruby are merely reflected light. And in this way we would see only light, though according to different dispositions and conditions of bodies inasmuch as it is reflected not just by higher bodies but also by lower ones. A certain light appears white and the same light, reflected by another body, appears red, and so on in other cases. From this a corollary is clear: that there is color in the dark only in potentiality, and in light it is made actual, because 'color' signifies not every manner of light, but light reflected by a body according to its disposition with respect to its primary qualities [i.e., the four elemental qualities: Hot, Cold, Wet, Dry]. And so [light] is varied by the alteration of the body that reflects it, and is strengthened or weakened.   (*Quaest. de anima* II.16, pp. 254–5)

After offering this as a "plausible" conclusion, Oresme explicitly says that for the remainder of the discussion he will nevertheless go back to the usual supposition that color and light are distinct (p. 255). Oresme's suggestion is not wholly unprecedented. John Buridan, in a discussion that undoubtedly would have influenced Oresme, considers various similarly adventuresome suggestions about the role of light (*Quaest. de anima* II.15). It is unclear to me whether Oresme's or Buridan's ideas had much influence on subsequent discussions, but it is notable that Suárez later considers and rejects the view that color is just light (*De anima* disp. 7 q. 2). For the view's subsequent triumph in the seventeenth century, see A. Mark Smith, *From Sight to Light*, pp. 400–8, who credits Descartes with understanding color as light for the first time and goes on to trace the idea through Hooke and Newton. (Note 10 here indicates that in 1654 Walter Charleton was presupposing that color is just light.)

The Quantitative Turn

Note 9 (p. 61). All the proper sense objects are real qualities, at least for most scholastic authors, but the list of real qualities is longer, strictly speaking, because the real qualities extend to everything in Aristotle's category of quality (see *Cat.* ch. 8), and hence include states like health and sickness, which are obviously not among the proper sensibles. For the metaphysics of real qualities, see my *Metaphysical Themes* chs. 19–23. In that work I argue that the year 1347 was critical in the history of debates over the sensible qualities. Through the first half of the fourteenth century, scholastic philosophy was on a path toward many of the ideas that would eventually characterize seventeenth-century thought; but it was stopped in its tracks by a series of condemnations at mid-century. Above all, scholastic philosophers were on track to call into question the reality of the proper sensibles as real qualities: both that they are metaphysically independent of their subjects and that they are natural kinds.

Within a framework that treats the proper sensibles as physically fundamental, it is possible to view the geometric–kinetic properties as secondary, and indeed perhaps as entirely nonreal. And so it is, for scholastic authors, that the only ultimate efficient causes are forms, and paradigmatically those forms in the category of quality. Thus Peter John Olivi in the late thirteenth century, bearing in mind particularly the case of local motion, takes himself to be stating the consensus view when he writes that "a natural agent causes nothing except through its likeness. But it does not cause local motion through its likeness, since everything that is caused in this way is a substantial or accidental form qualifying and denominating its subject" (quoted in Anneliese Maier, "Bewegung ohne Ursache," pp. 303–4). Olivi does not mean to suggest that bodies do not move other bodies. His point is one of ontology: he means to deny a robustly realist conception of motion on which a thing's being moved amounts to its acquiring some new entity within it—a motion. How the causal story about motion works is as much a puzzle for scholastic authors as it is in the seventeenth century. But the critical difference is that, whereas seventeenth-century authors assume that causation at the level of geometric–kinetic properties is the paradigm case, scholastic authors assume that causation among the proper sensibles is the paradigm. For further information, see my *Metaphysical Themes* §21.3.

In view of the causal primacy of the proper sensible qualities, scholastic authors can quite comfortably deny the reality of motion and geometric properties, as both Olivi and Ockham explicitly would. It is important to note, however, that "denying the reality of" comes in different flavors. In particular, it is one thing to take a reductive account of the kinetic and geometric properties and another to deny the very truth of claims like 'this body is moving' and 'this body is a sphere.' The first is a characteristic thesis of scholastic nominalism (see my *Metaphysical Themes* ch. 19), whereas the second seems merely paradoxical, as in Zeno. But Leibniz makes for an interesting case here: "Concerning bodies I can demonstrate that not merely light, heat, color, and similar qualities are apparent but also motion, shape, and extension." So what, for Leibniz, is ultimately real? He immediately continues: "And that if anything is real, it is solely the force of acting and suffering, and hence that the substance of a body consists in this (as if in matter and form)" ("On the Method of Distinguishing Real from Imaginary Phenomena," in *Phil. Papers*, p. 365). For an extended treatment of what such a story comes to, see Daniel Garber, *Leibniz*.

As goes motion, as a causal force, so go shape and size. Thus Franciscus Toletus, a fairly conservative Jesuit from the sixteenth century, takes it to be clear that "shapes are in no way active, neither in their own right nor in virtue of anything belonging to them, because they are not composed of the primary qualities" (*Comm. Phys.* VII.3.3). By "primary qualities" he still means the elemental qualities of hot, cold, wet, and dry. Accordingly, Aristotle's classification of the common sensibles as sensible *per se* was the subject of considerable puzzlement. This lecture (p. 60) invokes Aquinas's remarks on how common sensibles, like accidental sensibles, "are apprehended only insofar as proper sensibles are apprehended" (*Comm. De anima* II.13.75–9). But in that case it is hard to see why the one should be classed as *per se* and the other *per accidens*. Aquinas's story about this is that, although the common sensible are apprehended through the proper sensibles, the common sensibles still "make a difference in how the senses are altered" insofar as whether a body is large or small, and so on, makes a difference to the impression it makes on the senses (*Comm. De anima* II.13.125–59). John Buridan makes a similar suggestion but develops it somewhat more fully, by contending that the *per se* sensibles are those features that, if a thing is changed only in that feature, the change is sensible (*Quaest. de anima* II.13 n. 10). Given this test, it is not surprising that Buridan thinks that many more features of the world should count as *per se* sensibles than appear on the brief canonical lists of the proper and common sensibles (II.12 n. 13). But Buridan stresses that the common sensibles make no immediate impact on the senses: "the sensation of the common sensibles occurs on account of receiving no species other than those of the proper sensibles" (II.13 n. 14).

Further questions arise, among scholastic authors, about motion as a sense object, given that it is a successive entity, which exists through time rather than all at once, as a permanent entity exists. So if there is such a thing as motion as a successive entity, it cannot be perceived at any one given time (see, e.g., the remarks in Oresme, *Quaest. de anima* II.15).

Note 10 (p. 61). On the development of the familiar seventeenth-century distinction between primary and secondary qualities, see *Metaphysical Themes* chs. 21–2, and the papers in Lawrence Nolan, *Primary and Secondary Qualities*.

That distinction came under attack from all sides, almost as soon as it was formulated. On one side, the University of Paris, as late as 1691, can still be found censoring the Cartesian view that body is nothing more than *res extensa* (Des Chene, *Physiologia*, p. 3n). From the other side, even before Berkeley, figures like Malebranche, Simon Foucher, and Pierre Bayle were all calling into question the reality of the so-called primary qualities (see, e.g., Margaret Wilson, "Did Berkeley Completely Misunderstand?" pp. 220–1). One kind of complaint arose from the variability of primary quality perceptions, and this fueled Berkeley's famous arguments from sensory variability (e.g., *Three Dialogues*, dial. 1). The idea already appears in some detail in Malebranche, who argues that, at best, we can perceive relative size: "all we can know of size through sight is the relation between theirs and ours" (*Search after Truth*, p. 30, and see the passages quoted in note 1 above).

A deeper sort of complaint about primary qualities concerns the continuum. For Leibniz's views in this regard, see Samuel Levey, "Leibniz on Mathematics" and "Matter and Two Concepts of Continuity." Bayle delights in such paradoxes, and uses them to attack the very reality of extension (*Dictionary*, s.v. "Zeno," remarks G–H). Inevitably, the idea turns up in Berkeley, who reasons that "each body therefore, considered in itself, is infinitely extended [because infinitely divisible], and consequently void of all shape and figure" (*Principles of Human Knowledge* §47, in *Philosophical Writings*, p. 101). The destructive consequences are registered in Hume: "No priestly dogmas, invented on purpose to tame and subdue the rebellious reason of mankind, ever shocked common sense more than the doctrine of the infinitive divisibility of extension" (*Enquiry concerning Human Understanding* 12.2, p. 156).

Hume's reference to "priestly dogmas" is a sign of the providence of such ideas about infinite divisibility. The view is Aristotle's, and hence Aristotelian, though one does find medieval dissenters. For an overview, see John Murdoch, "Infinity and Continuity" and Rega Wood's introduction to Adam Wodeham's *Tractatus de indivisibilibus*. See also the papers in Norman Kretzmann, *Infinity and Continuity*. For authors in the Aristotelian tradition, however, the issue fails to have the sort of metaphysical or epistemic weight it had in the seventeenth and eighteenth centuries, when the corpuscularian philosophy expected the primary qualities to carry the whole weight of physical explanation.

Among the scholastics, all these debates over the status of the common sensibles count merely as interesting philosophical puzzles rather than as fundamental questions about physical reality. Today, conversely, one might say the same thing about the endless philosophical debates over the reality of color. This reflects the way we have shifted what counts as primary and secondary. Among seventeenth-century authors, once the common sensibles became primary qualities, what had once been merely puzzling took on the status of a foundational crisis, given that (a) these authors had no better idea than did the scholastics of how to handle such puzzles of infinite divisibility, and (b) now such questions really started to matter to these authors' basic theories.

That all physical causation would have to occur through local motion was widely taken for granted among the corpuscularians and might even be thought to define the movement. Thus Robert Boyle writes: "it is not easy to conceive either how one [body] can act upon the other, but by local motion ... or how by motion it can do any more than put the parts of the other body into motion too, and thereby produce in them a change of situation and texture, or of some other of its mechanical affections" (*Origin of Forms and Qualities*, in *Selected Papers*, p. 36). But, as for how such causation should be understood, this was notoriously contentious. (For a recent overview of the issues around causation in general, see the papers in Tad Schmaltz, *Efficient Causation*.) Boyle expressly contrasts the different junctures at which scholastic and corpuscularian views run into difficulty: "whilst, as the Aristotelians cannot particularly show how their Qualities are produced, so we cannot particularly explicate how they are perceived" (*Excellence of Theology*, in *Works* vol. 8: 69). This is to say that the

Aristotelian has no account of how such sensible qualities arise in the external world, whereas the corpuscularian, who puts such qualities into the mind, has no account of how they arise from the impact of bodies in motion. Once we draw this comparison, Boyle says, "it may keep us from boasting of the clearness and certainty of our knowledge about the operations of sensible objects" (p. 69).

Boyle was far from being the only one who felt such concerns. Walter Charleton, in his *Physiologia Epicuro-Gassendo-Charltoniana* (1654), frankly admits that his remarks on the process of vision should be treated as mere speculation:

This we judge expedient to profess, because we would not leave it in the mercy of censure to determine whether or no we pretend to understand what are the proper figures and other essential qualities of the insensible particles of light... what sort of reflection or refraction, whether simple or multiplied, is required to the creation of this or that colour... besides, had we a clear and apodictical theory of all these niceties, yet would it be a superlative difficulty for us to advance to the genuine reasons why light, in such a manner striking on the superfice of such a body therein... should be transformed into a vermillion, rather than a blue, green, or any other colour. Again, were our understanding arrived at this sublimity, yet it would come much short of the top of the mystery, and it might hazard a dangerous vertigo in our brains to aspire to the causes, why by the appulse of light so or so modified, there is caused in the eye so fair and delightful a sensation as that of vision. (*Physiologia* III.4, pp. 196–7)

The passage raises doubts at three levels. First, Charleton admits to the difficulties of giving a clear account of how particles of light, variously reflected, take on one color or another. (Newton would make progress here a few decades later.) Second, even if we had the first, he thinks it would be a further, "superlative" challenge to account for why certain surfaces cause light to take on a certain color. (This question would not truly be resolved until the development of quantum mechanics in the twentieth century.) Third, even if we could get a handle on these first two difficulties, we would still fall "much short" of the "mystery" of how light outside the eye gives rise within us to "so fair and delightful a sensation"—that is, to an experience with the distinctive qualitative feel of, say, seeing vermillion. Charleton seems to judge the difficulties here to be so great that his view amounts to a kind of mysterianism: he doubts, that is, whether a solution to such problems could ever be achieved. In any case, even if he and his allies were confident that the Aristotelian story had gone badly astray, they had little confidence in what they had to offer in its place. Glanvill, a decade later, borrows some of Charleton's exact phrases to make this same point (*Scepsis scientifica* ch. 5, pp. 20–3). Locke, several decades further on, is even more categorically doubtful about our prospects, holding that there is "no conceivable connection between any impulse of any sort of body, and any perception of a colour, or smell, which we find in our minds" (*Essay* IV.3.28).

Descartes's Three Paths

Note 11 (p. 62). When Descartes thinks like a natural philosopher, he puts significant weight on experience. A particularly developed discussion comes in Part Six of the *Discourse on Method*, where he writes: "I have noticed, regarding observations [*expériences*], that the further we advance in our knowledge [*connaissance*], the more necessary they become" (VI: 63). Then, after setting out how his method begins from innate "seeds of truth" and works its way to detailed observations of particulars, he concludes that "reviewing in my mind all the objects that have ever been present to my senses, I venture to say that I have never noticed anything in them which I could not explain quite easily by the principles I had discovered" (VI: 64). That makes it sound as if Descartes thinks there is no more work to be done in the sciences. But he immediately acknowledges that this is far from being the case. The passage is worth quoting at length:

But I must also admit that the power of nature is so ample and so vast, and these principles so simple and so general, that I notice hardly any particular effect of which I do not know at once that it can be deduced from these principles in many different ways; and my greatest difficulty is usually to discover in which of these ways it depends on them. I know no other means to discover this than by seeking further observations whose outcomes vary according to which of these ways provides the correct explanation. Moreover, I have now reached a point where I think I can see quite clearly what line we should follow in making most of the observations which serve this purpose; but I see also that they are of such a kind and so numerous that neither my dexterity nor my income (were it even a thousand times greater than it is) could suffice for all of them. And so the advances I make in the knowledge of nature will depend henceforth on the opportunities I get to make more or fewer of these observations. I resolved to make this known in the treatise I had written, and to show clearly how the public could benefit from such knowledge. This would oblige all who desire the general well-being of mankind—that is, all who are really virtuous, not virtuous only in appearance or merely in repute—both to communicate to me the observations they have already made and to assist me in seeking those that remain to be made.   (VI: 64–5)

This is the Descartes who might claim a place next to Galileo and Bacon as a founding father of modern scientific empiricism.

If Descartes is to assume the mantle of one of the champions of experience, then he needs to explain why he so often seems to disparage the senses. The balancing act he must perform is put nicely in a letter from 1642:

Being certain that I can have no grasp of what is outside me except by the mediation of the ideas within me of these things, I take great care not to relate my judgments immediately to things, and not to attribute to things anything positive that I do not previously perceive in the ideas of them. But I think also that whatever is to be found in these ideas is necessarily also in things.   (To Gibieuf, III: 474)

First he states the reason why experience is so essential: how else can we grasp what lies outside ourselves? But, given that experience is mediated by ideas, he then adds that we must be extremely careful not to misjudge the content of those ideas. Still, he concludes, provided that we are careful, the method works, because we can count on a guarantee: whatever genuinely is the content of the senses "is necessarily also in things." The senses do not misrepresent. Where there is error, it is because we have misjudged.

Descartes's often repeated verdict regarding how we are to judge is that we should trust the senses to show us the geometric–kinetic properties of things:

As to my ideas of corporeal things . . . the things that I perceive clearly and distinctly in them are very few. The list comprises size, or extension in length, breadth and depth, shape . . . position . . . and motion, or change in position. To these may be added substance, duration and number. But as for all the rest, including light and colors, sounds, odors, flavors, heat and cold, and the other tactile qualities, I think of these only in a very confused and obscure way, to the extent that I do not even know whether they are true or false—that is, whether the ideas I have of them are ideas of things or of nonthings.   (Med. 3, VII: 43)

It follows that corporeal things exist. They may not all exist in a way that exactly corresponds with my sensory grasp of them, for in many cases the grasp of the senses is very obscure and confused. But at least all those things are in them that I clearly and distinctly understand—that is, all the things that, viewed in general terms, are comprised within the subject-matter of pure mathematics.   (Med. 6, VII: 80)

Even in the case of such primary qualities (as they would soon be called), Descartes readily admits that sensory error is frequent. The point of these passages is not to say that we can always trust our sensory judgment in these cases, only that, when the senses yield ideas of these sorts about bodies, the ideas at least are clear and distinct. The senses are showing us bodies as they *can be*. (On Descartes's distinct treatment of primary-quality and secondary-quality perception, see Ann MacKenzie, "The Reconfiguration of Sensory Experience.")

This very limited endorsement of experience explains why Descartes often restricts the role of the senses to safeguarding the body's well-being. It is only here that Descartes is willing to express any real confidence in the deliverances of the senses: "in matters regarding the well-being of the body, all my senses report what is true much more frequently than what is false" (*Med.* 6, VII: 89). Citing *Principles* II.3 (a passage discussed in this lecture, p. 61), he tells Henry More: "As I warned . . . our senses do not always show us external bodies as they are, but only insofar as they are related to us and can benefit or harm us" (V: 271). In certain sorts of cases it is obvious what Descartes has in mind. Consider pain. Descartes thinks that we are liable to misinterpret pains, considering them to be located in the body rather than in the mind. The fault of misinterpretation is ours. But why are things arranged so as even to give us the opportunity to go wrong here? Why do pains seem to be located where they are not? The answer to this question is obvious as soon as it is asked, since it is so obviously useful to be able to use the pain sensation to determine the location of bodily harm.

It is less clear, however, how this line of thought might extend to a case like color. Here would be one story. Colors arise from the different speeds at which the surface particles of bodies rotate. We *could* have eyes sharp enough to see those movements, and if we did then the eyes would be more useful as guides to "external bodies as they are." This way of seeing, however, would—at best—be highly unwieldy and prone to error. It works much better, as a practical matter, for the different rotational speeds to cause within us vividly distinct color sensations, so that we may immediately and reliably detect differences on the surfaces of objects. This is conducive to our bodily well-being, because some of the physical differences associated with differences in color perception are things that "can benefit or harm us." For a careful and perceptive discussion of these issues, see Alison Simmons, "Are Cartesian Sensations Representational?"

Note 12 (p. 63). Whichever aspect of Descartes's theory of perception one focuses on, the story is inevitably highly intellectualist. It is the mind that recognizes the purely phenomenal status of colors and the mind that sees the connection to bodily well-being. Even geometric properties are grasped only at this higher level: "size, distance, and shape can be perceived by reasoning alone" (Sixth Replies, VII: 438). No wonder the Sixth Meditation holds that "to know what is true about external things seems to pertain to the mind alone, not to the composite" (VII: 82–3). On this intellectualism in his perceptual theory, see Margaret Wilson, "Descartes on the Perception of Primary Qualities."

By lodging all the deliverances of full-blown perception at the intellectual level, Descartes is also able to bring to bear his theory of error, from the Fourth Meditation, according to which "the scope of the will is wider than that of the intellect, but instead of restricting it within the same limits, I extend its use to matters that I do not understand" (VII: 58). That the error lies with our free will allows Descartes to insist that, when it comes to the lower parts of the perceptual story that run according to natural principles, "there can be no falsity" (Sixth Replies, VII: 438). Here is where, if we are to have any confidence in the senses at all, we have to embrace some kind of divinely guaranteed teleology. This is just a special case of the general principle that, "when I concentrate on the nature of God, it seems impossible that he should have placed in me a faculty that is not perfect of its kind, or which lacks some perfection that it ought to have" (*Med.* 4, VII: 55). On such "epistemic teleology," see Peter Machamer and J. E. McGuire, *Descartes's Changing Mind*, pp. 102–10. On teleology in Descartes more generally, see Simmons, "Sensible Ends" and Karen Detlefsen, "Teleology and Natures in Descartes' Sixth Meditation."

For doubts over whether Descartes's robust denial of falsity is compatible with his remarks about color and the other secondary qualities, see Pierre Bayle's remark that any proof for the existence of bodies based on God's not being a deceiver "proves too much":

Ever since the beginning of the world, all mankind, except perhaps one out of two hundred million, has firmly believed that bodies are colored, and this is an error. I ask, does God deceive mankind with regard to colors? If he deceives them about this, what prevents him from so doing with regard to extension? This second deception would be no less innocent, nor less compatible than the first with the nature of a supremely perfect being. If he does not deceive mankind with regard to colors, this is no doubt because he does not irresistibly force them to say, *These colors exist outside of my mind*, but only, *It seems to me there are colors there*. The same thing could be said with regard to extension. God does not irresistibly force you to say, *There is some*, but only to judge that you are having a sensation of it and that it seems to you that there is some.

(*Dictionary*, s.v. "Pyrrho," remark B, pp. 198–9)

Berkeley would take this line of thought to its logical conclusion.

Why is it, for Descartes, that color and other proper sensibles cannot be in the world? For an extended discussion of this question, see Lisa Downing, "Sensible Qualities and Material Bodies." Downing looks for a discrete argument in Descartes showing that the proper sensibles cannot be in the world. On my view, in contrast, he claims to have no such special argument. What he has is an empirical, best explanation style of general argument for the mechanical philosophy, from which it follows that colors and so on, as we perceive them, must be in the mind. For if we endorse the mechanical philosophy, and the irreducibility of the mental to the mechanical, then it follows that colors, as we perceive them, cannot be out in the world. Also on this topic, see Martha Bolton, "Confused and Obscure Ideas of Sense."

In saying that, for Descartes, colors cannot be out in the world, I am taking for granted a certain conception of what the colors are—colors as we perceive them. In a great many places, however, Descartes uses 'color' and other terms for proper sensibles to refer to the external-world counterparts to the sensations of color and the rest. Strictly speaking, then, one has to be somewhat cautious in saying that Descartes treats colors as sensations. I discuss this matter at some length in *Metaphysical Themes* §22.6. The further thought in this lecture is that, when Descartes does consider what we ought to say about colors as they are in the external world, his view is relational.

Note 13 (p. 65). There is tremendous scholarly disagreement over the representational content of sensation in Descartes's theory. Part of the problem is that Descartes is not always careful to insist on his no-representation thesis. For instance, in the Third Meditation's discussion of material falsity, Descartes appears to be saying that sensations of the proper sensibles do represent inasmuch as they misrepresent: "material falsity occurs in ideas when they represent non-things as things" (VII: 43). But the discussion of that passage in the Fourth Replies seems carefully to avoid this way of putting the point; it speaks instead of materially false ideas as ones that "furnish judgment with the material for error" (VII: 231). (The standard English translation inadvertently omits the critical word 'judgment.') A few pages later he writes that the ideas of color and cold "present [*exhibere*] nothing real" (VII: 234).

But the difficulties here arise not only from textual inconsistencies but from various internal tensions in the views to which Descartes is committed. Most obviously, his commitment to the God-given perfection of our faculties requires, as Martial Gueroult puts it, that he articulate "a new truth proper to the senses" (*Descartes' Philosophy Interpreted according to the Order of Reasons* vol. 2: 77). Yet it is not enough to make this new truth merely a subjective internal fact about one's perceptual experiences. For what would be the point of the senses' doing no more than that? The main point of the senses, Descartes insists, is to safeguard the body's well-being. But that requires that the senses show us what is happening in the world. It does not require high fidelity, but it does require reliability, and not just with regard to the common (primary) sensibles, but also with regard to the proper (secondary) ones. This is why it is natural for Descartes to have *a* use of the word 'color' that locates color out in the world, and why he can scarcely deny that, however obscurely and confusedly, vision represents *that*.

Gary Hatfield has recently argued that Descartes takes color perception to represent "the corporeal surface properties of objects" ("Descartes on Sensory Representation," p. 138), by which he means the corpuscular microstructure that is the cause of color perception. But it seems to me that we should not go nearly that far. The most that Descartes is willing to allow secondary-quality sensations to represent in the world is just a something we know not what, which is the cause of the sensation. Thus, gathering together in the Sixth Meditation the conclusions to which we are ultimately entitled, he writes: "From the fact that I sense widely different colors, sounds, odors, flavors, heat, hardness, and the like, I rightly conclude that in the bodies from which these various sensory perceptions arise there are assorted variations corresponding to them, even though they may not be similar to them" (VII: 81). This is the most we can claim to be contained in our secondary-quality sensations. So, when I come too close to a fire, "there is reason to suppose only that there is something in it, whatever it turns out to be, that produces in us these sensations of heat or pain" (VII: 83). And, again, in the *Principles*, "as long as we judge merely that there is something in objects (i.e., in the things from which sensations arise in us, whatever those things turn out to be like), something whose nature we do not know, then we avoid error" (I.70). This is an exercise in adhering to the rule stated in *Principles* I.66 (quoted in this lecture at p. 62) that our sensory judgments should "include no more than what is precisely contained in our perception."

If our perception contains the information that there is a something *je ne sais quoi*, we know not what, which causes the sensation, then I take it that the perception *represents* as much. But this, if we read closely, perhaps does not quite contradict the critical pronouncement of *Principles* I.71, that "what we call the sensations of tastes, smells, sounds, heat, cold, light, colors, and the like—these sensations represent nothing located outside our thought." For "what we call" these sensations is the phenomenal experience itself; and that experience, in its phenomenal character, represents nothing. In any event, whatever we ultimately want to say about *representation* in Descartes, it must be the case that even our sensations of color *somehow* show us the geometric features of the world with reasonable reliability. The disastrous mistake, for Descartes, is to suppose that anything like the color sensations is out there in the world. That would be like supposing that, when an artist paints a landscape, the paint itself is out there on the hills. We might thus say, borrowing a metaphor from Ned Block, that for Descartes the proper sensibles are the mental paint with which the senses show us the world. It is just a gross error—our fault and not that of the Artist Himself—if we take the phenomenal character of the experience to represent, with any kind of fidelity, how things are in the world.

Lecture Four takes this line of thought one step further, by arguing that mental content should be tied to what it represents with the greatest fidelity. So given that Descartes thinks that our primary-quality sensations represent external things with no fidelity at all but show us with perfectly high fidelity the character of our mental states, it is quite reasonable for him to suppose that what we immediately perceive is our own ideas. Although we can also say that these experiences represent the unknown external cause of those sensations, the manner in which they do so is quite derivative and remote.

There is an impressive secondary literature on the question of sensory representation in Descartes, and parties to the debate disagree quite dramatically about the proper conclusions to draw. For arguments that Descartes rejects sensory representation, see Laura Keating, "Mechanism and the Representational Nature of Sensation" and MacKenzie, "The Reconfiguration of Sensory Experience." For the argument in favor, see Raffaella De Rosa, "Myth of Cartesian Qualia." For attempts to give Descartes a coherent theory of sensory representation see Margaret Wilson, "Descartes on the Representationality of Sensation" and Simmons, "Are Cartesian Sensations Representational?" My own view, on which the perception of secondary qualities represents "something whose nature we do not know," is similar to that of Jean-Marie Beyssade, "Descartes on Material Falsity." For further remarks on what it means to speak of cognitive representation, see Lecture Four, note 1.

Note 14 (p. 65). To sort out Descartes's position on the objects of perception, one has to look carefully at the nuances of the original texts. As a cautionary example, consider *Principles* IV.198. The title of this section, as it is rendered in the standard English translation, is:

> By means of our senses we apprehend nothing in external objects beyond their shapes, sizes, and motions.
> (*Phil. Writings* vol. 1: 284)

On its face, this might seem like decisive evidence that Descartes denies that the senses represent secondary qualities. But problems abound. First, in the standard translation, these words are put in italics and set into the main text as if they were Descartes's own words. In the original, however, these titles occur in the margin, and even if Descartes wrote them (which is, so far as I can find, unknown), they are still just marginal glosses on the actual text. Second, although there is nothing really wrong with this translation, "we apprehend" translates *a nobis deprehendi*, which is not how one would make a point about the objects of perception. Rather, the question here is what we can discover about the world on the basis of the testimony of the senses, and Descartes's answer is that, contrary to how sensation might naïvely be interpreted, if in fact we base ourselves solely on what we can learn from sensory experience, there is "nothing in external objects beyond their shapes, sizes and motions." But again this is how the marginal gloss on this section of the *Principles* puts the conclusion. And when we look at how the section actually concludes, we run into still more trouble, because the actual conclusion of the section is as follows:

> In view of all this we must conclude that the things in external objects to which we apply the terms light, color, smell, taste, sound, heat, and cold . . . are, so far as we can recognize, nothing other than various dispositions of those objects, dispositions that make these bodies able to move our nerves in various ways.

To a modern reader (see, e.g., De Rosa, "Myth of Cartesian Qualia," p. 190), this is likely to look as if Descartes has reached quite a different conclusion from what the marginal gloss had promised: because now we have primary qualities *and dispositions*, and it is apparently these dispositions that are the objects of perception. But this is quite wrong, because *dispositio* in Latin simply means 'arrangement' or 'organization.' The very next section of the *Principles* makes this clearer by summarizing the conclusion of the previous section as follows:

> I have just demonstrated that these [light, color, etc.] are nothing else in the objects—or at least we do not apprehend [*a nobis deprehendi*] them as being anything else—but certain dispositions consisting in size, shape, and motion.   (*Principles* IV.199)

This is my translation, because here again the standard translation obscures Descartes's point, by rendering the key words as "dispositions *depending on* size, shape, and motion," which suggests two levels of things, one depending on the other. But the Latin makes it perfectly clear that all that Descartes is talking about is the way the parts are arranged. And the later French translation makes the point still clearer, by rendering the passage from IV.198 (quoted earlier) as follows:

> We have no apprehension of any sort that all the things in objects we call their light, color . . . [etc.] are anything else within them other than the various shapes, locations, sizes, and motions of their parts, which are disposed in such a way that they can move our nerves in all the various ways that are required to excite in our soul all the various sensations that exist there.

Here it is perfectly clear that the only things Descartes recognizes in the extended world are bodies and their geometric–kinetic modes. To be sure, we are on the brink of taking the step that Boyle and Locke would later take, that of giving theoretical significance to the identity of secondary qualities and dispositions. But Descartes is not taking that step. On the contrary, the express point here is to confine the world's contents within an austerely corpuscularian story.

A more interesting example of Descartes's sometimes relational approach to sensible qualities occurs in a discussion from the *Principles* of why only our intellect grasps bodies as they are. In themselves, bodies are simply extended things. Although we might suppose that we grasp a thing when we grasp its sensible qualities, in fact this is not so. His example is hardness:

> As regards hardness, sensation tells us no more than that the parts of a hard body resist the motion of our hands when they come into contact with them. For if, whenever our hands moved in a given direction, all the bodies in that area were to move away at the same speed as that of our approaching hands, we should never have any sensation of hardness. And since it is quite unintelligible to suppose that, if bodies did move away in this fashion, they would thereby lose their bodily nature, it follows that this nature cannot consist in hardness.
>
> (*Principles* II.4)

The passage takes for granted that hardness, the object of tactile sensation, is not some sort of real quality in bodies that causes us to have the corresponding sensation. Rather, as the first sentence explains, sensible hardness is the particles of a body resisting the influence of some part of our body. The argument for this comes in the second sentence: if a body were not to resist our approaching hand and were instead always to move away, we would never have the sensation of hardness. Hardness, then, when conceived of as the object of tactile sensation, is something relational, defined in terms of a certain response to observation. At this point the passage imagines what we might call the bashful body: one that, for some reason, always moves away rather than permit itself to be touched. We would have to say, on our relational account, that such a body is not hard. But, the passage concludes, it would be absurd to say that this body changed in any way with regard to its intrinsic nature merely in virtue of its strangely bashful character.

This is not an argument against a relational account of the sensible qualities. On the contrary, the argument presupposes that, if hardness is in the world as an object of perception, it will have to be defined in relation to perceivers. *That* is precisely why grasping a body's hardness shows us nothing about the body's nature. Moreover, Descartes immediately goes on to explain that a similar argument could be made about color and all the other nongeometric properties:

> By the same reasoning it can be shown that weight, color, and all other such qualities that are sensed in corporeal matter can be removed from it, while the matter itself remains unchanged [*integra*].   (*Principles* II.4)

This suggests that these qualities too, if located in the world, would have to be understood relationally. But there is room for interpretive disagreement here. The last word in the passage can be rendered "unchanged," as I have it, or it might be translated with the cognate "intact," which is how the standard translation does it. On that translation, however, it becomes unclear what Descartes means to say. On one reading, he might mean only that it is consistent with the nature of corporeal matter to cease having color, weight, and other such qualities. That is a natural claim to make about some secondary qualities, such as color, and one can see how Descartes believed it of weight, if we think of air, for instance, as lacking weight just as it normally lacks color. The more interesting reading, however, is that the sensible qualities can be removed from a body without *any* change at the level of corporeal matter. The bashful body, for instance, does not undergo intrinsic change, but just moves away whenever one's hand approaches. Cases of this kind have recently become popular as alleged counterexamples to relational theories of the sensible qualities, the best known such case being Saul Kripke's shade of yellow that instantaneously kills anyone who looks at it (see Gómez-Torrente, "Kripke on Color Words," pp. 305–7). Various proposals have been made regarding how to save a relational theory from these odd cases (see, e.g., David Lewis, "Naming the Colours").

Perhaps it was inevitable, in our fallen world, that murderous killer yellow rather than the charmingly bashful body would become the famous example. But the fault here lies partly with Descartes himself, because he does not seem truly committed to developing his example in the way I am advocating. In the French translation, the bashful body is still there, but the generalizing comment has been replaced by the claim that we can clearly and distinctly conceive of a body without any of the nongeometric qualities. This suggests that Descartes wants only the first, less interesting of the two readings mentioned above. And in a later discussion of this passage with Henry More he similarly seems to defend only the first interpretation of the passage (V: 268–9). This is perhaps all that Descartes really needs, given that his main purpose is to show that the nature of bodies consists exclusively of their geometric properties. And this reading fits better with the passage from IV: 198 discussed earlier in this note, which aims at a reductive understanding of the secondary qualities in terms of modes of extension. Moreover, it should be no surprise that Descartes would not insist on a reading of the argument that depends on a relational understanding of the sensible qualities, because, as this lecture argues, Descartes is not truly wedded to any such story.

Still, the relational strand in this passage cannot be dismissed, because without it the bashful body becomes a bad argument for Descartes's conclusion. For then one has to agree with Lisa Downing's verdict that this argument shows nothing more than that we can conceive of "a body whose hardness we cannot experience" ("Sensible Qualities," p. 112n). This is right if we are not thinking about the sensible qualities relationally, because then we can say that the bashful body and other such imperceptible bodies still have their various secondary qualities, as "dispositions" of their various primary qualities, even if these qualities never do—and perhaps cannot—relate to any observers.

In contrast with Descartes, who is reticent on this issue, Locke is quite explicit in understanding hardness relationally.

And indeed, hard and soft are names that we give to things only in relation to the constitutions of our own bodies; that being generally called hard by us, which will put us to pain, sooner than change figure by the pressure of any part of our bodies; and that, on the contrary, soft, which changes the situation of its parts upon an easy and unpainful touch. (*Essay* II.4.4)

Solidity, in contrast, he defines independently of our perceptions, as "that which thus hinders the approach of two bodies, when they are moving one towards another" (II.4.1). In fact, we continue to this day to think of hardness in relational terms. The Mohs scale of hardness, for instance, is defined in terms of one body's being able to scratch another. Here is where the case of the bashful body comes into its own again. For how hard is a body, on the Mohs scale, if that body never permits itself to be touched?

The Ideal of Fidelity

Note 15 (p. 68). Locke is often mocked for his allegedly botched account of secondary qualities, which seems on the face of it to waffle between locating them in the world and locating them in the mind. In light of the argument of this lecture, however, we can see why Locke, like Descartes, was pulled in different directions on this score, sometimes inclining more toward relationalism or reductivism, and sometimes more toward the subjectivism of his way of ideas. Each path is tempting, because each takes us closer to one ideal or another.

Locke develops a fairly sophisticated position on the epistemic value of our perceptions of secondary qualities, when those are taken as powers of bodies. In Cartesian terms, he holds that the simple ideas produced by secondary-quality perceptions are *clear*. Indeed, ideas of colors and the like would seem to be paradigms of clarity, because they so regularly meet the test of being "such as the objects themselves, from whence they were taken, did or might, in a well-ordered sensation or perception, present them" (*Essay* II.29.2). What his famous discussion of secondary qualities shows is that such ideas are prone to confusion—that is, to a lack of *distinctness*. For, even if the painter has the ideas of colors "clearly, perfectly and distinctly in his understanding," he is liable to confuse the idea and its cause (*Essay* II.8.3). On this terminology more generally, Locke writes as follows, invoking the scholastic vocabulary of 'evident':

As a clear idea is that whereof the mind has such a full and evident perception, as it does receive from an outward object operating duly on a well-disposed organ; so a distinct idea is that wherein the mind perceives a difference from all other; and a confused idea is such an one, as is not sufficiently distinguishable from another, from which it ought to be different.   (*Essay* II.29.4)

This usage of clearness and distinctness adheres fairly closely (though not without interesting differences) to the usage of Descartes (*Principles* I.45–6), who treats the perception of pain as a model of clarity but not of distinctness. See also note 8 here for the traditional scholastic link between distinctness and evidentness.

Another term of art Locke employs for the evaluation of our ideas is *adequacy*. For an idea to be adequate is for it to "perfectly represent those archetypes which the mind supposes them taken from, which it intends them to stand for, and to which it refers them" (*Essay* II.31.1). Surprisingly, Locke holds that all our simple ideas are adequate; and he defends this thesis particularly in the case of our secondary-quality ideas. Here is the argument:

All our simple ideas are adequate. Because being nothing but the effects of certain powers in things, fitted and ordained by God to produce such sensations in us, they cannot but be correspondent and adequate to those powers. And we are sure they agree to the reality of things. For if sugar produce in us the ideas which we call whiteness and sweetness, we are sure there is a power in sugar to produce those ideas in our minds, or else they could not have been produced by it. And so each sensation answering the power that operates on any of our senses, the idea so produced is a real idea, (and not a fiction of the mind, which has no power to produce any simple idea) and cannot but be adequate, since it ought only to answer that power. And so all simple ideas are adequate.   (*Essay* II.31.2)

The passage could hardly be more explicit about embracing the sort of relational strategy we first saw in Aristotle. What do the ideas of whiteness and sweetness represent, when we experience sugar? "A power in sugar to produce those ideas in our minds." When the situation is so conceived, then of course the idea *must* be adequate, because the reliability of its reference has been guaranteed by the terms of the theory. It further follows, on this view, that, if there were no perceivers able to perceive such qualities, the qualities would cease to exist. And this is precisely what Locke goes on to argue in this same section of the *Essay*: "were there no fit organs to receive the impressions . . . there would yet be no more light or heat in the world, than there would be pain if there were no sensible creature to feel it." The similarity with Aristotle is striking. The direct influence here, however, is Boyle, who makes similar remarks. On Boyle's version of relationalism, which seems to me even more nuanced than Locke's, see Dan Kaufman, "Locks, Schlocks, and Poisoned Peas" and my *Metaphysical Themes* ch. 23. For another gesture toward relationalism from this era, see Leibniz's *New Essays*, where, rather than concede that warmth is not in the water but in the hand (or mind) to which it feels warm, Leibniz writes that "that proves at most that warmth is not a sensible quality or power to make itself sensed that is entirely absolute, but that it is relative to its associated organs" (II.8, p. 132).

As this lecture argues (p. 68), Locke is more willing than Descartes to embrace relationalism as a path forward in understanding perception. Even so, he takes from Descartes various critical pieces of the theory. In the argument just quoted, he relies on the sort of epistemic teleology ("fitted and ordained by God") we saw in Descartes. Locke also relies on the Cartesian idea that "the great business of the senses" is to "make us take notice of what hurts or advantages the body" (*Essay* II.10.3). In taking this perspective, Locke partially absorbs the price of his relationalism: he is purchasing reliability at the cost of fidelity. Thus in various places Locke holds that our ideas of secondary qualities are "real and true" (II.30.2) and give rise to "real knowledge" (IV.4.4). Although these ideas do not show us things as they are in themselves, in high fidelity, it is enough that they serve as "marks of distinction in things" (II.32.14). *Essay* II.23.12 offers an extended meditation on this theme and on why perception in high fidelity would not be to our advantage.

For illuminating discussions of these issues in Locke, see Lisa Downing, "The 'Sensible Object,'" Martha Bolton, "Locke on the Semantic and Epistemic Role of Simple Ideas," and Lex Newman, "Locke on Sensitive Knowledge." I argue for an antirealist interpretation of both Boyle's and Locke's powers in *Metaphysical Themes* ch. 23.

Note 16 (p. 69). The distinction between reliability and fidelity illuminates the history of theorizing about perception, inasmuch as these ideals and the trade-offs between them lie behind many of the disagreements that run through the centuries.

Admittedly, however, it is not easy to draw a precise distinction between reliability and fidelity. The sound of my doorbell reliably tells me that someone is at the door, but not who is there. Yet it does tell me that a person is there, since nothing else—not my wife's cat, not the neighborhood bears—has yet figured out how to ring the bell. So that's some information on the *what* side. Does that count as fidelity? Precision at this point would require a theory of perceptual content, as well as a metaphysics well developed enough to specify just what whatness is at issue. Aristotle—who draws a similar distinction between the question of whether a thing exists and the question of what it is—has just such a metaphysics: the "what it is" question concerns the essences of things. Here I do not seek to enter into any substantive metaphysical commitments. But whether or not things have such natures or essences, there are, I assume, more or less accurate and comprehensive accounts of how things are. Fidelity can be understood as coming in degrees, in proportion to the extent to which this sort of accurate and comprehensive account is achieved. My doorbell is brilliant at signaling persons, but that is as far as it goes. The senses presumably do better, but what is at issue is just how much better they do.

So far as I have found, this distinction between reliability and fidelity has no close historical precedent. Just as this book goes to press, I have found Zed Adams suggesting that something like the ideal of fidelity motivates Descartes's resistance to a reductive theory of color (*On the Genealogy of Color*, p. 93). It is interesting, however, that, although Adams and I are similarly interested in untangling the various historical threads that run through theorizing about color, in most respects we reach quite different conclusions about how those threads are to be untangled.

What I am calling fidelity is related to what Mark Johnston, in modern times, has described as *revelation* ("How to Speak of the Colors"). But Johnston wants more than perception's showing us what its objects are like; he seems to want the qualitative features of visual experience *to be* the qualities of objects:

If external things are colored, then their colors must be tightly connected to the distinctive qualities which visual awareness alone reveals. Our immediate perceptual judgments about the colors of items in the environment do not systematically prescind from the qualities of surfaces ostensibly presented in sensory experience. Instead those judgments seem to predicate *those very sensed qualities* of environmental items ... The qualities predicated of objects in immediate perceptual judgment must be closely tied to the qualities which sensory awareness reveals. (That is to put it mildly: the close tie seems to be identity; we often judge things to be just the way the senses present them as being.)   ("Better than Mere Knowledge," p. 264)

A similar idea is characterized by David Chalmers as "an Edenic world in which we perfectly perceive objects and properties in that world." What would that be like? "Perfect perception of an object or property requires unmediated acquaintance with the object or the property, and perhaps also requires that the object or the property is itself a constituent of one's perceptual experience" ("Perception and the Fall from Eden," p. 94). This suggests my notion of fidelity, but is in other ways importantly different from how I understand the perceptual ideal. First, for reasons that Lecture Four explains, I do not think that immediacy is part of the perceptual ideal. Further, although I suppose that there are various ways of making sense of the strange idea that an external object might be a constituent of one's experience, I do not see any reason to regard such stories as part of the cognitive ideal—no more than an ideal marriage would be one in which my wife becomes a part of me.

Notes to Lecture Four

How Ideas Become Objects

Note 1 (p. 72). The hallmark of cognition is intentionality, which is to say that cognitive states are *about* things, or *refer* to things, or *represent* things. Inasmuch as this is so, cognition will always involve representations. Hence no special argument is required to show that, in thinking and perceiving, the mind contains representations of the things it thinks and perceives. This is necessarily true because of the very nature of cognition.

One might think that this alleged necessary truth will face certain sorts of counterexamples in cases where the things being thought and perceived are *themselves* within the mind, and so not in need of being *represented* by something else. Think of the case where the mind is aware of its own mental states, for instance, or where the mind is aware of God—who, Aquinas says, makes himself immediately present to the minds of the blessed and so is grasped by them directly, without any need for an intelligible species (*Summa theol.* 1a 12.2c).

Even in such cases, however, if there is an *awareness of* these inwardly present objects, then there is a cognitive act that *represents* these objects: that is part of what is involved in being *aware of* them. Hence the necessary truth stands.

These remarks help clarify what is at stake between proponents of the dual view and proponents of the simple view described in this lecture. Both parties agree, as they must, that perception and thought involve representation. Where they disagree is on whether there is any need for some sort of inner representation beyond the act itself. This disagreement, we can further see, will concern specific cases rather than running across the board. Hence Aquinas disagrees with Ockham about whether sensible species are required in ordinary cases—for example, in order to perceive colors. But Aquinas and Ockham agree about the case of perceiving God: both think that, when God makes himself immediately present to our minds, the act of awareness itself represents God, no further representational form being required. Even someone as committed to the dual view as Locke cannot think that all mental awareness requires ideas. For in that case how would we be aware of the ideas themselves? Through more ideas? How, in turn, would we be aware of those?

It is easy to find further examples of authors arguing for species or ideas on the basis of the need for something to take the place of distant objects. William of Ware (fl. *c.*1300), for instance, writes that, "because the object cannot be present to our intellect through its essence, its species must therefore be present to our intellect, so that through its mediation the external thing that it represents can be understood" (quoted in Jacqueline Hamesse, "Idea," p. 131). John Buridan similarly argues that "we sense exterior qualities only if they impress on our senses or sensory organs some representative of them. For, since the object receives nothing from the senses, if that object were also to impress nothing on the senses, then there would be no reason why it would be sensed when present to the senses and not before. And this is something that everyone grants" (*Quaest. de anima* II.17 n. 10).

Compare Ockham's report that, "if species are posited for the sake of representation, this is only because a distant object cannot act at a distance" (*Reportatio* II.12–13, in *Opera theol.* vol. 5: 274; see also *Opera theol.* vol. 6: 59–60). But Ockham is one of the few who reject this line of thought, for he immediately goes on to deny the assumption that action at a distance is impossible. (This discussion is translated in Hyman, Walsh, and Williams, *Philosophy in the Middle Ages*, pp. 624–30.)

Looking ahead to the seventeenth century, Arnauld and Nicole begin the first part of the *Port-Royal Logic* with the following remark: "As we can have no knowledge of what is outside us except by the mediation [*entremise*] of the ideas that are in us, the reflections we can make on our ideas are perhaps the most important part of logic, since it is the foundation of everything else" (trans. p. 25).

Malebranche likewise appeals to the need for mediation at *Search after Truth* III.2.1:

I think everyone agrees that we do not perceive objects external to us by themselves. We see the sun, the stars, and an infinity of objects external to us; and it is not likely that the soul should leave the body to stroll about the heavens, as it were, in order to behold all these objects. Thus, it does not see them by themselves, and our mind's immediate object when it sees the sun, for example, is not the sun, but something that is intimately joined to our soul, and this is what I call an *idea*.   (*Search after Truth* III.2.1, trans. p. 217)

The passage continues as quoted in this lecture (p. 72), by defining 'idea' as the immediate object of perception. Although this talk of strolling about the heavens has received much puzzled attention—"striking and bizarre" says John Yolton ("The Term *Idea*," p. 248)—Malebranche in fact is simply repeating one of the most familiar arguments for cognitive intermediaries such as ideas or species.

Although Malebranche's remarks seem to be not far from what Arnauld and Nicole (just quoted) had themselves said about ideas, Arnauld would later attack Malebranche on these very grounds:

I am not surprised that the majority of philosophers have reasoned in this way, after blindly accepting these two principles as incontestable: that the soul can perceive only objects that are present to it, and that bodies can be present to it only through certain representative beings, called ideas or species, which take their place and are similar to them, and which in their stead are intimately united with the soul.

(*True and False Ideas* ch. 4, trans. p. 15)

Malebranche's response to Arnauld backs off from this sort of distant-object rationale for species or ideas. He describes the passage from the *Search* quoted here as "a kind of raillery." What the passage shows, Malebranche now says, is only that "there must be something different from the sun, in order to represent it to the soul" (*Réponse* 12.7, in *Oeuvres complètes* vol. 6: 95–96]). He goes on to indicate that the passage does not establish whether that thing is an idea in Malebranche's sense, a scholastic species, or, as Arnauld would argue, a mode of the soul. For this argument in Malebranche, see Steven Nadler, *Malebranche and Ideas*, pp. 67–79. On the argument more generally in the seventeenth century, see Reid, *Essays on the Intellectual Powers* II.14 (*Works* vol. 1: 300–2) and Yolton, *Perceptual Acquaintance*, pp. 58–61. The argument makes its way down to Kant, in this form: "If we let outer objects count as things in themselves, then it is absolutely impossible to comprehend how we are to acquire cognition of their reality outside us, since we base this merely on the representation, which is in us. For one cannot have sensation outside oneself, but only in oneself, and the whole of self-consciousness therefore provides nothing other than merely our own determinations" (*Critique of Pure Reason* A378).

The argument from distant objects helps highlight the fact that there are two distinct roles that species or ideas might play. First, they may be needed to play a causal role, moving information from a distant object into the cognitive agent. This role cannot be played by the cognitive act itself, because what we are looking for here is that which *causes* such an act. This is the role that Ockham thinks unnecessary in normal cases, where he invokes action at a distance, and that Aquinas thinks unnecessary for the blessed in heaven, because their object, God, acts directly on the mind. Second, the vehicle may be needed to play an intentional role, as that which bears the *representational content* of the cognitive act. This second role seems most central to the philosophy of perception, whereas the first role, that of causal intermediary, seems mainly of concern to natural philosophy. It is this second role that gives rise to the disagreement between simple and dual views as well, for it is quite unclear whether this role might be played by the cognitive act itself.

On the distinction between these two roles, see Scotus, who defends the need for species on the basis of the second role (see Pasnau, "Cognition," pp. 289–90), and Durand of Saint-Pourçain, who rejects species on the grounds that they are required for neither role (see Jean-Luc Solère, "Durand of Saint-Pourçain's Cognition Theory").

Among the scholastics, both Olivi and Ockham argue at great length that species are required neither as causal agents nor as the bearers of representational content over and above the act itself. For both, see Pasnau, *Theories of Cognition*; Dominik Perler, *Theorien der Intentionalität*; and Han Thomas Adriaenssen, *Representation and Scepticism*. For more on Ockham, see Eleonore Stump, "Mechanisms of Cognition," and André Goddu, "William of Ockham's Arguments for Action at a Distance." It is worth noting that Ockham goes one step farther than Olivi, in that he rejects not only sensible and intelligible species but also species *in medio*, whereas Olivi accepts the latter's existence but denies that they offer an adequate explanation of the connection between perceiver and object (see *Summa* II.72 and II.74, trans. Pasnau).

In the seventeenth century Arnauld gives the most prominent defense of the simple view, and note 10 here will discuss his position at greater length. Another example is Spinoza, *Ethics* II.43 schol.: "For to have a true idea means nothing other than knowing a thing perfectly, or in the best way. And of course no one can doubt this unless he thinks that an idea is something mute, like a picture on a tablet, and not a mode of thinking, namely, the very [act of] understanding" (and see also *Ethics* II def. 3). The Cartesian Pierre-Sylvain Régis is another case. Responding to the charge that Descartes's use of 'idea' is ambiguous between the act of thought and the object of that act, Régis responds: "By the word 'idea,' Mr. Descartes never understood the object of our thought, but only the action by which we think of that object" (*Réponse*, p. 191). Yet another example is Henry Lee (see Adriaenssen, "An Early Critic of Locke").

Hobbes's materialism and steadfast rejection of forms (see my *Metaphysical Themes*, pp. 116–17, 510–12) put him in a very different position from that of other authors under consideration, because they lead him to think about cognition in very reductive terms: "All which qualities called sensible are in the object that causes them but so many several motions of the matter, by which it presses our organs diversely. Neither in us that are pressed are they anything else but diverse motions (for motion produces nothing but motion)" (*Lev.* 1.4). Hobbes does fairly often speak of ideas—"those ideas, or mental images we have of all things we see, or remember" (*Lev.* 46.16). But he does not tend to think of them as objects of perception—not in the passage just quoted, and not even when he gives the argument from illusion, which he offers not as an argument for ideas as objects of perception but rather as an argument for the thesis "that the subject wherein colour and image are inherent is not the object or thing seen" (*Elements of Law* I.2.4–5). In both of these passages the things seen are out in the world. A possible exception is *Lev.* 4.17: "when any thing is *seen* by us, we reckon not the thing itself, but the *sight*, the *colour*, the *idea* of it in the fancy: and when any thing is *heard*, we reckon it not, but the *hearing* or *sound* only, which is our fancy or conception of it by the ear; and such are names of fancies." But, even here, it is external things that are seen and heard. I am inclined to read this passage as Hobbes's account of a mistake we are prone to make rather than as his considered view about how cognition works.

Descartes's Ideas as Forms

Note 2 (p. 72). Descartes very frequently and consistently describes ideas as forms. In addition to the passage from the Second Replies (VII: 160) quoted in this lecture (p. 72), see the Third Replies (VII: 188): "by 'idea' I mean whatever is the form of a given perception"; the Fourth Replies (VII: 232): "Since ideas are forms of a kind"; to Mesland in 1644 (IV: 113): "I regard the difference between the soul and its ideas as the same as that between a piece of wax and the various shapes it can take"; and his *Notae in programma* (VIIIB: 358): "I observed that there were certain thoughts within me . . . I applied the term 'innate' to the idea or notions that are the forms of these thoughts." David Clemenson remarks that "Descartes may have banished species from the extramental world, and even dropped the term 'species,' but the Scholastic notion expressed by that term played as large a role in his philosophy of thought as it did in Jesuit theory of cognition" (*Descartes' Theory of Ideas*, p. 33).

More cautiously, Anthony Kenny remarks of such passages that "no scholastic theory seems to be involved" and that speaking of ideas as forms seems to mean simply that they are "nonmaterial representations of things" (*Descartes*, pp. 110–11). I agree that Descartes does not mean to be invoking a distinctively scholastic doctrine and that his talk of forms may be intended to carry the implications Kenny suggests. My point is only that Descartes is using, without apology, what was well known to be a scholastic way of characterizing ideas and mental representations in general, and that here—unlike in so many other contexts—he shows not the least reluctance to do so.

Perhaps part of the reason why Descartes happily refers to ideas as forms is that the usage is not only scholastic but also Augustinian. In *De trinitate* XI.2, Augustine discusses the triad object–vision–power. He never uses the word 'idea' here but speaks repeatedly of the object's impressing a form or species on the power. The power, once informed, gives rise to vision.

Mediation in the Seventeenth Century

Note 3 (p. 72). As for the principal question of this lecture—Why do ideas become the immediate objects of perception?—the textual evidence that this *is* Descartes's view seems unimpeachable. In addition to the Second Replies definition (VII: 160) quoted in this lecture (p. 72), see the Third Replies (VII: 181): "I am taking the word 'idea' to refer to whatever is immediately perceived by the mind"; the Fifth Replies (VII: 366): "You restrict the term 'idea' to only images depicted in phantasia, whereas I extend the term to everything that is thought"; and a marginal note Descartes added to the Latin edition of the *Discourse* (VI: 559): "Note that here, and everywhere that follows, the term 'idea' is taken in general for every thing cognized, insofar as it has any objective being in the intellect." (On *objective being*, see note 15 to this lecture.)

Janet Broughton observes that Descartes's skeptic does not rely on the mediation of ideas to derive his conclusions. Nowhere do those skeptical arguments assume, in her words, that "the ultimate grounds of justification are the contents of his own mind" ("Cartesian Skeptics," p. 31). To me, however, this shows not that Descartes himself rejects such an assumption, but only that he cannot very well make his opening skeptical gambit depend on it, given that no such thing would have been accepted by Descartes's audience. It is only *after* Descartes—above all in Locke, Berkeley, and Hume—that a doctrine of this kind came to be accepted as self-evidently true.

My explanation of why Descartes starts talking this way is, in broad outlines, hardly original. Many others have seen Descartes as the founder of inward theories of perception, and some have even suggested that the theory of secondary qualities played a role. (For both claims, see, e.g., Hilary Putnam, "Sense, Nonsense, and the Senses," pp. 467–8. More recently, John Campbell, *Berkeley's Puzzle*, p. 4 has remarked that "physics drove sensory experience inside the head," which is, to be sure, a tendentious way to put the point but gets the history roughly right.) But our knowledge of the history of philosophy has, until recently, been too impoverished for us to attempt a truly satisfying explanation of what happened in the seventeenth century. And the situation has been further complicated by the strenuous effort of some recent scholars to deny that there is anything to be explained. Michael Ayers, for instance, begins an essay on ideas in the seventeenth century with a remarkable denunciation of the sort of picture I am offering:

It has often been taught, and may in dark corners still be taught, that in the seventeenth century epistemology was transformed by a new notion of 'ideas' as the immediate objects of perception and thought . . . Recent (and some less recent) work on theories of ideas has undermined this influential story . . . [T]here was no sudden, radical departure, least of all by Descartes, from traditional frameworks for dealing with the relation between thought and its objects. As his own explanations emphasise, Descartes's use of the old term 'idea' was only mildly innovative.   ("Ideas and Objective Being," p. 1062)

Perhaps I have been living too long in the shadows of the Rocky Mountains, but this reprobate story is precisely my view. I do think that seventeenth-century epistemology was "transformed by a new notion of ideas," and I do think that Descartes, above all, was responsible for this "sudden, radical departure." Ayers goes on to show that various elements of the seventeenth-century story can be found in scholastic thought. But he provides no evidence whatsoever that authors before Descartes accept the notion that ideas (or anything of the kind) are the immediate objects of perception and thought. And it is precisely here where something radically new happens in the seventeenth century. Despite looking very hard, I have found virtually no one before Descartes who embraces anything like an idea or species or image as the object of perception. The following note provides more information on scholastic and ancient discussions, and the few exceptions I know of. Here let me mention some of the earlier seventeenth-century figures who might have seemed the best candidates for having set such a precedent, but who did not.

Francis Bacon's reduction of heat to motion is important to the story of secondary qualities (see my *Metaphysical Themes* ch. 21 sct. 4). But Bacon is explicit that heat is out in the world, and not to be identified with sensations (*Novum organum* II.20). Hence this famous discussion provides no impetus toward relocating the objects of perception within the mind. Galileo's *Assayer* (1623), in contrast, does argue that sensible qualities should be located within the perceiver (*Discoveries*, pp. 273–9). But, even so, Galileo does not make the further claim that the objects of perception are internal to us. Hobbes, similarly, when he offers the argument from illusion, concludes that colors and other sensible qualities are in the perceiver, but continues to treat the thing out in the world as the thing seen (see note 1 here).

Marin Mersenne, back in 1624, considers in some detail the skeptical arguments from sensory illusion and variation but shows no sign of wanting to put the objects of perception inside the mind. The farthest he is willing to go is this pregnant remark, which he leaves unexplored: "although the animals perceive objects differently from us, we must not worry about that . . . because it is enough to know things according to how they are proportioned to us" (*La vérité des sciences* I.4, p. 20; trans. Ariew, Cottingham, and Sorell, *Descartes' Meditations: Background Source Materials*, p. 160).

Gassendi's *Exercitationes paradoxicae* (1624) concludes with a lengthy rejection of Aristotelian *scientia* that enjoins us to stick with the appearances rather than to profess a knowledge of the deeper natures and causes of things (II.6). But it is not clear here that he understands the appearances to be something within us. The appearances may just as well be the fleeting superficial properties of things, which is the best we can hope to understand of the world around us. In his mature atomistic writings he discusses at length the topic of "visible, sensible, intentional species, or forms" (*Syntagma* II [Physics] I.6.13, in *Opera* vol. 1: 441–9). But here too he shows no signs of wanting to conceive of these "simulacra or images" as themselves the objects of perception. Compare the similar story in Charleton, *Physiologia* Book III, ch. 3.

One gets a somewhat different picture from the logical part of Gassendi's *Syntagma*, where simple mental operations get initially labeled "the simple imagination of things." We are then told that "an image is what appears to the mind and is, as it were, made its object, when we are thinking about anything." From the many alternative terms that might be used, Gassendi then says that he will most often use the term 'idea,' on the grounds that this is "an expression that is by now familiar and common" (*Syntagma*, Institutio logica pt. 1, in *Opera* 1: 92). Here I take Gassendi (who was writing in the 1640s and 1650s) to show Descartes's influence. But, even so, Gassendi puts little weight on ideas as objects. Correspondingly, his atomism about sensible qualities is of the Epicurean sort, one that locates them in the world rather than in the mind. (On this, see Antonia LoLordo, "Gassendi and the Seventeenth-Century Atomists.")

For the rise of mediated theories in the decades after Descartes, see, most recently, Adriaenssen, *Representation and Scepticism*. For the Cartesian history in particular, see Richard Watson, *The Breakdown of Cartesian Metaphysics*. On varying usages of 'idea' more generally in the post-scholastic era, see Yolton, "The Term *Idea*."

Authors who are more or less under Descartes's influence differ greatly in how they develop the doctrine. The case of Spinoza has been briefly mentioned in note 1 here and Arnauld will be discussed further in note 10. Malebranche offers a particularly complex hybrid approach, because he distinguishes between ideas as the objects of perception and the sensible features of our perceptions. The former belong to God—but are nevertheless the immediate objects of perception—whereas the latter belong to us. But it is only the former that represent things outside the soul. As for the latter—color, sound, pleasure, pain, and so on—"none of the soul's sensations and passions represent anything resembling them outside the soul, and are but modifications of which a mind is capable" (*Search after Truth* III.2.5, trans. p. 228).

Nadler has argued in detail that Malebranche does not treat sensory perception as mediated by ideas (*Malebranche and Ideas*, pp. 152–82), but this is, distinctly, a minority reading and, as Nadler himself admits, it flies in the face of much textual evidence. For a detailed response, see David Scott, "Malebranche's Indirect Realism."

Locke's treatment of ideas as the immediate objects of perception is so well known that it will perhaps be tedious to document it further, but here are just a few more examples, beyond the passage from *Essay* I.1.8 quoted in the Lecture:

Since the mind, in all its thoughts and reasonings, has no other immediate object but its own ideas, which it alone does or can contemplate, it is evident that our knowledge is only conversant about them.   (*Essay* IV.1.1)

[F]or the thing signified by [the term] ideas is nothing but the immediate objects of our minds in thinking: so that unless any one can oppose the article your lordship defends, without thinking on something, he must use the things signified by ideas: for he that thinks must have some immediate object of his mind in thinking, i.e. must have ideas.   (Reply to Stillingfleet, in *Works* vol. 3: 130–1)

But since the word idea has the ill luck to be so constantly opposed by your lordship to reason, permit me if you please, instead of it, to put what I mean by it, viz. the immediate objects of the mind in thinking (for that is it which I would signify by the word ideas).   (Reply to Stillingfleet, in *Works* vol. 3: 233)

If you [i.e., Locke himself] once mention ideas you must be presently called to an account [i.e., by Norris] what kind of things you make these same ideas to be, though perhaps you [Locke] have no design to consider them any further than as the immediate objects of perception.

(First Reply to John Norris, in Acworth, "Locke's First Reply," p. 10)

It is also worth noting that Locke's definition of 'idea' as the object of understanding appears verbatim in Draft B of the *Essay* from 1671 (*Drafts for the Essay*, p. 103), which shows that this aspect of the theory is fundamental to his earliest conceptions of the *Essay*, quite independently of subsequent discussions of this topic in Malebranche, Arnauld, Spinoza, and others.

By the turn of the eighteenth century, such claims were widely taken for granted. For instance, according to Pierre-Daniel Huet, "we must confess that our senses do not sense external objects, but only the impression of the species or images that proceed from outside things" (*Philosophical Treatise* I.3, p. 31). And Berkeley, in addition to the passage quoted in this lecture (p. 72), reports in the *Three Dialogues* that "the word *idea* . . . is now commonly used by philosophers to denote the immediate objects of the understanding" (dialogue 3, *Works* vol. 2: 235–6).

Mediation before the Seventeenth Century

Note 4 (p. 73). I know of only two clearly mediated accounts before the seventeenth century. One is that of William Crathorn, to be discussed in note 21 here. The other is that of the Cyrenaics (fourth and third centuries BC). Although our knowledge of their teachings is extremely indirect and limited, it is fairly well attested that one of their core doctrines was that "we have sensation of our affections [πάθη] alone" (see Voula Tsouna, *The Epistemology of the Cyrenaic School*, p. 31). It is not entirely clear how such claims are to be understood (for doubts, see Burnyeat, "Idealism and Greek Philosophy," pp. 27–8). But I am prepared to concede that such remarks point to the view that we perceive not external things, but our inner experiential states. (Tsouna's volume analyzes in detail the surviving testimonies.) That the view could be stated so early in the history of philosophy and that subsequent ancient philosophers, all the way to Augustine, had at least a passing familiarity with it only sharpens the question of why it was almost universally rejected for so long, only to be embraced as scarcely controversial in the later seventeenth century and early eighteenth century.

There is scholarly consensus that the Epicureans, despite their insistence that "all impressions are true," did not embrace a mediated view. For some key texts, see Lucretius in Long and Sedley, *Hellenistic Philosophers* 15C1 (vol. 1, p. 74, with commentary at p. 77 of vol. 2). For discussion, see Stephen Everson, "Epicurus on the Truth of the Senses"; C. C. W. Taylor, "All Perceptions Are True"; and Gisela Striker, "Epicurus on the Truth of Sense Impressions," who remarks that, "to be consistent, the Epicureans *ought* to have adopted the Cyrenaic position and said that only the affections of the senses can be known, while nothing can be said about their causes in the external world" (p. 141, my emphasis).

Perhaps Democritus earlier on did embrace mediation. This is suggested by the testimony of Theophrastus, who reports that, at least in the case of heat, flavor, and color, Democritus holds that "none of these other sensibles has any nature of its own, but all are states of a sense that is undergoing the alteration that results in an appearance" (*De sensibus* n. 63). Although I have argued in "Democritus and Secondary Qualities" that the balance of proof favors this interpretation, the textual evidence is fragmentary and points in many different directions.

Historically, the ancient skeptics have often been associated with mediation. Pierre Bayle, for instance, remarks that "no good philosopher any longer doubts that the skeptics were right to maintain that the qualities of bodies that strike our senses are only appearances" (*Dictionary*, s.v. "Pyrrho" note b, trans. p. 197). Hylas's very last sentence, in Berkeley's *Three Dialogues*, begins with the remark: "You set out upon the same principles that Academics, Cartesians, and the like sects usually do." And indeed one can find mediation among the ancient skeptics. Most prominently, Sextus Empiricus invokes mediated views, for example at *Outlines* II.vii.72: "the senses do not apprehend external existing objects but only—if anything—their own feelings." But this is hardly one of their doctrines. For it would, of course, be objectionably dogmatic for the

Pyrrhonists to insist on mediation as a positive thesis. Unsurprisingly, then, Sextus immediately goes on to consider the case where we do apprehend external objects. See also *Against the Logicians* I.354–8. On ancient skepticism's general lack of interest in securing knowledge at the level of appearances, see Myles Burnyeat, "Idealism and Greek Philosophy," pp. 26–7.

As noted in note 5 to Lecture Three, some modern readers have taken Aristotle's doctrine that the senses "cannot be deceived" about the proper sensibles (e.g., *De an.* II.6, 418^{a}12) as evidence of a mediated view on which the proper sensibles are the inner objects. But this fits poorly with the vast majority of texts and the later Aristotelian tradition almost uniformly fails to head in this direction, taking it for granted instead that the objects of sensation are external.

Surprisingly, Norman Kretzmann ("Infallibility, Error, and Ignorance," pp. 171–2) suggests that Thomas Aquinas's invocation of the "cannot be deceived" doctrine commits him as well to inner sense objects. But this seems to me definitely unfounded, as I have argued in *Thomas Aquinas on Human Nature*, pp. 188–9.

A somewhat more promising medieval candidate is Avicenna. In *Thomas Aquinas on Human Nature* (p. 186), I translated from the Latin version of his *De anima* as follows:

The thing that is sensed most certainly and immediately is that through which the one sensing is informed by the form of the thing sensed.   (Avicenna, *De anima*, ed. Van Riet, p. 129)

But if I had then been able to consult the Arabic, I would have found that in fact Avicenna says something rather different:

والمحسوس بالحقيقة القريب هو ما يتصور به الحاس من صورة المحسوس....

The thing sensed that is in truth closest is that through which the one sensing is informed by the form of the thing sensed.   (Avicenna, *De anima* [*al-Shifāʾ*] II.2, ed. Marmura, p. 66)

Contrary to what the Latin Avicenna suggests, *certainty* is not at issue. Avicenna is willing to speak here of the inner form as a sense object, which takes him an important step toward mediated views, but what he immediately goes on to say backs away from that doctrine:

Thus the one sensing, in a certain way, senses himself and not the body that is sensed, because that which is formed by the form is the closest thing sensed.

Thus, although in one respect we can think of the inner form as the "closest thing sensed," if we conceive of perception in this way then we have in fact switched topics, because we are no longer talking about the cognitive process by which we sense external things but rather about the process by which we sense *ourselves*. Accordingly, these remarks occur only in passing, as part of a much longer discussion of how we perceive the sensible qualities of external things.

The novelty of seventeenth-century views is understated by Thomas Reid, who writes that "all philosophers, from Plato to Mr. Hume, agree in this, that we do not perceive external objects immediately, and that the immediate objects of perception must be some image present to the mind" (*Essays on the Intellectual Powers* II.7, in *Works* vol. 1: 263a). In his nineteenth-century edition of Reid's *Works*, William Hamilton sagely remarks in a note here: "This is not correct. There were philosophers who held a purer and preciser doctrine of immediate perception than Reid himself contemplated." But the real focus of Reid's historical account is on what happens from Descartes forward, when he thinks that philosophers took a new skeptical turn not because they began treating ideas as objects but because these inner objects came to overshadow external objects and thus to render the existence of an external world doubtful.

The novelty of post-scholastic views is wildly overstated in Richard Rorty's *Philosophy and the Mirror of Nature*, which makes the most outrageous generalizations about what is new in the seventeenth century without displaying the slightest knowledge of philosophy prior to that century.

Note 5 (p. 74). I called attention to scholastic worries about the veil of perception in *Theories of Cognition*, which gave particular attention to Peter John Olivi; see especially pp. 236–47, which quote many more passages from Olivi, such as this one:

> A species will never actually represent an object to the cognitive power unless the power attends to the species in such a way that it turns and fixes its attention on the species. But that to which the power's attention is turned has the character of an object, and that to which it is first turned has the character of a first object. Therefore these species will have the character of an object more than the character of an intermediary or representative principle.   (*Summa* II.58 ad 14 [vol. 2: 469])

Gerard of Bologna's discussion (in Paris, 1309) has only recently become available in print. Gerard also draws the distinction, noted earlier, between species as causal agents and species as representational vehicles. The remark quoted briefly in this lecture (p. 74) runs more fully as follows:

> If a species is posited in the intellect, it is posted as a principle either of acting, or of being acted on, or of representing . . . If the third, then the species must be cognized before the object, in the order of nature, because to represent to the intellect is nothing other than to make it understand, which a species cannot do through its inhering in intellect, because then for the same reason a disposition [*habitus*] would do this. Therefore it is done through the species' representing the object. But that which represents something is first cognized in itself . . . But everyone holds that the species is not cognized before the object. Therefore no such species should be posited in the intellect.   (*Quodlibet* I.17, nn. 18–20)

Compare Ockham, a few years later: "when several things are of the same character (*ratio*), that which more immediately causes the vision is more immediately seen. Therefore if the species of whiteness is of the same character as whiteness, and according to you more immediately causes the act of seeing, then the species is more immediately seen, *which is manifestly false*" (*Reportatio* III.2, in *Opera theol.* vol. 6: 48). I discussed Ockham's case in some detail in *Theories of Cognition*, pp. 247–53.

Durand of St.-Pourçain (*c.*1320) likewise gives the familiar argument against species that, if they are to represent other things, then they themselves would have to be the first thing cognized. That they are not "is of itself manifest, for the species of a color existing in the eye is in no way seen, nor can it be seen by the eye—as everyone experiences" (*Sent.* [3rd vers.] II.3.6 n. 10). For further discussion, see Solère, "Durand of Saint-Pourçain's Cognition Theory" and Peter Hartman, "Durand and Aquinas on Representation."

Yet another example is that of John of Mirecourt (in 1344): "if such a *fictum* or image distinct from the act or disposition is to be posited, this would seem to be so that it would either terminate the act of understanding or be a likeness of singulars. Not the first, because the singulars themselves are the things that terminate the intellect, just as they are the things that are understood" (*Sent.* q. 4, p. 421).

All these authors were in the minority in insisting that species, to serve as representational vehicles, would have to be themselves the immediate objects of perception. But the minor premise of these arguments—that species are in fact *not* the immediate objects—was accepted by virtually everyone as self-evident. Hence, again, the puzzle arises over what changed from Descartes forward.

Admittedly, early scholastic discussions can be found to waffle a bit on the question of whether species are objects of perception. Aquinas, most notably, even while insisting that "the species of color in the eye is not that which is seen" (*Summa contra gentiles* II.75.1550), sometimes describes the relation between sense power and species in perceptual terms and talks of our "apprehending" species, "turning toward" species, and considering external things in virtue of "considering species" in a certain way. For an inventory and discussion of these passages, most of which occur in Aquinas's earlier writings, see my *Theories of Cognition* ch. 6. More recently, see Adriaenssen, *Representation and Scepticism* ch. 1.

Similarly, just a few years after Aquinas, Henry of Ghent confronts the skeptical worry that

One who does not perceive the essence and quiddity of a thing, but only its image, cannot know the thing. For one who has seen only a picture of Hercules does not know Hercules. A human being, however, perceives nothing of a thing, except only its image, that is, a species received through the senses, which is an image of the thing and not the thing itself.   (*Summa* 1.1 obj. 7)

His response is not to deny that species are perceived, but rather to distinguish two ways of perceiving a thing: as the object of cognition; and as the *ratio* (the basis or vehicle) of cognition (ad 7). See my translation in *Cambridge Translations* (pp. 95, 107), and my discussion in *Theories of Cognition*, pp. 221–9.

Scotus is another case where it is possible sometimes to take species as objects of cognition. See *Lectura* I.3.3 (Vatican edn. vol. 16, n. 392), where it is "perhaps better" to say that an act of thought is terminated not at the intelligible species but at "the object according to the intelligible being that it has in the actual thought." But see Richard Cross, *Duns Scotus's Theory of Cognition*, p. 166n, who rejects a mediation reading.

From the fourteenth century on, scholastic discussions are generally much more careful to avoid the suggestion that species are themselves perceived. See, for instance, Walter Burley, *De formis*, p. 71 [pars posterior]: "an intention is a likeness of a thing, representing the thing naturally and not directly represented to the power cognizing the thing through that intention. From this description it is apparent that the intention or species is not directly cognized and yet it leads to a cognition of the thing of which it is the intention." Or see Nicole Oresme's very careful discussion of whether every cognition is a cognition of itself (*Quaest. de anima* III.12), which distinguishes two kinds of signs: "those from whose objective cognition we arrive discursively at the cognition of other things, and these must be cognized ... Others are signs by means of which we cognize without argument, and these may even dispose the cognitive power. They serve as instrumental agents, and they need not be cognized" (p. 406).

Especially impressive is John Buridan's attack on those who would treat the species as an object of perception. His first argument against this view is what we might by now expect: "if the species of color existing in the perceiver were sensed or seen, it would follow that sight would judge these species just as certainly and evidently—indeed, more certainly and evidently—than it judges external colors. The consequent is false; therefore so is the antecedent" (*Quaest. de anima* II.17 n. 16). Whereas other authors rest content with taking the falsity of the consequent here for granted, Buridan goes on to argue for it at length (nn. 17–19).

Further examples might easily be adduced, not just from the Latin but also from the Arabic tradition (e.g., in Suhrawardī's theory of knowledge by presence). Here, though, let me skip ahead to sixteenth-century Europe. Not even a thoroughgoing skeptic like Francisco Sanches, in his *Quod nihil scitur* (1576), is willing to argue from the assumption of mediation. The closest he comes is when, arguing against the knowability of accidents, he writes that "not they themselves but only their images reach the mind" (p. 245). This is just a passing remark and, notably, it entails not that the images are the things we see but only that they are distorting intermediaries. It would not have been credible to say that we *see* the images, because this is something that no one at the time accepted.

One can see as much from the leading scholastic authorities of the era. Francisco Suárez, for instance, is very careful to deny that species are in any sense the objects of perception. As he says in the passage quoted in the lecture (p. 76), if species were perceived, they would be the things perceived "most evidently," which he takes for granted to be false. Hence they are grasped only indirectly, by inference from our acts of perception. Elsewhere he rejects the sort of move favored by some earlier scholastic authors (including sometimes Aquinas, e.g., at *Sent.* IV.49.2.7 ad 8), according to which species are perceived *qua* representation but not *qua* real being. Suárez writes: "To be representational is to be real...so if a species is seen as representing, then it is seen as having some being" (*De anima* disp. 5 q. 2 n. 15).

Suárez's Italian contemporary, Jacob Zabarella, is similarly clear that "we say that the real color is seen, not its species." It is precisely because species are not perceived that certain *idiotae homines* have denied their existence, "allowing nothing other than the real color to be seen by itself." But Zabarella insists that some such representational vehicle is required for distant objects to be perceived at all. The species is a real being, but it counts as visible only in the sense that the thing it represents is seen (*De rebus naturalibus* XXV.7, p. 1029).

These are all instances of what I call diaphanous views. Of course there is other, more familiar terminology. I prefer not to use the well-known term 'representationalism,' because that term is so variously understood that its use threatens to obscure more than it clarifies. (Adding to the confusion is the unfortunate fact that 'representationalism' has become widely used for an entirely different thesis in the philosophy of perception: the thesis that phenomenal properties can be accounted for wholly in terms of intentional properties.)

For diaphanousness, see G. E. Moore, "The Refutation of Idealism," p. 25. One often finds this view under the label 'transparency,' but in the context of the seventeenth century that usage is confusing, because there it usually serves to pick out precisely the opposite view: the doctrine that the contents of the mind are open to introspection. For my usage as well as for an exceptionally clear discussion of the surrounding issues, see Daniel Stoljar, "The Argument from Diaphanousness."

Simple versus Dual Views

Note 6 (p. 74). One basis for disputing the story I am telling about ideas in the later seventeenth century is to deny that these authors hold a dual view. With respect to both Descartes and Locke, the case has been made that their talk of *ideas* commits them to nothing more than *acts* of perception. This is to say that they hold simple rather than dual views. For me, this is a peripheral point, because, regardless of whether the view is dual or simple, what is radically new in their accounts is that it is mediated. Still, it is worth reviewing some of the literature on this issue.

In Descartes's case, I grant that there is a strong argument to be made that his ideas simply are themselves acts of thought. A particularly important passage occurs in the preface to the *Meditations*, where Descartes says that 'idea' is ambiguous between the material sense, according to which an idea is an "operation of the intellect," and an objective sense, according to which it is "the thing [*res*] represented by that operation" (VII: 8; see also VII: 232). This tells us that, at least sometimes, Cartesian ideas just are acts of thought. But what about when they are described as objects? Is this the objective sense? Are ideas, in this sense, distinct from the act of mind? Vere Chappell argues, to the contrary, that "these are not distinct entities at all" ("The Theory of Ideas," p. 179). See also Nadler, *Arnauld and the Cartesian Philosophy of Ideas*, pp. 126–30, who reaches a similar conclusion and cites much literature. This interpretation goes back to Arnauld, whose *On True and False Ideas* offers an extended argument, on textual and philosophical grounds, for developing Cartesianism along simple lines. I am not sure what to think of this issue, inasmuch as it seems to me quite difficult to reconcile Descartes's various ways of talking about ideas. Hence the only point on which I insist in this lecture is that he does unapologetically think of ideas as *forms* of thought (see note 2 here) and thinks of them as *objects* of thought. (But, for a vigorous dissent from even this much, see Andrew Pessin, "Mental Transparency.")

Locke has also been read sometimes as maintaining a simple view, on which his talk of ideas commits him to nothing more than mental acts. This is an interpretation that John Yolton has pushed to the fore (e.g., in *Perceptual Acquaintance* ch. 5) by focusing on passages where Locke describes ideas as perceptions (e.g., at *Essay* II.1.9: "ideas and perceptions being the same thing"). But this interpretation is much less plausible for Locke than for Descartes, because these seemingly clear texts lose their force once one sees that, in Locke, 'perception' sometimes refers to an act of perceiving and sometimes to the inner perceived object. For criticisms of Yolton's reading, see for instance Ayers, *Locke* vol. 1 ch. 7, Roland Hall, "*Idea* in Locke's Work," and Chappell, "Locke's Theory of Ideas," who notably rejects this reading of Locke even though he accepts it in Descartes's case.

Jonathan Bennett suggests that the best thing to say about Locke is that he simply does not take a stand on the ontology of ideas and on whether they are distinct from acts (*Learning from Six Philosophers* vol. 2: 10–12). One might—with even more justice, I think—say the same about Descartes, perhaps about Berkeley (see Keota Fields, *Berkeley*), and also about Hume, who seems to fluctuate considerably in how he thinks about ideas. Although Hume is generally thought of as having embraced some version of the Lockean notion of ideas, in fact his view is different in several respects. For one thing, the *Treatise* distinguishes between *ideas* and *impressions* and reserves 'idea' for the faint images left behind from initial impressions. Hence it is the term 'impression' that corresponds in many cases to what seventeenth-century authors had been describing as ideas. This usage is perhaps based on Malebranche's distinction between ideas and sensations (*Search after Truth* III.2.6, trans. p. 234), or on Locke's *Examination* of Malebranche, which draws particular attention to this terminology and puzzles over its meaning (nn. 38–42, in *Works* vol. 9: 232–7). In any event, the *Treatise* begins as if Hume is going to follow not Locke but instead Arnauld, by insisting on ideas as acts of the mind. For he tells us in the very first sentence that ideas and impressions are the two kinds of "perceptions" there are and then goes on to say, of impressions, "under this name I comprehend all our sensations, passions and emotions" (I.1.1, p. 1). This looks like the simple view. The pages that follow, however, make for a vertiginous ride—at least for a reader alert to the difference between the simple and the dual view—because Hume sometimes seems to adhere quite carefully to the simple view, and then other times falls headlong into formulations that require the dual view. For an instance of the latter, see *Treatise* I.1.2, pp. 7–8: "An impression first strikes upon the senses, and makes us perceive hot or cold." (But isn't the impression identical to the perception?) And *Treatise* I.4.2, p. 191: "Properly speaking, 'tis not our body we perceive, when we regard our limbs and members, but certain impressions, which enter by the senses." The corresponding pages in the *Enquiry* are similarly conflicted.

I suspect that these texts fluctuate so wildly because for Hume, given his concerns, the difference scarcely matters. Metaphysical niceties aside, the lessons Hume wants to draw can all be reached perfectly well on either the simple or the dual view. For here as in other cases, regardless of whether the view is simple or dual, it clearly is mediated, inasmuch as ideas and impressions serve as inner objects of sensation and thought. Hence Kenneth Winkler can remark that "Hume himself divided all the mind's objects (which he called *perceptions*) into impressions . . . and ideas" ("Perception and Ideas," p. 241).

Hume's case provides another cautionary example, then, of how we should be on our guard against the thought that because a view is simple it cannot count as mediated. (Compare Paul Hoffman on Nadler: "he seems to conclude at one point that Descartes is a direct realist simply on the grounds that Descartes thinks of ideas as acts of perception": "Direct Realism," p. 172.) The debate over simple versus dual views is interesting because it raises the question of just how parsimonious our ontology of the mind should be. This is the debate over whether we ought to "reify" ideas. If this is the issue we want to pursue, then it is better not to argue over the indeterminate texts we find in the post-scholastic era—as if all the great philosophers must have a well-developed view about every aspect of every topic they touch. If it is this debate over reification one wants, then it is the scholastic era we should be considering—a time when such ontological questions were discussed in loving detail. Or we might look at that most scholastic of post-scholastic authors, Leibniz, who expressly considers and rejects the possibility that an idea is merely an act of the mind. Instead, he says, it must be some sort of standing dispositional state within the mind, expressing the object of thought and ready to lead the mind to an actual contemplation of the thing ("What Is an Idea?" in *Phil. Papers*, pp. 207–8). In effect, Leibniz accepts Jonathan Bennett's challenge that we should postulate distinct entities only when we can conceive of their existing separately (*Learning from Six Philosophers* vol. 1: 9). Leibniz's response to the challenge is that we not only can but must so conceive of ideas, because we need ideas to endure between episodes of occurrent thought: "we are said to have an idea of a thing even if we are not thinking of it, provided that, when given the occasion, we can think of it" (*Phil. Papers*, p. 207). Elsewhere he writes: "If anyone wants to take ideas to be men's actual thoughts, he may; but he will be gratuitously going against accepted ways of speaking" (*New Essays* III.4, p. 300).

　Arguments of this same form can be found throughout scholastic texts. Paul of Venice, for instance, argues that the intelligible species must be really distinct from the act of thought, or otherwise there would be nothing remaining when the thought ceases (*Summa philosophiae naturalis*, De anima ch. 41 concl. 1). And if one looks closely one can see that the same point lies behind Locke's thinking: "whatever idea is in the mind is either an actual perception or else, having been an actual perception, is so in the mind that by the memory it can be made an actual perception again" (*Essay* I.4.21). (Here is a case where, as noted just above, 'perception' refers not to an act of perceiving but to a thing perceived.) Implicit in Locke, then, and explicit in Leibniz and many others, is a reason why ideas must be reified as entities distinct from occurrent mental acts: they must endure in between such acts. Of course, this reasoning might be disputed, as it already had been by critics of the species theory like Olivi and Ockham. But in any case the debate needs to go much deeper than simply throwing around 'reification' as a term of opprobrium.

Idea—Species—Verbum

Note 7 (p. 74). Descartes's role as the founder of the way of ideas is familiar enough. Jean-Robert Armogathe writes: "The cardinal importance in Descartes of the word *idée*/*idea* needs no demonstration: directly and indirectly (through Locke), Descartes determined the modern sense and use of the word" ("Sémantèse," p. 187). L. J. Beck writes that "it is notorious that Descartes's use of the word 'idea' is peculiar to himself" (*Metaphysics of Descartes*, p. 151). Roger Ariew and Marjorie Grene quote this as a typical remark, and then declare their intention to "challenge the standard reading" ("Ideas," p. 59). One thing they show is that the term 'idea' already had a wide nontechnical usage, both in French and in English, in something like Descartes's sense. Indeed, one need go no farther than the *Oxford English Dictionary* to find this passage from a 1616 English lexicon: "Idea, the form or figure of anything conceived in the mind." Ariew and Grene also show that the term was commonly used by late scholastic authors. (On this background, see also Norman Wells, "Descartes' *Idea*" and, for a marvelously detailed account of the term's pre-scholastic Latin origins, Hamesse, "*Idea*.") But Ariew and Grene's discussion of scholastic material serves mainly to highlight how thoroughly original Descartes's usage actually is. Indeed, they conclude that what Descartes did was to "borrow the term 'idea' but remove it almost altogether from its traditional context and import" ("Ideas," p. 75). On the significant development that Descartes's own usage of the word undergoes from his earliest work, see Armogathe, "Sémantèse."

This lecture argues that the change in terminology from 'species' to 'idea' is partly motivated by the desire to have a term that could designate the *object* of perception and thought. Clearly this was not the only consideration. In part, the term 'idea' owed its success to the fact that it was not a distinctively scholastic term of art, and so could safely be used by post-scholastic authors who sought to avoid technical school terminology, such as 'species.' In addition, many have taken the remark on 'idea' from the Third Replies (VII: 181), with its reference to the divine mind (see p. 74 of this lecture), to show that Descartes liked the unmistakably intellectual connotations of 'idea' and wanted to avoid the association of 'species' with the bodily organs of sense and imagination. (For this reading, see, e.g., Ayers, *Locke* vol. 1: 45; Ariew and Grene, "Ideas," pp. 75–6; and Peter Machamer and J. E. McGuire, *Descartes's Changing Mind*, p. 173.) No doubt this, too, is part of the story, especially given the context of this remark as a reply to Hobbes, who was focused on the sensory level. But Descartes knew full well that there were also wholly immaterial, intelligible species, inhering in the intellect, and it would have been easy enough to stipulate that species, in his system, are always forms of the immaterial mind. Moreover, as Ariew and Grene show ("Ideas," pp. 59, 60), the French term *idée* had some currency in Descartes's day as a term for sensory images, a usage that Descartes explicitly has to warn against. Judging from the historical context, then, it looks like the main justification for Descartes's usage was the unambiguous status of the word's referent as an object of thought and perception, a feature that Ariew and Grene also show to pervade late scholastic discussions (though they themselves do not highlight this point).

The full story of why, for Aquinas, God must have ideas, not species, is too subtle to take up in detail here, but in a nutshell Aquinas thinks that, if the divine ideas were species, then they would have to be forms actualizing God and hence would clearly violate the doctrine of divine simplicity. As objects of the divine mind, however, they can in a certain way (this is the subtle part) be outside of God (see esp. *Summa theol.* 1a 15.2 ad 1 and *Summa contra gentiles* I.54).

For another scholastic discussion of ideas that takes for granted their status as *objects* of thought rather than as *means by which*, see Ockham, *Ordinatio* I.35.5 ad arg. princ.: "An idea is not the basis [*ratio*] of cognizing, but is that which is cognized" (*Opera theol.* vol. 4: 507).

Another kind of inner object that plays a role in scholastic discussions is the *verbum*, which is often allowed to be an inner object of intellect. So, although Aquinas, for instance, denies that the sensible species is the thing seen or the intelligible object the thing thought, he allows the inner mental word or *verbum* to be the *primum intellectum*, the first thing understood (see e.g. *Quaestiones de potentia* 9.5c [= *On the Power of God*], *Quaestiones de veritate* 4.2c [= *Truth*], and my discussion in *Theories of Cognition*, pp. 254–71). Indeed, that mental word is the original model for the Berkeleian maxim that to be is to be perceived; in the case of the *verbum*, says Aquinas, *esse sit ipsum intelligi*—its existence is its being conceived (*Summa contra gentiles* IV.11, n. 11). Such views were not uncontroversial but were, at the level of intellect, quite common, for the reason that *something* is evidently required as the object of abstract thought, and yet everything outside the mind is supposed to be concrete and particular. That scholastic authors would identify the *verbum* as the inner object of thought is another mark of Augustine's influence, inasmuch as the *verbum* plays the central role in *De trinitate*'s attempt to find an inner trinity that could serve as a model for the divine persons.

Even Ockham, despite his fierce insistence on direct realism at the sensory level, was initially inclined to think that the objects of intellect must be something within the mind. Although he eventually gave this up, he always continued to conceive of propositional knowledge in terms of a higher order thought, such that, when we think about a proposition, we are thinking about our own complex thoughts (see, e.g., *Expositio in librum Perihermeneias* I, proem sct. 6, in *Opera phil.* vol. 2: 358). The general principle here is that thought must always be about something. Thus he writes:

> Take the common or confused cognition that corresponds to the spoken word 'man' or 'animal.' I ask: either something is understood by this cognition, or nothing is. It cannot be said that nothing is, since just as it is impossible for there to be a vision and for nothing to be seen, or for there to be love and nothing to be loved, so it is impossible for there to be a cognition and nothing to be cognized by that cognition.
>
> (*Opera phil.* vol. 2: 352–3; and see *Ordinatio* I.2.8, in *Opera theol.* vol. 2: 268)

Ockham's views about the nature of these intellectual objects changed dramatically over time and have been the subject of considerable study. See, for example, my *Theories of Cognition*, pp. 277–89, Claude Panaccio, *Ockham on Concepts*, and Susan Brower-Toland, "Ockham on Judgment."

As a term of art, *verbum* was *too* narrowly intellectual to be suitable for Descartes's purposes, as well as too theologically laden, in view of its associations with the divine Word. Still, the willingness of scholastic authors to treat the *verbum* as an inner object is quite closely analogous to what happens with ideas in the seventeenth century. Those authors, confronted with a similar dearth of plausible candidates fit to serve as external objects for sensation, made the analogous move of looking inward for their objects.

Introspection
Scholastic Conceptions of Self-Knowledge

Note 8 (p. 77). To get a clearer grip on the range of scholastic opinions regarding self-knowledge, we might distinguish these five increasingly strong positions:

(1) I have no privileged self-knowledge of my mind's states and operations.
(2) Self-knowledge is possible only indirectly, through inference from my knowledge of external things.
(3) Self-knowledge is possible by reflecting directly on occurrent acts of thought and perception.
(4) Self-knowledge is a constitutive part of my occurrent acts of thought and perception.
(5) Self-knowledge is immediate and prior to externally directed thought and perception.

These formulations are rough and capture just one dimension of the scholastic debate, but they help illuminate the relationship between self-knowledge and mediation.

The implausible-looking position (1), so far as I know, has had no defenders until recent years. Position (2) is the view that this lecture (pp. 76–7) ascribes to Aquinas: thought and perception are diaphanous even to oneself, and can be grasped only by inference. This does not collapse into (1) because it allows that I may have very extensive privileged knowledge of what is going on inside me just in virtue of having conscious awareness of the world around me and of thereby reaching the obvious conclusion that my mind is perceiving such and such and thinking such and such. Still, the nature of the privilege is rather thin, according to (2), since it comes only through an inference that, in principle, others can draw about me just as well as I can.

Positions (3)–(5) share the view, contrary to (1) and (2), that we are capable of grasping our inner psychological states directly. Where they disagree is on the dependence relation between such reflective cognition and our ordinary outward-directed cognition. According to (3), the outward-directed cognition is prior but can itself become an object through a higher order, inwardly aimed act of cognition. According to (4), the two acts are codependent, inasmuch as the ordinary outward-directed perception (say, of a blue house) contains a self-reflexive component: one is aware both of the house and of the character of one's perception. According to (5), the inwardly aimed act is prior: one perceives some sort of inner object and thereby perceives the external object that the inner object represents.

Position (5) corresponds to the sort of mediated theory of perception that one virtually never finds before the seventeenth century. It requires supposing not just that we have noninferential access to our inner states, but that it is only in virtue of grasping something inside us that we are able to grasp the external world at all. This is the implication, in the context of self-knowledge, of making ideas the "immediate" object of perception.

The most developed scholastic defense of (3) that I know of is found in Ockham (e.g., at *Quodlibet* I.14 and II.12). His position comes under attack from his contemporary Walter Chatton, who defends (4) with the remark that "the mind experiences something in two ways: it experiences it as an object, and it experiences it as a living subject experiences its own act... To experience in this [second] way is nothing other than a living subject's receiving its own act" (*Sent.* prol. q. 2 art. 5, p. 121). This seems to mean that the experience of self-awareness is not something over and above the experience of an external object but comes along with that experience, as a constitutive part. For the debate between Ockham and Chatton, see Mikko Yrjönsuuri, "The Structure of Self-Consciousness," Brower-Toland, "Medieval Approaches to Consciousness," and Sonja Schierbaum, "Subject Experience."

Both Ockham and Chatton reflect a more Augustinian strand in the scholastic debate, one that gives much greater scope to self-knowledge than does a view like Aquinas's. (For Augustine's views, see the following note.) A view in the vicinity of Ockham's can already be found in the late thirteenth century, in Matthew of Aquasparta, who distinguishes between the initial and the ultimate stage of cognition. Initially, the objects of cognition are external: "if we are speaking of the initial and inchoate stage of knowledge or cognition, then I say without doubt that the soul can intuit neither itself nor the dispositions existing within itself, nor can the first act of cognition be of itself or the things that are in it." But after this initial and outwardly directed act, the mind "by a certain spiritual conversion... can, through its direct attention, discern and intuit itself, its internal states, and the things that are internal to it" (*Quaestiones disputatae de cognitione* q. 5, p. 304). This explicitly embraces (3) and rejects the competing views, insisting, against (1), that the soul can grasp its own states and, against (2), that it does so directly, but that its doing so depends on a prior outwardly directed act—which runs against (4) and (5). For Aquasparta and similar late thirteenth-century views in Olivi and Roger Marston, see François-Xavier Putallaz, *La connaissance de soi*.

Olivi expressly rejects (2), like Aquasparta, on the grounds that "through this way we could never be certain that we exist, live, and understand. For although we may be certain that these acts arise from a certain power and exist in a certain subject, how do we know through this that *we* are that subject and that that power is *ours*?" ("Impugnatio" art. 19, n. 10). Olivi, however, defends not (3) but rather (4), insisting that "there is no object or act that it can actually know or consider without its always there knowing and sensing that it is the subject of the act by which it knows and considers those things" (*Summa* II.76 [vol. 3: 146]). See Christopher Martin, "Self-Knowledge and Cognitive Assent"; Brower-Toland, "Olivi on Consciousness"; and Christian Rode, "Olivi on Representation." More recently, Rode has published *Zugänge zum Selbst*, a comprehensive discussion of changing conceptions of self-knowledge from Aquinas to Descartes.

Some recent discussions of this topic suppose that scholastic theories of knowledge can be understood as theories of consciousness. For a very developed statement of this view, see Brower-Toland, "Olivi on Consciousness," pp. 150–3. Her discussion makes a persuasive case that type-4 theories, that is, theories such as Olivi's, which adopt position (4), are in effect theories of consciousness. But it should not be supposed that rival scholastic theories of self-knowledge are therefore rival theories of consciousness. In particular, theories that adopt position (2)—type-2 theories—can scarcely be understood as supposing that consciousness is inferential. Rather those theories are best understood as arguing that in normal cases consciousness is not to be thought of as *self*-consciousness but as consciousness *of external things*. Whatever that is, it is not a matter of self-knowledge. One might similarly wonder whether Ockham's version of (3) is a theory of phenomenal consciousness in the usual philosophical sense or a theory of a more elevated introspective awareness, available only to beings capable of reflection.

Although this lecture (pp. 76–7) associates the mediated position (2) with Aquinas, there are disagreements over how to characterize Aquinas's position. For my own reading, see my *Thomas Aquinas on Human Nature* ch. 11, but that should be compared with Putallaz, *Le sens de la réflexion*, Deborah Brown, "Aquinas's Missing Flying Man," and Therese Scarpelli Cory, *Aquinas on Human Self-Knowledge*.

It is always tempting to think of Aquinas's view as the standard scholastic view, but this is a domain where that assumption is questionable. Here as in many other places, it is in fact unclear how one might even decide what counts as the standard scholastic view. Even so, other defenders of (2) are not hard to find. Predictably, one finds it among Thomists such as Thomas of Sutton (on whom see Putallaz, *Connaissance de soi*). One finds much the same view, moreover, in Scotus:

according to this mode of exposition, the intellect is moved by imaginable objects, and once these have been cognized, it can from these cognize the common natures [*rationes*], both immaterial and material, and by so reflecting it cognizes itself under the nature [*ratio*] common to itself and imaginable things. It cannot, however, immediately [*statim*] understand itself, without understanding anything else, because it cannot immediately (*statim*) be moved by itself, on account of its necessary order, in this state, to imaginables.

(*Ordinatio* II.3.2.1 [Vatican edn. vol. 7: n. 293])

Classification is tricky, however, because it is not always clear whether an author means to say that only the soul's very nature is not available to direct introspection, which was fairly uncontentious, or that even the soul's *acts* are unavailable to direct introspection. Position (2), as I understand it, is committed even to the second of these claims.

A clear statement of (2) in this strong sense, from the mid-fourteenth century, can be found in John of Mirecourt, who defends the conclusion that "no intellection or cognition of the soul can be distinctly cognized by the soul through itself" (*Sent.* q. 5 concl. 4). Here he makes the argument that self-knowledge, like all knowledge, requires a likeness of the thing grasped. But when the soul thinks about something, the thought is a likeness of what it is thinking about, not a likeness of itself (p. 430). Mirecourt gladly embraces the implication of his position: "it can naturally happen that the soul cognizes an external object without actually cognizing anything interior" (p. 430). Nicholas of Autrecourt also finds something like (2) in Bernard of Arezzo, to whom he ascribes the view that "our intellect does not have intuitive awareness of its own acts" because "every intuitive awareness is clear, but the awareness that our intellect has of its own acts is not clear" (first letter, n. 11). Bernard's original works are not extant.

Position (2) endures into the fifteenth century through leading figures such as Paul of Venice, who argues at length for the indirectness of self-knowledge: "we cognize the sensible prior to the sensation, because we cognize the sensation only because we cognize the color" (*Summa philosophiae naturalis*, De anima, ch. 6 concl. 1; see also ch. 41 concl. 3). A key part of this discussion involves refuting the suggestion that species, if they are to serve as representations, must themselves be immediate objects of cognition. In the sixteenth century it is telling that the Jesuits—committed as they are to following the *opinio communis*—likewise line up behind (2). This lecture (p. 76) quotes from Suárez (on whom see also Yrjönsuuri, "Self-Knowledge and Renaissance Skeptics"). Another instance is the Coimbran commentary on the *De anima*:

Our soul cannot conceive of itself primarily and immediately, but is led to grasp itself through the perception of other things. For first it conceives of that whose species it has drawn from the senses (e.g., the nature of humanity), then it reflects on its act and perceives it, and from that it cognizes both the image and the power from which it elicited the act. (Collegium Conimbricense, *Comm. De an.* III.8.7.2)

Or consider Gervaise Waim, from early in the sixteenth century: "If a soul intuits its acts it does not follow that by virtue of that intuitive notion it can cognize all the truths cognizable concerning such acts. It suffices that by virtue of the intuitive notion of its acts it judges that it cognizes this object, hates this one, and loves this one" (quoted in Broadie, *Notion and Object*, p. 87). Waim's point seems to be that reflection is quite limited in its scope: we grasp that we hold a particular propositional attitude toward a particular object, but the many other "truths cognizable concerning such acts" are unavailable to reflection.

On this sort of view, reflection is not like a reveal-code command that toggles between world and mind, showing us the mind's operations directly. Instead, the species is a diaphanous vehicle for grasping external things and provides only a thin and inferential basis for self-knowledge. As the Coimbrans put it, "that which is understood through its proper species is understood *directly*. Experience testifies, however, that we come to a knowledge of our own soul only through a *reflective* act, by inferring [*arguendo*] one thing from another" (*Comm. De an.* III.8.7.2). Reflection is thus an inferential activity, not a matter of literal introspection. This is of course radically different from the mediated view—position (5)—that only a century later would prevail, according to which the species or idea has itself become the direct object of perception, a position that makes self-knowledge prior and requires that our knowledge of the *external* world be achieved through inference.

Such disputes over self-knowledge quickly become entangled with the debate over the mediation of species. Durand of Saint-Pourçain, for instance, wielded a more Augustinian conception of self-knowledge in order to argue that, if there were species serving as representational vehicles, then they would inevitably be perceived:

the intellect, since it is a reflexive power, cognizes itself and the things that are in it with certainty and as it were [*quasi*] experientially. Thus we experience ourselves to think and to have within us a principle by which we think. Therefore if there were some such species within our intellect, it is evident that we could with certainty cognize that it is within us.   (*Sent.* [3rd vers.] II.3.6 n. 13)

Like almost all his contemporaries, however, Durand takes for granted that this conclusion is absurd. So, by rejecting (2) in favor of a stronger position on self-knowledge, he is able to make trouble for the theory of species. But that this line of argument might push him all the way to (5)—to the view that we do have species and they are the immediate objects of perception and thought—seems never to have occurred to Durand. So here we have Augustinianism, without mediation. The gulf looks almost unbridgeable from here to the opening words of Locke's *Essay* Book II: "Every man being conscious to himself that he thinks, and that which his mind is employed about while thinking being the ideas that are there, it is past doubt that men have in their minds several ideas."

Augustine on Self-Knowledge

Note 9 (p. 78). The importance of Augustine in the story I am telling has been stressed by others. Gareth Matthews, for instance, writes as follows:

The picture of human beings as having, in this way, both an 'inside' and an 'outside' is so commonplace, so (as it may seem to us) commonsensical that we find it hard to realize how strikingly modern it is. But to appreciate its modernity one need only cast about for statements of it earlier than Descartes. One does find interesting anticipations of it in Augustine, but not much earlier, and not much between the time of Augustine and that of Descartes.   ("Consciousness and Life," p. 25)

Myles Burnyeat cites Matthews's paper approvingly and concurs: "So far as I can discover, the first philosopher who picks out as something we know what are unambiguously subjective states, and picks them out as giving certain knowledge because they are subjective states, is Augustine . . . in this as in other things a precursor of Descartes" ("Idealism and Greek

Philosophy," p. 28). Both scholars cite *Contra academicos* III.11.26, where Augustine argues, against the skeptic, that we can have knowledge at least of appearances.

I would not myself want to claim that Augustine is breaking new conceptual ground in articulating the notion of our "inside" or "subjective states." This concept is, I think, clearly enough present in Cyrenaic and skeptical texts (see note 4 to this lecture) and fairly evident in Democritus, and thus part of the overt background to Aristotle's theory of perception, as Lecture Three argues. But what is novel in Augustine is the emphasis he puts on these notions. His own version of the *cogito* is itself an instance of his inward orientation (see, e.g., *De trinitate* X.10.14, XV.12.21; *On Free Choice* II.3; *City of God* XI.26) and is, for him, the leading example of how the skeptic is to be refuted:

There are two kinds of things that are known: those that the mind perceives through the senses of the body, and those that it perceives through itself. These [skeptical] philosophers have babbled on and on against the senses of the body; but they have been utterly unable to cast doubt upon the mind's most firm perceptions, through its very self, of things that are true, such as the aforesaid *I know that I live*.   (*De trinitate* XV.12.21)

The reason why these inner states loom so large in Augustine, I believe, is that he has such a robust conception of self-knowledge: "The mind knows nothing so well as that which is present to itself, and nothing is more present to the mind than it is to itself" (*De trinitate* XIV.4.7). This is radically different from the sort of diaphanous views that prevailed both before and after him. (For recent discussion of the first-person case in Augustine, see Blake Dutton, *Augustine and Academic Skepticism* ch. 11.)

Yet despite this inward orientation, Augustine clearly does not defend a mediated theory of perception. The things known fall into two kinds (as quoted in the previous paragraph), inward and outward, and he shows not the slightest temptation to say that we get at outer things through a more immediate grasp of inner things. His most careful treatment of these issues comes in *De trinitate* XI, which stresses that what we see in ordinary cases is the form of external bodies, not the form impressed on the sense organ:

We do not by the same sense distinguish the form of the body that we see and the form that arises from it in the sense of the one who sees, because they are so conjoined that there is no room for distinguishing them. But through reason we conclude that it would have been utterly impossible to sense anything unless some likeness of the perceived body arose in our sense.   (*De trinitate* XI.2.3)

In ordinary veridical cases, then, we do not see the inner species but infer through reason that it must be there. It is striking, however, that Augustine does not categorically dismiss here the possibility of our seeing the inner form (or species or likeness). It is rather that the inner form is ordinarily eclipsed by the external form. In illusory cases, however, we *do* see the inner form. Hence the very next section of *De trinitate* discusses afterimages and double vision: two cases where we are able to see the inner form.

It might look as if Augustine's approach were disjunctive in the way in which some later scholastic accounts clearly are. But I think Augustine supposes that vision works in funda-mentally the same way in veridical and nonveridical cases. In each sort of case there is an inner likeness, and that likeness is in some sense available to the perceiver. It plays the same role in each case. The difference is that, in veridical cases, the inner likeness makes us see the external object, whereas if there is no external object then we see just the likeness. Speaking of the inner forms that become manifest in afterimages, Augustine writes that "this form was also there while we were seeing, and it was even clearer and more distinct. But it was so conjoined with the form of the thing we saw that it could not be discerned at all" (*De trinitate* XI.2.4). Again, it is as if the inner species were eclipsed in veridical cases by the external object. Why it seems natural to Augustine to describe the situation in these terms—rather than to say that in both cases the inner form is the immediate object of perception—is not at all clear from his discussion. My suspicion is that something like the Fidelity Constraint, as described in this lecture (p. 90), makes it seem plausible to say that in the veridical case we see external things, whereas in illusory cases we see the inner form. But in any event it is striking that, even in Augustine, the mediated theory of perception does not seem a salient possibility.

Although Augustine is not the source for the seventeenth-century rise of mediated theories, his influence more generally on the turn to a first-personal philosophical perspective is clear. For his influence on Descartes in particular, see Gareth Matthews, *Thought's Ego*, and Stephen Menn, *Descartes and Augustine*. His influence on Malebranche is even more pervasive and explicit. And it is notable that, when Arnauld asserts the mind's self-reflexivity, he explicitly invokes the *De trinitate* as an inspiration (*True and False Ideas* ch. 6, trans. p. 25).

Arnauld's Simple but Mediated View

Note 10 (p. 78). My understanding of Arnauld is controversial in several ways. First, in conceiving of the dispute with Malebranche as largely revolving around the ontological question of whether ideas are something more than acts of perception, I am essentially embracing Malebranche's side of the debate. (See too, on this ontological dimension, Marc Hight, *Idea and Ontology*, pp. 72–3.) Arnauld, in contrast, takes himself to be offering an importantly improved epistemic story. In arguing that Arnauld's view is every bit as mediated as Malebranche's, I am, again, taking Malebranche's side (see, e.g., the passages quoted in Nadler, *Arnauld and the Cartesian Philosophy of Ideas*, p. 103). This was also the verdict of Thomas Reid: "what he [Arnauld] had given up with one hand he takes back with the other" (*Essays on the Intellectual Powers* II.13, in *Works* vol. 1: 297a).

Among recent commentators, Arnauld's defense of the simple view has generally been treated as decisive evidence that he rejected the mediated view of perception, despite his explicit avowals of mediation. For a reading of this sort, see the extensive discussion in Nadler, on whose account of Arnauld "external things are perceived directly, without the mediation of any third thing" (*Arnauld and the Cartesian Philosophy of Ideas*, p. 113). Nadler takes Arnauld to endorse mediation merely as a *façon de parler* rather than as something he strictly believes in; and he takes the mind's self-reflection to be something the mind does *in addition* to its direct perception of external objects. Thus Nadler writes: "Every perception, in addition to being the perception of some object, also has itself (an idea-perception) as its object" (p. 119). For an extended critical attack on Nadler's view, in accord with my own reading, see Hoffman, "Direct Realism."

Once we understand that there is conceptual room for a view that is both simple and mediated, it is hard to see why we should dismiss Arnauld's apparently quite sincere embrace of Cartesian mediation. To dismiss those remarks requires us to suppose that he postulates, alongside our direct awareness of external objects, a separate reflexive awareness of our perceptual acts. But if we are to read him in that way, then he himself becomes vulnerable to the objection he put to Malebranche: we never find "the least trace" of any sort of reflexive perception, distinct from our perception of external bodies. So, if perception is, as Arnauld thinks, "essentially reflexive upon itself," it had better not be something that happens alongside our perception of external things; it had better be the way in which we perceive external things. And this is in fact what Arnauld says, as quoted in this lecture (p. 78), when he insists, first, that "I see this intelligible sun immediately by means of the virtual reflection that I have of my perception" and then immediately adds that "this same perception in which I see this intelligible sun makes me see, at the same time, the material sun that God has created" (*True and False Ideas* ch. 11, trans. p. 52). There are not two perceptions here in sequence, but one perception that is at once reflexive and, "by means of" such reflexivity, directed outward, at material things.

In thinking about the details of this account, it is important to consider what exactly Arnauld means when he says that thought is "reflexive upon itself." Such talk of the intellect's ability to reflect upon itself runs all throughout scholastic discussions, but in these earlier contexts it does not always mean that an act of thought literally reflects back on itself as an object, as if in a mirror. Ockham, for instance, argues that "properly and strictly speaking there is no reflexive intellection" (*Ordinatio* prol. 1.1 [*Opera theol.* vol. 1: 65]) and that self-knowledge involves instead a higher order act of thinking about a distinct lower order act. Ockham still refers to this as reflection, but it counts as such, he says, only in a loose sense. Arnauld, in contrast, makes it clear that an act of thought literally has itself as an object. For when he asserts that "thought or perception is essentially reflexive upon itself," he goes on to say that, "beyond this reflection, which one could call virtual, and which one finds in all our perceptions, there is another, more explicit reflection, through which we examine our perception through another perception, as everyone can easily verify" (ch. 6, trans. p. 25). This explicit reflection is a higher order introspection of our thoughts. But Arnauld wants to distinguish such occasional efforts from the constant "virtual" way in which thoughts are self-reflexively aware of themselves.

Such literal self-reflexivity deserves more attention than it has received. It is invoked by Descartes, for instance, in the Seventh Replies, in response to Bourdin's suggestion that the distinctive feature of thought is "to intuit and consider your thought by a reflexive act, so that when you think, you know and consider that you are thinking (and this truly is to be conscious and to have consciousness of some act)" (VII: 533–4). Bourdin goes on to say that, although this thesis is without doubt true, it is wholly unoriginal. Descartes, however, flatly denies its truth, seeing in the thesis the postulation of a wholly unnecessary second act: on such a view "it is not sufficient for the mind to think; it is further required that it should think that it is thinking, by means of a reflexive act" (VII: 559). Although Bourdin speaks of this act as reflection, it is so only in Ockham's weak sense. Descartes rejects such an account and instead advocates literal reflection: "the initial thought through which we become aware of something does not differ from the second thought through which we become aware that we were aware of it" (VII: 559). The first thought, then, is reflexively self-aware in the strict sense: it is aware *of its very act*. So if Descartes's own view is simple, as Arnauld and many modern commentators suppose, then this passage becomes important to understanding how his view can yet be mediated. (Also relevant here is *Passions of the Soul* I.19.)

For another example of this sort of approach, see Jean Pierre de Crousaz in the early eighteenth century: "[thought] is its own immediate object, and by that self-consciousness it represents to itself at the same time things different from itself" (as quoted in Yolton, *Perceptual Acquaintance*, p. 116).

Once one sees what literal self-reflection involves, questions arise over whether it is intelligible, or whether Ockham might have been right to rule it out as incoherent. One might suppose that this sort of literal self-reflection, rather than serving as a means of grasping the external world, would instead engender an endless feedback loop that lacks any representational content. Presumably the act's entire representational content cannot be self-reflexive, because then it would seem to have the structure of a dog's chasing its own tail: the act would be thinking about its own thinking about its own thinking . . . If that is possible at all, it is at any rate not how we ought to analyze our everyday acts of thought. So perhaps a view like this needs to distinguish, within a single act, between two components: its outwardly directed representational content; and its self-reflexive content, which is aimed at that outwardly directed component. (A view like this has recently been propounded by Uriah Kriegel, *Subjective Consciousness*.) This makes the view more intelligible, but then the question arises of whether we have abandoned literal reflexivity and in effect moved to a two-level view, like Ockham's.

Supposing that we can somehow hold on to literal self-reflexivity, a further question of priority arises: is the outwardly directed component prior or posterior to the self-reflexive component? Arnauld (as quoted in this lecture at p. 78) seems to make the self-reflexive component prior, not temporally but causally, inasmuch as he says that it is "by means of" the reflexive awareness of the idea (act) that one grasps the external thing. Hence he takes position (5) out of the five positions listed in note 8. But, again, questions of coherence arise, this time of a chicken-and-egg kind. If we say that the self-reflexive component is prior in some explanatory sense, then the question arises of what it is we are self-reflexively grasping. The answer is supposed to be: the externally directed idea component of the act of thought. But to say that self-reflection is *prior* makes it hard to understand how the externally directed idea can be available to be grasped, because that is the component that is supposed to be *posterior* to self-reflection.

The unfamiliarity of the self-reflexive account helps to bring such puzzles to the fore, but worries of this general kind can be raised for mediated views in general. Consider Locke. The immediate objects of perception, Locke says, are ideas, and in virtue of perceiving ideas we perceive external things. But if the perceiving of ideas is to be prior, then of course the idea must already be present. And if the idea is already present, then we can ask what it represents, and presumably the answer is that it already represents external things. But then it looks like our mental representation of external objects, via ideas, must in fact be prior to our perceiving those ideas. In that case, however, it is not clear what we gain by perceiving our own ideas, since we *already* have the ideas in virtue of which our cognitive faculties are representing external objects. I do not mean to suggest that there is no way out of this puzzle. On the contrary, several solutions suggest themselves immediately. But I see no sign that these difficulties were grappled with during the seventeenth century. The puzzle is the fruit of a novel way of conceiving of cognition, via the mediation of ideas, and it should be no surprise that such innovations brought in their wake further, unnoticed complications.

The Argument from Illusion

Note 11 (p. 79). Although the argument from illusion is very prominent in ancient skepticism and other Hellenistic schools, it is notably not taken to establish that perception is mediated by inner objects. Even the Epicureans, despite their insistence that "all impressions are true," think that illusions and in general sensory variation can be explained in terms of the senses' accurately detecting the different "images" that external objects generate in the external world. These images are not properties of the object, and hence the same object can give off a variety of images with contradictory properties. The senses of variously placed individuals accurately detect that variety. For a particularly full discussion of this, see Sextus Empiricus's account of Epicurus's views at *Against the Logicians* I.206–10 (= Long and Sedley, *Hellenistic Philosophers* 16E). See also Augustine, *De trinitate* XI.1.4.

Appeals to illusion remain commonplace in scholastic texts. See, for example, Siger of Brabant, *Impossibilia* II, which describes supporters of such an argument as "believing that everything that appears in any vision is a mere appearance" (*Écrits*, pp. 74–5). A mere appearance (*apparentia tantum*) would seem to be an inner object of sensation, but Siger denies that one can generalize from bad cases to all cases. As note 21 here discusses, William Crathorn in the fourteenth century is the unusual scholastic author who *is* willing to generalize from a bad case to all cases, and hence to defend mediation.

Hans Thijssen ("Quest for Certain Knowledge," pp. 212–16) shows that many of the illusions commonly discussed in scholastic texts are ultimately due to Aristotle. Others, particularly some of the more elaborate illusions discussed by Peter Auriol, have their origins in the perspectivist tradition, which runs from Ibn al-Haytham (Alhazen) through Witelo and

Roger Bacon (see Katherine Tachau, *Vision and Certitude*, pp. 91–8). Still others, such as an oar bent in the water and the apparent colors on a pigeon's neck, appear in Cicero, *Academica* II.7.19 and II.25.79. For a great many historical references to oars and sticks in water, see Stephen McCluskey, *Nicole Oresme on Light, Color, and the Rainbow*, p. 410 n. 29.

Malebranche's version of the argument from illusion comes in the context of a description of what Arnauld is committed to, but it seems clear that Malebranche takes the claim to be common ground between them; see also *Search after Truth* III.2.1, p. 217. For further discussion of this line of argument in Malebranche, see Nadler, *Malebranche and Ideas*, pp. 79–92. For Arnauld's reply, see Nadler, *Arnauld and the Cartesian Philosophy of Ideas*, pp. 130–1. For the argument later in Hume, see *Treatise* I.4.2, pp. 210–11.

A. J. Ayer is the best known modern proponent of the argument from illusion, up through his later work, for instance "Has Austin Refuted the Sense-Datum Theory?" The leading recent critic is Michael Huemer, *Skepticism and the Veil of Perception*. See also John Searle, *Seeing Things as They Are*. Searle is on firm ground when he contends that mediation is the most distinctive and far-reaching philosophical doctrine of post-scholastic thought. But he hardly gives a satisfying answer to the central question of this lecture—why mediated views became ascendant—when he invokes the argument from illusion. For, given that Searle thinks the argument from illusion is itself obviously flawed, his explanation for why philosophers from Descartes forward embraced mediation amounts to little more than the suggestion that these dead old guys were not very smart.

Disjunctivism

Note 12 (p. 81). Going back to the thirteenth century, Peter John Olivi is very clear that, in cases of veridical perception, there is no need for any representational vehicle other than the act of cognition itself: "when an object on its own sufficiently presents itself to the cognitive attention, it is not necessary that it be represented to it through another; nevertheless it is indeed necessary that the actual cognition of it be an actual and cognitive representation of it, since without this it would not be a cognition" (*Summa* II.74 [vol. 3: 130]). For Olivi's account of memory, where species are required as inner objects, see Juhana Toivanen, *Perception and the Internal Senses*, esp. p. 310: "Olivian memory species are images, similitudes, or representations of external objects. They are not formal or efficient causes of cognitive acts. Rather they serve as the objects of intentional cognitive acts ... Their role in the cognitive process of imagining and remembering is similar to the role of external objects in perceptual acts." See also Adriaenssen, *Representation and Scepticism* ch. 2.

As with Olivi, Scotus's form of disjunctivism does not arise out of worries about illusion but rather from various nonillusory cases where we represent things to be as they are not: cases of memory, imagination, and abstraction. It is not until Peter Auriol that cases of illusion take on a special prominence in these discussions. Scotus's grasp of the intuitive–abstractive distinction is not easy to understand, but interpretation is helped by the fact that he sets out the distinction in quite a few different places. See *Lectura* II.3.2.2 (Vatican edn. vol. 18: n. 285); *Ordinatio* I.1.1.2 (Vatican edn. vol. 2: nn. 34–6); *Ordinatio* II.3.2.2 (Vatican edn. vol. 7: n. 321; trans. Hyman, Walsh, and Williams, *Philosophy in the Middle Ages*, pp. 581–2); *Quodlibet* VI, nn. 18–19; *Quaest. meta.* VII.15, in *Opera phil.* vol. 4: n. 18. I discuss Scotus's cognitive theory at greater length in the chapter "Cognition" in the *Cambridge Companion to Scotus*. For more details, see Cross, *Duns Scotus's Theory of Cognition* ch. 2. Broad surveys of the intuitive–abstractive distinction can be had in Sebastian Day, *Intuitive Cognition* and Tachau, *Vision and Certitude*. For a helpful discussion of some late scholastic views, see Alexander Broadie, *Notion and Object*, pp. 38–49.

As far as I can find, I am the first to understand the debate over intuitive and abstractive cognition as centrally concerned with the philosophy of perception and, more specifically, with disjunctive approaches to perception. I do not mean to suggest, however, that the debate concerns only this. Inasmuch as the distinction is applied not only to the sensory level, but also to the intellectual level, another strand of the argument concerns the objects of abstract, conceptual thought, and so becomes entangled with the debate over universals. John Boler has suggested that the intuitive–abstractive distinction arose initially out of earlier debates over our intellectual grasp of particulars as opposed to universals ("Intuitive and Abstractive Cognition," p. 463). Aquinas, for instance, had denied any intellectual grasp of material individuals, whereas many of his contemporaries had insisted on this possibility. Boler may be right about the origins of the distinction. But it hardly looks as if the fourteenth-century debate is centrally concerned with this issue. The more pressing issue, as this lecture discusses, is what to do with the apparent grasp of individuals that do not exist, or at least do not exist the way they seem to exist. The centrality of such cases seems to have led many commentators to suppose that the intuitive–abstractive distinction is centrally concerned with the skeptical problems that might arise from illusion. To be sure, the threat of skepticism lurks throughout these discussions. But to think of it as the *central* issue seems to reflect our modern preoccupations rather than to represent accurately the historical debate.

That the intuitive–abstractive distinction might be used to mark off a species-free zone of intuitive cognition was obvious from early on. Even in Scotus there are passages that suggest this possibility, though in fact he seems to retain species throughout his cognitive theory (see my "Cognition," pp. 298–300). Gerard of Bologna also notes that "someone could set out the nature of intuitive cognition by saying that it is a cognition by which a thing is cognized entirely immediately, not mediated by a species, exemplar, image, or object other than the thing itself" (*Quodlibet* II.6, n. 17). But Gerard himself, despite being opposed to species, rejects this view (see David Piché, "Gerard of Bologna and Hervaeus Natalis on the Intuition of Non-Existents"). Other places where such a view is considered and rejected include Francis of Meyronnes, *Tractatus de notitia intuitiva* nn. 1–8 and John Rodington, *Sent.* prol. q. 2 (in Tweedale, *John of Rodynton*, p. 315).

A view of this kind is expressly defended by Gregory of Rimini, according to whom "an intuitive cognition is a simple cognition by which, formally, something is immediately cognized in itself, whereas abstractive is a simple cognition by which, formally, something is cognized in some representative medium" (*Sent.* I.3.3 art. 1 [vol. 1: 389–90]). This makes it look as if Rimini rejected species entirely in the case of intuitive cognition, but that is in fact not his view. Rimini thinks that species play a causal role in intuitive cognition but do not interfere with the external object's being cognized "immediately in itself," whereas in abstractive cognition—whether this be a dream, a memory, imagination, or certain kinds of illusions—the species serves as the immediate object (see *Sent.* I.3.1 concl. 2 [vol. 1: 306–9]; *Sent.* II.7.3, and Tachau, *Vision and Certitude*, pp. 358–68). The view is thus disjunctive in that it postulates fundamentally different objects in the two kinds of cases. Rimini's position is followed verbatim by Peter of Ailly, *Tractatus de anima* ch. 11 and *Sent.* I, d. 2 q. 1 art. 1 (1490 edn., quire g4vb, at L). See Joël Biard, "Présence et représentation chez Pierre d'Ailly."

Auriol's Apparent Being

Note 13 (p. 82). Peter Auriol's revisionary understanding of the intuitive–abstractive distinction as a phenomenal difference in how the object appears amounts to something much like the distinction that Malebranche would later draw between *sentiment* and *idée*, or Hume between impression and idea (see note 6 to this lecture). Marilyn Adams points out the similarity with Hume (*William Ockham* 1: 501) but wrongly applies the comparison to Scotus's version of the distinction, which is quite different. Not surprisingly, given how much Auriol transforms Scotus's original, he does not much like the terminology of 'abstractive' and 'intuitive,' describing it as *non multum proprium* and suggesting that abstractive cognition "can more suitably be called quasi-imaginary" and intuitive "quasi-visual and quasi-intuitive" (*Scriptum* proem 2, n. 154; trans. Pasnau, *Cambridge Translations*, p. 218).

Auriol's full account lists four distinctive features of intuitive cognition: directness, presence, actualizing, and existence-positing (nn. 103–11; trans. pp. 205–7). The last three of these are summarized in the passage quoted in this lecture (p. 82). The directness requirement might suggest the sort of view described in the previous note, on which only abstractive cognition involves species. But Auriol rejects species across the board, both in intuitive and in abstractive cases. He makes, in particular, the familiar arguments against species that they would veil our grasp of things in the world (see e.g. *Scriptum* d. 3 q. 3 [sct. 14] n. 31, trans. p. 225 at 5a; *Scriptum* d. 27 q. 2 art. 2 [ms. Vat. Borgh. 329, ff. 301–2]). And in the later books of his *Sentences* commentary he makes it explicit that he rejects the species theory in favor of a simple account: "a species and an intellection, both in us and in the angels, are really the same as an act of thought" (*Sent.* II d. 11 q. 3 art. 1 [Rome edn. vol. 2: 127bF]). For discussion of Auriol's views on species, see Russell Friedman, "Act, Species, and Appearance," Adriaenssen, "Peter John Olivi and Peter Auriol on Conceptual Thought," and Lukáš Lička, "Perception and Objective Being."

For discussion of Auriol's intuitive–abstractive distinction, see Philotheus Boehner, "*Notitia intuitiva*"; Tachau, *Vision and Certitude*, pp. 104–12; and Friedman, "Peter Auriol," who aptly remarks that "what is central to Auriol's distinction between intuitive and abstractive cognition is the character of the cognition as it appears to us. The distinction between them is phenomenologically determined" (§4). For a broad overview of Auriol's cognitive theory, focused on the intellectual level, see Onorato Grassi, *Intenzionalità*. For a still broader overview of these debates across the fourteenth century, see Tachau, *Vision and Certitude*.

Note 14 (p. 83). Although Auriol's theory is hard to understand, some parts of it are clear enough. It is clear, for instance, that he defines cognition by the presence of apparent being:

> If nothing were to appear objectively to the mind, then no one would say that he is thinking about anything— on the contrary, he would be in a state like someone asleep ... Likewise if, through a picture hanging on a wall, the depicted Caesar were to appear to the wall, then the wall would be said to cognize Caesar. Therefore it clearly appears that there is nothing more to the formal character of thinking, or cognizing in general, than to have something present as an appearance [*per modum apparentis*].
>
> (*Scriptum* dist. 35 q. 1 [ms. Vat. Borgh. 329, f. 359rb-va])

It is also clear that apparent beings are *somehow* the same as external objects. As Friedman carefully puts it, "this *esse apparens* is not a representation of the thing with its own real being; rather it *is* the thing itself merely placed in another type of existence. The *esse apparens* of a sensed object is merely that object as sensed" ("Peter Auriol," §3).

Yet given the obscurity of Auriol's account, it is no surprise that recent commentators have reached very different conclusions about the details of his view, and in particular have disagreed over how this sameness is to be understood. On one line of interpretation, apparent beings, at least in illusory cases, exist within the soul. According to Tachau, for instance, Auriol's appearances "have no extramental existence" (*Vision and Certitude*, p. 98) and his illusion cases in general "constitute evidence of naturally occurring cognition of an object either not present or non-existent" (p. 106). Similarly, Dallas Denery, even though he notices that Auriol puts illusory objects out in the world, cannot believe that this is the view: "Despite this statement placing the circle in the air, Aureol consistently asserts that apparent being has no existence apart from and outside the soul" (*Seeing and Being Seen*, p. 131). But Denery provides no textual support for this last claim.

At the other extreme, Perler treats the apparent being as nothing more than an "aspect" of the external object: "this aspect ... is not a 'double' of the real thing but something in the real thing, grasped through the intellect's acts" ("What Am I Thinking About?" p. 87). Alternatively, he describes it as a mere "function" of the external object, writing that objective existence characterizes "the real thing itself insofar as this thing assumes a certain function, namely to be the intellect's object. That is why the objective existence is a mode of being [*modus essendi*] of the real thing rather than an existence of its own" (p. 84). Perler here is focused especially on the intellect's grasping universal concepts, but he seems to think that this characterization of apparent being holds in the sensory case as well.

I do not think that either of these interpretations is tenable. Against the first are Auriol's explicit claims, cited in this lecture (p. 82), that the apparent being exists out in the world where it seems to exist. Moreover, the larger contours of Auriol's thought require him to say this, because the very point of apparent beings is that such entities have all the features they seem to have. If the apparent circle in the air does not, in fact, exist in the air, then its whole *raison d'être* disappears. And this is certainly how Ockham understands the view: he criticizes Auriol for endorsing the inference that "It is judged to be in the air; therefore it is in the air" (*Ord.* I.27.3, in *Opera theol.* vol. 4: 247).

The second interpretation seems, conversely, to bring apparent being into too close a connection with real things. For if apparent beings are merely an aspect or function of real things, then Auriol's account of illusions seems to collapse. What will the circle in the air be an aspect of? The air? The flaming stick? What about the mirror image of my face located behind the mirror? Is that an aspect of my face? It is better, I think, at least in these cases, to admit that Auriol does just what Perler denies: that in fact he postulates a "double" of reality—not of course a *real* double, but a double all the same, existing in its own special, intentional, apparent mode. And if one reads Auriol this way, the claim must be extended beyond illusory cases, to all cognition. Illusions thus point to the true structure of the world, which contains not only real, concrete beings, but also apparent beings.

In some sense, to be sure, these two domains are supposed to count as one: thus Auriol says, for instance, that "a thing placed in formed [i.e., apparent] existence is nothing other than the external thing (*res*) under a different mode of being" (*Scriptum* dist. 27 q. 2 art. 2 [ms. Vat. Borgh., f. 302vb]). Again, the difficult passage quoted in this lecture (p. 83) denies that the two modes of being are wholly distinct, but speaks not of identity but rather of "an intrinsic and indistinguishable relation." Perler invokes this discussion in support of his aspectual interpretation. But in this passage Auriol expressly considers what we should say about an afterimage or about a supernatural case where God has annihilated the wall and yet conserves my vision. In such a case "the wall would remain as an object and as seen in intentional being that is such, and so much, and in the same place as that in which before it really existed" (*Scriptum* dist. 27 q. 2 art. 2 [ms. Vat. Borgh., f. 302rb]). If the wall can continue to exist out in the world as an intentional, apparent being even after the real wall has been annihilated, then the apparent being cannot be some mere aspect or function of that real wall.

Another case that Perler's interpretation cannot account for is imagination. Here too Auriol invokes apparent beings as the object of inner sense. For instance, "my father, imagined by me, is himself put into intentional being" (*Scriptum* dist. 3 q. 3 [sct. 14] n. 31 [trans. Pasnau, *Cambridge Translations*, p. 224]). So long as my father really exists, Perler's interpretation is an option. But what if my father is no longer alive? And, since Auriol rejects any sort of disjunctive approach, what goes for the one case must go for the other. So, again, the theory is much more extravagant than Perler allows. In perceiving or thinking about the world, Auriol holds that we in some sense double it, inasmuch as we make the very same things exist twice over.

Recently Lička has argued that, for Auriol, "it does not make good sense to ask whether *esse apparens* is a mental or extramental entity: it is *both* extramental . . . and mental" ("Perception and Objective Being," p. 67n). It is both, Lička thinks, because it is to be understood as a relation. But to my mind this interpretation inherits all the problems of both the internal and the external interpretation.

Note 15 (p. 83). The phrase 'apparent being' (*esse apparens*) is distinctive of Auriol, but the general idea of a distinction between two modes of existence, real versus apparent or intentional or objective or diminished, can be found throughout the fourteenth century. Scotus is often thought of as the fountainhead of this tradition, but it is controversial just how he understands it. Recently, Cross has argued for a wholly reductive understanding of Scotus's position: when Scotus speaks of a thing's having intentional being, says Cross, he does not mean to say that this thing has any being at all, but only that there is a cognitive representation of it (*Duns Scotus's Theory of Cognition* ch. 10).

Whether or not this is right about Scotus, it is certainly not Auriol's view, because Auriol makes the theory do far too much work for a reductive interpretation to be plausible. And Auriol's contemporaries certainly did not understand Auriol in this way either. Walter Chatton, for instance, attacks Auriol's view for having the consequence that "nothing external is cognized or seen, but instead a certain fictive being signifying the external thing" (*Sent.* prol. q. 2 art. 2, p. 88). This, however, obviously ignores many of the subtleties in Auriol's account, such as his insistence that it is the same thing in apparent being and in real being. (For discussion of Chatton versus Auriol, see Perler, "Can We Trust Our Senses?" and Grassi, *Intenzionalità*.)

Auriol himself, preoccupied as he is with illusions, has strikingly little interest in saving some kind of privileged domain for sensation. On the contrary, he is more concerned by the risk presented by a view that overstates the infallibility of the senses. The doctrine of apparent being is a solution to that temptation: "Generally, anyone who denies that many things have merely intentional and apparent being, and who holds that everything that is seen exists externally in its real nature, denies all deception and falls into the error of those who say that everything that appears is so" (*Scriptum* d. 3 q. 3 [sct. 14] n. 31 [trans. Pasnau, *Cambridge Translations*, p. 224]).

On earlier scholastic discussions of objective being, see e.g. L. M. De Rijk, "Un tournant important," Perler, "What Am I Thinking About?" Perler, "What Are Intentional Objects?" and Hamid Taieb, "The 'Intellected Thing.'" For the later history, into the seventeenth century, see e.g. Calvin Normore, "Meaning and Objective Being" and Nadler, *Arnauld and the Cartesian Philosophy of Ideas* §18.

The doctrine of objective being is often held up as a solution to the problem of our access to the external world, which it supposedly gives us by making external objects somehow *be* the things in the mind, existing there with a different, intentional mode of being. Descartes has been understood to employ objective being to this end (see, e.g., David Clemenson, *Descartes' Theory of Ideas* ch. 3, Perler, "Inside and Outside," Adriaenssen, *Representation and Scepticism* ch. 4) and so has Arnauld (see, e.g., Nadler, *Arnauld and the Cartesian Philosophy of Ideas*, pp. 271–5). The idea is similarly said to be in Aquinas (e.g., Perler, *Theorien der Intentionalität*, pp. 80–9).

I tried some time ago to show that the view is not Aquinas's (*Theories of Cognition*, appendix A). Here I think it is possible to see more generally why this maneuver would not have been well received by either scholastics or their seventeenth-century critics. Among the scholastics, there is no need to secure our access to external reality through its existing objectively within the soul, because, as we have seen, the scholastics generally have no inclination to think that the objects of perception are within the soul at all. For them, in general, inner representations are diaphanous, and so there is no need to insist on the identity of inner and outer object: at least as far as perception goes, scholastics simply do not embrace inner objects. Auriol is an exception here in his use of objective being, but he is the exception that proves the rule, because his objective beings are out into the world.

Once we come to the seventeenth century, it is easier to see why an author might want to treat inner and outer objects as formally identical and as differing only in their mode of existence. And indeed one can find authors saying this quite explicitly. John Sergeant, for instance, criticized Locke's way of ideas with the remark that, "unless Ideas, or Notions, or whatever else we please to call them, be the very things in our understanding, and not mere resemblances of them, they can never reach or engage the thing itself, or give us knowledge of it" (*Solid Philosophy*, p. 41; see Adriaenssen, *Representation and Scepticism* ch. 6). Sergeant takes himself to be criticizing the entire earlier way of ideas—in Locke, Descartes, and others—and for good reason, because those authors are in fact not interested in establishing the identity between inner and outer objects. Thus Locke can blithely say to Stillingfleet that "your lordship has immediate objects of your mind, which are not the very things themselves existing in your understanding" (*Works* vol. 4: 391). The case of Descartes and Arnauld is admittedly less clear, but we are still in a position to see why they would have no interest in identifying inner and outer objects: not because, like the scholastics, they have no inner objects, but because they want to *accentuate* the distinction between inner and outer, not conflate it. Both their corpuscularian physics and their Augustinian psychology push them toward magnifying the difference between inner and outer and making inner objects the things immediately perceived. Thus when Arnauld invokes objective being, he does so as a way of articulating the primacy of the mental: "if I think of the sun, the objective reality of the sun, which is present to my mind, is the immediate object of that perception, and the possible or existing sun, which is outside my mind, is so to speak its mediate object" (*True and False Ideas* ch. 6, trans. p. 26).

Ockham's Simply Unmediated View

Note 16 (p. 85). Ockham criticizes Auriol's approach to illusions at *Ordinatio* I.27.3 (trans. Pasnau, *Cambridge Translations* ch. 9). Part of his antipathy to Auriol's account of objective being comes from the austere metaphysics that he shares (at least in its general spirit) with seventeenth-century mechanists. This leads him to take for granted, against Auriol's talk of "a circle in the air with intentional being," that "nothing is conceivable in the air except for what is real," which he takes to preclude the presence of such entities outside the mind: "For if it has being in the air, this is either subjective or objective being. If subjective, it is real. If objective, this is impossible, because air is neither cognitive nor volitional" (*Ordinatio* I.27.3, in *Opera theol.* vol. 4: 246–7; trans. p. 233).

Ockham agrees with Auriol in rejecting disjunctivism, writing: "I do not hold that appearances occur differently in erroneous sensations, compared to others; rather, they ought to be granted in a uniform way" (p. 251; trans. p. 236]). Unlike Auriol, however, Ockham does not have a single strategy for dealing with every case of illusion, but instead deploys a range of strategies across different kinds of cases. One might, however, think of those strategies as coming in two broad kinds. One kind of strategy distinguishes between sensation and judgment and insists that there is no such thing as there appears to be, but that the fault lies with judgment. For this strategy as applied to the bent stick, see *Ordinatio* I.27.3 (*Opera theol.* vol. 4: 247; trans. p. 233). His remarks here are reminiscent of Augustine's suggestion that what looks bent in water looks just as it should look: "If it were to appear *straight* while dipped in the water, *then* with good reason I would blame my eyes for giving a false report" (*Contra academicos* III.11.26; see also Dutton, *Augustine and Academic Skepticism*, pp. 216–19, who traces the argument back to the Epicureans). It is unclear to me, however, how Ockham's embrace of action at a distance allows the intervening air and water to refract to different degrees the apparent location of the stick. If the distant object's action must pass through such intermediaries, then in what sense is it still acting "at a distance"? Ockham does not, so far as I have found, address the issue. (Perhaps action at a distance occurs only through air, not water?)

This first strategy gets applied generally to illusions of *quantity*: shape, motion, and the like. The second kind of strategy, which applies generally to illusions of *quality*, is to find some sort of real object for the senses to detect. Ockham holds, for instance, that the apparent colors on the neck of a pigeon really are out in the world. And, as this lecture (pp. 84–5) discusses, he thinks an afterimage of the sun is a real quality within our sensory faculty (see *Ordinatio* I.27.3 [*Opera theol.* vol. 4: 250; trans. Pasnau, p. 235] and *Reportatio* III.3 [*Opera theol.* vol. 6: 105–7]).

Even in cases of memory and imagination, Ockham denies mediation: "the very same singular thing that first terminates a corporeal act of seeing is itself, entirely without distinction, the terminus for the act of phantasia and abstractive understanding. No species serves as terminus" (*Reportatio* III.3, in *Opera theol.* vol. 6: 121–2). For extended discussion of Ockham's reply to Auriol, see Adams, *William Ockham* ch. 3; Tachau, *Vision and Certitude*, pp. 135–48; Perler, "Can We Trust Our Senses?"; and Grassi, *Intenzionalità*. Somewhat similar arguments against Auriol can be found in Adam Wodeham, *Lectura secunda* prol. q. 4.

Note 17 (p. 85). Ockham's rejection of both Scotus's and Auriol's conception of the intuitive–abstractive distinction is so thoroughgoing that one might have expected him to dismiss the distinction altogether. That he retains it is a puzzle that requires some explaining. A first element of the story is that Ockham wants the category of intuitive cognition because he wants to identify the basis for our evident judgments about the existence of things. All and only intuitive cognitions are capable of grounding such judgments.

This connection between intuition and evidentness or certainty in the empirical domain is something that Scotus himself had suggested, albeit only in passing. Sebastian Day's influential but by now quite old discussion begins with the remark that "it is precisely in his discussions of this problem [of intuitive cognition] that Scotus develops his doctrine of immediate experience as the basis for certitude" (*Intuitive Cognition*, p. 39). Peter Vier offers further textual support for this claim (*Evidence and Its Function*, pp. 44–7, 118–20). Inspection of these passages in newer critical editions, however, reveals that the textual support is much thinner than either of these authors realized. Tachau, more recently, flags "existential certainty" as "one of the functions Scotus most explicitly gave *notitia intuitiva*" (*Vision and Certitude*, p. 75), but she rightly concludes that "the problem of existential certitude was nevertheless relatively peripheral in Scotus's epistemology" (p. 76). Ockham is, therefore, building on a feature of Scotus's account, but he does so in a way that renders the connection between intuition and evidentness wholly explicit and central to the theory. (For useful discussions of this linkage in Ockham, see T. K. Scott, "Ockham on Evidence," and Lilli Alanen and Mikko Yrjönsuuri, "Intuition, judgement et évidence").

In Ockham's contemporary Walter Chatton the association between intuitive cognition and evident certainty becomes fully explicit when Chatton protests that, if an intuitive cognition can occur in the absence of an object, then "all our certainty would perish" (*Sent.* prol. q. 2 art. 2, p. 89). Tachau seems to be right to conclude that early fourteenth-century authors had not taken for granted the connection between intuitive cognition and certainty, but that beginning with Ockham and Chatton "Oxford theologians increasingly took for granted...that the *primary* function of the intuitive mode of cognition was to yield existential certainty" (*Vision and Certitude*, pp. 209–10).

Ockham sets out his account of the intuitive–abstractive distinction most carefully in *Ordinatio* prol. q. 1 (*Opera theol.* vol. 1: 30–9; partly translated in *Phil. Writings*, pp. 22–5). His canonical formulation of the distinction there runs as follows:

Abstractive cognition is taken in another way insofar as it abstracts from existence and non-existence and from other conditions that contingently obtain [*accidunt*] in a thing or are predicated of a thing. Not that there is anything cognized through an intuitive awareness [*notitiam*] that is not cognized through an abstractive awareness. Rather, the same thing entirely, under all the same character [*ratione*], is cognized through each awareness. But they are distinguished in this manner: that an intuitive awareness of a thing is such an awareness in virtue of which it can be known [*sciri*] whether or not a thing exists, so that if the thing exists, the intellect right away [*statim*] judges that it exists and evidently cognizes that it exists, unless it happens to be impeded by the imperfection of that [intuitive] awareness. And in the same way if, by divine power, such a perfect awareness were conserved of a non-existent thing, then by virtue of that non-complex awareness, [the intellect] would evidently cognize that that thing does not exist.   (*Ord.* prol. q. 1 [*Opera theol.* vol. 1: 31; *Phil. Writings*, p. 23])

Some notable features of this account are that (a) the distinction is understood functionally, in terms of the causal role that such awarenesses play at the level of intellectual judgment; (b) what intuitive cognition generates at the intellectual level is an *evident* judgment, which means for Ockham that (b1) the judgment cannot be false, given that it is evident, and (b2) the judgment is compulsory, given the antecedent intuitive cognition (see Lecture Two, note 13); (c) Ockham is careful to say, not that intuitive cognitions *always* generate an evident judgment but that they *can* do so, whereas abstractive judgments *cannot* (as he later makes explicit: see p. 32, lines 4–5); (d) the passage suggests that intuitive cognitions always *will* generate an evident judgment, "right away," provided that the intuition is not imperfect.

A close reading of this passage helps adjudicate an interesting debate between Elizabeth Karger and Eleonore Stump in the *Cambridge Companion to Ockham*. They disagree over whether intuitive cognitions, for Ockham, are infallible in the sense that, when they lead to existential intellectual judgments, those judgments are always evident (and hence always true). The traditional view, which Stump upholds, is that they are infallible, and there are certainly good textual reasons to take this view. For instance, Ockham elsewhere briefly characterizes an intuitive cognition as "one by means of which a thing is cognized to be when it is, and not to be when it is not" (*Reportatio* II.12–13, in *Opera theol.* vol. 5: 256). This at least suggests a guarantee of correctness. And later in that same discussion, referring back to this passage, he remarks that "when any sort of intuitive awareness is had, I can immediately form the proposition *This thing exists* or *This thing does not exist*, and in virtue of the intuitive cognition I can assent to the proposition if the thing is, or dissent if it is not, as was said above. And thus [an intuition] in no way puts the intellect in error" (p. 287). Moreover, Ockham repeatedly and notoriously insists, as he does at the end of the canonical passage quoted here, that, if God were to preserve an intuitive cognition of something, e.g. a star, even while destroying that star, then the judgment that would result would be an evident judgment that the star *does not* exist. (For the death star case itself, see *Ord.* prol. q. 1 [*Opera theol.* vol. 1: 38–9].) But why would he insist that *this* is the only outcome, unless he thinks that intuitive cognitions lead infallibly to true judgments?

Now, as Karger herself stresses ("Ockham's Misunderstood Theory"), the fruits of an intuitive cognition are *evident* judgments, which by definition cannot be false. (On the factive character of evidentness, see Lecture Two, note 13.) Hence, in the death star case, there would be an outright contradiction in that intuition's generating an evident judgment that *This star exists*. Not even God could make that happen, because, on Ockham's usage, a false judgment cannot be an evident judgment. Hence either the death star case will yield no evident judgment one way or the other or, if it is to yield an evident judgment, it would have to be an evident judgment of nonexistence. Ockham thinks that both outcomes are possible (see *Quod.* V.5). So far, then, nothing in the death star case shows Ockham to be committed to the infallibility of intuitive cognition. But what makes it look as if Ockham is committed to infallibility here is that he seems steadfastly to disallow the possibility—urged upon him by Chatton (*Sent.* prol. q. 2 art. 3, pp. 98–9), to whom Ockham replies at *Quodlibet* V.5—that God might sustain an illusory intuitive cognition and that this cognition might give rise to the false (and hence nonevident) judgment "This thing exists." Karger is unwilling to acknowledge that Ockham does disallow this possibility but, as Stump stresses ("Mechanisms of Cognition," pp. 186–7), the texts seem clear enough. (For a painstaking recent discussion that reaches effectively the same conclusion, see Lorenz Demey, "Ockham on the (In)fallibility of Intuitive Cognition.")

Where Karger is on stronger ground, however, is in her discussion of ordinary sensory illusions ("Ockham's Misunderstood Theory," pp. 216–20). As we have seen, Ockham takes these cases seriously. His various ways of dealing with them yield the result that there always is an object of sensation, and so a cautious observer may always come to the correct intellectual judgment that "the stick in water is in fact straight" and that "there is an afterimage of the sun in my eye." The trouble, however, is that although a cautious observer *may* reach the right result, such perceptions do not *infallibly* yield the right judgment, nor do they yield the sort of *evident* judgment where assent is compulsory. (See *Ord.* I.27.3 [*Opera theol.* vol. 4: 247; trans. Pasnau, *Cambridge Translations*, p. 233] for the bent stick and double-vision cases, where the sensation gives rise to a false judgment because it is "equivalent" to the sensation of a truly bent stick or of two candles.) More generally, there are a great many perceptions, even in cases we do not think of as illusory, where it is quite doubtful and so not at all evident what judgment ought to be reached. One tempting way of handling such cases is to expel this whole class of perceptions from the rank of intuitive cognitions. But, although the texts here are not entirely clear, I think Karger is correct to argue that Ockham wants all sensations (that is, all the operations of the external senses) to fall into the category of intuitive cognition. This is what leads her to conclude that "contrary to current scholarly consensus, Ockham admitted there to be cases where an intuitive cognition causes a false judgment" ("Ockham's Misunderstood Theory," p. 219). But the trouble again is that, if this is right, then why are there so many indications that Ockham does want to insist on infallibility?

Here is where a close reading of the long canonical passage quoted at pp. 278–9 is helpful. Although not all of Ockham's formulations of the intuitive–abstractive distinction are equally careful, in this passage he takes pains to stress that he is distinguishing between the class of cognitions that *can* yield evident existential judgments and the class that *cannot*. This leaves room for the possibility that some intuitive cognitions in fact do not generate evident existential judgments. One sort of case, as noted already, will be the one where the intellect simply does not render any judgment either way, and of course this sort of thing happens all the time, since most of what we take in through the senses does not give rise to any propositional judgment. But the canonical passage also explicitly leaves room for another kind of case, where the intellect is "impeded by the imperfection of that [intuitive] awareness." In these cases, Ockham explicitly says, there is no guarantee that "the intellect right away . . . evidently cognizes that it exists." A few paragraphs later he expands on what these imperfect cases are like: "It should be noted that sometimes, because of the imperfection of the intuitive awareness, namely because it is quite imperfect and obscure, or because of certain impediments on the part of the object, or because of certain other impediments, it can happen that either no or few contingent truths about the thing so intuitively cognized can be cognized" (*Opera theol.* vol. 1: 33). This makes it clear that there will be intuitive cognitions that yield "no" evident judgments because of their obscurity. Ockham notably declines to expel these from the class of intuitive cognitions; instead he makes them *imperfect* intuitive cognitions. My suggestion, although the texts do not make this explicit, is that this is where we should put cases of sensory illusion. Yes, they are intuitive cognitions, but they are not sufficiently close to perfection to generate evident existential judgments. The careful observer will refrain from judgment in such a case; but not everyone is careful, and indeed sometimes even the most careful observer will be tricked. Hence Karger is right that there is no guarantee of infallibility across the whole domain of intuitive cognitions. But Stump and the traditional interpretation she defends are correct when we limit ourselves to cases of perfect intuitive cognitions.

This may seem to be just a terminological quibble over whether to call a certain class of perceptions abstractive or imperfectly intuitive. But the choice we make has a considerable bearing on what we think Ockham is trying to achieve with the intuitive–abstractive distinction. On one reading, he is marking off by definition a certain domain of sensory privilege, to which he gives the label intuitive and which he regards as infallible. This is Adams's view: "according to Ockham, it is true by the definition of 'intuitive cognition' that any judgment caused by an intuitive cognition is evident and therefore true" (*William Ockham* 1: 589; see also her more general discussion at pp. 501–9 in the same volume). Quibbling, we might limit this claim to cases of *perfect* intuitive cognition. But then we should wonder why imperfect instances fall into this category at all. And that leads to the deeper question about why Ockham would care about this sort of gerrymandered definition. As Adams herself stresses at some length (pp. 588–601), Ockham has no epistemic pretensions when it comes to establishing a criterion to mark off the domain of perfect intuitive cognitions. So the exercise of stipulating such a domain by definition would seem, from an epistemic point of view, quite pointless. In our modern jargon, it would be rather like contending that yes, we have empirical knowledge in all and only those cases where the belief is grounded on knowledge-generating perceptions, and then saying nothing more about which perceptions those might be.

Rather than think of the category of intuitive cognition as a purely definitional attempt to construct a privileged sensory domain, we would do better to think of Ockham as concerned with demarcating a natural kind within the sphere of cognition. He is, as we would now put it, advancing a thesis in psychology rather than in epistemology. Looking over the range of cognitive activities, Ockham observes that there is a class—paradigmatically including sensory perception—where the occurrence of such cognitions *can* (and ordinary *does*) give rise at once to an evident existential judgment. There is no guarantee that this will happen, either because we may not be paying enough attention to bother with such a judgment or because the intuition may be imperfect for one reason or another. Hence Stump is off the mark when she asserts, against Karger, that "on Ockham's view, then, built into the soul is an infallibly correct detector of the presentness of things" ("Mechanisms of Cognition," p. 188). Yet there is something right about the spirit of this way of putting things, because Ockham is trying to make a point about the sort of hardware—the kind of "detector"—that we have "built into the soul." As Lecture Three discusses, medieval Aristotelians do not take at face value Aristotle's claims that the senses never err with respect to their proper sensibles (e.g., *De an.* II.6, 418^{a}12). Even when the domain of privilege is limited to the proper sensibles, one cannot even approach infallibility unless the case is limited to normal perceivers in normal, unimpeded conditions. Ockham is tacitly drawing on that background here. *Of course* the senses are not infallible in every case, but if we set aside the manifest imperfections that plague us on all sides and look at the core feature of what perception makes possible, it is plausible to say that the most striking characterization of our perceptual capacities is that they directly yield evident judgments about the existence of things in the world outside us. Considered as a natural kind, this is what the five senses do. (And then, starting from this point, Ockham is particularly interested in wondering how far the class extends. What about introspection? Yes. What about a purely intellectual intuition of God and other immaterial entities? Yes, in principle.)

With this in mind, we can return, finally, to Ockham's puzzling treatment of the death star case. Why not allow that a divinely conserved illusory intuition might generate a false existential judgment? If my interpretation is correct, then Ockham could perfectly well allow this, provided that the intuition is somehow imperfect. But if one looks again at the last sentence of the long canonical passage quoted at p. 279, one will see that Ockham very carefully stipulates that, in the case in question, what God conserves is a *perfect* intuitive cognition. Here is where there is a guarantee of infallibility, and so if the intuition is to generate a judgment, it will be an evident (and hence true) judgment. Moreover, this is not just a cheap logical guarantee, as I understand Ockham's position, but a substantive claim about our natural capacities. When the senses have an unimpeded perception under just the right conditions—the thing is, as it were, right in front of you—then Ockham thinks that there is a natural guarantee that we will get it right intellectually, by arriving immediately at an evident judgment about the thing's existence. But what if, as in the death star case, God supernaturally removes the thing and conserves the intuition? The obvious answer is that, in such a case, we would continue to judge the object to exist, and thus we would be deceived by God. Ockham's answer is entirely unobvious and extremely puzzling: that this perfect but nonveridical intuition would yield an evident judgment of nonexistence. This seems quite incredible, since the case stipulates that the intuition itself remains intrinsically unchanged as it goes from being veridical to nonveridical. So why would the judgment change? Accordingly, later scholastic authors uniformly reject Ockham's view, and indeed it is hard to see how his position can be ultimately defensible. But in his favor it should be noted that the question cannot be settled on the basis of experience, since in truth we have no idea what would happen in a supernatural case such as this. We are asking how the human soul would perform under conditions we cannot test, and though it is natural to assume that we would fail the test, it cannot be ruled out that there might be some mechanism within us that would generate the correct judgment. Ockham's puzzling treatment of the death star case, then, reflects his confidence that our faculties are so finely designed that somehow, even in the face of supernatural deception, it would be evident to the intellect that the case is illusory. The guarantee of infallibility still holds, even under these conditions.

Autrecourt's Platonism

Note 18 (p. 86). Given the prominent role that illusions play in early fourteenth-century discussions, it is surprising to see Nicholas of Autrecourt committing himself to the unpromising-looking thesis that all appearances are true. On this, see Lecture Two, note 7.

Given the truth of appearances thesis, it is tempting to suppose that Autrecourt does subscribe to some sort of inner, mediating objects. Indeed, the initial course of the discussion might seem to confirm that impression. Invoking Auriol's illusions, he tells us that we need to distinguish between cases where we see a thing in its own light and cases where we see a thing "in the light of its image" (*Tractatus* ch. 6, p. 231.26). For instance, when we take the sun to be two-feet wide, "we see an image that is the image of the sun, and when this image is seen the sun is said in a certain way to be seen" (p. 231.34–6). Similarly, in the case of a stick that appears bent in water, "the appearance is of a certain image that *is* of such a condition as it appears" (p. 231.44). The truth of appearances is accordingly saved, even in these cases, because the image of the thing is as it appears to be.

If Autrecourt had said only this much, he might seem to be anticipating the seventeenth century's deployment of ideas as mediating inner objects of perception. But it soon becomes clear that his view is closer to Auriol's, in that he takes these images not to be species or ideas within the mind but to exist out in the world, where they seem to be. The image of the stick, for instance, is not only bent, but also half-submerged in the water. The distance from mediated views appears starkly when Autrecourt later considers whether these images— which by now he has taken to calling objective beings—should be identified with acts of perception. Here is the start of his response:

> Take the example of whiteness when it is seen. There is something external, to which we give the name 'whiteness,' and there is something internal. Otherwise, it would not be said that we see the whiteness that belongs to the stone. For we experience the external whiteness in the manner of an object, and we experience the internal whiteness in the manner of an act. (*Tractatus* ch. 7, p. 242.45–9)

Autrecourt is thus willing to accept that there are two whitenesses, one internal and one external, and he seems to be saying that we have to postulate both of them: the internal act is required if we are to be perceiving whiteness, and the external object if we are to be perceiving the whiteness of a stone. So far this looks fairly consistent with the mediated views of the seventeenth century. But look at what comes next:

> If one is asked what that act is, there is no better account than if one were asked "what is whiteness?" and one were to offer the thing being pointed to that you see here. Likewise [if asked 'what is the act of vision?'], the vision is what you have when you say that you see whiteness.   (*Tractatus* ch. 7, pp. 242.49–50.3)

In effect, Autrecourt claims here that the inner act of perception is diaphanous. Although in some sense there is an inner whiteness (he speaks of the act as a "configuration" of its external object), and although we somehow experience ourselves to be engaged in that act, we still have no way of characterizing what that act is like other than by pointing to the external object that is seen. But this is not to say that we are even within our rights to regard that inner act as *similar* to the external object. As he immediately goes on to explain:

> And that such a thing that we call a cognition is a likeness of its object, we have no knowledge of this by way of experience. For when we intuit the act of seeing whiteness, it is not apparent to us that it is whiteness or something similar to whiteness.   (*Tractatus* ch. 7, p. 243.3–6)

There may, then, be theoretical reasons to think that the act of cognition resembles its external object. But there is no way to know this from experience, because all that experience shows us is the external object. Although we are aware of being engaged in the act of seeing, the character of that act is diaphanous.

Interpreting Autrecourt is made still more complicated by the fact that his view seems to change over the course of the *Tractatus*. Perler describes him as holding the view that inner, objectively existing sensations are identical to outer, real objects ("Relations nécessaires ou contingentes?" p. 96), and this may well capture a stage in the *Tractatus*'s developing position. But it seems to me that Autrecourt's ultimate view puts objective beings in the world and makes them quite distinct from real, subjective being. A particularly clear indication of this, from relatively early in the discussion, is this remark: "It should be said that, when sight sees whiteness, it is certain that it sees something. Its appearance indicates this, and also that it is outside the eye and at such a location. And I grant that these are all true" (*Tractatus* ch. 6, p. 232.4–6).

What holds for veridically perceived whiteness seems to hold as well, in Autrecourt, for all clear and evident appearances, even "illusory" ones. When someone ill misperceives flavors, there are qualities in the tongue that serve as the object, and the sense of taste is right about these (p. 230.8–10). When an object that is white looks red, one can appeal to "atomalia" in the medium or in the organ (p. 230.10–12). In illusions of this kind, the objects may be within the organs of perception (as in some of Ockham's cases), but they are still distinct from the inner sensation. For discussion of such cases, see Thijssen, "Quest for Certain Knowledge," who concludes that "Autrecourt's theory of perception should be considered a form of direct realism" (p. 208).

Still, one has to be cautious in interpreting the *Tractatus*, because these later chapters in particular seem to offer a view in flux and development, and it is not clear that we should privilege the ideas that come later just because they come later. On the evolution of views, see Christophe Grellard, "The Nature of Intentional Objects" and "*Sicut specula sine macula*."

Note 19 (p. 87). Autrecourt's ultimate embrace of Platonism is only hinted at in the early pages of the *Tractatus*, but at least there are hints, particularly at *Tractatus* ch. 1 (pp. 199–200), where he offers Platonism as one of three ways of saving the thesis that nothing comes into or goes out of existence (see my discussion in *Metaphysical Themes* §28.2). At this early stage in the treatise, Autrecourt does not commit himself to this metaphysics, but his sympathies are clear.

On Auriol's contrastingly strict nominalism regarding universals, see *In librum Sententiarum* II.9.2, and the summary in Friedman, "Peter Auriol" §3.

The crucial role of internalism in Autrecourt's argument has gone completely unnoticed, so far as I have found. But it is no surprise that such views about mental representation play a role here, because these issues were very extensively debated among earlier scholastics. The best known discussion is in Ockham (e.g., *Reportatio* II.12–13 [*Opera theol.* vol. 5: 287–91] and *Quodlibet* I.13 [*Opera theol.* vol. 9: 76]), who had defended externalism on the grounds that a mental representation equally similar to two individuals, one nearby and one far away, would surely represent only the nearby object. Autrecourt's way around Ockham's externalist conclusion is to embrace universals. For various different accounts of Ockham's position, see Brower-Toland, "Intuition, Externalism, and Direct Reference"; Panaccio, "Ockham's Externalism"; and Philip Choi, "Ockham's Weak Externalism."

Note 20 (p. 88). It is extremely hard to get clear about just how Autrecourt thinks of the objective–subjective distinction, in part because he does not seem to make up his mind. That he does not commit himself to the radical monism he sets out toward the end of the *Tractatus* is clear from the closing lines of the discussion, which still leave it open whether we should say that there is one or multiple subjective beings (p. 266.22–3). The reason for this uncertainty, I take it, is that he does endorse at least the general picture on which the reality of subjective being is hidden behind the objective being with which we are acquainted. See, for example, p. 262.8–10: "that which they both seek to see, when they look, is the same in number subjectively, but it comes to them according to distinct objective beings."

The pressure to identify subjective being with God comes out clearly in chapter 7 of the *Tractatus* (p. 242.33–43), where Autrecourt considers what would follow if subjective being were nothing more than just another finite, created level of reality, beyond the objective beings we are acquainted with. If this were so,

> then there would have to be some finite objective being beyond which, if one goes on to grasp the thing still more clearly, the thing would be grasped according to its subjective being. And, since all this can be done by a finite power, just as the thing in itself has finite being, then either God is not infinite or he will not grasp such a thing, in virtue of the state of his own nature—unless one wants to say that the being of each most clear thing [viz., the subjective beings] is the one infinite being that is God. And the mind seems to find more persuasive [*magis se intimare*] the thought that God grasps none of the things outside him except insofar as they are reflected in his essence.   (*Tractatus*, p. 242.34–41)

This argument depends on Autrecourt's internalism: that facts about mental representation depend entirely on internal facts about the state of the representing mind. He reasons that if subjective being is finite, then a finite mind can grasp it, in which case an infinite mind cannot grasp it. Since it seems unacceptable to say that God does not grasp subjective being, we are driven toward the traditional theological notion that the object of the divine mind is God himself, and that he sees other things through himself (compare, e.g., Aquinas, *Summa theol.* 1a 14.5). God, on this picture, is subjective being, and everything else is just objective being.

If Autrecourt reasons in the way I describe, then I fear his argument contains a fatal flaw. Internalism tells us, in modern jargon, that the content of our mental representations supervenes on the qualitative character of our inner mental states. From this it follows that, if two minds have qualitatively the same mental states, then their contents are identical. This is how Autrecourt runs his quite interesting argument, discussed in this lecture (p. 86), that objective beings must be universals. But, in order to get his conclusion that God cannot grasp the finite, he has to run the inference invalidly in the other direction: that if two minds do not have qualitatively the same mental states (i.e., God and creatures), then their contents are not identical. Internalism does not license this inference. For all internalism says, a Martian and a human might have minds with exactly the same mental content, and the same holds for God and creatures.

The Quest for Fidelity
Caricatures of the Scholastic View

Note 21 (p. 89). Although the nominalistic tendencies of scholastic Aristotelianism put pressure on scholastics to find inner objects of intellectual thought (see the discussion on the *verbum* in note 7 above), these philosophers felt absolutely no pressure at the sensory level, because they simply never doubted that the senses are well suited to detecting qualities in the external world. Thus Avicenna begins a discussion of accidental qualities with this remark: "We now discuss qualities. As for the sensible and corporeal qualities, there is no doubt with regard to their existence" (*Metaphysics* [*al-Shifā'*] III.7, p. 102). Indeed, if one goes back to Aristotle, one finds that his method for deducing the four elemental qualities in the natural world is to consider what qualities are revealed by sensation, focusing on what he took to be the most fundamental sense modality, touch (*Gen. et cor.* II.2). Despite the relationalism that runs through Aristotle, he nevertheless takes for granted that, at least in some cases, the senses track the fundamental qualities of bodies (see Lecture Three, note 6).

If seventeenth-century authors had focused their criticisms of the scholastics here, they would have been on firm ground. For as Lecture Three considers in some detail, the scholastics clearly did take for granted that the senses show us the fundamental natural qualities of the physical world. But much of the attack made by Descartes and others depends on saddling scholastic authors with an absurd reduplication of phenomenal qualities, both out in the world and within the mind. In addition to the passages quoted in this lecture (p. 89), consider Malebranche:

> When philosophers say that fire is hot, grass green, sugar sweet, and so on, they mean, like children and the common man, that fire contains what they feel when they are warm; that grass has on it the colors they believe they see there; that sugar contains the sweetness that they sense in eating it, and so on of all things we see or feel. It is impossible to doubt this in reading their writings. They speak of sensible qualities as sensations; they take motion for heat; and they thus confuse, because of the equivocation of the terms, the modes of bodies with those of minds. Only since Descartes do we respond . . . by distinguishing the equivocation of the sensible terms. (*Search after Truth* VI.2.2, trans. p. 441)

The equivocation that Malebranche speaks of here is one that arises only within the terms of seventeenth-century mediated accounts. That "sugar contains the sweetness that they sense" is unproblematically true for philosophers prior to Descartes, because what was thought to be sensed was a quality of the sugar, its sweetness. The idea that we might sense something within the mind is a seventeenth-century development, a development that *creates* the equivocation that Malebranche describes. No wonder that it is "only since Descartes" that philosophers have drawn the necessary distinction. Until then, the distinction was not necessary.

The most extreme version of this post-scholastic line of criticism is Hume's: " 'Tis certain that almost all mankind and even philosophers themselves, for the greatest part of their lives, take their perceptions to be their only objects, and suppose that the very being which is intimately present to the mind is the real body or material existence" (*Treatise* I.4.2, p. 206). Hume describes an intellectual disaster: that for our whole lives we have been supposing ourselves to perceive the external world, but that in fact we have been confusing that world with our inner perceptions. Extreme though it is, Hume's criticism is in fact a more credible diagnosis than Malebranche's of what is wrong with premodern theories: it is not that they equivocated between inner and outer objects and thus confused the two, but that, at least in the case of perception, they never drew such a distinction at all and insisted instead that perception shows us things in the world. In effect, Hume inverts the scholastic doctrine of diaphanousness. Like Aquinas and most other scholastics, Hume insists that there is just one sort of object of perception and no immediate access to what lies beneath it. But, whereas the usual scholastic view was that the things we cannot see are our inner states, Hume concludes that these are *all* we see. When it comes to the external world, Hume thinks, we are blind and, worse yet, we mostly do not even realize that we are blind.

These critiques of scholastic realism, driven by the presupposition of mediation, have come to seem so natural that it is difficult even to see just how odd a picture it gives. Instead, the diaphanous scholastic view is the one that has come to look odd. Thus Margaret Atherton writes of Descartes that "the move that he is resisting is one that takes the sensuous green color we sense out into the world" ("Green Is Like Bread," p. 32). As Atherton tells the story, scholastic authors are bizarrely exporting into the world features of the mind. But, as familiar a narrative as this is, it gets the history of these discussions exactly backwards. For the scholastics, the "color we sense" is out in the world from the start, which makes it quite unnecessary to move it out there. Their view looks puzzling only if one begins from what is in fact a very idiosyncratic position: the later seventeenth-century conception of perception as mediated by inner ideas. I discuss these issues further, focusing on the status of secondary qualities, in *Metaphysical Themes* chs. 21–3.

Another way to see the oddness of this common misinterpretation is to consider the one exception I can find to the general rule that scholastic authors reject mediated accounts of perception. That one exception is an Oxford philosopher from the 1330s by the name of William Crathorn:

When an external thing (one that is outside the perceiver) is seen by the perceiver mediated by the species, the vision of the species and of that of which it is a species are numerically the same thing. For example, when someone sees whiteness mediated by a species, he sees in the same vision the species immediately and the whiteness mediately, since the species mediates.

(*Sentences* Bk. I q. 1 concl. 4; trans. Pasnau, *Cambridge Translations*, p. 269)

This is a remarkable conclusion to reach before the seventeenth century. But what makes it particularly remarkable and illuminating for our purposes is that Crathorn, unlike seventeenth-century proponents of mediation, is perfectly content with the usual scholastic realism about colors and other sensible qualities: they exist out in the world, perceived in high fidelity. This leads him to conclude that sensible species—the things we directly perceive— exactly resemble the things in the world that we indirectly perceive. As he puts it, "a soul seeing and understanding color is truly colored, not by any color existing outside the soul but by its likeness, which is a true color" (concl. 7 ad 2, trans. p. 288). With this we have the sort of reduplication that Locke and others caricatured, on which ideas are "the perfect resemblance" of bodies, "as they are in a mirror" (*Essay* II.8.16; see this lecture, p. 89).

Crathorn himself has been the subject of considerable mockery, even among his own contemporaries—such as Robert Holcot, who accused him of turning the soul into a chameleon (*Sex articuli* art. 3, p. 106). But we should ask ourselves which part of Crathorn's view is supposed to be absurd. Is it absurd because he thinks colors are in the mind? Or is it absurd because he thinks colors are in the world? In fact, trouble arises only because of the conjunction of these views. If colors are in the world, as scholastic authors always held, then they can serve as the objects of vision and they need not be in the mind. But if we cannot find a place for them in the world, then it hardly seems absurd to locate them in the mind. Either view is defensible by itself. What seems absurd is to postulate color twice over. It is not, then, the usual scholastic view that is absurd, nor is it the usual post-scholastic view. Absurdity arises from their combination.

Crathorn does not expressly say *why* he defends a mediated view, but it would seem from the context that the argument from illusion looms large in his thinking. For the previous conclusion had just discussed Auriol's illusions at length, in order to establish that "the aforesaid likeness existing within the cognizer, which is the word and natural likeness of a sensible quality existing outside the cognizer, is sometimes cognized and sensed when the thing of which it is a likeness is not intuitively cognized or sensed" (*Sentences* Bk. I q. 1 concl. 3, trans. p. 264). From this Crathorn seems to treat it as obvious that, if species are perceived in illusory cases, they are also perceived in veridical cases.

But why, then, does Crathorn insist on literal resemblance? His reasoning begins with what might look like a fairly innocuous claim, at least for an Aristotelian: that "the quality that is a word and natural likeness of the cognized thing existing outside the soul is of the same species as the thing of which it is a likeness" (concl. 7, trans. p. 285). The boldness of this claim emerges when he goes on to insist that we should consequently hold that the soul is literally colored (as quoted above). In *Theories of Cognition* I was quick to brand this view "absurd and confused" (p. 90). More recently, Aurélien Robert wrote: "Incredibly, Crathorn affirms that whenever one is thinking of a white thing, the mind of that person actually becomes white" ("William Crathorn" §3). I now think that the thesis deserves at least a little more respect. Although Crathorn is obviously framing his thesis in provocative ways, there is something to the point that, on the scholastic theory, the species *in medio* and the species in the sensory power need to be forms of the same specific kind as the sensible quality they represent. This is plausible not for any reason to do with perceptual theory, but because in general the underlying Aristotelian causal theory should lead us to expect it, just as it leads us to expect that the heat of the fire produces in other things forms of the same kind: it produces, univocally, *heat*. But, once we accept that much, should we not also say that any subject that receives such a form of ϕ becomes, univocally, ϕ? Of course, to say this does not require saying that all such subjects will receive ϕ in exactly the same way. Crathorn is perfectly happy to admit, for instance, that the soul's sensory power is immaterial and that, hence, the color received will be extensionless (*Sentences* Bk. I q. 1 concl. 7 ad 1, trans. pp. 287–8). And he is even happy to apply his conclusion to the immaterial human intellect and to an angelic intellect (pp. 287–8). They too, on his view, become *colored*, but of course they cannot be colored in the way physical surfaces are colored. So it is not as if Crathorn thinks that you could *see* the color of my soul if you were to look at the right place inside me.

Once we recognize that Crathorn is not willing to go all the way to these absurdly incoherent results, it may seem wrong to describe his view as attributing color to the soul at all. We now tend to mark the extension of 'color' in response-dependent terms—that is, in terms of what is visible to standard observers in standard conditions. From this perspective, it looks incoherent to think that something extensionless and so invisible could be colored. But if we take seriously the scholastic idea that colors are real qualities in the world, and if we think of causation in the usual Aristotelian way, in terms of ϕ-forms making other things ϕ, then we can at least see why Crathorn found his conclusion tempting. Indeed, if we accept this much, then the most natural way to reject Crathorn's conclusions may be to reject the theory of species entirely. This is how Crathorn's fellow Dominican, Durand of Saint-Pourçain, had reasoned a decade earlier. Just like Crathorn, Durand insists that "a species representing a thing and the thing of which it is a species are of the same specific nature [*rationis*] even if they differ in their mode of being" (*Sent.* [3rd vers.] II.3.6 n. 17; cf. IV.49.2 nn. 13–19). But for Durand this is a powerful argument against species, precisely because it is absurd to think that an intellect takes on the very species of the substances that it thinks about—especially given that species are *accidents* rather than substances (II.3.6 n. 17). Rather than be forced into this conclusion and into the conclusion that species are the objects of cognition, Durand rejects species entirely (see notes 5 and 8 here). I suspect Crathorn has Durand's precise arguments in mind here, and is simply hugging the monstrous consequences that Durand had brought forward. (For a different sort of reply to Durand on these points, see Suárez, *De anima* disp. 9 q. 2 n. 13: Suárez insists that a *representational* likeness does not require specific sameness and need not itself be perceived.)

Mediation and Skepticism

Note 22 (p. 91). It is one of the most familiar ideas in the history of philosophy that mediated views run afoul of skepticism. For a representative recent example, see Perler: "It is clear that such a characterization of ideas has devastating consequences. For if ideas are indeed inner objects, set apart from external things and if they are the only objects to which we have immediate access, we are out of touch with external things" ("Inside and Outside," pp. 70–1). And see also Searle:

> I said the denial of Direct Realism was disastrous and I want now briefly to say how. The whole epistemic tradition was based on the false premise that we can never perceive the real world directly ... But if you deny Direct Realism, you can never directly perceive objects and states of affairs in the world; how then is it possible to get knowledge of facts in the world?   (*Seeing Things as They Are*, p. 29)

Adriaenssen, in contrast, rightly stresses that skeptical arguments can be posed just as readily against simple diaphanous views such as Ockham's (*Representation and Scepticism* ch. 3).

The classic statement of the skeptical worry about mediation is Reid's long discussion of the theory of ideas in Book II of his *Essays on the Intellectual Powers of Man*. Throughout that discussion, he always takes for granted that such mediation will obscure the external world, and so make external objects ineligible as themselves objects of perception. But there is no reason why the mediation of inner objects must necessary obscure external things, rather than provide a faithful picture of them. One could think that perception provides a great deal of reliable information, in high fidelity, about both our inner states and external states. If things had been like that, then we would surely want to say that we perceive at once both our ideas and the world outside us. Despite such mediation, skeptical worries would never arise; indeed, under those circumstances the science of both mind and world would have been much easier. This shows that directness, in and of itself, is no part of the epistemic ideal. What matters is reliability and fidelity.

For the case of photography, see Kendall Walton's argument that, despite the mediation involved, "we see, quite literally, our dead relatives themselves when we look at photographs of them" ("Transparent Pictures," p. 252).

The Allure of Inward Fidelity

Note 23 (p. 93). Historically, those who turn inward to find a privileged domain of sensation in high fidelity very often entwine that view with a dualism of mind and body. Descartes is a particularly clear example of this. The main thesis of the Second Meditation, that "the mind is better known than the body," is used to leverage the distinction between mind and body. Our difficulties with grasping body begin with the senses: "I use the senses as reliable touchstones for immediate judgments about the essences of the bodies located outside us, about which in fact they signify only very obscurely and confusedly" (Sixth Meditation, VII: 83). Such conclusions encourage the thought that, if the external world is problematic as the domain of sensation, we should expect to find a more satisfactory domain within, in the immaterial mind. As note 9 here discusses, this is a fundamentally Augustinian notion, but stripped now of Augustine's confidence that veridical sensation yields a faithful picture of the external world. For Descartes, the only place where such confidence is warranted is within the mind.

Although Descartes connects such claims with his dualism, the story need not go that way. Even in Locke, dualism is by no means taken for granted. Locke tells us from the start of the *Essay* that he will set aside as unnecessary all such speculation about "whether those ideas...depend on matter" (*Essay* I.1.2). This move is not just strategic, but epistemically forced upon Locke, because we "perhaps shall never be able to know whether any mere material being thinks" (IV.3.6), even if immateriality is "the more probable opinion" (II.27.25). But Locke does subscribe to the critical assumption behind the mediation doctrine: that, even when perception does not show us external things as they are, it still shows us inner things as they are. Thus in the *Essay*'s initial Epistle to the Reader, which explains how he uses "determinate or determined" in place of Descartes's "clear and distinct," Locke writes that "by those denominations, I mean some object in the mind, and consequently *determined*, i.e., such as it is there seen and perceived to be" (p. 13). Again, the inversion of views is striking. Whereas the scholastics are mocked for supposing that external things are just as they are perceived to be, Locke is able to take it entirely for granted that the senses show us ideas just as they are perceived to be.

Among modern philosophers, even those who are avowedly materialists, one can still find the view that perception reveals our inner mental states. David Papineau provides a particularly vivid example in his recent presidential address to the Aristotelian Society:

From my perspective, then, our conscious sensory properties, the ones we are aware of when we introspect, are intrinsic properties of us, and metaphysically quite distinct from the properties of objects that successful sensory experience enable[s] us to perceive. The 'blueness' that I know to be present when I introspect my sense experience is a property of me, not of the object out there. Of course there is a perfectly good sense in which I perceive the external blueness of my shirt itself in the good case. But I so perceive that external blueness in virtue of having a different property of conscious sensory 'blueness.'   ("Sensory Experience," p. 26)

Although Papineau makes it clear that he does not mean to commit himself to dualism, and although he wishes to reserve 'perception' for external objects, the view he presents is in its essential details just a modern version of the seventeenth-century way of ideas. I discuss this and other modern cases at greater length in "Therapeutic Reflections."

Another way of holding on to the ideal of high fidelity in perception is to follow the lead of scholastic authors such as Auriol and Autrecourt by positioning sensible qualities out in the world. The neutral monism of William James and Bertrand Russell attempts something like this approach. Instead of reducing the sensible world to physics and thereby introducing a gap between experience and reality, they try to understand everything that exists as the world of experience, thus allowing the mind to grasp things fully as they are (on this movement, see Erik Banks, *The Realistic Empiricism of Mach, James and Russell*). For a more measured attempt to find sensible qualities in the world, in something like the way they seem to be there, see Mark Johnston, "Better than Mere Knowledge," who holds: "If external things are colored, then their colors must be tightly connected to the distinctive qualities which visual awareness alone reveals" (p. 264). Interestingly, Peter Alexander understands Locke himself to hold this sort of view. He takes Locke's ideas to be *dependent* on the mind, but to be *located* out in the world (*Ideas, Qualities and Corpuscles*, pp. 103–13). As an interpretation of Locke, this has not met with much approval, but it illustrates how what is mainly at stake in mediated theories of perception is the question of *what* we perceive with the greatest fidelity. The location question is incidental.

The Fidelity Constraint has affinities with Dretske's appeal to information carried as the test for what counts as the objects of perception (*Knowledge and the Flow of Information*, pp. 153–68). It would take more space than is appropriate to assess here the precise relationship between these two approaches, but it seems worth mentioning in particular the weight Dretske puts on object constancy effects. The senses normally represent color, shape, and size as constant, even while the inner impression changes. Hence they track external things more closely than they track what is happening within the perceiver. Hence we should conclude that the objects of perception are external. The Fidelity Constraint might likewise take object constancy into effect, but only as one consideration among many. And this might be desirable. For, as Dretske notes (p. 166), we can train ourselves to override object constancy effects and see color, shape, and size as varying. When we do that, are we seeing our inner impressions? Dretske embraces that result, but this seems like a dubious conclusion.

Notes to Lecture Five
Many Thoughts at Once
The Medieval Debate

Note 1 (p. 97). Although the question of how much we can think at once has not recently received much attention in philosophy, medieval authors debated these issues quite extensively, disputing over not just *whether* we need to grasp a whole proposition or argument at once (the principal focus of this lecture), but *how* the mind is capable of grasping multiple things at once. Aquinas's "one thought at a time" constraint seems to have been the majority view among Latin-writing authors through the thirteenth century and into the fourteenth. See Albert the Great, *Sentences* III.30.4, and Thomas of Sutton, *Quaestiones ordinariae* 23, though Sutton has little to say that is not already in Aquinas. Both Albert and Aquinas cite a remark from Aristotle's *Topics*: "it is possible to know many things but it is not possible to think about many things" (II.10, 114^{b}34–5). This is a natural English translation of the standard Latin text (as given by Boethius): *contingit enim plura scire, intelligere autem non*—and the Latin is, in turn, a word-for-word translation of the Greek, which uses ἐπίστασθαι and διανοεῖσθαι. On inspection of the context, however, it looks as if Aristotle may have meant only the weaker, uncontroversial claim that "it is possible to know many things without thinking of them all."

Aquinas, at *Quodlibet* VII.1.2c, also refers to al-Ghazālī's *Metaphysics* (from his *Maqāṣid al-falāsifa*): "knowledge [*scientia*, العلم] is like an engraving in the soul: for just as we cannot imagine two engravings or two shapes in the same wax at the same time in the same way and in the same respect, so it cannot be imagined that in the soul there are two distinct knowledges present at the same time and in the same way" (I.3.4 [p. 68 Muckle; p. 230 Dunya]).

Albert's discussion alludes to opponents who seem to have rejected the one-thought constraint. But the first scholastic author I have been able to find who in fact makes such a denial is Peter John Olivi, in the 1270s. He dedicates an entire question to the topic (*Summa* II.78), and in his characteristically brilliant and iconoclastic way distinguishes three ways in which composition can be found in the soul's acts (vol. 3: 161–2):

- virtual extension, either spatial or temporal, for example in our ordinary perception of extended bodies or of temporally unfolding processes, such as circular motion;
- the composition of intensity, inasmuch as a more intense cognitive act is explained in terms of compiled grades of forms;
- the composition of discrete acts, as when the common sense compares hearing to seeing.

The last occurs at the intellectual level too, Olivi contends, when we apprehend the terms of a proposition.

I owe this reference to Richard Cross (*Duns Scotus's Theory of Cognition*, p. 175). Cross (pp. 57–9, 174–8) shows that John Duns Scotus, a few decades later, similarly rejects the one-thought constraint. Scotus makes the intriguing comparison (explicit in Olivi's discussion as well) between the "multiple distinct visions" that constitute our perfectly ordinary perception of an extended visual field and the multiple "indistinct and imperfect" intellections that occur at the same time in the intellect (*Reportatio* II.42.1 [ed. Wadding vol. 11.1, n. 13]).

Henry of Harclay also rejects the one-thought constraint in his *Ordinary Question 25* (argued in Oxford between 1310 and 1317); on this, see Charles Bolyard, "Harclay on Knowing Many Things." Thomas Wylton does the same in Paris, in 1312–13. Wylton's principal text on the subject has been edited in Stella, "Quaestiones de libero arbitrio," pp. 506–17, and has received further attention in Dumont, "New Questions" and in Friedman, "On the Trail" and "Mental Propositions." Wylton's discussion is evidently not the first statement of his position, since it is a response to Durand of St.-Pourçain, a Parisian contemporary who was already arguing against him in a text from the same year (also edited in Stella, "Quaestiones de libero arbitrio"). Wylton himself says that he is arguing against "that which is commonly [*communiter*] accepted as a principle: that the intellect cannot at the same time think about distinct things under their proper aspects [*rationes*]" (in Dumont, "New Questions," p. 371).

Dumont refers to Wylton's view as "notorious" and says that his debate with Durand was "famous" ("New Questions," p. 367). Fame here may seem unlikely, but in fact it is suggested by the large number of subsequent discussions we find, many of which quote extensively from both Wylton and Durand. At first, common opinion remains on Durand's side. John Baconthorpe, for instance, sets out the debate at length in the mid-1320s and continues to characterize Durand's side as the *opinio communis* (in Friedman, "On the Trail," p. 435 n. 9). But the one-thought constraint would come to meet with growing resistance. Ockham, not long after Wylton, seems to see no difficulty in allowing the intellect to have multiple intellectual acts at once (see *Opera phil.* vol. 2: 356–7, *Opera phil.* vol. 6: 408–9, *Opera theol.* vol. 5: 390–3, *Opera theol.* vol. 9: 695). Francis of Marchia takes Wylton's side in around 1320 (as this lecture considers at p. 101), as do Gregory of Rimini in the 1340s (see Friedman, "Mental Propositions," pp. 114–15) and John Buridan just a little later (*Quaest. de anima* III.16).

The debate between Wylton and Durand makes explicit that we need to distinguish between (i) the weaker claim that the intellect can think about more than one thing at once and (ii) the stronger claim that the intellect can have multiple acts of thought at once. Aquinas does not explicitly draw this distinction. It is clear, however, that Aquinas denies (ii) entirely and accepts (i) only in the sorts of cases described in this lecture (pp. 96–7), where a complex object can be thought of in virtue of a single intelligible species. Wylton, in contrast, expressly defends (i) in virtue of the possibility of (ii): he thinks the intellect can take on multiple intelligible forms or species and thereby have multiple intellectual acts, each with its own object. Durand, in contrast, stoutly denies (ii) but stresses the intellect's ability to grasp many things in a single act: "It should be granted, then, that the intellect thinks at the same time about discrete things [*divisa*] that it distinguishes: both a conclusion with its premises, and opposites taken not just relatively but in any sort of way as having an order or relation [*habitudo*] between them. But it does this not through distinct acts of thought, but through one" (in Stella, "Quaestiones de libero arbitrio," p. 491, lines 26–30). This seems close to Aquinas's view.

When viewed within the apparatus of scholastic metaphysics, the debates are clear enough: can a single intellect be informed by two distinct intelligible species? Can it be doubly actualized? But if one tries to extract the fragile substance of the debate from the skeleton of that metaphysical framework—that is, if one directly considers the question of what the mind is capable of—then the issues threaten to dissolve in our hands. After all, all parties to the dispute want the intellect to have some ability to form complex thoughts. Whether that be described as a single complex act or as a complex of concurrent simple acts looks like quite a rarified issue, even by scholastic standards. Wylton himself, for instance, grants that the intellect cannot think at the same time about two wholly distinct subjects (in Stella, "Quaestiones de libero arbitrio," pp. 513.41–514.3). And when he describes the intellect's complex grasp of the parts of a proposition, he speaks sometimes of multiple concurrent acts of thought and sometimes of a single composite act (see the texts in Dumont, "New Questions," pp. 371–2). When Ockham discusses these issues (see reference at p. 99), he seems quite indifferent as to whether an occurrent mental proposition is a single complex act of thought or several acts of thought, concurrent but distinct, provided that we can make sense of how the intellect grasps at once a whole proposition and even a whole syllogism.

It would be natural to expect views about whether the mind can think more than one thought at once to depend critically on whether one is a dualist or materialist. From a dualistic point of view, the mind could be expected to be simple, and hence capable of only one thought at a time. Once the mind is conceived of as realized in *res extensa*—the brain—it would seem natural for it to be capable of multiple parallel thoughts. In fact, however, the history does not go this way. Although Aquinas is a prominent instance of a dualist who accepts the "one thought at a time" constraint, other dualists do not, as the case of Wylton shows. One can see why dualists might go either way on this question by considering their broader commitments. For, although dualists have often treated the mind as simple in some way or another, they have also recognized both that it has various faculties, each giving rise to distinct operations, and that it holds a vast store of memories and dispositions. These features evidently require *some* kind of complexity. And if the mind is capable of holding in storage more than one thought at once, it is not clear why it could not also *think* more than one thought at once. (Henry of Harclay in fact advances an argument of this form against Aquinas's prohibition on the intellect's taking on more than a single intelligible species: see *Ordinary Questions* 25.14.) So it should not be surprising that Descartes rejects the one-thought constraint, as this lecture discusses (p. 106). But around the same time Pascal insists on the constraint: "A single thought occupies us. We cannot think of two things at the same time" (*Pensées* n. 453, trans. p. 142). Burge provides a modern instance of a materialist who seems to take for granted this one-thought constraint, both in the works cited in this lecture (p. 96) and in his more recent Dewey Lectures, where he continues to insist that memory is critical to whether an inference is warranted ("Self and Self-Understanding," pp. 330–3). Another recent example is Susanna Rinard ("Reasoning One's Way Out of Skepticism"), who relies on the diachronic character of complex reasoning to make the following intriguing argument: someone who is skeptical about the external world should also be skeptical about the reality of the past. But skeptics must rely on the reality of the past to take their own arguments seriously. Hence skepticism is inconsistent.

Support for the one-thought constraint obviously comes in part from introspection. But the phenomenology here is murky enough to call for some further explanation. My suspicion is that these views share a tacit commitment to what Daniel Dennett mocked as the Cartesian Theater: "a central . . . Theater where 'it all comes together' . . . a crucial finish line or boundary somewhere in the brain . . . *what happens* there is what you are conscious of" (*Consciousness Explained*, p. 107). Both materialists and dualists are liable to conceive of thought in this way, which in turn makes it natural to think that the theater of the mind has room for only a single thought at a time. If one abandons this sort of picture, the one-thought constraint immediately looks less attractive.

Working Memory

Note 2 (p. 98). Rather than treat conscious events as happening in a theater, Bernard Baars treats the whole mind as the theater and argues that consciousness takes place on the extended platform of the stage, which is his metaphor for working memory (*In the Theater of Consciousness* passim). Elsewhere he characterizes consciousness in terms of a shared workspace and, again, thinks of working memory as a central component of consciousness. But, although consciousness can spread over multiple objects at once, it remains highly constrained in comparison with the mind as a whole:

> [The brain] is a massive collection of neural assemblies, cells, layers, and connections, each specialized in some specific task... The great bulk of these functions happen at the same time, in parallel, as one great 'society of the mind.' Together, their processing capacity is enormous, though unconscious. The great puzzle is, why is the conscious aspect of the brain so limited when the unconscious part is so vast?
>
> (Baars, "Global Workspace Theory," p. 238)

To a philosophical reader, the psychological literature on working memory looks shockingly confused over what the phenomenon even is. Alan Baddeley, an acknowledged leader in the field, begins his principal work on the subject with this definition: "working memory is assumed to be a temporary storage system under attentional control that underpins our capacity for complex thought" (*Working Memory*, p. 1). Compare that with Brad Postle: "Working memory refers to the retention of information in conscious awareness when this information is not present in the environment" ("Working Memory as Emergent Property," p. 23). So is working memory a matter of "storage" or is it a matter of "conscious awareness"? See, too, Jackie Andrade: "working memory refers to a system that enables temporary storage of the intermediate products of cognition" ("Introduction," p. 5). In contrast, Atkinson and Shiffrin ("Control of Short-Term Memory," p. 83) remark that they "tend to equate the short-term store with 'consciousness,' that is, the thoughts and information of which we are currently aware can be considered part of the contents of the short-term store." Such foundational disagreements look quite embarrassing, on their face, for the cogency of the psychological literature. But these authors might respond by blaming the philosophers for foisting on them a wretchedly crude conceptual framework, in which thoughts must be either conscious or not, and either stored in memory or not. The psychologists might say that *they* know well enough what they are talking about, inasmuch as they have identified a phenomenon they can study empirically. If they lack a clear conceptual framework in which to describe this phenomenon, and so must constantly appeal to metaphors, this is perhaps the philosophers' fault.

Evidential Force

Note 3 (p. 99). The case for treating *understanding* as a central part of our epistemic framework has been made most prominently in Jonathan Kvanvig, *The Value of Knowledge*. See, for example, p. 192: "Understanding requires the grasping of explanatory and other coherence-making relationships in a large and comprehensive body of information. One can know many unrelated pieces of information, but understanding is achieved only when informational items are pieced together by the subject in question." His subsequent discussion argues for the value of such a cognitive state, and these remarks might be applied a fortiori to the Anselmian glance. See also, more recently, Duncan Pritchard, "Knowledge and Understanding."

In her paper "Explanation as Orgasm," Alison Gopnik proposes a more provocative framework for thinking about the sort of understanding involved in the Anselmian glance. She takes as her epigraph Hobbes's words on curiosity:

> Desire to know why, and how, CURIOSITY; such as is in no living creature but man: so that man is distinguished, not only by his reason, but also by this singular passion from other animals; in whom the appetite of food, and other pleasures of sense, by predominance, take away the care of knowing causes; which is a lust of the mind, that by a perseverance of delight in the continual and indefatigable generation of knowledge, exceeds the short vehemence of any carnal pleasure. (*Leviathan* 6.35)

Ockham appeals not to the sensual but to the sapiential. I have found no decisive evidence for whether he thinks that *scientia* of some conclusion *must* be accompanied by a concurrent grasp of the premises, but he makes it clear that it *can* be: "with respect to premises and conclusion there can be a single act, because a single act of understanding is no more contradictory in the case of a syllogism composed of many propositions than in the case of a proposition composed of many terms" (*Ordinatio* I prol. q. 8, in *Opera theol.* vol. 1: 218–19). Here he speaks of "a single act"; but, as noted earlier, he often does not seem to put much weight on the difference between a single mental act and multiple concurrent mental acts. In any case, he proposes *sapientia* (as cited in this lecture, p. 99) as the correct term for the mental disposition (*habitus*) that gets imprinted from an all-at-once grasp of the whole syllogism. In contrast, on the basis of these premises, the *habitus* of the conclusion alone is properly described as *scientia* (*Opera theol.* vol. 1: 222). In proposing this usage, Ockham is tacitly following the lead of Aristotle's discussion of intellectual virtues at *Nicomachean Ethics* VI.3–7, which treats σοφία as "the most finished of the forms of knowledge" (ἀκριβεστάτη ἂν τῶν ἐπιστημῶν, 1141ᵃ16), involving a grasp of both conclusions and principles. But Ockham is offering a rather imaginative extension of that terminology, since Aristotle's discussion makes no reference to anything in the vicinity of the Anselmian glance. Still, this usage gives us an explanation of why one might prefer to say that the epistemic ideal, strictly speaking, is not ἐπιστήμη or *scientia* but rather σοφία or *sapientia*. But, as a matter of historical development, this is not how the epistemic ideal would usually get understood, and for several reasons. First, Aristotle, as just quoted, is content to think of σοφία as a kind of ἐπιστήμη, which licenses using the latter term for the ideal. Second, there was competition here from Augustine, who thought of *sapientia* as the grasp of eternal things (*De trinitate* XII.14.22), a usage that heavily influenced later Christian authors and pulled *sapientia* into a different conceptual orbit.

It is unclear to what extent Ockham endorses the claim that *scientia* must be based on an actual, or even dispositional, grasp of the premises. A relevant text is *Quaestiones variae* 5 (*Opera theol.* vol. 8: 189–90), which discusses believing a proposition that one remembers to have been demonstrated, but where one has forgotten the details of the syllogism. Ockham's verdict is that, in such a case, there can be an act of assenting "without any evidentness." Given that *scientia* is almost always linked to evidentness, in Ockham and others (see Lecture Two, note 12), we might conclude that Ockham does not allow *scientia* in such a case, and he seems to say as much there. But Ockham sometimes does allow *scientia* without evidentness, as in the passage quoted at the end of Lecture Two, note 12. His examples there concern testimony, not forgotten syllogisms, but if one thinks of the memory of a conclusion as analogous to another's testimony, then one might think a forgotten syllogism can yield *scientia* in this weak sense.

Note 4 (p. 101). Peter Auriol's insistence that a whole argument must be grasped simultaneously calls to mind Thomas Wylton's argument, just a few years earlier, for why we must be able to think multiple things at once (see note 1 to this lecture). Wylton had offered this as the leading argument for his thesis: "Someone who knows a conclusion actually, for that same measure [of time], understands the principles, not just in themselves, but also in connection to the conclusion" (in Stella, "Quaestiones de libero arbitrio," p. 516). (Wylton's other main argument is our ability to think at once of a whole proposition.)

In fact, however, Auriol is not on Wylton's side in this debate, but on the side of Wylton's opponent, Durand. Durand agrees that we have to be able to grasp a whole argument at once. He insists only that we can and must do so through a single act of intellect (see note 1 to this lecture). So, when Auriol says (as quoted in this lecture, p. 100) that we must grasp a whole argument in a "singular and simple" act of intellect, he is in fact taking Durand's side on the question of how the Anselmian glance is possible. Indeed he is not just in accord with Durand's position but is further extending it, inasmuch as he is claiming that multiple concurrent acts would not even achieve the purpose of the Anselmian glance. For if we grasp premises and conclusion through distinct acts, then, even if they are temporally concurrent, they still are distinct, and so we fail to achieve the very thing we are after, which is to see the argument as a whole.

Since Auriol was revising these lectures in Paris around 1316, it seems likely that he knew of this debate between Durand and Wylton. In any case, it is clear elsewhere that Auriol's position is in accord with Durand's (and so with the *opinio communis* of the time, going back to Aquinas). But the accord comes in a surprising way. For when Auriol takes up the question of whether the angels can think about multiple things at once, he argues—against what he says is held *communiter*—that the angels can actually think about many things at once. Indeed, he goes so far as to say that, at one and the same time, the angels can actually think about *everything* that they have a species of in their mind. This is to say that they can actually think at once about everything they hold dispositionally in memory. Obviously this is not something we can do. So whence does the impossibility arise for us? Not, as Durand and Aquinas thought, from general metaphysical considerations about how forms actualize an intellect, but from the way we think in conjunction with a body:

our intellect cannot think about multiple things at once not from the nature of intellect in itself, but because of the way it is conjoined with a body and tied to a bodily power, namely through a phantasm—for we do not think about anything that we are not actually forming a phantasm of. But it is repugnant to phantasms for us to form more than one phantasm at once. (*Reportatio* II.11.3.3, in Rome edn. vol. 2: 139bD)

This is to say that our thoughts are limited by our inability to have more than one sensory image at the same time. Here it is the *materiality* of the process, rather than its *immateriality*, that drives the argument.

Even if Auriol finds himself, via this argument, in agreement with the *opinio communis* about human thought, he still insists, in a way Durand and others did not, on the importance of grasping a whole argument at once. In fact he builds this requirement into his account of *scientia*, contending that "*scientia* is something [a] determining intellect to [b] a simple intellection that [c] reaches some truth on account of another prior truth, something [d] distinct from the demonstration retained by memory, and [e] embedded in intellect" (*Scriptum* proem 4, n. 41). It is not clear whether Auriol intends this as a definition of *scientia*. The usual Aristotelian definition of *scientia*, canonically formulated by Aristotle at *Post. An.* 71^{b}10, is invoked by Auriol himself in this very discussion (n. 44), in support of his own characterization of *scientia*. Hence one might think that he intends these five clauses as consistent with the usual Aristotelian definition, but also as making an improvement upon them. In any case, the (b)–(d) clauses ensure that *scientia* must somehow involve just what Auriol says it does: an all-at-once, simple Anselmian glance over the whole argument.

A few decades later, in Paris, John Buridan similarly supposes that, when we grasp an argument, we not only can but must do so all at once. See *Summulae* VIII.3.7 (esp. trans. pp. 693–4). Buridan, however (as cited in note 1 here), takes Wylton's side on the question of thinking many things at once.

Both Buridan and Auriol frame their arguments in terms of what is required for the premises to compel the intellect to endorse an argument's conclusion, which signals that they have in mind the sort of subjective indubitability that arises from evidentness (see Lecture Two, note 13). Admittedly, neither actually speaks of *evidentia* in these particular discussions. But it seems clear enough that they are thinking of the issues in very much this way, and when we arrive at Marchia and Wodeham we find the term itself playing a central role.

Note 5 (p. 101). Francis of Marchia illustrates just how confusingly cross-cutting the various issues in play are. Like Wylton, Marchia allows that the intellect can have multiple acts of thought at once, as when it grasps a proposition in virtue of grasping simultaneously, through distinct acts of thought, the individual terms of the proposition. (Marchia argues for this thesis at *Reportatio* I.1.1 art. 1, esp. n. 35, and in a reworked form at *Scriptum* I.1.7 art. 1 [in *Quodlibet*, esp. p. 531 lines 230–36]). Turning next to the case of a whole argument, Marchia, again, aligns with Wylton against Durand and Auriol, denying that the intellect could grasp premises and conclusion in a single thought (*Reportatio* I.1.1 art. 2; *Scriptum* I.I.7 art. 2). Then, in the next article, Marchia reaches an analogous conclusion in the case of means–end reasoning: "just as the intellect cannot think about premise and conclusion by the same act, so the will cannot, by the same act, will the end and the means to the end" (*Scriptum* I.I.7 art. 3 [p. 542, lines 619–21]). For this strand of Marchia's view, see Friedman, "Mental Propositions," pp. 106–12, and "On the Trail," pp. 454–6. Marchia does not explicitly name Auriol as a target of this discussion, but since Auriol's influence on Marchia in many other places is quite explicit, a connection here seems probable as well.

What makes Marchia especially distinctive, however, is that he does not take the obvious next step of following Wylton's view that we grasp a proposition all at once in virtue of having multiple concurrent thoughts. Instead, his next question rejects the *opinio communis* that Durand, Wylton, and Auriol all share: that is, he denies that in reasoning we grasp a whole argument all at once. Marchia claims, on the contrary, that demonstration requires a *motion* from premises to the conclusion, and so the argument is not held in the mind all at once. This makes the grasp of an argument fundamentally unlike the grasp of a proposition. In addition to the passage quoted in this lecture (p. 101), consider the following text, which allows an all-at-once grasp of the terms of a proposition but then denies it for the premises of an argument:

The intellect, in understanding multiple terms at once, is not moved from one term to another term, but rather understands each one on its own. So in such an act of understanding multiple terms, the intellect does not come to rest in one term, nor is it moved by another, because it is not moved from one term to another term. If this were the case, it could not apprehend multiple terms at once. But the situation is otherwise for principle and conclusion, because the intellect is moved from the principle to the conclusion, since the inference to the conclusion is a kind of motion of reason, instantaneously advancing from principle to conclusion. Hence it cannot understand both at once.   (*Scriptum* I.1.8 [pp. 310–11])

On this sort of movement through an argument, see also *Scriptum* I.1.7 art. 2 (p. 539, lines 505–40).

Like Auriol, Marchia relies on the analogy with volition; but he takes its lesson differently: he takes it to be clear that we *can* be moved by an end for which we do not presently, occurrently, actually have any volition (see, e.g., *Reportatio* I.1.2 art. 2, n. 54; *Scriptum* I.1.8 [p. 308, lines 142–53]). Auriol grants that much, as this lecture makes clear (p. 100); but Auriol insists that the motivational force of desire requires there to be a point where means and end are desired concurrently. Marchia explicitly denies this (*Reportatio* I.1.3; *Scriptum* I.1.8 [pp. 313–16]) and denies, analogously, that premises and conclusion must at any point be grasped simultaneously. Indeed, Marchia's view is not just that they *need not* but that they *cannot* be grasped at the same time. On his view, as noted already, premises and conclusion cannot be grasped concurrently in a single act of thought (*Reportatio* I.1.1 art. 2; *Scriptum* I.I.7 art. 2). His further, more distinctive claim is that they cannot be concurrently grasped even through multiple acts, in a case where "we are actually understanding the conclusion as the endpoint of discursive reasoning" (*Reportatio* I.1.2 art. 2, n. 55). His argument, again, is that discursive reasoning requires a motion from premises to the conclusion. This claim gets applied even to the case of the angels (n. 58).

In this lecture (p. 101) I claim rather tentatively that Marchia thinks it may be possible to apprehend a whole argument at once. The basis for this is *Scriptum* I.1.8 (p. 311, lines 259–63), where he says:

although the intellect cannot understand [*intelligere*] premises and conclusion at once [*simul*], it can nevertheless apprehend [*apprehendere*] both at once, because it does not apprehend one through the other, but each on its own, and so in the act of apprehending there is no motion from one to the other, in the way that in an act of understanding the intellect is moved from one to the other.

But matters are not as clear as this suggests; for, not long after making that remark, he argues that limitations on the number of phantasms we can simultaneously entertain block the possibility of grasping a whole argument at once (*Reportatio* I.1.2 art. 2, nn. 59–60; *Scriptum* I.1.8 [pp. 311–12]). This argument seems to be taken from Auriol (see note 4 here). In any case, it would seem to block any sort of apprehension of a whole argument. And indeed, in the *Reportatio* discussion he goes on to say that "from this [argument from phantasms] it can be concluded that our intellect, in this life, cannot naturally have an actual understanding [*intelligere*] of multiple complex objects at once—which I grant" (I.1.2 art. 2, n. 63). Perhaps Marchia grants this point with an eye to the distinction between understanding and apprehension. Even so, it would seem that his arguments work just as well against any simultaneous grasp of premises and conclusion. So Marchia's exact position on these issues remains somewhat unclear.

Note 6 (p. 103). With regard to the justificational force of an argument, Marchia is in accord with Wodeham in thinking of evidentness (*evidentia*) as the critical factor. He writes: "Someone can judge only about what is evident to him. Therefore, with respect to what is evident through another rather than through itself, someone can judge only through that by means of which the thing is evident to him. But a conclusion is evident to the intellect not through itself, but rather through its premises. Therefore etc." (*Reportatio* I.1.2 art. 2, n. 48 [excluding Mariani's emendation]). But, whereas Wodeham takes it to be clear that a simultaneous grasp of premises and conclusions would enhance such evidentness, Marchia thinks that this misunderstands how arguments do their work. The evidentness we seek through syllogisms, according to Marchia, requires a discursive process that must unfold in time. Hence the debate comes to turn on a disagreement over how the mind reasons. (For Wodeham, in addition to the discussion in *Lectura secunda* dist. 1 q. 1 §§11–14, see the supplementary discussion in dist. 1 q. 2 §7.)

   Another significant discussion of Auriol's position is found in John of Reading, a contemporary of Marchia's and a fellow Franciscan, who lectured in Oxford and then, like Marchia, in Avignon. In the prologue to his *Sentences* commentary (q. 10, primum dubium), he recites Auriol at length and then argues against him. Although Reading thinks that we *can* have a single act of cognition that virtually contains two propositions, both the conclusion and the reason for it, he thinks that in practice it is implausible to suppose that all *scientia* must take that form, in view of the complexity of the arguments that often must be marshaled for a given conclusion (edited in Livesey, *Theology and Science*, pp. 184–8 and 191–8).

   Regarding Aristotle's remark from *De anima* I.3, 407^{a}32–4 (in this lecture, p. 102), Ross's edition insightfully offers the gloss that "even in a syllogism the connexion of the premises with the conclusion is grasped in a single act of thought" (p. 191). Aristotle is expressly discussing Plato, albeit not the *Theaetetus* but rather Plato's account of the world soul in the *Timaeus*, according to which the eternal god made the world soul spin continuously around itself in the same place, "the one of the seven motions that is especially associated with understanding and intelligence" (34a). Aristotle's complaint is that reasoning should not be thought of in terms of motion at all. I have not found medieval Latin authors invoking either this passage from Aristotle or the *Timaeus*. They did not have access to the *Theaetetus*.

For a useful discussion of some late scholastic debates over whether cognition occurs at an instant or over time, see Alexander Broadie, *Notion and Object*, pp. 118–24.

Descartes's Privileged Now

Note 7 (p. 104). Descartes particularly stresses the importance of getting the main argument of the *Meditations* into one's head all at once. The initial dedicatory letter, for instance, cautions that "although the proofs I employ here are in my view as certain and evident as the proofs of geometry, if not more so, it will, I fear, be impossible for many people to achieve an adequate perception of them, because they are rather long and some depend on others" (VII: 4). A 1640 letter urges Constantijn Huygens to read the first five Meditations "all in one breath" (III: 242). Mersenne was very much alive to this concern, when in the Second Objections he asked for the argument to be presented *more geometrico*: "so that at a single glance, as it were, from each reader, you would fill their minds" (VII: 128). Descartes took the bait, and constructed such an argument, acknowledging "how difficult it will be to intuit [*intueri*] the whole body of my *Meditations*, and at the same time [*simul*] to distinguish its individual members, two things that I think need to be done at once [*simul*] in order to derive the full benefit therefrom" (Second Replies, VII: 159).

Although Descartes does not fuss over the metaphysical details that so engaged the scholastics on whether thought is synchronic or diachronic, there are various indications in his work of how he regards the matter. It may be, however, that his view changed over time. As this lecture says (p. 106), he is reported in the conversation with Burman from 1648 to have held that even a single act of thought unfolds over time: "it is false that thought occurs instantaneously, for all my acts occur in time." And in a letter to Arnauld from that same year Descartes writes that "a successiveness is manifestly recognized in our own thoughts, whereas no such thing can be allowed in God's thoughts" (V: 193). Around twenty years earlier, however, in the *Rules*, he distinguishes between deduction and intuition, allowing that deductions take time, whereas in a clear and distinct intuition "the whole proposition must be understood all at once [*tota simul*], and not successively" (Rule 11, X: 407). And it is natural to think that it is this earlier idea that informs the *Meditations'* account of the *cogito* as a simple, all-at-once intuition. For we could then make good sense of why Descartes insists that the *cogito* is not a syllogism: "When someone says 'I think, therefore I am,' he does not deduce existence from thought by means of a syllogism, but rather recognizes it as something self-evident by a simple intuition of the mind" (Second Replies, VII: 140). On the all-at-once character of the *cogito*, see Peter Machamer and J. E. McGuire, *Descartes's Changing Mind*, pp. 69–71.

The enduring impact of these issues on the seventeenth century can be gauged by the number of other places where they arise. For instance, just after Galileo makes his striking remark in the *Dialogue* (1632) that a human being can equal the divine mind in certainty (see Lecture Two, p. 30), he adds that the manner in which we grasp such truths is quite different, inasmuch as "our method proceeds discursively by steps from one conclusion to another, whereas God's is one of simple intuition" (*Dialogue*, first day; trans. Drake, p. 118). The best we can do, then, is to "master some conclusions and get them so firmly demonstrated and so readily in our possession that we can run over them very rapidly."

Pascal would seem to show Descartes's influence when he writes in *Pensées* (c.1658) that "the metaphysical proofs of God are so remote from people's reasoning and so complicated that they make little impression. And when they are of service to some, it is only for the instant during which they see this demonstration. But an hour later they fear they have been mistaken" (n. 222, trans. pp. 55–6). The moral he draws, quite unlike Descartes's, is not that we need simpler and better proofs, but that we need to supplant reason with faith: "Reason acts slowly, and with so many perspectives, on so many principles, which must always be present, that it constantly falls asleep or wanders, when it fails to have all its principles present. Feeling does not act in this way; it acts instantaneously, and is always ready to act. We must then put our faith in feeling; otherwise it will always be vacillating" (n. 661, trans. p. 202). For more on Pascal in this domain, see Lecture Six, note 15.

Leibniz, in his *New Essays* (1704) offers a similar rationale for the importance of faith:

God, it is true, never bestows this faith unless what he is making one believe is grounded in reason . . . but it is not necessary that all who possess this divine faith should know those reasons, and still less that they should have them perpetually before their eyes. Otherwise none of the unsophisticated . . . would have the true faith, and the most enlightened people might not have it when they most needed it, since no one can always remember his reasons for believing. (IV.18, p. 497)

Lecture Six will return to the role that faith might play in our story.

The distinction between an all-at-once intuition and deduction over time shows up again in Locke. He distinguishes the degrees of knowledge in terms of degrees of evidentness or clarity. There are, he says initially, just two degrees of evidentness that are sufficient for knowledge: intuition and demonstration. The difference is entirely a matter of how much can be grasped at once. In the case of intuition, we immediately grasp the agreement or disagreement between two ideas: "such kind of truths, the mind perceives at the first sight of the ideas together, by bare intuition, without the intervention of any other idea, and this kind of knowledge is the clearest and most certain that human frailty is capable of" (*Essay* IV.2.1). Locke treats it as entirely unproblematic that we can, at an instant, compare two ideas. But because the mind cannot always "so bring its ideas together, as by their immediate comparison, and as it were juxtaposition or application one to another, to perceive their agreement or disagreement, it is fain, by the intervention of other ideas (one or more, as it happens) to discover the agreement or disagreement which it searches" (IV.2.2). This, in general, is reasoning, and if every step along the way counts as intuitively known, then the whole counts as a demonstration. See also *Essay* IV.17.15:

one simple intuition, wherein there is no room for any the least mistake or doubt: the truth is seen all perfectly at once. In demonstration, 'tis true, there is intuition too, but not altogether at once; for there must be a remembrance of the intuition of the agreement of the medium, or intermediate idea, with that we compared it with before, when we compare it with the other.

This suggests that Locke, like Burge, thinks it impossible to grasp a whole argument all at once, without relying on "remembrance." In the *Conduct of the Understanding* §3, he compares our case with that of the angels:

we may imagine a vast and almost infinite advantage that angels and separate spirits may have over us . . . some of them perhaps have perfect and exact views of all finite beings that come under their consideration, [and] can, as it were, in the twinkling of an eye, collect together all their scattered and almost boundless relations. A mind so furnished, what reason has it to acquiesce in the certainty of its conclusions!

The importance of synchronically grasping an argument appears again in Joseph Butler's *Analogy of Religion* (1736), who urges that the accumulation of arguments for Christianity, if it is to achieve evidentness, must be grasped all together: "Thus the evidence of Christianity will be a long series of things . . . making up all of them together one argument; the conviction arising from which kind of proof may be compared to what they call the effect in architecture or other works of art, a result from a great number of things so and so disposed and taken into one view" (*Analogy* II.7, p. 224). Why is this important? Because "it is easy to show . . . that this and another thing is of little weight in itself, but impossible to show in like manner the united force of the whole argument in one view" (p. 261).

At around this same time, Hume, at *Treatise* I.3.1, so takes for granted the distinction between synchronic intuition and diachronic demonstration that he does not even bother to explain it. Hume gets it from Locke, no doubt, and perhaps Locke gets it from Descartes. The term 'intuition' seems to be commonly in use throughout the seventeenth century, and I suspect that it has its origins in the ultimately Scotistic distinction between intuitive and abstractive cognition described in Lecture Four. This terminology, however, undergoes a startling transformation in the seventeenth century: whereas for scholastic authors the paradigm case of intuitive cognition had been a direct perceptual grasp of things in the world, for later seventeenth-century authors the paradigm of intuition becomes the direct comparison of ideas (see Lilli Alanen and Mikko Yrjönsuuri, "Intuition, judgement et evidence," p. 169). Descartes remarks in *Rules* 3 that he is not using 'intuition' as it has been "usurped in recent times in the Schools" (X: 369), which helpfully marks both his awareness of the earlier tradition and his distance from it.

Looking ahead to the twentieth century, Bertrand Russell also argues for the importance of getting an argument into the privileged now, not because of the greater evidential force of such an argument but because this is required in order to preserve, across an argument, sameness of reference, which otherwise is liable to shift as our sense data shift:

Question: If the proper name of a thing, a "this," varies from instant to instant, how is it possible to make any argument?

Mr. Russell: You can keep "this" going for about a minute or two. I made that dot and talked about it for some little time. I mean it varies often. If you argue quickly, you can get some little way before it is finished.
                    ("Philosophy of Logical Atomism," p. 203; I owe this reference to Hilary Kornblith)

Russell is talking about spoken discourse, but the point presumably applies to thinking as well. He does not here suppose that a whole argument needs to be grasped in a single instant, but still, for his own idiosyncratic reasons, he sees the need to "argue quickly."

Returning to Descartes, whatever the case may be for simple intuitions, it is clear in general that, for him, demonstrative arguments are not grasped in an instant, let alone in a single thought. Accordingly, his remark to Huygens (above) about "one breath" fits with the *Rules'* talk of "a continuous and wholly uninterrupted sweep of thought" (as quoted in this lecture, p. 103). Given his diachronic picture of how thought works, this sort of rapid and continuous inspection of the whole is as good as we can hope for. To seek the Anselmian glance in some stronger sense would be to hope for a more-than-human ideal.

The Cartesian Circle

Note 8 (p. 106). That the Cartesian epistemic ideal requires the knowledge of God's existence is amply attested elsewhere. Compare Descartes's remark, just before the long Meditation Five passage quoted in this lecture (p. 104), that "the certainty of all other things so depends on this [the certainty of God's existence] that without it there can never be perfect *scientia* of anything" (VII: 69). In Meditation Three he had already announced that "if I do not have *scientia* of God's existence, then it seems I can never be quite certain about anything else" (VII: 36). And in the Second Replies the atheist "will never be free of this doubt until he acknowledges that God exists" (VII: 141).

The privileged-now reading of Descartes's position, which rests on a distinction between the synchronic and the diachronic ideals of inquiry, would be bolstered if he were to flag more clearly the distinction between the sort of epistemic achievement that is an occurrent, clear and distinct grasp of a conclusion on the basis of its premises and the resulting *scientia* that is a stable disposition to affirm that conclusion. The second is the ultimate goal of inquiry, but it cannot be reached without the first. One place where Descartes suggests this picture is a 1640 letter to Regius (III: 64–5) where he says that we can have *persuasio* of conclusions "at the moment when we deduced them from those principles," but we cannot have *scientia* until we recognize that God exists and is no deceiver. Then we have the kind of *persuasio* that is "based on a reason so strong that it can never be shaken by any stronger reason"—and such a *scientia* can endure even after the premises are no longer being considered.

As I understand this remark to Regius, he does not mean to say that, at the moment of deduction, *persuasio* is anything less than certain. Admittedly, the letter is less than clear on this point, inasmuch as it characterizes *persuasio* as a case where "there remains [*superest*] some reason that could push us toward doubt" (V: 65). I have to understand this as referring to a reason that could arise only once the clear and distinct perception has faded away. For textual support on this point, see the Seventh Replies (VII: 460):

So long as we attend to a truth that we perceive very clearly, we cannot doubt it. But when, as so often happens, we are not attending to any truth in this way, even though we remember that we have perceived many things very clearly, nevertheless there will be nothing which we may not justly doubt so long as we do not know that whatever we clearly perceive is true.

So the reason, in the letter to Regius, why *persuasio* not grounded in God does not count as *scientia* is not that—at that moment—it can "be shaken by any stronger reason," but rather that it inevitably *will* be shakable once the clarity of the whole deduction falls out of view. Without the background story about God, then, mere *persuasio* does not satisfy the requirement that "it can *never* be shaken."

A passage reported in the conversation with Burman sets out the whole story nicely:

If we were unaware that all truth has its origin in God, then however clear our ideas were, we would not have *scientia* that they were true, or that we were not mistaken—I mean, of course, when we were not paying attention to them, and when we merely remembered that we had clearly and distinctly perceived them. For on other occasions, when we do pay attention to the truths themselves, even if we do not have *scientia* that God exists, we cannot be in any doubt about them. For otherwise, we could not prove that God exists.   (V: 178)

With this distinction between an all-at-once clear and distinct *persuasio* and a stable dispositional *scientia*, the solution to the Cartesian circle becomes clear in terms of the special status, for Descartes, of the privileged now. Although I hope to have helped situate this line of thought in its broader historical and philosophical context, I do not take any particular credit for the privileged-now solution to the circle, since one can find roughly the same sort of story in a great many other recent scholars. See, for instance (in chronological order), James Van Cleve, "Foundationalism," Bernard Williams, "Descartes's Use of Skepticism," pp. 349–50, John Cottingham, *Descartes*, pp. 66–73, Michael Della Rocca, "Descartes, the Cartesian Circle," John Carriero, *Between Two Worlds*, pp. 337–58, Baron Reed, "Knowledge, Doubt, and Circularity," pp. 277–81, and Thomas Lennon and Michael Hickson, "Skepticism of the First Meditation," pp. 18–20. There is indeed such consensus among scholars about how to handle the notorious puzzle of the circle that I think this is one problem in Cartesian scholarship we should simply declare solved.

Memory's Testimony

Note 9 (p. 108). The privileged-now account is quite distinct from the "memory gambit," which has long and rightly been rejected as a solution to the circle (the decisive arguments go back to Frankfurt, "Memory and the Cartesian Circle"). For a succinct statement of the difference between appealing to memory and appealing to the privileged now, I can do no better than to quote Van Cleve ("Foundationalism," p. 57):

Consider the following sequence of propositions:

(1) I remember clearly and distinctly perceiving *p*.
(2) So, I did clearly and distinctly perceive *p*.
(3) So, *p* is true.

Descartes says that the atheist cannot argue from (1) to (3). According to the Memory Gambit, this is because he cannot take the step from (1) to (2). But another possible explanation is that he cannot take the step from (2) to (3).

Like Van Cleve, I take it that the inference from (2) to (3) is what needs to be rejected, inasmuch as Descartes accepts this inference only when (2) is framed in the present tense. Here is precisely where his dogmatism lies.

There is decisive textual evidence showing that Descartes is not mainly concerned with memory. For instance, the long passage from Meditation Five quoted in this lecture (p. 104) is prepared to grant the reliability of memory: "as soon as I turn my mind's eye away from the demonstration, then *in spite of still remembering that I perceived it with complete clarity*, I can easily fall into doubt about its truth" (VII: 70, emphasis added). Pressed by Burman to address memory's reliability, Descartes is reported as having remarked: "I can say nothing about memory, since each of us should each test ourselves as to whether we are good at remembering. If one has any doubts on that score, then he should make use of written notes and so forth to help him" (V: 148).

For an intricate recent philosophical discussion of the relationship between memory and testimony, see David James Barnett, "Is Memory Merely Testimony?".

Note 10 (p. 110). Exactly how much do we have to remember in order to have the sort of *scientia* that Descartes promises? Clearly, we have to remember the conclusion of the Reliability Proof:

(CD)   Everything I clearly and distinctly perceive is true.

And, since we need this claim to extend to past cases, we also need to remember

(CD+)   Everything I have clearly and distinctly perceived is true.

But perhaps we do not need to remember the argument that got us to CD and CD+? So Descartes might seem to say in the long Fifth Meditation passage quoted in this lecture (p. 104):

Now, however, I have perceived that God exists, and at the same time I have understood that everything else depends on him, and that he is no deceiver. From this I have drawn the conclusion that everything I clearly and distinctly perceive is of necessity true [= CD]. Accordingly, *even if I am no longer attending to the arguments on account of which I have judged that this is true*, as long as I remember that I clearly and distinctly perceived, no counter-argument can be adduced to make me doubt. On the contrary, I have true and certain *scientia* of it.   (VII: 70, emphasis added)

A precise understanding of this passage is impeded by unclarity regarding what the referent of the underlined 'this' is. He is, I take it, referring at least in part to CD. But he might also be referring to

(GD)   God is no deceiver.

Given Descartes's insistence that *scientia* requires a recognition of God's existence, one would expect GD to be among the things we must remember. And the 1640 letter to Regius (discussed in note 8 here) confirms this point:

When someone has once clearly understood the reasons that persuade us that God exists and is not a deceiver, even if he no longer attends to those reasons, *so long as he remembers just the conclusion "God is no deceiver,"* there will remain in him not just the *persuasio* but also the true *scientia* both of this and also of all other conclusions whose reasons he remembers himself to have at some time clearly perceived.   (III: 65)

Descartes says, in both of these passages, that I must "remember" CD and GD. That cannot mean, absurdly, that I am constantly thinking about these theses at Grade A (see p. 107), but just that they are at Grade B, on hand for immediate recall when the question arises. What about the rest of the details of the Reliability Proof? Descartes certainly seems to be saying that these details can slip down to a lower grade. But how far? He does not say, in either of these passages, that *scientia* would be compatible with wholly forgetting the full Reliability Proof that gets us to GD and ultimately to CD and CD+. What he says, in both passages, is that I need not presently "attend" to that proof. This is consistent with the lecture's claim that the details of the proof must be able to be recalled. My suggestion is that CD and GD must remain at Grade B, ready for immediate recall should doubts arise. The remaining details of the Reliability Proof might not be attended to even then, but we still have to be able to access them too, if pushed hard enough by doubt. So these details must remain at Grade C, accessible albeit it with effort. On the privileged-now interpretation, this is as low as the Reliability Proof can go. The proof cannot slip down to Grade D, becoming unrecallable, because the whole system depends on according a special sort of privilege to occurrent clear and distinct perceptions. What we want is *scientia*, a stable disposition, and this requires the sort of indubitability such that "no counterargument can be adduced to make me doubt" (VII: 70). Since the only ultimate recourse against doubt is clear and distinct perception in the privileged now, we must be able to get that whole Reliability Proof in our mind all at once, in as close to a single Anselmian glance as is humanly possible. If we lose the ability to do that, we lose the ideal indubitability of *scientia*.

Another passage relevant to these issues comes from the end of Meditation Four:

Although I experience within myself the weakness of being unable to keep my attention always fixed on one and the same thought [*cognitio*], still I am able, by attentive and regularly repeated meditation, to make myself remember this same thought as often as the need arises, and thus get into the habit of avoiding error.   (VII: 62)

Christia Mercer, in an erudite discussion of the role of meditation in the *Meditations*, points out the significance of this passage to Descartes's method ("Methodology," p. 38). The unreliable "weakness" of our fugitive thoughts requires something other than the usual philosophical approach—it requires that the reader join in a meditation that will make a lasting difference to our understanding of the world.

Disprivileging the Present Self

Note 11 (p. 112). To understand why Descartes puts such weight on the privileged now, it helps considerably to keep in mind the idealized framework described in the first two lectures: that he is describing not a perfectly unassailable absolute ideal, but simply the best position we can be expected to achieve, given our capacities and the world in which we live. Still, even within that framework, I contend that his view is simply a mistake. For, even if we follow Descartes in according special weight to what is clear and distinct, there should be nothing epistemically privileged, for me, about *my* clear and distinct perceptions *now*.

In assessing Descartes's brand of dogmatism, there is little to be learned from the recent secondary literature, which has not dwelt in any detail on these issues, let alone recognized that Descartes's views are continuous with earlier scholastic debates. But we might compare a similar line of thought that Richard Foley has recently advanced. Foley argues that, in cases of conflict between present and past views, our present views should be given special weight, because of "the banal truth that at the current moment, if I am to have opinions at all, they will be current opinions." Accordingly, "it cannot be a demand of rationality that I shed my current perspective and adopt a vantage point from which I treat all of my temporal selves and their opinions identically" (*Intellectual Trust*, p. 149).

We should distinguish, though, between the truly banal claim that, necessarily, what I now believe is what I now believe, and the substantial claim that my present opinions must give special weight to how things seem to me now, in preference to how they seemed to me at some earlier time. The first claim is trivial, but the second describes a contingent and significant doxastic practice. You might decide to adhere, in every case, to how things seem to you now. But this is likely to be a bad general policy. It may seem to you, for instance, that something you have written is a brilliant piece of philosophy, but if your dissertation director says otherwise, it is probably rational for you to abandon that self-confident belief, even if the paper still *seems* brilliant. Conversely, a certain complex thesis may no longer seem right to you. But if you have previously considered the matter carefully and found it to be true, then it may make sense to continue believing it, even if it does not presently seem right. Rationality does not require that your beliefs track how things intellectually seem to you any more than your perceptual beliefs must track how things visually appear. (I do not *believe* that the stick is bent, despite its *looking* that way.) To be sure, your present self controls (or at least should control) what you believe. But this does not entail that your present self must give special weight to how things seem to you now.

In denying that there is anything epistemically privileged about the first-person now, we should allow our past perspectives, and the perspectives of others, to receive equal consideration in our ultimate determination of what is the case. Of course, that ultimate determination must happen in the now. As things *ultimately* seem to be, so one must (or at least should) believe. In that sense, the now is privileged. The very decision to reject Cartesian dogmatism about the first-person now is, after all, a decision that one makes *now*. In this sense, Foley is quite correct that I cannot treat the views of my past selves "identically" with those of my present self. The present self ultimately determines (or should determine) what I think. But it need not be incoherent for me to decide that what *now* seems best is to give my past views weight equal to my current ones. I might even decide that I used to be much wiser, and hence I might treat my past self as a kind of guru controlling my present beliefs within a certain domain.

The previous remarks concern a case of intrapersonal disagreement over time. But the more common intrapersonal case is not one of disagreement but of a failure to remember even as much as would be needed for me to be sure whether or not I disagree with my past self. Here the question arises whether I should trust the fragments I do remember, even though I no longer remember the grounds on which those fragments were based. Modern authors have taken a range of views on this subject. Norman Malcolm thinks that those forgotten reasons wholly retain their epistemic force: "If a man previously had grounds for being sure that *p*, and he now remembers that *p*, but does not remember what his grounds were, then he nonetheless has the same grounds he previously had" (*Knowledge and Certainty*, p. 230).

Andrew Moon ("Knowing without Evidence") has recently taken the converse view that, in cases where the evidence for a belief no longer survives, it is no longer the case that this belief is based upon that evidence. But rather than hug the monster that lurks here and admit that a great deal of what we believe is unwarranted, Moon concludes instead that one can have knowledge without evidence.

Tyler Burge takes a compromise view. *Justification*, he thinks, requires that one be able to recall the premises to a justifying argument. But he identifies a weaker notion of *entitlement*, and argues that someone "can be entitled to believe a theorem she believes because of a preservative memory even if she cannot remember the proof she gave long ago, and even if she cannot remember that she gave a proof" ("Interlocution," p. 38). Indeed, "most of what one is entitled to believe . . . derives from sources and warrants that one has forgotten" (p. 38). (This is effectively what we saw Adam Wodeham claim in this lecture, pp. 102–3, when he distinguished between two grades of *scientia*.)

Gilbert Harman (*Change in View* ch. 4) discusses in detail the problem of forgotten evidence and contends that so much has slipped into (what I call) Grade D that it is simply hopeless to conceive of knowledge as grounded in evidence. The best one can hope for (what I call the normative ideal) is to hold beliefs that are coherent with other things one believes. Ralph Wedgwood ("Justified Inference") builds upon this idea but distinguishes between enduring beliefs (where something like Harman's view is right) and occurrent mental events, where some more evidentialist account can be given.

Note 12 (p. 113). Locke regards the problem of forgotten evidence (or lost evidentness) as critical to a comprehensive theory of knowledge, because he thinks it is the usual case. Although the ideal is the Anselmian glance that occurs in what he calls intuition (see note 7 here), reasoning of any complexity requires memory, which is severely limited. One might conclude from this that, as the evidentness of our conclusions fades, we should reduce our credences accordingly. But Locke expressly formulates the principle of proportionality so that it calls for our retaining our original credences, even after the evidence has been forgotten:

> I confess, in the opinions men have and firmly stick to in the world, their assent is not always from an actual view of the reasons that at first prevailed with them: It being in many cases almost impossible, and in most very hard, even for those who have very admirable memories, to retain all the proofs which upon a due examination made them embrace that side of the question. It suffices that they have once with care and fairness sifted the matter as far as they could . . . and thus having once found on which side the probability appeared to them, after as full and exact an enquiry as they can make, they lay up the conclusion in their memories, as a truth they have discovered; and for the future they remain satisfied with the testimony of their memories, that this is the opinion that by the proofs they have once seen of it deserves such a degree of their assent as they afford it. (*Essay* IV.16.1)

It is debatable, as the previous note considered, whether forgotten evidence still counts as evidence in our modern sense of that term. But, given Locke's usage of 'evidence' to mean *evidentness*, the passage just quoted requires a significant adjustment to the principle of proportionality described in Lecture Two (p. 40), according to which one ought to proportion one's assent to the evidence. A conclusion retained after its proof has faded away does not have the evidentness it once had. So, contrary to his usual formulations—for example: "It is very easily said, and nobody questions it, that giving and withholding our assent, and the degrees of it, should be regulated by the evidence which things carry with them" (*Conduct of the Understanding* §33)—Locke is telling us here that very often we should not proportion our assent to a proposition's current evidentness, but should tie that assent to the evidentness it had at the time of "due examination."

Descartes, as we have seen, acknowledged the difficulty of holding on to a complex argument over time. But he was clearly much less tolerant than Locke of such imperfections. One might wonder whether part of what accounts for this disagreement, and for the pronounced divergence in their philosophical styles, is a difference in their relative abilities to keep their own complex theories in mind all at once. Locke, perhaps because he was more thoroughly immersed in practical affairs, struggled to hold together the complexities of a theory that he built up over many years. His famously loose and repetitive manner is the symptom of a mind that finds it difficult to get the whole account under the control of a single

Anselmian glance. Descartes, in contrast, displays throughout his work a masterfully systematic control over the many intricate details of his account. This, I suspect, was possible for him because he had a remarkable ability to keep in his head a much fuller picture of his whole theory—perhaps in part just because he had fewer distractions in his life. Unsurprisingly, then, Descartes tended to stress the importance of others' doing the same, whereas Locke was much more forgiving.

This difference shows up again in their contrasting attitudes to disagreement. It is not exactly the case that Descartes was so solipsistic that he never learned from criticism. He did enlarge and clarify many of his positions in response to correspondence with others, and occasionally he asked for corrections to be made to his work. (For discussion, see Roger Ariew, "The *Meditations* and the *Objections* and *Replies*.") But Descartes thought that having *scientia* entails a kind of invulnerability to criticism, and indeed that it ultimately should put an end to disagreement:

> Whenever two persons make opposite judgments about the same thing, it is certain that at least one of them is deceived, and it seems that neither has *scientia*. For if the reasoning of one of them were certain and evident, he would be able to lay it before the other in such a way as eventually to convince the other's intellect as well.
>
> (*Rules* 2, X: 363)

Those who are in possession of *scientia* grasp the reasons for their beliefs in a way that ought "eventually" to settle all disagreement. Locke thinks no such thing. Because he holds that assent on the basis of forgotten reasons can still count as "in effect true knowledge" (*Essay* IV.1.9), he cannot suppose that knowledge dispels disagreement. On the contrary, his resolution of the problem of forgotten evidence leads directly to his conclusion that disagreement must inevitably be widespread and that our best recourse is "to commiserate our mutual ignorance . . . and not instantly treat others ill, as obstinate and perverse, because they will not renounce their own, and receive our opinions" (*Essay* IV.16.4). No sentiment could be more foreign to Descartes's combative manner.

On individualism as a working method in the seventeenth century, see Stevin Shapin, "The Mind in Its Own Place." For a handy overview of the sorts of dogmatism one finds in recent epistemology, see Ali Hasan and Richard Fumerton, "Foundationalist Theories" §4. I discuss these issues somewhat further in Lecture Six, note 15.

Note 13 (p. 114). There has been considerable recent work on the epistemology of disagreement, going well beyond the fairly superficial remarks of Descartes and Locke. On one prominent line of thought, often known as the "equal weight view," we should show no partiality to our own judgments about what is right, in cases where we are confronted with others who seem equally well positioned to get at the truth (our "epistemic peers"). On this view, we should not only be tolerant of disagreement (as Locke would have it), but we should adjust our own views to take into account the divergent views of others (something Locke does not expect of us). This is what we should do, according to this line of thought, not only on Locke's relatively tolerant picture of what knowledge requires, but even on Descartes's stricter version. For, even if we were to get ourselves into an ideal state of Cartesian certainty, grounded in occurrent clear and distinct perceptions, we ought to adjust our beliefs downward in the face of a dissenter who seems equally well positioned. Of course, Descartes would insist that such disagreement is impossible: that is the whole point of the guarantee provided by clear and distinct perceptions. But surely we have seen enough philosophy go by, at this stage in its history, to acknowledge that there is no such privileged state of truth-guaranteeing mental clarity.

Influential statements of the equal weight view can be found, for example, in David Christensen, "Epistemology of Disagreement" and Adam Elga, "Reflection and Disagreement."

Elga also makes some interesting remarks on the question of trusting one's future self. This is a problem that largely gets ignored in the seventeenth century, but would be invoked in Condorcet's notes for his 1782 inaugural address to the *Académie française*, where he wondered about what confidence we should have that our present certainty over a mathematical proposition such as 2 + 2 = 4 will carry on into the future (see Popkin, "Scepticism," p. 436).

It seems to me that, if one's only concern is with epistemic rationality—roughly, with getting at the truth—then the equal weight view is correct, as applied both to interpersonal disagreement and to intrapersonal disagreement over time. But it also seems to me that recognizing this leads directly to a deeper and more interesting point, which is that epistemic rationality is not and should not be the only thing we care about when it comes to forming beliefs. One other thing we do and should value, I believe, is self-trust—the sort of doxastic tendency that makes Descartes's boldness and confidence so admirable in many ways, even if we might think that he exhibits this trait to an extent that goes somewhat past the golden mean. (I have written about self-trust in the face of disagreement in "Disagreement and the Value of Self-Trust.")

Lecture Six considers the value of faith and hope as grounds for belief in cases where epistemic rationality seems to yield doubt.

Hume's Privileged Now

Note 14 (p. 116). For reasons that Lecture Six discusses, I find in Hume some inspiration for taking the ethics of belief beyond the narrowly epistemic. But my argument there is that he merely opens the door and does not arrive at anything approaching a satisfactory account of what our cognitive aspirations should be, once the prospects of rationality prove disappointing. Here, though, my concern is with just one feature of Hume's position: the significance he gives to an all-at-once Anselmian glance. Although commentators have barely noticed the issue (let alone situated it in its proper historical context), it arises over and over. The very last paragraph of *Treatise* Book I, for instance, offers Hume's blessing on the philosophical enterprise: it is "proper we should in general indulge our inclination in the most elaborate philosophical researches, notwithstanding our sceptical principles." Moreover, he immediately continues, "we should yield to that propensity, which inclines us to be positive and certain in *particular points*, according to that light, in which we survey them in any *particular instant*" (I.4.7, p. 273). The italics are Hume's, because he wants to stress that the enterprise of philosophy rests on grasping conclusions at a time and cannot be counted upon to endure beyond that time. Thus the famous backgammon passage concludes: "when, after three or four hour's amusement, I would return to these speculations, they appear so cold, and strained, and ridiculous, that I cannot find in my heart to enter into them any farther" (p. 269). The start of Book III of the *Treatise* returns to this theme, reminding the reader of the "inconvenience which attends all abstruse reasoning . . . When we leave our closet, and engage in the common affairs of life, its conclusions seem to vanish, like the phantoms of the night on the appearance of the morning; and 'tis difficult for us to retain even that conviction, which we had attained with difficulty" (p. 455; cf. *Enquiry concerning Human Understanding* section 1, p. 7). In Descartes, this "inconvenience" is both recognized and guarded against by an extended meditation that ultimately appeals to a divine guarantee. But in Hume the failing is seen as working in part to our advantage, inasmuch as it allows us to escape a skepticism that would otherwise be inescapable: "this [skeptical] difficulty is seldom or never thought of; and even when it has once been present to the mind, is quickly forgot, and leaves but a small impression behind it" (*Treatise* I.4.7, p. 268). If Hume had felt obliged to subject himself to a Cartesian regime of philosophical meditation, or if he had taken Locke's view that we ought to govern our assent according to the probability of conclusions reached in the past from premises now forgotten, then his "abstruse reasoning" would have forced him into full-blown, debilitating skepticism. But instead Hume thinks that we *cannot* maintain such credences in cases where they conflict so sharply with our natures. Hence the *ought* of Locke's principle of proportionality becomes otiose.

In note 12 here I speculated that perhaps Descartes's and Locke's contrasting attitudes to the privileged now arise from their differing capacities to hold in mind at once a complex train of thought. As it happens, we have autobiographical evidence that this was a concern of Hume's. In a letter from 1734, addressed to a physician and written while he was working out the ideas that would become the *Treatise of Human Nature*, Hume lodges the following complaint about his condition:

> But my disease was a cruel incumbrance on me. I found that I was not able to follow out any train of thought, by one continued stretch of view, but by repeated interruptions, and by refreshing my eye from time to time upon other objects. Yet with this inconvenience I have collected the rude materials for many volumes; but in reducing these to words, when one must bring the Idea he comprehended in gross, nearer to him, so as to contemplate its minutest parts, and keep it steadily in his eye, so as to copy these parts in order, this I found impracticable for me, nor were my spirits equal to so severe an employment. Here lay my greatest calamity.
>
> (*Letters* I: 16)

What Hume is looking for is, precisely, the Anselmian glance. Perhaps he was later able to do better, or perhaps he simply came to realize that his condition was indeed the human condition. In any case, what he here describes as his "calamity" takes on a leading role in the argument of the *Treatise*.

Understanding the role of the privileged now allows a more nuanced understanding of the relationship between reason and passion for Hume. According to Norman Kemp Smith, "his attitude in ethics—that 'reason is, and ought only to be the slave of the passions . . .'—has its exact counterpart in his theory of knowledge" ("Naturalism of Hume," p. 156). This is not right. In Hume's theory of knowledge, reason can override our sensory natures under the right circumstances, that is, in the calm of one's study, when the grounds for belief can be drawn together under a single Anselmian glance. Reason's power in that context is what precipitates the skeptical crisis of the *Treatise*. The sensory part does indeed dominate, and even does so by an "absolute and uncontrollable necessity" (*Treatise* I.4.1 p. 183), but this is so not through brute enslavement, but simply through its outlasting the fleeting power of reason. Kemp Smith cites in his favor a passage from the first *Enquiry* in which Hume is talking about causal beliefs reached in the face of constant conjunction: "All these operations are a species of natural instincts, which no reasoning or process of the thought and understanding is able either to produce or prevent" (5.1, pp. 46–7). But the context shows this remark to be limited in its application. The previous sentence says: "It is an operation of the soul, *when we are so situated*, as unavoidable as to feel the passion of love, *when we receive benefits*; or hatred, *when we meet with injuries*." The clauses I have emphasized make clear that Hume thinks that it is only in certain circumstances that "no reasoning" is able to influence these beliefs. In the cool calm of one's study, matters may be quite different. Indeed, things must be different there, or otherwise Hume would have been unable to write about causation as he did, and we would be unable to grasp the force of his argument.

David Owen's discussion of these issues strikes me as getting closer to the heart of things (*Hume's Reason*, pp. 193–6). Owen stresses that, for Hume, reason has little force against habitual belief in cases where it must rely on long chains of reasoning (see, e.g., *Treatise* I.3.13, pp. 145–6; I.4.1, p. 185). This is an important piece of the story. But to see why this matters so much, we need to supply the further piece I am describing here. Hume is not saying that long arguments have any less force intrinsically, but that they fail to have lasting force on minds such as ours, because they are simply too complex to get into our heads all at once. They represent the opposite extreme of the cognitive continuum that has, at its other end, the case of belief produced by an immediate sensory impression or remembered idea: "to believe is in this case to feel an immediate impression of the senses, or a repetition of that impression in the memory" (*Treatise* I.3.5, p. 86). In such a case the cognitive side of our nature is relatively secure against passion and sentiment, because the impression leads directly to belief. Some rational arguments can be like that too—perhaps the *cogito* is the best example—and, again, in such cases the cognitive is more secure against the sensitive side of our nature. But in philosophy matters quickly and inevitably get much more complex, and when that happens reason cannot hold out. From the start, such reasoning is too fragile to survive distraction: "the first and most trivial event in life will put to flight all his doubts and scruples" (*Enquiry* 12.2, p. 160). Subsequently, abstruse arguments, once lost, cannot easily be recalled to mind: "we enter with difficulty into remote views of things, and are not able to accompany them with so sensible an impression, as we do those which are more easy and natural" (*Treatise* I.4.7, p. 268). So much weight does Hume put on these considerations that he remarks, of this last cognitive limitation, that it is "only by means of that singular and seemingly trivial property of the fancy" that "we save ourselves from this total scepticism" (p. 268).

Annette Baier approaches the ideas I am developing in an intriguingly different way. For her, *Treatise* I.4 describes not an ideal we sadly cannot achieve (the reading I develop in Lecture Six), but a failed picture of how reason ought to work, due ultimately to Descartes, which Hume recognizes as a failure and attempts to supersede. Part of what needs rejecting in *Treatise* I.4, Baier thinks, is the very idea of an Anselmian glance, or what she calls "a static consistent system." In its place, Hume gives us "an instructive series of mutually contradicting self-correcting theses" (*Progress of Sentiments*, p. 26). The very title of Baier's book refers to a model of reasoning that unfolds over time and does not attempt to grasp the whole all at once. The picture she proposes deserves much more discussion (and see Lecture Six, notes 11–12, for further remarks), but it seems to me that, at least as a reading of Hume, it misses much of the poignancy of his position. Baier takes as her slogan Hume's invitation to join him in studying philosophy "in this careless manner" (*Treatise* I.4.7, p. 273), remarking that Hume uses this word in the older sense of "carefree rather than negligent" (*Progress of Sentiments*, p. 1). Hume does, in his *History of England*, occasionally use the word 'careless' in what is unmistakably that older sense, as in praising Charles II for a temper that is "cheerful, careless, and sociable" (VI: 77). But the overwhelming preponderance of the dozens of occurrences of this word in Hume is negative, as when he refers to "the universal carelessness and stupidity of men with regard to a future state, where they shew as obstinate an incredulity, as they do a blind credulity on other occasions" (*Treatise* I.3.9, p. 113). Moreover, the carelessness he recommends at I.4.7 as being "more truly skeptical" is just a reframing of his less sanguine reference, four pages earlier, to a "blind submission [in which] I show most perfectly my sceptical disposition and principles" (I.4.7, p. 269). So, even if the carelessness of the manner that Hume recommends is officially offered as a commendation, we should bear in mind the irony behind his choice of words—a reminder that, in pursuing philosophy in this manner, we betray an ideal that we might have hoped to achieve.

Notes to Lecture Six

God the Deceiver

Note 1 (p. 118). Like so many of the ideas associated with skepticism, the possibility of divine deception is so obvious and natural that its constant recurrence in the history of philosophy requires no special explanation. Even if this and other skeptical scenarios had been somehow lost from the historical record, it would take about five minutes for some clever philosopher to come along and reinvent them. So I do not find it very interesting to comb the historical record for information about when exactly this or that skeptical text reemerged. No one needed Sextus Empiricus, for example, to see that deception and error might pose an obstacle to knowledge. (With Aristotle and Plato matters are quite different: if we had lost their work, we would have lost philosophical ideas that might never have been reinvented.) The *fortuna* of Sextus and other such skeptical texts over the centuries is interesting, then, less because of what it shows about when certain ideas might have been transmitted, and more because it shows us when skepticism was and was not taken seriously enough to want to have these skeptical works readily available.

And indeed it is interesting to see how the worry about divine deception gets taken more seriously at some times than at others. In antiquity, Cicero invokes it at *Academica* 2.15.47, as a staple of Academic skepticism (see Leo Groarke, "Descartes' First Meditation," pp. 286–7). Among earlier scholastic authors, in contrast, the possibility is not particularly prominent. Aquinas, for one, is more interested in how angels and demons might influence our thoughts for better and worse (see, e.g., *Quaest. de malo* 16.12, and the discussion in Dominik Perler, *Zweifel und Gewissheit*, pp. 123–35). On demonic deception more generally, see Geoffrey Scarre, "Demons." For a sense of how demonic deception figures among ordinary folk more generally in thirteenth-century Europe, see *Dialogus miraculorum*, an immensely popular collection of miracle stories assembled in the early thirteenth century by Caesarius of Heisterbach, particularly Book V on demons.

In the fourteenth century quite an extensive discussion of divine deception emerges. Ockham seems to have been the starting point, not because he regarded divine deception as a threat, but precisely because he was puzzlingly dismissive of it, insisting that, if God were to cause in me the perception of an object that does not exist, then what would seem evident to me is precisely that the object does not exist (e.g., *Reportatio* II.12–13, in *Opera theol.* vol. 5: 260). On this, see Lecture Four, note 17.

Ockham's position provoked a widespread response and was generally rejected even by subsequent Franciscan authors. Adam Wodeham, for instance, held that all human certainty is hostage to the assumption that God is not deceiving us (see, e.g., *Lectura secunda* prol. q. 6 [vol. 1: 169–70]). Similar remarks can be found in Walter Chatton (*Sent.* prol. q. 2 art. 2, p. 92) and John Rodington (see this lecture, p. 118). For some of the details, see Elizabeth Karger, "Ockham and Wodeham," who characterizes Ockham's thesis as an "astonishing claim" (p. 229). For an account of other fourteenth-century discussions in this domain, see Anneliese Maier, "Problem der Evidenz." For more information on John Rodington, see Martin Twee-dale, *John of Rodynton*.

Among Dominicans, Robert Holcot's discussion of the issue seems to have been influential. He argued for the possibility of divine deception, but stressed that God could deceive only in a beneficial way (*Sent.* III q. 1). William Crathorn had similarly stressed the possibility of deception (*Sent.* q. 1 concl. 9–10), but then argued that certainty could be attained when sensory cognition is supplemented by the proposition, known *per se*, that "God or the first cause does nothing groundlessly or supernaturally so as to lead human beings into error" (concl. 12, trans. Pasnau, *Cambridge Translations*, p. 295; see Perler, *Zweifel und Gewissheit*, pp. 179–91).

Autrecourt's letters (mid-1330s) may have contributed to the growing notoriety of the divine deception hypothesis, and by the 1340s one finds authors attempting to show that deception is impossible. John of Mirecourt, as discussed in this lecture (p. 119), is one example. A slightly earlier case is Gregory of Rimini, whose *Sentences* commentary (1343–4) argues that "God cannot say something false to someone, willing thereby that the one to whom he speaks assents to what he says" (*Sent.* I dd. 42–4 q. 2 [vol. 3: 391]; see Perler, "Does God Deceive Us?" pp. 182–4). In the notes to Rimini's text at this point, the editors quote Adam Wodeham and Richard Fitzralph, whom they take to be the targets of Rimini's account.

Around 1348, Peter Ceffons felt that authority required him to deny the possibility of divine deception. Jean-François Genest, "Pierre de Ceffons," takes this to show that divine deception was among the condemned doctrines of 1347, which makes a kind of sense, given that the main targets of those condemnations, Autrecourt and Mirecourt, both took such deception quite seriously—even if they both, in the end, proposed subtle philosophical strategies for dealing with the possibility. John Buridan is another relevant example from around this time. In *Questions on the Metaphysics* II.1 he gives prominent attention to the possibility of divine deception and responds not by denying it, but by insisting (like Wodeham and others) that conditional certainty is good enough.

It is of course Descartes whom we now associate most closely with the possibility of divine deception. The question arises in the First Meditation (VII: 21), then gets diverted to the prospect of an evil demon, and then recurs in Meditation Three, where we are invited to imagine that "perhaps some God could have given me a nature such that I was deceived even in matters that seemed most evident" (VII: 36). Mersenne queries this possibility in the Second Objections and reminds Descartes of the scholastic tradition I have just sketched (VII: 125). But Mersenne does not quite get it right, inasmuch as he mentions Gregory of Rimini and Gabriel Biel as proponents of the view that God can lie, when in fact that was neither man's position (see Perler, "Does God Deceive Us?" p. 183). Interestingly, though, Descartes's reply to Mersenne arrives at much the sort of view that Holcot defended, according to which God might "produce verbal untruths which, like the lies of doctors who deceive their patients in order to cure them, are free of any malicious intent to deceive" (VII: 143). As for malicious deception, Descartes seems to reject the view that it is only God's ordained power that precludes deception. For in the Second Replies (VII: 144) he speaks of a "contradiction" in God's allowing systematic deception. This suggests a logical impossibility—that is, a conflict with God's absolute power.

Note 2 (p. 119). The literature on John of Mirecourt is unfortunately quite limited. As regards his epistemic views, the fullest discussion remains Maier, "Problem der Evidenz." Mirecourt's conclusion regarding our lack of evident knowledge runs as follows: "No one evidently knows [*scit*], with the aforesaid evidentness, that anything other than oneself exists. One does not know, for instance, that whiteness exists, that a human being exists, that two things or many things exist, and on and on, or that a human being is different from a donkey, and so forth" (*Sent.* q. 6, concl. 5, p. 445.337–40). After invoking the possibility of supernatural interference, Mirecourt expressly considers the response that God is not a deceiver and accepts this thesis, but insists that God might still interfere with nature in a way that produces false beliefs, remarking that, "although it may be that God indisposes things in this way either by himself by means of a secondary cause, still he does not deceive, because he does not make things otherwise than they ought to be" (p. 446.395–7).

In *Sentences* question 21, Mirecourt discusses at length the case of God's existence. His handling of that question gave rise to a queried proposition in the proceedings against him, which provided the occasion for Mirecourt's fullest account of the different degrees of *evidentia* (First Apology, n. 44). There he stands by his claim that God's existence cannot be proved with the evidentness of first principles, but stresses that nevertheless he takes God's existence to be both evident and known (*scita*). He also insists that he does not regard God's existence as any more to be "doubted" than the truth of first principles. The cost of trying to have it both ways here is that he violates Lockean proportionality.

Note 3 (p. 120). Mirecourt's argument against the impossibility of divine deception looks quite plausible as a response to the sort of Cartesian scenario familiar from undergraduate classes. What Descartes imagines—that God or an evil demon might reach into my mind and cause me to have new, false thoughts—seems not a case of *my* falsely thinking something, but of my mind's undergoing alien possession. Mirecourt compares the situation to a case where God, rather than the sun, causes there to be light: "that would not count as the sun's illuminating, if it is not caused by the sun" (First Apology, n. 45). Thus Mirecourt concludes that "God cannot by himself cause a thought within the soul" (*Sent.* q. 6, p. 440.118). This leaves plenty of room for deception when it comes to judgments about the existence of contingent entities, like the dragon that might or might not lie ahead. But we get infallibility, or so Mirecourt thinks, when it comes to the principle of noncontradiction (and presumably other self-evident principles), because here the only way to induce error would be through direct imposition of an alien thought. "God cannot by means of secondary causes cause an error by which someone dissents from the first principle, because the most powerful way he has to do this is through something's being cognized, but this cannot be, because every cognition is suited to cause *assent* to the first principle" (*Sent.* q. 6, p. 440.126–9). So, no matter what God makes happen in the world and what thoughts this gives rise to in my mind, there is nothing that could lead me to doubt the principle of noncontradiction.

To see the character of the infallibility Mirecourt achieves here and its limitations, it is helpful to appeal to higher order certainty along the lines discussed in Lecture Two, note 7. Following the suggestion made in this lecture (p. 120), one might say that, even if I cannot be wrong in judging that *p*, I can be wrong in judging that I am judging with certainty that *p*. I can go wrong at the second order, because I am aware that God might have implanted a false judgment in my head, and I am aware that, if he had done so, I would not be able to tell the difference. In view of this possibility, I arguably ought to suspend judgment across the board at the second-order level. Accordingly, Mirecourt perhaps makes a mistake elsewhere in endorsing the principle that "it is absurd for someone to know [*sciat*] and consider actually whether he knows and not know that he knows" (*Sent.* q. 5, p. 437). Or, if Mirecourt wishes to stand by this principle of higher order knowledge, then that restores considerable leverage to divine deception as a skeptical tool.

In a way it is obvious that no argument can be wholly effective in securing infallibility. After all, even with respect to the most basic principles, it is certainly *possible* for people to have doubts. Buridan describes having asked "many old women" whether they could eat and not eat at the same time, which they of course deny, and then asking them whether the Almighty God could make this the case, to which they reply, "I don't know" (*Quaest. ethic.* VI.11, f. 127vb). Autrecourt imagines that "someone could, through custom or other reasons, refuse to affirm undoubtingly that the first principle is true. For instance, someone might be brought up so as to be told that there is an omnipotent agent who can bring about contraries" (*Tractatus* ch. 6, p. 237.25–8). So, even if Mirecourt's argument against *direct* divine deception is successful, his assertion of complete infallibility with regard to first principles goes too far. People can be brought up from an early age to believe pretty well anything, and can be influenced by figures of authority to change their beliefs in drastic ways. God might indirectly deceive us, and so might charismatic professors and real-estate magnates. Thus, even in that most favorable of cases, the principle of noncontradiction, there is no guarantee of even subjective indubitability.

So far as I know, no modern scholar has ever discussed Mirecourt's interesting argument against divine deception. Part of the problem, beyond the general neglect of his work, is that the discussion is scarcely intelligible as it appears in his *Sentences* commentary. It emerges fairly clearly, however, in his First Apology. Here, then, let me say a bit more about the textual details.

Mirecourt's *Sentences* commentary considers three different accounts of what a thought or an intellection (*intellectio*) is. On the standard view that he wants to reject, "an intellection is a certain quality subjectively existing in the soul, which God could cause by himself and place wherever he wants" (*Sent.* q. 2, p. 330.331–3). Here he may well have in mind Robert Holcot (*Sent.* III.1, quire n.iii rb-va BBB), whose chief argument for the possibility of divine deception had rested precisely on God's ability to add and subtract thoughts within us, independently of how the world is. (Another potential target is Scotus, who likewise treats intellections as qualities and allows that God can impress on me a thought that then becomes *my* thought; see Giorgio Pini, "Can God Create My Thoughts?" p. 61.) Mirecourt contrasts this view with two alternatives. The first, which he characterizes as "more pleasing to many modern authors" (p. 330.338), denies the very existence of thoughts as entities over and above the thing that is thinking. This view calls into question the whole category of what is known as "successive entities" (*entia successiva*)—especially actions and motions—which exist through time, part by part, rather than wholly enduring through time (see my *Metaphysical Themes* ch. 18). For a person to have a thought, on this view, is simply to have an intellectual power so constituted that the person would be thinking in a certain way. The second alternative, like the first, refuses to identify thought with the possession of a quality but instead treats thoughts as *modes*—modes of the power of thought. Mirecourt characterizes this modal view as "highly plausible" (*Sent.* q. 2, p. 329.323–4) and says that this is the view "he would gladly assert if he dared" (p. 330.338–9). He knows that the view is risky, however, because it threatens to replace real qualities with modes, a doctrine for which he would indeed be condemned in 1347.

Mirecourt's discussion, however, is still more confusing than this brief summary indicates. He introduces the topic in *Sentences* question 2, at the start of article 3, where he "sets forward several assumptions that, whether they are true or false, are conceded by many" (p. 327.207–8). This turns out to be a statement of what I call the first alternative view, on which there are no successive entities but only permanent ones, which he takes to yield the view that a thought, since it is an action, must be a permanent thing and hence must be the thing that thinks—that is, the power of intellect. Then, after a long series of extremely intricate arguments, he reminds the reader that all of these arguments are based on that original assumption and proceeds to distinguish the two other views described, beginning at p. 329.319 (*Ista sint dicta tendendo*), which is unfortunately not punctuated in the printed edition as a new line of thought.

Matters are more complicated still in the first of his subsequent *apologiae* (n. 45), where he offers a discussion of this threefold distinction that seems to differ in important ways from the original discussion in his *Sentences* commentary. This new discussion puts greater weight on the presence of qualities on all three accounts but insists that qualities cannot be identified with mental states. Perhaps this stress on the presence of qualities is a way of trying to avoid the condemnation he saw coming over his flirtation with the denial of real qualities. I have discussed Mirecourt's view of qualities in some detail in *Metaphysical Themes* §19.3. There I argued that his occasional talk of modes should be understood as wholly reductive: modes, for Mirecourt, are not entities of any kind. But this is itself unclear. Others (e.g., Stefano Caroti, "Les *modi rerum*") take Mirecourt to be committed to modes as entities of some sort.

Interestingly, Mirecourt applies his remarks on divine deception to volitional states. On either of the alternative approaches to what a mental state is, God could perhaps cause there to be certain sorts of love and hate in my soul, but God cannot directly cause *me* to love and hate anything. In contrast, on the standard view, on which a volition is a distinct quality existing within the soul, God could directly make it the case that I hate my neighbor, or even God, simply by implanting such a quality within me (First Apology, n. 45).

As in the case of cognitions, it would presumably be a straightforward matter for God to cause me to have certain volitions *indirectly*. God could, for instance, create some sort of visual simulacrum of my next-door neighbor as doing horrible things and thus cause me to have a certain sensory experience, which would in turn give rise to certain volitional states toward my neighbor. But, again analogously, we might think that there are volitional first principles—such as loving the good—that God could not cause me to reject.

Mirecourt's argument against divine deception seems indebted to Robert Holcot's discussion at the start of his *Sentences* commentary (Bk. I q. 1 art. 3, quire a.iiii ra), where he argues that "God cannot, in any rational creature, cause an assent or dissent of intellect or will without that creature's co-producing or co-causing that assent or dissent." Holcot's rationale is much the same as Mirecourt's would later be: although God could produce such a state of mind, it would not be the *creature's* assent or dissent unless the creature is the one who does it. Holcot's interest here is in meritorious and demeritorious action, which makes this a fairly natural conclusion to reach. It is Mirecourt's insight that this point could be extended to the domain of skepticism and divine deception.

Peter of Ailly recites Mirecourt's argument and reaches just the same conclusion (*Sent.* prol. q. 1. art. 1, pp. 151–2; see Perler, "Does God Deceive Us?" pp. 186–7). Ailly credits the idea not to Mirecourt but to Holcot, and cites the passage just discussed. But this does not show very much, because Ailly regularly borrows from Mirecourt without acknowledgement (see, e.g., the example mentioned in Lecture Two, note 7). He could not safely acknowledge his debt, given that so many of Mirecourt's views had been condemned.

God the Deceived

Note 4 (p. 121). It seems clear that Mirecourt thought that human beings, in the limited case of first principles, could achieve a certainty that is the equivalent of God's. See his First Apology, n. 44, p. 66.11ff., which begins by setting out the case of divine evidentness and then sets out the human case as attaining that level in part. The passage is not nearly as explicit as Galileo's later remarks would be (as discussed in Lecture Two, p. 30), but Mirecourt's implicit suggestion is that we and God are on a par with respect to first principles.

Interestingly, Peter of Ailly sees the worry that a view along Mirecourt's line makes our certainty the equal of God's. He puts this as an objection to the view: "nothing is equally evident to us as it is to God and the angels" (*Sent.* prol. q. 1 art. 1, p. 147). In response he argues that the implication is not that our certainty is equal to God's, but that it is "the maximal certainty naturally possible for us" (p. 155).

This is where Descartes, too, would arrive, under pressure from Mersenne, who asks: "if God were to show us the pure truth, what eye, what mental vision, could endure it?" (Mersenne, Second Objections, VII: 126). Descartes begins his reply by arguing that no malicious verbal deception is possible on God's part (see note 1 here). But then he turns to what he calls the "greater" issue of whether our God-given natural instincts might be systematically misleading (Second Replies, VII: 143). This is in effect the same as Tillotson's worry, as quoted in this lecture (p. 120), over whether errors might be possible in "the perfection of nature." The only way for Descartes to avoid having to take recourse in the sort of dogmatism I charged him with in Lecture Five (p. 111) would be to deny the possibility of such errors. And indeed, he invokes here God's goodness in predictable ways, to insist on the reliability of our faculties, at least when used correctly. But ultimately Descartes recognizes that his argument must stop somewhere, and at that point he makes the concession discussed already in Lecture Two, note 8: "What is it to us if someone imagines that something whose truth we are so firmly convinced of appears false to God or to an angel, and so *is* false, absolutely speaking? What do we care about this 'absolute falsity,' given that we do not in any way believe it or even have the slightest suspicion of it?" (VII: 145). In effect this is equivalent to Ailly's view (quoted in this note), on which the ideal to be achieved is merely the maximum humanly possible; and this is conditional on an assumption that cannot be independently established. There seems to be no escaping some hard kernel of dogmatism in which infallible certainty gives way to mere indubitability: our inability to "believe" or even to have "the slightest suspicion."

Note 5 (p. 125). Discussions of God's knowledge are commonplace historically, along with some perfunctory remarks about the perfection of such knowledge (see, e.g., Aquinas, *Summa theol.* 1a 14.1c, Bonaventure, *Sent.* I.39 [*Opera* vol. 1], Ockham, *Ord.* I.35 [*Opera theol.* vol. 4]). Less usual is to find this registered as a critical premise in religious faith. For an example, perhaps, see Kenelm Digby, in his *Conference with a Lady about Choice of Religion*, who stresses that God's "goodness and knowledge we can no ways doubt of, by which two perfections in him, we may be secure that he neither can be deceived himself, nor will deceive us" (pp. 35–6). Of course, the second point, stemming from God's goodness, is routinely stressed in these contexts, but it is unusual to find anyone stressing the first point.

The possibility that God might be subject to epistemic limitations is hardly ever considered, but is not without precedent. See Robert Nozick, "Testament," and William Alston's remarks in *Reliability of Sense Perception*, p. 125n, where an idea in this vicinity is credited to Alvin Plantinga.

The Dismal Verdict

Cartesian Skepticism

Note 6 (p. 127). Descartes's skeptical arguments from the First Meditation are the most prominent historical example of the mild brand of skepticism that insists only that our beliefs lack certainty and so cannot count as knowledge. This form of skepticism is consistent with allowing that our beliefs have some degree of evidential support. Consider for instance this passage from the middle of the First Meditation:

> I shall never get out of the habit of confidently assenting to these opinions, so long as I suppose them to be what they in fact are, namely highly probable opinions—opinions which, despite the fact that they are doubtful in a way, as has just been shown, it is still much more reasonable to believe than to deny. In view of this, I think I will not go wrong if I turn my will in completely the opposite direction and deceive myself, by pretending for a time that these former opinions are utterly false and imaginary. (VII: 22)

This is a puzzling passage in at least two ways. First, despite coming in the midst of Descartes's most extended effort to motivate skepticism, the passage concedes that the opinions in question are "highly probable" and "much more reasonable to believe than to deny." Such remarks hardly seem on message. What Descartes is trying to do, however, is to put one foot into the epistemology room, where all beliefs receive heightened scrutiny, even while keeping his other foot in the ordinary world. Out in the world, our regular beliefs about the external world are of course "much more reasonable" than not. Even there, Descartes is perhaps a kind of skeptic, inasmuch as he thinks that—prior to his arrival on the stage of human history—such opinions have always been merely "probable," lacking the sort of certainty required for the highest sort of knowledge (*scientia*). The ambition of the *Meditations* is to elevate such ordinary beliefs to that exalted level, thereby achieving ideal knowledge regarding God, the soul, and physical bodies. His strategy for achieving that goal is to lock himself and his readers into the epistemology room for the duration of six meditations. While so encloistered, we might have expected him to argue for the stronger skeptical thesis that we have no good reason to embrace any of our beliefs. But instead he follows the weaker strategy of introducing scenarios that he acknowledges to yield only a slight basis for doubt—the dreaming doubt, the evil demon, and so on—and then to insist as a matter of methodology that, where there is any doubt at all, we should suspend belief. (Points similar to these were made in Lecture Two, p. 25 but were used there to argue that the *scientia* Descartes targets in the *Meditations* and elsewhere should not be understood as knowledge in anything like our modern sense of the term.)

A second puzzling feature of the above passage is that he does not say there that he will suspend his credences, but rather that he will invert them, going "in completely the opposite direction" and endorsing as true the various skeptical scenarios that he has been working his way through. This seems, on its face, strange: if Descartes is provisionally accepting that his "former opinions are utterly false," then he is not endorsing skepticism, but rather some strange sort of credence inversion. This is, however, a short-term strategy of overcompensating for years of carelessness. Like a selfish man who vows to be overly generous for a time so as to escape from his vice, Descartes wants us to commit to the falseness of our ordinary beliefs, at least for a time, so that we can escape "the habit of confidently assenting," and thus arrive at the familiar skeptical attitude of suspending belief. Indeed, a page later, at the start of the Second Meditation, the goal of suspension seems to be squarely in view: "anything that admits of the least doubt I will set aside just as if I had found it to be wholly false" (VII: 24). In this way *all* beliefs get provisionally suspended, until we find something that cannot be doubted. See also the start of Descartes's next major work, the *Principles of Philosophy*: "it seems that the only way we are able to free ourselves from these opinions is to make the effort, once in the course of our life, to doubt everything that we find to contain even the least suspicion of uncertainty." For another instance of overcompensation, see a letter to Mersenne from 1637: "I consider almost as false whatever is only a matter of probability [*vraisemblable*]" (I: 450).

Descartes's view is, however, even more elusive than these remarks suggest, for reasons that note 4 here hints at. For, even while the arguments of the First Meditation are not intended to show that our beliefs lack all plausibility, they cannot be understood to turn on quite the claim that we have just seen Descartes make: that we should doubt anything that is even slightly uncertain. The well-known passage from the Second Replies quoted in note 4— "what do we care about this 'absolute falsity'?"—seems to show that Descartes recognizes that he cannot rule out every possible ground for uncertainty. So it would seem that his skeptical arguments have to hit just the right target: not be so strong as to suggest, absurdly, that our ordinary beliefs are entirely unreasonable, but not be so weak as to raise merely the sorts of negligible possibilities we do not "care about." Whether there is a stable middle ground here could no doubt be the subject of much ingenious interpretive subtlety. But, as interesting as that might be in its own right, I doubt it would really have much to do with Descartes. These skeptical arguments are, after all, ones that he himself does not really take seriously, and so there is no reason to think that he has, or needs, a fully worked out and coherent skeptical position. As many recent interpreters have urged, Descartes's interest in skepticism is methodological: he is not genuinely worried about some sort of skeptical crisis but rather uses the discussion simply as a tool to motivate his own positive arguments for *scientia*. (For this perspective, see, e.g., John Carriero, *Between Two Worlds*, pp. 2–3.)

On the distinction between two kinds of skepticism, stronger and weaker, see for instance Michael Huemer, *Skepticism and the Veil of Perception*, pp. 20–1, and Michael Williams, "The Agrippan Argument," pp. 123–4.

Ancient Skepticism

Note 7 (p. 127). Ancient Pyrrhonism is the most famous version of a full-throated defense of skepticism in its strong form. And, since Sextus Empiricus's writings record the only extensive defenses of Pyrrhonism that survive from antiquity, any discussions of the view must inevitably give considerable weight to his writings. It is sometimes suggested (e.g., by

Montaigne, as quoted in the following note, or in the *Port-Royal Logic* IV.1, trans. p. 228) that only the Pyrrhonian form of ancient skepticism defends the central thesis of strong skepticism—that ultimately there are no good, noncircular, non-question-begging reasons for anything. But in fact proponents of Academic skepticism can also be found advancing the Pyrrhonian strategy of balancing argument against counterargument. Such a procedure, wielded for skeptical ends, seems to go back to Arcesilaus, who assumed charge of the Academy around 273 BC (see David Sedley, "The Motivation of Greek Skepticism," pp. 10–11). Cicero's *Academica* offers an extensive statement of ancient skepticism in its Academic form. For a collection of key fragments from a range of sources pertaining both to Pyrrhonian and Academic skepticism, see Long and Sedley, *The Hellenistic Philosophers*. It seems likely that the Academic's association with a watered-down form of skepticism can be traced back to Philo of Larissa, the last skeptical leader of the Platonic Academy, who seems to have argued for a heavily mitigated version of skepticism (see Charles Brittain, *Philo of Larissa*). For an extensive seventeenth-century argument in favor of treating Academic and Pyrrhonian skepticism as essentially the same, see Pierre-Daniel Huet, *Philosophical Treatise* I.14. For discussion of the mistake on this score in Hume, see Julia Annas, "Hume and Ancient Skepticism," pp. 277–9. But I disagree with Annas, as this lecture makes clear, in that I regard Hume's skepticism as fundamentally akin to that of the ancients. Although Annas is right to characterize Hume as a kind of dogmatist, his achievement (if we can call it that) is to acknowledge just how utterly dogmatic all of his claims ultimately are. Although this is not how the ancient skeptics proceed, it is a strategy that arises out of the same fundamental embrace of epistemic defeat.

One of the most complete surviving reports of the views of Pyrrho describes how "we should be unopinionated, uncommitted and unwavering." For those who achieve this attitude, the outcomes "will be first speechlessness, then tranquility and, says Aenesidemus, pleasure." (This is from Aristocles, quoting Timon's report on Pyrrho, in Long and Sedley 1F, translation modified. Aenesidemus, about whom we have little information, is the founder of Pyrrhonian skepticism.) Sextus, for his part, does not aspire to pleasure, but thinks that the whole aim of Pyrrhonism is the achievement of tranquility: he describes how, just by chance, early skeptics discovered that the suspension of belief brought an end to their being "perpetually troubled" over worldly affairs. Once the Pyrrhonists made that fortuitous discovery, their ambition is to show others how they can achieve that end too (*Outlines* I.xii.25–30).

A History of Epistemic Defeatism

Note 8 (p. 128). It is contentious whether Pyrrhonism recommends suspension of belief. According to Sextus, "the main point is this: in uttering these phrases they [the Pyrrhonists] say what is apparent to themselves and report their own feelings without holding opinions [δόξα], affirming nothing about external objects" (*Outlines* I.vii.15). But it has been questioned whether this means quite what it seems to, given the Pyrrhonists' insistence that they can lead ordinary lives just like other people. See in particular the dispute between Myles Burnyeat and Michael Frede, reprinted in their *The Original Sceptics*. In this lecture I take for granted the usual understanding of Pyrrhonism as demanding suspension of belief.

It is striking how little Sextus has to say about knowledge—so little that the standard Annas and Barnes English translation of Sextus's *Outlines* uses the word 'knowledge' and its cognates only a handful of times, and always in passing, in a nontechnical sense. Accordingly, the word does not even appear in their comprehensive glossary of terms. This is not to say that Sextus might concede that we have knowledge in our usual sense of the term. For if, as the usual interpretation has it, he thinks that we should not form beliefs, then presumably he thinks that our beliefs are unjustified, and hence cannot count as knowledge (in our usual sense). One might say that Pyrrhonian skepticism is so radical that to speak of its denying knowledge does not begin to do it justice.

On Augustine's response to ancient skepticism, see Blake Dutton's recent *Augustine and Academic Skepticism*. Dutton speaks of "radical skepticism" in relation to a view like the one that I label epistemic defeatism.

In looking for historical instances of epistemic defeatism beyond antiquity, one has to be clear about exactly what sort of views one is looking for. According to Manfred Kuehn, "others went so far as to argue that no ground of belief is intrinsically better than any other ground of belief. But most philosophers in the Western tradition, including those called skeptics, have insisted that their enterprise had to do with exposing bad grounds of belief and replacing them with good ones" ("Knowledge and Belief," p. 389). The negative view Kuehn describes is in fact much stronger than epistemic defeatism, which holds only that no *evidential* grounds are ultimately better than any other. One may think that and yet also think that there are *other* sorts of good grounds for holding a belief. Relying on God, as al-Ghazālī proposes (see this lecture, p.128), would be one sort of ground; appealing to sentiment or custom, as Hume does, would be another. Perhaps some ancient skeptics believed that *no* ground of belief is better than any other (hence we should suspend belief), but I am not aware of any later authors who did so, and Kuehn does not offer any instances.

So what about epistemic defeatism—the view that no evidence ultimately carries any weight? Many so-called skeptics do not go even this far. For instance, John of Salisbury is often described as a medieval skeptic. His prologue to the *Policraticus* (c.1156) offers what might have served as an epigraph to Lecture Five:

> The shortness of life, our obtuseness, our careless indifference and our sterile activities permit us to know [*scire*] but little; and even this is straightaway driven and torn from our minds by she who is the thief of knowledge, the ever hostile and faithless stepmother of memory—forgetfulness. (*Policraticus* trans. p. 3)

But, although Salisbury proclaims himself a follower of the Academics, this is so only in matters that are disputed by the wise. Where the wise are in agreement, Salisbury thinks that we can have a "probable" grasp of things; he is using *probabilis* to refer to what we can achieve through dialectical methods, following the consensus views of the wise or of the many. On this sense of *probabilis*, see Lecture Two, note 11. On Salisbury's form of skepticism, see Dallas Denery, "Uncertainty and Deception in the Medieval and Early Modern Court," Christophe Grellard, *Jean de Salisbury et la renaissance médiévale du scepticisme*, and Cary Nederman, "Beyond Stoicism and Aristotelianism."

For al-Ghazālī and the broader Islamic tradition, see Paul Heck, *Skepticism in Classical Islam* chs. 2–3, which documents the extent to which something like epistemic defeatism is widely discussed among Islamic authors, even if rarely defended.

Petrarch does not say nearly enough to make it clear whether he would actually embrace epistemic defeatism. But other figures, usually considered Renaissance skeptics, clearly do not. For instance, although Gianfrancesco Pico attacks Aristotelianism at mind-numbing length for its inability to achieve the highest level of certainty, his *Examen vanitatis doctrinae gentium* (1520) nevertheless acknowledges that Aristotelianism can be treated as plausible (see Lecture Two, notes 9 and 16). Francisco Sanches is similarly modest in his claims. Despite having penned a treatise *Quod nihil scitur* (1581), he too means only to attack the certainty of Aristotelian *scientia*. And he holds on to the aspiration of "establishing, as far as I am able, a kind of *scientia* that is both sound and as easy as possible to obtain" (p. 290).

Montaigne, however, writing a year before Sanches, clearly does endorse epistemic defeatism. He criticizes the Academic skeptics for not going far enough, for "admitting that some things were more probable than others" ("Apology for Raymond Sebond," in *Complete Essays*, p. 422). (But see the previous notes for doubts about whether this is right about Academic skepticism.) He mocks philosophy as "but sophisticated poetry" (p. 401), and invokes the standard skeptical strategy of impugning both the senses and reason, leaving nothing that we can guide ourselves by: "Since the senses cannot decide our dispute, being themselves full of uncertainty, it must be reason that does so. No reason can be established without another reason: there we go retreating back to infinity" (p. 454). For more information, see Richard Popkin, *History of Scepticism*, pp. 44–57. Montaigne's linking of philosophy and poetry would later show up in Hume: "All probable reasoning is nothing but a species of sensation. 'Tis not solely in poetry and music, we must follow our taste and sentiment, but likewise in philosophy" (*Treatise* I.3.8, p. 103).

Pierre Charron was Montaigne's adopted son. Popkin describes him as simply a system-atizer of Montaigne, but this seems somewhat unjust, inasmuch as there is a great deal in Charron that is nowhere to be found in Montaigne. Indeed, for long stretches of his very long *De la sagesse*, Charron looks to hold only to a very moderate and mitigated form of skepticism, on which our awareness of our own fallibility leads us to hold our beliefs with a certain measure of diffidence. Popkin, however, writes that "the major theme here is that man is unable to discover any truth except by revelation" (*History of Scepticism*, p. 59), and in fact such strong claims can in places be found, for example: "We try all the means capable of assisting us, but in the end all our efforts fall short, because the truth is not to be acquired (*n'est pas un acquêt*), nor a thing that lets itself be taken in hand, and still less be possessed by the human spirit" (*De la sagesse* I.14.13, in *Oeuvres* 1: 55). Charron questions whether the great philosophers of antiquity actually meant to advance their "pleasant inventions" as definite assertions—except perhaps for "Aristotle, the most resolute of all, the prince of the dogmatists and yes-men, the God of pedants" (II.2.5, in *Oeuvres* 2: 18). He recommends the skeptical philosophy as best suited to piety and religion: "an Academic or Pyrrhonian will never be a heretic" (II.2.6, in *Oeuvres* 2: 22). Curiously, this last remark is entirely missing from the 1697 translation by George Stanhope, which in general cannot be trusted for anything like a faithful rendering of the French. The 1608 translation by Samson Lennard is much more accurate. For a modern translation of excerpts from II.2, see Ariew, Cottingham, and Sorell, *Descartes' Meditations: Background Source Materials* ch. 5. On Charron's originality and influence, see José Neto, *Academic Skepticism*.

Bayle credits Pierre Gassendi with opening the eyes of philosophers to Sextus Empiricus, but Gassendi himself rejects Pyrrhonism in favor of a middle path between skepticism and dogmatism, denying that the skeptics are right to call everything into question but recognizing that the dogmatists know far less than they claim, especially in natural philosophy, where "we should be happy if we achieve not what is true, but what is truth-like [*verisimile*]" (*Syntagma* pt. I, De logicae fine ch. 5, in *Opera* 1: 79b). Gassendi's much earlier *Exercitationes paradoxicae adversus Aristoteleos* (1624) concedes more to the skeptics, but still insists that there can be *scientia* that is not Aristotelian *scientia* and certainty that falls short of Aristotelian certainty (II.6.6).

The later seventeenth century sees a flourishing of views that degrade the level of certainty that can be acquired. We saw in Lecture Two how the English tradition from Chillingworth forward abandoned the prospect of infallible certainty, settling instead for indubitability. Henry More, a prominent part of that tradition, goes one step farther and remarks: "as for perfect scepticism, it is a disease incurable, and a thing rather to be pitied or laughed at, than seriously opposed. For when a man is so fugitive and unsettled that he will not stand to the verdict of his own faculties, one can no more fasten anything upon him, than he can write in the water, or tie knots of the wind" (*Immortality of the Soul*, p. 5). Yet More seems hardly defeated by this remark. On the contrary, he takes himself to be in possession of very strong— even if not strictly demonstrative—arguments both for God's existence and for the soul's immortality. (For more on More's skepticism, see Alan Gabbey, "A Disease Incurable.")

Pierre-Daniel Huet is reputed to have been one of the great figures of late seventeenth-century skepticism, but on inspection it turns out that he, too, is very far from embracing epistemic defeatism. His principal work, *Traité philosophique de la foiblesse de l'esprit humain*, begins by distinguishing the different degrees of certainty (1.1), then goes on to contend that we lack only certainty in its purest form: "Neither do I say that man can have no knowledge at all of the truth; I say only that he cannot know it thoroughly, clearly, and with such an entire certitude as that it shall want nothing to make it perfect" (*Philosophical Treatise* II.1, trans. p. 134). This is such a mild conclusion that hardly anyone would have denied it. Moreover, Huet goes on to say in the next chapter that this highest sort of certainty can be had through faith. And, as for cases where faith cannot guide us, there Huet says that it is adequate to rely on "likelihoods and probabilities" (II.4, trans. p. 153). Indeed, once one disambiguates the two meanings of *savoir*—one requiring perfect certainty, the other mere probability—it turns out that we can all have knowledge in the latter sense (III.10). This is a feeble sort of skepticism indeed.

Bayle is quite a different matter. Describing how the arguments of the skeptic must eventually turn on themselves and render the skepticism itself a matter of doubt, he remarks:

> How great a chaos, and how great a torment for the human mind! It seems therefore that this unfortunate state is the most proper one of all for convincing us that our reason is a path that leads us astray since, when it displays itself with the greatest subtlety, it plunges us into such an abyss. The natural conclusion of this ought to be to renounce this guide and to implore the cause of all things to give us a better one. This is a great step toward the Christian religion; for it requires that we look to God for knowledge of what we ought to believe and what we ought to do, and that we enslave our understanding to the obeisance of faith.
>
> (*Dictionary*, s.v. "Pyrrho" note C, trans. p. 206)

This looks very much like epistemic defeatism; indeed, it is often said that Hume's skepticism comes straight from Bayle (see, e.g., John Passmore, *Hume's Intentions*, p. 133: "the scepticism which Hume learnt from Bayle"). As for Bayle's apparent fideism, there remains much disagreement as to whether it could have been sincere. On this, see for example Popkin, *History of Scepticism*, pp. 290–301 and Ruth Whelan, "The Wisdom of Simonides," as well as Bayle's own long discussion in his "Third Clarification" to the *Dictionary*.

As for Hume, the closest he comes to appealing to the divine is in the heavily ironic conclusion to his posthumously published essay "The Immortality of the Soul." After calling for a "new species of logic" that might be able to prove the soul's immortality and "new faculties of the mind" to "comprehend that logic," Hume concludes by handing the case for immortality over to God. "Nothing could set in a fuller light the infinite obligations which mankind have to Divine revelation, since we find that no other medium could ascertain this great and important truth" (*Selected Essays*, p. 331).

Skepticism and Religious Belief

Note 9 (p. 129). In view of all this history, I want to revisit two sweeping claims I have made elsewhere. First, in *Metaphysical Themes*, speaking of the seventeenth century, I wrote that "skepticism is a view that no one held" (p. 84), and on that ground I dismissed the familiar appeal to skepticism as an organizing concept for thinking about the rise of "modern" philosophy. I promised there to say more about it elsewhere, so let me defend that brief remark now. As this lecture argues, *skepticism* is a notion spun from three different threads: (1) the denial of knowledge, (2) the suspension of belief, and (3) the repudiation of evidence. What I have been claiming here is that we do find a very extensive historical tradition in support of (3), which in its most radical form becomes the view I call epistemic defeatism. So, if (3) alone is sufficient for skepticism, then one finds ample instances of it, beginning in the sixteenth century, and it would not be unreasonable to see this as a hallmark of "modern" thought. (In effect, this is the main idea behind Popkin's work.) If, however, one thinks of (1) and/or (2) as definitive of skepticism, then skepticism is a view that no one held. This is obvious in the case of (2), since no prominent figure during the Middle Ages and throughout the seventeenth century was willing to express disbelief in God and in the various articles of faith, if only because to do so would have met with harsh social and institutional censure. (Historians have found professions of atheism in obscure places during this time; see, e.g., my *Metaphysical Themes* p. 434 n. 8, and Dorothea Weltecke, *Der Narr spricht*.) The case of (1) is trickier on account of the widely varying and unstable range of meanings given to 'knowledge' over the centuries and of the diversity of languages in which the correct counterpart to 'knowledge' has to be identified. If we use 'knowledge' very strictly, then it is easy to find those who deny that we have it. Lecture Two (p. 24) finds even Descartes denying that anyone before him had knowledge (i.e., *scientia*) of anything other than a few claims in mathematics. Using the English word itself, both Locke and Hume think that, despite Descartes's best efforts, our knowledge remains severely limited (see Lecture Two, note 22). But all these authors think that, short of this epistemic ideal, our beliefs can have some kind of positive epistemic status, enough for us today to speak of it as knowledge, even if they do not offer an explicitly developed theory of what this good enough state consists of. Hence it is very hard to find anyone during this period who denies that we have knowledge in our modern sense of the term.

Second, in the *Cambridge Companion to Medieval Philosophy*, I wrote: "One might be a Christian and a Platonist, like Augustine, or a Christian and an Aristotelian, like Aquinas, or conceivably even a Christian and a Stoic. But it is hard to see how the beliefs of a Christian could be reconciled with a skeptic's suspension of all belief" ("Human Nature," pp. 213–14). There is, naturally, much more to be said here too. Thinking of the various schools of antiquity, I was assuming that (2) above would count as an essential part of what it is to be a skeptic, and so it seemed obvious that skepticism and Christianity would have to be incompatible. But what, then, are we to make of those authors from the sixteenth and seventeenth centuries who argued specifically for Pyrrhonian skepticism, complete with its suspension of belief, as a path toward the Christian faith? In addition to Montaigne, Charron, and Bayle, consider Henry Cornelius Agrippa, whose *Of the Vanity and Uncertainty of Arts and Sciences* (1526) argues that "there is nothing that is as repugnant to the Christian religion and faith as is knowledge [*scientia*], and that less agree with one another" (ch. 101, trans. p. 182v)? Even better, take François de la Mothe le Vayer. He advocates skepticism, by comparison to the other ancient schools of philosophy, as the straightest path to Christianity: "there are none of them which come to terms so easily with Christianity as Skepticism, respectful towards heaven and submissive to faith" (as quoted in Popkin, *History of Scepticism*, pp. 84–5). How so? Because "the soul of a Christian Skeptic is like a field cleared and cleansed of bad plants . . . which then receives the dew drops of divine grace much more happily than it would do if it were still occupied and filled with a vain presumption of knowing everything with certainty and doubting nothing" (p. 85). Such very common post-scholastic views fly in the face of my claim that skepticism and Christianity are incompatible. Similar remarks from le Vayer can be found in Ariew, Cottingham, and Sorell, *Descartes' Meditations: Background Source Materials*, pp. 206–7. For an analogous case in Islam, see the discussion of al-Ghazālī in Heck, *Skepticism in Classical Islam*, p. 136.

The natural reply for me is to hold that such fideistic skepticism is incoherent. It plainly does not advocate *full* suspension of belief, but only a selective suspension that stops at the door of religious belief. Moreover, such a stopping point looks incoherent, inasmuch as the tropes that destroy belief elsewhere seem to apply just as readily to the religious domain. Appealing to the grace of God seems to help not at all, because if one has skeptical grounds for doubting sensory experience, then surely there will also be skeptical grounds for doubting putative religious experiences. So it looks to be just painfully obvious that fideistic skepticism cannot be coherently maintained. Either one should suspend *all* belief or one should trust one's ordinary cognitive faculties from the start. Perhaps this is why it is so hard to take such fideistic skeptics at their word. Popkin tells us that "it has been difficult to assess the sincerity of La Mothe le Vayer" (*History of Scepticism*, p. 85), and similar remarks hold for other figures in this tradition. How could they seriously hold such a view, one ought to wonder, given that it looks to be just obviously incoherent?

Popkin's own solution to this puzzle is to treat evidentialism as an optional thesis for the Pyrrhonian: "the principle that one should believe only those propositions for which there is adequate evidence does not follow from any sceptical reflection" (p. 86). But this is too easy a way out, because, although the careful skeptic will certainly not *assert* the truth of evidentialism, practical adherence to evidentialism is a constitutive part of what it is to be a Pyrrhonian skeptic (see note 8 to this lecture). So all that Popkin is really suggesting is that the fideist can selectively abandon Pyrrhonism. And, if that is the strategy, then it is again unclear why Pyrrhonism ought to be abandoned in the religious domain and yet maintained in other cases. We still have not found a consistent way for one to be a fideistic skeptic.

A better way out is to see that the incoherence of fideistic skepticism arises only given an internalist epistemic perspective—that is, it arises when one asks what beliefs an agent ought to form, given the evidence available to her. For the committed Pyrrhonian skeptic, there is no coherent way to stop the train of doubts at the door of religion. But what this ignores is the possibility that *God* might stop the train. This requires us to think of grace not as just another piece of evidence—another kind of experience—to which the epistemic agent must decide how to respond, but rather as an event that might force a certain outcome. If the committed skeptic is permitted to choose, then her skeptical tropes must commit her to suspend belief all the way down the track, no matter what "dew drops of divine grace" fall on her head. But what if those drops of grace, instead of being further evidence to be evaluated internally, give her no choice but to believe? From an internalist perspective, such beliefs are epistemically indefensible. But someone in the grips of such grace will believe all the same. And this kind of belief may lead to salvation. The economy of grace, in other words, may be externalist—it may be that saving grace works not by giving us good, internally accessible reasons to believe, but just by making us believe, through a veridical (and salvific) mechanism that we are unable to evaluate internally. Charron is in fact very clear about this. To the objection that the Academic skeptic or the Pyrrhonian skeptic will be neither Christian nor Catholic, he responds that "this misunderstands what has been said, which is that there is no suspension, no place from which to judge, no liberty in what comes from God. We must allow him to deposit and engrave whatever pleases him and nothing else" (*De la sagesse* II.2.6, in *Oeuvres* vol. 2: 22; the passage is critically mistranslated in Ariew, Cottingham, and Sorell, p. 62). Although Charron does not work out the implications of this response, we can now see why, on this line of thought, it becomes entirely intelligible how a skeptic might come to have religious beliefs. And it might even be, as this tradition urges, that skepticism is the doctrine that best prepares a philosopher to receive grace. One would, however, perhaps not want to say that skepticism is the best doctrine for *everyone*. The point would be that, for a *philosopher* faced with the various bad options available to human reason, the best path is to embrace skeptical disbelief and wait for God to force the issue. And, if that never happens, then again so much the better for skepticism. (See note 16 to this lecture for more on these issues from Aquinas's perspective.)

So can a Christian be a skeptic? One who remains gracelessly locked in Pyrrhonian belief suspension cannot, since a Christian must believe. But a Christian can embrace epistemic defeat, and can even accept the stronger claim (described by Kuehn in note 8) that there are no good reasons of any sort to believe. For, even if she thinks this, she might in fact still believe, thanks to the grace of God. And now we can see that what is new in Hume is not the seemingly odd combination of epistemic defeatism with sustained belief, but rather that, in place of grace as the force that sustains our beliefs, Hume posits mere sentiment and custom.

Turning now to our modern era, it is harder still to find anyone who might be counted as a skeptic. Even so, there has been some measure of attention paid to the dismal Pyrrhonian verdict of epistemic defeatism. One prominent voice is Robert Fogelin, who draws on Pyrrhonian arguments to set out standards for a successful theory of justification that he thinks no theory has met. Instead, epistemologists tend to ignore the problem: "There exists what might be called 'the Epistemologists' Agreement' not to hold each other to such standards, perhaps because it is tacitly understood that no theory can meet them" (*Pyrrhonian Reflections*, p. 119). Another case is Richard Foley: "Regardless of how we marshal our intellectual resources, there can be no non-question-begging assurances that the resulting inquiry is reliable" (*Intellectual Trust*, p. 8; compare note 17 below). There is also William Alston, whose *Reliability of Sense Perception* argues at length that "we are unable to give a noncircular demonstration, or even a strong supporting argument, for the reliability of SP [our sense perceptual practices]" (p. 115)—a verdict he thinks likely to extend "to all our most fundamental belief-forming practices" (p. 118). Even so, Alston remains optimistic about the ultimate prospects for epistemic success, arguing that it can still be shown "that it is rational to take SP to be reliable" (p. 132). In *Perceiving God*, Alston seeks to leverage these sorts of remarks into a defense of the practice of adhering to religious experience. Similarly, Alvin Plantinga argues that the improbability of warranted belief in a world without design leaves theism as the only intellectually coherent option for us as rational beings (*Warrant and Proper Function* chs. 11–12). In effect, this approach reverse-engineers our epistemic Panglossianism, relying on it to draw us back toward the theism we thought we had abandoned after Hume.

Hume's Quietism

Note 10 (p. 129). The analogy drawn in this lecture (p.129) between epistemic defeatism and moral antirealism is strong enough for me to have originally wanted to speak here of "epistemic antirealism." But 'antirealism' in the epistemic domain is best reserved for views that argue for expressivism or some other form of antirealism with regard to specifically epistemic norms— for example, a claim such as *We ought to believe in accord with the evidence*. For this sort of antirealism, see Hartry Field, "Epistemology without Metaphysics."

Interesting questions arise about the relationship between such epistemic antirealism and epistemic defeatism. Field (p. 287) suggests that skeptical questions go away on his version of antirealism, but that is not quite the case. What is true is that it may be *easier* for the epistemic antirealist to respond to the skeptic, depending on the epistemic framework the antirealist prefers. If there are no objective facts about the correct epistemic framework, then one is free, in principle, to choose a framework in which worries about evidence do not arise. By the same token, it is harder to argue for epistemic defeatism against an epistemic antirealist, because one has to be prepared to argue for the view against whatever framework one's interlocutor might prefer to adopt. Even so, doubts about evidence may well arise, because epistemic defeatism does not need to make its case relative to every imaginable framework, but only relative to the ones *we* find preferable. Who counts as "we" may of course prove contentious.

In seeing an analogy between Hume's ethics and his epistemology, I am following a path made familiar by Norman Kemp Smith, who argued for "a complete analogy" between belief and the evaluative domains of taste and morality ("Naturalism of Hume," p. 339). At note 14 to Lecture Five I took issue with one aspect of this analogy. But Kemp Smith goes farther than I would in another respect: he treats belief as entirely a matter of sentiment, and so not subjected to evaluation in other terms. This is too strong. Any full account of Book I of the

Treatise must make sense of how Hume can eschew our ability to supply adequate reasons (in Part 4) while yet thinking (especially in Part 3) that we have some basis, beyond merely subjective sentiment and custom, for preferring some beliefs over others. I have no settled view about exactly what this basis is, but I recommend recent scholarship on this question. Louis Loeb, for instance, argues that the key basis of evaluation is stability (see especially his *Stability and Justification*). For Frederick Schmitt (*Hume's Epistemology*), it is reliability. For Don Garrett, it is a "sense of probability" (*Hume*, pp. 137–43). My own suggestion is limited to a negative point about what Hume thinks we cannot have. Our beliefs may in fact be stable—may even be reliable—and, if so, we may have a kind of reason for maintaining them, but all the same we lack *good evidence* for the truth of these beliefs, as that phrase is defined in this lecture (p. 128).

Note 11 (p. 131). Whether or not Hume should count as a skeptic is a slippery question, for reasons I have already suggested in these notes. Given the strict way in which he uses 'knowledge' (see Lecture Two, note 22), he counts among those who think that we know almost nothing. This looks like skepticism, but in this regard he is not so different from Locke, who likewise thinks that we only rarely have knowledge and who is surely not a skeptic. Also, the *Treatise*'s discussion of skepticism seems to embrace without qualification many of the central skeptical arguments, and hence Hume looks to be a skeptic, but then, again, he dismisses skepticism as absurd.

My view is that the difficulties in understanding Hume on this point largely dissolve once we mark off the doctrine of epistemic defeatism. *That* is what Hume thinks. It causes him to despair while inside the epistemology room, but it does not cause him to abandon his larger aim to understand human nature; and thus his project in the remainder of the *Treatise* and elsewhere is to carry on in whatever way seems most natural, even while recognizing that his beliefs are ultimately unsupported by reason. Critical to the story is Hume's insistence that we are by nature unable to retain these defeating reflections in our minds for very long. For, as long as we do find ourselves enmeshed in a skeptical philosophical perspective, our beliefs are undermined in a way that is inconsistent not just with knowledge but even with any lesser degree of justification. Fortunately we find it easy to set aside such worries, not just insofar as we can forget about them for a time, but furthermore—and critically—insofar as, outside the epistemology room, the arguments of the skeptics look "cold and strained and ridiculous" (*Treatise* I.4.7, p. 269). Thus nature defeats the skeptic's defeaters and replaces them with a propensity to believe that serves as its own kind of justification. (From this point of view, interestingly, God might be in a *worse* epistemic predicament than we are, because the divine mind has no way to escape the skeptic's defeaters.)

This is a contentious reading of Hume, because it puts more weight on his skeptical side than many commentators do. (For recent examples of readings that downplay the extent of his skepticism, see Garrett, "A Small Tincture of Pyrrhonism" and Donald Ainslie, *Hume's True Scepticism*). In arguing that Hume accepts the arguments of *Treatise* I.4 and despairs of answering them, I am sympathetic with Richard Popkin, who describes Hume's philosophy as "schizophrenic," unable to reconcile its two different worlds ("David Hume," p. 98n). See also Ira Singer, who speaks of his "split epistemic personality" ("Hume's Extreme Skepticism," p. 609), and Passmore, who refers to "the unresolved tension between the sceptic and the scientist" (*Hume's Intentions*, p. 64). Obviously claims of such irresolution serve as red flags to any self-respectingly bullish Hume scholar. But it seems to me that this is effectively Hume's predicament, provided that this split personality is understood diachronically, along the lines I have developed in Lectures Five and Six. The conviction that there must be some clever reading of Hume that makes everything come out just fine is just another symptom of epistemic Panglossianism. Our world, as Hume sees it, is very far from being the best of all epistemic worlds.

To say that Hume despairs does not mean saying that he thinks that inquiry must come to an end. Clearly, he thinks there is much that one can go on to say about our belief-forming practices. So I am also sympathetic to those who have argued that Hume has interesting and well-developed positive views about how to develop a defeat-friendly epistemology—see for instance the references to Loeb, Schmitt, and Garrett in the previous note. Where he despairs, or so I claim, is in how to reconcile that positive project with his embrace of epistemic defeatism. Even this much puts me at odds with Loeb, Schmitt, and Garrett, however, insofar as they find in Hume epistemic values that override the value of rational confirmation (even supposing we could have that). For these scholars, then, there is no basis for despair, because Hume gets what he ultimately wants. But, if so, then why does Hume seem so dismayed in Part 4? Is he just play-acting?

That is essentially what Annette Baier thinks: she characterizes the arguments of *Treatise* I.4 as nothing more than an "experiment" (*Progress of Sentiments*, p. 32), or a "persona" that Hume tries on (p. 101), the point of which is simply to warn us away from a certain misguidedly solipsistic and overconstrained notion of reasoning. This, it seems to me, ignores the genuine price that Hume takes those reflections to exact. There is an ideal there that human beings naturally and reasonably take themselves to be able to achieve—to form beliefs on the basis of well-founded reasons—and it turns out that we cannot achieve this. Baier offers her own intriguing account of where Hume heads once he sees what we cannot have. Whatever the merits of her reading of Hume's constructive side, I wish to argue only that what he destroys represents a horrible loss for our epistemic prospects. (See Lecture Five, note 14, for further remarks on Baier's reading of Hume.)

For a recent attempt to offer a reading of Hume like Baier's, but one that acknowledges something of the validity of the skeptic's demands, see Ainslie, *Hume's True Scepticism*, especially ch. 7. But, whereas Ainslie thinks that the skeptic demands something that is self-defeating, I think that the skeptic demands only something that we cannot sustain.

Note 12 (p. 132). The central interpretive question at issue in my reading of Hume is whether he is committed to evidentialism in the following sense: Ought we to form our beliefs in accord with the sort of evidence that *Treatise* I.4 tells us we cannot have? Recent scholars generally say "no," arguing instead that Hume rejects that standard for belief and replaces it with another (although they disagree about what that revised standard is). I argue "yes," and that this explains why Hume is so despairing of any satisfying outcome. He is committed to a standard that he thinks we cannot achieve. But, since life must go on and suspension of belief is impossible for us, the task of the philosopher is to find some standard for belief that we can satisfy.

Here are two objections to my reading. First, it seems that ought implies can. So, if we cannot adhere to evidentialism as just defined, then neither is it the case that we ought to do so. Fair enough. But then let such evidentialism be not a normative ideal but merely an absolute one (following the distinction at Lecture One, p. 10). Hume, along with virtually the entire history of philosophy before him, is invested in this absolute ideal. Its unattainability may not be an ethical crisis (since ought implies can), but it is a cognitive disaster: the disaster of our lacking "measures of truth and falsehood" (*Treatise* I.4.1, p. 183). Here is where others read Hume differently, seeing nothing desirable in the sort of rational evidence that *Treatise* I.4 finds us unable to achieve. Of course, much depends at this point on just what conception of rationality one finds to be at stake in that part of the *Treatise*. But here I will just say that this alternative reading of the text strikes me as strained and Panglossian: persuaded of Hume's arguments that we cannot have such rationality, commentators strive to reassure us that there is nothing to worry about—that we don't want that sort of rationality anyway!

Second objection: would it not be disingenuous for Hume to adhere to evidentialism, deem its realization impossible, and yet continue to form beliefs? For that charge, see Baier, *A Progress of Sentiments* ch. 3, who sees "bad faith" and "hypocrisy" as the outcome of a reading on which Hume conjoins such views. This would be tantamount to his holding that "all causal inferences [are] without warrant" even while he "continues to make them" (p. 57). Add the word 'rational' in front of warrant, and I think this is precisely Hume's view; but I see no bad faith there. Instead, I see Hume attempting to articulate an epistemology grounded in something other than rationality and good evidence. Even if our beliefs ultimately lack evidential support, they can be evaluated in other ways that allow us to judge that some of them are more warranted than others. If this is the basic structure of his thinking, then the charge of bad faith would be appropriate only if he had not written Part 4 of Book I of the *Treatise*. As it is, he could scarcely have put us on notice more forcefully.

In focusing on that notorious stretch of text, I am able to present Hume at his most skeptical and most despairing. To my mind, however, the later *Enquiry concerning the Human Understanding* takes broadly the same view in substance, and is different only in tone. Whereas *Treatise* I.4 seems to express genuine intellectual anguish regarding our "malady which can never be radically cured, but must return upon us every moment" (I.4.2, p. 218), the more grown-up *Enquiry* takes an urbane attitude of lighthearted resignation:

When he [a Pyrrhonian] awakes from his dream, he will be the first to join in the laugh against himself, and to confess that all his objections are mere amusement, and can have no other tendency than to show the whimsical condition of mankind, who must act and reason and believe; though they are not able, by their most diligent enquiry, to satisfy themselves concerning the foundation of these operations, or to remove the objections which may be raised against them. (*Enquiry* 12.2, p. 160)

This leads into Hume's discussion of the usefulness of "a more mitigated scepticism." In my terms, the *Enquiry* sees evidentialism not as a live prospect whose unattainability is to be mourned, but simply as a remote absolute ideal that only the naïve would still hope to achieve. See Fogelin, "Tendency of Hume's Skepticism," for a similar verdict on the relationship between the *Treatise* and the *Enquiry*. Miriam McCormick, "A Change in Manner," likewise sees the two works as offering a similar response, but she downplays Hume's commitment to anything in the vicinity of skepticism. For yet another perspective, see Passmore, who reads what I call genuine intellectual anguish as "a stagey, melodramatic tone" and urges that we focus on the first *Enquiry*, where "his feelings, his ideas, and his 'literary' impulses were under better control" (*Hume's Intentions*, p. 133). One's reading of these passages may depend in large part on one's attitude toward what Hume is relinquishing. To my mind, Hume is announcing nearly the worst news that could befall philosophy. No room for melodrama there.

Hume could have arrived at a less conflicted position had he simply abandoned the search for truth. Yet he clearly does not abandon it, as one can see from the extensive discussion, in *Treatise* II.3.10, of "that love of truth, which was the first source of all our enquiries" (p. 448). For Hume, this is a passion with an "origin in human nature" (p. 448), and so we should not expect that any amount of skeptical reflection will cause us to forsake it. But, even at this later juncture in the *Treatise*, Hume's attitude to the philosophical pursuit of truth is shaped by the dismal results obtained earlier. Thus, when he seeks an analogy for our pursuit of the truth in philosophy, the examples he offers are hunting and gambling (pp. 451–2), two cases where the rewards are, in themselves, of the most doubtful value but where we still derive tremendous enjoyment because we persuade ourselves that something important is at stake. (For a very different reading of this section of the *Treatise*, see Garrett, *Hume*, pp. 152–9.)

I should note that the term 'evidentialism' is used in various ways. Here I broadly follow Andrew Chignell, "Ethics of Belief," who defines it as "the position, roughly, that we are obliged to form beliefs always and only on the basis of sufficient evidence that is in our possession" (§1.1).

Note 13 (p. 133). In announcing the disastrous news of our epistemic defeat, Hume is doing nothing at all new, as we have seen, and it is debatable whether his arguments for that conclusion are even an improvement on previous versions. (For a discussion of their merits, see Fogelin, *Hume's Skepticism in the Treatise*, esp. ch. 2.) Hume's novelty arises from his attempt to advance science anyway, despite the arguments of *Treatise* I.4. But even here there are a great many anticipations of Hume's shift toward a naturalistic account of the necessities of our cognitive nature. Among scholastic authors, one finds some precedent in the notion that evidentness is to be understood as the intellect's natural inability to doubt (see Lecture Two, note 13). Buridan is perhaps the clearest example of this approach, because he combines such indubitability with the acknowledgement that infallibility can be had only *ex suppositione*. Accordingly, Grellard speaks of *le naturalisme qu'il défend en épistémologie* (*De la certitude volontaire*, p. 57). Grellard finds the same sort of naturalistic approach in Ockham, with the difference that, for Ockham, faith requires a basic and ungrounded act of will, through which we assent to what is not evident (p. 74).

In the seventeenth century, Wilkins's turn away from what is strictly infallible toward what in fact our natures do not allow us to doubt can also be found in Joseph Glanvill, who writes that, "though we are certain of many things, yet that certainty is not absolute infallibility; there still remains the possibility of our being mistaken in all matters of humane belief and inquiry. But this bare possibility (as I said) moves us not, nor does it in the least weaken our assent to those things that we clearly and distinctly perceive" (*Essays*, p. 50). Locke too, when he rules that perceptual beliefs can count as knowledge, does not insist on the complete infallibility of such empirical judgments but rather remarks that "we are provided with an evidence that puts us past doubting" (*Essay* IV.2.14). He rests his case, in other words, on what in fact we are and are not able to believe.

Locke uses this naturalizing strategy to shoehorn perceptual beliefs into the domain of knowledge. Wilkins, as Lecture Two discusses (p. 43), goes farther and encompasses even things that are merely morally certain. Epistemologists today go farther still, and have developed countless analyses of knowledge that allow this word to range as widely as ordinary language licenses. There are analyses in terms of reliability, security, safety, and an adequate possession of the epistemic virtues—any and all of which might be satisfied even if epistemic defeatism is true. (They *might* be, provided that epistemic defeatism does not violate some additional "no defeat" clause that these accounts might have built into them.) Such a wide repertoire of potential analyses of 'knowledge' makes it natural for recent scholars to suggest that Hume does have a positive epistemology, and indeed a theory of knowledge, though he himself does not call it by that name. I have no wish to dispute any of these suggestions, provided that such results are not then used to dismiss the seriousness of what gets lost in *Treatise* I.4.

What goes for knowledge goes for science as well, especially since Hume himself wants to use the term 'science' to describe his positive achievements. But, again, our willingness to retrench our expectations of what counts as science should not lead us to suppose that Hume cannot be serious about his skepticism. Compare Passmore: "Unless scepticism can be refuted, the science of man must be destroyed along with every other form of reasoning" (*Hume's Intentions*, p. 137). This would of course be true on many ideal conceptions of what science requires. But it is the central feature of Hume's epistemology to set aside any such ideal and to aspire to science even while conceding nearly everything to the skeptics.

Believing Hopefully

Idealism and Naturalism

Note 14 (p. 134). The form of idealism that might be thought best suited to respond to epistemic defeatism is Kant's. On the usual understanding, Kant distinguishes between our epistemic defeat at the transcendental level and the epistemic success that is possible empirically. Depending on one's sympathies, his distinction between the phenomenal and the noumenal amounts either to a brilliant escape from the *seems–is* gap or merely to an alternative description of it. The labyrinths of the First Critique yield a systematic account of our seemings—of what is empirically real—in consolation for our inability to say anything about what is transcendentally real. Part of the appeal of Kant is that he offers a way forward in philosophy that fully honors epistemic defeatism. We form no beliefs about the mind-independent world, and yet there still is a great deal we can say about how things are. How Kant's views should be understood in light of Hume (or Berkeley) is of course a matter of endless controversy. For a clear down-the-middle account, see Barry Stroud, "Kant and Skepticism."

Kant's embrace of epistemic defeatism regarding the external world must be qualified by his claim that he can *prove* the existence of that world. As a footnote to the second-edition preface to the *Critique of Pure Reason* famously remarks, "it always remains a scandal of philosophy and universal human reason that the existence of things outside us . . . should have to be assumed merely on faith, and that if it occurs to anyone to doubt it, we should be unable to answer him with a satisfactory proof" (B xxxix). I prefer Heidegger's wry recognition that this is an ideal best abandoned: "The 'scandal of philosophy' is not that this proof has yet to be given, but that such proofs are expected and attempted again and again" (*Being and Time* I.6).

For a good overview of naturalized epistemology, see Hilary Kornblith, "In Defense of a Naturalized Epistemology." It should be noted that Quine himself denies that his naturalized approach is intended to remove normative questions from epistemology (see e.g. *Pursuit of Truth*, pp. 19–21; see also Lecture Two, note 13). Another instance of the turn toward naturalism is Peter Strawson, who advocates "naturalism" in the face of skepticism: "having given up the unreal project of wholesale validation, the naturalist philosopher will embrace the real project of investigating the connections between the major structural elements of our conceptual scheme" (*Skepticism and Naturalism*, p. 22).

Belief through Faith

Note 15 (p. 135). If naturalism and idealism are rejected on the grounds that they merely evade the real issue, then the obvious next thought is that we must have recourse to some kind of faith. It seems most natural to develop such fideism in geometric terms. We would consider which axioms—not self-evident axioms, as Euclid hoped for, but unargued, dogmatically embraced axioms—might yield the most comprehensive system of beliefs. In God's case, this is easy: the only axiom He needs is that He *is* God. From this, the rest follows as a matter of logic. In the human case, it is less clear how to proceed. Some have taken as axiomatic the analogous principle that we are the creations of a good and all-powerful God. Others have proposed to cross the *seems–is* gap directly, by embracing a principle according to which a thing's seeming to be so yields *prima facie* good evidence for taking it to be so. In general, once we let faith into the game, interesting questions arise about the most effective strategies here. The geometric model suggests that parsimony will weigh quite heavily and that the ideal approach will take for granted as little as possible. But one might think that it scarcely matters whether we believe just one thing on faith, or dozens of things. After all, if even one faith-based proposition is foundational for the whole system, then there is an obvious sense in which *everything* is based on faith. And if this is how things are, then perhaps we should take seriously the way in which faith seems to play a role in our everyday epistemic practices: our faith in friends and family, even in oneself. Clearly, however, this is a dangerous path; for, once the constraints are loosened on what may be embraced through faith, we risk epistemic chaos. How any constraints might be maintained is a central challenge for any fideistic response to epistemic defeat.

If something must be taken on faith, then the most direct solution, as just noted, is to embrace what Huemer calls "phenomenal conservativism," according to which a thing's seeming to be so yields *prima facie* good evidence for taking it to be so. Huemer himself has no truck with faith: he argues that phenomenal conservativism is "self-evident" (*Skepticism and the Veil of Perception*, pp. 103ff). But perhaps James Pryor's "dogmatism" is a case where a similar principle is embraced, in effect, on faith (see "The Skeptic and the Dogmatist"). Lecture Five (p. 111) suggests that Descartes adheres to a restricted dogmatism with regard to clear and distinct perceptions made in the privileged present. Descartes would presumably resist the charge that there is anything dogmatic or faith-based in that. But what other basis would he offer? In effect, I think Descartes relies on the same Panglossian principle that this Lecture (p. 134) finds in Berkeley: that God surely would not leave us so badly off in the epistemic domain. And before Berkeley (but after Descartes), here is John Tillotson: "Were it not for the veracity of God, we might, for anything we know, be under a constant delusion; and no man could demonstrate the contrary, but that this is our make, and our temper, and the very frame of our understandings, to be then most of all deceived, when we think ourselves to be most certain" (*Works* vol. 2: 583). But what entitles us to have confidence in divine "veracity"? That, presumably, is where faith comes in.

For an account of faith *more geometrico*, one could hardly hope to do better than Pascal, who is reputed to have discovered on his own the principles of geometry at the age of twelve (see Popkin, *History of Scepticism*, p. 180). Pascal writes:

> The most powerful argument of the Pyrrhonians (setting aside the lesser ones) is that we have no certainty of the truth of these principles, apart from faith and revelation, except insofar as we naturally perceive them in ourselves. But this natural sensation is not a convincing proof of their truth. For there is no certainty, apart from faith, as to whether man was created by a good God, by an evil demon, or by chance. Hence, depending on our origin, it is doubtful whether these principles given us are true, or false, or uncertain.
>
> (*Pensées* n. 164, trans. p. 34)

Anticipating Hume, Pascal goes on to say that "there never has been a fully effective Pyrrhonian. Nature sustains our feeble reason and prevents it from ranting so wildly" (p. 36). But this is not a response to skepticism. On the contrary, we are stuck in "paradox": "You cannot be a Pyrrhonian without stifling nature; you cannot be a dogmatist without repudiating reason. Nature confounds the Pyrrhonians, and reason confounds the dogmatists" (p. 36). So what are we to do? "Listen to God" (p. 36). "It is not through the proud exertions of our reason, but through its simple submission, that we can truly know ourselves" (p. 37). This leads Pascal to set down "two equally constant truths of faith": that grace lifts us up to participate in divinity; and that in a state of sin we are made similar to beasts (p. 37). For more on Pascal in this domain, see Lecture Five, note 7.

What is new in Hume is his willingness—perhaps for the first time since antiquity—to confront how the whole story collapses once God is taken out of the picture. Hume, however, offers no true way forward, only a form of quietism. Not the sort of spiritual quietism fashionable in the later seventeenth century, according to which one hands one's volition over to God (see Popkin, *History of Scepticism*, pp. 184–8), but a secular quietism that, in place of mystical practices, extols dinner and a game of backgammon.

Note 16 (p. 136). It may seem odd, in looking for a way forward from Hume, to turn back toward the pious Middle Ages. But, if we think of Hume as showing us that Enlightenment rationality is a dead end, then it makes perfectly good sense to look back to an era that offered a broader menu of options.

Aquinas offers a usefully brief and systematic discussion of the territory in his commentary on Hebrews. Intellectual assent, he says there, comes in two kinds. The first comes when we assent because of the evidentness of the object, which Aquinas takes to yield the certainty of *scientia*. The second comes when the object of assent is insufficiently evident to move the intellect. This could yield a state of doubt, when one is balanced between possibilities. Or, if there is assent, it will yield a state of opinion: "The intellect forms an opinion, if it has an argument [*ratio*] for one side that does not entirely quiet it, but comes with fear of the opposite side" (*Commentary on Hebrews* 11.1). Faith, Aquinas goes on to explain, is an odd sort of middle case. "Faith yields neither of these entirely, because neither is it evident as the first ones are [i.e., *scientia*], nor is it doubtful as the latter ones are [i.e., doubt and opinion], but it is determined to one side with a certainty and firm adherence, through a choice of will." But can we simply *will* such certainty (even subjective certainty) in the absence of sufficient evidence? Is that what faith requires: willing ourselves not to worry about the other side? To some extent Aquinas thinks the will can play such a role. He elsewhere describes our choosing to believe what someone says, because doing so "seems proper [*decens*] or useful" (*Quaest. de veritate* 14.1c). But the virtue of faith is a theological virtue, infused by God. So here in the Hebrews commentary Aquinas immediately goes on to say that the will in question is supplied by God: "Divine authority makes this choice, and through this choice the intellect is determined to adhere firmly to matters of the faith, and to assent most certainly to them" (11.1). See also *Quaestiones de veritate* 14.1 ad 7: "with respect to firmness of adherence, faith is more certain than any understanding or *scientia*, because the first truth [God], which causes faith's assent, is a stronger cause than the light of reason, which causes the assent of understanding or *scientia*." This is a delicate matter, however, both because Aquinas wants to say that faith is something *we* choose (since faith is meritorious) and because he wants intellect to have primacy over will in their interactions.

On the role of will in belief for Aquinas, see James Ross, "Aquinas on Belief and Knowledge," and Claudia Eisen Murphy, "Aquinas on Voluntary Beliefs." More generally, for the Middle Ages, see Grellard, *De la certitude volontaire* and the papers in Laurent Jaffro, *Croit-on comme on veut?* For a useful history of *opinio* in the Latin tradition, see Gabriele Gualdo, *Tractatus probabilitatis* ch. 2. More recently, see Rudolf Schüssler, *Moral im Zweifel* I: 54–7. On Aquinas in particular, see Edmund Byrne, *Probability and Opinion*, esp. pp. 63–9.

Aquinas very often analyzes *opinio* in terms of "fear of the opposite"—the Latin, most often, is *cum formidine alterius*. (See e.g. *Summa theol.* 1a 79.9 ad 4, 1a2ae 67.3c, *Comm. Post an.* I.1 n. 6.) Essentially the same expression appears frequently not just in later scholastic authors but also in earlier ones, including Albert the Great (as cited in this lecture, p. 136), Bonaventure (*Sent.* III.24.2.2 resp.) Alexander of Hales (e.g. *Summa* II.161.1) and William of Auvergne (*De fide* ch. 1, in *Opera*, p. 4bG). (Thanks here to Nicolas Faucher.) This is a decidedly different sense of *opinio* from what is found in Augustine, according to whom "those hold opinions who take themselves to know [*scire*] what they do not know" (*Advantage of Believing* 11.25). Augustine's pejorative usage of *opinio* was abandoned by these later scholastic authors, for whom holding a mere opinion might be a reasonable response to the available evidence. Predictably, this neutral scholastic usage seems to have its ultimate origins in the *Posterior Analytics*, where opinion (δόξα; *opinio*) concerns what is thought to be possibly otherwise. The story takes a surprising twist, however, in Avicenna's *De anima*, the Latin version of which defines opinion as "a conception that is accepted with fear [*cum formidine*] of the other side" (*De anima* VI.1 [vol. 2: 79]). This, very clearly, is the origin of the standard scholastic definition of opinion. But it turns out that the word 'fear' is based on a misreading of the Arabic, which speaks not of "fear" but of the "possibility" of the other side. (The Latin translator seems likely to have read تخويف instead of تجويز. Thanks here to Deborah Black.) All Avicenna meant to do, then, was to reiterate Aristotle's account. As is often the case, however, misinterpretation is the mother of philosophical invention.

Having been bequeathed this affective component of belief, authors hastened to deploy it in interesting ways. According to Buridan, an absence of fear is necessary for *scientia*: "If someone assents to a proposition while fearing the opposite, he would never say that he knows [*scire*] that it is true, but rather that he takes it or believes [*putat vel credit*] that it is" (*Summulae* VIII.4.4, trans. p. 707). According to Isaac Barrow (three centuries later), an absence of fear is sufficient for the certainty of knowledge: "what else signifies a certainty of knowledge, but that the thing known seems evidently true to the mind of the knower, so that all dread of the contrary is entirely excluded" (*Usefulness of Mathematical Learning*, lecture 5, trans. p. 69). Barrow holds that only a fool could reject the first principles of mathematics. Normal people, he says, cannot avoid assenting to such principles, not because they necessarily possess good supporting evidence, but just because they are unable to muster any worry about the possibility of their denial. Indeed, it does not matter *why* people fail to have any such fear: "whatsoever other way it is attained, it is sufficient that we are intimately conscious of it, and find it impressed upon the mind in an indelible character" (p. 69). This context makes it clear that Barrow has in mind "dread" as a distinctively affective state that precludes certainty. This bears a close resemblance to Wilkins's appeal to the frame of human nature in defending our absolute belief in what is morally certain. See the passaged quoted in this lecture (p. 132), which continues as follows: "Why, doubt is a kind of fear, and is commonly styled *formido oppositi*, and 'tis the same kind of madness for a man to doubt of anything, as to hope for or fear it upon a mere possibility" (*Principles* I.3, p. 30). As it happens, Barrow and Wilkins were colleagues at Trinity College in Cambridge.

Not everyone understood this notion of "fearing the opposite" in a way that is friendly to anti-evidentialism. Consider Siger of Brabant (*c*.1274): "if the knowledge of truth is the resolution of doubts, it does not appear that anyone can apprehend the truth and not know how to refute the arguments opposed to it" (*Quaest. meta.*, p. 165). The idea is close to Buridan's, but Siger makes it clear that what matters is not simply an absence of doubt (cognitive) or fear (affective), but rather an ability to give decisive reasons against the opposite view. This is the evidential route to escaping fear of the contrary. Compare Descartes's similar standard (as quoted in Lecture Two, p. 23): "Whenever two persons make opposite judgments about the same thing, it is certain that at least one of them is deceived, and it seems that neither has *scientia*. For if the reasoning of one of them were certain and evident, he would be able to lay it before the other in such a way as eventually to convince the other's intellect as well" (*Rules* 2, X: 363).

On 'expectation' in the seventeenth century, see Lorraine Daston, "Probabilistic Expect-ation." She shows that, in appealing to "expectations," Bernoulli follows Huygens, whose foundational treatise on probability was itself formulated as a theory of expectations. Accord-ing to Daston, the focus of probability treatises on expectation is a reflection of their interest in establishing a standard for reasonableness. If that is right, then the rise of this mathematical literature proceeds in step with the seventeenth century's rising interest in treating knowledge in terms of reasonably evident, or justified, true belief (see Lecture Two for details).

On beliefs versus credences, see Lecture Two, note 27.

Note 17 (p. 137). The discussion of Petrarch's letter to Francesco Bruni (see Petrarca, *Res seniles* I.5) in this lecture (p. 136) relies on Hans Nachod's translation (in Cassirer, Kristeller, and Herman, *Renaissance Philosophy of Man*). Unfortunately for my purposes, it is Nachod and not Petrarch who speaks of "fear"—all that Petrarch literally says is "lest I be entangled in error" (*ne erroribut implicer*). But I use the published translation because, even if it is not literally correct, it does capture the spirit of what Petrarch is saying. He *is* afraid of error, and that is why he has embraced skepticism.

The link between affective states and beliefs is widely discussed by medieval authors. It is said to be characteristic of rhetoric, for instance, that it generates belief through passion rather than through intellectual considerations (see Rita Copeland, "Living with Uncertainty"). Buridan thinks that emotion plays a large role in popular beliefs. For instance, "that devils have appeared to women and others with horns, or as naked black men is, I believe, a mere fantasy, an error assisted by the passions of fear and anxiety" (*Quaest. meta.* 3.2; see Grellard, "How Is It Possible to Believe Falsely?").

It is crucial to my purposes, however, to distinguish the idea that passion can cause someone to have a certain belief from the idea that a certain sort of passion is a constitutive element in belief. The sense in which scholastic authors say the latter has to be spelled out with some care. On one common way of setting out the territory (e.g., in Aquinas, *Comm. on Hebrews* 11.1, and Buridan, *Quaest. meta.* II.1), the broad genus that roughly corresponds to belief is dubbed 'assent' (*assensus*). This kind of belief might be caused by passion (as in the examples just given), but the assent itself does not have an affective component. Affect enters the scene (on these accounts) when assent gets distinguished into its various kinds: opinion involves fear of the alternative, whereas a state of subjective certainty involves confidence that is free from fear. Roughly, then, making allowances for the vagaries of how Latin and English psychological terms line up, we might say, on this approach, that belief in general does not have an affective component, but that the specific doxastic state necessary for knowledge does. (See Lecture Two, note 25, for further remarks on where to locate 'belief' within scholastic terminology.)

Hume's account of belief in terms of sentiment is, so far as I can tell, quite uninfluenced by this earlier history. Even so, the essential lines of thought are interestingly similar. Hume's puzzle is to understand what it is to believe a proposition, beyond our simply conceiving of the relevant ideas. (He regularly speaks of "belief or assent," e.g., *Treatise* I.3.5, p. 86, which helps bridge the gap between scholastic and modern vocabulary.) His answer is that belief is such a conception of ideas, when conceived through a certain "manner" or "feeling." More precisely,

This different feeling I endeavor to explain by calling it a superior *force*, or *vivacity*, or *solidity*, or *firmness*, or *steadiness*. This variety of terms, which may seem so unphilosophical, is intended only to express that act of the mind, which renders realities more present to us than fictions, causes them to weigh more in the thought, and gives them a superior influence on the passions and imagination.   (*Treatise*, p. 629 [appendix])

The common medieval view makes a similar move, but understands the "feeling" at issue in terms of presence or absence of fear concerning rival hypotheses. Hume seems not to have considered this possibility.

Whether or not either of these accounts is plausible, severally or jointly, they take on special importance because of the opportunity they allow to make sense of our epistemic predicament. Among medieval authors, this opportunity is mainly tacit, but in Hume the point becomes quite explicit. He tells us that, if belief were not an act of the "sensitive . . . part of our natures," then the force of the skeptical arguments would compel us to suspend belief (see this lecture, p. 137, quoting *Treatise* I.4.1, p. 184). Hume thinks that nature compels us to believe, but what bears stressing is that the method nature deploys to accomplish this necessary task is to direct our sentiments: "as experience will sufficiently convince anyone, who thinks it worthwhile to try, that *though he can find no error in the foregoing arguments*, yet he still continues to believe, and think, and reason as usual, he may safely conclude that his reasoning and belief is some sensation or peculiar manner of conception, *which 'tis impossible for mere ideas and reflections to destroy*" (*Treatise* I.4.1, p. 184, emphasis added). The skeptical arguments are sound, then, which is to say that epistemic defeatism is true. But, as discussed in note 14 to Lecture Five, such arguments are too abstruse to be sustained for very long against the influence of sentiment. As Hume famously stresses elsewhere, it is sentiment that controls reason, not the other way around. And what controls sentiment? That is where we depend on nature's "absolute and uncontrollable necessity" (p. 183).

The link between skepticism and affective attitudes shows up again, recently, in Richard Foley, although without adverting to any of this history. Foley describes how one's attitude to skepticism is like the grading of a test:

> You yourself determine the special cost of error. If your distaste of error is great, the scoring range of the test is enlarged on the negative side … If the distaste is great enough, it may be unwise for you to answer any of the questions. You will then find yourself in a skeptical position, but it is your own attitude, your own horror of error, that has put you in this position. Thus, the solution to this kind of skepticism must also be one of attitude. The trick is not to find a better argument but rather a better attitude.   (*Working without a Net*, p. 200)

Foley says little more, however, about the character of these attitudes, nor does he defend the assumption that we can choose our own attitude.

For other recent treatments of belief that stress its affective component, see Christopher Hookway, "Doubt," and Karen Jones, "The Politics of Intellectual Self-Trust."

Belief through Hope

Note 18 (p. 138). In suggesting that our hopes be allowed to influence our beliefs, I am flying in the face of one of the main preoccupations of philosophy ever since the seventeenth century. Locke's principle of proportionality is one early example of a rule that I would violate, and others can be found in Arnauld and Nicole's *Port Royal Logic*, whose probabilistic strictures on reasoning are aimed at "making us more reasonable in our hopes and fears" (IV.16, trans. p. 274).

In contrast to these confident Enlightenment-era bids to have reason govern hope, medieval theories of hope offer a rich model for the sort of affective state that might permit belief without sufficient evidence. But the model would have to be qualified and reshaped in quite a few ways. Here I will mention just a few salient issues, focusing on Aquinas's theory. As explained in this lecture (p. 137), Aquinas treats hope as an affective state: a habit of the will. It is, however, not simply a standing rational desire, but a desire that "tends with certainty towards its end" (*Summa theol.* 2a2ae 18.4c). Hence Aquinas regularly uses 'expectation' to describe the mental state of hope. As a theological virtue, it is "the expectation of future beatitude" (2a2ae 17.6 arg. 2). Someone who is hopeful, then, fixes her expectations not according to the rule Bernoulli would later describe, as proportioned to the evidence (see this lecture, pp. 135–6), but in the hope of achieving the best outcome. Yet whence does this sort of certain expectation arise? Aquinas's answer is that it rises out of faith:

> Faith absolutely precedes hope. For the object of hope is a future good that is difficult but possible to obtain. Therefore, for someone to hope, the object of hope must be given to him as possible. But the object of faith in one way is eternal beatitude, and in another way it is divine assistance … Each of these is given to us through faith.   (2a2ae 17.7c)

Hence the certitude without evidentness that is characteristic of faith on the cognitive side (see note 16 to this lecture) gives rise within the will to an affective certitude.

But here things get tricky, because Aquinas thinks that hope, if it is to be a virtue, must be balanced against the countervailing affective state of fear—the fear of divine justice. Thus, in a virtuous person, "God is the object of hope *and* fear" (2a2ae 19.1 ad 2). Given this, one might wonder about the sense in which Aquinas can speak of the "certainty" of hope. Plainly he does not mean that our "expectation of future beatitude" is such as to remove all worries about the contrary. Nor is there any reason why faith would produce such an outcome. After all, the articles of faith tell us only that God's benevolent concern for us makes it *possible* for us to achieve beatitude. This leaves quite open the possibility that we will not merit such a reward, and hence even the most faithful should be worried—not about how things stand with God, but about how things stand with us. We should worry about our own failure, and so be afraid that, instead of receiving the reward of divine mercy, we will receive the punishment of divine justice (see 2a2ae 19.1 ad 1). The certitude of faith, then, gives rise to simultaneous counter-vailing certainties on the affective side, of both hope and fear. How we can be said to be *certain* in our hope is not at all clear from Aquinas's discussion, but gets a remarkable and extensive contemporary treatment from Bonaventure, who concludes that the certainty of hope is neither propositional nor cognitive but is a kind of affective firmness, or lack of hesitation, with respect to its object: eternal life. "It is not the certainty of perpetual confirmation, but of a kind of forceful adherence" (Bonaventure, *Sentences* III.26.1.5, in *Opera* vol. 3: 565–8). (Here I am indebted to discussion with Luc Bovens.)

I am not sure about Bonaventure, but Aquinas at least is too much of an intellectualist to allow what I am proposing: that we should encourage our expectations on the affective side to run free of our credences on the cognitive side. To let this happen is to indulge in vice. Indeed, "every appetitive motion which conforms itself to a false intellect is in itself evil and a sin" (Aquinas, *Summa theol.* 2a2ae 21.2c). If fear crowds out hope, then we have succumbed to despair. If hope crowds out fear, then we have acquired the vice of presumption. This last option, however, is exactly what I recommend. Moreover, I must part ways with Aquinas not only on the question of whether this option leads to vice, but also on whether the attitude I describe is psychologically possible. Aquinas thinks that these two affect-side vices are typically the result of one or another mistake on the cognitive side. We might, for instance, lose faith in God's benevolence and, in consequence, despair. But Aquinas is not such a strict intellectualist as to dismiss the possibility of *akrasia*: that the will might go wrong *despite* the intellect's counsel. He thinks, for instance, that one can despair even while remaining constant in one's faith, if one fails to apply the universal principles of the faith to one's own particular case (2a2ae 20.2). (This coheres with his broader analysis of *akrasia* at *Summa theol.* 2a2ae 155–6.) Yet for my story to work I need more than this. I need a case where the intellect's considered judgment is that we have no good basis for *p*, neither in general nor in this particular case, and nevertheless I reach the affect-side hope that *p*. This, all by itself, violates Aquinas's intellectualism, since it requires the will to take a stand that runs contrary to intellect's guidance. The intellect is saying in effect that ~*p* is entirely possible, and yet the will is refusing to take it seriously. Matters get still worse when I suggest that such hope can give rise to belief, because now we have the affective side taking priority over the cognitive side in a way that Aquinas regards as flatly impossible at the rational level. For even if, as we have seen (note 16 here), Aquinas accepts that belief involves the pseudo-Avicennian feature of not fearing the opposite, he takes this to be a *consequence* of our cognitive-side state rather than a *cause* of it.

Here is one final obstacle to the way I would employ hope. Aquinas thinks that hope must be regulated not only by cognitive-side faith, but also by affect-side charity or love: "Hope, and every appetitive motion, arises from some love, by which someone loves the good that he expects" (*Summa theol.* 2a2ae 17.8 ad 2). Combine this with the Augustinian dictum that love requires knowledge: "Who loves that which he does not know? For something can be known and not loved, but what I am asking is whether something can be loved that is not known?" (Augustine, *De trinitate* VIII.4.6; cf. X.1.1) The result is that hope cannot give rise to know-ledge, as I suggest, because hope presupposes knowledge. In the theological context, this creates a genuine puzzle, because it is hard to see how one can know God sufficiently to love him and to hope for eternal life with him, unless one has already achieved the sort of illumination that presupposes hope and charity. But in my secular context there is no real puzzle, only an equivocation about kinds of knowledge. To hope that the world around us has at least roughly the character our cognitive faculties indicate requires that we know *what* that character is, at least roughly. To hope that the world is like this, we must know what it is that we hope for. Such hope can then give rise to belief that, under the right circumstances, can constitute knowledge *that* the world is this way. But, because *knowing what* is quite different from *knowing that*, there is no paralyzing circularity here.

In focusing on Aquinas I do not mean to suggest that his views describe the medieval consensus on these matters. If, for instance, one looks instead at Ockham, one finds a different conception of hope (see *Quodlibet* III.9) and a much more voluntaristic conception of the relation between will and belief (see *Quaest. var. 5*). Moreover, although it lies beyond the scope of this study to consider these topics in their broader cultural context, the topic of hope is a particularly fertile one in medieval literature. Dante, for instance, tells us that the shades in limbo suffer in just one thing: "cut off from hope, we live on in desire" (*Inferno* IV.41–2). Or, to take a very different sort of example, medieval romantic poetry is full of discussions about the hopes, futile or not, of the lover for his beloved. For a philosophically sophisticated exploration of this topic, see Helen Swift, "The Merits of Not Knowing." For a comparison of Aquinas and Ockham on hope, see Dominik Perler, "Die kognitive Struktur von Hoffnung." More generally, see Jacques Bougerol, *La théologie de l'espérance*.

Another place to look for something like hope as an affective attitude impinging on our cognitive attitudes is in the recent literature on trust. Karen Jones, in particular, has argued that "to trust someone is to have an attitude of optimism about her goodwill and to have the confident expectation that, when the need arises, the one trusted will be directly and favorably moved by the thought that you are counting on her" ("Trust as an Affective Attitude," pp. 5–6). My own suggestion, in effect, is that we think of such affective attitudes as foundational quite generally in epistemology.

Note 19 (p. 138). Can we simply choose our affective attitudes, and thereby choose our beliefs? Augustine *prays* for the three theological virtues—faith, hope, charity—because he does not suppose that these are things we are able to acquire for ourselves. This increasingly appears to be true in the religious domain today, inasmuch as trust in God seems to be something the human mind easily rejects, once it is no longer embedded as a cultural expectation. But trust in other people seems to have a firmer hold on our nature, and trust in the fundamental posit of epistemology—that the external world is (roughly) as it seems to be—looks quite unshakeable. No grace needed.

Matters become much murkier, however, when one tries to combine this native attitude of trust with the explicit embrace of epistemic defeatism. The lecture's suggestion is that we can embrace both these notions if we distinguish between credence and belief, letting our rational expectations track the dismal reality of epistemic defeat and yet optimistically believing all the same. Of course, this proposal cries out for more substantial development, which I will not attempt here. But, lest the very notion seems flatly incoherent, think of a professional gambler whose affective states swing wildly from night to night, with the result that sometimes he believes he will win and at other times he believes he will lose. Even so, professional that he is, he deploys the same strategy night after night, remorselessly playing the odds as reflected in his credences. Or, for a real-life case of someone displaying this sort of doubleness of mind, consider this recent pronouncement from the University of Colorado's athletic director: "I'm optimistic that it will be done and have every belief that it will be done but something could happen outside of our control. But we plan on it being done" (*Daily Camera* Sept. 5, 2014, p. C1). Let none of us be judged by how we are quoted in the newspaper. Still, the state of mind should be familiar.

Cases such as this one might call to mind Tamar Gendler's distinction between belief and alief, where the latter is an action-generating representational state that falls short of belief because it does not involve the agent's accepting the proposition in question. Thus we *believe* that the bridge will support us, but we *alieve* that we might well fall (see Gendler, "Alief and Belief"). For this distinction to apply here, however, it would seem most natural to count the gambler's steady credences as beliefs, leaving the swings between optimism and pessimism to give rise to less explicit aliefs. One could tell the story in something like that way and then argue that hope makes possible not knowledge in the usual belief-involving sense, but alief knowledge. On my version, however, it is the fluctuating states of mind that are better candidates for belief: the gambler, as I am thinking of him, really does believe, on many a night, that he is going to win. So the sort of distinction that I require would need to be developed in a different way.

As is the case with Gendler's distinction, I am supposing that an agent's behavior may follow the credences or may follow the beliefs. The epistemic defeatist, then, may hopefully believe that there is an external world much as it appears to be and may act on that belief, but may at the very same time issue skeptical-sounding proclamations about the poverty of the evidence. What sort of behavior counts as rational, in such a circumstance, will depend partly on what is at stake in one's actions. Given that there is no practical alternative to a generalized trust in one's senses, there is little at stake in one's trusting them. Hope, at this general level, seems therefore easy to defend. But pragmatic considerations will encroach on particular cases, where workable alternatives to trust are at hand and the cost of making the wrong choice is immediate and dire. Here is where hope can become clearly irrational, because the cost of not following one's credences is so severe as to outweigh whatever advantages might accrue to a policy of cheerful hopefulness. (On such pragmatic influences, see e.g. Mark Schroeder, "Stakes, Withholding, and Pragmatic Encroachment.")

The evidentialist pressure I am resisting—to give the utmost weight to conforming our beliefs to how the world seems most likely to be—has an interesting counterpart in the domain of values. Here you might think it of paramount importance that your evaluative attitudes match up with what really is of value. But what if nothing has ultimate value, or what if it turns out that what matters is things that leave you quite cold? In the face of such value-skeptical scenarios, you might well just shrug and go on caring about the things that in fact you care about. Indeed, much more than in the epistemic case, this is how I suspect many philosophers do position themselves. Unable to rebut the familiar antirealist arguments in the moral domain, we nevertheless go on caring about the things we care about. We might do so out of faith, which would consist in unsupported confidence in the falsity of antirealism. But a better attitude would be one of hopefulness: that of continuing on the affective side to care about the things we care about, in the hope that these things really do matter, but without having any cognitive confidence that in fact they do matter. Such a stance is far from ideal, but it may be the best we can do.

ACKNOWLEDGMENTS

My first debt is to the faculties of Philosophy and History at the University of Oxford, for the privilege of serving as the Isaiah Berlin Visiting Professor in 2014. It was my additional fortune, during this time, to be welcomed at Corpus Christi College as a visiting fellow.

Among the many who attended my lectures from beginning to end, I owe special thanks, for their hard questions and encouraging advice, to Gail Fine, Terry Irwin, Anna Marmodoro, Giorgio Pini, and Cecilia Trifogli. I also learned much, while in Oxford, from long conversations with Charity Anderson, Anita Avramides, Peter J. Graham, John Greco, Tony Kenny, Steffen Koch, Maria Lasonen-Aarnio, Paul Lodge, Dani Rabinowitz, Miriam Schoenfield, and Helen Swift. Many of these conversations were made possible by my association with John Hawthorne's project on New Insights and Directions for Religious Epistemology, supported by the Templeton Foundation. Finally, and above all, for his unflagging support and friendship during my time in Oxford, I am grateful to Christopher Shields.

Some of the ideas from various lectures have appeared in other places. The first two lectures draw on "Epistemology Idealized." Some material in Lecture Four is developed further in "Therapeutic Reflections." Lecture Six serves as the starting point for "Snatching Hope." All these papers develop the philosophical implications of the more narrowly historical treatment pursued here.

For help over the years with various aspects of this project, thanks also to Dominic Bailey, Don Baxter, Justin Broackes, Herman Cappelen, Victor Caston, Patrick Connolly, Mary Domski, Blake Dutton, John Heil, Dan Kaufman, Hilary Kornblith, Mitzi Lee, Jon McGinnis, Thomas Metcalf, Bradley Monton, Joseph Moore, Claude Panaccio, Elliot Paul, Sydney Penner, Susanna Rinard, Beth Robertson, Robert Rupert, Michael Sechman, and Katia Vavova. Two readers for OUP, one of whom was Tad Schmaltz, offered much helpful advice on a complete draft of the book. Mark Boespflug and Philip Choi provided very helpful comments on all six lectures in their late stages. Manuela Tecusan edited the whole typescript with tremendous care and erudition.

Finally, thanks to my family for tolerating my various absences of mind and body, and especially to Josie, who has waited patiently for so many years now, while I have been absorbed by one thing or another. Now that this book is done, girl, we'll go on some nice gentle walks in the mountains. I promise.

BIBLIOGRAPHY

Sources prior to the twentieth century count as primary. Christian authors active before 1600 are alphabetized by first name. English translations are listed where available, though the translations in the lectures are generally my own. Where confusion might arise over how to understand a citation, a brief annotation is appended to the relevant bibliographical entry.

Readers should bear in mind that most of the medieval material I discuss remains, to this day, untranslated. Where no translation is mentioned below, it is very likely that no translation has yet been made. On the other hand, books published before 1923 are likely to be available on the internet for free, which makes all of the early English material readily accessible even without a modern edition.

Primary Sources

Adam Wodeham. *Lectura secunda in librum primum Sententiarum*, ed. R. Wood and G. Gál (St. Bonaventure, NY: St. Bonaventure University, 1990).

Adam Wodeham. *Tractatus de indivisibilibus*, ed. and trans. R. Wood (Dordrecht: Kluwer, 1988).

Albert of Saxony. *Expositio et quaestiones in Aristotelis libros Physicorum ad Albertum de Saxonia attributae*, ed. B. Patar (Leuven: Peeters, 1999).

Albert of Saxony. *Questiones subtilissime in libros de generatione* (Venice, 1505; repr. Frankfurt: Minerva, 1970).

Albert the Great. *Opera omnia*, ed. E. Borgnet (Paris: Vivès, 1890–9).

Albert the Great. *Opera omnia*, ed. B. Geyer et al. [Cologne] (Münster: Aschendorff, 1951–).

Albert the Great. *Opera omnia*, ed. P. Jammy (Lyon, 1651).

Alexander of Hales et al. *Summa theologica* (Quaracchi: Editiones Collegii S. Bonaventurae, 1924–48).

Anselm. *Basic Writings*, trans. T. Williams (Indianapolis, IN: Hackett, 2007).

Anselm. *Opera omnia*, ed. F. S. Schmitt (Edinburgh: Nelson, 1946; repr. Stuttgart: Frommann, 1968).

Antoninus of Florence. *Summa theologica* (Verona, 1740; repr. Graz: Akademische Druck, 1959).

Aristotle. *Arisṭūṭālīs fī al-nafs*, ed. A. Badawi (Cairo: Imprimerie Misr S.A.E., 1954; repr. Beirut, 1980).

Aristotle. *The Complete Works of Aristotle: The Revised Oxford Translation*, ed. J. Barnes (Princeton: Princeton University Press, 1984).

Aristotle. *De anima*, ed. D. Ross (Oxford: Oxford University Press, 1961).

Aristotle. *De generatione et corruptione*, trans. C. J. F. Williams (Oxford: Clarendon, 1982).

Aristotle. *Ethica Nicomachea*, ed. I. Bywater (Oxford: Clarendon, 1991).

Aristotle. *Metaphysics*, 2 vols., ed. W. D. Ross (Oxford: Clarendon, 1924).

Aristotle. *Physics*, ed. W. D. Ross (Oxford: Clarendon, 1936).

Aristotle. *Posterior Analytics*, trans. J. Barnes, 2nd edn. (Oxford: Clarendon, 1993).

Aristotle. *Prior and Posterior Analytics*, ed. W. D. Ross (Oxford: Clarendon, 1957).

Aristotle. *Topica et Sophistici elenchi*, ed. W. D. Ross (Oxford: Clarendon, 1958).

Arnauld, Antoine. *Des vraies et des fausses idées*, ed. D. Moreau (Paris: Vrin, 2011).

Arnauld, Antoine. *On True and False Ideas*, trans. E. J. Kremer (Lewiston, NY: Edwin Mellen Press, 1990).

Arnauld, Antoine and Pierre Nicole. *La logique ou l'art de penser*, ed. P. Clair and F. Girbal, rev. edn. (Paris: Vrin, 1981).

Arnauld, Antoine and Pierre Nicole. *Logic or the Art of Thinking* [*Port-Royal Logic*], trans. J. V. Buroker (Cambridge: Cambridge University Press, 1996).

Augustine. *The Advantage of Believing*, trans. L. Meagher (New York: Fathers of the Church, 1947).

Augustine. *Against the Academicians and The Teacher*, trans. P. King (Indianapolis, IN: Hackett, 1995).

Augustine. *Concerning the City of God against the Pagans*, trans. H. Bettenson (Harmondsworth: Penguin Books, 1984).

Augustine. *De vera religione / Of True Religion*, trans. J. H. S. Burleigh (Chicago, IL: Regnery, 1964).

Augustine. *On Free Choice of the Will*, trans. T. Williams (Indianapolis, IN: Hackett, 1993).

Augustine. *On the Trinity: Books 8–15*, ed. G. B. Matthews, trans. S. McKenna (Cambridge: Cambridge University Press, 2002).

Augustine. *Opera* (Corpus Christianorum, series latina) (Turnhout: Brepols, 1954–81).

Augustine. *The Retractations*, trans. M. I. Bogan (Washington, DC: Catholic University of America Press, 1968).

Augustine. *Soliloquies*, in J. H. S. Burleigh (tr.), *Earlier Writings* (Louisville: Westminster Press, 1953).

Averroes. *Commentaria in Aristotelis Metaphysicorum libri XIIII*, vol. 8 of *Aristotelis opera* (Venice: apud Iunctas, 1562; repr. Frankfurt: Minerva, 1962).

Averroes. *Commentarium magnum in Aristotelis De anima libros*, ed. F. S. Crawford (Cambridge, MA: Mediaeval Academy of America, 1953).

Averroes. *Long Commentary on the* De anima *of Aristotle*, trans. R. C. Taylor (New Haven, CT: Yale University Press, 2008).

Averroes. *Middle Commentary on Aristotle's* De anima, ed. A. Ivry (Provo, UT: Brigham Young University Press, 2002).

Averroes. *Tafsīr mā baʿd al-ṭabīʿa / Metaphysics*, ed. M. Bouyges (Beirut: Imprimerie Catholique, 1938–52).

Averroes. *Tahāfut al-tahāfut (The Incoherence of the Incoherence)*, trans. S. Van den Bergh (London: Luzac, 1954).

Averroes. *Tahāfut al-tahāfut*, ed. M. Bouyges (Beirut: Imprimerie Catholique, 1930).

Avicenna. *Avicenna's De anima (Arabic Text): Being the Psychological Part of Kitab al-Shifāʾ;*, ed. F. Rahman (London: Oxford University Press, 1959).

Avicenna. *Liber de anima seu Sextus de naturalibus* (Avicenna Latinus 1.1), ed. S. Van Riet (Leiden: Brill, 1968–72).

Avicenna. *The Metaphysics of 'The Healing' [al-Shifāʾ]*, trans. M. E. Marmura (Provo, UT: Brigham Young University Press, 2005).

Avicenna. *Remarks and Admonitions, Part I: Logic*, trans. S. C. Inati (Toronto: Pontifical Institute for Mediaeval Studies, 1984).

Bacon, Francis. *The Instauratio magna, Part II: Novum organum and Associated Texts* (The Oxford Francis Bacon 11), ed. and trans. G. Rees with M. Wakely (Oxford: Clarendon, 2004).

Bacon, Francis. *The Major Works*, ed. B. Vickers (Oxford: Oxford University Press, 2002).

Bacon, Francis. *Philosophical Studies c.1611–c.1619* (The Oxford Francis Bacon 6), ed. G. Rees (Oxford: Clarendon Press, 1996).

Bacon, Francis. *The Works of Francis Bacon*, 14 vols., ed. J. Spedding, R. L. Ellis, and D. D. Heath (London: Longman, 1857–74).

Barrow, Isaac. *Lectiones mathematicae XXIII* (London: J. Playford, 1685).

Barrow, Isaac. *The Usefulness of Mathematical Learning*, trans. J. Kirkby (London: Stephen Austen, 1734).

Bayhaqī, Aḥmad ibn al-Ḥusayn. *Shuʿab al-īmān*, 7 vols. (Beirut: Dār al-Kutub al-ʿIlmīyah, 1990).

Bayle, Pierre. *Dictionnaire historique et critique*, 16 vols. (Paris: Desoer, 1820).

Bayle, Pierre. *Historical and Critical Dictionary: Selections*, trans. R. H. Popkin (Indianapolis, IN: Hackett, 1991).

Benedictus Pererius. *De communibus omnium rerum naturalium principiis et affectionibus* (Paris: Michael Sonnius, 1579).

Berkeley, George. *Philosophical Writings*, ed. D. M. Clarke (Cambridge: Cambridge University Press, 2008).

Berkeley, George. *Works*, 9 vols., ed. A. A. Luce and T. E. Jessop (London: Nelson, 1948–57).

References to Berkeley's *Three Dialogues* cite the page numbers of the Luce and Jessop edition, which are indicated in the margin of Clarke's edition.

Bernoulli, Jacob. *Ars conjectandi* (Basel: Thurnisii fratres, 1713).

Bernoulli, Jacob. *The Art of Conjecturing*, trans. E. D. Sylla (Baltimore, MD: Johns Hopkins University Press, 2006).

Biancani, Giuseppe. *De mathematicarum natura dissertatio* (Bologna, 1615).

Blasius of Parma. *Le "Quaestiones de anima*,*"* ed. G. Federici Vescovini (Florence: Olschki, 1974).

Boethius. *Chaucer's Translation of Boethius's "De consolatione philosophiae*,*"* ed. R. Morris (London: N. Trübner, 1868).

Boethius. *The Consolation of Queen Elizabeth I: The Queen's Translation of Boethius's* De consolatione philosophiae, ed. N. H. Kaylor, Jr. and P. E. Phillips (Tempe, AZ: Arizona Center for Medieval and Renaissance Studies, 2009).

Boethius. *In Porphyrii Isagogen commentorum editio duplex* (Corpus Scriptorum Ecclesiasticorum Latinorum 48), ed. S. Brandt (Vienna: F. Tempsky, 1906).

Boethius. *The Old English Boethius, with Verse Prologues and Epilogues associated with King Alfred*, ed. and trans. S. Irvine and M. Godden (Cambridge, MA: Harvard University Press, 2012).

Bonaventure. *Opera omnia* (Quaracchi: Editiones Collegii S. Bonaventurae, 1882–1902).

Bonaventure. *Sermones de diversis*, ed. J. G. Bougerol (Paris: Editions Franciscaines, 1993).

Boyle, Robert. *Selected Philosophical Papers of Robert Boyle*, ed. M. A. Stewart (Manchester: Manchester University Press, 1979).

Boyle, Robert. *The Works of Robert Boyle*, ed. M. Hunter and E. B. Davis (London: Pickering & Chatto, 1999–2000).

Buffon, Georges Le Clerc. *Essais d'arithmétique morale*, in idem, *Suppléments à l'histoire naturelle*, vol. 4 (Paris: L'Imprimerie Royale, 1777).

Burgersdijk, Franco. *Collegium physicum, disputationibus XXXII absolutum*, 3rd edn. (Cambridge, 1650).

Burgersdijk, Franco. *Monitio logica or An Abstract and Translation of Burgersdicius: His Logick* (London: R. Cumberland, 1697).

Butler, Joseph. *The Analogy of Religion Natural and Revealed to the Constitution and Course of Nature*, 6th edn. (London: John Beecroft, 1771).

Caesarius of Heisterbach. *The Dialogue on Miracles*, 2 vols, trans. H. von E. Scott and C. C. Swinton Bland (London: Routledge, 1929).

Cavendish, William (ed.). *Letters and Poems in Honour of the Incomparable Princess, Margaret, Dutchess of Newcastle* (London: Thomas Newcombe, 1676).

Charleton, Walter. *The Immortality of the Human Soul* (London: William Wilson for Henry Herringman, 1657).

Charleton, Walter. *Physiologia Epicuro-Gassendo-Charltoniana* (London, 1654; repr. New York: Johnson, 1966).

Chillingworth, William. *The Religion of the Protestants a Safe Way to Salvation* (Oxford: Leonard Lichfield, 1638).

Chillingworth, William. *Works* (Philadelphia, PA: H. Hooker, 1840).

Cicero. *Academica* (Loeb Classical Library), trans. H. Rackham (Cambridge, MA: Harvard University Press, 1967).

Collegium Conimbricense. *Commentarii Collegii Conimbricensis in octo libros Physicorum Aristotelis* (Lyon, 1594; repr. Hildesheim: G. Olms, 1984).

Collegium Conimbricense. *Commentarii Collegii Conimbricensis in tres libros De anima* (Cologne, 1609; repr. Hildesheim: G. Olms, 2006).

Craig, John. *Theologiae christianae principia mathematica* (London, 1699).

Dabillon, André. *Nouveau cours de philosophie en François* (Paris: Sebastien Piquet, 1643).

Dante Alighieri. *The Inferno*, trans. R. Hollander and J. Hollander (New York: Doubleday, 2000).

Descartes, René. *Oeuvres de Descartes*, ed. C. Adam and P. Tannery (Paris: Cerf, 1897; repr. Paris: Vrin, 1996).

Descartes, René. *The Philosophical Writings of Descartes*, 3 vols., trans. J. Cottingham, R. Stoothoff, D. Murdoch, and A. Kenny (Cambridge: Cambridge University Press, 1984–91).

References to Descartes supply the volume and page number in the standard Adam–Tannery edition, which are printed in the margins of the standard Cottingham et al. translation.

Diderot, Denis and Jean le Rond d'Alembert. *Encyclopédie, ou dictionnaire raisonné des sciences, des arts et des métiers* (Paris, 1751–72).

Digby, Kenelm. *Conference with a Lady about Choice of Religion* (Paris: [Widow of J. Blagaert], 1638).

Digby, Kenelm. *A Late Discourse . . . Touching the Cure of Wounds by the Powder of Sympathy; With Instructions How to Make the Said Powder; Whereby Many Other Secrets of Nature are Unfolded*, trans. R. White (London: R. Lownes and T. Davies, 1658).

Digby, Kenelm. *Two Treatises: In the One of Which the Nature of Bodies; In the Other, the Nature of Mans Soule; Is Looked into: In Way of Discovery, of the Immortality of Reasonable Soules* (Paris: G. Blaizot, 1644).

Diogenes Laertius. *Lives of Eminent Philosophers* (Loeb Classical Library), 2 vols., trans. H. D. Hicks (London: Heinemann, 1925).

Domingo de Soto. *In Porphyrii Isagogen, Aristotelis Categorias, librosque De demonstratione absolutissima commentaria* (Venice, 1587; repr. Frankfurt: Minerva, 1967).

Dominicus Gundisalvi. *De divisione philosophie*, ed. L. Baur (Münster: Aschendorff, 1903).

Du Châtelet, Émilie. *Selected Philosophical and Scientific Writings*, trans. I. Bour and J. P. Zinsser (Chicago, IL: University of Chicago Press, 2009).

Durand of St.-Pourçain. *In Petri Lombardi Sententias theologicas commentarium libri quatuor* (Venice: ex typographia Guerraea, 1571; repr. Ridgewood, NJ: Gregg, 1964).

Elias. *In Porphyrii Isagogen et Aristotelis Categorias commentaria* (Commentaria in Aristotelem Graeca 18.2), ed. A. Busse (Berlin: G. Reimer, 1900).

al-Fārābī. *Kitāb al-burhān*, in *Al-Manṭiq ʿinda al-Fārābī*, 4 vols., ed. R. al-ʿAjam and M. Fakhry (Beirut: Dār al-Mashriq, 1986–7).

al-Fārābī. *Kitāb al-ḥurūf*, ed. M. Mahdī (Beirut: Dār al-Mashriq, 1969).

Francesco Petrarca. *Res seniles*, 2 vols., ed. S. Rizzo (Florence: Le lettere, 2006–9).

Francis of Marchia. *Commentarius in IV libros Sententiarum Petri Lombardi: Distinctiones primi libri prima ad decimam [Reportatio]*, ed. N. Mariani (Grottaferrata: Editiones Collegii S. Bonaventurae, 2006).

Francis of Marchia. *Quodlibet cum quaestionibus selectis ex commentario in librum Sententiarum [Scriptum]*, ed. N. Mariani (Grottaferrata: Editiones Collegii S. Bonaventurae, 1997).

Francis of Meyronnes. *Tractatus de notitia intuitiva*, in G. J. Etzkorn (ed.), "Franciscus de Mayronis: A Newly Discovered Treatise on Intuitive and Abstractive Cognition," *Franciscan Studies* 54 (1994–7): 15–50.

Francisco Sanches. *That Nothing Is Known / Quod nihil scitur*, ed. and trans. E. Limbrick and D. F. S. Thomson (Cambridge: Cambridge University Press, 1988).

Francisco Suárez. *De anima: Commentaria una cum quaestionibus in libros Aristotelis De anima*, 3 vols., ed. S. Castellote (Madrid: Sociedad de Estudios y Publicaciones, 1978–91).

Francisco Suárez. *Disputationes metaphysicae* (Paris: Vivès, 1866; repr. Hildesheim: G. Olms, 1965).

Francisco Suárez. *Opera omnia*, 28 vols., ed. D. M. André and C. Berton (Paris: Vivès, 1856–78).

Franciscus Toletus. *Commentaria una cum quaestionibus in octo libros Aristotelis de physica auscultatione* (Cologne: Birckmann, 1579).

Frege, Gottlob. *Basic Laws of Arithmetic, Derived Using Concept-Script*, vols. 1–2, trans. P. A. Ebert and M. Rossberg (Oxford: Oxford University Press, 2013).

Galilei, Galileo. *Dialogue concerning the Two Chief World Systems*, trans. S. Drake (New York: Modern Library, 2001).

Galilei, Galileo. *Discourse on Bodies in Water*, trans. T. Salusbury (London: W. Leybourn, 1663; repr. Urbana: University of Illinois Press, 1960).

Galilei, Galileo. *Discoveries and Opinions of Galileo*, trans. S. Drake (Garden City, NY: Doubleday Anchor, 1957).

Galilei, Galileo. *Le opere di Galileo Galilei*, 20 vols., ed. A. Favaro (Florence: G. Barbèra, 1890–1909).

Galilei, Galileo. *Two New Sciences*, trans. S. Drake, 2nd edn. (Toronto: Wall & Emerson, 1989).

Gassendi, Pierre. *Dissertations en forme de paradoxes contre les Aristotéliciens / Exercitationes paradoxicae adversus Aristoteleos: Livres I et II*, ed. B. Rochot (Paris: Vrin, 1959).

Gassendi, Pierre. *Syntagmatis philosophici*, in *Opera omnia* (Lyon, 1658; repr. Stuttgart-Bad Cannstatt: Frommann-Holzboog, 1964).

Gerard of Bologna. *La théorie de la connaissance intellectuele de Gérard de Bologne (ca. 1240/50–1317): Édition critique et étude doctrinale de quatorze Quodlibeta*, ed. D. Piché (Leuven: Peeters, 2014).

al-Ghazālī. *Algazel's Methaphysics: A Medieval Translation*, ed. J. T. Muckle (Toronto: St. Michael's College, 1933).

al-Ghazālī. *al-Munqidh min al-ḍalāl / Rescuer from Error*, ed. J. Ṣalībā and K. ʿAyyād (Damascus: Maktab al-Nashr al-ʿArabī, 1934).

al-Ghazālī. *Maqāṣid al-falāsifa*, ed. S. Dunya (Cairo: Dār al-Maʿārif, 1961).

Gianfrancesco Pico della Mirandola. *Examen vanitatis doctrinae gentium, et veritatis Christianae doctrinae*, in Giovanni Pico della Mirandola, *Opera omnia* (Basel, 1557; repr. Hildesheim: Olms, 1969), vol. 2: 710–1264.

Gilbert, William. *De magnete* (London: P. Short, 1600).

Gilbert, William. *De magnete*, trans. P. F. Mottelay (New York: Dover, 1958).

Glanvill, Joseph. *Essays on Several Important Subjects in Philosophy and Religion* (London, 1676).

Glanvill, Joseph. *A Praefatory Answer to Mr. Henry Stubbe* (London, 1671).

Glanvill, Joseph. *Scepsis scientifica: Or, Confest Ignorance, the Way of Science* (London, 1665).

Glanvill, Joseph. *The Vanity of Dogmatizing: Or Confidence in Opinions, Manifested in a Discourse of the Shortness and Uncertainty of our Knowledge and Its Causes, with Some Reflections on Peripateticism, and an Apology for Philosophy* (London, 1661).

Gregory of Rimini. *Lectura super primum et secundum Sententiarum*, ed. D. Trapp et al. (Berlin: De Gruyter, 1979–84).

Grotius, Hugo. *De veritate religionis Christianae*, 2nd edn. (Leiden: J. Maire, 1629).

Grotius, Hugo. *The Truth of the Christian Religion*, trans. J. Clarke (London: J. F. Dove, 1827).

Gualdo, Gabriele [as Nicolao Peguleti]. *Tractatus probabilitatis ex principiis antiquorum compositus* (Leuven, 1707).

Guidobaldo dal Monte. *Mechanicorum liber* (Pisa, 1577).

Hale, Matthew. *The Primitive Origination of Mankind, Considered and Examined according to the Light of Nature* (London: W. Godbid for W. Shrowsbery, 1677).

Henry Cornelius Agrippa. *De incertitudine et vanitate scientiarum declamatio* (Cologne: apud Eucharium Agrippinatem, 1531).

Henry Cornelius Agrippa. *Of the Vanity and Uncertainty of Arts and Sciences* (London, 1569).

Henry of Ghent. *Opera omnia*, ed. R. Macken et al. (Leiden: Brill, 1979–).

Henry of Ghent. *Summa of Ordinary Questions, Article One: On the Possibility of Knowing*, trans. R. J. Teske (South Bend, IN: St. Augustine's Press, 2008).

Henry of Harclay. *Ordinary Questions*, 2 vols, ed. M. G. Henninger, trans. R. Edwards and M. H. Henninger (Oxford: Oxford University Press, 2008).

Hobbes, Thomas. *De corpore*, in idem, *Opera latina*, vol. 1 (London: John Bohn, 1845).

Hobbes, Thomas. *De principiis et ratiocinatione geometrarum* (London: Andrew Crooke, 1666).

Hobbes, Thomas. *Elements of Law*, ed. F. Tönnies (London: Simpkin & Marshall, 1889).

Hobbes, Thomas. *The English Works*, 11 vols., ed. W. Molesworth (London: J. Bohn, 1839–45).

Hobbes, Thomas. *Leviathan*, ed. E. Curley (Indianapolis, IN: Hackett, 1994).

Hobbes's work can be confusing to navigate because it has been published under confoundingly various titles. The *De corpore*, written in Latin, was badly translated into English in 1656 as the first section of the *Elements of Philosophy*. And the first part of the *Elements of Law*, written in English, was initially published in 1650 under the title *Human Nature: Or the Fundamental Elements of Policy*.

Holden, Henry. *The Analysis of Divine Faith* (Paris, 1658).

Holden, Henry. *Divinae fidei analysis* (Paris, 1652).

Hooke, Robert. *Micrographia* (London, 1665).

Hooke, Robert. *The Posthumous Works* (London: R. Waller, 1705).

Huet, Pierre-Daniel. *An Essay concerning the Weakness of Human Understanding*, trans. E. Combe, 2nd edn. (London: M. de Varenne, 1725).

Huet, Pierre-Daniel. *A Philosophical Treatise concerning the Weakness of Human Understanding* (London: G. Dommer, 1725).

Huet, Pierre-Daniel. *Traité philosophique de la foiblesse de l'esprit humain* (London: J. Nourse, 1741).

Hugh of Saint-Victor. *Didascalicon de studio legendi*, ed. C. H. Buttimer (Washington, DC: Catholic University of America Press, 1939).

Hugh of Saint-Victor. *Didascalicon: A Medieval Guide to the Arts*, trans. J. Taylor (New York: Columbia University Press, 1961).

Hume, David. *A Treatise of Human Nature*, ed. L. A. Selby-Bigge, 2nd edn. rev. by P. H. Nidditch (Oxford: Clarendon, 1978).

Hume, David. *A Treatise of Human Nature*, ed. D. F. Norton and M. J. Norton (Oxford: Oxford University Press, 2000).

References to Hume's *Treatise* supply the page numbers of the Nidditch edition, which are indicated in the margin of the Norton edition.

Hume, David. *Enquiries concerning the Human Understanding and concerning the Principles of Morals*, ed. L. A. Selby-Bigge, 3rd edn. rev. by P. H. Nidditch (Oxford: Clarendon, 1975).

Hume, David. *The History of England: From the Invasion of Julius Caesar to the Revolution in 1688* (Indianapolis, IN: Liberty Classics, 1983).

Hume, David. *The Letters of David Hume*, 2 vols., ed. J. Y. T. Greig (Oxford: Clarendon, 1932).

Hume, David. *Selected Essays*, ed. S. Copley and A. Edgar (Oxford: Oxford University Press, 1993).

Huygens, Christiaan. *Oeuvres complètes*, 22 vols., ed. Société hollandaise des sciences (La Haye: M. Nijhoff, 1888–1950).

Ibn al-Haytham. *The Optics of Ibn al-Haytham, Books I–II–III: On Direct Vision: The Arabic Text*, ed. A. I. Sabra (Kuwait: National Council for Culture, Arts and Letters, 1983).

Ibn al-Haytham. *The Optics of Ibn al-Haytham. Books I–III: On Direct Vision*, trans. A. I. Sabra (London: Warburg Institute, 1989).

Jacob Zabarella. *De rebus naturalibus*, 2 vols., ed. J. M. García Valverde (Leiden: Brill, 2016).

Jacob Zabarella. *Opera logica* (Cologne, 1597; repr. Hildesheim: G. Olms, 1966).

James, William. *The Principles of Psychology*, 2 vols. (New York: Holt, 1890).

John Buridan. *In Metaphysicam Aristotelis quaestiones* (Paris, 1518; repr. Frankfurt: Minerva, 1964).

John Buridan. *Quaestiones in duos Aristotilis libros Posteriorum analyticorum*, ed. H. Hubien (n.d.). http://individual.utoronto.ca/pking/resources/buridan/QQ_in_Post_An.txt

John Buridan. *Quaestiones super decem libros Ethicorum Aristotelis ad Nicomachum* (Paris, 1513; repr. Frankfurt: Minerva, 1968).

John Buridan. *Quaestiones super octo libros Physicorum Aristotelis (secundum ultimam lecturam): Libri I–II*, ed. M. Streijger and P. J. J. M. Bakker (Leiden: Brill, 2015).

John Buridan. *Quaestiones super octo Physicorum* (Venice, 1509: repr. Frankfurt: Minerva, 1964).

John Buridan. *Questions on Aristotle's 'De anima', Books I–III*, ed. and trans. G. Klima, P. Hartman, P. King, P. G. Sobol, and J. Zupko (Dordrecht: Springer, forthcoming).

John Buridan. *Summulae de demonstrationibus*, ed. L. M. de Rijk (Groningen: Ingenium, 2001).

John Buridan. *Summulae de dialectica*, trans. G. Klima (New Haven, CT: Yale University Press, 2001).

John Case. *Summa veterum interpretum in universam dialecticam Aristotelis* (London: T. Vautrollerius, 1584).

John Duns Scotus. *Cuestiones Cuodlibetales*, ed. and trans. F. Alluntis (Madrid: Biblioteca de Autores Cristianos, 1968).

John Duns Scotus. *God and Creatures: The Quodlibetal Questions*, trans. F. Alluntis and A. B. Wolter (Princeton, NJ: Princeton University Press, 1975; repr. Washington, DC: Catholic University of America Press, 1987).

John Duns Scotus. *On Being and Cognition: Ordinatio 1.3*, trans. J. van den Bercken (New York: Fordham, 2016).

John Duns Scotus. *Opera omnia*, 21 vols., ed. C. Balić et al. (Vatican City: Typis Polyglottis Vaticanis, 1950–2013).

John Duns Scotus. *Opera omnia*, 12 vols., ed. L. Wadding (Lyon: L. Durand, 1639; repr. Hildesheim: Olms, 1968).

John Duns Scotus. *Opera philosophica*, 5 vols., ed. T. Noone et al. (St. Bonaventure, NY: Franciscan Institute, 1997–2006).

John Duns Scotus. *Questions on the Metaphysics of Aristotle*, 2 vols., trans. G. J. Etzkorn and A. B. Wolter (St. Bonaventure, NY: Franciscan Institute, 1997–8).

John Duns Scotus. *Reportatio I-A*, 2 vols., ed. A. B. Wolter and O. V. Bychkov (St. Bonaventure, NY: Franciscan Institute, 2004–8).

Scotus's writings are notoriously difficult to navigate. There are three main versions of his principal work, his commentary on Lombard's *Sentences*. Two of these versions, the *Ordinatio* and the *Lectura*, are fully available in the modern Vatican edition, but are almost entirely untranslated. The third version, the *Reportatio*, is partly available in the Latin–English edition of Wolter and Bychkov.

John Gerson. *The Consolation of Theology*, trans. C. L. Miller (New York: Abaris Books, 1998).

John Gerson. *Oeuvres complètes*, ed. P. Glorieux (Paris: Desclée de Brouwer, 1960–73).

John Lydgate. *Fall of Princes*, 4 vols., ed. H. Bergen (Oxford: Oxford University Press, 1924–7).

John Major. *In primum Sententiarum* (Paris, 1519).

John of Jandun. *Super octo libros Aristotelis de physico auditu subtilissimae quaestiones* (Venice, 1587; repr. Frankfurt: Minerva, 1969).

John of Mirecourt. *Commento alle* Sentenze *(libro I): Edizione on-line provvisoria*, ed. M. Parodi. http://www.filosofia.unimi.it/mparodi/mirecourt/home.htm.

John of Mirecourt. "Questioni inedite di Giovanni di Mirecourt sulla conoscenza" [*Quaestiones in librum primum Sententiarum* qq. 2–6], ed. A. Franzinelli, *Rivista critica di storia della filosofia* 13 (1958): 319–40, 415–49.

John of Mirecourt. "Die zwei Apologien des Jean de Mirecourt," ed. F. Stegmüller, *Recherches de théologie ancienne et médiévale* 5 (1933): 40–78, 192–204.

> Franzinelli's printed text of the key epistemological questions from John of Mirecourt's *Sentences* commentary are cited here, but should be compared against the provisional online edition of the whole work. No English translations have yet been made.

John of Salisbury. *Metalogicon*, ed. J. B. Hall and K. S. B. Keats-Rohan (Turnhout: Brepols, 1991).

John of Salisbury. *The Metalogicon*, trans. D. McGarry (Berkeley: University of California Press, 1962).

John of Salisbury. *Policraticus*, trans. C. J. Nederman (Cambridge: Cambridge University Press, 1990).

John of Salisbury. *Policraticus I–IV*, ed. K. S. B. Keats-Rohan (Turnhout: Brepols, 1993).

John Wyclif. *Tractatus de logica*, 3 vols., ed. M. H. Dziewicki (London: Trübner, 1893–9).

Juan de Lugo. *Disputationes scholasticae et morales* (Lyon, 1656).

Kant, Immanuel. *Critique of Pure Reason*, trans. P. Guyer and A. Wood (Cambridge: Cambridge University Press, 1998).

Kant, Immanuel. *Critique of the Power of Judgment*, trans. P. Guyer and E. Matthews (Cambridge: Cambridge University Press, 2000).

Kant, Immanuel. *Kritik der reinen Vernunft*, ed. R. Schmidt (Hamburg: F. Meiner, 1956).

Kant, Immanuel. *Metaphysical Foundations of Natural Science*, trans. M. Friedman (Cambridge: Cambridge University Press, 2004).

al-Kindī. *The Philosophical Works of al-Kindī*, trans. P. Adamson and P. E. Pormann (Karachi: Oxford University Press, 2012).

al-Kindī. *Rasāʾil al-falsafiyya*, ed. M. Abū Rīda (Cairo: Dār al-Fikr al-ʿArabī, 1950–3).

Lactantius. *Divinarum institutionum libri septem*, 4 vols., ed. E. Heck and A. Wlosok (Munich: Saur, 2005–11).

Leibniz, Gottfried Wilhelm. *New Essays on Human Understanding*, trans. P. Remnant and J. Bennett (Cambridge: Cambridge University Press, 1996).

Leibniz, Gottfried Wilhelm. *Nouveaux essais sur l'entendement humain*, ed. A. Robinet and H. Schepers (Berlin: Akademie-Verlag, 1962).

Leibniz, Gottfried Wilhelm. *Philosophical Essays*, trans. R. Ariew and D. Garber (Indianapolis, IN: Hackett Publishing Co., 1989).

Leibniz, Gottfried Wilhelm. *Philosophical Papers and Letters*, ed. L. E. Loemker, 2nd edn. (Dordrecht: Reidel, 1969).

Leibniz, Gottfried Wilhelm. *Die philosophischen Schriften*, 7 vols., ed. C. I. Gerhardt (Berlin: Wiedmann, 1875–90; repr. Hildesheim: Olms, 1965).

Locke, John. *Drafts for the Essay concerning Human Understanding, and Other Philosophical Writings*. vol. 1: *Drafts A and B*, ed. P. H. Nidditch and G. A. J. Rogers (Oxford: Clarendon, 1990).

Locke, John. *An Essay concerning Human Understanding*, ed. P. H. Nidditch (Oxford: Clarendon, 1975).

Locke, John. *Some Thoughts concerning Education and Of the Conduct of the Understanding*, ed. R. W. Grant and N. Tarcov (Indianapolis, IN: Hackett, 1996).

Locke, John. *The Works of John Locke*, 11th edn. (London: W. Otrige, 1812).

Lucretius. *De rerum natura*, ed. M. F. Smith, trans. W. H. D. Rouse (Cambridge, MA: Harvard University Press, 1982).

Lucretius. *On the Nature of the Universe*, trans. R. E. Latham (Baltimore, MD: Penguin, 1951).

Malebranche, Nicolas. *De la recherche de la vérité*, ed. J.-C. Bardout (Paris: Vrin, 2006).

Malebranche, Nicolas. *Oeuvres complètes*, 20 vols., ed. A. Robinet (Paris: Vrin, 1959–66).

Malebranche, Nicolas. *Philosophical Selections*, ed. S. Nadler (Indianapolis, IN: Hackett, 1992).

Malebranche, Nicolas. *The Search after Truth*, trans. T. M. Lennon and P. J. Olscamp (Cambridge: Cambridge University Press, 1997).

Marsilius of Inghen. *Quaestiones de generatione et corruptione* (Venice, 1505; repr. Frankfurt: Minerva, 1970).

Marsilius of Inghen (Pseudo-). *Quaestiones subtilissimae super octo libros Physicorum secundum nominalium viam* (Lyon: J. Marion, 1518; repr. Frankfurt: Minerva, 1964).

Matthew of Aquasparta. *Quaestiones disputatae de fide et cognitione* (Quaracchi: Collegium S. Bonaventurae, 1957).

Maxwell, James Clerk. *The Scientific Letters and Papers of James Clerk Maxwell*, ed. P. M. Harman (Cambridge: Cambridge University Press, 1990–).

Mersenne, Marin. *Traité des mouvemens* (Paris: J. Villery, 1634).

Mersenne, Marin. *La vérité des sciences: Contre les sceptiques ou pyrrhoniens* (Paris, 1625; repr. Stuttgart-Bad Cannstatt: Frommann, 1969).

Michel de Montaigne. *The Complete Essays of Montaigne*, trans. D. M. Frame (Stanford, CA: Stanford University Press, 1958).

Michel de Montaigne. *Les Essais*, ed. J. Balsamo, C. Magnien-Simonin, and M. Magnien (Paris: Gallimard, 2007).

More, Henry. *An Antidote against Atheism* (London: J. Flesher, 1655).

More, Henry. *The Immortality of the Soul* (London: J. Flesher, 1659).

Moses Maimonides. *Dalālat al-ḥāʿirīn*, ed. S. Munk (Paris: A. Franck, 1856; repr. Osnabrück: Zeller, 1964).

Moses Maimonides. *The Guide of the Perplexed*, trans. S. Pines (Chicago, IL: University of Chicago Press, 1963; repr. 1974).

Newton, Isaac. *The Mathematical Papers of Isaac Newton*, 8 vols., ed. D. T. Whiteside (Cambridge: Cambridge University Press, 1967–81).

Newton, Isaac. *Optice: Sive de reflexionibus, refractionibus, inflexionibus et coloribus lucis libri tres*, trans. S. Clarke (London: Smith and Walford, 1706).

Newton, Isaac. *Opticks, or A Treatise of the Reflections, Refractions, Inflections and Colors of Light* (New York: Dover, 1952).

Newton, Isaac. *Philosophiae naturalis principia mathematica*, 2 vols. (Glasgow: Tegg and Griffin, 1833).

Newton, Isaac. *Philosophical Writings*, ed. A. Janiak (Cambridge: Cambridge University Press, 2004).

Newton, Isaac. *The Principia: Mathematical Principles of Natural Philosophy*, trans. I. B. Cohen and A. Whitman (Berkeley: University of California Press, 1999).

Nicholas of Autrecourt. *Nicholas of Autrecourt, His Correspondence with Master Giles and Bernard of Arezzo: A Critical Edition and English Translation*, ed. L. M. de Rijk (Leiden: Brill, 1994).

Nicholas of Autrecourt. *Tractatus utilis ad videndum an sermones peripateticorum fuerint demonstrativi*, in J. R. O'Donnell (ed.), "Nicholas of Autrecourt," *Mediaeval Studies* 1 (1939): 179–267.

Nicholas of Autrecourt. *The Universal Treatise*, trans. L. A. Kennedy, R. E. Arnold, and A. E. Millward (Milwaukee, WI: Marquette University Press, 1971).

References to Autrecourt's *Tractatus* are to the page numbers and line numbers of the O'Donnell edition, which are indicated in the margin of the Kennedy et al. translation.

Nicholas of Cusa. *Nicholas of Cusa on Wisdom and Knowledge* [*Idiota de mente*], trans. J. Hopkins (Minneapolis: Banning, 1996).

Nicolaus Copernicus. *De revolutionibus libri sex*, ed. H. M. Nobis and B. Sticker (Hildesheim: Gerstenberg, 1984).

Nicole Oresme. *Expositio et quaestiones in Aristotelis De anima*, ed. B. Patar (Leuven: Peeters, 1995).

Nicole Oresme. *Le livre du ciel et du monde*, ed. A. D. Menut and A. J. Denomy (Madison: University of Wisconsin Press, 1968).

Nicole Oresme. *Nicole Oresme and the Marvels of Nature: A Study of His* De causis mirabilium *with Critical Edition, Translation and Commentary*, ed. B. Hansen (Toronto: Pontifical Institute of Mediaeval Studies, 1985).

Nicole Oresme. *Nicole Oresme and the Kinematics of Circular Motion: Tractatus de commensurabilitate vel incommensurabilitate motuum caeli*, ed. E. Grant (Madison: University of Wisconsin Press, 1971).

Oldenburg, Henry. *Correspondence*, edited by A. R. Hall and M. B. Hall (Madison: University of Wisconsin Press, 1965).

Pascal, Blaise. *Pensées*, ed. P. Sellier (Paris: Classiques Garnier, 1999).

Pascal, Blaise. *Pensées*, trans. R. Ariew (Indianapolis, IN: Hackett, 2005).

There are many editions and translations of Pascal's *Pensées*, each with its own preferred numbering and ordering of passages, which makes it very difficult to compare references across different versions of the work. The references here supply Sellier's enumeration and Ariew's pagination.

Paul of Venice. *Expositio in libros Posteriorum Aristotelis* (Venice, 1477; repr. Hildesheim: Olms, 1976).

Paul of Venice. *Summa philosophiae naturalis* (Venice, 1503; repr. Hildesheim: Olms, 1974).

Peter Abaelard. *Dialectica*, ed. L. M. de Rijk, 2nd edn. (Assen: Van Gorcum 1970).

Peter Abelard. *Des intellections* [*Tractatus de intellectibus*], ed. P. Morin (Paris: Vrin 1994).

Peter Abelard. *Logica "Nostrorum petitioni sociorum,"* ed. B. Geyer (Münster: Aschendorff, 1933).

Peter Auriol. *Commentariorum in primum[-quartum] librum Sententiarum* (Rome, 1596–1605).

Peter Auriol. *Scriptum super primum Sententiarum*, 2 vols., ed. E. M. Buytaert (St. Bonaventure, NY: Franciscan Institute, 1952–6).

Peter Auriol. *Scriptum super primum Sententiarum*, in ms. Vat. Borgh. lat. 329, transcribed by R. Friedman et al. http://www.peterauriol.net

While we await a critical edition of Peter Auriol's work, scholars use Buytaert's edition for Book I through distinction 8. Beyond that, there is the highly unreliable Rome edition or, for some stretches of the text, provisional online transcriptions collected by Friedman.

Peter John Olivi. "Impugnatio quorundam articulorum Arnaldi Galliardi, art. 19," ed. S. Piron, in idem, *Pierre de Jean Olivi: Philosophe et théologien* (Berlin: De Gruyter, 2010), 453–62.

Peter John Olivi. *Quaestiones in secundum librum Sententiarum* [*Summa*], 3 vols., ed. B. Jansen (Quaracchi: Editiones Collegii S. Bonaventurae, 1922–6).

Peter John Olivi. "Question 72: Can Bodies Act on the Spirit and On Its Apprehensive Powers?" trans. R. Pasnau. http://spot.colorado.edu/~pasnau/research/olivi72.htm

Peter John Olivi. "Question 74: Is the Effective Principle of a Cognitive Act a Species, a Habit, or the Cognitive Power?" trans. R. Pasnau. http://spot.colorado.edu/~pasnau/research/olivi74.htm

Peter of Ailly. *Quaestiones super libros Sententiarum cum quibusdam in fine adjunctis* (Strassburg, 1490; repr. Frankfurt: Minerva, 1968).

Peter of Ailly. *Questiones super primum, tertium et quartum librum Sententiarum* (Corpus Christianorum, Continuatio Mediaevalis 258), ed. M. Brinzei (Turnhout: Brepols, 2013–).

Peter of Ailly. *Tractatus de anima*, in O. Pluta (ed.), *Die philosophische Psychologie des Peter von Ailly* (Amsterdam: B. R. Grüner, 1987), 1–111.

Philoponus. *In Aristotelis Analytica posteriora commentaria* (Commentaria in Aristotelem Graeca 13.3), ed. M. Wallies (Berlin: G. Reimer, 1909).

Philoponus. *On Aristotle, Posterior Analytics 1.1–8*, trans. R. McKirahan (London: Duckworth, 2008).

Pierre Charron. *Of Wisdom*, trans. S. Lennard (London: Blount and Aspley, 1608).

Pierre Charron. *Of Wisdom*, trans. G. Stanhope (London, 1697).

Pierre Charron. *Toutes les oeuvres de Pierre Charron* (Paris: J. Villery, 1635).

Plato. *Complete Works*, ed. J. M. Cooper (Indianapolis, IN: Hackett, 1997).

Plato. *Opera*, ed. J. Burnet (Oxford: Clarendon, 1905–13).

Ptolemy. *Almagest*, trans. G. J. Toomer (New York: Springer, 1984; repr. Princeton, NJ: Princeton University Press, 1998).

Ptolomy. *Opera quae exstant omnia*, ed. J. L. Heiberg (Leipzig: Teubner, 1898–1907).

Reginald Pecock. *The Folewer to the Donet*, ed. E. V. Hitchcock (London: Early English Text Society, 1924).

Régis, Pierre-Sylvain. *Cours entier de philosophie, ou système général selon les principes de M. Descartes* (Amsterdam: Huguetan, 1691).

Régis, Pierre-Sylvain. *Réponse au livre qui a pour titre P. Danielis Huetii, Episcopi Suessionensis designati, Censura philosophiae Cartesianae* (Paris: J. Cusson, 1691).

Régis, Pierre-Sylvain. *Système de philosophie* (Paris, 1690).

Reid, Thomas. *Works*, ed. W. Hamilton, 6th edn. (Edinburgh: Maclachlan and Stewart, 1863).

Richard Hooker. *Of the Lawes of Ecclesiasticall Politie* (London: J. Windet, 1593).

Robert Grosseteste. *Commentarius in Posteriorum analyticorum libros*, ed. P. Rossi (Florence: L. S. Olschki, 1981).

Robert Holcot. *In quatuor libros Sententiarum quaestiones* (Lyon 1518; repr. Frankfurt: Minerva, 1967).

Robert Holcot. *Sex articuli*, in F. Hoffmann (ed.), *Die "Conferentiae" des Robert Holcot OP und die akademischen Auseinandersetzungen an der Universität Oxford 1330–1332* (Münster: Aschendorff, 1993), 65–127.

Roger Bacon. *Opus maius*, ed. J. H. Bridges (Oxford: Clarendon, 1897–1900; repr. Frankfurt: Minerva, 1964).

Roger Bacon. *The Opus Majus*, trans. R. B. Burke (Philadelphia, PA: University of Pennsylvania Press, 1928; repr. New York: Russell, 1962).

Rushworth, William. *Rushworth's Dialogues, or The Judgement of Common Sense in the Choyce of Religion*, corrected and enlarged by Thomas White (Paris: J. Billaine, 1654).

Sennert, Daniel. *Hypomnemata physica* (Frankfurt, 1636).

Sennert, Daniel. *Thirteen Books of Natural Philosophy* (London: Peter and Edward Cole, 1661).

Sergeant, John. *Solid Philosophy Asserted against the Fancies of the Ideists* (London, 1697).

Sextus Empiricus. *Outlines of Scepticism*, trans. J. Annas and J. Barnes (Cambridge: Cambridge University Press, 2000).

Sextus Empiricus. *Sextus Empiricus* (Loeb Classical Library), 4 vols., trans. R. G. Bury (Cambridge, MA: Harvard University Press, 1933–49).

Siger of Brabant. *Écrits de logique, de morale, et de physique: Édition critique*, ed. B. C. Bazán (Leuven: Publications universitaires, 1974).

Siger of Brabant. *Questions sur la métaphysique: Texte inédit*, ed. C. A. Graiff (Louvain: Éditions de l'Institut supérieur de philosophie, 1948).

Silhon, Jean de. *De l'immortalité de l'ame* (Paris, 1634).

Spinoza, Benedict de. *Opera*, 5 vols., ed. C. Gebhardt (Heidelberg: Carl Winters, 1925–87).

Spinoza, Benedict de. *The Collected Works of Spinoza*, 2 vols., trans. E. Curley (Princeton, NJ: Princeton University Press, 1985–2016).

Starkey, Thomas. *England in the Reign of King Henry the Eighth: Life and Letters and a Dialogue between Cardinal Pole and Lupset* (London: N. Trübner, 1871–8).

Themistius. *Analyticorum posteriorum paraphrasis* (Commentaria in Aristotelem Graeca 5.1), ed. M. Wallies (Berlin: G. Reimer, 1900).

Themistius. *In De anima paraphrasis* (Commentaria in Aristotelem Graeca 5.3), ed. R. Heinze (Berlin: G. Reimer, 1899).

Themistius. *On Aristotle's "On the Soul 1–2.4"* (Ancient Commentators on Aristotle), trans. R. B. Todd (Ithaca, NY: Cornell University Press, 1996).

Themistius. *Paraphrasis of the Posterior Analytics in Gerard of Cremona's Translation*, ed. J. R. O'Donnell, *Mediaeval Studies* 20 (1958): 239–315.

Theophrastus. *Theophrastus and the Greek Physiological Psychology before Aristotle* [*De sensibus*], ed. G. M. Stratton (London: George Allen & Unwin, 1917).

Thomas Aquinas. *Commentary on Aristotle's* De anima, trans. R. Pasnau (New Haven, CT: Yale University Press, 1999).

Thomas Aquinas. *Commentary on the Epistle to the Hebrews*, trans. C. Baer (South Bend, IN: St. Augustine's Press, 2006).

Thomas Aquinas. *Commentary on the Posterior Analytics of Aristotle*, trans. F. R. Larcher (Albany, NY: Magi Books, 1970).

Thomas Aquinas. *Disputed Question On Evil*, trans. J. A. Oesterle and J. T. Oesterle (Notre Dame, IN: University of Notre Dame Press, 1995).

Thomas Aquinas. *Exposition of Aristotle's Treatise On the Heavens*, trans. F. R. Larcher and P. Conway (Columbus: College of St. Mary of the Springs, 1963–4).

Thomas Aquinas. *In duodecim libros Metaphysicorum Aristotelis expositio*, ed. M. R. Cathala and R. M. Spiazzi (Rome: Marietti, 1971).

Thomas Aquinas. *On the Power of God*, trans. L. Shapcote (London: Burns, Oates & Washbourne, 1932–4).

Thomas Aquinas. *Opera omnia*, ed. Leonine Commission (Rome: Commissio Leonina, 1882–).

Most of Aquinas's Latin texts are now available in the critical Leonine edition, though in practice scholars use the searchable texts at www.corpusthomisticum.org. Most texts have also been translated into English, and the two *Summae* are readily available in tolerably good online translations.

Thomas Aquinas. *Opuscula theologica*, ed. M. Calcaterra, R. Spiazzi, and R. A. Verardo (Rome: Marietti, 1954).

Thomas Aquinas. *Scriptum super libros Sententiarum*, ed. P. Mandonnet and M. F. Moos (Paris: P. Lethielleux, 1929–56).

Thomas Aquinas. *Summa contra gentiles*, trans. A. C. Pegis et al. (Notre Dame, IN: University of Notre Dame Press, 1975). http://dhspriory.org/thomas/ContraGentiles.htm

Thomas Aquinas. *Summa theologiae*, trans. L. Shapcote (New York: Benzinger, 1947–8). http://www.newadvent.org/summa

Thomas Aquinas. *Super Epistolas S. Pauli lectura*, ed. R. Cai (Turin: Marietti, 1953).

Thomas Aquinas. *Super Evangelium S. Ioannis lectura*, ed. R. Cai (Rome: Marietti, 1952).

Thomas Aquinas. *Truth*, trans. J. V. McGlynn, R. W. Mulligan, and R. W. Schmidt (Chicago, IL: Henry Regnery, 1954; repr. Indianapolis, IN: Hackett, 1994).

Thomas of Sutton. *Quaestiones ordinariae*, ed. J. Schneider (Munich: Bayerische Akademie der Wissenschaften, 1977).

Tillotson. John. *The Works of the Most Reverend Dr. John Tillotson*, ed. R. Barker, 4th edn. (London, 1728).

Toland, John. *Christianity Not Mysterious* (London, 1696).

Virgil. *The Georgics*, trans. L. P. Wilkinson (Harmondsworth: Penguin, 1982).

Voltaire (François-Marie d'Arouet). *Les oeuvres complètes*, ed. T. Besterman et al. (Geneva: Institut et Musée Voltaire, 1968–).

Voltaire (François-Marie d'Arouet). *Oeuvres complètes*, 52 vols., ed. L. E. D. Moland and G. Bengesco (Paris: Garnier Frères, 1877–85).

Voltaire (François-Marie d'Arouet). *A Philosophical Dictionary*, 6 vols. (London: J. and H. L. Hunt, 1824).

Walter Burley. *Treatise "De formis,"* ed. F. J. D. Scott (Munich: Bayerische Akademie der Wissenschaften, 1970).

Walter Chatton. *Reportatio et lectura super Sententias: Collatio ad librum primum et Prologus*, ed. J. Wey (Toronto: Pontifical Institute of Mediaeval Studies, 1989).

Ward, Seth. *A Philosophical Essay*, 4th edn. (Oxford, 1667).

Whewell, William. *History of the Inductive Sciences from the Earliest to the Present Times*, 3 vols. (London: J. Parker, 1837).

Whewell, William. *History of Scientific Ideas*, 2 vols., 3rd edn. (London: Parker and Son, 1858).

White, Thomas. *An Exclusion of Scepticks from All Title to Dispute: Being an Answer to the Vanity of Dogmatizing* (London: J. Williams, 1665).

White, Thomas. *Peripateticall Institutions in the Way of That Eminent Person and Excellent Philosopher, Sir Kenelm Digby* (London, 1656).

Wilkins, John. *A Discourse concerning a New World and Another Planet* (London: John Maynard, 1640).

Wilkins, John. *Of the Principles and Duties of Natural Religion* (London, 1675).

William Crathorn. *Quästionen zum ersten sentenzenbuch*, ed. F. Hoffmann (Münster: Aschendorff, 1988).

William Ockham. *Opera philosophica et theologica* (St. Bonaventure, NY: Franciscan Institute, 1967–89).

William Ockham. *Philosophical Writings*, trans. P. Boehner, rev. S. Brown (Indianapolis, IN: Hackett, 1990).

William Ockham. *Quodlibetal Questions*, trans. A. Freddoso and F. Kelley (New Haven, CT: Yale University Press, 1991).

All of Ockham's non-political works are edited in the *Opera philosophica et theologica*. Most of his works remain untranslated.

William of Auvergne. *Opera omnia*, ed. B. Le Feron (Paris, 1674; repr. Frankfurt: Minerva, 1963).

Secondary Sources

Acworth, Richard. "Locke's First Reply to John Norris," *Locke Newsletter* 2 (1971): 7–11.

Adams, Marilyn McCord. *William Ockham* (Notre Dame, IN: University of Notre Dame Press, 1987).

Adams, Zed. *On the Genealogy of Color: A Case Study in Historicized Conceptual Analysis* (New York: Routledge, 2016).

Adamson, Peter. *Al-Kindī* (Oxford: Oxford University Press, 2007).

Adriaenssen, Han Thomas. "An Early Critic of Locke: The Anti-Scepticism of Henry Lee," *Locke Studies* 11 (2011): 17–47.

Adriaenssen, Han Thomas. "Peter John Olivi and Peter Auriol on Conceptual Thought," *Oxford Studies in Medieval Philosophy* 2 (2014): 67–97.

Adriaenssen, Han Thomas. *Representation and Scepticism from Aquinas to Descartes* (Cambridge: Cambridge University Press, 2017).

Ainslie, Donald C. *Hume's True Scepticism* (Oxford: Oxford University Press, 2015).

Alanen, Lilli and Mikko Yrjönsuuri. "Intuition, judgement et évidence chez Ockham et Descartes," in J. Biard and R. Rashed (eds.), *Descartes et le Moyen Age* (Paris: Vrin, 1997), 155–74.

Alexander, Peter. *Ideas, Qualities and Corpuscles: Locke and Boyle on the External World* (Cambridge: Cambridge University Press, 1985).

Alston, William P. *Beyond "Justification": Dimensions of Epistemic Evaluation* (Ithaca, NY: Cornell University Press, 2005).

Alston, William P. *Perceiving God: A Study in the Epistemology of Religious Experience* (Ithaca, NY: Cornell University Press, 1991).

Alston, William P. *The Reliability of Sense Perception* (Ithaca, NY: Cornell University Press, 1993).

Anagnostopoulos, Georgios. *Aristotle on the Goals and Exactness of Ethics* (Berkeley: University of California Press, 1994).

Andrade, Jackie. "An Introduction to Working Memory," in eadem (ed.), *Working Memory in Perspective* (New York: Taylor and Francis, 2001), 3–30.

Annas, Julia. "Hume and Ancient Skepticism," in J. Sihvola (ed.), *Ancient Scepticism and the Sceptical Tradition* (Helsinki: Societas Philosophica Fennica, 2000), 271–85.

Annas, Julia and Jonathan Barnes. *The Modes of Scepticism: Ancient Texts and Modern Interpretations* (Cambridge: Cambridge University Press, 1985).

Anstey, Peter R. "Experimental versus Speculative Natural Philosophy," in P. R. Anstey and J. A. Schuster (eds.), *The Science of Nature in the Seventeenth Century* (Dordrecht: Springer, 2005), 215–42.

Antognazza, Maria Rosa. "The Benefit to Philosophy of the Study of Its History," *British Journal for the History of Philosophy* 23 (2015): 161–84.

Ariew, Roger. "The Mathematization of Nature in Descartes and the First Cartesians," in G. Gorham et al. (eds.), *The Language of Nature: Reassessing the Mathematization of Natural Philosophy in the Seventeenth Century* (Minneapolis, MN: University of Minnesota Press, 2016), 112–33.

Ariew, Roger. "The *Meditations* and the *Objections* and *Replies*," in S. Gaukroger (ed.), *The Blackwell Guide to Descartes' Meditations* (Oxford: Blackwell, 2006), 6–16.

Ariew, Roger, John Cottingham, and Tom Sorell (eds.). *Descartes' Mediations: Background Source Materials* (Cambridge: Cambridge University Press, 1998).

Ariew, Roger and Marjorie Grene. "Ideas, in and before Descartes," in R. Ariew (ed.), *Descartes and the Last Scholastics* (Ithaca, NY: Cornell University Press, 1999), 58–76.

Armogathe, Jean-Robert. "Sémantèse d'*idée*/*idea* chez Descartes," in M. Fattori and M. L. Bianchi (eds.), *Idea: VI Colloquio Internazionale del Lessico Intellettuale Europeo* (Rome: Edizioni dell'Ateno, 1989), 187–205.

Ashcraft, Richard. "Faith and Knowledge in Locke's Philosophy," in J. W. Yolton (ed.), *John Locke: Problems and Perspectives: A Collection of New Essays* (London: Cambridge University Press, 1969), 194–223.

Atherton, Margaret L. "Green Is Like Bread: The Nature of Descartes's Account of Color Perception," in R. Schumacher (ed.), *Perception and Reality: From Descartes to the Present* (Paderborn: Mentis, 2004), 27–42.

Atkinson, Richard C. and Richard M. Shiffrin. "The Control of Short-Term Memory," *Scientific American* 225 (1971): 82–90.

Ayer, A. J. "Has Austin Refuted the Sense-Datum Theory?" *Synthese* 17 (1967): 117–40.

Ayers, Michael. "Ideas and Objective Being," in D. Garber and M. Ayers (eds.), *The Cambridge History of Seventeenth-Century Philosophy* (Cambridge: Cambridge University Press, 1998), 1062–107.

Ayers, Michael. *Locke: Epistemology and Ontology* (London: Routledge, 1991).

Baars, Bernard J. "The Global Workspace Theory of Consciousness," in M. Velmans and S. Schneider (eds.), *The Blackwell Companion to Consciousness* (Oxford: Blackwell, 2007), 236–46.

Baars, Bernard J. *In the Theater of Consciousness: The Workspace of the Mind* (New York: Oxford University Press, 1997).

Baddeley, Alan. *Working Memory, Thought, and Action* (Oxford: Oxford University Press, 2007).

Baier, Annette C. *A Progress of Sentiments: Reflections on Hume's Treatise* (Cambridge, MA: Harvard University Press, 1991).

Banks, Erik C. *The Realistic Empiricism of Mach, James and Russell: Neutral Monism Reconceived* (Cambridge: Cambridge University Press, 2014).

Barker, Peter and Bernard R. Goldstein, "Realism and Instrumentalism in Sixteenth-Century Astronomy: A Reappraisal," *Perspectives on Science* 6 (1999): 232–58.

Barnes, Jonathan. "Aristotle's Theory of Demonstration," *Phronesis* 14 (1969): 123–52.

Barnett, David James. "Is Memory Merely Testimony from One's Former Self?" *Philosophical Review* 124 (2015): 353–92.

Beck, L. J. *The Metaphysics of Descartes: A Study of the* Meditations (Oxford: Clarendon, 1965).

Beiser, Frederick C. *The Sovereignty of Reason: The Defense of Rationality in the Early English Enlightenment* (Princeton, NJ: Princeton University Press, 1996).

Bennett, Jonathan. *Learning from Six Philosophers: Descartes, Spinoza, Leibniz, Locke, Berkeley, Hume* (Oxford: Clarendon, 2001).

Benson, Hugh H. *Socratic Wisdom: The Model of Knowledge in Plato's Early Dialogues* (New York: Oxford University Press, 2000).

Berchielli, Laura. "Color, Space and Figure in Locke: An Interpretation of the Molyneux Problem," *Journal of the History of Philosophy* 40 (2002): 47–65.

Berlin, Isaiah. *Concepts and Categories: Philosophical Essays*, ed. H. Hardy (Harmondsworth: Penguin, 1981).

Berlin, Isaiah. *Four Essays on Liberty* (London: Oxford University Press, 1969).

Bertoloni Meli, Domenico. *Thinking with Objects: The Transformation of Mechanics in the Seventeenth Century* (Baltimore, MD: Johns Hopkins University Press, 2006).

Beyssade, Jean-Marie. "Descartes on Material Falsity," in P. D. Cummins and G. Zoeller (eds.), *Minds, Ideas, and Objects: Essays on the Theory of Representation in Modern Philosophy* (Atascadero, CA: Ridgeview, 1992), 5–20.

Biard, Joël. "Certitudo," in I. Atucha et al. (eds.), *Mots médiévaux offerts à Ruedi Imbach* (Turnhout: Brepols, 2011), 153–62.

Biard, Joël. "Présence et représentation chez Pierre d'Ailly: Quelques problèmes de théorie de la connaissance au XIVe siècle," *Dialogue* 31 (1992): 459–74.

Biard, Joël. *Science et nature: La théorie buridanienne du savoir* (Paris: Vrin, 2011).

Biro, John. "Hume's New Science of the Mind," in D. F. Norton and J. Taylor (eds.), *The Cambridge Companion to Hume*, 2nd edn. (Cambridge: Cambridge University Press, 2008), 40–69.

Black, Deborah L. "Avicenna on Self-Awareness and Knowing that One Knows," in S. Rahman, T. Street, and H. Tahiri (eds.), *The Unity of Science in the Arabic Tradition: Science, Logic, Epistemology and their Interactions* (Dordrecht: Springer, 2008), 63–87.

Black, Deborah L. "Certitude, Justification, and the Principles of Knowledge in Avicenna's Epistemology," in P. Adamson (ed.), *Interpreting Avicenna: Critical Essays* (Cambridge: Cambridge University Press, 2013), 120–42.

Black, Deborah L. "Knowledge (ʿilm) and Certitude (yaqīn) in al-Fārābī's Epistemology," *Arabic Sciences and Philosophy* 16 (2006): 11–45.

Bloch, David. "Aristotle on the Exactness or Certainty of Knowledge in *Posterior Analytics* I.27," in B. Bydén and C. T. Thörnqvist (eds.), *The Aristotelian Tradition: Aristotle's Works on Logic and*

Metaphysics and Their Reception in the Middle Ages (Toronto: Pontifical Institute of Mediaeval Studies, 2017), 151–61.

Block, Irving. "Truth and Error in Aristotle's Theory of Sense Perception," *Philosophical Quarterly* 11 (1961): 1–9.

Block, Ned. "Mental Paint," in M. Hahn and B. Ramberg (eds.), *Reflections and Replies: Essays on the Philosophy of Tyler Burge* (Cambridge, MA: MIT Press, 2003), 165–200.

Boehner, Philotheus. "*Notitia intuitiva* of Non Existents according to Peter Aureoli, O.F.M. (1322)," *Franciscan Studies* 8 (1948): 388–416.

Boespflug, Mark. "Locke's Principle of Proportionality," *Archiv für Geschichte der Philosophie* (forthcoming).

Boler, John F. "Intuitive and Abstractive Cognition," in N. Kretzmann et al. (eds.), *The Cambridge History of Later Medieval Philosophy* (Cambridge: Cambridge University Press, 1982), 460–78.

Bolton, Martha Brandt. "Confused and Obscure Ideas of Sense," in A. O. Rorty (ed.), *Essays on Descartes' Meditations* (Berkeley: University of California Press, 1986), 389–403.

Bolton, Martha Brandt. "Locke on the Semantic and Epistemic Role of Simple Ideas of Sensation," *Pacific Philosophical Quarterly* 85 (2004): 301–21.

Bolton, Martha Brandt. "The Real Molyneux Problem and the Basis of Locke's Answer," in G. A. J. Rogers (ed.), *Locke's Philosophy: Content and Context* (New York: Oxford University Press, 1994), 75–99.

Bolyard, Charles. "Henry of Harclay on Knowing Many Things at Once," *Recherches de théologie et philosophie médiévales* 81 (2014): 75–93.

BonJour, Laurence. "The Myth of Knowledge," *Philosophical Perspectives* 24 (2010): 57–83.

Bougerol, Jacques. *La théologie de l'espérance aux XIIe et XIIIe siècles* (Paris: Etudes Augustiniennes, 1985).

Brittain, Charles. *Philo of Larissa: The Last of the Academic Sceptics* (Oxford: Oxford University Press, 2001).

Broackes, Justin. "Aristotle, Objectivity, and Perception," *Oxford Studies in Ancient Philosophy* 17 (1999): 57–113.

Broadie, Alexander. *Notion and Object* (Oxford: Clarendon, 1989).

Broadie, Sarah. "Aristotle's Perceptual Realism," *Southern Journal of Philosophy* 31 (1993): 137–59.

Broughton, Janet. "Cartesian Skeptics," in W. Sinnott-Armstrong (ed.), *Pyrrhonian Skepticism* (Oxford: Oxford University Press, 2004), 25–39.

Broughton, Janet. *Descartes's Method of Doubt* (Princeton, NJ: Princeton University Press, 2002).

Brower-Toland, Susan. "Intuition, Externalism, and Direct Reference in Ockham," *History of Philosophy Quarterly* 24 (2007): 317–35.

Brower-Toland, Susan. "Medieval Approaches to Consciousness: Ockham and Chatton," *Philosophers' Imprint* 12.17 (2012): 1–29.

Brower-Toland, Susan. "Ockham on Judgment, Concepts, and the Problem of Intentionality," *Canadian Journal of Philosophy* 37 (2007): 67–110.

Brower-Toland, Susan. "Olivi on Consciousness and Self-Knowledge: The Phenomenology, Metaphysics, and Epistemology of the Mind's Reflexivity," *Oxford Studies in Medieval Philosophy* 1 (2013): 136–71.

Brown, Deborah J. "Aquinas's Missing Flying Man," *Sophia* 40 (2001): 17–31.

Bruno, Michael and Eric Mandelbaum. "Locke's Answer to Molyneux's Thought Experiment," *History of Philosophy Quarterly* 27 (2010): 165–80.

Burge, Tyler. "Content Preservation," *Philosophical Review* 102 (1993): 457–88.

Burge, Tyler. "Interlocution, Perception, and Memory," *Philosophical Studies* 86 (1997): 21–47.

Burge, Tyler. "Self and Self-Understanding," *Journal of Philosophy* 108 (2011): 287–383.

Burnyeat, Myles F. "Aristotle on Understanding Knowledge," in E. Berti (ed.), *Aristotle on Science: The Posterior Analytics* (Padua: Edizioni Antenori, 1981), 97–139.

Burnyeat, Myles F. "Idealism and Greek Philosophy: What Descartes Saw and Berkeley Missed," *Philosophical Review* 91 (1982): 3–40.

Burnyeat, Myles F. and Michael Frede. *The Original Sceptics: A Controversy* (Indianapolis, IN: Hackett, 1997).

Burtt, Edwin A. *The Metaphysical Foundations of Modern Physical Science* (Garden City, NY: Doubleday, 1954).

Byrne, Edmund F. *Probability and Opinion: A Study in the Medieval Presuppositions of Post-Medieval Theories of Probability* (The Hague: Martinus Nijhoff, 1968).

Campbell, John and Quassim Cassam. *Berkeley's Puzzle: What Does Experience Teach Us?* (Oxford: Oxford University Press, 2014).

Caroti, Stefano. "Les *modi rerum* . . . Encore une fois. Une source possible de Nicole Oresme: Le commentaire sur le livre 1er des *Sentences* de Jean de Mirecourt," in S. Caroti and J. Celeyrette (eds.), *Quia inter doctores est magna dissensio: Les débats de philosophie naturelle à Paris au XIVe siècle* (Florence: Olschki, 2004), 195–222.

Carriero, John. *Between Two Worlds: A Reading of Descartes's* Meditations (Princeton, NJ: Princeton University Press, 2009).

Carriero, John. "Epistemology Past and Present," *Proceedings of the Aristotelian Society* 113 (2013): 175–200.

Cassirer, Ernst, Paul Oskar Kristeller, and John Herman Randall Jr. (eds.). *The Renaissance Philosophy of Man* (Chicago, IL: University of Chicago Press, 1948).

Chalmers, David. "Perception and the Fall from Eden," in T. S. Gendler and J. Hawthorne (eds.), *Perceptual Experience* (Oxford: Clarendon, 2006), 49–125.

Chappell, Vere. "Locke's Theory of Ideas," in idem (ed.), *The Cambridge Companion to Locke* (Cambridge: Cambridge University Press, 1994), 26–55.

Chappell, Vere. "The Theory of Ideas," in A. O. Rorty (ed.), *Essays on Descartes'* Meditations (Berkeley: University of California Press, 1986), 177–98.

Chignell, Andrew. "The Ethics of Belief," in E. N. Zalta (ed.), *The Stanford Encyclopedia of Philosophy* (Winter 2016). http://plato.stanford.edu/archives/win2016/entries/ethics-belief

Chignell, Andrew. "Rational Hope, Possibility, and Divine Action," in G. E. Michalson (ed.), *Kant's* Religion within the Boundaries of Mere Reason: *A Critical Guide* (Cambridge: Cambridge University Press, 2014), 98–117.

Choi, Philip. "Ockham's Weak Externalism," *British Journal for the History of Philosophy* 24 (2016): 1075–96.

Christensen, David. "Epistemology of Disagreement: The Good News," *Philosophical Review* 116 (2007): 187–217.

Clavelin, Maurice. *The Natural Philosophy of Galileo: Essay on the Origins and Formation of Classical Mechanics*, trans. A. J. Pomerans (Cambridge: MIT Press, 1974).

Clemenson, David. *Descartes' Theory of Ideas* (London: Continuum, 2007).

Clifford, W. K. *The Ethics of Belief and Other Essays* (Amherst: Prometheus Books, 1999).

Clucas, Stephen. "*Scientia* and *inductio scientifica* in the *Logica Hamburgensis* of Joachim Jungius," in T. Sorell, G. A. J. Rogers, and J. Kraye (eds.), Scientia in Early Modern Philosophy: Seventeenth-Century Thinkers on Demonstrative Knowledge from First Principles (Dordrecht: Springer, 2010), 53–70.

Cohen, I. Bernard. *The Newtonian Revolution* (Cambridge: Cambridge University Press, 1980).

Copeland, Rita. "Living with Uncertainty: Reactions to Aristotle's *Rhetoric* in the Later Middle Ages," in D. G. Denery II, K. Ghosh, and N. Zeeman (eds.), *Uncertain Knowledge: Scepticism, Relativism, and Doubt in the Middle Ages* (Turnhout: Brepols, 2014), 115–33.

Corbini, Amos. *La teoria della scienza nel XIII secolo: I commenti agli* Analitici secondi (Florence: SISMEL, 2006).

Cory, Therese Scarpelli. *Aquinas on Human Self-Knowledge* (Cambridge: Cambridge University Press, 2014).

Cottingham, John. *Descartes* (Oxford: Blackwell, 1986).

Cowan, Nelson. *Working Memory Capacity* (New York: Psychology Press, 2005).

Craig, Edward. *Knowledge and the State of Nature: An Essay in Conceptual Synthesis* (Oxford: Oxford University Press, 1990).

Crombie, A. C. *Robert Grosseteste and the Origins of Experimental Science, 1100–1700* (Oxford: Clarendon, 1953).

Crombie, A. C. "Sources of Galileo's Early Natural Philosophy," in M. L. Righini Bonelli and W. R. Shea (eds.), *Reason, Experiment, and Mysticism in the Scientific Revolution* (New York: Science History Publications, 1975), 157–75.

Cross, Richard. *Duns Scotus's Theory of Cognition* (Oxford: Oxford University Press, 2014).

Curley, Edwin. "Certainty: Psychological, Moral, and Metaphysical," in S. Voss (ed.), *Essays on the Philosophy and Science of René Descartes* (New York: Oxford University Press, 1993), 11–30.

Daston, Lorraine. *Classical Probability in the Englightenment* (Princeton, NJ: Princeton University Press, 1988).

Daston, Lorraine. "Probabilistic Expectation and Rationality in Classical Probability Theory," *Historia Mathematica* 7 (1980): 234–60.

Daston, Lorraine. "Probability and Evidence," in D. Garber and M. Ayers (eds.), *The Cambridge History of Seventeenth-Century Philosophy* (Cambridge: Cambridge University Press, 1998), vol. 2: 1108–44.

Davis, Lennard J. "Constructing Normalcy," in idem (ed.), *The Disabilities Studies Reader*, 3rd edn. (New York: Routledge, 2010), 3–19.

Day, Sebastian. *Intuitive Cognition: A Key to the Significance of the Later Scholastics* (St. Bonaventure, NY: Franciscan Institute, 1947).

De Pace, Anna. *Le matematiche e il mondo: Ricerche su un dibattito in Italia nella seconda metà del Cinquecento* (Milan: FrancoAngeli, 1993).

De Rijk, L. M. "Un tournant important dans l'usage du mot idea chez Henri de Gand," in M. Fattori and M. L. Bianchi (eds.), *Idea: VI Colloquio Internazionale del Lessico Intellettuale Europeo* (Rome: Edizioni dell'Ateneo, 1989), 89–98.

De Rosa, Raffaella. "The Myth of Cartesian Qualia," *Pacific Philosophical Quarterly* 88 (2007): 181–207.

Dear, Peter. *Discipline and Experience: The Mathematical Way in the Scientific Revolution* (Chicago, IL: University of Chicago Press, 1995).

Dear, Peter. *Mersenne and the Learning of the Schools* (Ithaca, NY: Cornell University Press, 1988).

Degenaar, Marjolein. *Molyneux's Problem: Three Centuries of Discussion on the Perception of Forms*, trans. M. J. Collins (Dordrecht: Kluwer, 1996).

Della Rocca, Michael. "Descartes, the Cartesian Circle, and Epistemology without God," *Philosophy and Phenomenological Research* 70 (2005): 1–33.

Deman, Thomas. "Probabilisme," in A. Vacant and E. Mangenot (eds.), *Dictionnaire de théologie catholique* (Paris: Letouzey, 1936), vol. 13.1: 417–619.

Demey, Lorenz. "Ockham on the (In)fallibility of Intuitive Cognition," *Logical Analysis and History of Philosophy* 17 (2014): 193–209.

Denery, Dallas G. II. "Nicholas of Autrecourt on Saving the Appearances," in S. Caroti and C. Grellard (eds.), *Nicolas d'Autrécourt philosophe* (Cesena: Stilgraf editrice, 2006), 65–84.

Denery, Dallas G. II. *Seeing and Being Seen in the Later Medieval World: Optics, Theology and Religious Life* (Cambridge: Cambridge University Press, 2005).

Denery, Dallas G. II. "Uncertainty and Deception in the Medieval and Early Modern Court," in Dallas G. Denery II, Kantik Ghosh, and Nicolette Zeeman (eds.), *Uncertain Knowledge: Scepticism, Relativism, and Doubt in the Middle Ages* (Turnhout: Brepols, 2014), 13–36.

Dennett, Daniel C. *Consciousness Explained* (Boston, MA: Little, Brown, 1991).

Des Chene, Dennis. *Physiologia: Natural Philosophy in Late Aristotelian and Cartesian Thought* (Ithaca, NY: Cornell University Press, 1996).

Detlefsen, Karen. "Du Châtelet and Descartes on the Roles of Hypothesis and Metaphysics in Science," in E. O'Neill and M. Lascano (eds.), *Feminist History of Philosophy: The Recovery and Evaluation of Women's Philosophical Thought* (Dordrecht: Springer, forthcoming).

Detlefsen, Karen. "Émilie du Châtelet," in E. N. Zalta (ed.), *The Stanford Encyclopedia of Philosophy* (Summer 2014). http://plato.stanford.edu/archives/sum2014/entries/emilie-du-chatelet

Detlefsen, Karen. "Teleology and Natures in Descartes' Sixth Meditation," in eadem (ed.), *Descartes' Meditations: A Critical Guide* (Cambridge: Cambridge University Press, 2013), 153–75.

Dewender, Thomas. "Imaginary Experiments (*procedere secundum imaginationem*) in Later Medieval Natural Philosophy," in M. Cândida Pacheco and J. F. Meirinhos (eds.), *Intellect et imagination dans la philosophie médiévale: Actes du XIe Congrès International de Philosophie Médiévale de la Société Internationale pour l'Étude de la Philosophie Médiévale* (Turnhout: Brepols, 2006), 1823–33.

Diels, Hermann and Walther Kranz. *Die Fragmente der Vorsokratiker* (Dublin: Weidmann, 1966).

Dijksterhuis, E. J. *The Mechanization of the World Picture*, trans. C. Dikshoorn (Oxford: Clarendon, 1964).

Downing, Lisa. "The 'Sensible Object' and the 'Uncertain Philosophical Cause,'" in D. Garber and B. Longuenesse (eds.), *Kant and the Early Moderns* (Princeton, NJ: Princeton University Press, 2008), 100–16.

Downing, Lisa. "Sensible Qualities and Material Bodies in Descartes and Boyle," in L. Nolan (ed.), *Primary and Secondary Qualities: The Historical and Ongoing Debate* (Oxford: Oxford University Press, 2011), 103–35.

Drake, Stillman. "Galileo's New Science of Motion," in M. L. Righini Bonelli and W. R. Shea (eds), *Reason, Experiment and Mysticism in the Scientific Revolution* (New York: Science History Publications, 1975), 131–56.

Drake, Stillman and I. E. Drabkin. *Mechanics in Sixteenth-Century Italy: Selections from Tartaglia, Benedetti, Guido Ubaldo, and Galileo* (Madison: University of Wisconsin Press, 1969).

Dretske, Fred. *Knowledge and the Flow of Information* (Cambridge, MA: MIT Press, 1981).

Ducheyne, Steffen. *The Main Business of Natural Philosophy: Isaac Newton's Natural-Philosophical Methodology* (Dordrecht: Springer, 2012).

Dummett, Michael. "Testimony and Memory," in B. K. Matilal and A. Chakrabarti (eds.), *Knowing from Words* (Dordrecht: Reidel, 1994), 1–23.

Dumont, Stephen D. "New Questions by Thomas Wylton," *Documenti e studi sulla tradizione filosofica medievale* 9 (1998): 341–79.

Dunlop, Katherine. "What Geometry Postulates: Newton and Barrow on the Relationship of Mathematics to Nature," in A. Janiak and E. Schliesser (eds.), *Interpreting Newton: Critical Essays* (Cambridge: Cambridge University Press, 2012), 69–101.

Dutant, Julien. "The Legend of the Justified True Belief Analysis," *Philosophical Perspectives* 29 (2015): 95–145.

Dutton, Blake D. *Augustine and Academic Skepticism: A Philosophical Study* (Ithaca, NY: Cornell University Press, 2016).

Dyson, Freeman. "What Can You Really Know?" *New York Review of Books* 59 (November 8, 2012). http://www.nybooks.com/articles/archives/2012/nov/08/what-can-you-really-know

Elga, Adam. "Reflection and Disagreement," *Nous* 41 (2007): 478–502.

Embry, Brian. "Descartes on Free Will and Moral Possibility," *Philosophy and Phenomenological Research* (forthcoming).

Everson, Stephen. *Aristotle on Perception* (Oxford: Clarendon, 1997).

Everson, Stephen. "Epicurus on the Truth of the Senses," in S. Everson (ed.), *Epistemology* (Cambridge: Cambridge University Press, 1990), 161–83.

Feingold, Mordechai. *The Newtonian Moment: Isaac Newton and the Making of Modern Culture* (New York: New York Public Library, 2004).

Ferejohn, Michael T. *Formal Causes: Definition, Explanation, and Primacy in Socratic and Aristotelian Thought* (Oxford: Oxford University Press, 2013).

Ferreira, Jamie M. *Scepticism and Reasonable Doubt: The British Naturalist Tradition in Wilkins, Hume, Reid and Newman* (Oxford: Clarendon, 1986).

Field, Hartry. "Epistemology without Metaphysics" *Philosophical Studies* 143 (2009): 249–90.

Fields, Keota. *Berkeley: Ideas, Immaterialism and Objective Presence* (Lanham, MD: Lexington Books, 2011).

Fine, Gail. "Descartes and Ancient Skepticism: Reheated Cabbage?" *Philosophical Review* 109 (2000): 195–234.

Fine, Gail. "Knowledge and Belief in *Republic* V–VII," in S. Everson (ed.), *Epistemology* (Cambridge: Cambridge University Press, 1990), 85–115.

Fogelin, Robert J. *Hume's Skepticism in the Treatise of Human Nature* (London: Routledge, 1985).

Fogelin, Robert J. *Pyrrhonian Reflections on Knowledge and Justification* (Oxford: Oxford University Press, 1994).

Fogelin, Robert J. "The Tendency of Hume's Skepticism," in M. Burnyeat (ed.), *The Skeptical Tradition* (Berkeley: University of California Press, 1983), 397–412.

Foley, Richard. "The Epistemology of Belief and the Epistemology of Degrees of Belief," *American Philosophical Quarterly* 29 (1992): 111–24.

Foley, Richard. *Intellectual Trust in Oneself and Others* (Cambridge: Cambridge University Press, 2001).

Foley, Richard. *The Theory of Epistemic Rationality* (Cambridge, MA: Harvard University Press, 1987).

Foley, Richard. *Working without a Net: A Study of Egocentric Epistemology* (New York: Oxford University Press, 1993).

Forde, Steven. *Locke, Science, and Politics* (Cambridge: Cambridge University Press, 2013).

Frankfurt, Harry. "Memory and the Cartesian Circle," *Philosophical Review* 71 (1962): 504–11.

Frankish, Keith. "Partial Belief and Flat-Out Belief," in F. Huber and C. Schmidt-Petri (eds.), *Degrees of Belief: An Anthology* (Dordrecht: Springer, 2009), 75–93.

Franklin, James. *The Science of Conjecture* (Baltimore, MD: Johns Hopkins University Press, 2001).

Friedman, Russell L. "Act, Species, and Appearance: Peter Auriol on Intellectual Cognition and Consciousness," in G. Klima (ed.), *Intentionality, Cognition, and Mental Representation in Medieval Philosophy* (New York: Fordham University Press, 2014), 141–65.

Friedman, Russell L. "Mental Propositions before Mental Language," in J. Biard (ed.), *Le langage mental du Moyen Âge à l'âge classique* (Leuven: Peeters, 2009), 95–115.

Friedman, Russell L. "On the Trail of a Philosophical Debate: Durandus of St.-Pourçain vs. Thomas Wylton on Simultaneous Acts in the Intellect," in S. F. Brown, T. Dewender, and T. Kobusch (eds.), *Philosophical Debates at Paris in the Early Fourteenth Century* (Leiden: Brill, 2009), 433–61.

Friedman, Russell L. "Peter Auriol," in E. N. Zalta (ed.), *The Stanford Encyclopedia of Philosophy* (Spring 2014). http://plato.stanford.edu/archives/spr2014/entries/auriol

Frost, Robert. *The Poetry of Robert Frost*, ed. E. C. Lathem (New York: Henry Holt, 1969).

Gabbey, Alan. "Between *ars* and *philosophia naturalis*: Reflections on the Historiography of Early Modern Mechanics," in J. V. Field and F. A. J. L. James (eds.), *Renaissance and Revolution: Humanists, Scholars, Craftsmen and Natural Philosophers in Early Modern Europe* (Cambridge: Cambridge University Press, 1993), 133–45.

Gabbey, Alan. "'A Disease Incurable': Scepticism and the Cambridge Platonists," in R. H. Popkin and A. Vanderjagt (eds.), *Scepticism and Irreligion in the Seventeenth and Eighteenth Centuries* (Leiden: Brill, 1993), 71–91.

Gabbey, Alan. "Newton's *Mathematical Principles of Natural Philosophy*: A Treatise on 'Mechanics'?" in P. M. Harman and A. E. Shapiro (eds.), *The Investigation of Difficult Things: Essays on Newton and the History of the Exact Sciences in Honour of D. T. Whiteside* (Cambridge: Cambridge University Press, 1992), 305–22.

Garber, Daniel. "Descartes, Mechanics, and the Mechanical Philosophy," *Midwest Studies in Philosophy* 26 (2002): 185–204.

Garber, Daniel. "Descartes on Knowledge and Certainty: From the *Discours* to the *Principia*," in idem, *Descartes Embodied* (Cambridge: Cambridge University Press, 2001), 111–29.

Garber, Daniel. *Leibniz: Body, Substance, Monad* (Oxford: Oxford University Press, 2009).

Garber, Daniel. "Leibniz, Newton and Force," in A. Janiak and E. Schliesser (eds.), *Interpreting Newton: Critical Essays* (Cambridge: Cambridge University Press, 2012), 33–47.

Garber, Daniel. "Natural Philosophy in Seventeenth-Century Context," in A. P. Martinich and K. Hoekstra (eds.), *The Oxford Handbook of Hobbes* (Oxford: Oxford University Press, 2016), 106–33.

Garber, Daniel. "On the Frontlines of the Scientific Revolution: How Mersenne Learned to Love Galileo," *Perspectives on Science* 12 (2004): 135–63.

Garber, Daniel. *What Happens after Pascal's Wager: Living Faith and Rational Belief* (Milwaukee, WI: Marquette University Press, 2009).

Garber, Daniel and Sandy Zabell. "On the Emergence of Probability," *Archive for History of Exact Sciences* 21 (1979): 33–53.

Garrett, Don. *Hume* (London: Routledge, 2015).

Garrett, Don. "'A Small Tincture of Pyrrhonism': Skepticism and Naturalism in Hume's Science of Man," in W. Sinnott-Armstrong (ed.), *Pyrrhonian Skepticism* (New York: Oxford University Press, 2004), 68–98.

Gaukroger, Stephen. "Aristotle on the Function of Sense Perception," *Studies in History and Philosophy of Science Part A* 12 (1981): 75–89.

Gendler, Tamar Szabó. "Alief and Belief," *Journal of Philosophy* 105 (2008): 634–63.

Genest, Jean-François. "Pierre de Ceffons et l'hypothèse du Dieu trompeur," in Z. Kaluza and P. Vignaux (eds.), *Preuve et raisons à l'Université de Paris: Logique, ontologie et théologie au XIVe siècle* (Paris: Vrin, 1984), 197–214.

Gerson, Lloyd P. *Ancient Epistemology* (Cambridge: Cambridge University Press, 2009).

Geyser, Joseph. "Zur Einführung in das Problem der Evidenz in der Scholastik," in *Festschrift für Clemens Bäumker* (Beiträge zur Geschichte der Philosophie des Mittelalters suppl. 2) (Münster: Aschendorff, 1923), 161–82.

Gilbert, Neal Ward. *Renaissance Concepts of Method* (New York: Columbia University Press, 1960).

Gingras, Yves. "What Did Mathematics Do to Physics?" *History of Science* 29 (2001): 383–416.

Goddard, Cliff. "Universals and Variation in the Lexicon of Mental State Concepts," in B. Malt and P. Wolff (eds.), *Words and the Mind* (New York: Oxford University Press, 2010), 72–93.

Goddu, André. "William of Ockham's Arguments for Action at a Distance," *Franciscan Studies* 44 (1984): 227–44.

Goldenbaum, Ursula. "The Geometrical Method as a New Standard of Truth, Based on the Mathematization of Nature," in G. Gorham et al. (eds.), *The Language of Nature: Reassessing the Mathematization of Natural Philosophy in the Seventeenth Century* (Minneapolis, MN: University of Minnesota Press, 2016), 274–307.

Gómez-Torrente, Mario. "Kripke on Color Words and the Primary/Secondary Quality Distinction," in A. Berger (ed.), *Saul Kripke* (Cambridge: Cambridge University Press, 2011), 290–323.

Gopnik, Alison. "Explanation as Orgasm and the Drive for Causal Understanding: The Evolution, Function and Phenomenology of the Theory-Formation System," in F. Keil and R. Wilson (eds.), *Cognition and Explanation* (Cambridge, MA: MIT Press, 2000), 299–323.

Gorham, Geoffrey, Benjamin Hill, Edward Slowik, and C. Kenneth Waters (eds.). *The Language of Nature: Reassessing the Mathematization of Natural Philosophy in the Seventeenth Century* (Minneapolis, MN: University of Minnesota Press, 2016).

Gotthelf, Allan. "First Principles in Aristotle's *Parts of Animals*," in A. Gotthelf and J. G. Lennox (eds.), *Philosophical Issues in Aristotle's Biology* (Cambridge: Cambridge University Press, 1987), 167–98.

Gottlieb, Paula. "Aristotle versus Protagoras on Relatives and the Objects of Perception," *Oxford Studies in Ancient Philosophy* 11 (1993): 101–19.

Grant, Edward. "John Buridan and Nicole Oresme on Natural Knowledge," *Vivarium* 31 (1993): 84–105.

Grant, Edward. "Late Medieval Thought, Copernicus and the Scientific Revolution," *Journal of the History of Ideas* 23 (1962): 197–220.

Grant, Edward (ed.). *A Source Book in Medieval Science* (Cambridge, MA: Havard University Press, 1974).

Grassi, Onorato. *Intenzionalità: La dottrina dell' "esse apparens" nel secolo xiv* (Genoa: Marietti, 2005).

Grellard, Christophe. *Croire et savoir: Les principes de la connaissance selon Nicolas d'Autrécourt* (Paris: Vrin, 2005).

Grellard, Christophe. *De la certitude volontaire: Débats nominalistes sur la foi à la fin du moyen âge* (Paris: Sorbonne, 2014).

Grellard, Christophe. "How Is It Possible to Believe Falsely? John Buridan, the *Vetula* and the Psychology of Error," in D. G. Denery II, K. Ghosh, and N. Zeeman (eds.), *Uncertain Knowledge: Scepticism, Relativism, and Doubt in the Middle Ages* (Turnhout: Brepols, 2014), 91–113.

Grellard, Christophe. *Jean de Salisbury et la renaissance médiévale du scepticisme* (Paris: Les Belles Lettres, 2013).

Grellard, Christophe. "The Nature of Intentional Objects in Nicholas of Autrecourt's Theory of Knowledge," in G. Klima (ed.), *Intentionality, Cognition, and Mental Representation in Medieval Philosophy* (New York: Fordham University Press, 2014), 235–50.

Grellard, Christophe. "Science et opinion dans les *Quaestiones super Analyticorum posteriorum* de Jean Buridan," in J. Biard (ed.), *Raison et démonstration: Les commentaires médiévaux sur les Seconds analytiques* (Turnhout: Brepols, 2015), 131–50.

Grellard, Christophe. "*Sicut specula sine macula*: La perception et son objet chez Nicolas d'Autrécourt," *Chôra: Revue d'études anciennes et médiévales* 3 (2005–6): 229–50.

Grellard, Christophe. "La théorie de la croyance de Nicole Oresme," in J. Celeyrette and C. Grellard (eds.), *Nicole Oresme philosophe: Philosophie de la nature et philosophie de la connaissance à Paris au XIVe siècle* (Turnhout: Brepols, 2014), 203–23.

Groarke, Leo. "Descartes' First Meditation: Something Old, Something New, Something Borrowed," *Journal of the History of Philosophy* 22 (1984): 281–301.

Grosse, Sven. *Heilsungewißheit und Scrupulositas im späten Mittelalter: Studien zu Johannes Gerson und Gattungen der Frömmigkeitstheologie seiner Zeit* (Tübingen: Mohr, 1994).

Gueroult, Martial. *Descartes' Philosophy Interpreted according to the Order of Reasons*, 2 vols., trans. R. Ariew (Minneapolis, MN: University of Minnesota Press, 1984).

Gutas, Dimitri. *Greek Thought, Arabic Culture: The Graeco-Arabic Translation Movement in Baghdad and Early ʿAbbāsid Society (2nd–4th/8th–10th Centuries)* (London: Routledge, 1998).

Gutas, Dimitri. "Paul the Persian on the Classification of the Parts of Aristotle's Philosophy: A Milestone between Alexandria and Bagdâd," *Der Islam* 60 (1983): 231–67.

Hacking, Ian. *The Emergence of Probability: A Philosophical Study of Early Ideas about Probability, Induction and Statistical Inference*, 2nd edn. (Cambridge: Cambridge University Press, 2006).

Hald, Anders. *A History of Probability and Statistics and Their Application before 1750* (New York: Wiley, 1990).

Hall, Roland. "*Idea* in Locke's Works," in M. Fattori and M. L. Bianchi (eds.), *Idea: VI Colloquio Internazionale del Lessico Intellettuale Europeo* (Rome: Edizioni dell'Ateno, 1989), 255–63.

Hamesse, Jacqueline. "*Idea* chez les auteurs philosophiques des 12 et 13 siècles," in M. Fattori and M. L. Bianchi (eds.), *Idea: VI Colloquio Internazionale del Lessico Intellettuale Europeo* (Rome: Edizioni dell'Ateno, 1989), 99–135.

Hankins, Thomas L. "Newton's 'Mathematical Way' a Century after the *Principia*," in F. Durham and R. D. Purrington (eds.), *Some Truer Method: Reflections on the Heritage of Newton* (New York: Columbia University Press, 1990), 89–112.

Harari, Orna. "Proclus' Account of Explanatory Demonstrations in Mathematics and Its Context," *Archiv für Geschichte der Philosophie* 90 (2008): 137–64.

Harman, Gilbert. *Change in View: Principles of Reasoning* (Cambridge, MA: MIT Press, 1986).

Harper, William L. *Isaac Newton's Scientific Method: Turning Data into Evidence about Gravity and Cosmology* (Oxford: Oxford University Press, 2011).

Hartman, Peter John. "Durand of St.-Pourçain and Thomas Aquinas on Representation," *History of Philosophy Quarterly* 30 (2013): 19–34.

Hasan, Ali and Richard Fumerton. "Foundationalist Theories of Epistemic Justification," in E. N. Zalta (ed.), *The Stanford Encyclopedia of Philosophy* (Winter 2016). http://plato.stanford.edu/archives/win2016/entries/justep-foundational

Hatfield, Gary. "Descartes on Sensory Representation, Objective Reality, and Material Falsity," in K. Detlefsen (ed.), *Descartes' Meditations: A Critical Guide* (Cambridge: Cambridge University Press, 2013), 127–50.

Hawking, Stephen and Leonard Mlodinow. *The Grand Design* (New York: Bantam Books, 2010).

Hawthorne, John and Jason Stanley. "Knowledge and Action," *Journal of Philosophy* 105 (2008): 571–90.

Hazony, Yoram. "Newtonian Explanatory Reduction and Hume's System of the Sciences," in Z. Biener and E. Schliesser (eds.), *Newton and Empiricism* (Oxford: Oxford University Press, 2014), 138–70.

Heck, Paul L. *Skepticism in Classical Islam: Moments of Confusion* (Abingdon: Routledge, 2014).

Heidegger, Martin. *Being and Time*, trans. J. Macquarrie and E. Robinson (Oxford: Blackwell, 1962).

Hein, Christel. *Definition und Einteilung der Philosophie von der spätantiken Einleitungsliteratur zur arabischen Enzyklopädie* (Frankfurt: Lang, 1985).

Held, Richard et al. "The Newly Sighted Fail to Match Seen with Felt," *Nature Neuroscience* 14 (2001): 551–3.

Henry, John. "Testimony and Empiricism: John Sergeant, John Locke, and the Social History of Truth," in T. Demeter, K. Murphy, and C. Zittel (eds.), *Conflicting Values of Inquiry: Ideologies of Epistemology in Early Modern Europe* (Leiden: Brill, 2015), 95–124.

Herrtage, Sidney J. (ed.). *England in the Reign of King Henry the Eighth, Part 1: Starkey's Life and Letters* (London: Early English Text Society, 1878).

Hight, Marc A. *Idea and Ontology: An Essay in Early Modern Metaphysics of Ideas* (University Park, PA: Pennsylvania State University Press, 2008).

Hoffman, Paul. "Direct Realism, Intentionality, and the Objective Being of Ideas," *Pacific Philosophical Quarterly* 83 (2002): 163–79.

Holton, Richard. "Intention as a Model for Belief," in M. Vargas and G. Yaffe (eds.), *Rational and Social Agency: The Philosophy of Michael Bratman* (Oxford: Oxford University Press, 2014), 12–37.

Hookway, Christopher. "Doubt: Affective States and the Regulation of Inquiry," *Canadian Journal of Philosophy*, suppl. 24 (1998): 203–25.

Hookway, Christopher. "How to be a Virtue Epistemologist," in M. DePaul and L. Zagzebski (eds.), *Intellectual Virtue: Perspectives from Ethics and Epistemology* (Oxford: Clarendon, 2003), 183–202.

Huemer, Michael. *Skepticism and the Veil of Perception* (Lanham, MD: Rowman & Littlefield, 2001).

Hyman, Arthur, James J. Walsh, and Thomas Williams (eds.). *Philosophy in the Middle Ages: The Christian, Islamic, and Jewish Traditions*, 3rd edn. (Indianapolis, IN: Hackett, 2010).

Ierodiakonou, Katerina. "The Notion of Enargeia in Hellenistic Philosophy," in B. Morison and K. Ierodiakonou (eds.), *Episteme, etc.: Essays in Honour of Jonathan Barnes* (Oxford: Oxford University Press, 2011), 60–73.

Inwood, Brad and L. P. Gerson (trans.). *Hellenistic Philosophy: Introductory Readings*, 2nd edn. (Indianapolis, IN: Hackett, 1997).

Irwin, Terence. *Aristotle's First Principles* (Oxford: Clarendon, 1988).

Jabre, Farid. *La notion de certitude selon Ghazali dans ses origines psychologiques et historiques* (Paris: Vrin, 1958).

Jacomuzzi, Alessandra, Pietro Kobau, and Nicola Bruno. "Molyneux's Question Redux," *Phenomenology and the Cognitive Sciences* 2 (2003): 255–80.

Jacovides, Michael. "Locke on Perception," in M. Stuart (ed.), *A Companion to Locke* (Oxford: Blackwell, 2015), 175–92.

Jaffro, Laurent (ed.). *Croit-on comme on veut? Histoire d'une controverse* (Paris: Vrin, 2014).

James, William. *The Principles of Psychology*, 2 vols. (New York: Holt, 1890).

Janiak, Andrew. *Newton* (Malden, MA: Wiley Blackwell, 2015).

Janiak, Andrew. "Newton and the Reality of Force," *Journal of the History of Philosophy* 45 (2007): 127–47.

Jardine, Nicholas. "Demonstration, Dialectic, and Rhetoric in Galileo's *Dialogue*," in D. R. Kelley and R. H. Popkin (eds.), *The Shapes of Knowledge from the Renaissance to the Enlightenment* (Dordrecht: Springer, 1991), 101–21.

Jardine, Nicholas. "Epistemology of the Sciences," in C. B. Schmitt et al. (eds.), *The Cambridge History of Renaissance Philosophy* (Cambridge: Cambridge University Press, 1988), 685–711.

Jeffrey, Richard. "Dracula Meets Wolfman: Acceptance vs. Partial Belief," in M. Swain (ed.), *Induction, Acceptance, and Rational Belief* (Dordrecht: Reidel, 1970), 157–85.

Jesseph, Douglas M. "Hobbes and the Method of Natural Science," in T. Sorell (ed.), *The Cambridge Companion to Hobbes* (Cambridge: Cambridge University Press, 1996), 86–107.

Jesseph, Douglas M. "Hobbesian Mechanics," *Oxford Studies in Early Modern Philosophy* 3 (2006): 119–52.

Jesseph, Douglas M. "Scientia in Hobbes," in T. Sorell, G. A. J. Rogers, and J. Kraye (eds.), *Scientia in Early Modern Philosophy: Seventeenth-Century Thinkers on Demonstrative Knowledge from First Principles* (Dordrecht: Springer, 2010), 117–27.

Jesseph, Douglas M. *Squaring the Circle: The War between Hobbes and Wallis* (Chicago, IL: University of Chicago Press, 1999).

Johnston, Mark. "Better than Mere Knowledge? The Function of Sensory Awareness," in T. S. Gendler and J. Hawthorne (eds.), *Perceptual Experience* (Oxford: Clarendon, 2006), 260–90.

Johnston, Mark. "How to Speak of the Colors," *Philosophical Studies* 68 (1992): 221–63.

Jones, Karen. "The Politics of Intellectual Self-Trust," *Social Epistemology* 26 (2012): 237–51.

Jones, Karen. "Trust as an Affective Attitude," *Ethics* 107 (1996): 4–25.

Jones, Steve. "The Set Within the Skull," *New York Review of Books* 44 (November 6, 1997), 13–16.

Jordan, Jeff. *Pascal's Wager: Pragmatic Arguments and Belief in God* (Oxford: Clarendon, 2006).

Joy, Lynn Sumida. *Gassendi the Atomist: Advocate of History in an Age of Science* (Cambridge: Cambridge University Press, 1987).

Kantola, Ilkka. *Probability and Moral Uncertainty in Late Medieval and Early Modern Times* (Helsinki: Luther-Agricola Society, 1994).

Kaplan, Mark. "It's Not What You Know that Counts," *Journal of Philosophy* 82 (1985): 350–63.

Kaplan, Mark. *Decision Theory as Philosophy* (Cambridge: Cambridge University Press, 1996).

Karger, Elizabeth. "Ockham and Wodeham on Divine Deception as a Skeptical Hypothesis," *Vivarium* 42 (2004): 225–36.

Karger, Elizabeth. "Ockham's Misunderstood Theory of Intuitive and Abstractive Cognition," in P. V. Spade (ed.), *The Cambridge Companion to Ockham* (New York: Cambridge University Press, 1999), 204–26.

Kaufman, Dan. "Locks, Schlocks, and Poisoned Peas: Boyle on Actual and Dispositive Qualities," *Oxford Studies in Early Modern Philosophy* 3 (2006): 153–98.

Kaye, Joel. *A History of Balance, 1250–1375: The Emergence of a New Model of Equilibrium and its Impact on Thought* (Cambridge: Cambridge University Press, 2014).

Keating, Laura. "Mechanism and the Representational Nature of Sensation in Descartes," *Canadian Journal of Philosophy* 29 (1999): 411–30.

Kemp Smith, Norman. "The Naturalism of Hume," *Mind* 14 (1905): 149–73, 335–47.

Kemp Smith, Norman. *The Philosophy of David Hume: A Critical Study of Its Origins and Central Doctrines* (London: Macmillan, 1941).

Kenny, Anthony. *Descartes: A Study of His Philosophy* (New York: Random House, 1968).

Keynes, John Maynard. *A Treatise on Probability* (London: Macmillan, 1921).

Khalidi, Muhammad Ali (trans.). *Medieval Islamic Philosophical Writings* (Cambridge: Cambridge University Press, 2005).

King, Peter. "Jean Buridan's Philosophy of Science," *Studies in History and Philosophy of Science* 18 (1987): 109–32.

Kitcher, Philip. *The Advancement of Science: Science without Legend, Objectivity without Illusions* (New York: Oxford University Press, 1993).

Klima, Gyula. *John Buridan* (New York: Oxford University Press, 2009).

Klima, Gyula, with Fritz Allhoff and Anand Jayprakash Vaidya (eds.). *Medieval Philosophy: Essential Readings with Commentary* (Malden, MA: Wiley Blackwell, 2007).

Knebel, Sven K. *Wille, Würfel und Wahrscheinlichkeit: Das System der moralischen Notwendigkeit in der Jesuitenscholastik 1550–1700* (Hamburg: Meiner, 2000).

Kornblith, Hilary. "In Defense of a Naturalized Epistemology," in J. Greco and E. Sosa (eds.), *The Blackwell Guide to Epistemology* (Oxford: Blackwell, 1999), 158–69.

Koyré, Alexandre. "An Experiment in Measurement," *Metaphysics and Measurement: Essays in Scientific Revolution* (Cambridge, MA: Harvard University Press, 1968), 89–117.

Koyré, Alexandre. *Newtonian Studies* (London: Chapman & Hall, 1965).

Kretzmann, Norman. "Infallibility, Error, and Ignorance," in *Aristotle and His Medieval Interpreters* (*Canadian Journal of Philosophy* suppl. vol. 17), ed. R. Bosley and M. Tweedale (Calgary: University of Calgary Press, 1992), 159–94.

Kretzmann, Norman (ed.). *Infinity and Continuity in Ancient and Medieval Thought* (Ithaca, NY: Cornell University Press, 1982).

Kriegel, Uriah. *Subjective Consciousness: A Self-Representational Theory* (Oxford: Oxford University Press, 2009).

Kuehn, Manfred. "Knowledge and Belief," in K. Haakonssen (ed.), *The Cambridge History of Eighteenth-Century Philosophy* (Cambridge: Cambridge University Press, 2006), 389–425.

Kurath, Hans (ed.) and Sherman M. Kuhn (associate ed.). *Middle English Dictionary*, 23 vols. (Ann Arbor, MI: University of Michigan Press, 1952–2000) http://quod.lib.umich.edu/m/med

Kurz, Dietrich. *AKPIBEIA: Das Ideal der Exaktheit bei den Griechen bis Aristoteles* (Göppingen: Kümmerle, 1970).

Kvanvig, Jonathan L. *The Value of Knowledge and the Pursuit of Understanding* (Cambridge: Cambridge University Press, 2003).

Lähteenmäki, Vili. "Locke and Active Perception," *Studies in the History of Philosophy of Mind* 14 (2014): 223–39.

Larmore, Charles. "Descartes' Psychologistic Theory of Assent," *History of Philosophy Quarterly* 1 (1984): 61–74.

Laudan, Larry. "The Demise of the Demarcation Problem," in R. S. Cohen and L. Laudan (eds.), *Physics, Philosophy and Psychoanalysis: Essays in Honor of Adolf Grünbaum* (Dordrecht: Reidel, 1983), 111–27.

Laudan, Larry. "The Nature and Sources of Locke's Views on Hypotheses," in I. C. Tipton (ed.), *Locke on Human Understanding* (Oxford: Oxford University Press, 1977).

Lee, Mi-Kyoung. *Epistemology after Protagoras: Responses to Relativism in Plato, Aristotle, and Democritus* (Oxford: Clarendon, 2005).

Lennon, Thomas M. and Michael W. Hickson. "The Skepticism of the First Meditation," in K. Detlefsen (ed.), *Descartes' Meditations: A Critical Guide* (Cambridge: Cambridge University Press, 2013), 9–24.

Lennox, James G. "Aristotle, Galileo, and 'Mixed Sciences,'" in W. A. Wallace (ed.), *Reinterpreting Galileo* (Washington, DC: Catholic University of America Press, 1986), 29–51.

Lesher, J. H. "On Aristotelian ἐπιστήμη as 'Understanding,'" *Ancient Philosophy* 21 (2001): 45–55.

Levey, Samuel. "Leibniz on Mathematics and the Actually Infinite Division of Matter," *Philosophical Review* 107 (1998): 49–96.

Levey, Samuel. "Matter and Two Concepts of Continuity in Leibniz," *Philosophical Studies* 94 (1999): 81–118.

Lewis, David. "Naming the Colours," *Papers in Metaphysics and Epistemology* (Cambridge: Cambridge University Press, 1999), 332–58.

Lewis, John Michael. *Galileo in France: French Reactions to the Theories and Trial of Galileo* (New York: Peter Lang, 2006).

Lička, Lukáš. "Perception and Objective Being: Peter Auriol on Perceptual Acts and Their Objects," *American Catholic Philosophical Quarterly* 90 (2016): 49–76.

Livesey, Steven J. *Theology and Science in the Fourteenth Century: Three Questions on the Unity and Subalternation of the Sciences from John of Reading's Commentary on the Sentences* (Leiden: Brill, 1989).

Lloyd, G. E. R. *The Ideals of Inquiry: An Ancient History* (Oxford: Oxford University Press, 2014).

Lloyd, G. E. R. "The Theories and Practices of Demonstration," *Aristotelian Explorations* (Cambridge: Cambridge University Press, 1996), 7–37.

Loeb, Louis E. *From Descartes to Hume: Continental Metaphysics and the Development of Modern Philosophy* (Ithaca, NY: Cornell University Press, 1981).

Loeb, Louis E. *Stability and Justification in Hume's* Treatise (New York: Oxford University Press, 2002).

LoLordo, Antonia. "Gassendi and the Seventeenth-Century Atomists on Primary and Secondary Qualities," in L. Nolan (ed.), *Primary and Secondary Qualities: The Historical and Ongoing Debate* (Oxford: Oxford University Press, 2011), 62–80.

LoLordo, Antonia. *Pierre Gassendi and the Birth of Early Modern Philosophy* (New York: Cambridge University Press, 2007).

Long, A. A. and Sedley, D. N. *The Hellenistic Philosophers* (Cambridge: Cambridge University Press, 1987).

Ludlow, Peter. "Contextualism and the New Linguistic Turn in Epistemology," in G. Preyer and G. Peter (eds.), *Contextualism in Philosophy: Knowledge, Meaning, and Truth* (Oxford: Clarendon, 2005), 11–50.

Machamer, Peter. "Galileo and the Causes," in R. E. Butts and J. C. Pitt (eds.), *New Perspectives on Galileo* (Dordrecht: Reidel, 1978), 161–80.

Machamer, Peter and J. E. McGuire. *Descartes's Changing Mind* (Princeton, NJ: Princeton University Press, 2009).

MacKenzie, Ann Wilbur. "The Reconfiguration of Sensory Experience," in J. Cottingham (ed.), *Reason, Will, and Sensation: Studies in Descartes's Metaphysics* (Oxford: Clarendon, 1994), 251–72.

Maclean, Ian. *Logic, Signs and Nature in the Renaissance: The Case of Learned Medicine* (Cambridge: Cambridge University Press, 2002).

Mahoney, Michael S. "The Mathematical Realm of Nature," in D. Garber and M. Ayers (eds.), *The Cambridge History of Seventeenth-Century Philosophy* (Cambridge: Cambridge University Press, 1998), 702–55.

Maier, Anneliese. "Bewegung ohne Ursache," in eadem, *Zwischen Philosophie und Mechanik: Studien zur Naturphilosophie der Spätscholastik* (Rome: Edizioni di Storia e Letteratura, 1958), 289–339.

Maier, Anneliese. *Metaphysische Hintergründe der spätscholastischen Naturphilosophie* (Rome: Edizioni di Storia e Letteratura, 1955).

Maier, Anneliese. *On the Threshold of Exact Science: Selected Writings of Anneliese Maier on Late Medieval Natural Philosophy*, trans. S. Sargent (Philadelphia, PA: University of Pennsylvania Press, 1982).

Maier, Anneliese. "Das Problem der Evidenz in der Philosophie des 14. Jahrhunderts," in eadem, *Ausgehendes Mittelalter: gesammelte Aufsätze zur Geistesgeschichte des 14. Jahrhunderts* (Rome: Edizioni di Storia e Letteratura, 1967), vol. 2: 367–418.

Maier, Anneliese. *Zwischen Philosophie und Mechanik: Studien zur Naturphilosophie der Spätscholastik* (Rome: Edizioni di Storia e Letteratura, 1958).

Malcolm, Norman. *Knowledge and Certainty* (Englewood Cliffs, NJ: Prentice Hall, 1963).

Mancosu, Paolo. *Philosophy of Mathematics and Mathematical Practice in the Seventeenth Century* (New York: Oxford University Press, 1996).

Markie, Peter. *Descartes's Gambit* (Ithaca, NY: Cornell University Press, 1986).

Marmodoro, Anna. *Aristotle on Perceiving Objects* (New York: Oxford University Press, 2014).

Marmura, Michael E. "The *fortuna* of the *Posterior Analytics* in the Arabic Middle Ages," in M. Asztalos, J. E. Murdoch, and I. Niiniluoto (eds.), *Knowledge and the Sciences in Medieval Philosophy* (Helsinki: Yliopistopaino, 1990), vol. 1: 85–103.

Martin, Christopher J. "Self-Knowledge and Cognitive Ascent: Thomas Aquinas and Peter Olivi on the KK-Thesis," in H. Lagerlund (ed.), *Forming the Mind: Essays on the Internal Senses and the Mind/Body Problem from Avicenna to Medical Enlightenment* (Dordrecht: Springer, 2007), 93–108.

Matson, Wallace. *Grand Theories and Everyday Beliefs: Science, Philosophy, and Their Histories* (Oxford: Oxford University Press, 2011).

Matthews, Gareth B. "Consciousness and Life," *Philosophy* 52 (1977): 13–26.

Matthews, Gareth B. *Thought's Ego in Augustine and Descartes* (Ithaca, NY: Cornell University Press, 1992).

McCluskey, Stephen C. *Nicole Oresme on Light, Color, and the Rainbow: An Edition and Translation, with Introduction and Critical Notes, of Part of Book Three of His* Questiones super quatuor libros meteororum (PhD dissertation, University of Wisconsin, 1974).

McCormick, Miriam. "A Change in Manner: Hume's Scepticism in the *Treatise* and the First *Enquiry*," *Canadian Journal of Philosophy* 29 (1999): 431–48.

McGinnis, Jon. "Avicenna's Naturalized Epistemology and Scientific Method," in S. Rahman, T. Street, and H. Tahiri (eds.), *The Unity of Science in the Arabic Tradition* (Dordrecht: Springer, 2008), 129–52.

McGinnis, Jon. "Scientific Methodologies in Medieval Islam," *Journal of the History of Philosophy* 41 (2003): 307–27.

McGinnis, Jon and David C. Reisman. *Classical Arabic Philosophy: An Anthology of Sources* (Indianapolis, IN: Hackett, 2007).

McKeown-Green, Jonathan, Glen Pettigrove, and Aness Webster. "Conjuring Ethics from Words," *Nous* 49 (2015): 71–93.

McMullin, Ernan. "The Conception of Science in Galileo's Work," in R. E. Butts and J. C. Pitt (eds.), *New Perspectives on Galileo* (Dordrecht: Reidel, 1978), 209–58.

McMullin, Ernan. "Conceptions of Science in the Scientific Revolution," in D. C. Lindberg and R. S. Westman (eds.), *Reappraisals of the Scientific Revolution* (Cambridge: Cambridge University Press, 1990), 27–92.

McMullin, Ernan. "The Impact of Newton's *Principia* on the Philosophy of Science," *Philosophy of Science* 68 (2001): 279–310.

Meinel, Christoph. *In physicis futurum saeculum respicio: Joachim Jungius und die Naturwissenschaftliche Revolution des 17. Jahrhunderts* (Göttingen: Vandenhoeck und Ruprecht, 1984).

Menn, Stephen. *Descartes and Augustine* (Cambridge: Cambridge University Press, 1998).

Mercer, Christia. "The Methodology of the *Meditations*: Tradition and Innovation," in D. Cunning (ed.), *The Cambridge Companion to Descartes'* Meditations (Cambridge: Cambridge University Press, 2014), 23–47.

Miller, George A. "The Magical Number Seven, Plus or Minus Two: Some Limits on Our Capacity for Processing Information," *Psychological Review* 63 (1956): 81–97.

Mills, Charles W. "'Ideal Theory' as Ideology," *Hypatia* 20 (2005): 165–83.

Mills, Charles W. "Lost in Rawlsland," *The New York Times* (November 16, 2014). http://opinionator.blogs.nytimes.com/2014/11/16/lost-in-rawlsland

Milton, J. R. "Laws of Nature," in D. Garber and M. Ayers (eds.), *Cambridge History of Seventeenth-Century Philosophy* (Cambridge: Cambridge University Press, 1998), 680–701.

Moon, Andrew. "Knowing without Evidence," *Mind* 121 (2012): 309–31.

Moore, G. E. "The Refutation of Idealism," in *Philosophical Studies* (London: Routledge, 1922), 1–30.

Morris, John. "Descartes and Probable Knowledge," *Journal of the History of Philosophy* 8 (1970): 303–12.

Murdoch, John E. "Infinity and Continuity," in N. Kretzmann et al. (eds.), *Cambridge History of Later Medieval Philosophy* (Cambridge: Cambridge University Press, 1982), 564–91.

Murphy, Claudia Eisen. "Aquinas on Voluntary Beliefs," *American Catholic Philosophical Quarterly* 74 (2000): 569–97.

Murray, Michael. "Pre-Leibnizian Moral Necessity," *Leibniz Review* 14 (2004): 1–28.

Nadler, Steven. *Arnauld and the Cartesian Philosophy of Ideas* (Princeton, NJ: Princeton University Press, 1989).

Nadler, Steven. *Malebranche and Ideas* (New York: Oxford University Press, 1992).

Nagel, Jennifer. "Defending the Evidential Value of Epistemic Intuitions: A Reply to Stich," *Philosophy and Phenomenological Research* 87 (2013): 179–99.

Nardi, Bruno. *Soggetto e oggetto del conoscere nella filosofia antica e medievale* (Rome: Edizioni dell'Ateneo, 1952).

Nederman, Cary J. "Beyond Stoicism and Aristotelianism: John of Salisbury's Skepticism and Twelfth-Century Moral Philosophy," in I. Bejczy (ed.), *Virtue and Ethics in the Twelfth Century* (Leiden: Brill, 2005), 177–84.

Neto, José R. Maia. *Academic Skepticism in Seventeenth-Century French Philosophy: The Charronian Legacy, 1601–1662* (Dordrecht: Springer, 2015).

Newman, Lex. "Descartes' Epistemology," in E. N. Zalta (ed.), *The Stanford Encyclopedia of Philosophy* (Winter 2014). http://plato.stanford.edu/archives/win2014/entries/descartes-epistemology

Newman, Lex. "Locke on Sensitive Knowledge and the Veil of Perception: Four Misconceptions," *Pacific Philosophical Quarterly* 85 (2004): 273–300.

Nolan, Lawrence (ed.). *Primary and Secondary Qualities: The Historical and Ongoing Debate* (Oxford: Oxford University Press, 2011).

Norcross, Alastair. "Reasons without Demands: Rethinking Rightness," in J. Dreier (ed.), *Blackwell Contemporary Debates in Moral Theory* (Oxford: Blackwell, 2006), 38–53.

Normore, Calvin G. "Meaning and Objective Being: Descartes and his Sources," in A. O. Rorty (ed.), *Essays on Descartes Meditations* (Berkeley: University of California Press, 1986), 223–42.

Nozick, Robert. "Testament," in *Socratic Puzzles* (Cambridge, MA: Harvard University Press, 1997), 324–8.

Nuchelmans, Gabriel. *Judgment and Proposition from Descartes to Kant* (Amsterdam: North-Holland, 1983).

Nuchelmans, Gabriel. *Late-Scholastic and Humanistic Theories of the Proposition* (Amsterdam: North-Holland, 1980).

Nuchelmans, Gabriel. *Theories of the Proposition: Ancient and Medieval Conceptions of the Bearers of Truth and Falsity* (Amsterdam: North-Holland, 1973).

Olson, Philip R. "Putting Knowledge in Its Place: Virtue, Value, and the Internalism/Externalism Debate," *Philosophical Studies* 159 (2012): 241–61.

Orr, Robert R. *Reason and Authority: The Thought of William Chillingworth* (Oxford: Clarendon, 1967).

Osler, Margaret J. "John Locke and the Changing Ideal of Scientific Knowledge," *Journal of the History of Ideas* 3 (1970): 3–16.

Ott, Walter R. *Causation and Laws of Nature in Early Modern Philosophy* (Oxford: Oxford University Press, 2009).

Owen, David. *Hume's Reason* (Oxford: Oxford University Press, 1999).

Owens, David. "Descartes's Use of Doubt," in J. Broughton and J. Carriero (eds.), *A Companion to Descartes* (Oxford: Blackwell, 2008), 164–78.

Panaccio, Claude. *Ockham on Concepts* (Aldershot: Ashgate, 2004).

Panaccio, Claude. "Ockham's Externalism," in G. Klima (ed.), *Intentionality, Cognition, and Mental Representation in Medieval Philosophy* (New York: Fordham University Press, 2014), 166–85.

Panaccio, Claude. "Le savoir selon Guillaume d'Ockham," in R. Nadeau (ed.), *Philosophies de la connaissance* (Quebec: Presses de l'Université Laval, 2009), 91–109.

Papineau, David. "Sensory Experience and Representational Properties," *Proceedings of the Aristotelian Society* 114 (2014): 1–33.

Pasnau, Robert (trans.). *Cambridge Translations of Medieval Philosophical Texts*, vol. 3: *Mind and Knowledge* (New York: Cambridge University Press, 2002).

Pasnau, Robert. "Cognition," in T. Williams (ed.), *The Cambridge Companion to Duns Scotus* (Cambridge: Cambridge University Press, 2003), 285–311.

Pasnau, Robert. "Democritus and Secondary Qualities," *Archiv für Geschichte der Philosophie* 89 (2007): 99–121.

Pasnau, Robert. "Disagreement and the Value of Self-Trust," *Philosophical Studies* 172 (2015): 2315–39.

Pasnau, Robert. "Epistemology Idealized," *Mind* 122 (2014): 987–1021.

Pasnau, Robert. "Human Nature," in A. S. McGrade (ed.), *The Cambridge Companion to Medieval Philosophy* (Cambridge: Cambridge University Press, 2003), 208–30.

Pasnau, Robert. "Medieval Social Epistemology: *Scientia* for Mere Mortals," *Episteme* 7 (2010): 25–41.

Pasnau, Robert. *Metaphysical Themes 1274–1671* (Oxford: Clarendon, 2011).

Pasnau, Robert. "Snatching Hope from the Jaws of Epistemic Defeat," *Journal of the American Philosophical Association* 1 (2015): 257–75.

Pasnau, Robert. *Theories of Cognition in the Later Middle Ages* (New York: Cambridge University Press, 1997).

Pasnau, Robert. "Therapeutic Reflections on Our Bipolar History of Perception," *Analytic Philosophy* 57 (2016): 253–84.

Pasnau, Robert. *Thomas Aquinas on Human Nature: A Philosophical Study of* Summa theologiae 1a 75–89 (New York: Cambridge University Press, 2002).

Passmore, John. *Hume's Intentions*, rev. edn. (New York: Basic Books, 1968).

Pearse, Harry. "Historical Faith and Philosophical Theology: The Case of Thomas White," *Intellectual History Review* 26 (2016): 221–43.

Perfetti, Stefano. "Pietro Pomponazzi," in E. N. Zalta (ed.), *The Stanford Encyclopedia of Philosophy* (Winter 2012). http://plato.stanford.edu/archives/win2012/entries/pomponazzi

Perler, Dominik. "Can We Trust Our Senses? Fourteenth-Century Debates on Sensory Illusion," in D. G. Denery II, K. Ghosh, and N. Zeeman (eds.), *Uncertain Knowledge: Scepticism, Relativism, and Doubt in the Middle Ages* (Turnhout: Brepols, 2014), 63–90.

Perler, Dominik. "Does God Deceive Us? Skeptical Hypotheses in Late Medieval Epistemology," in H. Lagerlund (ed.), *Rethinking the History of Skepticism: The Missing Medieval Background* (Leiden: Brill, 2010), 171–92.

Perler, Dominik. "Inside and Outside the Mind: Cartesian Representations Reconsidered," in R. Schumacher (ed.), *Perception and Reality: From Descartes to the Present* (Paderborn: Mentis, 2004), 69–87.

Perler, Dominik. "Die kognitive Struktur von Hoffnung: Zwei mittelalterliche Erklärungsmodelle," *Deutsche Zeitschrift für Philosophie* 60 (2012): 73–89.

Perler, Dominik. "Relations nécessaires ou contingentes? Nicolas d'Autrécourt et la controverse sur la nature des relations cognitives," in S. Caroti and C. Grellard (eds.), *Nicolas d'Autrécourt philosophe* (Cesena: Stilgraf editrice, 2006), 85–111.

Perler, Dominik. "Seeing and Judging: Ockham and Wodeham on Sensory Cognition," in S. Knuuttila and P. Kärkkäinen (eds.), *Theories of Perception in Medieval and Early Modern Philosophy* (Dordrecht: Springer, 2008), 151–69.

Perler, Dominik. "Skepticism," in R. Pasnau (ed.) and C. Van Dyke (assoc. ed.), *The Cambridge History of Medieval Philosophy* (Cambridge: Cambridge University Press, 2010), 384–96.

Perler, Dominik. *Theorien der Intentionalität im Mittelalter* (Frankfurt: Klostermann, 2002).

Perler, Dominik. "Was There a 'Pyrrhonian Crisis' in Early Modern Philosophy? A Critical Notice of Richard H. Popkin," *Archiv für Geschichte der Philosophie* 86 (2004): 209–20.

Perler, Dominik. "What Am I Thinking About? John Duns Scotus and Peter Aureol on Intentional Objects," *Vivarium* 32 (1994): 72–89.

Perler, Dominik. "What Are Intentional Objects? A Controversy among Early Scotists," in D. Perler (ed.), *Ancient and Medieval Theories of Intentionality* (Leiden: Brill, 2001), 203–26.

Perler, Dominik. *Zweifel und Gewissheit: Skeptische Debatten im Mittelalter* (Frankfurt: Klostermann, 2006).

Pessin, Andrew. "Mental Transparency, Direct Sensation, and the Unity of the Cartesian Mind," in J. Miller (ed.), *Topics in Early Modern Philosophy of Mind* (Dordrecht: Springer, 2009), 1–37.

Piché, David. "Gerard of Bologna and Hervaeus Natalis on the Intuition of Non-Existents," *Quaestio* 10 (2010): 207–18.

Pini, Giorgio. "Can God Create My Thoughts? Scotus's Case against the Causal Account of Intentionality," *Journal of the History of Philosophy* 49 (2010): 39–63.

Pitt, Joseph C. "Galileo: Causation and the Use of Geometry," in R. E. Butts and J. C. Pitt (eds.), *New Perspectives on Galileo* (Dordrecht: Reidel, 1978), 181–96.

Plantinga, Alvin. *Warrant and Proper Function* (Oxford: Oxford University Press, 1993).

Popkin, Richard H. "David Hume: His Pyrrhonism and His Critique of Pyrrhonism," in V. C. Chappell (ed.), *Hume: A Collection of Critical Essays* (Garden City, NY: Anchor Books, 1966), 53–98.

Popkin, Richard H. *The History of Scepticism from Savonarola to Bayle*, rev. edn. (Oxford: Oxford University Press, 2003).

Popkin, Richard H. "Scepticism," in K. Haakonssen (ed.), *The Cambridge History of Eighteenth-Century Philosophy* (Cambridge: Cambridge University Press, 2006), 426–50.

Postle, B. R. "Working Memory as an Emergent Property of the Mind and Brain," *Neuroscience* 139 (2006): 23–38.

Pritchard, Duncan. "Knowledge and Understanding," in D. Pritchard, A. Millar, and A. Haddock (eds.), *The Nature and Value of Knowledge: Three Investigations* (Oxford: Oxford University Press, 2010), 3–88.

Pryor, James. "The Skeptic and the Dogmatist," *Nous* 34 (2000): 517–49.

Putallaz, François-Xavier. *La connaissance de soi au XIIIe siècle: de Matthieu d'Aquasparta à Thierry de Freiberg* (Paris: Vrin, 1991).

Putallaz, François-Xavier. *Le sens de la réflexion chez Thomas d'Aquin* (Paris: Vrin, 1991).

Putnam, Hilary. "Sense, Nonsense, and the Senses: An Inquiry into the Powers of the Human Mind," *Journal of Philosophy* 91 (1994): 445–517.

Quine, W. V. O. "Epistemology Naturalized," in idem, *Ontological Relativity and Other Essays* (New York: Columbia University Press, 1969), 69–90.

Quine, W. V. O. *Pursuit of Truth* (Cambridge, MA: Harvard University Press, 1990).

Quine, W. V. O. *Theories and Things* (Cambridge, MA: Harvard University Press, 1981).

Ragland, C. P. "Descartes on the Principle of Alternative Possibilities," *Journal of the History of Philosophy* 44 (2006): 377–94.

Rashed, Roshdi. "Al-Kindī's Commentary on Archimedes' 'The Measurement of the Circle,'" *Arabic Sciences and Philosophy* 3 (1993): 7–53.

Rashed, Roshdi. "The Philosophy of Mathematics," in S. Rahman, T. Street, and H. Tahiri (eds.), *The Unity of Science in the Arabic Tradition* (Dordrecht: Springer, 2008), 153–82.

Rawls, John. *A Theory of Justice* (Cambridge, MA: Belknap Press, 1971).

Reed, Baron. "Knowledge, Doubt, and Circularity," *Synthese* 188 (2012): 273–87.

Reisman, David C. "Al-Fārābī and the Philosophical Curriculum," in P. Adamson and R. C. Taylor (eds.), *The Cambridge Companion to Arabic Philosophy* (Cambridge: Cambridge University Press, 2005), 52–71.

Reynolds, Philip L. "The Infants of Eden: Scholastic Theologians on Early Childhood and Cognitive Development," *Mediaeval Studies* 68 (2006): 89–132.

Reynolds, Philip L. "Properties, Causality, and Epistemic Optimism in Thomas Aquinas," *Recherches de théologie et philosophie médiévales* 68 (2001): 270–309.

Rinard, Susanna. "Reasoning One's Way Out of Skepticism," in K. McCain and T. Poston (eds.), *The Mystery of Skepticism* (Leiden: Brill, forthcoming).

Robert, Aurélien. "William Crathorn," in E. N. Zalta (ed.), *The Stanford Encyclopedia of Philosophy* (Winter 2015). http://plato.stanford.edu/archives/win2015/entries/crathorn

Rochot, Bernard. "Gassendi et les mathématiques," *Revue d'histoire des sciences* 10 (1957): 69–78.

Rode, Christian. "Peter of John Olivi on Representation and Self-Representation," *Quaestio* 10 (2010): 155–66.

Rode, Christian. *Zugänge zum Selbst: Innere Erfahrung in Spätmittelalter und früher Neuzeit* (Münster: Aschendorff, 2015).

Rorty, Richard. *Philosophy and the Mirror of Nature* (Princeton, NJ: Princeton University Press, 1979).

Ross, Jacob and Mark Schroeder. "Belief, Credence, and Pragmatic Encroachment," *Philosophy and Phenomenological Research* 88 (2014): 259–88.

Ross, James F. "Aquinas on Belief and Knowledge," in W. A. Frank and G. J. Etzkorn (eds.), *Essays Honoring Allan B. Wolter* (St. Bonaventure, NY: Franciscan Institute, 1985), 245–69.

Rossi, Pietro. "Robert Grosseteste and the Object of Scientific Knowledge," in J. McEvoy (ed.), *Robert Grosseteste: New Perspectives on his Thought and Scholarship* (Turnhout: Brepols, 1995), 53–76.

Russell, Bertrand. "The Philosophy of Logical Atomism," in R. C. Marsh (ed.), *Logic and Knowledge: Essays 1901–1950* (New York: Capricorn Books, 1956), 177–281.

Ryle, Gilbert. *Collected Papers*, vol. 1: *Critical Essays* (London: Hutchinson, 1971).

Rysiew, Patrick. "Making It Evident: Evidence and Evidentness, Justification, and Belief," in T. Dougherty (ed.), *Evidentialism and Its Discontents* (Oxford: Oxford University Press, 2011), 207–25.

Scarre, Geoffrey. "Demons, Demonologists and Descartes," *Heythrop Journal* 31 (1990): 3–22.

Schierbaum, Sonja. "Subject Experience and Self-Knowledge: Chatton's Approach and Its Problems," in J. Kaukua and T. Ekenberg (eds.), *Subjectivity and Selfhood in Medieval and Early Modern Philosophy* (Dordrecht: Springer, 2016), 143–56.

Schmaltz, Tad M. (ed.). *Efficient Causation: A History* (New York: Oxford University Press, 2014).

Schmitt, Frederick F. *Hume's Epistemology in the* Treatise: *A Veritistic Interpretation* (Oxford: Oxford University Press, 2014).

Schrimm-Heins, Andrea. "Gewißheit und Sicherheit: Geschichte und Bedeutungswandel der Begriffe 'certitudo' und 'securitas,'" *Archiv für Begriffsgeschichte* 34 (1991): 123–213 and 35 (1992): 115–213.

Schroeder, Mark. "Stakes, Withholding, and Pragmatic Encroachment on Knowledge," *Philosophical Studies* 160 (2012): 265–85.

Schüssler, Rudolf. *Moral im Zweifel*, 2 vols. (Paderborn: Mentis, 2003–6).

Schüssler, Rudolf. "On the Anatomy of Probabilism," in J. Kraye and R. Saarinen (eds.), *Moral Philosophy on the Threshold of Modernity* (Dordrecht: Springer, 2005), 91–114.

Schüssler, Rudolf. "Probability in Medieval and Renaissance Philosophy," in E. N. Zalta (ed.), *The Stanford Encyclopedia of Philosophy* (Spring 2015). http://plato.stanford.edu/archives/spr2015/entries/probability-medieval-renaissance

Schüssler, Rudolf. "Scholastic Probability as Rational Assertability: The Rise of Theories of Reasonable Disagreement," *Archiv für Geschichte der Philosophie* 96 (2014): 202–31.

Schumacher, Ralph. "What Are the Direct Objects of Sight? Locke on the Molyneux Question," *Locke Studies* 3 (2003): 41–61.

Schwenkler, John. "Do Things Look the Way They Feel?" *Analysis* 73 (2013): 86–96.

Schwitzgebel, Eric. "A Phenomenal, Dispositional Account of Belief," *Nous* 36 (2002): 249–75.

Scott, David. "Malebranche's Indirect Realism: A Reply to Steven Nadler," *British Journal for the History of Philosophy* 4 (1996): 53–78.

Scott, T. K. "Ockham on Evidence, Necessity and Intuition," *Journal of the History of Philosophy* 7 (1969): 27–49.

Searle, John R. *Seeing Things as They Are: A Theory of Perception* (Oxford: Oxford University Press, 2015).

Sedley, David N. "The Motivation of Greek Skepticism," in M. Burnyeat (ed.), *The Skeptical Tradition* (Berkeley: University of California Press, 1983), 9–29.

Serene, Eileen. "Demonstrative Science," in N. Kretzmann et al. (eds.), *The Cambridge History of Later Medieval Philosophy* (Cambridge: Cambridge University Press, 1982), 496–517.

Shank, J. B. "Voltaire," in E. N. Zalta (ed.), *The Stanford Encyclopedia of Philosophy* (Fall 2015). http://plato.stanford.edu/archives/fall2015/entries/voltaire

Shapin, Steven. "'The Mind in Its Own Place': Science and Solitude in Seventeenth-Century England," *Science in Context* 4 (1991): 191–218.

Shapin, Steven. *A Social History of Truth: Civility and Science in Seventeenth-Century England* (Chicago, IL: University of Chicago Press, 1994).

Shapin, Steven and Simon Schaffer. *Leviathan and the Air-Pump: Hobbes, Boyle, and the Experimental Life* (Princeton, NJ: Princeton University Press, 1985).

Shapiro, Barbara J. *"Beyond Reasonable Doubt" and "Probable Cause": Historical Perspectives on the Anglo-American Law of Evidence* (Berkeley: University of California Press, 1991).

Shapiro, Barbara J. *A Culture of Fact: England, 1550–1720* (Ithaca, NY: Cornell University Press, 2000).

Shapiro, Barbara J. *John Wilkins, 1614–1672: An Intellectual Biography* (Berkeley: University of California Press, 1969).

Shapiro, Barbara J. *Probability and Certainty in Seventeenth-Century England: A Study of the Relationships between Natural Science, Religion, History, Law, and Literature* (Princeton, NJ: Princeton University Press, 1983).

Shea, William R. "Descartes as a Critic of Galileo," in R. E. Butts and J. C. Pitt (eds.), *New Perspectives on Galileo* (Dordrecht: Reidel, 1978), 139–59.

Silverman, Allan. "Color and Color-Perception in Aristotle's *De anima*," *Ancient Philosophy* 9 (1989): 271–92.

Simmons, Alison. "Are Cartesian Sensations Representational?" *Nous* 33 (1999): 347–69.

Simmons, Alison. "Sensible Ends: Latent Teleology in Descartes' Account of Sensation," *Journal of the History of Philosophy* 39 (2001): 49–75.

Simpson, John A. and Edmund S. C. Weiner (eds.). *The Oxford English Dictionary*, 2nd edn. (Oxford: Clarendon, 1989).

Singer, Ira. "Hume's Extreme Skepticism in *Treatise* I.iv.7," *Canadian Journal of Philosophy* 25 (1995): 595–622.

Smith, A. D. "Space and Sight," *Mind* 109 (2000): 481–518.

Smith, A. Mark. *From Sight to Light: The Passage from Ancient to Modern Optics* (Chicago, IL: University of Chicago Press, 2015).

Smith, George E. "How Newton's *Principia* Changed Physics," in A. Janiak and E. Schliesser (eds.), *Interpreting Newton: Critical Essays* (Cambridge: Cambridge University Press, 2012), 360–95.

Solère, Jean-Luc. "Durand of Saint-Pourçain's Cognition Theory: Its Fundamental Principles," in R. L. Friedman and J.-M. Counet (eds.), *Medieval Perspectives on Aristotle's* De anima (Louvain-la-Neuve: Éditions de l'Institut supérieur de philosophie, 2013), 185–248.

Sorell, Tom. "Hobbes's Scheme of the Sciences," in idem (ed.), *The Cambridge Companion to Hobbes* (Cambridge: Cambridge University Press, 1996), 45–61.

Sorell, Tom, G. A. J. Rogers, and Jill Kraye (eds.). *Scientia in Early Modern Philosophy: Seventeenth-Century Thinkers on Demonstrative Knowledge from First Principles* (Dordrecht: Springer, 2010).

Sorensen, Roy A. "The Metaphysics of Precision and Scientific Language," *Philosophical Perspectives* 11 (1997): 349–74.

Sosa, Ernest. "How to Resolve the Pyrrhonian Problematic: A Lesson from Descartes," *Philosophical Studies* 85 (1997): 229–49.

Sosa, Ernest. "Replies to Brown, Prichard and Conee," *Philosophical Studies* 143 (2009): 427–40.

Sosa, Ernest. *A Virtue Epistemology*, vol. 1: *Apt Belief and Reflective Knowledge* (Oxford: Clarendon, 2007).

Southgate, Beverley C. "'Beating down Scepticism': The Solid Philosophy of John Sergeant, 1623–1707," in M. A. Stewart (ed.), *English Philosophy in the Age of Locke* (Oxford: Clarendon, 2000), 281–315.

Southgate, Beverley C. *"Covetous of Truth": The Life and Work of Thomas White, 1593–1676* (Dordrecht: Kluwer, 1993).

Stella, Prospero T. "Le 'Quaestiones de libero arbitrio' di Durando da S. Porciano," *Salesianum* 24 (1962): 450–524.

Stern, Josef. *The Matter and Form of Maimonides'* Guide (Cambridge, MA: Harvard University Press, 2013).

Stich, Stephen. *The Fragmentation of Reason: Preface to a Pragmatic Theory of Cognitive Evaluation* (Cambridge, MA: MIT Press, 1990).

Stoljar, Daniel. "The Argument from Diaphanousness," in M. Escurdia, R. J. Stainton, and C. D. Viger (eds.), *Language, Mind and World: Special Issue of the Canadian Journal of Philosophy* (Alberta: University of Alberta Press, 2004), 341–90.

Strawson, P. F. *Skepticism and Naturalism: Some Varieties* (New York: Columbia University Press, 1985).

Striker, Gisela. "Epicurus on the Truth of Sense-Impressions," *Archiv für Geschichte der Philosophie* 59 (1977): 125–42.

Striker, Gisela. "Sceptical Strategies," in M. Schofield, M. Burnyeat, and J. Barnes (eds.), *Doubt and Dogmatism: Studies in Hellenistic Epistemology* (Oxford: Oxford University Press, 1980), 54–83.

Stroud, Barry. "Kant and Skepticism," in M. Burnyeat (ed.), *The Skeptical Tradition* (Berkeley: University of California Press, 1983), 413–34.

Stump, Eleonore. *Aquinas* (Arguments of the Philosophers) (London: Routledge, 2003).

Stump, Eleonore. "The Mechanisms of Cognition: Ockham on Mediating Species," in P. V. Spade (ed.), *The Cambridge Companion to Ockham* (New York: Cambridge University Press, 1999), 168–203.

Swift, Helen. "The Merits of Not Knowing: The Paradox of *espoir certain* in Late-Medieval French Narrative Poetry," in D. G. Denery II, K. Ghosh, and N. Zeeman (eds.), *Uncertain Knowledge: Scepticism, Relativism, and Doubt in the Middle Ages* (Turnhout: Brepols, 2014), 185–212.

Sylla, Edith Dudley. "Galileo and Probable Arguments," in D. O. Dahlstrom (ed.), *Nature and Scientific Method* (Washington, DC: Catholic University of America Press, 1991), 211–34.

Sylla, Edith Dudley. "Oxford Calculators," in E. Craig (ed.), *Routledge Encyclopedia of Philosophy* (London: Routledge, 1998), vol. 7: 179–83.

Tachau, Katherine H. *Vision and Certitude in the Age of Ockham: Optics, Epistemology and the Foundations of Semantics, 1250–1345* (Leiden: Brill, 1988).

Tachau, Katherine H. "What Senses and Intellect Do: Argument and Judgment in Late Medieval Theories of Knowledge," in K. Jacobi (ed.), *Argumentationstheorie: Scholastische Forschungen zu den logischen und semantischen Regeln korrekten Folgerns* (Leiden: Brill, 1993), 653–68.

Taieb, Hamid. "The 'Intellected Thing' (*res intellecta*) in Hervaeus Natalis," *Vivarium* 53 (2015): 26–44.

Taylor, C. C. W. "'All Perceptions Are True,'" in M. Schofield, M. Burnyeat, and J. Barnes (eds.), *Doubt and Dogmatism: Studies in Hellenistic Epistemology* (Oxford: Oxford University Press, 1980), 105–24.

Taylor, C. C. W. "Aristotle's Epistemology," in S. Everson (ed.), *Epistemology* (Cambridge: Cambridge University Press, 1990), 116–42.

Taylor, C. C. W. *The Atomists: Leucippus and Democritus* (Toronto: University of Toronto Press, 1999).

Thayer, H. S. "Aristotle on the Meaning of Science," *Philosophical Inquiry* 1 (1979): 87–104.

Thijssen, Johannes M. M. H. "John Buridan and Nicholas of Autrecourt on Causality and Induction," *Traditio* 43 (1987): 237–55.

Thijssen, Johannes M. M. H. "The Quest for Certain Knowledge in the Fourteenth Century: Nicholas of Autrecourt against the Academics," in J. Sihvola (ed.), *Ancient Scepticism and the Sceptical Tradition* (Helsinki: Societas Philosophica Fennica, 2000), 199–223.

Toivanen, Juhana. *Perception and the Internal Senses: Peter of John Olivi and the Cognitive Functions of the Sensitive Soul* (Leiden: Brill, 2013).

Tsouna, Voula. *The Epistemology of the Cyrenaic School* (Cambridge: Cambridge University Press, 1998).

Tutino, Stefania. *Thomas White and the Blackloists: Between Politics and Theology during the English Civil War* (Aldershot: Ashgate, 2008).

Tweedale, Martin. *John of Rodynton on Knowledge, Science, and Theology* (Ph.D. dissertation: University of California, Los Angeles, 1965).

Unger, Peter. *Ignorance: A Case for Scepticism* (Oxford: Clarendon, 1975).

Van Cleve, James. "Foundationalism, Epistemic Principles, and the Cartesian Circle," *The Philosophical Review* 88 (1979): 55–91.

Van Leeuwen, Henry G. *The Problem of Certainty in English Thought: 1630–1690* (The Hague: Martinus Nijhoff, 1970).

Vier, Peter C. *Evidence and Its Function according to John Duns Scotus* (St. Bonaventure, NY: Franciscan Institute, 1951).

Waldman, Theodore. "Origins of the Legal Doctrine of Reasonable Doubt," *Journal of the History of Ideas* 20 (1959): 299–316.

Wallace, William A. *Causality and Scientific Explanation*, 2 vols. (Ann Arbor, MI: University of Michigan Press, 1972–4).

Wallace, William A. "The Certitude of Science in Late Medieval and Renaissance Thought," *History of Philosophy Quarterly* 3 (1986): 281–91.

Wallace, William A. "The Problem of Causality in Galileo's Science," *Review of Metaphysics* 36 (1983): 607–32.

Walton, Kendall L. "Transparent Pictures: On the Nature of Photographic Realism," *Critical Inquiry* 11 (1984): 246–77.

Watson, Richard A. *The Breakdown of Cartesian Metaphysics* (Atlantic Highlands, NJ: Humanities Press, 1987).

Watts, Edward J. *City and School in Late Antique Athens and Alexandria* (Berkeley: University of California Press, 2006).

Wedgwood, Ralph. "Against Ideal Theory," Ralph Wedgwood's Blog, May 2, 2014. http://ralphwedgwood.typepad.com/blog/2014/05/against-ideal-theory.html

Wedgwood, Ralph. "Justified Inference," *Synthese* 189 (2012): 273–95.

Weisheipl, James A. "Classification of the Sciences in Medieval Thought," *Mediaeval Studies* 27 (1965): 54–90.

Weisheipl, James A. "The Place of John Dumbleton in the Merton School," *Isis* 50 (1959): 439–54.

Wells, Norman J. "Descartes' *Idea* and Its Sources," *American Catholic Philosophical Quarterly* 67 (1993): 514–35.

Weltecke, Dorothea. *"Der Narr spricht: es ist kein Gott." Atheismus: Unglauben und Glaubenszweifel vom 12. Jahrhundert bis zur Neuzeit* (Frankfurt: Campus Verlag, 2010).

Westfall, Richard S. *The Construction of Modern Science: Mechanisms and Mechanics* (Cambridge: Cambridge University Press, 1977).

Westfall, Richard S. *Force in Newton's Physics* (London: MacDonald, 1971).

Westtfall, Richard S. "Making a World of Precision: Newton and the Construction of a Quantitative World View," in F. Durham and R. D. Purrington (eds.), *Some Truer Method: Reflections on the Heritage of Newton* (New York: Columbia University Press, 1990), 59–87.

Westfall, Richard S. "Newton and the Fudge Factor," *Science* 179 (1973): 751–8.

Whelan, Ruth. "The Wisdom of Simonides: Bayle and La Mothe Le Vayer," in R. H. Popkin and A. Vanderjagt (eds.), *Scepticism and Irreligion in the Seventeenth and Eighteenth Centuries* (Leiden: Brill, 1993), 230–53.

Williams, Bernard. "Descartes's Use of Skepticism," in M. Burnyeat (ed.), *The Skeptical Tradition* (Berkeley: University of California Press, 1983), 337–52.

Williams, Michael. "The Agrippan Argument and Two Forms of Skepticism," in W. Sinnott-Armstrong (ed.), *Pyrrhonian Skepticism* (New York: Oxford University Press, 2004), 121–46.

Williamson, Timothy. *Knowledge and Its Limits* (Oxford: Oxford University Press, 2000).

Wilson, Margaret Dauler. "Descartes on the Perception of Primary Qualities," in eadem, *Ideas and Mechanism: Essays on Early Modern Philosophy* (Princeton, NJ: Princeton University Press, 1999), 26–40.

Wilson, Margaret Dauler. "Descartes on the Representationality of Sensation," in eadem, *Ideas and Mechanism: Essays on Early Modern Philosophy* (Princeton, NJ: Princeton University Press, 1999), 69–83.

Wilson, Margaret Dauler. "Did Berkeley Completely Misunderstand the Basis of the Primary-Secondary Quality Distinction in Locke?" in eadem, *Ideas and Mechanism: Essays on Early Modern Philosophy* (Princeton, NJ: Princeton University Press, 1999), 215–28.

Winkler, Kenneth P. "Perception and Ideas, Judgement," in K. Haakonssen (ed.), *The Cambridge History of Eighteenth-Century Philosophy* (Cambridge: Cambridge University Press, 2006), 234–85.

Wise, M. Norton (ed.). *The Values of Precision* (Princeton, NJ: Princeton University Press, 1995).

Wittgenstein, Ludwig. *Philosophical Investigations*, trans. G. E. M. Anscombe (Oxford: Blackwell, 1953).

Wittgenstein, Ludwig. *Tractatus Logico-Philosophicus*, trans. F. Ramsey and C. K. Ogden (London, Routledge, 1961).

Wolterstorff, Nicholas. *John Locke and the Ethics of Belief* (Cambridge: Cambridge University Press, 1996).

Yolton, John W. *Perceptual Acquaintance from Descartes to Reid* (Minneapolis, MN: University of Minnesota Press, 1984).

Yolton, John W. "The Term *Idea* in Seventeenth and Eighteenth-Century British Philosophy," in M. Fattori and M. L. Bianchi (eds.), *Idea: VI Colloquio Internazionale del Lessico Intellettuale Europeo* (Rome: Edizioni dell'Ateno, 1989), 237–54.

Yrjönsuuri, Mikko. "Self-Knowledge and Renaissance Skeptics," in J. Sihvola (ed.), *Ancient Scepticism and the Sceptical Tradition* (Helsinki: Societas Philosophica Fennica, 2000), 225–53.

Yrjönsuuri, Mikko. "The Structure of Self-Consciousness: A Fourteenth-Century Debate," in S. Heinämaa, V. Lähteenmäki, and P. Reimes (eds.), *Consciousness: From Perception to Reflection in the History of Philosophy* (Dordrecht: Springer, 2007), 141–52.

Zemplén, Gábor Áron. "Newton's Strategic Manoeuvring with Simple Colours, Categories, and Descriptions," in T. Demeter, K. Murphy, and C. Zittel (eds.), *Conflicting Values of Inquiry: Ideologies of Epistemology in Early Modern Europe* (Leiden: Brill, 2015), 223–45.

Zupko, Jack. "On Certitude," in J. Thijssen and J. Zupko (eds.), *The Metaphysics and Natural Philosophy of John Buridan* (Leiden: Brill, 2001), 165–82.

Zupko, Jack. *John Buridan: Portrait of a Fourteenth-Century Arts Master* (Notre Dame, IN: University of Notre Dame Press, 2003).

INDEX OF NAMES

Christian authors active before 1600 are alphabetized by first name.

SUBJECT INDEX

a priori 104, 123, 159–60
action at a distance 71, 251–2, 277
Adam and Eve 7
adequacy 248
afterimage 81, 84–5, 268, 275, 278, 280
akrasia 334
Alexandria 27, 140, 161, 176–7
angels and demons 101, 118, 121, 124, 183, 199, 203, 274, 287, 295, 296, 299, 310, 311, 314
animals (nonrational) 223, 254
Anselmian glance 94–115, 293–8, 300, 303, 305–9
antirealism, moral and epistemic 129–30, 323, 336
apparent being 82–4, 86–8, 92, 273–7, 282–3, 284–5
arguments
    all-at-once grasp of, *see* Anselmian glance
    and evidential force 100–3, 105, 110–11, 297
    and understanding 99, 105
assent, *see* belief
astronomy 27, 30, 153–4
atomism 14, 20, 54, 155, 255
authority, *see* first-person authority; testimony

Bayesianism, *see* belief, absolute vs. degrees of
belief
    absolute vs. degrees of 40–5, 135–6, 172, 211–12, 216–22, 335–6
    as opposed to knowledge 218–19
    and passion 115, 137–8, 308–9, 318–19, 323–4, 332–5
    voluntary control of 138, 333; *see also* indubitability; will and belief
    see also faith; opinion; skepticism and belief
brain 72, 73, 90, 92, 98, 236, 292–3

Cartesian circle 105–6, 110, 300–2
causation
    efficient 14, 155, 237–8
    final 14
    formal 14; *see also* essences
    requirement for knowledge 6, 7, 12, 13–16, 150–1, 153–60, 165–9, 181–3, 214–15
    theories of 157, 287, 308
certainty
    absolute 29, 32, 35, 36–8, 44–5, 119–21, 174, 197, 202–4, 207–9, 216, 220, 314–15
    conditional 32, 34, 36, 37, 38–9, 118–19, 128, 132, 183, 195, 198, 203, 209–13, 224, 311, 315, 327
    degrees of 29, 32, 35, 36, 42–3, 118–19, 178–9, 184, 185–6, 191, 197–201, 216, 320; *see also* probability
    as epistemic ideal 22–30, 45, 111, 161, 172, 174–7, 183–5
    higher order 179–81, 194, 312
    limits to 29–30, 37–45, 111–16, 117–29, 131, 319–20
    moral 32, 34–7, 42–4, 49, 132, 179, 197–201, 202, 203, 204, 205, 206, 207, 209, 217, 218–21
    natural 32, 34, 37, 118–19, 183, 195, 198, 327
    objective vs. subjective 28–30, 32, 38, 178, 179, 184, 211–12
charity 134–5, 334–5

chemistry 158–9
clarity and distinctness 62, 104–6, 109–14, 191, 193, 236, 241, 247–8, 300–3, 306
cogito ergo sum 104, 119, 190, 268, 298, 309
color 50, 52, 54, 55–6, 63, 64–5, 92, 159, 226–7, 232–5, 237, 239–40, 242, 243–4, 287
condemnations of 1347 57, 201, 237
confusion, sensory 58, 235–6, 241, 248
consciousness 97, 98, 265–6, 292–3
continuum, puzzles of 60, 239
corpuscularianism, *see* mechanical philosophy
credence, *see* belief, absolute vs. degrees of
curiosity 293
Cyrenaics 256, 268

defeaters 128, 134–5, 324, 327; *see also* epistemic defeat
demonstration 3–4, 8, 27, 99–106, 142, 154, 161, 177, 188, 203, 213–14, 299
desire, *see* belief and passion; will
dialectic 8, 145, 188, 213, 318
diaphanous, *see* perception, mediated vs. diaphanous
directness, *see* perception, directness of
disability 147
disagreement 24, 114, 306–7
disposition 65, 67–8, 98, 99, 100, 105, 107, 135, 144, 174, 190, 210–11, 221, 245–7, 258, 262, 265, 292, 294–5, 301, 303
distinctness, *see* clarity and distinctness
dogmatism 111–12, 119, 129–30, 133, 197, 302–6, 314–15, 317, 319, 329
dreams 79–82, 117, 191, 273, 315
dualism 288–9, 292

earth, motion of 158, 190
education 145
elements, *see* qualities, elemental
empiricism 20, 47, 222–3, 241
Epicureans 47, 73, 223, 224, 255, 256, 271, 277
epistēmē 3–6, 26, 142–3, 153, 175–6, 210, 294
epistemic defeat 176, 128–38, 317–28, 332, 335–6
epistemology
    as foundational 1, 3, 10, 19–20, 139
    naturalized 133–4, 196, 328
    origins of 1–3, 19–20, 21–2, 42–5, 139–41, 206–7
    see also idealized epistemology; knowledge; science
essences 10–14, 17, 22, 39, 125, 152, 155–6, 157–8, 209, 249
ethics 1, 129, 153, 214, 323–4, 336
events 70
exactness, *see* precision
expectation 135–6, 331, 333–4
experiment 166
explanation, *see* causation, requirement for knowledge
external world, knowledge of 41, 65, 222, 276, 328
externalism, *see* internalism
evidence 33, 38–40, 43–4, 109–11, 126–8, 130–2, 135, 138, 191–2, 210–13, 304–6, 322, 324; *see also* evidentness

Printed and bound by CPI Group (UK) Ltd, Croydon, CR0 4YY